Business Management

Robert Erskine

Business Management

PRENTICE HALL

New York · London · Toronto · Sydney · Tokyo · Singapore

First published 1991 by
Prentice Hall International (UK) Ltd,
66 Wood Lane End, Hemel Hempstead,
Hertfordshire, HP2 4RG
A division of
Simon & Schuster International Group

Printed and bound in Great Britain at
the University Press, Cambridge

British Library Cataloguing in Publication Data

Erskine, Robert K.
  Business management.
  I. Title
  658

  ISBN 0-13-552027-4

1 2 3 4 5 95 94 93 92 91

Contents

Part 6   An integrated view of management systems in a reach for excellence 457

Figures

Foreword

Professor W.J. Reddin

The key thing in this book is its enormous novelty and therefore interest. An absolutely central feature of the book is its multidisciplinary approach. This approach flourishes in an innovative course in Risk Management, developed at Glasgow and taught by Robert Erskine. This is not one of your dull books on management. The areas of emphasis include management information, business policy, organisational behaviour, information technology and of course effectiveness generally.

This book is well designed for the discriminating reader who believes that there is much more to management than Peters and Waterman, 'In Search for Excellence'; and who also believes that Peter Drucker gave us, bountifully, the philosophy of management effectiveness but also believes his ideas deserve to be supplemented, as in this book, by more specificity and more case studies.

Surely, with our wired society and such concepts as the world global matrix it is obvious that we are living in an information society. A Canadian, Marshall McLuhan, who created the concept of the world as a global village, would have liked this book because it brings the impact of information technology to the organisational and managerial level.

Robert Erskine and I both recognise the clear centrality of managerial effectiveness, though our routes to this common goal are different. Cool logic must lead to the conclusion that it is the manager's only job.

While, I expect, the book will be much used in both introductory and advanced courses in management, there is no doubt that it has to be simply a good read for any practising manager. The reason for this is its novel combination of chapter and section structure which could help any good manager summarise thinking around core themes.

Fortunately, the book is long enough that not all teachers will have to require all students to read all chapters. The book is clearly designed for flexibility in application in a teaching situation. Some of the case studies border on the brilliant.

Professor Reddin is author of 22 management textbooks and an international expert on the theme of 'Managerial Effectiveness'.

XV

It will be quite clear to anyone reading this book that it has been written by someone with a solid educational base, plus a substantial industrial base — always, I think, a good combination.

This book is not traditional. It is comprehensive and it certainly is multidisciplinary. For all these reasons it is also refreshing and therefore is a superb introduction to management. This book will at least nudge and in some cases shape the framework of management teaching. It is a breath of fresh air.

Preface

Readership

Students of management

The key readerships will be: undergraduate students doing a BA in business studies or management studies; post-experience students doing a Diploma in Management Studies or Master of Business Administration; professional students qualifying in banking, insurance, accounting and engineering, where their programmes of study have a component of management; students studying management via open learning programmes from the Open University or Open College; and students studying Scottish HND or English BTEC courses in business studies.

Practising managers

Once anyone has reached the level of supervision, he or she will need to acquire competence in the theory, practice and skills of management to plan, organise, control and change the work environment. Supervisors, middle managers and senior managers in both the public and private sectors would benefit from this book by learning the basic skills to do this. In addition, there are managers from specialist functions, corporate planners, data processing specialists, personnel managers with responsibility for staff assessment and management development and business consultants involved in trouble-shooting who would find particular sections of the book useful.

Structure of the book

Part 1 provides an overview of the theory of management and methods for studying management.

Part 2 provides an introduction to policy-making, planning and objective-setting.

Part 3 covers the development of management skills and the functions of management.

Part 4 covers the information society environment and the deployment of systems for tactical and strategic management.

Part 5 looks at management, organisation and change with input from the behavioural sciences.

Part 6 offers an integrated view of management systems in a search for excellence.

Rationale of structure

A supposition about the study of management might be that there is a natural beginning point and a natural optimum sequence of developing the various topics of the subject. However, a detailed look at the works of several theorists of management reveals a lack of standardisation, though one author, Mintzberg (1973) warns his readers to adopt his sequence 'or else', if they want to benefit from his presentation.

Unlike Euclidean geometry, management is inherently multidisciplinary (it relates to other established academic disciplines such as accounting) and interdisciplinary (it develops an integrated, problem-solving approach to understand better and respond to unstructured but realistic situations in organisations). There is much contemporary debate on the relationships among subject headings and topics. Furthermore, a common observation of tutors of management is that students of management come to their courses with a variety of initial expertise and familiarity from their life and work experiences, and their need in a textbook is to study selectively. That means they will use the index and chapter headings to help them find the points of greatest interest. Browsing is such a creative and essential activity in fast and enjoyable learning!

However, a sequence of a textbook must be defined and in this textbook it reflects what the author believes is the most meaningful way for the subject to make an impact on the reader. Many academics are obsessed with logical rigour in their selection of topics and their sequence, and the need to build the material from first principles becomes an end in itself. Does a car driver need to know first the principles of mending punctures or to flavour the new horizons which are open to life if there is a mastery of the techniques of driving? My bet is that there is greater satisfaction to be derived from the experience of driving than from mending punctures. In any event a novice, on encountering a puncture, can be particularly good at the art of playing *actus patheticus* at the roadside and a knight in shining armour will invariably volunteer to change the offending wheel!

Likewise the student of management is not particularly interested in the technology of the computer or in the involved and time-consuming methods used to design a modern, computerised management information system. Nevertheless, it is indeed a real thrill to be exposed to a sophisticated working management information system and be given the opportunity to participate in the creative manipulation of this, redefining its policy rules and refocusing its power to scrutinise areas of real business concern in time to elicit a managerial response. But to introduce the reader to this thrill one needs early in a text to offer the power of modern management approaches in the information society.

Later chapters can develop an understanding of the theory behind such approaches and their articulation by specialists. But one must first paint a picture to attract the attention of the generalist, who can view business from the high-level perspective of the boardroom.

To support this approach one needs a text which goes quickly to the heart of the strategic management process and from this moves to seek out the supporting disciplines as economics, accounting and behavioural science, and puts the student into a position where these support disciplines are the tools and techniques which enable top-level management to build a stronger business. It seems a tactical error to let a subject such as organisational design be dominant in its own right. It is much healthier to take the position that the structure of a firm should reflect the business strategy of that firm. As the strategy changes so the structure should adapt; the most important variables to be aware of therefore are those of strategy. These provide the building-blocks from which variations in the support disciplines become meaningful. Likewise, computer methods should not be dominant in their own right. Management needs to articulate a computing strategy that supports the business strategy.

The scene for the book is set in Part 1 with a brief review of the process of management. It has been the common observation of the author that first-time students find much difficulty in conceptualising management into an intelligible framework; furthermore, courses are littered with poorly defined syllabuses on management, which add to this confusion. Part 1 gives an opportunity to sketch a wide framework of the branches of the theory of management. The purpose is to enable the student to have a conceptual map from which the topics of management can be recognised in syllabuses, in the chapters of this book and also in other writers' books.

This book relies heavily on interactive exercises, which are embedded in the text and offered frequently in the form of case problems. A case essentially offers a situation requiring appreciation, analysis and response. In the text the writer offers not only the case situation and typical tasks, but also reflects on typical student responses and then interposes a good practice solution. With practice the reader gets as skilled at this process as the author, so the cases become a creative fulcrum on which to try out their ideas as though the tutor were actually present! Learning through cases is generally a novel experience, particularly to the undergraduate, and for this reason chapter 2 develops a case methodology. This has been used and tested by the author with some very successful results.

Cases are often criticised by management tutors as being so long that much time is wasted at the assimilation stage before real learning can take place. In this book the author has deliberately offered concise case material, typically amenable for analysis and response well within a two-hour study period. There are, however, a few exceptions where the material based on live action research sequences will require a longer time for analysis. Whenever cases are adopted in the text it is because they are considered to be the most efficient vehicle for communicating applied principles of management. Cases can take the student into the fascination of real situations and the unusual manifestations of human nature.

With the framework of management theory sketched and a practical case methodology outlined it is possible to develop in Part 2 the substance of this book. Policy-making, planning and objective-setting are the very core of strategic management practice, so let us get to grips with these basic concepts quickly and start using them. The key topic here is the corporate planning process, recognised initially as long ago as 1965 by Ansoff, but very rapidly developed and refined in the 1970s and 1980s. The good practice norms from this development provide a powerful analytical tool of management situations. We need norms of good practice to shine brightly as they enable us to recognise bad practice for what it is, for real management situations are loaded with bad practice and missed opportunities.

We also need a mechanism to transmit policy and objectives vertically and laterally throughout the organisation. Peter Drucker offered the managing by objectives (MbO) philosophy as long ago as 1954, but this approach needed a lot of refinement to be refocused into a role supportive of modern corporate planning methods and practice. Drucker initially confused the situation by presenting MbO as though it were a manifestation of corporate planning practice in its own right, rather than as an instrument of a higher-level discipline. This book presents MbO refined to this new supportive, creative and acceptable role.

In Part 3 attention is focused on particular skills and functions of management. This part could be a book in itself, but with a keen sense of selection of topics, delegation, decision-making, communication and chairmanship, planning and control are perceived as the most fundamental and useful topics worthy of developing. Some theoretical frameworks and guidelines of good practice are offered and cases again pose situational problems. These need a proper analysis and give some coaching by offering a comparison with the writer's solutions.

This approach offers another bonus — that of exposing the reader to multidisciplinary problems at an early stage. Some of these will inevitably relate to topics whose theory has not yet been developed. Exercises thus take on a detective element, which makes them more interesting in analysis, and develop in the participant a tolerance for the unexpected — a deliberate ploy to encourage a generalist management attitude. Furthermore, it enables the writer to approach the more difficult topics gradually by offering several exposures to their treatment, with some unobtrusive signposting to other sections of the book. By the time we get to Part 5, which deals with organisation structure and change, there are many situational models already discussed, so the framework for organisation design does not have to start from first principles.

The writer increases the scope and coverage of the text from the public sector to the private sector by flavouring the narrative with a balance of cases and problems taken from both sectors.

In Part 4 we look in some depth at the manifestation of the information society, which is recognised as the predominant environment of contemporary management. The mid-1980s was perhaps a watershed with personal computers coming on to the market cheaper than the office typewriter, a wide exposure of middle management to computing skills and the real spill-over of this approach into the boardroom. No longer could senior executives rely on specialists to advise them on computer methods, these methods themselves were being dramatically upgraded into the normally accepted skills of generalist line management, but this would still be a painful learning process for many senior executives. Decisions relating to communication networks and adoption of major elements of hardware and computerised systems were increasingly of a strategic nature, and the very competitive effectiveness of the organisation would depend on its ability to find points of leverage in the organisation which could yield dramatic improvements in their financial performance. The new technology would also offer ways of dramatically speeding up the product life development cycle, and delivery methods for getting to the customer and improving after-sales service.

Where there is an opportunity there is also a challenge, the challenge to overcome organisational inertia. Computerised systems and methods signify change in many dimensions in the organisation — social, political, economic, organisational. Top management needs to know how to structure the organisation to get the benefit of the new methods.

Part 4 relates to the deployment of both tactical and strategic systems, and thus its target is all levels of management. The theory is not developed from first principles. We start from the analysis of finished successful applications of systems and learn to appreciate what they do in a managerial sense. Then the finished design is taken apart to reveal the design decisions and the organisational moves that secured the implementation. The intention is to develop ways in which user line management can develop an empathy with computer specialists so that the design decisions are those with a balance of input from users and specialists, but with a greater influence from the users.

Two topics are emphasised. The first is managing by exception. This puts a conscious emphasis on policies, targets and standards emanating from the corporate planning process and written into the effectiveness standards of every executive, and the deliberate direction of the computer systems to focus on the planning and monitoring of these, particularly where they are areas of concern. The second major topic is that of appreciating and applying the concept of leverage in the use of computing equipment and systems.

The text offers many examples of successful design of computerised systems based on action research in a computer manufacturer, the computer manufacturer's clients and that achieved within the public sector environment of a college. But it also offers some disaster sequences for analysis (very rare in the published literature) to reinforce notions of good practice in the organisation and management of the computing facility. An original case is presented where an analyst is able to 'hijack' his organisation for a cool £3 million from hospital!

The text in Part 5 takes us to the behavioural sciences, choices in organisational design and the key topic of the management of change. In earlier parts of the text two opportunities have been unveiled; the power of the modern corporate planning process and the need to take advantage of the information society and absorb technological change without pain and trauma.

The opportunities are lost, however, unless people and groups can be persuaded to adopt the new methods and anticipate and manage the very wide-ranging implications that fundamental change brings. At last the behavioural sciences are beginning to deliver profiles of the process consultant competent at intervening in organisations to facilitate a process of planned change. Recent researchers do, however, sound a note of warning that change is also a matter of playing power politics within the organisation and finding a project champion to advance the change process.

A book must have an ending and conclusion, so an attempt is made in Part 6 to summarise and rationalise the previous sequences. To add to the credibility of this notion these conclusions are directly related to a long programme of management research completed by the author in Scotland. This suggests that effective management may be articulated by introducing good practice in four fundamental systems in any business and ensuring that each such system is interfaced and compatible with the other systems. The four systems contemplated are: corporate planning, objective-setting, strategic deployment of computerised management information systems and organisation development to accomplish the change process. The chapter here offers the logic of this model and suggests from action research an implementation sequence and method.

In putting the final pieces together from the building-blocks of the earlier chapters, the author follows a final Euclidean logic to repackage the principles of organisation and management with a new look and awareness of the environment and implications of the information society.

The author finds some rapport with the ideas of Peters and Waterman (1982), but consolidates the principles and guidelines of management into a more coherent and implementable set of concepts.

Book development process

The book was put together over three academic sessions. As each section was completed it was used in trial runs with two main groups of management students: an undergraduate class and a post-experience group studying for the Diploma in Management Studies. At the end of their courses the students offered their comments, which were most favourable. A book of this nature and structure with the self-help exercises was just what the market needed. In the final editing of the text the student comments were taken into account. All the main exercise feedback discussions are organised at the end of the text in Appendix 1.

Exercise and case study feedbacks

Note: Some exercise feedbacks were deliberately included in the chapter text as demonstration material. The exercise and case study feedbacks in Appendix 1 are provided to enable to student to explore further and compare his or her own solution with the author's. There will be differences, but hopefully the dialogue will be improved by this technique to assist self-study.

Feedback on the following can be found in the Appendix:

References

Mintzberg, H. (1973), *The Nature of Managerial Work*, Harper & Row.
Peters, T.J. and Waterman, R.H. (1982), *In Search of Excellence. Lessons from America's best-run companies*, Harper & Row.

Acknowledgements

Thanks are due to the following for their role in the preparation of this text:

The editors of Prentice Hall International, Cathy Peck and Maggie MacDougall, for their initial encouragement of me to tackle such an ambitious publishing project in just two-and-a-half years.

The external reviewers and the copy editors for their many helpful suggestions, most of which were adopted.

Allan Kinross, an internal reviewer and colleague, who made many useful suggestions in connection with an MBA/DMS readership.

Norrie Train, a very supportive colleague, who pointed me to many of the research results which became adopted as text material.

Undergraduate students from BA Risk Management at Glasgow College and post-experience students from the Diploma in Management Studies course, who participated enthusiastically in trials of the material and gave valuable feedback on their reactions.

To Susan, my wife, for her constant support and encouragement, and Iona, Hamish and Sandy, who tolerated the publishing contract.

To Gwen, Lady Edmonstone, my generous mother-in-law, who gave me my first word processor, which enabled me to write quickly and maintain my publisher's deadlines.

To the many companies and other organisations that provided me with the facilities and access from which to write up the action research studies contained in the text.

To the many fellow authors who granted me permission to publish their copyright material, often at no charge.

Part 1
Studying management

Chapter 1

The nature and process of management

Overview

This chapter identifies the evolution of management thought and the assumptions that underlie this process. It includes a review of the salient ideas of such figures as Fayol (1916), Mayo (1933), Gullick (1939), Drucker (1954), Reddin (1968, 1971), Belbin (1981), Mintzberg (1973), Glueck (1976), Lucey (1981) and Davies (1974).

The chapter highlights the action verbs of management and the variety of management roles and techniques; suggests the need for skills in objective-setting and teamwork; and emphasises the concept of leadership.

Learning objectives

The student should be able to recognise the different approaches to management and should have some idea of the schools of thought from which they were developed. The basic understanding of the nature and process of management gained from this chapter should provide a useful framework for further study.

A common technique used in this book is to invite participation, even in the early stages of learning. This is a means of demonstrating that management is not a set of theories derived from some ivory tower, but an evolving set of principles recognised in the practice of doing ordinary things in an exceptionally effective way.

Definitions of the process of management

A simple exercise (Exercise 1.1, p. 12) starts the enquiry going by getting the individual or group to identify the *management components* of some twelve selected position titles, to which students can readily relate. When the resulting components are put together they reveal the richness and complexity of the management process. Data from this exercise are used to develop a simple appreciation of some of the leading writers of management.

A final, short exercise, Exercise 1.2, p. 13, examines two management heresies couched in anti-management terms. The reader or group is invited to confront these heresies. This brings out the influence of values and culture on the application of management in any environment — something which makes the search for good practice even harder.

Subjective approach

Identify the management role of each of the following and the management process through which they operate.

1. The economist.
2. The local government official.
3. The data processing manager.
4. The chief executive.
5. The production manager.
6. The marketing manager.
7. The accountant.
8. The management consultant.
9. The amateur gardener.
10. The priest.
11. The engineer.
12. The personnel officer.

Note: This may be used as the basis of a group exercise, in which each student may be asked to define one of the management roles.

Some typical responses

The economist
This person is a professional, who advises organisations or governments on better ways to use scarce resources. The management method is to gather data, interpret and analyse them according to good professional practice, and offer reports of appreciation and recommendation.

Comment: We notice that the economist is an adviser and that generally there is an assumption about an objective function, that of profit-maximisation, derived from the notion of using scarce resources.

The local government official
This person is a bureaucrat. The dominant influence in what is done and how it is done is laid down by statute, bye-law, committee minute or resolution. Whenever any problem arises the emphasis is on selecting and interpreting the right rule or referring the issue

to a higher competent authority for a ruling. The emphasis is on consistently implementing policy, whose rationale has been decided elsewhere, and if the rules have an unfortunate effect on others, then that is tough luck. If the matter at issue relates to money, then it is most important to operate within the framework of the official budget.

Comment: Notice the absence of the profit motive and the predominance of rules, controls, budgets and higher levels of authority. Unfortunately, most job positions, even in the private sector, and particularly in large organisations, have a bureaucratic component to ensure a standardisation of practice. However, this can give rise to some very bad practice. For example, one month before the end of the financial year, there may be money left unspent in the budget which cannot be carried forward to the next accounting year, resulting in wasteful spending sprees.

The data processing manager

This executive is a staff manager, responsible for providing a service to the other members of the management team. The central focus of this service is the provision of information systems to assist other managers in their decision-making and help them monitor and control the business. There is also responsibility for managing a high-technology department and coordinating the work of many different specialists.

Comment: Note the reference to 'staff' manager. This is in contrast to a 'line' manager, who is responsible for the core work of the organisation and its profit — generally manufacturing and marketing.

Note, too, the central objective function is provision of management systems for other managers, which is the unique factor in this position. The running of a department is a secondary role, but one common to many other managers.

The chief executive

The chief executive's role is to lead the board and develop and implement objectives and policies in line with the expectations of the stakeholders in the business. The stakeholders consist of shareholders, banks, other managers, employees at different levels, customers, suppliers and government. The overall planning and monitoring function is carried out through an executive team and the long-term aim is one of profit-maximisation.

Comment: Note the selectivity of the functions of the chief executive. The work is done through others and concentrates on planning and policy. There is a wide-ranging responsibility to many stakeholders, though in the United Kingdom the legal responsibility to shareholders is the predominant one.

The production manager

This executive is a line manager, responsible for the core activity of the business, and has major objectives relating to profit, volume, quality and meeting delivery dates. The operation has to be scheduled taking account of scarce resources and is generally directed through a chain of command, and with the aid of specialists from staff departments. Lateral links, particularly with marketing, are particularly important to ensure that the 'right' products are made.

Comment: There is a tendency to think of high volumes and efficient production at the expense of the human element. Insufficient emphasis is often placed on contact with marketing. But if the wrong products are made the result is dissatisfied customers and uneconomic inventory levels.

The marketing manager

This executive is a line manager responsible for a core activity in the business — profit, volume sales, market research, forecasting and product development. There is the need to coordinate many different specialists and an organisation which is often dispersed over a wide geographic area.

The accountant

The accountant is a staff member of the executive team. Accountancy covers three broad roles: (1) there is a book-keeping—policing role, to ensure that financial controls and standards are in place; (2) management accountants use special techniques to focus financial advice for management decisions and tax problems; (3) there is responsibility for the cash flow and financial resources of the organisation.

Comment: Commonly the book-keeping—policing role is the one most emphasised and this often gives rise to tensions at branch level in an organisation. Staff may look upon the local accountant as the head office 'spy' rather than as a staff member willing to provide a service on request.

The management consultant

This is a specialist manager, who might operate as an internal or external consultant. Selection and briefing is done on the basis of the consultant's expertise and he or she will then activate a problem-solving methodology. From an analysis of the points of concern that brought about the consultancy assignment, there will follow an investigation to appraise the situation and make a specification of the real problems. These problems are generally defined as deviations from good practice and the consultant through expertise knows what is good practice. From this specification data are reviewed with the client and alternative courses of action are explored, giving rise to conclusions and recommendations for implementation.

Comment: The crucial factor is the problem-solving methodology and the technique for developing empathy with the client. The consultant must facilitate the understanding of bad practice and its causes, without allowing the client to lose face in the process.

An internal consultant is often unable to take a fresh look at the problem situation as he or she will probably have been institutionalised by current practice. It can be difficult for an internal consultant to 'rock the boat'.

An external consultant is not at this disadvantage and will more easily recognise bad practice. He or she will bring to bear a wide experience of practice from many other organisations and will report to the client at a senior level. However, it is possible to misjudge some key situational considerations in the client organisation, which can then render the conclusions impossible to implement. Nearly all managers at some time are called upon to play the role of internal consultant and will need to have skills in the methodology of problem-solving.

The amateur gardener

The amateur gardener has limited space and time resources. He or she has a desire to create colourful groups of plants and shrubs and to grow vegetables successfully. This activity provides pleasure for both the gardener and his or her family.

Comment: Notice the absence of the profit motive here. The aim might well be to give the gardener exercise, but there is still a need to be productive and to plan ahead. Feeding, digging, sowing, weeding, disease prevention, harvesting and pruning are probably the main activities, but if the scheduling of these is misjudged then much productivity and pleasure will be lost!

The priest

This person is the leader of a local unit, a parish, and his overall objective is to bring care and spiritual sustenance to the parishioners. At a local level such parishioners generally have a choice and so they are 'voluntary' members of the 'flock'. Much of the management structure locally is overseen by the priest who exercises a persuasive leadership, but funds still have to be raised, events organised and buildings maintained, all of which requires considerable management gifts and careful handling of volunteers. However, the priest also relates to his denominational masters, and when dealing with these there are precise rules which he must follow very closely or face the threat of being defrocked. Before becoming a priest he undertakes a long professional training.

Comment: We do not normally associate management with this role but on analysis we see a complex managerial environment with a great need for flexibility. In fact, the priest seems to work simultaneously within two different organisational structures — the flexible, locally-based, voluntary one and the more rigid, bureaucratic, denominational one.

The engineer

The prime driving force of the engineer is to develop satisfying and elegant design. A secondary aim may be to increase automation in design and remove the need for human intervention in the process. Complication in design may be an end in itself, as this will ensure the continued need for engineers.

Comment: Notice the lack of a prime profit objective. Cost is probably regarded as a tiresome constraint. Notice too the prevalence of complication in design as a means of furthering the influence of the engineer and the love of automation at the expense of providing a rewarding occupation for the operator.

The personnel officer

The personnel officer concentrates on recruitment, selection, training and industrial relations. He or she is concerned about morale and good communications throughout the organisation. A major asset of any organisation is its people, and although they do not have a formal place in the company balance sheet, the health of the company may reflect the continued quality of its people and its ability to retain them in a competitive employment market.

Comment: Notice how the personnel officer is almost the opposite of the engineer. The one relates strongly to people and qualitative measurements, and hardly at all with things; the other is mainly interested in things and quantitative measurements, and only indirectly interested in people.

Classical approach

Author's note: The concepts of this chapter are examined more fully in chapter 18. This chapter is only intended to offer the reader an overview.

The classical approach is so called because it connotes a traditional wisdom, particularly that perceived in the early twentieth century. 'Classical' seems to evoke the idea of age, but as management is a newly accepted academic discipline, we only need to go back to the beginning of the twentieth century.

Henri Fayol

Henri Fayol (1916) is a recognised authority of this approach. He was the head of a large French industrial and mining group and was considered to be very successful in his field. He believed that he could declare some universal principles of management from a synthesis of his own experiences. He established fourteen principles of management and six verbs of the management process: command, control, coordinate, forecast, plan, organise.

These verbs suggest much activity by the manager himself through a defined structure, which was assumed to be hierarchical. Everyone would know their position and defer to higher levels of authority. The verbs also imply that management is always right and can instruct downwards through the organisation, without needing to be over-concerned about communication being fed back up through the structure. At that time there was little expectation of the junior manager being involved in important decision-making. Senior managers were the educated class and did not expect or value advice from below. There did not seem to be a place for staff specialists. If more labour were required then the foreman of the line would probably hire them; personnel departments did not exist and selection techniques were crude in the extreme.

However, many readers may still recognise in Fayol's verbs a picture of the bureaucrat, and his emphasis on *planning*, *control* and *forecasting* is still appreciated, although many of the techniques for doing these things have since developed considerably. Fayol did not give any serious recognition to the human dimension of management — communication, training or motivation. It seemed as though labour was just another factor of production!

Fayol's verbs were extended by Gullick (1939, 1965) to: plan, organise, staff, control, report, budget.

Staffing was a full recognition of the importance of the personnel department and of techniques for selection, training and management development. *Budgeting* gave a proper recognition to the newer techniques of the management accountant and the arrival of professional accountants in the management team. Much of the *controlling* already recognised was now assisted by special techniques and accounting systems. *Reporting* was a recognition of the arrival of staff members who did consultancy work, often work study to improve productivity on the shop floor, or organisation and methods which were intended to define clerical systems and enable a regular flow of reports to management. The emphasis had moved away from the intuition and wisdom of the chief executive. In its place came the credible idea of executives working in a team and staff specialists being valued for their expertise and contribution.

Human relations approach

Disenchantment was setting in during the 1920s with the development of assembly-lines and large industrial units, and unrest manifested itself in increasingly frequent strikes and absenteeism. Some observers hypothesised that the apparent alienation between management and labour was caused by a hostile working environment and an over-specialisation of jobs. There was a need for a concept which could do justice to the human element and human spirit as part of the management process, thus supplanting the view that labour was just another factor of production.

Elton Mayo

Elton Mayo was a respected researcher in the field of social science. His studies of the Hawthorn Electric Company were published in 1933. He wrote: 'Management is the art of unifying economic man with social man to harness his unique ability to grow when his motivational needs are satisfied.'

The importance of the social environment was shown in one experiment where initial research results appeared to defy current wisdom. The experiment set out to study the connection between working conditions and productivity for a group of workers. As the work conditions were improved in stages, productivity went up. Then the experiment was put into reverse and the quality of the working conditions reduced, but productivity continued to rise. Later a debriefing questionnaire revealed that the group felt important with so many senior university people watching them and so much attention from senior management, who had previously not singled them out for special treatment.

Many researchers followed the path opened up by Mayo to define and develop a theory of motivation and gain a better understanding of how to encourage effective work in groups. At last there was an appreciation of the inhumanity of an 'over-engineered' assembly-line environment. People were demanding occupations which were rewarding, and pay, although important, was no longer assumed to be the predominant motivator at work — people would live to work rather than work to live.

Peter Drucker

Peter Drucker extended this approach: 'Management is the art of getting the right results through other people.' He defined eight result areas: profitability, productivity, physical assets and return on financial resources, worker performance and attitude, innovation, manager performance and attitude, market standing, social responsibility.

Drucker kept the *people* aspect at the very centre of the management process, but he introduced a new and novel idea — that there were multiple objectives in management. These should be reviewed regularly and comprehensively or the organisation would ossify, deteriorate and die.

He was particularly interested in the need to reconcile a range of internal and external influences and find a mechanism for balancing these conflicting pressures. Conventional wisdom was that the financial shareholder was the predominant influence. Drucker suggested that the major influence for a healthy business was the customer. If there is no continuity of custom there is no continuity of business. This is now referred to as the marketing concept.

Looking inside the business, Drucker saw that its strength was dependent on the sustained quality of its people. Management was a special group whose skills needed nurturing, and other employees needed training and development too. If they could visualise a relevant set of objectives for an organisational level higher than their own, they could suggest to management a much wider framework for their own contribution than if they waited to be told what to do by traditional instructional methods. Drucker called this novel approach 'managing by objectives', but later writers have emphasised the importance of managing through a 'framework of expectancy' to promote group work and to reconcile individual ambition with the legitimate objectives of the organisation. This approach also highlighted the importance of delegation.

Bill Reddin

Bill Reddin extended Drucker's ideas, highlighting: innovation, planning, systems, superior/subordinate relationship, organising and controlling. The central feature of his views was the notion of leadership style.

Reddin was much influenced by Drucker's concept of managing by objectives, but as a behavioural scientist he was acutely aware of how very difficult this style of management had been to implement. To Reddin there were three major difficulties with MbO.

Firstly, there was a need to emphasise innovation in objective-setting (reinforcing what Drucker had already pointed out).

Secondly, there was a need to provide a better environment for the objective-setting exchanges to take place. This environment he defined as the superior/subordinate relationship. He developed a framework of leadership style definitions, and with these offered a language from which more informed exchanges could take place during objective-setting sessions and the sessions that followed, i.e. the sessions monitoring progress and performance. With these concepts it was much easier to emphasise the participative role of the junior manager and the contribution both managers expect. This was to overcome a common abuse of MbO — its ritualisation or use as a manipulative, authoritarian device. The main focus of Reddin's leadership style models was to develop in the manager 'style flexibility' and 'situation sensitivity'. These were the two skills necessary to manage change successfully.

Thirdly, Reddin highlighted the fact that management was increasingly making use of contributions from new technology. That is summarised in the one word 'systems'.

Computers, however, were not Reddin's forte and it is necessary to seek out other authors for detailed analysis.

Systems approach

This approach stems from the late 1950s and began to grow in its importance once a serious attempt was made to convert commercial procedures by defining them in terms of a very detailed set of rules which a computer can execute. The main authorities are Simon (1957), Davies, (1974) and Lucey (1981). The ideas that summarise the notion of 'systems' in the context of the process of management are summed up in the following paragraph.

Management is the art of getting relevant and timely information to decision-makers to improve the quality and effectiveness of their decision-making. The organisation is perceived as a set of systems and sub-systems interacting with one another and the environment. Relationships, boundaries, decision-making points all require analysis and clarification. From the systems approach Management Information Systems (MIS) are developed.

In the 1980s people first started suggesting that we were entering a post-industrial society, an 'information society', in which electronic communications and intelligence stored in chips and systems would profoundly influence the way managers and others would do their jobs.

Role approach

Henry Mintzberg

In 1973 Henry Mintzberg published research findings from a set of diary studies. These were aimed at chief executives, and initially the purpose was to confirm that managers did indeed spend their time in the type of verb and process activities envisaged by writers such as Fayol.

Mintzberg's findings profoundly challenged current beliefs about the process of management. He found that management — particularly senior management — was a most unstructured activity, with many breaks in continuity and a huge number of informal contacts and decisions being made in a typical day. However, he was able to define the ten key roles of a chief executive as: figurehead, leader, liaison, monitor, disseminator, entrepreneur, spokesperson, disturbance-handler, resource allocator and negotiator.

This was to be exceptionally useful for defining the needs and qualities of executive teams, in team selection and team development. More ambitiously, the concept could be used for executive development and succession training, where it was recognised that particular skills were important for expected future management positions or task assignments. Mintzberg's ideas on management or leadership roles appeared to complement Reddin's concepts of leadership styles.

R.M. Belbin

Belbin's research (1981) focused on project work. He suggested that much executive work in the exciting areas of product innovation and the introduction of new technology was often done within the environment of a multidisciplinary project team, and the secret of success was to have a balanced team competent to deal with all stages of the project. Belbin identified eight distinct but useful roles for people to adopt in successful project teams. They were: company worker, chairman, shaper, plant, resource investigator, monitor evaluator, teamworker, completer-finisher. Belbin pointed out that for success, completer-finisher team types are needed, as well as gifted boffins. Indeed, Belbin found that teams overloaded with too many clever people were not effective. They tended to give rise to personality clashes and unresolved conflicts.

Summary

From the opening section of this chapter, which involved defining the management components of twelve positions, it became obvious that management is indeed a complicated process though the layman can still, without difficulty, identify components of that process.

The literature shows that during the twentieth century the concepts of management have evolved from simplistic roots to sophisticated attempts to integrate the various approaches. Each new generation of writers on management develops more refined and sophisticated approaches to understanding the management process.

Exercise 1.1
The process of management

This exercise offers a structured attempt at rationalising the process of management. Develop the following framework:

1. Management is a set of action verbs and if these are mastered by the manager, then he or she will be able to grow in competence. What are these verbs?
2. Management is an integration of the disciplines of separate specialists and each specialist exercises a functional role and expertise. What are the relevant functions (or departments) within a manufacturing company?
3. Management attempts at integration of other established academic disciplines. What are they?
4. Management is a study of how to develop useful skills, roles and techniques. What are they?

For a discussion of possible feedback, see Appendix 1, p. 494.

Exercise 1.2
Two heresies

Consider the following two quotations and develop counter-arguments. Could the statements be partially true in certain environments? If so, describe these environments.

Heresy 1

Sir John Toothill, Chief Executive, Ferranti, 1974: 'Management development is a waste of time. Let managers be self-selecting.'

Heresy 2

Alistair Mant, *The Rise and Fall of the British Manager* (1977): 'The prime role of business is business at the sharp end. Management is incidental to this process; if emphasised it creates barriers, class systems and privileges, "us and them" attitudes with a vengeance.'

For a discussion of possible feedback, see Appendix 1, p. 495.

References

Belbin, R.M. (1981), *Management Teams — Why they Succeed or Fail*, Heinemann.

Davis, G.B. (1974), *Management Information Systems — Conceptual foundations, structure and development*, McGraw-Hill.

Drucker, P. (1954), *The Practice of Management*, Harper.

Fayol, H. (1916), *General and Industrial Management*, translated from the French by C. Storrs, Pitman and Sons, 1949.

Glueck, W.F. (1976), *Business Policy*, McGraw-Hill.

Gullick, L. (1965), 'Management is a science', *Academy of Management Journal*, vol. 8, no. 1, pp. 7–13, from findings of 1939.

Lucey, T. (1981), *Management Information Systems*, Smiths.

Mant, A. (1977), *The Rise and Fall of the British Manager*, Macmillan.

Mayo, E. (1933), *The Human Problems of an Industrial Civilisation*, Macmillan.

Mintzberg, H. (1973), *The Nature of Managerial Work*, Harper & Row.

Reddin, W.J. (1968), *Effective Management*, McGraw-Hill.

Reddin, W.J. (1971), *Effective MbO*, BIM.

Simon, H.A. (1957), *Administrative Behaviour*, Collier-Macmillan.

Further reading

Murdick, R.G., Ross, J.E. and Claggett, J.R. (1984), *Information Systems for Modern Management*, Prentice Hall.

Chapter 2

Case studies for management

Overview and definition of case studies

Chapter 1 looked at definitions of the boundaries and processes of management. Historically, management was conceived as an art and skill developed through experience and relying to a large extent on innate abilities. The contemporary view is that management is a profession with an underpinning theoretical framework, which is rapidly evolving as a legitimate field of academic study. This suggests that by studying management the student may gain the appropriate skills faster than would be possible by relying solely on experience.

Chapter 1 also showed that managers need to be effective in a variety of different roles. No one could expect real-life experience in more than just a few of these, but to be effective in any one role it will probably be necessary to communicate and cooperate with managers in other roles. The study of synthetic situations allows this deeper understanding about roles and attitudes to emerge. Management case studies are a useful vehicle for analysing such hypothetical situations and gaining experience of good and bad practice.

The management case study may take a variety of forms. Some situations can be illustrated via film or video, which makes it possible to portray the attitudes of the characters as well as the dilemmas which they face. More commonly, a case is presented in written form. This has the advantage of flexibility and adaptability.

The written case study may contain straightforward descriptions of actions and problems which require analysis, and it may also be presented as a set of correspondence files from a company's executives, together with reports and statistics. The instructor may introduce the case in an unstructured manner, leaving the student to define problems and suggest solutions, or he or she may draw attention to particular questions of interest. He or she may also introduce a written case as a simulated video script, allocating reading parts of characters to individuals and discussing issues raised in particular speeches.

Alternatively, the instructor may simply offer a situation definition and role specifications and get the group to analyse problems from within the assigned roles. This helps to illustrate decision-making and leadership skills.

Lastly, the instructor may assign a case study as a group project for written analysis and oral presentation after a significant amount of group work, over perhaps a fortnight. This will enable the more complex problems of multidisciplinary work to be accomplished.

Learning objectives

The aim of this chapter is to offer the reader some insights into the place and relevance of management case studies in the study of management practice. In many management courses case studies form a significant proportion of the teaching programme, allowing both for individual work and work in teams. Some courses, too, provide case studies as an integral part of the assessment, so skills in case analysis are a precondition for passing the course.

Case studies require an approach different from that used in other forms of learning and can be frustrating for the novice. The object of this chapter is to show how the case study experience may be a rewarding one, both for the student and for those who are designing and using case studies for teaching purposes.

From chapter 3 onwards, case studies are offered for analysis. The methods of analysis required are specified alongside the case brief. The tasks assigned are then discussed in order to demonstrate the methodologies used.

Case study approaches

Harvard method

Under the traditional Harvard method the business case was the predominant method of instruction. At each session a particular student would be asked to lead the analysis of the case and would be required to defend his or her diagnosis and recommendations. As no one knew when they would be required to lead, this put pressure on students to assimilate large quantities of case material, causing some information overload for the students.

This early approach still assumed that management skills were based on experience alone. Later, the management theorists developed cases to illustrate specific aspects of management theory. These were used to support the teaching, rather than as the predominant learning method.

Harvard developed an international reputation for the quality of its Business School, and many of the case studies used there were published in texts or made available to teachers of business management through 'Case Clearing Houses'. These offered the original case study material, generally based on real action research or consultancy, supplemented with notes for an instructor.

Seven-step method

In the United Kingdom a major contribution to the case study approach was developed by Geoff Easton in *Learning from Case Studies* (1982). Easton specialised in marketing. His approach may be called the problem-solving approach and this is summarised in *seven steps*. These are as follows:

1. Understanding the situation.
2. Diagnosing the problems.
3. Creating alternative solutions.
4. Predicting outcomes.
5. Choosing among alternatives.
6. Rounding out the analysis.
7. Communicating the results.

The chapters illustrating choosing among alternatives, and the well-developed quantitative analyses which support this phase, are especially valuable. However, it is a pity that Easton's work is mainly directed at the specialist and functional area of marketing, rather than at general issues of business policy and management.

Simple business picture method

In this book a simpler but more wide-ranging approach is taken. The central idea is that business situations are a composite of elements requiring interpretation, which together form business pictures. These pictures require analysis and from such analysis there is the need for a response. The method is then reduced to three phases of case analysis:

1. Interpretation,
2. Analysis,
3. Response.

In this text there is an emphasis on the central role of management processes and systems and the assertion of norms of good practice. The business pictures thus result from examining situations against such norms of good practice, in order to highlight the bad practice for treatment. As the text progresses into further topics and techniques of management they all offer some form of 'good practice', and therefore it is possible to construct a richer form of business picture and response.

Case study methodology with business pictures

1. Read the text, underlining all key phrases of business significance in order to build up the elements of a business picture. Interpretation of all these elements will suggest a total picture for analysis.
2. Working as a small group, begin an analysis using several relevant analysis techniques to put the business pictures into relief.
3. Discuss and share in the outcomes of the analysis to suggest alternative courses

of action and the appropriate responses to perceived problems and opportunities. The management models should reveal variances. Most corrective action is effectively one of 'gap closing' these variances to fit the circumstances and environment of the organisation. This requires development of alternative courses of action, selection of a particular course, then implementation by adjusting structure to fit strategy and allocating the necessary resources. The core of the response should lie in compatibility with the good practice of the corporate planning process.

Relevant analysis techniques

Use of the following analysis techniques is gradually developed as students become more aware of the theory behind them.

Corporate appraisal (see chapter 3)

1. Look at external influences and analyse along the lines of the factors — *political, economic, social, technological*. Relate the analysis to your own industry, the industries of your suppliers and the industries of your key customers, as well as to the transport and other relevant support systems affecting your industry. Identify and analyse the key resources and systems of the firm.
2. Next develop a SWOT analysis. SWOT stands for: *s*trengths, *w*eaknesses, *o*pportunities, *t*hreats. Now apply this analysis to the key functional areas of the business: production, marketing, finance, management services, research and development, personnel.
3. Analyse the data through the theoretical management model of *long-range corporate planning*. Is there a corporate planning team and process in action? Are the winners and loses in terms of products and customers being analysed? Does the company know its growth direction and strategy? Is it supported by market research and forecasting systems?

Financial appraisal

The aim of financial appraisal (see chapter 4) is to analyse the financial state of the organisation. Firstly, analyse the financial structure. This determines who has the power in the organisation. Look at the legal structure of the company and the groupings of the major shareholders, particularly those who together control more than 30 per cent of the equity capital. Consider the options for financing further expansion should there be an attractive business opportunity.

Secondly, analyse financial performance and the cash-flow situation, using the norms of the financial performance ratios as a guide.

Thirdly, use the appropriate financial techniques such as budgeting, standard costing and contribution analysis to highlight segments of the business with financial strengths and weaknesses. Use discounted cash flow as a technique for appraising capital and business ventures.

Managing by objectives — MbO

The MbO model (see chapters 5 and 6) indicates how objectives are transmitted vertically and laterally and then used as a basis for feedback and the appraisal process, leading to management development and promotion on the basis of competence. MbO requires clarity of role, priority of objectives and a spirit of expectancy. Are there any mismatches with these norms? Common problems include a lack of coordination, untreated managerial incompetence and ritualising of the appraisal process.

Management information systems (MIS)

Are there any mismatches with the norms of good practice of MIS? Exception information should be directed to decision-makers by tracking variances with plans, policies and targets. The rules and policies written into the MIS should reflect the reality of the business and be congruent with the corporate planning process. (See chapters 12−17.)

Other management models

A case study often contains a variety of issues, some of which are difficult to put into perspective. It is essential to refer to what one would expect if good practice were applied to those issues which are crucial. (See chapters 1 and 18.)

Classical approach   Examine the structure of the organisation, particularly for compliance with the norms about span of control. Watch out for the tendency of an organisation to become a 'one-man band', lacking delegation and teamwork.

Identify the relevant quantitative techniques which are being used. Are they being used correctly? Are the fourteen principles outlined by Fayol (p. 363) being adopted?

Human relations approach   What is the employee relations climate like? Does management take account of motivation theory in selecting and deploying employees? Is there a separate management development programme for managers? Is this based on an analysis of the real needs of the employees? Is there evidence of management activating a 'consultative process' when taking decisions which affect employees or does management take major decisions unilaterally? Does management take account of relevant theory regarding the working of groups and embrace this to develop management talent?

Systems approach   If coordination seems to be a problem in the organisation, check for the development and use of the appropriate systems. The main systems to look for are those relating to: corporate planning (LRCP), the articulation and transmission of objectives (MbO); and quantitative feedback (MIS). Most organisations have fundamental weaknesses here and the recognition of that weakness is a major diagnostic tool. Systems theory helps to bring clarity to complex organisations through the rigorous analysis of boundaries and of the interrelationships between systems.

Comments on the business picture methodology

Within just a few hours the novice can acquire a remarkable fluency in this technique. The tutor will offer a rich mix of case situations to stimulate what is effectively a multidisciplinary analysis. The method enables a dynamic situation to be reviewed as a series of snapshots. Each time feedback is offered by the group it is compared with a 'good' solution, and the differences become the debating points from which real learning is internalised. This method gives group members the opportunity to speak about their analysis and findings, make a case and offer solutions.

This method develops confidence in the novice and is also fun. An initial major benefit accrues in the interpretation phase as events and problems are gradually put into perspective, provoking many questions: Is this good practice in industrial relations? Do the accounting ratios reveal a cash-flow problem? Is the product range healthy? If new products are vital, are the financial resources available to develop these new products? Is there a research and development group which is capable of developing a new product? Is the organisation structure appropriate for the current developments suggested by the chief executive?

This business picture analysis approach was adopted by the author with collaboration of a colleague, Dick Weaver, in the 1980s for two separate student groups. The first was a group of sixty students preparing for the Scottish Higher National Diploma in Business Studies. The pass rate for this segment of the course rose to over 95 per cent, far above the national average for this subject. The second group was for the final year of a degree course in risk management, validated by the Council for National Academic Awards. The external examiner reported very favourably on the final standard achieved in the analysis of business situations as a result of using this case method.

A major strength of the business picture methodology, and its execution in the three phases of interpretation, analysis and response, is its basic elasticity. As the group's management knowledge grows, so too is the case methodology enhanced. The methodology focuses naturally on the key systems of the business, corporate planning, managing by objectives, management information systems, financial analysis and some key elements taken from the behavioural sciences. Once a student has mastered the workings of those main systems, a very critical and penetrating view and analysis of business situations is possible!

Variations in timescales and impact on choice of case material

The major disadvantage of adopting the case study approach to learning management is the amount of time required to become sufficiently familiar with the business situation portrayed. The length of teaching sessions varies considerably. Most commonly sessions last an hour, but for subjects such as business policy there are some three-hour sessions, and with the possibility of residential study at a weekend, sessions can be as long as fifteen hours over three days. With the BA in Risk Management there are two fortnightly case study slots in the final year of this full-time course when all other teaching is suspended. This forms part of the assessment. For day-release students there are often discontinuities. This suggests that cases are used most efficiently when the whole analysis can be completed within a single session and the forgetting cycle can have no impact!

In theory, students should come to class well prepared to discuss a case previously issued; this was the Harvard approach. However, day-release students, who are practising managers, generally have limited opportunity to prepare before class. This again suggests that the whole analysis should be able to be completed within the single session. The implication is that case material needs to be very compact for learning efficiency and that there is some skill involved in the selection and making of case material. Tutors will always need to select material, with learning objectives uppermost in mind, to suit the length of the planned session. Many of the cases in this book can be completed within an hour, and none requires longer than three hours.

Getting the most out of cases

In this text cases are used to demonstrate the application of theory to real situations. They provide a vehicle for sharing in the analysis of business situations as a device for assessing management competence. The aim is that by developing skills to handle the hypothetical situations portrayed in cases, students will develop the skills needed for dealing with situations in real life. The case study approach will promote both writing and speaking skills and the experience of working fluently as a member of a management team. However, students will gain these advantages and skills only if full commitment is made to the material. It is helpful if the cases analysed are fully incorporated in students' subject notes and they should complete a short commentary on each case studied. This might cover the following points:

1. What was the curriculum aim of the case?
2. In what way was its objective achieved or not achieved?
3. What theory and methods were being exercised?
4. What learning did I achieve in methods of interpretation, analysis and response or in the application of the theory or technique of management?
5. What insights did I gain into the workings of the group of which I was a member during the analysis?
6. To what extent did I agree with the solutions of other groups and the tutor's interventions and suggestions?

References

Easton, G. (1982), *Learning from Case Studies*, Prentice Hall.

Part 2
Policy-making, planning and objective-setting

Chapter 3
The corporate planning process

Overview

This chapter is placed very early in the book because it will allow the reader quickly to grasp and cope with an analytical approach to business situations, bringing out the strengths, weaknesses, opportunities and threats. It will demonstrate the need to refer to specialist managers and specialist techniques, providing a framework for further study.

The core of this chapter is what is known as the Glueck model of the corporate planning process (1976), simplified into the three phases of *interpretation, analysis, response.*

This theoretical standpoint is the basis for a simple method of applied case analysis, suitable either for use in a class group or for the individual working through the exercises alone.

Three simple, one-page case situations are used to reveal the phases of interpretation, analysis and response. Students complete each phase in a group of three, and the tutor invites feedback in forms of business pictures.

Learning objectives

After working through this chapter the novice should be aware of the rudiments of *interpretation, analysis* and *response* and should have had some practice in applying this theory to simply stated corporate situations. This should lead to an awareness of priorities, choice and key result areas. The *key result areas* are of major significance to the structuring of the organisation and to the transmission of objectives, both vertically and laterally.

Chapter 4 develops a framework for a critical financial appraisal and analysis of a company. A later chapter, chapter 17, offers a criticism of Glueck (1976) and develops a more powerful set of profiles of good practice, known as the 'dynamic open systems model', drawing on the ideas and concepts of several leading authorities.

Long-range corporate planning

Definitions of corporate planning and strategic planning

The terms 'corporate planning' and 'strategic planning' are considered in this text as conveying the same central idea. Corporate planning is the process of planning for the corporation as a whole. In the absence of this capability a firm may be said to be reacting to its environment or responding to the entrepreneurial flair of its chief executive. Both of these alternatives have severe disadvantages.

Reaction to the environment may be ineffectual because the response is too late. To adopt a new technology, to seek a new merger partner and manage an acquisition, to direct a new product from laboratory to volume production, to set up a dealer network, to establish a management information system — these are all major objectives which will take several years to complete. Corporate planning offers a set of processes and disciplines which make it possible to live within time constraints and provide in-depth support for their successful management.

Reacting only to the entrepreneurial flair of the chief executive has other significant dangers. Firstly, there is the question of continuity and succession. What happens when he or she becomes ill, retires or becomes isolated from colleagues? When the firm has reached a position of size, complexity and maturity, will it respond better to leadership by an executive team or to one-person rule? The corporate planning process may be regarded as the prime vehicle by which the executive team may identify and evaluate the various options of policy and strategy and manage the implementation of those which are appropriate.

One of the first writers to draw academic attention to corporate planning was Igor Ansoff in his classic work *Business Strategy* (1965). He outlined a process of disciplined and comprehensive analysis, originally to determine the question of when a firm should begin diversifying its activities.

Prior to this it was thought that corporate planning concerned objective-setting (Drucker, 1954), or that it was synonymous with entrepreneurship. Entrepreneurship somehow defied a systematic analysis, though it would yield to the general guidance of economics. The weakness in this economics approach was that it lacked any conception of how a firm could organise itself to carry out the corporate planning process. The weakness of Drucker's early approach was that it was not sufficiently comprehensive to cover the whole of the management process, including implementation.

The board and the corporate planning team

The main board is always responsible for policy and the strategic decisions of a company. Its members are not involved in all the staff work which precedes most changes in corporate direction. They may well rely for advice on the board's functional executives or on special task groups set up for particular purposes, but they do need a staff group that can look regularly at the overall company position. Through this work the company should benefit from a wider range of options and a more confident assessment of viability of any new proposals.

When the corporate planning team is working well it is effectively giving the overall policy and strategy of the firm a critical audit — just as important as a financial audit!

Much thought needs to be given to how the corporate planning group is organised. There is often a tendency for the chief executive to see this group as a simple extension of his or her own immediate staff, but such a very close involvement with the chief executive would in fact take away much of the value and purpose of having such a group!

The corporate planning team should support the executive team as a whole. It should not be attached to the chief executive's office, as it may then act as a device for isolating the chief executive from line management.

A similar principle applies in cabinet government. If many influential advisers are attached to the prime minister's office this undermines the authority of the key ministers of state. In 1989 the British prime minister, Margaret Thatcher, was confronted with the resignation of her Chancellor, Nigel Lawson, over his irritation at the presence in her office of a key economic adviser, Sir Alan Walters.

A previous prime minister, Harold Wilson, was also much criticised for over-reliance on advisers at 10 Downing Street. The group of advisers was dubbed the 'kitchen cabinet', i.e. an unofficial cabinet which was not accountable to Parliament. A most prominent adviser of the kitchen cabinet was his private secretary Lady Falkender. She was the cause of very unhealthy tensions between Wilson and many of his senior cabinet ministers. Richard Crossman revealed this friction in his *The Diaries of a Cabinet Minister* (1979).

In the business organisation a corporate planning staff group needs multidisciplinary talents. The exact nature and mix will depend on the way in which the corporate planning process is activated and on the particular nature of the assignments given to this group by the main board.

Policy and strategy

Before examining a long-range corporate planning model it is necessary to explain the terms 'policy' and 'strategy'. Policy refers to the overall objectives of a business which reflect its culture and values. A strategy is normally regarded as a complex package of actions and decisions to achieve a particular objective. Whereas a policy is a guide to action, the strategy is the action itself.

Strategic decisions are normally important decisions, taken at the summit of the business, which have an element of irreversibility. For example, the decision of Honeywell in 1960 to enter the computer market was a strategic decision to adopt a new technology. It took Honeywell some ten years to achieve a profit in this new venture. The decision of Ferranti in 1988 to take over a US company in the defence industry to widen its international operation was also a strategic decision. (This decision gave rise to complications in 1989 when the US operation reported losses which threatened the viability of Ferranti.) The strategic decision is likely to affect fundamentally the structure and culture of a business, its portfolio of products and markets and its expertise in particular technologies.

Glueck's model of corporate planning

Figure 3.1 shows Glueck's model of the corporate planning process, which represents a logical, stage-by-stage approach. In its simplest form it covers the verbs *appraisal, choice, implementation, evaluation.* Another way of looking at this sequence is to describe the process as that of *interpretation, analysis, response.* In order to make a company stronger and more capable of maintaining growth, it is necessary to identify 'winners and losers' in the company portfolio of products and markets. With an effective response the winners should be consolidated and improved and the losers should be rationalised or discontinued, releasing resources to improve the winners!

The starting point in Glueck's analysis is a critical review of the strategic planning elements. These are the existing enterprise objectives and the existing enterprise strategies. Objectives connote direction; strategy comprises the set of coordinated responses for getting there.

Corporate appraisal

The next stage is corporate appraisal. Firstly, an analysis is made to identify some key influences of the external environment. The environment has the following four dimensions:

1. Political,
2. Economic,
3. Social,
4. Technological.

These are known as the PEST factors. In the turbulent environment of the 1980s change was expected in each dimension. For instance, *political* decisions radically affected UK trade with Middle Eastern countries, such as Libya.

In the United Kingdom legislation affects the structure of certain industries through privatisation, local authority spending and regulations, which may fundamentally affect trading conditions. Many of these influences are not sudden events, but are discernible in advance through interpreting party manifestos and the provisions outlined in the Queen's Speech at the opening of each new session of Parliament.

Economic factors of significance include interest rates, tariffs, the cost of energy, the boom/slump conditions of particular industries, the cost of labour and the availability of investment grants.

Social factors relate to the changing expectations of people at work; for example, the desire for job satisfaction, reduced hours or the changing perceptions of career opportunities for women and the changing tastes of consumers. This has a major implication for marketing policy and product design.

Technology affects the firm, its industry and the industries of suppliers and customers.

The corporate planning process for developing a business policy

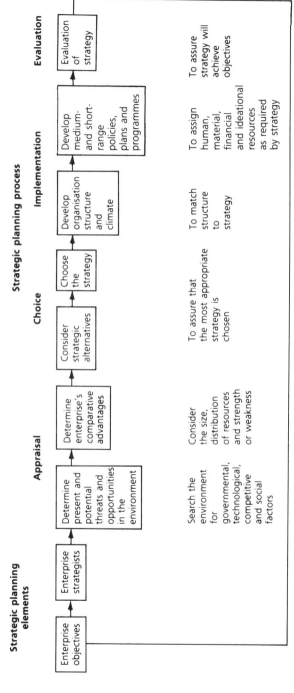

Figure 3.1 *Glueck's model*
(Source: Glueck (1976), p. 36. Reprinted with permission of McGraw-Hill)

Technological change can have fundamental effects, some of which are very difficult to predict without an effective industrial intelligence organisation and appropriate channels through which this information may be brought to the notice of the planners. The research and development group should offer an appreciation of the technology of their own industry; the purchasing group should offer an appreciation of the technology of their suppliers; marketing should offer intelligence and market research about the technology of customers and their changing tastes and needs. Such intelligence needs interpretation by the corporate planning staff group to weigh up the significance of such change. If this intelligence is gathered and interpreted regularly, the full impact of technological change should not be unexpected. The pace of technological change is mitigated by high-quality intelligence, and it is well within the power of the company to equip itself to get that intelligence.

However, the ability of the firm to gather, interpret and pass on such intelligence depends crucially on the effectiveness of *information technology*-based systems and the company communications network.

Information technology may have other fundamental influences on the products and services developed and delivered by the firm. For instance, the inspired use of information technology transformed Reuters from a news-gathering agency into one of the major providers of real-time information for dealers in commodities. The company capitalisation rose from £1 million in 1970 to £100 million in 1985 as a result of this development.

As part of the corporate appraisal phase of Glueck's model it is important to consider the enterprise's comparative advantages *vis-à-vis* competing organisations taking account of the distribution of resources. This part of the analysis is called a SWOT analysis (see p. 37). This analysis relates to the company as a whole but places particular emphasis on those threats directed at its customer or supplier base, and on threats to its financial independence through takeover.

Choice of strategy

This leads to the analysis of the next stage — the choice of a new strategy following a review of a number of possible alternative courses of action. Having adopted a new strategy the implementation process begins and plans are developed throughout the organisation to achieve the desired results. A key part of this process involves matching the organisation's structure to the new strategy and redeploying financial, managerial and material resources to ensure the viability of the implementation process.

An excellent example of this process of bringing together strategy and structure is shown in IBM's decision to enter the personal computer market. Traditionally, IBM's business was with mainframe computers and these were sold by a sales team. However, the value of a personal computer is much lower than a mainframe, and IBM decided that the sales team approach was not cost-effective in this new market. They decided to sell instead through distributors and agents. However, they realised that customers would be concerned about after-sales service when the product was as sophisticated as a computer. The IBM response was to set up an enquiry/response service located in their plants and area offices, thus retaining direct contact with customers for vital after-sales service and advice. Once the new business strategy had been decided, the organisation structure was modelled to fit precisely. Other firms might have been tempted to let the status quo prevail and allow the mainframe sales forces extend their roles — a very expensive solution.

Evaluation

Finally, there is the need to evaluate the strategy to establish whether predicted outcomes and actual outcomes are in line, taking into account any other changes which have taken place in the environment.

The cycle is then repeated regularly covering all these strategic planning phases. The strategic planning process should become integrated within the organisation's management culture.

Why a company might adopt a corporate planning approach

A company might adopt a corporate planning approach for the following reasons:

1. The adoption of an LRCP approach gives a company a regular and systematic way of taking stock of its strategic position and renewing this in the light of the changing environment.
2. Techniques of corporate planning help companies anticipate trouble in time to take corrective action.
3. Techniques of corporate planning help to identify winners and losers both in the product catalogue and customer base, and to detect when a change in strategy is called for.
4. Evaluative techniques of corporate planning help assist in the screening process of possible strategic changes to improve their prospects of viability.
5. The corporate planning approach encourages teamwork in groups working for the board, with emphasis on forecasting.
6. With careful implementation the corporate planning staff group should be able to clarify issues for the board without a functional bias. The group should assist the board in achieving unity in expressing corporate policy.
7. A credible output from the corporate planning process leads to a solid definition of *key result areas* for transmission via the managing by objectives approach to integrate activity throughout the business.

Glossary of corporate planning terms

This section provides brief definitions and explanations of some of the main terms used in corporate planning.

Consultative processes

Corporate planning does not take place in a vacuum. Line and staff management groups need to work together to develop plans through the exercise of good teamwork. Consultative processes facilitate successful teamwork. The corporate planning staff may be expected to work for a board of directors. This staff group, following the brief of the board, will propose a company plan for adoption or otherwise by that board, who must of course take managerial responsibility for its acceptability and implementation.

A large company, however, is likely to have divisions. Each division may be considered as a separate business entity. As such, each separate business will also have a corporate planning staff reporting to the divisional board. A dilemma often arises. When the overall corporate planning group meets, do they have the divisional director as representative or the divisional planning staff as representative? Consultative processes iron out the problems of etiquette to enable the headquarters to relate effectively to its constituent parts in the overall planning process.

Gap analysis

This technique was developed by John Argenti in the late 1960s. He recognised that inertia killed most attempts at setting up a corporate planning capability. His technique was to start with the crude assumption that the organisation would undertake no new developments for the next five years. He would then analyse the firm by projecting cash flow from existing product lines and product markets, taking account of expected return on capital already invested in the business. The result of this projection would almost inevitably show a decline in return on investment over the five-year period, owing to the normal effects of the product life-cycle. He would then quantify the gap as the difference between normal return on investment (ROI) and the projection. The gap would indicate the amount to be done as a minimum to maintain ROI. This would provide the input to the decision-making process relating to new products and new markets. The technique is a useful indicator to help management plan the timing of new product initiatives. It concentrates the minds of management on the features of the environment which affect profit in the most simplistic terms — prices, costs and competitiveness. (A fuller definition of ROI is given later in the glossary.)

Key result areas

This concept was developed by John Humble in 1972. There are specific areas within any business where meeting standards of effectiveness are vital for the continuity of the business. These may be quality standards, delivery standards, market share figures or absentee ratios. In a college environment key result areas will relate to monitoring the quality of courses. The key result areas are the vital standards within the organisation which should reflect the very excellence of that business, and these become self-evident on completion of the corporate planning process. They reflect the points in the organisation where improvements will have significant impact.

Objectives

Objectives are the most important single concept in the corporate planning process. Objectives relate to the aims and targets which give the organisation a sense of identity and direction. Drucker (1954) is well known for posing the fundamental question: 'What business are we in?' At the highest level, objectives are concerned with direction and identity. Hicks and Gullett (1981) label these objectives *visionary*. Other writers prefer the phrase *mission statement*. Hicks and Gullett relate the notion of objectives to a hierarchy of levels and time-scales in the framework 'visionary, attainable, immediate'.

Much literature on objectives is concerned with the approach of management by objectives. This concept stresses the need to quantify and qualify objectives to make them as specific as possible. An objective would be defined as 'a result to be achieved at a cost not to exceed £x by [date]'. This formula is widely used among managers at the operating level of a business. Drucker's view is that all managers should be prepared to set panoramic objectives which relate their realistic contribution to the next higher level of management. His approach is often called the bottom-up method, and he gives an appropriate emphasis to qualitative objectives which relate to management development, social responsibility and innovation.

Policy

Policy may be defined as a set of guidelines. These may be stated generally in the form: 'If X, then Y'. Policy permeates an organisation's culture. Those who are familiar with the culture will know what the policies are. Some firms write them down in elaborate policy statements, other firms express policy informally and orally. When plans are being made they need to be verified against current policy. If they go against current policy, consultative processes may need activating to ensure that the change is smooth and planned.

Modern management relies to a large extent on management systems. Systems in turn reflect management policy. If the system does not reflect management policy then it is perceived as being rigid and bureaucratic. Any designer of a system must start at the drawing board with questions relating to management policy. Without such self-discipline a system may reflect a technological concept at the expense of a business policy concept. Policies abound in computerised systems. Policy is also the mechanism through which a balance can be achieved in the reconciliation of conflicting objectives. The classic case is stock control, where there is a need to balance the advantages of high stocks in terms of economies of scale in production and good customer services, against the accountant's desire to minimise cost by keeping stocks low. Policy rules based on judgement and pragmatism will help to achieve this balance. At the highest level of an organisation policies will relate to growth and direction — whether growth by acquisition or growth from internally generated profits. Policies relate to the contingencies foreseen by management. Policies on growth direction in turn relate to the organisation's concept of its range of products and services.

Product life-cycle

Products and services have a natural development cycle, as follows:

1. Research,
2. A pilot run or mock-up,
3. Production runs,
4. Launch on the market,
5. Acceptance and development within the market-place,
6. Consolidation in the market, possibly with several phases of modification and improvement,
7. Product decline,
8. Product obsolescence.

As businesses want continuity, much of their business forecasting will relate to product life-cycles and appropriate funding so that research and development teams can produce new products at the right time in order to maintain adequate cash flows.

Product market strategy

This concept was developed by Drucker (1954) and Ansoff (1965) and simply states that any business is making a range of products but each product is related to specific markets. Profit analysis is determined by looking at distinct product markets and then managing these for growth. Ansoff uses the concept specifically to suggest the times when a policy of diversification is desirable. Ansoff's analysis begins by projecting the existing product market strategy some five years into the future to see the impact on profit. If projected profit is unsatisfactory he advocates an internal appraisal of the firm to suggest improvements in products and markets and reductions in costs. If the result of this exercise still does not give an adequate profit projection then he advocates an external appraisal to take the firm into new products with new technologies in new markets. He suggests that a firm should minimise risk by diversifying into related technology or related markets. When the firm diversifies through acquisition and merger these concepts of related technologies and related markets should ensure that such combinations have a synergistic effect. (Synergy is defined later in this glossary.)

Return on investment (ROI)

This term often causes confusion and there are many different and valid interpretations. However, for the purposes of this book the viewpoint is primarily that of the generalist when considering investment decisions for a company and overall performance figures for inter-company comparison. ROI is defined as the *net profit after tax* divided by the total sunk capital in the business, taken from the balance sheet. As a rule of thumb the expected figure is usually above the net rate from a building society, where there is virtually no risk. The greater the risk involved in the business, the greater ROI figure the investor would normally expect to compensate for the risk.

Strategy

A strategy is normally regarded as a complex package of actions and decisions required to achieve a particular objective. Strategy also connotes important, decisive moves which have an element of irreversibility in them. Whereas a policy is a guide to action, the strategy is the action itself.

Strategic decisions

Strategic decisions are normally those decisions taken at the summit of the business which have an element of irreversibility. The strategic decision is likely to affect fundamentally the structure, identity and culture of a business. Acquisitions or divestments are typically strategic decisions.

Strategic management

Strategic management is the art of making successful strategic decisions. Well-founded strategic decisions make good use of planning information, timing and the combination of resources. When strategic management is being practised, strategic decisions will tend to be synergistic.

Strategic plans

Strategic plans will be the mechanism for putting into effect strategic decisions. Strategic planning is also the development and revision of a five-year rolling plan. Strategic plans also reflect the contingencies of the business as defined by realistic business scenarios, and are articulated by senior management.

Strategic structure

Argenti (1968) is the leading author on this concept. The organisational structure is the means through which management gets people to work in harmony. A specific organisational pattern which fits the firm's strategic planning position is known as the strategic structure. In simplistic terms this relates to whether a firm adopts a centralised or decentralised structure and whether it adopts a line/staff, a project or even a matrix structure. Structure relates to the power base of various business functions such as research and development, marketing, management services. Organisation structure reflects the business culture, which may cause resistance to change or alternatively may facilitate it. The strategic structure should be the means through which management attempts to achieve corporate objectives using corporate plans. The topic of strategic structure is developed further in chapter 19.

Strategic management information systems

This concept has developed since the early 1970s and relates to the projection and testing of corporate plans. This topic is developed in chapters 12–17. Management information systems should not be just historical book-keeping systems. The modern idea of strategic MIS involves creating an operational model of the business in an attempt to get realistic future projections of the existing product market strategy. Most examples of strategic MIS are fashioned on realistic models of the production planning and control process then projected on a 3–5-year base. Once a particular corporate plan is adopted the model will take in data on costs and prices and engineering data on resource requirements and will be able to compute manpower, plant, profit profiles for the period in question. The strategic MIS can be used directly for monitoring an existing corporate plan and also for suggesting likely outcomes to possible alternative corporate plans. Strategic MIS can thus be the vehicle through which corporate planners 'brainstorm' various alternative strategies. The key strength of strategic MIS is its ability to evaluate and predict outcomes. There are several companies in Scotland which have achieved some success with strategic MIS. The Honeywell organisation in the 1970s computerised the production planning and control function and linked it with corporate planning. Scottish and Newcastle Breweries have modelled their production processes to enable management to see many different alternatives in their corporate planning process. The literature on strategic MIS is as yet rather weak, but chapters are appearing in the leading books on business policy and in the periodical literature the topic is very active. *Management Today* has a regular monthly column on strategic use of MIS and information technology equipment and techniques.

Synergy

This concept is used by Ansoff (1965) to describe a desirable phenomenon in organisations — that the whole may be greater than the sum of the parts. Mergers are often inspired by this principle. There are several possibilities for achieving synergy in business. It may be achieved through economies of scale with related technology and research and development capability or through marketing and distribution. An example taken from the early 1970s was the merger of Honeywell with the computer interests of GEC. Honeywell had a well-developed world-wide marketing organisation, but a weak product. GEC had a well-developed and well-engineered product range of computers, but weaknesses in marketing. After the merger the product line of both companies was rationalised; GEC's came out on top, but could then be much more widely marketed. The combination was generally welcomed as having synergy, a '2 + 2 = 5' effect.

The subject of synergy is, however, a controversial one. There have been examples of mergers with 'diseconomies of scale' and such difficulty in getting the necessary rationalisation implemented that the results were disappointing. Two weak firms coming together may well make a super 'lame duck'.

Tactics

Tactics are the subset of actions and plans which together make up a strategy. Tactics tend to be short-term in their orientation and are generally adopted at the operational level. Whereas there will be a strategy for winning a war, there will be tactics for winning a battle. The firm which indulges in a strategic acquisition policy will very possibly set up a tactical group who investigate potential acquisition victims and gather data for evaluation and analysis.

Summary

Good practice in corporate planning involves two groups working fluently together. The board of directors has responsibility for policy and strategy for the company as a whole. In general the board looks for growth and opportunity and is assisted in the 'leg-work' and planning of this process by a corporate planning staff group. This attempts at least once a year a critical audit of the company's products and markets, with a view to identifying winners and losers. The winners are singled out for consolidation and improvement and the losers for rationalisation or divestment, allowing the reallocation of resources to the winners. The corporate planning process involves the phases of interpretation, analysis, response. The techniques used are a PEST analysis of the environment and a SWOT analysis of the firm and its competitors/rivals. When a new corporate direction has been developed the structure and resources are refashioned so that they are compatible with the new strategy.

Case Study 3.1
Britcan

(Case used with permission of Scottish Vocational Education Council, Glasgow).

The financial year 1980/1 was not a good one for Britcan, Britain's major multinational can manufacturing company. As early as July 1980, Denis Smallwood, the Chairman and Chief Executive, was hinting at a 'disappointing' year. By the end of 1980 the message was much grimmer. An interim dividend was slashed by half and a 5 per cent drop in UK sales was announced along with redundancy and reorganisation costs of £9.4 million. Pre-tax profits tumbled from £34 million to £10.5 million, and even so were largely due to profits from overseas sales and earnings, particularly in South Africa which accounted for no less than 65 per cent of overseas trading profits. Less cheerful, however, was the almost total loss of the company's canning plant in the Italian earthquake zone. Taking everything into account, the company's shares slumped by 24p to 178p during the last week of November 1980. The Britcan board was clearly taken unawares by the slump in demand, particularly for drink cans, their crucial market.

'It was not till about August that we saw the extent to which the steel strike earlier in the year has disguised what was happening in the market-place,' said Smallwood. 'We didn't believe the beverage business would turn down as much as it did. Stocks were higher than anticipated, and then we had the worst summer on record.'

But Britcan were under other pressures. On top of poor demand, US giants such as Continental Can and National Can were bringing in products already canned, taking advantage of cheap American steel, aluminium and energy. In mid-1980 Continental Can opened a new plant at Wrexham making the new two-piece cans which, they claimed, cut raw material costs by 20 per cent compared with the old style three-piece cans used by Britcan.

'We agree that the new can represents the future of the industry,' said Smallwood. 'But unless we can persuade the unions to agree to continuous four-shift working, the capital investment in a new plant would not be justified.'

Task

Give an appraisal of Britcan, and suggest possible strategies for securing its future.

Britcan feedback

Interpretation

In the first reading every point in the case is scrutinised for its business significance and consequence. Each such point is a business element, and together they make up the business picture for further analysis.

1. Interim dividend slashed.
2. Drop of 5 per cent in UK sales.
3. Redundancy and reorganisation costs £9.4 million.
4. Pre-tax profits plunge from £34 million to £10.5 million.
5. South Africa is responsible for 65 per cent of overseas trading profit. Not stated what percentage of overall trade this represents.
6. Italian factory facility destroyed. Insurance claims?
7. Shares slump during one week from 201 to 178. City confidence low.

8. Home demand weak. Blame attached to wet summer and steel strike.
9. High stocks left. How should this be financed?
10. Competition — National Can and Continental Can. Cost reduction of 20 per cent through simpler product, the two-piece can. Continental Can also has the advantage of low aluminium cost and low energy cost.
11. Continental Can has new technology plant at Wrexham.
12. Britcan could join new technology given investment and four-shift working agreement with unions.

Analysis

PEST analysis

Political Trade with South Africa is an emotional and political issue. Institutional shareholders may by policy not be willing to invest in such a company. South Africa is a large market and there is no suggestion that Britcan has a manufacturing plant there. Sanctions could close this outlet. Are there pressures from Italy to re-establish a factory facility in Italy? If aid is forthcoming from the Italian government, then this would be useful. A new plant could take account of the new two-can technology.

International competition from Continental Can is severe. Could Britcan lobby for control of this subsidiary in the United Kingdom against unfair competition? Britcan could seek price concessions for electricity and aluminium.

Economic Britcan is currently at a disadvantage in the economy of scale stakes through not having continuous four-shift working. Major problems exist with falling profit and share price. New investment would be difficult to get. Current technology involves a 20 per cent higher cost than the new technology.

Social Labour practices in the United Kingdom seem to be at variance with those in other firms in this industry. Is the labour relations climate warm enough to offer chances of adopting four-shift continuous working in a year following reorganisation and redundancies? Why did the reorganisation not utilise the four-shift working idea? There are social implications too for the Italian workers, with their plant out of action.

Technological What new plant and labour skills would be required to operate a two-piece can technology? Would this technology be protected by patent? If it is, would it be possible to negotiate for a licence to produce? Would this be a good business proposition? Would a joint venture agreement be possible with Continental Can allowing Britcan to market a two-piece can in the rest of the world? Could Britcan's R & D develop a one-piece can and outdo everyone?

SWOT analysis

Strengths Britcan is a major United Kingdom multinational can manufacturer and assumed to have significant market share. It has established a manufacturing base in the United Kingdom and Italy. It has established markets in the United Kingdom and overseas. In a good year the group can make a profit of £34 million.

Weaknesses   These include a falling dividend and profit, increased competition from other multinationals and denial of access to cheap raw material or low-cost energy. The loss of the Italian manufacturing facility probably threatens overseas markets. There is a high demand on working capital to finance high stocks of cans not yet sold through weak demand. Britcan lacks any credible forecasting system and cannot mobilise the company into new technology ahead of the competition. Corporate planning is not much in evidence in the text.

Opportunities   Britcan could use the insurance money from Italy to invest in new technology, and while the labour force is weak from redundancies negotiate four-shift continuous working in new technology plant. It could seek a merger with Continental Can on favourable terms, although this might lead to problems with the Monopolies Commission. Another opportunity would be to liquidate Britcan interests in Italy and South Africa and use the money to develop a programme of diversification into areas of related markets or technologies.

Threats   The better trading position of Continental Can could give them a greater market share and possibly the opportunity to mount a takeover bid for Britcan. The attitude of the Monopolies Commission could pose a threat. The rapid collapse of Britcan's profit position would make it very difficult to raise further risk capital to finance the adoption of new technology.

Response

The main problems threatening Britcan seem to be those of the market and of technology. These may be very difficult to solve in the existing company structure, so some form of re-grouping or diversification may be necessary. Distasteful as it may seem a merger with one of the US competitors may be necessary if the new technology cannot be introduced in any other way. There is a need to take advantage of the principle of synergy in this very competitive market, and synergy is often related to similarities in technology and markets.

Many other improvements to the internal management of Britcan are possible. Forecasting and planning manifest some real weaknesses, but these are treatable given leadership and some goodwill. Following on from establishing these, and techniques such as managing by objectives and computerised management, information systems would offer much clearer feedback of information and transmission of objectives vertically and laterally throughout Britcan to the general benefit of the company.

Case Study 3.2
Sykes Industries

(Case used with permission of Scottish Vocational Education Council, Glasgow).

Geoff Sykes rose to commercial power in the classic mould of the self-made man, starting in a back-street workshop in the 1920s and building his business through the 1930s, until wartime expansion saw the real growth of Sykes Industries. But Sykes knew that post-war deceleration would pose problems. His plan — and it worked — was to diversify into demolition and construction. He bought a fleet of army surplus lorries to service his projects, and in the end transport became a major part of his business in its own right. In the years that followed, his transport operations were themselves split into a heavy transport hire service to industry and a trans-European fleet operating between England, Europe and the Middle East.

Meanwhile his original and wartime engineering enterprises continued to grow, mainly in defence-related projects, although more recently the company had opened a factory producing precision toys (Sykes himself was a fanatical railway modeller and an enthusiastic student of railway systems). By the late 1970s Sykes had control of a huge, diverse commercial enterprise: two construction companies, one specialising in civil engineering projects (motorways, bridges, etc.), the other in housing, office blocks, etc.: a transport hire company with depots in Stirling, Glasgow, Newcastle, Sheffield, London and Bristol; and a London-based firm operating trans-European heavy goods vehicles. Each of the construction companies and the transport companies were run by general managers. All the general managers met with Sykes periodically to discuss the overall running of Sykes Industries, but Sykes himself was effectively in total command and was fond of indulging his enthusiasm for railways by travelling the country, arriving unannounced at any of his factories or depots. This kept the organisation on its toes, but was not popular.

Sykes was now 73, however, and unknown to him, three of the general managers were drawing up plans for the future without him. Unknown to them and to Sykes, Peter McGarry (Sykes' personal assistant at head office) was collaborating in the same way with the other two general managers. Unknown to all of them, Sykes himself had sounded out an old friend, a well-known head of a nationalised industry.

On 30 April 1979, in the middle of a general managers' meeting which had already discussed the refusal of Austria and Germany to grant more transit permits to Sykes Trucks and the much publicised collapse of a Sykes bridge in Wales, and while waiting for the arrival of the National Secretary of the Transport Workers' Union to discuss a strike in the transport depots, Sykes collapsed and died.

Tasks

1. Give an appreciation of the current company position.
2. Develop an outline plan for the long term for the company stating clearly any assumptions on which this is based.
3. Suggest a set of priorities of action to cope with any immediate problems, and suggest what further analysis might be done in Sykes.

For discussion of exercise feedback see Appendix 1, p. 497.

Case Study 3.3
Peter Dunn Tyres

(Case used with permission of Scottish Vocational Education Council, Glasgow.)

The Peter Dunn Tyres factory near Edinburgh is regarded as one of the most modern in Europe. Until the end of August 1982 it was rolling out Radial XY4 tyres for the British car industry at the rate of 100,000 a month. Then, on 28 August, the company announced that its 500-strong workforce would be joining 1,000 other Peter Dunn employees in England and Ireland on two weeks' enforced holiday.

The lay-offs were blamed in part on British Leyland's decision to stop production of the Mini and Metro for two weeks. At the same time, Lucas Car Components announced that many of its 12,000 workers were to go on short time while Automotive Products of Leamington placed 6,000 workers on a short week which they believed would last until the spring of 1983.

Peter Dunn maintained that their lay-offs were due to false optimism in the car industry in 1982. An expected upturn in sales caused Peter Dunn to go on a four-shift system working round the clock seven days a week. By August 700,000 tyres were stockpiled, according to works convener Ian Sanderson, who said the figure was given to union representatives at a meeting with management. Peter Dunn's Director of Tyres, Simon Charity, denied that the figure was high and insisted that they were 'right in step with demand'.

Certainly the demand for new Y registration cars in August 1982 must have been encouraging. The new Y registration attracted more than 250,000 car sales in that month alone. British Leyland's policies, however, held a real threat for all the companies associated with the car industry. British Leyland was convinced that its own policies for improving efficiency had worked and the only way that they could save more was by tackling the costs of components, such as tyres, batteries and brake parts. Such components represent about 60 per cent of the cost of a finished car, or some £600 million per year. On average, according to British Leyland, British components were 20 per cent more expensive than the same items from European manufacturers. As a result, the Jaguar Division of British Leyland announced in August 1982 that they would be reducing British components in their cars from 82 per cent to around 70 per cent. British Leyland, according to the head of Jaguar Cars, had suffered trauma as a result of introducing new technology and dramatically cutting the workforce. Why, then, should they subsidise the less efficient component companies?

Peter Dunn, among others, was angered by such attitudes and by British Leyland's stop—go production. One brake drum manufacturer pointed out that British Leyland had been his sole customer for twenty years and was now prepared to get rid of him at a moment's notice.

'How can we compete with the Europeans?' he asked. 'We make a brake drum for £6, but the finished product comes in from Italy at only £4.'

Tasks

1. Give a critical appraisal of the situation at Peter Dunn Tyres.
2. Suggest a possible future for Peter Dunn Tyres.

For a discussion of this exercise see Appendix 1, p. 499.

References

Ansoff, I. (1965), *Corporate Strategy*, McGraw-Hill.
Argenti, J. (1968), *A Practical Guide to Corporate Planning*, Allen & Unwin.
Crossman, R.H.S. (1979), *Diaries of a Cabinet Minister 1964–70*, edited by A. Howard, Hamilton.
Drucker, P. (1954), *The Practice of Management*, Harper.
Glueck, W.F. (1976), *Business Policy and Strategic Management*, 3rd edition, McGraw-Hill.
Hicks, H.G. and Gullett, C.R. (1981), *Management*, McGraw-Hill.
Humble, J.W. (1972), *Management by Objectives*, Teakfield.

Chapter 4

Financial appraisal of the corporation

Overview

This chapter will focus on the interpretation of the crucial ratios from profit and loss account and balance sheets. A simple case study is used to bring to life a practical example of the material and its manipulation. See Case Study 4.1, 'M and N Company Limited'.

The material in this chapter is of special value to any students who are required to analyse business policy situations through case studies as part of their courses, as a financial appraisal will nearly always be a key component of the overall company appraisal.

Many other managers who work in a specialist field such as operational research, organisation and methods or risk management, also need to be aware of the background financial climate of their organisations when making specialist proposals to more senior management. As most of them will require some funding they will need to know what is expected in terms of pay-off periods, internal rate of return expectations for projects, and the preference of the organisation to fund by revenue or capital expenditures. Of course, when there is a cash-flow crisis then funding via capital is not an option at all.

One group of risk managers proposed to a board of directors a scheme to spend £70,000 on a sprinkler system for a company which was nearly bankrupt. There was an alternative method of coping with the same risk, at a marginally lower level of thoroughness, costing only £5,000 a year. Yet they had available a balance sheet, which they should have interpreted properly before finalising their proposals. They would then have had a captive audience instead of a hostile one to deal with.

The material in this chapter is treated from the viewpoint of those wishing not to be dominated by the detailed mechanics of the accounting process. The policy-maker wishes to shed light on the fruits and outputs of the accounting system, to be able to see 'the wood for the trees', and get quickly to the more fundamental questions. These may include the following:

1. Would the company under scrutiny be worth buying and rescuing? What is its return on investment status and its liquidity status?

2. What are the priorities financial planning must tackle?
3. Which assets are being poorly utilised?
4. Where are the sick profit margins?
5. What could be done to a few significant cost components to treat these disaster areas?
6. Should part of the company be liquidated to generate investment cash for its areas of strength?
7. In any event, what opportunities are there for further borrowing on the basis of existing financial resources?
8. If the company is in a cash-flow crisis, how could it be managed for cash to get breathing space for recovery?

Learning outcome

The aim of this chapter is to give the reader an appreciation of systematically posing the eight critical questions above in a company situation and interpreting the results. Reference will also be made to some modern techniques of analysis using spreadsheet packages now widely available on microcomputers. These offer very useful techniques for calculating key ratios and then examining change opportunities and likely effects. This is known as a 'what if' capability. The microcomputer aspects will be developed more fully in chapters 12–17.

Analysis of financial ratios to assess internal performance

The balance sheet and a profit and loss account give a useful framework for assessing the vital statistics of a company. The corporate planning analyst may well be interested in the following measures and their interpretation in particular business situations. Their usefulness lies in that each statistic is easy to calculate, and there is a set of useful norms for each measure, so that identification of a variance against the norm should immediately alert attention to any financial weak spots in the company. (*Note*: the terminology used in describing and defining ratios may vary slightly from writer to writer.)

Return on investment (ROI)

Return on investment (ROI) is net profit after tax divided by total net assets. It represents the average rate of return for sunk capital and is generally regarded as the most important single ratio of the 'bottom line', with the greatest influence on potential investors and lenders to the company. This figure is normally higher than the net building society rate where risk is very low. If the company is in a high-risk industry or market then the investor would expect a greater return to make up for such risk.

Percentage margin on sales turnover

This ratio makes it possible to assess whether an active business is also a profit-conscious one. This ratio is calculated by total net profit after tax divided by gross sales revenue. It is useful when the corporate planning analyst wishes to compare performance between profit centres or between companies — a real 'bottom line' figure of comparison. However, the sales mark-up varies from industry to industry and will vary too from manufacturing to distribution. To get a normative figure when analysing a particular company one also needs the industry figures. At the lowest level the mark-up may be 3 per cent for a very high volume, fast-moving, homogeneous product such as manufacturing cigarettes, with very low risk of obsolescence and perishability, while that on retailing luxury or customised products may be as much as 30 per cent. A common rule of thumb for manufacturing is 10 per cent.

Stock turnover times

This measure is primarily an indication of the effectiveness of internal company systems. Every time the raw material, work-in-process and finished inventory turn around there is an opportunity for profit. The definition of this measure is gross sales divided by total stock. In most manufacturing businesses it may be expected that the stock turns over at least four times a year. In some retail businesses one might expect a turnover of as much as 52, i.e. once a week. There are generally well-established norms for this measure by industry.

Sometimes stock turnover time is given in terms of the number of weeks of trading. Thus a business with a stock turnover of four times a year has thirteen weeks of stock. Better still is the division into the number of days of trading, with total stock broken down into work-in-process, raw material and finished goods. As each such category is part of a separate system, figures by each separate category will point more directly to where any weakness in the company system lies.

Asset turnover times

This measure is intended to assess the effectiveness of the use of sunk capital in the business. Industry norms are generally well established for this measure. Its definition is gross sales divided by total net assets.

Collection period for receivables

The purpose of this measure is to assess the effectiveness of the organisation's debt collection system. Commonly, a company trades on terms of monthly credit, with at any one time some thirty days' money not yet collected from customers. Any hold-ups here mean that the business is unnecessarily financing its customers. Why can't they finance their own business? The collection period is calculated as follows: take gross annual sales divided by debtors. This gives the number of times a year the debtor money is turning. Divide 365 (days) by the answer and that will give the collection period.

Open purchase payment time in days

The assumption is that we can maintain good relationships with vendors, but that does mean not keeping them waiting for their money. If the terms of credit are not respected a bad relationship may develop, and if the waiting period gets beyond a level of tolerance then actions for payment could trigger liquidation proceedings. The normal period of credit is commonly thirty days. Calculation of the payment period is obtained by dividing the annual material purchases by the current creditor amount. Then 365 days is divided by this figure, giving the needed purchase payment time in days.

The current ratio

This is calculated as current assets divided by total current liabilities, and is one measure to assess liquidity. It must be greater than 1, and is normally in excess of 1.5.

The quick ratio

This is calculated as current assets less stock divided by current liability. It is also known as the 'liquid ratio'. It should be greater than one. In this ratio stock is not taken account of as in a liquidation the stock might be obsolete and worthless, so it is a more stringent test.

Overdraft cover

To minimise lending risk, banks often require some collateral behind an overdraft. Collateral has to be something which is realisable — property and buildings generally fall into this category. Sometimes equipment may be considered suitable for collateral, but this will depend on its saleability. To compute this measure it is necessary to identify the unmortgaged fixed assets and divide this figure by the current overdraft. It must exceed one, or the lender is likely to charge premium interest rates. Banks are, however, unlikely to be prepared to increase the overdraft unless there is at least 1.5 times of cover, or they can get some other security in the form of personal guarantees, etc.

This overdraft cover measure is crucial whenever a company is attempting to undertake investment projects from its existing financial resources.

Net profit after tax per employee

This measure is an indicator of productivity and becomes most meaningful when used in industry comparisons. It can also be used to detect a management strategy to preserve continuity in employment figures. Large international firms such as IBM deliberately subcontract much of their component and assembly manufacture and preserve resources to fund critical research and development, which is much more difficult to subcontract. Thus as trade expands and contracts with new product launches, etc., it is the subcontractors who take the shock of the ups and downs, leaving the parent company in a state of relative stability.

Ratios of financial structure and investment

(These ratios are to guide potential investors and are common parlance with investment advisers and stockbrokers.)

Gearing

This is a concept developed from Holmes and Sugden (1982). The idea is important to any investor who is contemplating gaining control of a company by acquiring a majority holding of the equity stock. It may be defined as debt divided by equity or borrowings divided by shareholder's capital.

Borrowings include capital raised with fixed interest obligations. Most observers thus consider overdraft as a liability, not a borrowing in the capital structure, but if the business is not a seasonal one and there is always a substantial average overdraft then it makes more sense to consider the overdraft as though it were capitalised, and thus as fixed interest capital.

Low geared is where the equity is predominant. The shareholders take the normal risk of trade fluctuations.

Highly geared is where most of the capital invested is raised through other borrowings. The equity-holder only gets a dividend after fixed interest capital has been paid and thus there will be much greater fluctuations in dividend availability when there are fluctuations in trade. In a highly geared company the purchase of a relatively small amount of equity will enable the investor to win control over much larger assets, and this increases opportunities of being taken over.

Leverage effect is the percentage change in earnings available for ordinary shareholders brought about by a 1 per cent change in earnings before interest and tax.

Price earnings ratio (PER)

PER is calculated as share price divided by earnings per share (EPS).

EPS is calculated as the profit attributable to ordinary shareholders divided by the average number of ordinary shares in issue during the year.

Dividend yield

This is expressed as a percentage and calculated as gross dividend multiplied by 100 divided by the share price.

The 'pyramid of ratios': a review of Figure 4.1

In reviewing Figure 4.1 it is necessary to read from right to left to see the eventual build-up of the vital ROI figure. The figure is helpful in revealing the relationships between the different components which go to make up the ratios.

Company value?

There are three general approaches to the question of company value as follows:

1. The company may be viewed as a *going concern*. This is primarily related to its current profit-earning capacity. A common measure is to take some ten times the current net profit after tax figure. In Figure 4.1 this would give a value of just £2,000,000.
2. The value may be attributed to the total net assets. In Figure 4.1 this amounts to £5,000,000. This figure is significantly influenced by the fixed asset figure of £4,000,000 which is a book figure, i.e. it represents original cost less depreciation. The *liquidation* value of such assets to another business might be very different.
3. The value may be the *synergy* value which a takeover predator would place on the company. To get to a figure here one would need to make an estimate of what the increase in net profit after tax for the combined group would be after takeover and multiply this figure by 10, thus reflecting the potential extra profit.

The takeover could be inspired for a variety of reasons. The bidding company may covet the property assets, the patents, the marketing organisation, the manufacturing capacity, the product range, the management talent or a number of other aspects. When considering the *price* to be paid the key factor tends to be whether there is more than one predator to make a market in any takeover battle. There might also be a variety of motives among companies contemplating a takeover. If the takeover is part of an offensive strategy then the outcome is likely to be some rationalisation as a bigger unit of organisation, followed by a greater market share, and general dominance of the market. Alternatively, the takeover might be inspired by a defensive strategy, where it would be convenient to liquidate assets on purchase in a move to silence unwelcome competition. It is possible too that the takeover victim might actively court a suitor in order to become a willing part of a larger group.

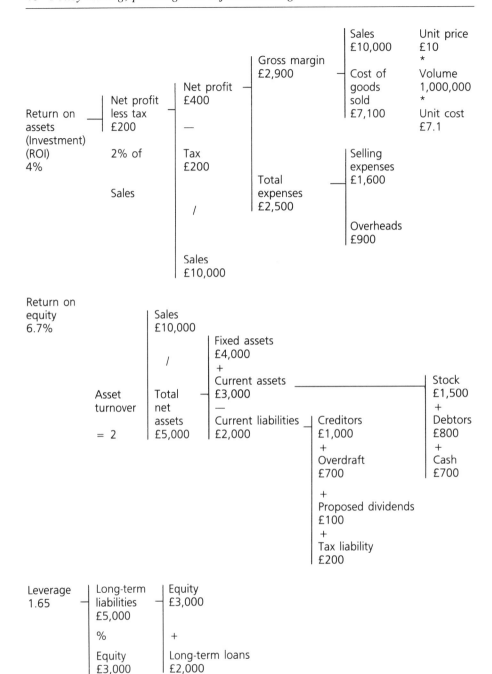

Figure 4.1 *Structure of financial ratios (money figures given in 000s)*
(Source: Johnson and Scholes (1984))

Cost of company acquisition

Control normally results from ownership of more than 50 per cent of the equity capital of a company. However, the current share price would probably be inflated if a takeover predator indulged in extensive dealings on the stock market, consequently it is necessary to mount a formal takeover offer. Merchant bankers are normally retained as specialist advisers on the terms of an offer to gain control. Tactics may be influenced by a knowledge of the pattern of the current shareholding, which may be determined from inspection of the company share register.

Summary

This section has reviewed the main ratios of significance in a financial analysis. Return on investment (ROI) is the most basic of these measures in a capitalistic economy. The structure of data, relationships and ratios which go to make up this 'bottom line' measure was traced through Figure 4.1, adapted from Johnson and Scholes (1984). The ROI figure is of particular interest to those who manage a company, work in it, supply it, invest in it and those who lend to it. ROI is the principal measure of economic effectiveness.

Other ratios were examined which threw light on the City view of a company, its worth and its share price. Next the ratios of liquidity were examined to determine the short-term viability of the company and some normative values were suggested to anticipate a possible liquidity crisis.

Case Study 4.1
M and N Limited

(Case printed with permission from Scottish Vocational Education Council, Glasgow.)

M and N Limited is a private company employing just over 200 people in the Edinburgh area. The company has three manufacturing sections, each associated with the timber and furniture trade. These three sections are:

1. Doors and windows for the building industry,
2. Office furniture,
3. Domestic furniture, mainly dining room furniture and three-piece suites.

The company has a small sawmill attached to the doors and windows section but, due to the limited capacity, buys in 90 per cent of its total requirements of wood raw materials in a semi-finished state from other sawmills. The finished products of the doors and windows section are sold to two Scottish companies in the construction industry. The products of the office furniture and domestic furniture sections are sold direct to retail outlets; previously all these outlets were in the Edinburgh and Glasgow areas, but this year the company has been able to sell its products in other areas of Scotland and in the North of England.

The accounts provided represent the results and position of M and N Limited for the last two years ending 31 December. The business has been following a policy of expansion and intends to continue this in the future. The figures for three years ago did not ostensibly differ from those of two years ago, indeed the profit and stock figures were exactly the same.

The company's expansion in year 2 has been mostly in the area of domestic furniture, while the other areas have remained fairly constant. This expansion has been achieved by an aggressive marketing policy, especially in the newer geographical areas previously mentioned.

The figures relating to the three product areas for year 2 are shown in Figure 4.2, Figure 4.3 shows the profit and loss account, Figure 4.4 the ratio analysis and Figure 4.5 the contribution analysis

The managing director of M and N Limited, John, feels that the company should give up its production of doors and windows for the construction industry, because of the loss-making situation. He feels that this would also release resources for further expansion in the domestic furniture sector. Factory space is particularly scarce as a result of the expansion. John's plan is to use about half of the space given up by the 'doors and windows' for assembly of domestic furniture and to use the rest of the space for building a modern sawmill, so that the company could become self-sufficient in processing its own wood raw materials. The company's chief accountant estimates that this would reduce the cost of the semi-finished wood raw materials by 20 per cent, although the establishment of a sawmill would cost in the region of £1,200,000.

The extra space allocated to assembly would allow production of domestic furniture to expand by 30 per cent. Further expansion beyond this would not be possible in the existing premises.

	Doors and windows	Office furniture	Domestic furniture	Total
Sales	500,000	1,500,000	2,500,000	4,500,000
Wages	110,000	340,000	550,000	1,000,000
Materials	350,000	850,000	1,300,000	2,500,000
Depreciation	15,000	45,000	70,000	130,000
Other production overheads	20,000	60,000	70,000	150,000
Selling	15,000	35,000	200,000	250,000
Administration and loan interest	28,000	84,000	138,000	250,000
Total cost	538,000	1,414,000	2,328,000	4,280,000
Profit before tax	− 38,000	86,000	172,000	220,000

Figure 4.2 *M and N Limited — product areas for year 2*

	Year 1		Year 2	
Sales		3,100,000		4,500,000
Less expenses				
Wages	500,000		1,000,000	
Materials	2,000,000		2,500,000	
Depreciation	100,000		130,000	
Other production				
overheads	100,000		150,000	
Selling	150,000		250,000	
Administration	50,000		150,000	
Loan interest	100,000	3,000,000	100,000	4,280,000
Profit before tax		100,000		220,000
Corporation tax		55,000		100,000
Net profit after tax		45,000		120,000

M and N Limited balance sheets as at 31 December

	Year 1		Year 2	
Fixed assets:				
Property (at cost)		1,500,000		1,500,000
Equipment (at cost)	1,000,000		1,300,000	
Less depreciation	400,000	600,000	530,000	770,000
Current assets:				
Stocks	450,000		700,000	
Debtors	500,000		690,000	
Cash	50,000		10,000	
	1,000,000		1,400,000	
Less current liabilities:				
Corporation tax	55,000		100,000	
Creditors	495,000		595,000	
Overdraft	100,000		405,000	
	650,000		1,100,000	
Net working capital		350,000		300,000
Total net assets		2,450,000		2,570,000
Financed by:				
Issued share capital		800,000		800,000
Revenue reserves		650,000		770,000
Loan capital				
secured on property		1,000,000		1,000,000
		2,450,000		2,570,000

Figure 4.3 *M and N Limited — profit and loss account for the years ended 31 December*

		Year 1	Year 2
(a) ROI	45,000/2,450,000	= 1.8%	4.6%
(b) % margin of sales	45,000/3,100,000	= 1.4%	2.6%
(c) Stock turnover times	3,100,000/450,000	= 6.8	6.4
(d) Asset turnover times	3,100,000/2,450,000	= 1.26	1.75
(e) Collection period for receivables		58 days	55.3 days
(f) Open purchase payment time		90.3 days	86.8 days
(g) Current assets/total current liability	1,000,000/650,000	= 1.5	1.3
(h) Current assets less stock/total current liability	(1,000,000−450,000)/650,000	= 0.85	0.64
(i) Overdraft cover	(1,500,000−1,000,000)/100,000	= 5 times	1.23 times

Figure 4.4 *M and N Limited — ratio analysis*

	Doors and windows	Office furniture	Domestic furniture	John's proposal 30% expansion
Variable				
Direct wages	110,000	340,000	550,000	715,000
Materials	350,000	850,000	1,300,000	1,352,000
Selling expenses	15,000	35,000	200,000	260,000
Loan interest	28,000	84,000	138,000	179,000
	503,000	1,309,000	2,188,000	2,506,000
Fixed				
Overhead	20,000	60,000	70,000	70,000
Depreciation	15,000	45,000	70,000	70,000
	35,000	105,000	140,000	140,000
Revenue	500,000	1,500,000	2,500,000	3,250,000
Contribution	−3,000	191,000	312,000	746,600
Contribution increase*		170,000		431,600
				**170,000
				601,000
New investment				1,200,000
ROI on new investment				50%
Payoff period from new investment based on contribution impact				2 years

* Contribution increase
The calculation of this element was achieved by increasing revenue by 30 per cent, leaving other costs as they were except material costs, which were reduced by 20 per cent.

** This figure of 170,000 was transferred from the office furniture section.

Figure 4.5 *M and N Limited — contribution analysis*

The production manager, Bill, feels that it would not be a good idea to abandon the production of doors and windows, since the loss-making situation is due to low output. Profits would be possible if the construction industry were to recover, which it is expected to do within the next twelve months. He also feels that the company would be wasting resources by abandoning doors and windows, since only a small proportion of the equipment and labour is transferable to other areas of manufacturing. Inevitably, this would cause redundancies for production operators of certain job grades, unless they could be re-trained; it is considered that many because of their age, could not be successfully re-trained. John, however, believes that transfer and re-training would be possible.

Bill takes the view that the goodwill lost by redundancies would never be recovered. And in any event the change in policy away from doors and windows is based on past history rather than future demand.

Interpretation

A very dismal picture emerges from this analysis. ROI is so weak that it would be hard to attract outside investors to the company. Liquidity is also at crisis level. It has been so bad for so long it is amazing that the company has coped. Suppliers are kept waiting ninety days for payment and could easily initiate legal debt proceedings. The threat of liquidation is strong. Internal company systems appear weak. Receivables are well outside normal levels. The overdraft situation is also at crisis level. There is hardly any surplus cover should the bank demand collateral. Indeed the bank would be trying to reduce overdraft. There is no chance for John and his sawmill expansion plans, but some further light might emerge from doing a contribution analysis.

Analysis

The objective of doing a contribution analysis is to assess what the situation would be if one of the sections were discontinued, and all disposable resources either liquidated or transferred to another section. This is a typical 'what if' exercise, based on the premise in corporate planning that management should be keen to back winners rather than let losers attract so much survival money that they become a black hole which drags the parent organisation into liquidation.

The principle behind a contribution analysis (Figure 4.5) is to assess whether closure of a section would improve, in the short term, the profitability of the firm as a whole. It is based on the assumption that sections of a firm may in bad times temporarily fail to achieve profit, but that liquidation would still be too drastic an action, reducing the base from which overheads were allocated and aggravating the situation.

The general rule is that the section should be allowed to survive if it generates some excess of revenue over variable costs. That excess is called contribution and means a contribution to overheads. If revenue is less than variable costs the situation is much more serious, i.e. the more the company manufactures the more it loses, so when a section is identified as making a negative contribution, that section must close unless there are very real possibilities of reducing costs and returning in the immediate future to a positive contribution situation, or other very compelling business reasons for keeping the unit open.

Much controversy, however, surrounds the interpretation of the term 'fixed cost'. The management accountant has a tendency to argue that elements such as 'selling and administration' and 'loan interest' are fixed cost items. A corporate planning analyst is likely to go further and pose such questions as: 'If doors and windows were closed could the salesmen be reallocated to another section, or could the total establishment of salesmen be reduced?' If the answer is yes to either of these, then sales and administration is a variable cost, not a fixed cost. Similarly, the analyst may ask: 'If doors and windows were closed would it still require loan interest to finance its working capital needs?' If the answer is no, then loan interest is a variable cost, not a fixed cost.

In the M and N Company analysis we noticed that the doors and windows section has a negative contribution of £3,000, so it is very much a prospect for closure, unless special mitigating circumstances can be pleaded. As other sections are much healthier and short of resources such as space, it looks as though a decision to close the section is likely.

John's expansion proposal

It is necessary to assess the possible impact of John's proposal to expand the other two sections by 30 per cent, reducing material costs in each by 20 per cent and investing £1,200,000 in a sawmill. This would result in a contribution increase of £431,000 for the domestic furniture section and a further £170,000 for office furniture. This gives a remarkable extra contribution of £601,000 for the above investment project, and does look very attractive. However, from the analysis of critical ratios it is clear that with a poor liquid situation and a poor overall ROI, neither banks nor investors will be enthusiastic about funding this proposition. At this point in the analysis most observers would conclude that there is no long-term future for M and N Limited, but the corporate planning analyst cannot give up that easily!

A 'what if' exercise

A business analyst contemplating a company rescue would probably look at the very weakest points and attempt some change here. Two possibilities emerge for experimentation.

Let us devise a 'simulation rate', initially, say, 10 per cent, and see what impact that would have on the ROI figure. Two critical factors influence ROI — the sales revenue and the material cost. With a keener purchasing practice in action and a 10 per cent reduction may be negotiated. As demand is so strong in some parts of the business, this is not an unreasonable assumption to simulate.

Finally, we might experiment with this 'simulation rate' to find out what value is required to bring ROI up to an acceptable 10 per cent. This latter application is called 'goal-seeking'.

The simulation on the M and N Limited model

Initially we will do the simulation on the year 2 figures. We will enter the balance sheet and profit and loss account into a computer spreadsheet and also use this to calculate critical ratios. Once this has been done for a first time an analyst can easily use such a model to reflect another balance sheet, so the spreadsheet model is a very useful tool for capturing the experience and technique of ratio analysis and simulation. Then we enter a simulation rate defined initially at 10 per cent. Next we alter formulas in the spreadsheet model to take account of the rise in revenue and reduction in material cost by the simulation rate and see what happens.

The first result is a mild sensation. The ROI figure is improved to over 19 per cent.

The simulation may now be repeated using different values of the simulation rate. It looks as though a simulation rate of 3.5 per cent gives an eventual ROI of 9.86 per cent, quite near a respectable ROI, which would no longer put off investors and lenders to the business.

It is amazing that with a mere 3.5 per cent change directed at two significant weak points in M and N Company, a firm which seemed hopeless could be rescued by concentrated action.

Another look at John's expansion proposal

Perhaps it is necessary to rethink one aspect of John's proposal. The argument behind establishing M and N's own sawmill is that economies of scale would enable substantial cost reductions in the basic raw material, which would have an immediate impact on sales margin and ROI. With an improved order book, the cash-flow situation would also improve. The flaw in John's thinking lies in the necessity for M and N to put up the capital for the sawmill, as capital is the one thing the company does not have. Instead, the purchasing manager could hunt around the Edinburgh/Glasgow area for a business with an underutilised sawmill and offer a large annual contract, *if prices can be reduced by 20 per cent*. There is still a practical snag here if the vendor presses the question of M and N's payment record, as no vendor would willingly accept a 90-day waiting period!

Manage for cash

In the short term the company will need to be managed *for cash* to get the liquidity restored. Closure of the doors and windows section should help here. However, it is important to avoid expensive redundancy payments, and every effort should be made to reassign labour to the remaining sections. As there is a buoyant market in these other sections there should be little difficulty in getting the labour reabsorbed. Another main target for action and attention in any 'manage for cash' initiative will be the high stock figures. The balance sheet shows over £700,000 of the assets tied up in stock in the year 2 figures. The problem with this approach is that it does require some expertise in the principles of stock control, and possibly the introduction of computerised methods, helpful for the long term, but not much use in the short term. Unless there is expertise available and a management team ready to accept the disciplines of change, meddling with the stock control routines could actually weaken the cash flow.

Other alternatives

An alternative strategy for M and N would be to seek a joint venture or merger with a suitable vendor who had the necessary sawmill or spare financial resources to rescue

M and N, though as the company is currently a private limited company the active cooperation of shareholders would be a precondition and M and N would then lose its independence.

Alternatively, the purchasing manager could negotiate a reduction of less than 20 per cent, as a mere 3.5 per cent reduction in material cost and a similar rise in sales price will bring the ROI up to 10 per cent. This would not seem to be an impossible way ahead. Yet just a few hours previously in our analysis it looked as though there were no future for M and N Limited.

References

Holmes, G. and Sugden, A. (1982), *Interpreting Company Reports and Accounts*, 2nd edition, Woodhead-Faulkner.
Johnson, G. and Scholes, K. (1984), *Exploring Corporate Strategy*, Prentice Hall.

Further reading

Parker, R.H. (1972), *Understanding Company Financial Statements*, Penguin Books.

Chapter 5
Objective-setting approaches

Overview

People often pose the question of how to distinguish an organisation which has adopted a managing by objectives approach from an organisation which has not. Two features are probably the most significant. In non-MbO environments the predominant culture is one of instruction from the top management group rather than a conscious attempt to share in objective-setting issues. In non-MbO environments there is a tendency to maintain the standards, budgets and establishments of the previous year, whereas in MbO environments there is a constant striving for new goals and levels of achievement and a critical review of existing resources and establishments. Some observers would suggest that the MbO approach is a direct antithesis of Parkinson's law of bureaucracy (Parkinson and Rowe, 1977), which states that work simply expands to fill the time of executives!

Chapter 3 showed the need to convert the priorities and key result areas of the response phase of the corporate plan into lower-level action plans and objectives for the rest of the business through an effective transmission or conversion process. The 'right' version of MbO can be developed to fit this need if we pick a dynamic responsive version which emphasises frequent objective-setting and review sessions with groups and superior/subordinate pairs, involving participation and consultation. Key result areas may be associated with organisational issues and position descriptions and this clarification process is aimed at 'managing within a framework of expectancy and collective responsibility — no nagging!' (Odiorne, 1972).

The approach of managing by objectives is a complex one and for that reason two chapters are devoted to it in an attempt to make the concepts more digestible. The process really falls into two phases — a planning phase and a feedback phase. In this context planning includes objective-setting for individuals and groups within the organisation. The feedback is described as 'the appraisal process'. This chapter gives an overview of the approach as a whole, but with most emphasis on the objective-setting, planning phase. One simple case study, 'On Target', is offered for analysis to demonstrate the MbO approach in a private sector environment.

An effective management approach should be valid in both the public and private sectors, and it has been in the public sector that most difficulties with the MbO approach have been encountered. Case Study 5.2 illustrates an effective deployment of the technique in a college. In this sequence, attention is devoted to the most basic college building-block, the course unit, run and managed by a course team.

Learning objectives

After reading this chapter the reader should be familiar with the main terms and principles of managing by objectives and have some appreciation of how they can be applied both in the private and public sectors. This understanding should be more complete after working through chapter 6, also devoted to MbO. The experience will be the more rewarding if the reader can identify with the issues and discussions developed in the case material of the two chapters.

Management by objectives

An organisation's objectives are its *raison d'être*, and its relative success or failure can be measured by the degree to which it achieves those objectives (Reddin, 1968). At the highest level of organisational hierarchy, objectives are an expression of the organisation's long-term direction and identity. Hicks and Gullett (1981) term these 'visionary' objectives. In this chapter it is assumed that the organisation has a corporate planning process from which are distilled the strategic objectives, mission statements or key result areas for refinement and use further down the hierarchy. At operational levels managerial objectives are said to be attainable and are defined as '*results to be achieved at cost not to exceed £x, by [date]*'. At the lower levels of operational management objectives are usually short-term or immediate and concern the day-to-day issues involved in running a business.

Another useful term in the theory of MbO is effectiveness standards. These relate to the norms of good business and professional practice that guide managers and professionals in all aspects of their work. Every organisation will have some special subset of effectiveness standards, which comprise excellence in the organisation. Managers will be expected to link their own work priorities to these.

Objectives are achieved through the organisation's members. It is a prerequisite for success, however defined, that members know what the objectives are and how their departmental, group and individual activities contribute to attaining them. Hence the emphasis of management theory and practice on developing effective objective-setting systems.

Objective-setting systems

Peter Drucker

Peter Drucker defined an objective-setting system as follows:

> A philosophy of managerial leadership which aims at bringing together the individual manager's objectives with those of his or her unit and creates an environment of free dialogue about the mutual expectations of a manager with his or her superior.

Drucker was the writer normally credited with initiating interest in objective-setting systems in *The Practice of Management*. Many writers further developed his ideas forming a school of management thought. These included George Odiorne in *The System of Managing by Objectives*, John Humble in *Managing by Objectives* and W. Reddin in *Effective MbO*. The *MbO Journal* was founded to report developments of the theory and offer research results from companies which had adopted MbO programmes. The journal ceased publication in the late 1970s in the wake of the criticisms of MbO, most of which focused on implementation difficulties. Nevertheless, in the United Kingdom, there was much establishment backing for the concept of MbO. When the Fulton Report on the Civil Service was published in 1968, MbO was to be the vehicle for establishing accountable units.

Much controversy has surrounded the theory, its interpretation, its orientation and the contingency aspects which relate to how particular organisations may adopt the model and get a 'fit' with reality and their own culture. However, this text contends that MbO, in its modern form, improved as a result of much research, can be a useful managerial tool for analysis and action.

Drucker's early work, published in 1954, was concerned with establishing the marketing concept. He observed that companies did not have the natural ability to react continuously and creatively to the external environment as manifested in changing customer demands. Somehow the bureaucracy separating the customer from the decision-makers in the organisation had to be galvanised into action. The way to achieve this was to establish a communication link from the customer contact point to the summit of the producing organisation so that decision-makers would manage the business with a greater sense of realism. There were to be two strands to this approach. First of all, a set of protocols and mechanisms would ensure that the individual could make a 'contribution'. Secondly, to effect an articulation of the notion of 'contribution', there would be a framework for focusing on specific objectives. Drucker identified eight areas where objective-setting performance was vital for the perpetuation of the business. These were: profitability, productivity, physical return on assets and financial resources, worker performance and attitude, innovation, manager performance and attitude, market standing and social responsibility.

The intention in including areas other than marketing was to reflect a comprehensive view of the ambit of objective-setting. Although in Drucker's view the customer was still the predominant stakeholder, he acknowledged that there were complementary supporting objectives which if not achieved would compromise the business, ignoring other stakeholders. Note that in this early rendition Drucker stressed qualitative objectives (e.g. market standing and social responsibility) as well as other objectives which could be rigorously quantified. Later writers, such as Stoner (1978), fell into the trap of suggesting that if an objective could not be quantified it could be ignored!

The problem of defining objectives is particularly evident in the public sector where public service rather than profit is the core activity. A French writer, Ruffat (1983), developed a trade-off model linking the three concepts of return on investment through public funding; value of service as perceived by the public; value of the compensation package as perceived by employees. He used this model as a useful guide for getting the necessary balance and providing a base from which performance trends could be measured. Other writers tend to emphasise the relevance and application of effectiveness standards for the public sector.

Drucker's ideas of contribution and the eight objective-setting areas are brought together in the MbO concept. To put this into practice Drucker suggested that the manager writes a letter to his or her superior stating the perception of the superior's position and the trade-off positions for reconciliation of the eight objective-setting areas for both superior and self. He or she invites discussion of points of difficulty or disagreement. The purpose is to ensure that his or her own contribution fits the needs of the organisation represented at a higher level. This pressure from lower levels in the hierarchy is intended to develop a free and creative dialogue between manager and superior within the setting of a problem-solving environment. Once this process is activated it may be expected that the manager will develop naturally, thus implementing the theories of managerial motivation which have been developed by Mayo (1933), Maslow (1970) and McGregor *et al.* (1960).

John Humble

John Humble (1972) sought to reinterpret Drucker's model specifically to fit his perception of UK culture. At that time Britain was still in the post-war boom and profits depended significantly on achieving growth. In Humble's view, as a starting point, one needed a corporate plan developed by policy-makers at the top of the business, using Drucker's eight areas of objective-setting as a guide. From this framework those areas which could be quantified would be quantified, and from this fixed set of figures managers would sit down together once a year in the superior/subordinate relationship throughout the hierarchy of the organisation, to break these down into a share of contribution perceived by the superior as being fair to the manager and consistent with accountability to higher levels.

Much criticism was applied to Humble's over-emphasis on quantifying objectives at the expense of the qualitative features of Drucker's model. Furthermore, the corporate planning process envisaged by Humble in the early 1970s was very much an authoritarian process. Later versions of corporate planning developed in the 1980s emphasise the staff role in corporate planning with a team approach at the summit of the organisation. (See chapters 3 and 17.)

Because Humble's process was activated by the senior member of each of the pairs, the dialogue tended to lack the fluency of dialogue envisaged in Drucker's approach. Humble's process tended to be perceived by lower-level managers as manipulative — a control mechanism to oblige them to toe the company's line which had been unilaterally decided in the boardroom. Wilkie described this approach as a *do-it-yourself hangman's kit* (Bradley and Wilkie, 1974). He thought that MbO could become a device for forcing middle managers into accepting impossible targets.

Many companies in the United Kingdom adopted Humble's version of MbO, claiming benefits for motivation, but such programmes tended not to last. There were four major difficulties. Firstly, MbO was initially very time-consuming and relatively inflexible, owing to the annual cycle of action. Secondly, the appraisal phase, again interpreted as an annual cycle, became a ritual and very demanding of time. Thirdly, there was a cultural problem. The MbO model required an openness of dialogue, but UK management had a tradition for secret decision-making. Fourthly, UK trade unions did not take kindly to the implications of appraisal, which was commonly regarded as a device for exploitation. If they succeeded in blocking feedback of the appraisal process then MbO programmes tended to be abandoned. Expression of such criticisms may be found in Froissart (1972).

Bill Reddin

Meanwhile, Reddin, a Canadian behavioural scientist, was building on the Drucker foundations. He saw the process of MbO as critically dependent on the fluency of dialogue at the time of both objective-setting and appraisal. He developed an elaborate leadership style model to provide some concise concepts which would describe manager relationships with one another and provide the framework for change targeted at his central idea of managerial effectiveness. His emphasis was on two points. Firstly, the manager's job description, which had to be concisely clarified and related to a real output fitting the organisation's needs. Secondly, for the appraisal phase he introduced the notion that a third party would be present to lock manager and superior into a creative problem-solving mode. This would overcome the tendency to whitewash one another and avoid issues of real substance. Furthermore, he encouraged objective-setting to be done by groups of managers rather than by pairs alone.

Several writers, are very favourable to MbO. Steidl (1974), in his article 'Seven successful years at Packaging Corporation of America', suggests that the assimilation of MbO into the normal culture of the organisation had led to considerable and sustained benefits.

French and Drexler (1984) emphasise the importance of teamwork throughout the MbO approach, both at the objective-setting and appraisal phases. They claim that Drucker referred to group work in objective-setting as far back as his work with Alfred G. Sloan with General Motors in the late 1920s. However, French and Drexler do admit that a group objective-setting approach is more demanding of skills and has significant other organisational preconditions for success, and this explains why there is much more literature available on the better known one-to-one approach in objective-setting. Real organisations in action show some diversity of approach. Some objective-setting activities are done in groups — the corporate planning process and probably also the product development process. Whereas in other spheres the natural forum for objective-setting is within a one-to-one dialogue.

Components of the MbO model

Further analysis of the literature suggests a credible framework for an objective setting system. Figure 5.1 illustrates the components of this model. It is neither a top-down model nor a bottom-up model, but rather, one embracing contributions from all levels of the organisation structure.

It is convenient to begin at the top left-hand corner, *organisation objectives from corporate plan*. This does, however, involve us in making the key assumption that organisations do indeed have objectives and that they are well articulated. The reality may be otherwise. According to organisation theory in so far as an organisation may be said to have objectives, they are those of top management. Typically in business top management is a board of directors, each of whom may perceive objectives differently in form, substance, balance and interpretation. They need to achieve a consensus so that clear objectives can be transmitted vertically and laterally throughout the organisation. Without this solid starting point the business has no common purpose: contradictory messages, resulting in conflict, will be created throughout the organisation. Drucker's framework of the vital eight objective-setting areas will not generally have been understood and implemented unless the organisation has already adopted a corporate planning approach.

This process may be compared with that which operates in political parties. The left and right wings may be at odds. However, following discussions, agreement is reached, a manifesto is published and the party unites behind it. When a party is in power priorities have to be established for the programme of legislation which is outlined in the Queen's Speech at the opening of the Parliamentary session. This again reflects a consensus of party view and much UK constitutional thinking is based on the doctrine of collective responsibility. However, in a business it is more difficult to identify those times when executives must unite behind their common definition of organisation objectives. One example is probably the Chairman's annual statement, preceded by a corporate plan, which has been discussed in relevant circles. Collective responsibility may then apply to the board as a whole. It may be noted that in the 1970s much progress was reported in the literature in defining corporate planning processes supported by consultation and many advanced management techniques.

MbO can be an efficient mechanism for transmission of objectives to other quarters once the unit's objectives have this solid base. Next an organisation structure is needed to sustain the transmission process. In an existing structure one may expect executive positions to be expressed as titles. It is important to create a framework of expectancy around each such job title to ensure the congruence of the roles with the organisation's objectives. To ensure this congruence the process of MbO recognises key result areas from the corporate planning process. This term refers to a limited number of areas

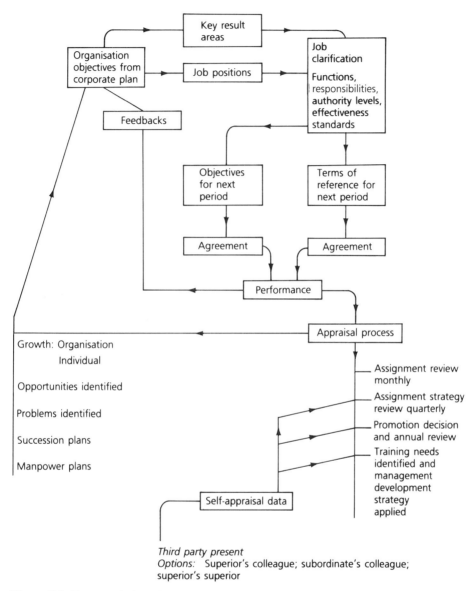

Figure 5.1 *Conceptual chart for managing by objectives*

of performance which are critical to the organisation's viability and growth. They are normally related to both the organisation as a whole and the operation of its constituent units as departments, divisions, profit centres, etc. A manager incorporates KRAs into his job. They are an input to the phase of job clarification down to the lowest level of management.

Job clarification is the process by which a manager and his superior identify the manager's functions, his specific responsibilities, and the delegation of authority commensurate with these responsibilities (see Figure 5.2). Job clarification begins at the point when a job is created and is continually reviewed as circumstances change. In large organisations the terms of reference ensuing from this process will often be in written form. However, within small and dynamic units the process may be completed satisfactorily through oral dialogue alone. Job clarification also includes setting terms of reference for a limited period to reflect agreed priorities and specific time-bounded assignments. (See Figure 5.3 for a typical assignment planning form.) This planning

A *function* is defined as a major sphere of activity.
A manager's functions may be given in priority sequence.
Each function may be subdivided into distinct areas of responsibility.
Each area of responsibility is commonly associated with norms of good practice, 'effectiveness standards'.

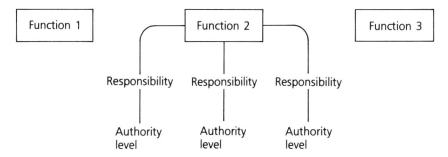

In a well-defined management position authority will equate with responsibility to establish a framework of mutual expectancy.

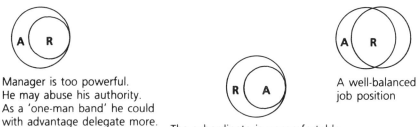

Manager is too powerful.
He may abuse his authority.
As a 'one-man band' he could
with advantage delegate more.

The subordinate is uncomfortable.
He has too little authority. He
risks being 'nagged' for failure
to satisfy his superior's
expectations, some of which
may be unknown to him.

A well-balanced
job position

Figure 5.2 *Authority and responsibility in job positions*

Department   *Subject*

Manager's name *Superior's*   *Starting*   *Anticipated*   *Actual*
          name   *date*   *completion*   *completion*
                                                date   *date*

Statement of objective in format
Result to be achieved by [date]
at a cost not to exceed £...

Terms of reference including any special *resources or authority* required
for *successful completion of this objective.*

Phases of assignment as planned by manager	Started	Completion target	Completion actual	Resource effort estimated by manager in man/days of his own commitment.	

Progress reports   Total

Figure 5.3 *A manager's assignment planning sheet*
(Source: adapted from a document used in Honeywell Ltd)

form is particularly useful for those managers who are working on projects and need to delegate parts of such projects to others.

Clarification of jobs should start at the top of the organisational hierarchies and work downwards to the lowest level of management. The underlying intention of job clarification is to set up jobs in which authority as a resource adequately balances the responsibility, seen as a burden for discharge. This locks in the notion of mutual expectancy. The reality in most jobs is that there are policy aspects which require the job-holder to consult other managers before acting. However, the very fact that on determining the need for more authority the manager has a route through which to direct his dialogue upwards assists in creating a natural problem-solving protocol. A practical way of implementing this idea is to code every identified responsibility with an authority classification. Ellis-Jones, Director of Management Development at Honeywell Limited, suggests such a classification:

A = act without reference above.

B = act and report back to superior to keep him or her in the picture.

C = treat as policy area. Consult with colleagues about the issues and approaches involved and suggest to superior a course of action, pending approval.

F = spend financial resources up to defined limit without further reference to higher levels.

Job clarification which fails to resolve the question of authority jeopardises the success of the objective-setting system (see Figure 5.2). Commonly, executives complete what they think is the process of job clarification with subordinates only to find later, much to their cost, that each had a different perception of discretion in the job, as they had not developed sufficiently their dialogue on authority levels. This may be regarded as a finer point in MbO implementation, but MbO is a very fragile approach without fluency in application of such finer points. Efficient MbO must achieve a real empathy in superior/subordinate relationships.

It is necessary to separate 'assignments for next period' from 'terms of reference for next period' in order to overcome the criticism that MbO is bureaucratic and takes up so much management time that it becomes unviable. This regular identification of assignments integrates objective-setting with the normal on-going management process, so that in time it becomes accepted as part of the normal management culture (Steidl, 1974). In contrast Humble's approach advocated an annual assessment which could take up to three hours per session but which could not easily be reviewed during the year.

To facilitate the understanding of 'assignments for next period' a planning document is reproduced in Figure 5.3. This is a document on which a manager may identify the phases and sub-phases for delegating downwards. He or she will, however, always record his or her own anticipated time input to prevent an overload. This document is normally kept in two portfolios — one copy in his or her own, the other in the superior's. Thus two minds can meet when discussing progress. Elaborate and complicated project assignments may be planned with an additional aid, the use of critical path networks, which will add precision to the timings and resource requirements. Although CPNs are not readily associated with objective-setting systems, they would appear to be complementary. Complex projects need breaking down and assigning to individuals. Individuals need assigning to roles in an organisation structure. This process allows precision in defining roles in the organisation structure and projects in the task structure and uniting these with priorities. This binds the framework of expectancy and is the very core of objective-setting systems.

The above process requires some 'organisational glue' to keep it together, to attain the motivational potential of the objective-setting system and to ensure business and organisational benefit. In essence, if commitment is required on the part of the manager to the plans and work of the superior then it is most important that there is real, not forced, agreement both to the 'terms of reference for next period' and to 'assignments for next period'. Indeed, in an organisation where objective-setting systems have become part of the firm's culture, it may be expected that the junior manager contributes as much to this process as his or her immediate superior. However, it should be stated that the more senior a manager becomes in the firm's hierarchy the more the pressure will be on him or her to generate the activity of objective-setting and rely less and less on the superior's initiative. If agreement is manipulated the approach ceases to be a genuine objective-setting system but becomes in contrast a system of instruction.

The MbO process should be dynamic rather than bureaucratic. This implies that it must adapt quickly to changing conditions and priorities and the effects of the external environment. Objective-setting must also be done frequently. The planning sheets offered in Figure 5.3 are activated on a continuous basis for objective-setting and progress review. However, corporate planning activities will often send shock-waves through the organisation and some response is obviously needed to changes from that source. Also, in time a manager's general terms of reference may become obsolete so that it is necessary to initiate an open door policy and seek an interview with the superior in order to re-clarify the job. This job clarification should be done at least once a year and more frequently if necessary. The general terms of reference which ensue are a means of giving clear delegation guidelines so that authority is confidently passed down the organisation.

The second major phase in the MbO model relates to the 'appraisal process', but discussion of theory and practice about this is delayed till the next chapter after some incidents have been analysed to get a feel of MbO in real life situations.

5.1 Case Study
'On target'

(The case was set in 1966 and developed from unpublished material, whose original source is unknown. For details of tasks see end of case text.)

The General Manager had left Bullock in no doubt as to what was wanted in the new Maidstone depot — 100 tons per man per week before the end of the half-year.

Bullock knew that this target had never been achieved before, but he had accepted the challenge. He was thrilled to have a real job and real responsibility at long last. The company had done a great deal for him; it had trained him, promoted him, helped him buy a house and offered him attractive prospects for the future. Indeed, Bullock felt a great loyalty to the organisation. Now he was to take over the management of the company's latest depot, which incorporated completely modern equipment set up under the Chairman's £1 million expansion scheme. Development was planned to take place over the next five years.

In the early capital proposals the General Manager had claimed that the throughput of Maidstone and similar new depots would be doubled from 50 tons to 100 tons a man within the first six months of opening. He had staked his reputation on this in many public speeches and now, having every confidence in Bullock, was asking him to go out and prove all his theories in practice.

Before Bullock left Head Office, he spent some time with the Assistant General Manager responsible for the immediate planning and opening of Maidstone. He was given a thorough briefing on the staffing of the place, the equipment available and the volume expected in and out of the depot over the next six months. It was evident straight away that this volume was less than Bullock had expected. Therefore, if the 100 tons per man was to be reached, there would have to be an overall reduction in the manual staff from twelve to nine men.

In passing, the Assistant General Manager made the point quite strongly that in his view three men could be 'wasted out' and the remainder extended to a new pace of working. Unfortunately, he felt that Bullock would get little support in this approach from Hooker, the depot supervisor. He was one of the wartime promotions and several people felt that he was not the man for the job. Hooker appeared to lack the vision and enthusiasm to achieve the new output figures required by Head Office. Still Hooker's appointment had been approved by the local Regional Manager and for the moment the company had to accept the situation. 'However, the sooner you transfer Hooker the sooner you will get the 100 tons per man, and believe me, the General Manager will be delighted,' were the parting words of the AGM to Bullock.

Soon after he arrived in Maidstone, Bullock met the Regional Manager who was to be his immediate superior. Early in their conversation they talked of the high output figures required by London. The prospect of achieving them within the next six months seemed to be remote to the Regional Manager. In his opinion, with careful, close management, the depot might achieve 80 tons per man, but no more. Bullock felt this view to be timid and conservative. The Regional Manager went on to say that Hooker, the supervisor, would need a good deal of help and support from his new manager. He had not yet adapted himself to the new ways of working and was finding snags in the system never anticipated by the planners at Head Office.

Two days after Bullock took over, Hooker informed him that one of the manual staff had decided to leave. However, he knew of a good man to replace him. Bullock took this opportunity to state quite firmly that there would be no replacement. In fact, Hooker would in time lose another two men and would be expected to operate on a basic staff of nine men. Somewhat shaken, Hooker pointed out that his staff had always contained a small surplus to allow for holidays and sickness — something approved by his previous managers and certainly by the present Regional Manager. It would be physically impossible to manage with nine men and maintain scheduled deliveries. Despite all the new handling devices, the deck loading last thing at night and first thing in the morning still had to be done manually. For this he needed his establishment of twelve men. Experience told him that nothing less was sensible.

Bullock felt that this attitude was unreasonable. He now began to see what the Assistant General Manager had meant about Hooker. As the days went by the rift between the two men widened. Bullock, moreover, began to feel that Hooker was now actively criticising his policy with the men. About a month later and purely by chance another of the dock loaders handed in his notice. Bullock welcomed the move and reaffirmed his policy of staff reduction to his supervisor, who received the news in stony silence.

Soon after the departure of the second man the General Manager paid a brief visit to Maidstone, when Bullock was able to announce his staff reductions and mention his high hopes for increasing output. He felt that he was on the right track.

But as the weeks went by, there was no appreciable increase. His figures remained as before in the low seventies and there had been an increase in complaints from customers owing to late deliveries. Overtime had risen and 'down time', often symptomatic of poor morale among the men, had increased. For Bullock, this was the signal really to put the 'squeeze' on Hooker; for instance he was not to operate any breakdown routines himself, but he was to report them to the manager who would personally make arrangements for repair. Somehow this did not achieve its objective. Breakdowns increased still more and Bullock was not always immediately available when something went wrong.

In desperation, he called Hooker to his office and bluntly pointed out that unless output figures improved he would have to replace him. After three or four weeks they did not improve and Bullock made an urgent request to his Regional Manager to transfer Hooker to another depot. The Regional Manager counselled caution. Had Bullock done everything to put across his policy to Hooker? Had he given his supervisor all the support he should have done? For Bullock these remarks only revealed the timid and conservative outlook of the Regional Manager. After more argument it was reluctantly agreed to transfer Hooker and ask Head Office for a new man.

Fortunately, so Bullock felt, he was allocated a man who was regarded as the best supervisor in the business. Bisley's reputation in depot operations was very high, particularly with the General Manager. He was admired for his frankness and honest way of tackling a job. With the men he was firm and they had a great respect for him. Bullock was delighted with this newcomer and saw early prospects of reaching the output figures he wanted.

In the very early days of the new regime he explained to Bisley his policy of staff reduction and sought his approval. Bisley's reply was non-committal. After about a week, Bisley came back to Bullock and pointed out that the overtime situation was very unsatisfactory. Not only was there too much but it was consistently excessive, day after day. Bullock gently reminded Bisley that it was his job to reduce the overtime. For the next four weeks, Bisley stayed with the men for the whole of their day, every day, from 7.00 a.m. till 7.00 p.m. Monday to Friday, and for six hours on Saturdays. At the end of this period a third man gave in his notice. Bullock called Bisley to his office and told him he did not propose to replace this third man. They would then have reached their objective in staff reduction and output figures would undoubtedly reach the 100 tons per man. Certainly, the shoe would pinch for a week or two, but everyone would adjust to the new rate of work.

Bisley's reaction was immediate and violent: 'Mr Bullock, you are crazy! You are ruining this depot. If you haven't the courage to tell the General Manager that his planning is fundamentally wrong I propose to do it for you. I should like your answer by lunchtime today!'

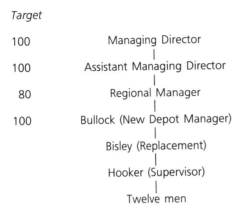

Target

100 Managing Director
|
100 Assistant Managing Director
|
80 Regional Manager
|
100 Bullock (New Depot Manager)
|
Bisley (Replacement)
|
Hooker (Supervisor)
|
Twelve men

Figure 5.4 *'On target' organisation chart*

Tasks

Figure 5.4 contains an organisation chart which may be helpful.

1. In formulating the objective of 100 tons per man-week what main principle of management by objectives was ignored and by whom?
2. Was the Assistant General Manager's attitude towards Hooker, the depot supervisor, justifiable?
3. If MbO were properly implemented what should the Assistant General Manager be doing about Hooker?
4. How did the Regional Manager (Bullock's superior) show his commitment (or lack of it) towards his objectives?
5. How did Bullock communicate his objectives to Hooker? Was this convincing?
6. Was Hooker committed to his firm's objectives?
7. Did Bullock's squeeze on Hooker work? If not, why not?
8. Is there any other prospect of breaking out of the deadlock of the under-achievement of the production figures?

For discussion of this case study see Appendix 1, p. 501.

Case Study 5.2
Effectiveness standards in a college environment

It has been suggested that in the public sector objectives are very difficult to quantify. Jean Ruffat (1983), a French researcher, did, however, offer a rather complex trade-off model, to reinforce the notion of value in the outcomes of people's jobs.

This case study will consider the concept of effectiveness standards in relation to college courses. In the college where this case study was developed there were 126 such courses, offered by a total of 24 departments. The course unit is a natural point of reference for effective management. Indeed, the college's reputation will depend much on the sum total of quality in its courses and supporting research, and if the units are really well managed there will be a synergy between such research and courses.

By developing a set of effectiveness standards and adopting an effective process for applying and monitoring these, we have a manifestation of group MbO in action. Initially we may suspect that this is just another bureaucratic process, marked by a lot of red tape, meetings and rituals. However, when the process is well managed, the course team should be seen to be responding to leadership, showing improvements, a problem-solving posture and a good record of validation feedbacks with bodies such as the Council for National Academic Awards (CNAA). This happened in practice and led to the granting of delegated powers, leaving the college with very near complete responsibility for the validation of its degree courses.

In this review of course management practice the process of development seemed initially to be very slow, looking back with hindsight, but in its eventual manifestation it showed some maturity of management and planning as well as acceptability for the college as a whole. It could be said to reflect the college culture. But the change of culture is a slow process and MbO principles are not learned and adopted overnight.

Stages of the management of course units

Stage 1   Setting up of course boards (year 1)
Firstly, a course team was appointed, and responsibilities assigned. A course organiser assumed managerial responsibility for the running of each course and was to be generally accountable to a head of department *vis-à-vis* line responsibility and to a course board, consisting of those who had a stake in the course and its success. These were the subject tutors, student class representatives, and in some cases a member representing an employer or professional institute. The course boards were to meet at least once a term.

In time these boards became unwieldy with a large membership and the meetings became ritualised. The eventual response was to narrow the membership, by calling in only subject leaders rather than every lecturer, and focus activity particularly on effectiveness standards as they became better understood.

Stage 2   Setting up an internal college validation structure, the Academic Practice Committee (year 3)
Higher-level management in the college wanted to know whether or not the courses were in a healthy state and set up a mechanism whereby the effectiveness standards for courses and their target numbers were made known. This became the role of the Academic Practice Committee, who would report to the main Academic Board.

The weakness of this was that there was no effective feedback process, except through line management as represented by heads of department.

Stage 3   Strengthening validation structure with the Faculty Practice Committee (year 9)

Twenty-four departments are a lot to monitor, so the college set up a faculty structure of three faculties and each faculty then developed its own Academic Practice Group to be more involved in the activity of course monitoring.

Stage 4   Design and implementation of the annual course board report (year 9)

Each course board team assumed responsibility for completing an annual course board report for scrutiny by another peer group of tutors from the faculty practice group. The course board report became the definitive focus of the college effectiveness standards. Summaries from faculty went to the main Academic Practice Committee for follow-up action and for decisions about the future of courses, particularly those perceived as 'weak'.

Early versions of the annual course board report included the following sections:

1. Analysis of first year admissions — actual number, target, differences, first choice applicants. Used to identify demand trends and unsatisfied demand.
2. Qualifications of first year admissions. This was broken down into a points system relating to grades of entry qualifications. Used for monitoring entry standard by year and course.
3. Student performance. Used to review progression rates.
4. Final outcomes. Used to monitor classes of honours awarded and categories of commendation and distinction.
5. Employment destinations of last year's graduates. Used to monitor employability of students from the college.
6. Analysis of student placements by type of employer for sandwich courses only. Used to monitor a problem area, particularly in times of recession.
7. External examiners' reports and responses by internal examiners to these comments.
8. Student representatives' reports, containing a wide range of items.
9. Curriculum arrangements — analysis of each department's contributions by hours. Forms the basis of staff establishment planning.

The system of feedback from Faculty was rather slow. There was a lack of back-up from research to underpin course development. Effectiveness standards needed reinforcing. Initially, course organisers complained about the time taken to prepare these reports and the boards about the time taken in reviewing them. After the second cycle, when it was better understood what was required and what degree of importance the college placed on this monitoring system, the quality of course board reports improved significantly.

Stage 5   Fine-tuning the report layout and content (year 10)

A new heading was introduced specifically on *course development*. This related to trends, relevant research of staff members to underpin teaching and expected future resource requirements to maintain course quality.

Stage 6 Fine-tuning the monitoring process (year 11)

Written reports may easily be misunderstood and misinterpreted by a faculty group, working alone on the annual course board reports. The practice was adopted of doing the review in the presence of the course organiser, who could easily clear up any such communication difficulty. This face-to-face contact gave the process a much greater credibility and avoided an earlier tendency of non-problems being given undue attention. With a face-to-face session the validating peer group and the representative of the course team could much more easily adopt a constructive problem-solving posture. A good deal of time was saved by this system, which also reinforced the line responsibility of the course organiser for the course team and its work.

The reader may find a similarity in this group assessment procedure and that behind the assessment process for individuals outlined in chapter 6. The aim in both cases is to overcome the tendency to ritualise what should be a creative, problem-solving interaction. In certain organisational cultures, particularly those in which professionals are in a majority, this group appraisal against effectiveness standards may be much easier to accept than processes which focus on the individual. In implementing MbO approaches it is prudent to be aware of organisational culture and to work as far as possible with it, rather than against it. In the end, the aim should simply be to strive for both good and acceptable management practice.

Stage 7 Use of annual course board data in college strategic planning and policy-making (year 11)

Once this monitoring process for the 124 courses was fully functioning it was natural to develop a summary which generated data on required resources and also offered opportunities to identify 'strong' and 'weak' courses. The policy-makers were then better able to formulate strategies regarding the course portfolio and to reallocate resources on the basis of course prioritisation. Many courses were dropped, but many imaginative course development initiatives were authorised. Research programmes and staff development could then be focused on areas of priority course development. The college was developing a sense of unity. A strategic management approach was being adopted, in the public sector, building on the solid foundations of effectiveness standards applied through the basic unit of the course team.

References

Bradley, D. and Wilkie, R. (1974), *The Concepts of Organisation*, Blackie.

Drucker, P. (1954), *The Practice of Management*, Harper.

Ellis-Jones, D. (1973), 'Director of Management Development', Honeywell, unpublished research.

French, W.L. and Drexler, J.A. (1984), 'A team approach to MbO: History and conditions for success', *Leadership and Organisation Development Journal*, vol. 5, no. 5, pp. 22−6.

Froissart, D. (1972), 'What can be learnt from MbO failures?', *MbO Journal*, vol. 2, no. 1, pp. 30−3.

Fulton, J.S. Lord (1968), *Civil Service. Report of Committee*. Cmd 3638, HMSO.

Hicks, H.G. and Gullett, C.R. (1981), *Management*, McGraw-Hill.

Humble, J.W. (1972), *Management by Objectives*, Teakfield.

McGregor, D. (1960), *The Human Side of Enterprise*, McGraw-Hill.

Maslow, A.H. (1970), *Motivation and Personality*, Harper.

Mayo, E. (1933), *The Human Problems of an Industrial Civilisation*, Macmillan.

Odiorne, G.S. (1972), *Management by Objectives: A System of Managerial Leadership*, Pitman.

Parkinson C.N. and Rowe N. (1977), *Parkinson's Formula for Business Survival*, Prentice Hall.

Reddin, W.J. (1968), *Effective Management*, McGraw-Hill.

Reddin, W.J. (1971), *Effective MbO*, BIM.

Ruffat J. (1983), 'Strategic management of public and non-market corporations', *Long-Range Planning Journal*, vol. 16, no. 2, pp. 74–85.

Steidl, J. W. (1974), 'Seven successful years at Packaging Corporation of America', *MbO Journal*, vol. 4, no. 1, pp. 6–10.

Stoner, J.A.F. (1978), *Management*, Prentice Hall.

Further reading

French, W.L. and Bell, C.H. (1978), *Organisation Development. Behavioural science interventions for organisation improvement*, Prentice Hall.

McGinnes, M.A. (1984), 'The key to strategic planning: integrating analysis and intuition', *Sloan Management Review*, Fall, pp. 45–52.

Chapter 6
The appraisal process

Overview

In this second chapter on the theory and practice of managing by objectives, attention is devoted to the feedback process known as the 'appraisal process'. In the early versions of MbO the feedback phase was the least understood and many MbO programmes foundered owing to the clumsy way in which it was handled. However, there has been much development in the literature of personnel management of the theory of performance review, sometimes coupled with an MbO approach and sometimes treated in isolation from MbO. It is the aim of this chapter to illustrate good practice in an appraisal process coupled fully to the MbO approach.

Learning objectives

By the end of the chapter, after being exposed to the case material, the reader should be able to recognise the main components of such good practice, but should also have an awareness of the obstacles to implementation of such principles.

The appraisal process

Objective-setting systems have a vital feedback phase, the 'appraisal process'. Note that it is a process, implying several components, and not an event. As a process it must be integrated with the normal feedback which is compatible with the firm's management culture. It should become the forum from which the manager/superior relationship is cultured to achieve mutual understanding and a framework of expectancy. It must embody interactions with a frequency that implies a real personal relationship. The process must not take up too much extra time as this will be costly and lead to resentment.

In practice, appraisal in organisations often involves three layers of management —

the manager, the manager's superior and the superior's superior, the latter being brought in as a counsellor after appraisal has been done at a lower level. Research suggests that this is not a successful approach. If a typical appraisal session lasts one hour and we assume a 10:1 relationship in the span of control, then over two tiers of management the superior's superior will be giving 100 hours to this activity. Organisations simply cannot afford that amount of time. If the interview is reduced to say 15 minutes it degenerates into a discipline interview and the opportunity for easy problem-solving dialogue is lost. The appraisal process must involve no more than two layers of management for each individual in order for the time requirements to be acceptable.

The key role of a third party

The model shown in Figure 5.1 (p. 63) highlights the usefulness of self-appraisal data and the presence of a third party during some of the sessions. Research, for example Torrington *et al.* (1989), generally recognises that the presence of a third party is beneficial to performance reviews. This third party role is to act as a catalyst and to encourage the development of a creative problem-solving environment. This is all directed at progress and development on the basis of merit and conscious choice, rather than luck, patronage and being a 'nice person' with some influential friends.

The third party may be a person associated with the work of the individual being appraised and should therefore have a natural empathy with the issues under discussion. As an 'interested outsider' he or she will attempt to bring to the session an objectivity that is very difficult to achieve between a manager and superior alone.

A management consultant or a member of a neutral department such as the personnel department may be the chosen third party. However, this is a very expensive approach in the long term, and organisations should be encouraged to get the superior's colleague to play this role as soon as possible. At the summit of the organisation, where there is no superior's colleague, then it is suggested that the subordinate's colleague becomes the third party.

Components of the appraisal process

Assignment review

It would appear that the most effective appraisal process has three separate components. The *assignment review* is a simple progress review session between the manager and superior alone to check status on all current assignments, and the operating issues arising from them. The frequency of this process will vary according to the level of the manager, but is unlikely to be less than once a month.

Assignment strategy review

The assignment strategy review is done in the presence of the recommended third party. Here the nature of the manager/superior dialogue is to probe the pattern of past and future assignments, to reveal problems and opportunities, resource deficiencies, delegation style and other organisational issues. The assignment strategy review may be expected to take place approximately every three months. It builds on the assignment review and is done with sufficient frequency to encourage the manager's continuous growth and personal development. This is a session where training needs are identified, which may require a manager's superior to commit resources. It may also call for a change of behaviour from the manager himself or herself or it may call for an organisational change affecting both. The management development aspect of MbO described here is, in Douglas McGregor's view (1960), the most important feature of MbO.

Promotional recommendation

The annual promotional recommendation is a consolidation process, done in the presence of the third party and building on the data from the other elements of the process, but with one important extra — a recommendation about the future. There are many possible outcomes. For a manager displaying significant strengths, promotion prospects could be considered with a plan for developing appropriate skills and experience. For many managers the emphasis will be on a consolidation of the existing position with an emphasis on widening the experience base. For those with an unsatisfactory performance there are two basic options: either a remedial management development programme to close the gap or a sideways (in extreme situations a downwards) move to a position better suited to the manager. If done sufficiently quickly, moving people sideways may be achieved relatively painlessly with the minimum loss of face. As this is the most sensitive process to manage, it is essential that it is done in the presence of a third party. At director level the third party will be a colleague of the subordinate, i.e. another director. At the highest level of an organisation that attainment of fluency in the appraisal process is the most important, for as a result of this process a natural teamwork and unity of purpose for the organisation as a whole may be communicated to lower levels. Nothing is more demoralising than having untreated incompetence at high levels in an organisation. Yet it is sometimes at the high levels that the greatest resistance to the appraisal process may be manifested, generally on the grounds that professionals communicate so well anyway that the appraisal process is superfluous. Dr Laurence Peter (1969), however, in his well-known work on the *Peter Principle*, asserts that executives rise to their level of incompetence in a bureaucracy and that the need for treatment in high places is almost universal! At lower levels of an organisation much of the work is easily measured and remedial action can be taken if necessary, but at higher levels this is much more difficult to achieve.

Research results suggest that the pressures on managers at senior levels in an organisation make them very vulnerable and they can easily become very isolated. Exposure to regular appraisal sessions can help to force them out of the ivory tower and into the reality of the problem-solving process.

In a research study on a Scottish manufacturer carried out by Erskine (1985), a senior production manager was interviewed who stated that appraisal would be unnecessary for him as he was in touch every day with his senior colleagues and could not but help being on the same wavelength as them. Three months later the researcher noticed that this senior manager had been demoted two levels, and then had a job at that level broken in half for him! The fall from grace had not been anticipated and the sudden action was very painful.

At levels lower than the board, the third party may be expected to be the superior's colleague. With the above process outlined there will be as much as sixteen appraisal snapshots done each year and with effective communication when the third party is present it should be unthinkable for a senior manager to be permitted to become deadwood over a period greater than two years. Salary adjustments too will depend to some extent on the outcome of the appraisal process.

Management inventory

Finally, if the appraisal process is competently managed it should yield valid data about the organisation's management inventory. The term management inventory refers to the total sum of management talent within the organisation as perceived by appraisers. The inventory provides vital data for corporate planning exercises. It is also the basis from which succession plans may be developed and personnel recruitment policy determined and implemented.

For a multi-division, multi-location organisation there are obvious advantages in having a managerial inventory for the planning of careers and resourcing new posts as the organisation grows and develops. This is not a particularly novel idea. Organisations with an international base of operations such as the armed forces and Shell Petroleum have for a long time had an inventory of management as part of the infrastructure of their personnel function.

Case Study 6.1
The Hudson-Lansing Company

(Material used and adapted with special permission of the copyright holder, BNA Communications Inc., 9439 Key West Avenue, Rockville, Maryland 20850, USA.)

Options for analysis

This case study consists of a transcript of the interviews between Peter Drucker and company executives, as a result of which he makes recommendations about the future of each of the three key executives. For tutorial purposes the MbO model is used to establish the issues relating to management development for the three executives. Drucker's solution, however, is open to debate in the climate of contemporary practice. Did he get it right?

Each interview sequence should be analysed separately.

This case may be analysed by individuals or groups. If working in a group, members may be asked to read the scripts of the characters. Alternatively the tutor may read all the script and pause for tutorial comment and questions as is required. If the case is being studied by an individual, the reader should analyse each interview sequence in turn and then compare this analysis with that offered in the exercise notes given in Appendix 1.

Company organisation

Hudson-Lansing has been trading for some thirty-four years and is still led by the owner/founder, Mr Lansing, who is Executive President. The firm currently employs some 1,000 people and calls in Peter Drucker as consultant to advise on executive development. Mr Lansing is 55, and although not immediately wishing to retire, he is anxious to leave behind him, when the time comes, a competent executive team. Currently he has serious problems with three senior members of his executive team.

Charlie Fisher is the Sales Manager. Young, ambitious, energetic, he falls out with his boss Lansing and gets the sack.

Bill Mathis holds the combined posts of Director of Research and Quality Control. He was recently promoted as a boffin from section leader in the research team and has the reputation of being the ablest bench scientist in the industry, but he does have some difficulty in coming to terms with the management components of his job. The double promotion has taken its toll.

Ralph Evans is the Controller (Financial Director) of the company and started with Lansing thirty-four years ago. There are some serious problems in the way he discharges his role.

Figure 6.1 shows an organisation chart for this case study.

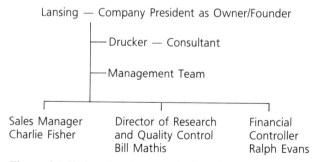

Figure 6.1 *Hudson-Lansing organisation chart*

Interview 1

Lansing: Margey, call Charlie Fisher and send him up here immediately, no matter what he is doing.

Fisher: (On the shop floor with Mathis). Your spot-check is just not accurate enough. Look, how the hell do you expect me to go out and get reorders when 11 per cent of those packs are faulty. How many are you checking out of every 100?

Mathis: Two.

Fisher: Then you ought to be pretty clear from the number of complaints which we have been getting that two just is not enough. No, you should be checking a dozen even twenty until we can be sure that we are getting the bugs out of production.

Mathis: I agree.

Fisher: Oh! That is all very nice. Boy, I wish you had to go out and sell those damn things after word goes round that they go off if somebody coughs near them. What the hell are you doing about the quality check?

Mathis: There is nothing I can do about it. To do the job you are talking about would take four to six highly-trained men, and the Controller will not approve it. Half the time I am out fixing the damn things myself.

Fisher: Supposing we send separate memos to Evans detailing our problems both in sales and quality control. Once we get them on paper I do not see how he can turn us down. I will see to it that those papers go right upstairs and then if he is still holding tight on us I will get help from the top desk. You see I did not read my Machiavelli for nothing!

Mathis: Okay let's go. There are some pencils and pads in my office.
Telephone rings. *Fisher* answers.
What is it Margey? No, no, I cannot. Tell him I will be there in 45 minutes . . . Oh, all right, all right, tell him I will be there right away. Right away, yes. I am sorry, Bill. When he says right away he means right away. I hope that he is happier with his next Sales Manager.

Mathis: Take it easy.

Fisher: Like hell I will. I am sick of taking it easy.

Lansing (now with Fisher in his office): What kind of excuse is that?

Fisher: An excuse! It's a reason.

Lansing: Now, Charlie, I did not call you up here to quibble. I have three letters this month from my oldest customers. Your sales people have not been near them for half a year or more. Now that is downright neglect and I will not have it.

Fisher: It isn't neglect, downright, upright or sideways. I simply told the boys not to waste time covering them.

Lansing: You told them? Phew. It would have been bad enough if they had done it on their own but to have my own sales manager go out of his way to offend my most reliable trade, the customers who helped me to build this business. Why all I can think it is is stupidity or . . . arrogance.

Fisher: Now look, Mr Lansing. I thought that when you gave me this job you were also giving me the authority to do it.

Lansing: I was.

Fisher: Then don't you think you ought to let me make the decisions about how my salesmen spend their time?

Lansing: I cannot let you make decisions, when your decisions are alienating my best customers.

Fisher: That is just the point, Mr Lansing, they are not your best customers, they are your worst customers. They are also your oldest customers. That is why there is not so much reason to cover them. I mean they are going to send in their reorders whether the boys see them or not.

Lansing: They are, huh? Take a look at this letter. Here is one who is not so darned ready to reorder. I was able to fix it with five phone calls, a golf weekend and a case of bourbon. But it won't be so easy next time. Now get this thing straight, Fisher. I want those firms serviced the way they always have been.

Fisher: I am sorry, Mr Lansing. I just cannot do it. In the first place I am short-handed. Two of my best men went over to RTR.

Lansing: And that is another thing I wanted to talk to you about. Why?

Fisher: Ask your Controller.

Lansing: What does that mean?

Fisher: The men got sick and tired having every item on their expense account being gone over with a microscope and a third of their vouchers disqualified. Sure they were fudging a little, and I knew it, but those men were worth it.

Lansing: I won't have stealing in my company. That is why I have a Controller.

Fisher: OK, you have got a Controller. But now you do not have two first-rate salesmen . . . now I was not going to bring this up but as long as you have Evans that is how we lost them. And I must say it couldn't have been handled in a more miserable fashion. I want my salesmen to report to me, not to the Controller.

Lansing: I do not approve of this. I won't have heads of departments carrying tales against each other. Evans has been with me since I started.

Fisher: Now you are asking straight questions; do you want straight answers or a lot of crap?

Lansing: Now just you listen, Fisher, I hesitated a long time before hiring you. I was warned that you had an extremely arrogant personality.

Fisher: What is the point of being a sales manager without one?

Lansing: I was my own Sales Manager while you were still wetting your pants. I do not think I need any lessons from you on how to deal with salesmen or customers.

Fisher: You have your way and I have mine. I did not leave a good job and come here because you have got a good business going in transformers. I came here because you also have some new and exciting things to sell and I would go where the action is. I am no sentimentalist. Look Mr Lansing if you want somebody who is going to make your old customers with $8,000 business per annum feel happy then I respectfully suggest that you hire your old Sales Manager back again.

Lansing: Well then, I am just going to take you up on your respectful suggestion. Just because you can get the sales does not mean that you are in charge. I think that we will both be a lot happier if you go elsewhere.

Fisher: OK, so be it. No hard feelings Mr Lansing. I could feel this coming for some time now. Now if you will allow yourself to take some advice next time you hire a man to do a job give him the authority to do it. Don't second guess him till he has a chance to prove his point. Maybe that's why you have had three Sales Managers in the last three years before I got here.

Issues involved in this first interview. Lansing/Fisher

There is a need to analyse how a bad relationship developed.

1. Job role of the Sales Manager — Was there a mutual agreement on what this role was?
2. Fisher's perception of his authority. Did this match Lansing's?
3. Salesmen who left after expenses were disqualified. Was this Fisher's fault?

(For discussion of feedback see Appendix 1, p. 504).

Interview 2

Lansing (now with Peter Drucker): Oh, it isn't just these squabbles, Peter. When we went into these new lines I thought that it was going to be the most exciting time of my life. You know, getting into the big leagues where there are growth possibilities. All I can tell you is that it is one big headache. I have stopped enjoying my work and I spend too much time at it to put up with these pressures and irritations. I am even having trouble with management personnel that I never had before. Suddenly everybody is a prima donna and my wife keeps reminding me that I am not getting any younger — a phrase that I find particularly irritating. Now she is beginning to talk about me retiring. Hell, I can't retire. I have just built an $11 million plant. What's more, I do not want to retire. Frankly, I would go out of my mind. Well, I have got to run now. A committee meeting about getting job opportunities for Blacks in the community and I have some plans.

Drucker: Well don't let me keep you, Mr Lansing. Would you mind if I talked to some of those people we have been discussing? I would like to start with Charlie Fisher.

Lansing: Hm, as far as I am concerned he's an ex-employee. Talk to anyone you please. Hm.

(Drucker is fully acquainted with the situation leading up to Fisher's dismissal.)

(Drucker comes in and asks Mathis how he sees his job.)

Mathis: Oh, well I need to do my job better. We could start with a forty-hour day and a ten-day week.

Drucker: Tell me Mr Mathis, why do you need a special calendar?

Mathis: There is just too much to do to fit into the one we have. I was going great as head lab researcher developing the computer memory system and then I found out that they liked my work. Now I get a lot more money and my name on the door. We all go to the Lansing's three times a year. Very nice, and I am not knocking it, but I am here sometimes fifteen hours a day, and my dog barks at me when I go home, so it doesn't impress him that I am Director of Research and Quality Control. And it doesn't impress me so much any more either. See, I haven't been near the research lab in a year now. That is what I like best. That is what I do best. You see I have a couple of bright Caltex boys there but I don't know how to tell them what to look for. I have always had to do that kind of thing myself. Just messing around till I come up with a lead. I have got four ideas that I have been wanting to explore, and they are good ideas I think . . . but there is no time to get to them. And the quality control. That's a real mess. Every time something goes wrong in Cleveland or Cincinnati one of the researchers is on a plane the same day, or one of the quality control men, or I have to go myself. And every time that I ask for more of something, especially manpower, well I don't want to go into that one. Just say I don't get it.

Drucker: And what are you going to do about it?

Mathis: Give it a little thought, see if it straightens out, and if it doesn't — what does one usually do about a situation like this?

Issues for discussion interview. Drucker/Mathis
1. How does Mathis see his managerial role and discharge it?
2. What are his training needs? How should they have been detected?
3. If the job is too big for Mathis how could it be redesigned?
4. Should Mathis be a target for management development?

For discussion of feedback see Appendix 1, p. 506.

Interview 3

(Drucker is now with Ralph Evans. He asks Ralph how he sees his job.)

Evans: I don't understand a question like that, Mr Drucker. I don't *think* that I know what my job is. I know perfectly well what my job is.

Drucker: Oh, I didn't mean to offend you. I am just trying to get a little information.

Evans: Now that was a strange question. I started thirty-four years ago as a book-keeper. I made my way up to head accountant, now I am Controller of the company. Now if Lansing is not a stupid man, if I did not know my job I would still be a book-keeper or would not be here at all.

Drucker: Well, what do you consider to be the most important functions?

Evans: Well, they are all important. For instance, I can tell you where we stand on

receivables, inventory, and of course there is payroll, taxes ... I suppose I have
saved this firm over $1.5 million in taxes. Now I am not a college man, Mr
Drucker, but I have taken every tax course they have at the university. I suppose
that I could be termed an expert in the field. As a matter of fact, some of my
friends in firms in the area call me in for advice when they have a particularly
nasty tax problem. If it were not for what I owe Lansing I could set up as an
independent tax consultant. I am sure that I could do pretty good. So you
asked me what my job was. I keep track of every dollar that comes in, every
dollar that goes out, and I make sure that no more goes out than is strictly
necessary.

Drucker: Who decides what is necessary?

Evans: Oh, Mr Lansing makes the big decisions over big expenditures and for the
week-to-week expenses and operating costs of the firm I take responsibility
myself. I enjoy it. I owe a loyalty to this company that some of these young hot
shots around here cannot understand. They would spend money like water if I
would let them. You know they will not make do with what they have.
Everything is more money, more men, more equipment. Of course they have a
different orientation to what I have. They do not know what hard times are.
Some of them were children in the depression, some were not even born. What
is the name of that book — *The Affluent Society*? That is these kids — the
affluent society. If I did not hold them down they would spend this firm into
bankruptcy.

Issues interview 3

1. What are the key roles of a financial controller?
2. Does Evans do well in all such roles? Some roles?
3. Role competence — When and how is it assessed? How should deviations be managed?
4. Would the appraisal process be appropriate?
5. Who would play the third party role?
6. Who did play the third party role?

For feedback see discussion in Appendix 1, p. 507.

Interview 4

Drucker: (now in Lansing's office) I have been spending quite a few days at
Hudson-Lansing talking with its people and I think I know quite a bit more
about the company than I really want to know. Well, three things stand out
quite clearly. First, they do not have the controls they need. And second, they
have been quite amazingly successful in shifting from a one-man company to a
management team, but the last point is that they don't yet know how to get
mileage out of that management team. Evans isn't really a Controller.
Receivables, inventories, production schedules and production costs are in pretty
poor shape. That is why they aren't doing well economically and do not get the

benefit of their products and of their sales. Evans knows where the pencils are but he does not know what the costs are. At the same time Lansing has been able to do what very few people can do who start out with nothing as he did and build a sizeable business. He has been able to shift gears from one-man control to having a management team of people who want to do a job. That's remarkable. That is a big man. I do not know many. But at the same time he is still trying to use what people cannot do. He is not trying to use the strengths of people. He sure has a lot to learn about how one uses people.

Lansing (enters the office): Terribly sorry Peter, but they let me out of the meeting fifteen minutes late. Well, let's get down to business. You have had a chance to talk to the men we discussed and I know that I have got to make some decisions pretty quickly.

Drucker: What do you propose to do with these key people?

Lansing: Well, let's start with Evans. I have thought a great deal about Ralph. He has been with the company as long as I have. But I realise that I cannot keep him on this day-to-day stuff, so I have just about decided to kick him upstairs to make him Treasurer, so that he can concentrate on financial policy. The promotion will work all right and it will take the pressure off that one.

Mathis has me baffled. He did such a beautiful job as a bench scientist. But I do not think that I am getting the most out of him as a manager. Yet if I pay him any less I will lose him. It is a real dilemma.

Charlie Fisher has given me some sleepless nights too. In a way I am sorry that I lost him. He was a hell of a salesman, and I am beginning to find out that he is a very hard man to replace. But I do not want any man on a team who won't play, and as far as I am concerned he's through. Now, what are your ideas, Peter?

Drucker: What you propose to do, nine out of every ten executives would do and all nine of you would be wrong! Take Evans first. Of course you have got to move him out from being Controller. He is not the Controller, and you do need one around here. If you kick him upstairs you are only buying trouble, next year, two years hence and much worse trouble. You do need a good financial man one of these days and Evans isn't. It never pays to kick a man upstairs into a bigger job for which he is even less competent. What can you do with him because you are quite right you cannot let him go? Thirty-four years create their obligation. Your organisation will judge you by the way you treat him. But let me say that if you leave him in there your organisation will also judge you by that. You have got to get him out, but you have got to treat him right. So let's find out what this fellow can do. Thank goodness he can do quite a bit. He is the best tax man around this area for the kind of business which you are in, and there are quite a few round here. Maybe you rent him an office down town next to your law firm, set him up as a tax consultant, make your company his first client, and underwrite his expenses, and drum up trade for him from your buddies around here. I think you will make him happy. I think that your organisation will appreciate it. I think that you will have done your duty.

Mathis is probably the best bench scientist in your entire industry. And you have just fallen victim to the oldest and hoariest myth of management. The myth that one cannot pay a scientist or any other professional more than one pays his manager. Nobody, but nobody says anything if Chris Evert makes more money than her coach. Why should that not apply in all other areas just as well? Put him back into the corner office where he belongs, ensure than nobody reports to him, and have him go back to designing and give him a 10 per cent raise for the agony he suffered trying to be a manager, which God in his infinite wisdom did not create him to be.

Then Fisher. Fisher belongs back here and he knows it. I think you will have no difficulty in getting him back here.

Drucker's summary

Let's go back to Evans. There is an Evans in every organisation. And what you do as a manager about your Evans will largely determine whether you have an organisation or not. If you leave him where he is not competent you will demoralise your entire organisation. But if your forget his thirty-four years full of loyal and dedicated service and throw him out you will also demoralise your organisation. You have got to find a way in which you can harmonise what seems at first quite impossible to do. You have got to find a way in which you can make use of what he can do. It will not always be as easy and as pat as in the little story we showed you today. Not everybody is a tax expert, but you would be surprised how often you will find the right solution if you work at it. The key question is always: 'What can the man do?'

Men like Mathis are a different case and they will be increasingly common. Increasingly, you will have people who are high knowledge people in all kinds of areas and kinds of specialisations, who perform, who deserve recognition but who should not be made managers. Increasingly, you will have to learn to give them the money they have earned and the recognition they have earned and yet keep them doing what they can do. Increasingly, you will have to accept that a first-rate professional may earn a great deal more than the manager and that that's a very much better way than ruining the professional by trying to make a manager out of him or her.

Well, the easiest one but also the most common is the Charlie Fisher case. There all you have to overcome is your natural tendency to judge a man by whether you like him or not. Just keep in mind that that is totally irrelevant. What matters is, does he perform? If he performs then he has earned the right to be disagreeable to you, his boss.

But let me say the most important lesson was not in this show you just saw . . . or did you see it there? The one person whose strengths are least used is the boss, it's Lansing, the ablest man in the company, the company's greatest resource. Could you figure out what he is doing? As far as I can see he is playing the assistant to every single one of his managers. He has not looked at himself. He has not asked: 'And what can I do?' An effective executive looks at every one of his subordinates and asks: 'What can he do?' He does not worry too much about what they cannot do. He is grateful to the good Lord for every ounce of strength he has in the organisation, but above all he looks at himself and asks: 'What is my strength, what do I have to apply, what can I do?' That to me is the main lesson.

Contentious Drucker offerings

Does the reader agree with him?

1. God in his infinite wisdom did not make Mathis into a manager. Save him the agony and put him into a small corner office where nobody reports to him and give him a salary rise.
2. An effective manager has earned the right to stick his tongue out at his boss. He should be judged only on performance, not personality.

For discussion of these issues see Appendix 1, p. 504.

Case Study 6.2
A service manager's problem

(Case adapted from unpublished material written by D. Ellis-Jones, edited by Robert Erskine.)

This case relates to incidents dealt with by a line manager, Jim Marshall, newly promoted to the senior staff position of National Service Manager in his company. The company is using MbO principles, but during the early stages of implementation there are several manifestations of weak practice, which form the basis of analysis. After reading the case study text, readers will analyse the following issues:

1. Jim Marshall seems to have some problems in getting the perspective of his new position, and setting the objectives. In what year should the *Service Manual* have been completed?
2. Why was the manual not completed until year 3?
3. An appraisal process has recently been introduced into the company, but there are question marks over its effective application. Does it reflect the norms of good appraisal practice?
4. Other contingent problems relate to the theory of organisation structure and organisational effectiveness. To what extent is the General Manager, Paul McKay, using the natural strengths of the company's organisation structure?

Much of the case is illustrated from a file of company correspondence relating to the late publication of a policy manual, the *Service Manual*. With the benefit of hindsight the reader may attribute many of the problems described in the later memos directly to the late publication of this manual. Figure 6.2 gives the company's organisation chart.

Jim Marshall's position

Jim Marshall is the National Service Manager for a division of a large diversified manufacturer of automated controls. His division specialises in installation and servicing

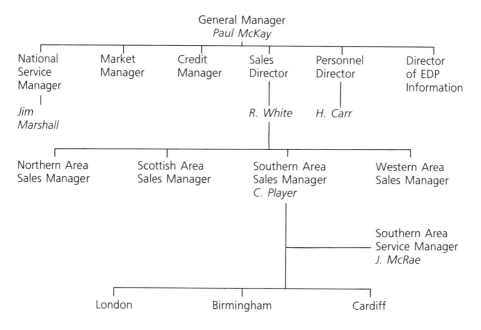

Figure 6.2 *Service group organisation chart*

automated controls of large industrial, commercial and residential facilities. Marshall's function is to provide advice and assistance to the field organisation, which sells and installs these systems. Marshall's department provides information and service to both regions and branches on methods of improving installation of controls, cost-saving procedures, systematising of records and statistics and improvements in branch operations.

Marshall had been promoted from the post of Area Manager, where he had earned a considerable reputation as an energetic 'doer'. His company has recently adopted a consultant's recommendation to manage by objectives. In his first year he participated in an objective-setting session with Paul McKay and the outcome of this was an agreed list of objectives to work on marked 'First Year Objectives'. Several memos which discuss his assignments and performance that year are attached. The reader will note that one objective, the *Service Manual*, was not completed that year. Many of the memos in this case relate directly or indirectly to the *Service Manual*.

Marshall, in developing his second-year objectives with his own boss, Paul McKay, carried over the *Service Manual* objective. Additional memos pertaining to the second year's work are attached, together with his appraisal record.

Marshall's third year objectives and various explanatory memos are also attached.

List of memos and other material

Memo no.	From	Subject
1.	Harry Carr	Request for help on the Union Contract. 15 April, year 1.
2.	Harry Carr	Thanks for help on Union Contract. 18 July, year 1.
3.	Tom Schmidt	Request for help from Birmingham after Jackson's termination. 4 August, year 1.
4.	Paul McKay	Authorisation for Jim to get involved with Birmingham, but no slippage expected on other assignments. 1 September, year 1.
5.	Jef McRae	Suggestions for Jim from National Conference for *Service Manual*. 10 October, year 1.
6.	Paul McKay	Jim Marshall's year 1 performance review. 20 December, year 1.
7.	Jim Marshall	Service contract escalation. 22 February, year 2.
8.	Paul McKay	Contract escalations. 25 February, year 2.
9.	Paul McKay	Computer problem, request for Jim's involvement. 12 June, year 2.
10.	Jim Marshall	Computer problem, report offered. 15 September, year 2.
11.	Dave Elliot	Apology for delay in reviewing *Service Manual* outline. 3 October, year 2.
12.	Rhoddie White	Serious concern about non-delivery of *Service Manual*. 22 November, year 2.
13.	Paul McKay	Jim Marshall's second year performance review. 20 December, year 2.
14.	Jef McRae	When will *Service Manual* be ready? 31 March, year 3.
15.	Pete Angel	Request for help from London. 19 June, year 3.
16.	Pete Angel	Thanks for Jim Marshall's help. 12 September, year 3.
17.	Jim Marshall	Circulation of final draft of *Service Manual*. 1 Nov, year 3.

Jim Marshall's first-year objectives

Priority

1. Review all branch service statements and evaluate their results against plan. List those off plan and recommend corrective action to branch managers. Weighting 30 per cent.
2. Provide and administer the following training schools:
   (a) computerised control systems;
   (b) advanced salesman's training;

(c) service selling school for new hires.
Weighting 20 per cent.
3. Complete and publish for distribution a *Service Manual* by the year end. Weighting 20 per cent.
4. Develop a set of standards to be used by field service managers in determining profitability of service contracts. Weighting 20 per cent.
5. Establish a specific estimating method for the new total maintenance package, to be in the field manager's possession by the third quarter. Weighting 10 per cent.

Inter-office correspondence — memo 1

To: Jim Marshall
From: Harry Carr, Bracknell
cc: P. McKay

Subject: Controls Division — Union Contract
15 April, Year 1

Dear Jim,
   As you are aware, the National Union Contract is coming up for negotiations next month and I will need your help in putting together a plan of action. Could you set aside the week of 3 May?

Thanks,
Harry

Inter-office correspondence — memo 2

To: Jim Marshall
From: Harry Carr, Bracknell
cc: P. McKay

Subject: Union contract
18 July, Year 1

Dear Jim,
   Just a note to let you know that we have finished the final draft on the union contract. Your help was really appreciated, both during the planning stage and the negotiations. Your contributions were instrumental in getting a very satisfactory contract. I had a gut reaction that you would be able to do much better than my own staff, such is your reputation from previous days!
   I owe you and Cathy a dinner on me for keeping you two apart for three weeks in London.

Best regards,
Harry

Inter-office correspondence — memo 3

To: Jim Marshall
From: Tom Schmidt, Birmingham
cc: C. Player, London; J. McRae, London

Subject: Dan Jones
4 August, Year 1

Dear Jim,

With Jack Jackson's termination four months ago, we now have a chance to evaluate the damage done to our service contract customers. To put it bluntly, we're in trouble! Here is just a sample of what went on while Jack was head of department:

1. XYZ Company called four times for service on our equipment, without results. An explosion occurred in which we were named defendants in a law suit for £15,000 damages.
2. Service contracts have not been escalated in the last three years to take account of inflation. The possible loss of branch income is £20,000.
3. Inventory equipment is completely chaotic. We have no idea as to what is new, exchanged, etc.

When Dan was brought in to replace Jack we had hopes that he could bring the service department up to a level of other service departments in our region. Although Dan is doing a commendable job, I believe that it may be a little too much for him to handle at this time. We need your expertise in getting our department back on the straight and narrow. Will you help?

Regards,
Tom

Inter-office correspondence — memo 4

To: Jim Marshall
From: Paul McKay, Bracknell

Subject: Tom Schmidt's memo
1 September, Year 1

Dear Jim,

It looks as though our people in Birmingham could use your experience as a former area manager in getting the service department back on the right track. As from now, why do you not plan on whatever time you deem necessary to get the job done.

I hope that you will be able to work on this special project without having to slip dates on any of the regular objectives. Good luck!

Regards,
Paul

Inter-office correspondence — memo 5

To: Jim Marshall
From: Jef McRae, London
cc: R. White Bracknell; C. Player, London

10 October, Year 1

Dear Jim,

   At our annual Southern managers' meeting last week, one of the topics on the agenda was that of the *Service Manual*. The managers came up with a number of suggestions which you might consider in the development of the material. I am attaching an outline of these suggestions for your review.

   The fellows are very enthusiastic about your manual, but the one question which keeps coming up is: 'When are we going to have the valuable manual in our hands?' As you know, we've been promised this manual ever since the matter was brought up two years ago. Can you give me an idea as to the timetable which you have planned, so that I can pass this on to our men?

   If there is anything I can do to expedite this matter please let me know.

Best regards,
Jef

Inter-office correspondence — memo 6

To: Jim Marshall's personnel file
From: Paul McKay

Subject: Year-end performance review
20 December, Year 1

   Today I discussed Jim's job performance with him. I pointed out that his attitude and accomplishments in this first year on the National Service Manager's job were very good.

   All the people with whom he works have high praise for his contribution to the Division's success. He is always ready to take on additional assignments and he usually does them well.

   During the year, Jim fell down on only one objective, the development of a *Service Manual*. I told Jim that this disappointed me, but that I understood how many other very important projects had come up which got him off the track.

   All in all, Jim's work has been very satisfactory.

Paul McKay

Jim Marshal's second-year objectives
Priority

1. Establish a short-range manpower scheduling procedure for service representatives. Once established, review with branch management for implementation. Weighting 25 per cent.

2. Develop and publish a Service Manager's Manual by the fourth quarter of this year. Weighting 25 per cent.
3. Prepare and have implemented by the third quarter a service sales contest for the area service salesmen. Weighting 25 per cent.
4. Review the present training programmes, and recommend changes to conform to present-day practices. Special emphasis should be placed on warehouse management. Weighting 15 per cent.
5. Revise the present method of estimating contracts requiring a fixed contract price. Completion and presentation to area service managers at annual autumn meeting. Weighting 10 per cent.

Inter-office correspondence — memo 7

To: Paul McKay, Bracknell
From: Jim Marshall, Bracknell
cc: R. White, Bracknell

Subject: Service contract escalation
22 February, Year 2

Dear Paul,

  Working with our auditors, we have come upon the fact that many of our service contracts have not been properly escalated over the past years to take account of inflation. Should this be the case, we could very easily have lost income estimated at £200,000 annually in the Division. As you can see, this is a sizeable sum of money involved and I therefore believe I should devote a major proportion of my time to this project. In most discussions with the auditors and accounting people, it appears as though it could take up to three months to get the wheels in motion to have the regional service managers correct this situation.

  I am sure that you will agree that a project of this magnitude will require my full attention. As a result, I might encounter a delay in the completion of the *Service Manual*. I know you concur that as of the moment the escalation of contracts certainly takes precedence over the manual.

  May I hear from you on this matter?

Regards,
Jim

Inter-office correspondence — memo 8

To: Jim Marshall
From: Paul McKay, Bracknell
cc: R. White, Bracknell

Subject: Contract escalations
25 February, Year 2

Dear Jim,

  With this year's pressure for an increase in sales revenue, I wholeheartedly agree with you that you should go after lost income on service contracts. Keep me posted on the progress you're making as I will want to keep our top executives informed as to our year-end projections.

Knowing that the *Service Manual* is foremost in the mind of our field area managers, is it possible to tie the service manual project and the escalation project together? See what you can do.

Regards,
Paul

Inter-office correspondence — memo 9
To: Jim Marshall, Bracknell
From: Paul McKay, Bracknell

Subject: Computer problem
12 June, Year 2

Dear Jim,

For the past six months, we have been receiving complaint after complaint on our computerised inventory control reports. I won't go into much detail on the problems but I want you to get together with the boys from our EDP Department and get it resolved. I know that your past experience in the area office will be invaluable in seeing this project through. I'm sure that you can appreciate what these managers put up with by having inaccurate reports.

This special project will put you behind on that manual but I have asked our National Construction Manager to give assistance as you see fit.

Regards,
Paul

Inter-office correspondence — memo 10
To: Paul McKay, Bracknell
From: Jim Marshall, Bracknell

Subject: Computer problem
15 September, Year 2

Dear Paul,

Attached is the report covering the problems which we found as a result of my working with our EDP group. In the summary of the report, I made certain recommendations which I believe merit your consideration.

Now to get to work on that *Service Manual*!

Best regards,
Jim

Inter-office correspondence — memo 11

To: Jim Marshall, Bracknell
From: Dave Elliot, London
cc: C. Player, London

Subject: My involvement in *Service Manual* contents
3 October, Year 2

Dear Jim,

Because of my immediate need to hire three new servicemen in the London area, I must postpone my visit to Bracknell. As a result I will not be able to go over your proposed outline for the *Service Manual*. There must be other service managers who are available, timewise, to give you assistance.

Sorry for any inconvenience this change may have caused.

Regards,
Dave

Inter-office correspondence — memo 12

To: Paul McKay, Bracknell
From: Rhoddie White, Sales Director, Bracknell

Subject: Outcomes of recent national sales conference
22 November, Year 2

Dear Paul,

I have just returned from our national sales meeting and thought that you would be interested in what was discussed.

Attached are the sales figures through the third quarter. As you can see, we are well ahead of plan in five regions, with the Western Region slightly behind plan. This deviation can be attributed to the lack of Government spending in Wales. May I suggest that we meet to go over these figures in detail?

Secondly, factory delivery of our goods is becoming atrocious. The regions are starting to stockpile their inventory as they can no longer trust the factory promises. I am certain that a lot of this is uncalled for; however, the movement appears to be snowballing. We must meet with our manufacturing people and somehow get the problems resolved.

Finally, the matter of the *Service Manual* came up again as it did last year. Our director suspects that the regional managers and branch managers are handling service by the seat of their pants. There appears to be inconsistency from one branch to another on the very basics of the service department. The Director would like to see that its publication becomes the number one priority for Jim Marshall. Based on what I hear from these managers, I would have to agree with them. My appreciation of the incidence of many service problems and contract escalations is simply that we do not have an operational *Service Manual* to guide our people. When I made the original case for the appointment of Jim Marshall the core of my argument was that he should bring orderliness to the service function, and this we have not achieved! He really does need some active coaching to enable him to tackle projects which have a significant element of consultation in them. I believe that we should adopt a third-party approach in the appraisal process to emphasise the aspects of management development in a supportive interactive environment.

I wish to get together with you sometime next week to go into more detail on this item and other matters which we discussed.

Regards,
Rhoddie

Inter-office correspondence — memo 13

To: Jim Marshall's personnel file
From: Paul McKay, Bracknell

Subject: Year-end performance check-up
20 December, Year 2

This memo recaps a performance review discussion held today with Jim Marshall.

Jim continues to perform very well. His manpower scheduling project has made a big impact on the field service department efficiency.

He successfully launched the service sales contest which is the talk of the field. In addition, he was able to put out several important 'fires' which came up during the year.

The only project he didn't complete was the *Service Manual* — once again. I have given it high priority for next year since it is so important.

Jim's attitude and results have demonstrated that he is very ripe for bigger things in the future.

Paul McKay

Jim Marshall's third-year objectives

Priority

1. Assist the area service managers in establishing standards for measurement of service personnel performance. Recommend review with Personnel Department on salary pay practices. Complete by second quarter. Weighting 30 per cent.
2. Publish a Service Manager's Manual. Complete by third quarter. Weighting 25 per cent.
3. Develop a comparative cost of our new method of servicing the electronic equipment versus the old method. Upon completion prepare to give presentations to our area managers. Weighting 20 per cent.
4. Provide a technical training course on the Mark XV Service Control Centre. To be complete by the fourth quarter. Weighting 15 per cent.

5. Conduct a study of cost comparison on service vehicles. Recommend type of vehicle and manner of financing. Complete by second quarter. Weighting 5 per cent.
6. Select and establish in Bracknell a database manager for compiling company reports by the second quarter. Weighting 5 per cent.

Inter-office correspondence — memo 14

To: Jim Marshall, Bracknell
From: Jef McRae

Subject: Service manual
31 March, Year 3

Dear Jim,

   I have just returned from the branches and the one question which each manager asked was, 'When can we expect the *Service Manual*?'

   We realise that you have spent many days with our managers and we do sincerely appreciate your efforts. We know that when the manual is finished, it will be a product of these and other projects which you have done so well.

Sincerely,
Jef

Inter-office correspondence — memo 15

To: Jim Marshall, Bracknell
From: Pete Angel, London
cc: D. Elliott, London

Subject: London visit
19 June, Year 3

Dear Jim,

   I am sure that you are aware that the London Branch has had a rather narrow profit margin on our total service sales. In order to improve this picture we took a number of measures hoping to improve our profit but without a great deal of success. Undoubtedly, much of our time was spent in pursuing what we thought were cost-saving areas; however, the end result was a fruitless waste of effort.

   I know that you are engrossed in any number of projects but would you find some time to spend with us? Your expertise in this area would be very beneficial to us.

Best regards,
Pete

Inter-office correspondence — memo 16

To: Paul McKay, Bracknell
From: Pet Angel, London
cc: R. White, Bracknell; D. Elliot, London; J. Marshall, Bracknell

Subject: Jim Marshall
12 September, Year 3

Dear Paul,

Some months ago, I requested that Jim Marshall spend some time with us in London to go over the profitability of our service department. With his help we were able to increase our profit by a welcome 5 per cent.

He should be complimented on a job well done.

Regards,
Pete

Inter-office correspondence — memo 17

To: All Regional Service Managers
From: Jim Marshall
cc: P. McKay, Bracknell; R. White, Bracknell

Subject: *Service Manager's Manual*
1 November, Year 3

Enclosed is your personal copy of the new *Service Manager's Manual*. Would you take time to review the contents and let me have your comments and suggestions for improvement. I would like to hear from you within a month, as we plan to put the finalised edition into your service managers' hands by the end of this year.

Regards,
Jim

Tasks for students

Review the four tasks stated at the beginning of this case study. A feedback of possible answers is in Appendix 1, p. 509.

Summary

Significant characteristics of MbO are:

1. The MbO approach provides the mechanism for reconciling the aims and objectives of individuals with the needs of the organisation and other stakeholders. It is thus the prime mechanism for transmitting a corporate plan

throughout an organisation and for assisting in the consultative processes involved in shaping the plan itself. Its commonest application is through a process of objective-setting in direct paired relationships, though some organisations have reported greater impact when the objective setting has been done on a group basis (French and Drexler, 1984).

2. It provides a framework for communication and clarification of roles and assignments for the manager so that he or she may operate within a framework of mutual expectancy with other managers and colleagues. This is much more difficult to achieve than may appear at first sight. Case Study 6.1 illustrates this point clearly.

3. MbO provides a basis from which competence in achieving organisational results is the main indicator for career advancement.

4. MbO offers a built-in management development opportunity for all those with development aspirations, and encourages good delegation practice. The quarterly assignment strategy review in the presence of a third party is a useful way to implement this idea.

5. MbO provides the mechanism for implementing accepted motivational theory.

6. MbO, in modern forms with a regular superior/subordinate dialogue, provides the basis from which quick organisational responses may be made to adapt to a hostile internal or external environment.

7. MbO provides a fair means of identification and treatment for those executives who have risen above their competence levels. The case studies of this chapter contain instances of the recognition of the need for such treatment and its application.

Difficulties of implementation

1. MbO relies heavily on fluency in face-to-face communication between managers in objective-setting sessions and also during the appraisal process, both of which require skill and sensitivity. There are also many barriers which may prevent objective problem-solving dialogue taking place between managers and their subordinates unless there is an established third party present.

2. MbO will not work well unless there is a credible corporate plan as a frame of reference for the formulation and transmission of objectives throughout the organisation. Otherwise managers may be keen to achieve personal or departmental objectives, but this may be at the expense of the organisational objectives. This has particular importance for public sector organisations, many of which have weaknesses in corporate planning.

3. MbO techniques and approaches may take years to be fully understood and properly used within an organisation. The literature does record many failures in implementation, for example Froissart (1972), though the weight of current research opinion is that such difficulties can be overcome. MbO does,

however, challenge certain points of culture (such as tenure, openness or consultation).

4. MbO may be difficult to implement where it is perceived as a threat to significant vested interests.

5. MbO techniques are very dependent on optimistic assumptions about human nature, for example about openness, desire for improvement and growth or professional practice.

6. Group objective-setting, much commended by some authorities, does require as a precondition a culture based on collaboration, not competition, and the organisational reward system must be compatible with this requirement (French and Drexler, 1984).

References

Erskine, R.K. (1985), 'Effective Management', M.Litt. thesis, Glasgow University.

French, W. L. and Drexler, John A. (1984), 'A team approach to MbO: history and conditions for success', *Leadership and Organisation Development Journal* vol. 5, no. 5, pp. 22−6.

Froissart, D. (1972), 'What can be learnt from MbO failures?', *MbO Journal*, vol. 2, no. 1, pp. 30−3.

Hertzberg, Frederick (1966), *Work and the Nature of Man*, Staples Press.

McGregor, Douglas (1960), *The Human Side of Enterprise*, McGraw-Hill.

Peter, Laurence J. *et al.* (1969), *The Peter Principle*, Pan.

Torrington, D. *et al.* (1989), *Effective Management: People and Organizations*, Prentice Hall.

Part 3

Skills and functions of management

Chapter 7
Effective delegation practice

Overview

The objective of this chapter is to emphasise the importance of acquiring the skills of delegation, to provide a set of guides for detecting poor delegation practice and to offer some typical but challenging case situations where the consequences of poor delegation styles are seen to be devastating. The reader is invited to join in the process of management development and become involved in coaching the characters in the cases, who manifest problems of delegation. The chapter uses and builds on the theory of MbO developed in chapters 5 and 6.

Learning objectives

The reader should be able to recognise delegation styles, diagnose reasons why delegation practice around them is poor and have some appreciation of what to do about it.

Delegation

Delegation is the core of the superior/subordinate relationship; an organisation can only operate through delegation. The effective manager gets results through other people (Drucker, 1954). We need, therefore, to consider the organisational and psychological barriers that need to be overcome in order for the discipline and practice of delegation to be applied.

A delegation checklist

This section contains a series of sometimes controversial statements, and comments are made on them. It is realised that there must be many contingencies attached to the principles; unfortunately universal rules are not easy to formulate.

The delegation pay-off

1. It equips subordinates to solve their own problems.
2. It gives subordinates more time for planning and taking the big decisions that cannot be delegated.
3. Being dispensable helps your own promotion.

In times of recession people tend to be concerned about job security above all else. Clearly, a job with much sophistication and difficulty could not easily be assumed by another in any rationalisation programme. However, when a manager is being considered for promotion two criteria predominate in the minds of higher management — is the candidate available and is the candidate suitable for the promotion?

If extensive training for a successor would be required then in the eyes of management the candidate is not available. The outcome may be that a less suitable but more available candidate is promoted. The response to this dilemma is to develop more purposefully the aspects of succession planning from the MbO approach.

Are you good at delegation?

This is an important question, yet it is not frequently asked. It strikes at the very heart of our own ego and self-image. It has been said that there is no such thing as a bad driver, a bad lover or a poor delegator. It is very difficult to be objective in answering this question, so there is a need to interpret what others say about us or how they react to us. If we have the courage and self-discipline to interpret that data then we should have useful clues about this difficult aspect of management, delegation style and skill. The following is a useful checklist of questions:

1. Are you satisfied that the long-term problems and the important aspects of your job receive a sufficient share of your time and attention?
2. Do you spend too much time 'putting out fires', dealing with constant emergencies demanding your personal attention and coping with the irritating details of day-to-day problems that keep you from working on the major issues?
3. Does your work face constant deadline crises, with some dates missed and others only just met?
4. Do you take work home?
5. Do you yield to the temptation to do the subordinate's job yourself?

The difficulty lies in distinguishing between being overburdened unnecessarily and being very highly committed.

Top management's assumption is that if a manager is always overburdened then there is likely to be a problem of poor delegation and lack of trust in the team. However, there are times of retrenchment when, for economic reasons, the organisation is working below its staff establishment; also, there are times of high activity when projects have been started but not yet fully resourced and their viability is dependent on particular and higher levels of commitment. For a time this may mean that work must be taken home.

Also those involved in part-time external courses (the most committed managers) will often need to take work home to keep on top of both the course and the job.

There is a further dilemma regarding the temptation for the manager to do the subordinate's job. There is a commitment to deliver work on time and to an acceptable quality, reflected in the pressures and key results of the job. At the same time, there is an obligation to ensure effective delegation and development of subordinate team members and a need to maintain an environment of stimulation and challenge. This suggests that help and intervention is not a first but a last resort. Independence and strength cannot be developed if the subordinate manager is always stifled.

What prevents managers delegating effectively?

1. The assumption that the carrot and stick are essential to ensure that every detailed sub-component of the assignment is done by an unwilling and work-shy subordinate. Douglas McGregor (1960), in his discussion of motivation theory, refers critically to this assumption as theory X. He also propounds a diametrically opposed theory — theory Y — and suggests that people behave according to the assumptions that have been made about them in the culture in which they operate. Within a trusting culture people will naturally strive through positive internal forces of self-control to achieve their objectives. Drucker (1954) states that with appropriate participation in objective-setting, self-control becomes the predominant force.
2. The manager's belief that he or she can do things better than any subordinates. The way round this is to recognise that:
   (a) managers employing specialists cannot possibly be expert in every field;
   (b) where subordinates really are inadequate, they will never improve if managers do their work for them; they must either be removed or improved by delegation.
3. Organisational weakness — there is no time to think about delegation, and no one to delegate to anyway. A lot of hard work will be needed here to make delegation possible — redesigning the organisation structure, defining jobs and the type of person required to fill them, recruitment, selection, training and appraisal to develop competent people who can accept delegation. All this is an investment of time and is accompanied by *a degree of risk*, which the manager must be prepared to take.
4. Escapism — managers do the easy things with which they feel more confident, although a subordinate should handle them, and avoid all the 'hot potatoes' which represent their real job. The escapist must realise that the tough decisions do not get any easier with delay, but they will be easier if the routine stuff is unloaded, because that leaves more time to analyse the real problems. The manager often finds it difficult to get a perspective on a new job and erroneously replicates what he or she did in the previous job. Some initial coaching may be appropriate to prevent escapism. This point was illustrated in chapter 6, Case Study 6.2, in the character of Jim Marshall.

5. Insecurity — sometimes when organisational weakness is quoted it really means that the manager is feeling insecure. He or she may be afraid of:
   (a) someone else taking credit;
   (b) admitting that others know more than you or can do some things better;
   (c) a subordinate getting ahead too fast;
   (d) insisting that everybody carries their fair share of the load;
   (e) losing face.

What should managers delegate?

Anything that someone can do in one of the following ways:

1. *Better* than ourself. Do managers take advantage of key persons with more knowledge and experience than themselves in certain aspects of the job?
2. At *less expense* than ourselves — e.g. in terms of time (because they are on the spot) and wages costs (because they are paid less).
3. With *better timing* — the less than ideal solution at the right time is better than the otherwise ideal solution at the wrong time.
4. As part of their *own stated function*. Supervisors should control their own labour, even if initially they do not handle things quite as well as their manager. Each job should be tackled at the *lowest* possible level.
5. As a contribution to their *training and development*. If a manager feels that a subordinate cannot be trusted with the jobs that he or she should be tackling, then you have a training problem; training includes delegation.
6. To demonstrate *suitability for promotion* — if their existing work is of a different type from the job to which they are being considered for promotion. Great care, however, has to be exercised here. The new responsibility or assignment must be a reasonable challenge, not an expectation of the impossible, as failure will disrupt the superior/subordinate relationship and may have other adverse consequences for the organisation. Again, there is some element of risk in the application of this principle.

What should managers not delegate?

1. Overall *policy* for the operation.
2. Overall *planning*. Both policy and planning are to some extent dependent on the level in the organisation from which one is operating. A managing director will delegate policy-making and planning assignments to divisional managers.
3. *Selection, training*, and *appraisal of immediate subordinates*. This principle is often disregarded in the public sector, where staff selection in particular is done via a bureaucratic process and the manager is obliged to accept the staff who are assigned. This does weaken accountability.
4. *Promotion, praise* and *disciplinary action* for immediate subordinates. Again, much of this action can be eroded by bureaucracy and the function of staff departments, particularly the personnel department.

How do managers delegate?

Managers can use the MbO model to clarify the central role of the job and the authority levels expected for each component, and to define more detailed assignments with appropriate dates and planning sheets. They must give appropriate discretion to the subordinate and adopt an open door policy if the subordinate requires more resources or help during the assignments. Or, if the environment changes the viability and relevance, they can use the appraisal process to review progress regularly, with appropriate emphasis on the development of delegation strategy and other management development activity within a problem-solving environment. They should strive to build on the superior/subordinate relationship to develop the necessary trust and empathy within the context of the problem-solving environment.

Some finer points of delegation

1. Delegation does not mean just giving somebody a task, without guidance, and then leaving them to sink or swim — that is *abdication*.
2. Delegation does not mean giving detailed instructions on exactly what is to be done and how, then breathing down the subordinate's neck.
3. Delegation *is* a matter of asking, 'What should I be doing and how can I best equip each subordinate to do what he or she should be doing?'
4. Delegation is a matter of allocating responsibility together with authority and accountability — although one's own accountability upwards to one's own manager remains.
5. Delegation is a matter of investing in time to develop an appropriate organisation structure, then staffing it with competent subordinates. Delegation is a matter of being prepared to take risks when developing people to new higher levels of achievement, and then having judgement to appraise the acceptability of such risk.
6. A manager should delegate *only* to his or her *own* subordinates.
7. A manager should delegate one level down only — if that is done properly it will be sufficient.

Case Study 7.1
Miss Clark

(This case is taken from unpublished material; the original source is unknown.)

In this case a newly promoted supervisor is invited to introduce her section to new, more advanced machinery and the adoption process runs into some snags. The case provides a useful situation from which to initiate tactics to secure change. It demonstrates difficulties in applying effective delegation practice.

List of characters

Mr Barker, *Head of Administration*
Mrs Cook, *Chief Administration Officer*
Miss Clark, *Supervisor of typing pool*
Mrs Reilly, *Assistant Supervisor*
Mr Yates, *Sales Engineer, Vetti*
Miss Rice, *Former Supervisor of typing pool*
Mr Holmes, *Sales Representative, Vetti*

Miss Clark, now 40 years of age, joined the Glasgow Hospital Board on leaving a secretarial college at the age of 17. Employed initially in the typing pool, she proved to be neat and efficient. She attended evening classes to improve her shorthand and after two years she was selected as private secretary to the Head of Administration, Mr Baker.

Three years later the typing pool, which had been under the supervision of Miss Rice, was reorganised as a new section dealing with all the general typing, including the typing of scripts, floor directions, etc. for the various programmes put out by the board. In addition, the section became responsible for the duplication of all such material. Miss Rice's responsibilities were to allocate work and to see that a high standard was maintained. She indented for all stationery requirements to Mrs Cook, Chief Administration Officer, whose responsibilities included the purchase of equipment and materials.

Miss Rice's staff included thirty-five typists and it was decided that she should have an assistant. Miss Clark knew the routine of the typing pool and had gained valuable knowledge and experience of administration while working as private secretary to the Head of Administration. At weekly conferences she had met doctors and senior nursing officers and had come to understand their problems and the particular requirements of their work. She was also well liked by Miss Rice and thus seemed to be an excellent choice for Assistant Section Head.

When offered the position she had accepted readily and, on Miss Rice's retirement two years later, she became Section Head. She ran the section with great efficiency and was considered firm but fair by the staff, who all enjoyed working for her. Those calling on the services of the section were impressed by the speed and standard of the work.

When ordering stationery supplies, Miss Clark followed the practice of her predecessor in ordering the makes of typewriter ribbon, carbon paper, etc., which she considered most satisfactory taking into account such factors as wear and economy. She was given a free hand to experiment with the products of new suppliers or with new types of product and dealt personally with the various sales representatives.

The first major problem arose six months after Miss Clark's promotion, when Mrs Cook decided to replace some of the duplicating equipment with machinery which was more versatile and sophisticated. Having seen the latest Vetti equipment advertised in the current issue of the *Nursing Times*, she sent away for further details. A representative called and convinced her that his firm's new equipment was ideally suited to the heavy volume of work handled by the Typing and Duplication Section — it would produce more copies, better copies and cheaper copies. In the hope of persuading the Chief Administration Officer to place orders for other office equipment and supplies manufactured by this firm, the representative was authorised to sell at a price very advantageous to the Glasgow Hospital Board.

Realising that this price reflected the hopes of Vetti to become a major supplier of the board and convinced of the superior merits of the equipment, Mrs Cook decided to order three of the new machines. First, however, she arranged for the representative to visit her again, and Miss Clark was asked to be present. Mrs Cook explained to her that she had noted her remarks made a few weeks earlier that some of the duplicating equipment would need replacement in the near future. She had seen the Vetti sales literature advertising their latest machines and she had since discussed such matters as performance, reliability, servicing and terms with Mr Holmes, the Vetti representative. She now had invited Miss Clark to raise with Mr Holmes any queries she might have.

Rather to Mrs Cook's surprise, Miss Clark asked few questions and said that if Mrs Cook considered the machines suitable that would be all right with her.

The three new machines were delivered promptly and the Vetti representative and sales engineer, Mr Yates, both travelled to the board offices to check the installation and demonstrate the correct operation of the equipment. Miss Clark had been advised of the date of their visit and had promised to be present when the typists were trained in the operation of the machines. The day before the visit, however, she told her assistant, Mrs Reilly, that she could not afford the time to watch the demonstration, particularly as a number of the staff would have to be freed from their work to enable them to attend. She suggested that Mrs Reilly should be present *and see that not too much time was wasted* — the typists had plenty of experience and one machine was pretty much like another.

The staff concerned were told by Miss Clark that Mrs Cook had decided to buy some new machines and they would be demonstrated by the Vetti representative. She hoped that they would be as good as the Chief Administration Officer had been led to believe.

Within three weeks of the new equipment going into service there were complaints by the staff. The main criticism was that the machines were difficult to handle, were liable to break down and gave poor results. Some minor criticisms of the work produced were voiced by departments requiring the duplicating service. Miss Clark had explained the inferior results by stating that the new machines were giving trouble. The staff's complaints were passed on by Miss Clark to the Chief Administrative Officer, who immediately telephoned Vetti.

Surprised by Mrs Cook's unexpected telephone call and anxious to retain the board's goodwill, Holmes promised to rearrange his week's programme so that he could see the equipment on the following day, and said he would bring the service engineer with him. He explained that the machines had been rigorously tested before being marketed and no major problems had been experienced with similar machines placed with other organisations.

Holmes and Yates called on Miss Clark before inspecting the equipment and expressed their surprise and concern at hearing of the trouble that she was experiencing with it.

Miss Clark said that she had been put to considerable inconvenience and regretted the Chief Administration Officer's decision to purchase. The board had had no trouble with the old equipment which had always proved reliable and efficient.

When they inspected the machines they found evidence of mishandling. Unnecessary adjustments had been made which should have been carried out only by the service engineer and certainly not by the operatives. With these adjustments corrected, Holmes asked to watch the operators on the machines. Many of them reiterated that they found the machines difficult to operate. Although the procedure was somewhat different from that used on other equipment, Holmes felt that a reasonably intelligent person should soon master the technique. When operated correctly the machines were producing excellent results.

Yates checked all the machines and Holmes ensured that all the operatives were capable of handling them correctly before they reported back to Miss Clark. She said that so far she had not been impressed with the performance of Vetti equipment and hoped that assurances that there would be no further trouble would prove correct. Holmes tactfully explained that the typists were probably experiencing a little more difficulty than was usual in adapting to the new equipment, but hastily dropped the subject when Miss Clark said that she hoped he wasn't trying to switch the blame from his firm's products to her staff. Holmes saw Mrs Cook before leaving, explained the situation as he saw it and said that he was sure there would be no more difficulties.

As a result of Holmes' remarks, Mrs Cook decided to take the matter up with Miss Clark. Not wishing to antagonise her, she decided to make an informal call on her to discuss the situation.

Passing through the section to Miss Clark's office, she felt conscious of a change in atmosphere among the staff. She mentioned the unauthorised interference with the machines, but Miss Clark maintained that any adjustments carried out had been made because the equipment was not functioning correctly. After an unfruitful 20 minutes, Miss Clark asked if there had been any complaints about herself or the work of her section since she had been placed in charge of it. Mrs Cook replied that Miss Clark knew perfectly well that the section had a good reputation for turning out work of the first quality. Miss Clark then observed that in view of Mrs Cook's reply she considered it unreasonable and unjust in the present situation to blame her staff when the new machines were clearly the cause of trouble. The board had not had dealings with the suppliers before and, by Mrs Cook's own admission, there had never been complaints about her section before.

Mrs Cook decided not to pursue the matter any further. Before leaving she asked Miss Clark if the machines were now working satisfactorily and she replied that as far as she knew they had been 'put to rights'. Mrs Cook said that she hoped their difficulties were now over. When she left, however, she was not entirely happy about the way the interview had gone and wondered if she should have taken a stronger line.

For the next few weeks complaints were few, but they then started to mount in number. Work was not being produced on time — partly as a result of the staff's apparent inability to use the machines properly, partly because some departmental heads were asking for their work to be done on the old-type equipment since the standards of work produced on the new equipment was not satisfactory.

Extremely angry at these continuing problems, Mrs Cook telephoned Holmes, who promised to make another visit, accompanied by Yates, to try to get to the root of the trouble. On inspection, Holmes was annoyed that there had been further unauthorised interference with the machines; he also found the attitude of the staff surly and uncooperative. Miss Clark said that she never wanted Vetti equipment in her section again. The Chief Administrative Officer should have kept to the type of equipment which had proved itself in the past and with which the staff were familiar. Yates overhauled the machines and checked that they were functioning properly. Holmes went over the operating instructions with the staff again and asked for questions on any particular difficulties encountered. No questions were forthcoming and all Holmes could get was a muttered comment that 'the machines were no good and the staff preferred using the other equipment'.

Holmes reported to Mrs Cook, informing her that the machines functioned perfectly if used according to the instructions and produced work which he had run off himself that afternoon on all three machines. The standard of production was excellent. He pointed out that the staff had not been following instructions and seemed to be making deliberately heavy weather of what was a relatively simple process. He commented on Miss Clark's attitude, which he considered prejudiced his firm's products, and suggested to Mrs Cook that the problem was a psychological rather than a mechanical one. His company was most anxious to give complete satisfaction and priority had been given to complaints received from the board. But, frankly, Holmes thought that Miss Clark had made up her mind that the machines were no good. Even though she may not have said this to her staff in so many words, her attitude had clearly communicated itself. Staff had interfered with machine parts but, as far as he could ascertain, had not been reprimanded. Any remarks about the conduct of the operatives were taken by Miss Clark as an attack upon herself.

Puzzled, angry and upset, Mrs Cook decided that she would have to thrash the matter out with Miss Clark.

Problems for discussion

Miss Clark

1. What reasons can you suggest for Miss Clark's failure to respond to the Chief Administration Officer's invitation to raise queries about the new machines with Holmes, the Vetti sales representative?
2. Comment on Miss Clark's instructions to Mrs Reilly and her remarks to her staff.
3. How far do you think that Miss Clark deliberately attempted to sabotage the efforts of Holmes and Yates? Attempt to explain her behaviour.

The staff

The staff of the Typing and Duplicating Section had earned a reputation for speed, efficiency and accuracy. Account for their present difficulties and low morale.

Mrs Cook

1. How far is Mrs Cook responsible for the present situation?
2. What action should she take now?

For feedback on this exercise see Appendix 1, p. 512.

Case Study 7.2
The foreman's dilemma

The purpose of this case study is to illustrate some of the problems of organisation, human relations, attitudes and principles of delegation to which a foreman may be exposed. Figure 7.1 gives a company organisation chart.

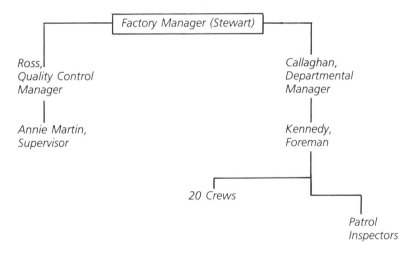

Figure 7.1 *Impgalgo factory organisation chart*

List of characters

Tom Stewart, *Factory Manager*
George Callaghan, *Department Manager*
Robert Kennedy, *Shop Foreman*
Annie Martin, *Supervisor of Quality Inspectors*
Tom Driver, *Shop Steward*
Jim Ross, *Quality Manager*

The scenario

The Impgalgo Company was long established in Britain and had its main base in Leicester. It had over 30 per cent of the market for both plain and filter-tipped cigarettes. The success of its brands had enabled it to expand away from the main Leicester base. For two years a modern shift factory had been producing cigarettes at a new location, Perth. The Perth factory employed some 500 people and at full production produced some 140 million cigarettes a week.

The most critical production unit within a tobacco factory is the machine room, which converts raw cut tobacco into trays of cigarettes. The Making Department at Perth had twenty modern cigarette-making machines. This was a much smaller unit than in the factory complex at Leicester, where there were four factories each with machine rooms of over eighty cigarette-making machines.

The factory manager appointed to run the Perth site was Tom Stewart. He was a man in his mid-fifties and he had a reputation as a very dominant personality. As a foreman himself, he had been a hard man and had been known as a stickler for quality. On one thing he was determined: to outperform the Leicester complex of factories on the quality standards of production.

The foreman of the Making Department was Robert Kennedy, a graduate of 25. He had recently been sent from Leicester to take up his first supervisory appointment after concluding his management training. He saw the Perth appointment as a real opportunity in a green field site. The labour force was new and he expected attitudes to be much more flexible than at headquarters. In the Cigarette Making Department Robert controlled twenty-five men and fifty women. He had no under-foreman to whom he could delegate any supervisory responsibility. Also in the department was a quality supervisor, Annie Martin. Annie reported to her own boss, the Quality Manager, Jim Ross. Robert Kennedy reported directly to George Callaghan, who had responsibility for two departments, Cigarette Making and Cigarette Packing. The quality group had been set up in all factories of Impgalgo following the advice of management consultants that they should operate independently from line production management. Jim Ross reported to a company quality control manager at Leicester.

Quality becomes an issue

Robert had been warned to expect Tom Stewart to be a tough and demanding factory manager. In his second week at Perth he was busy at 6.00 a.m. crewing up the machines with labour. Tom Stewart was already doing his early rounds. Tom went down the lines of machines inspecting the quality of the cigarettes as they were collected in trays. Every now and then he paused, made a comment to the machine operator and the machine was pulled up. That morning he pulled up three of the twenty machines. Robert was obliged to follow Tom and whenever a machine was pulled up he directed a senior mechanic to investigate it. After an hour's inspection Tom quizzed Robert on his attitude towards quality. The faults he had found in the cigarette had been to do with the shape. Tom insisted that a cigarette had to be perfectly round. He expected Robert to set a personal standard for quality above the quality standards laid down by the company head office. Roundness was not a recognised quality point in official company standards.

After this somewhat abrasive encounter between the factory manager and the foreman, Robert realised that he would have to watch quality like a hawk.

Each making machine for plain cigarettes was crewed by two people: an operator and a tray catcher. The operator was responsible for feeding the machine with material (reels of paper, sticky gum, printer ink). Cut tobacco was fed by pneumatic suction and the operator saw to it that the fine machine settings were correct. The operator also had to respond to the electronic devices on the machine which would warn of quality and weight defects of a basic nature. The catcher was responsible for removing completed trays of cigarettes from the machine, putting them into a trolley and inspecting random samples of cigarettes as they went down the belt of the machine. It was the catcher's responsibility to bring to the operator's attention any cigarettes which were below quality standards. These would then be investigated and a decision made whether to pull the machine up. An example of a serious fault was an interruption in the flow of gum down the seam, which might cause the cigarette to split on packing. There were in all twenty quality points relating to cosmetic blemishes such as a smudged stamp.

In addition to the catchers, who were full crew members, there were two departmental patrol inspectors who visited each machine every 10 minutes, constantly taking samples and putting them under powerful lights as a check against cosmetic faults. If they found any problems they had to inform the crew and the foreman immediately. The catchers and the patrol inspectors were all accountable to the foreman.

Independent quality checking

Lastly, the Quality Department had on the floor an independent quality supervisor, Annie Martin. Her responsibility was to take random samples from the production trolleys, each of which contained one hour's worth of production from one machine. She would put these samples under the powerful lights and scrutinise them against the full twenty quality points. Annie maintained a record of fault score by machine for each shift. These returns were summarised by month and then sent to head office.

This elaborate and in-depth system of checking and counter-checking of quality had been in operation for one year. Robert Kennedy realised that the quality assessments as made up through the independent samples by Annie was a key factor by which the factory manager would assess his own performance. Robert found the machine room a hectic place to run. His inexperience in the job, a large workforce of seventy-five to oversee and the quantity of clerical recording for payment schemes all made it difficult for him to give the attention needed to overcome the inherent problems of quality. Nevertheless, he made it a practice to check Annie's quality records at the end of each shift and match these results against the records that were being made on a continuous basis by the production catchers and his two patrol inspectors. If a fault was found by Annie but not by the production crews he would admonish them for neglect of duty. This often caused resentment. The crews tended to play down a quality fault, particularly the finer cosmetic ones, whereas Annie tended to seek out ruthlessly every minor defect she could possibly find. The twenty quality points she looked for required a reasonable interpretation of company standards. The production crews would tend to take notice of a significant deviation, whereas Annie would expect perfection. Robert Kennedy and the crews were also assessed for high machine utilisation — a production of 140 million cigarettes a week on full capacity.

A quality threat

The factory manager, Tom Stewart, was unhappy that his Perth factory had not done well against company averages as revealed by assessment from the Quality Department summaries of fault scores. His boss at Leicester hinted that if the quality standards reported did not improve, the Perth factory would not be expanded to include the production of filter-tipped cigarettes, which were a growth market. Furthermore, he made it plain that it was company policy to tie quality and production assessments together directly into a bonus payment scheme for the crews. However, he recognised that it would be difficult to implement such a bonus scheme until current assessment figures improved significantly.

Relationships between foreman and quality supervisor

In the first six months of Robert Kennedy's tenure as foreman he had many arguments with Annie over what was a real quality defect. He insisted that Annie should show him each reject as it happened, but often Annie would bring a batch of defects and Robert, having put them under the lights, could not see the fault complained of. He even took the disputed rejects to the quality manager, Jim Ross, and asked him why these had been rejected. He soon found, however, that Jim always backed Annie. No matter whether the standard was being liberally or tightly interpreted, Annie always won.

Labour relations overtones

Labour relations on the shop floor were getting more and more abrasive. The crews were feeling increasingly frustrated at the low quality assessments and the extent to which their machines were pulled up by the foreman or the factory manager for what seemed to them to be non-existent faults. Morale was low and all the production people were touchy at the very mention of quality. What grated further was the knowledge that the other shift in the factory did not appear to share these problems as their fault score was average, but then they had a different quality supervisor.

Robert did his best to maintain a reasonable relationship with Annie. It was obvious to her that he was displeased with the interpretation of standards. The attitude she expressed to him was that the crews would really have to work for a high quality assessment and she took pride in her role of enforcing a very high standard. This seemed to be reinforced by Jim Ross, her immediate manager, and by what she had seen of the factory manager and his public exhortations about perfect cigarettes, even perfectly round cigarettes. In an unguarded moment she also said that production workers were grossly over-paid and she was determined to give them a run for their money. She stated on a number of occasions that she was looking forward to the day when the quality assessment became a formal part of their bonus earnings, because it would increase her leve.:age over the crews. She seemed extremely irritated when Robert rejected some of her quality findings and instructed crews to continue production as he could not support her judgement. She felt that her word on quality should be final and she alone should be the arbiter on the interpretation of company standards. Robert Kennedy was mindful not only of quality but also of the quantity of production. He worked out that as the Cigarette Making Department had the scarcest and most capital-intensive resources in the total production line, production which was lost could never be made up in any other department of the factory. He thus calculated that opportunity cost of a machine pulled up amounted to £1,575 per hour. He felt that he too should be able to see standards of quality in perspective and reserved the right to stop the machines when in his judgement a significant quality defect occurred.

Some external quality statistics

Robert discussed his dilemma with George Callaghan, his own boss. He had some respect for George, who had had over thirty years' experience in the tobacco industry. George was sympathetic to Robert's discomfiture and showed him a report from head office which gave an analysis of all customer complaints for every branch of the company. To Robert's surprise and pleasure he found that his shift in the Perth factory had by far the best record in the company! Each cigarette is coded on its seam to indicate the machine number of manufacture and the date of packing. For the last eight months of operation his shift was getting one complaint from the public for every 800 million produced. This contrasted with the average Leicester performance which was one complaint per 60 million produced. George advised Robert to humour Annie. He told him, 'I know that you are doing everything reasonably possible to get this excellent external statistic but in this company we are judged by the internal reports and systems, implemented at great cost after management consultancy. You cannot beat that system in this factory. You will have to get Annie to eat out of your hand. It would be of no use to complain about the system to Tom Stewart as he would hunt you to death if he thought that you were not supporting the system on the shop floor. Indeed he will continue to harass you till there is an improvement in the recorded fault score for the shift.'

Six months later

Some six months elapsed. There was only a marginal improvement in the quality fault score figures. Meanwhile, head office had agreed to install four filter-tipped making machines in the department and they had been in production for two months. The technical problems of getting them into production had been very trying. The average up-time was only 50 per cent whereas the standard should have been 85 per cent. Annie Martin was making the most of the new situation. For the filter-tipped cigarettes she had no less than forty points of quality to assess. The scores she wrote down against the factory were dreadful.

A shop steward's warning

The shop steward, Tom Driver, approached Robert and warned him, 'That woman is costing the company thousands of pounds an hour. We would never accept a direct incentive bonus scheme in which she played a part in the assessment. Thank goodness we are currently paid by the hour. If we were paid by output that woman would surely ruin us.'

An unpopular suggestion

Relationships between Tom Stewart and Robert had recently deteriorated over another issue. Robert had observed to his surprise when analysing production figures over the previous eighteen months that in the weeks in which overtime had been worked on Saturday mornings (the only overtime possibility in a shift factory), that instead of production being increased by 5 per cent it actually fell by 10 per cent! On rationalising this unusual phenomenon he had produced a written explanation and presented a copy of this to Tom Stewart, stating his intention of processing it through the company committee dealing with suggestions. Stewart's reaction was most hostile. In the paper Robert had given the following explanation:

> On weeks in which overtime is planned the departments of Making and Packing (the most labour-intensive) are the only ones invited to participate in such overtime. The other departments — tobacco cutting and leaf blend — are perceived as capital-intensive and capable of building up enough buffer stock of cut tobacco to keep Making in business without the need for overtime. However, the Cutting Department foreman tends to panic over his ability to build up the buffer. His common response in these overtime weeks was to come through to Making, pleading that he needed men to make up the minimum crew to run his cutting/blending processes. As Making had no spare pool of labour a transfer effectively meant a whole making machine crew was stopped. Labour transfer thus immediately unbalanced the flow and had a disproportionate and disruptive effect, hence overall production was reduced. An evaluation of this idea may be done on the basis of opportunity/cost theory. Under this some eight million cigarettes of lost production is incurred per overtime week and this represents a loss of £16,800 per week. A suggestion is put that the factory either hire a pool of labour or change policy so that all four departments do overtime in unison with one another.

Tom was furious and demanded that Robert withdraw the suggestion, saying that the suggestion scheme was for technical ideas, and no way would it be a platform for telling him, Tom, how to run the factory. Robert had shared the idea with George, but George, anticipating Tom's reaction, had shown indifference. Robert felt frustrated as his two years of management training had included a spell of work study in which critical analysis and the creative ability to challenge culture and history had been encouraged. Robert felt humiliated at the way Tom came into his department pulling up machines and that his authority was being undermined. He did not wish to withdraw his suggestion unless he could get an acknowledgement, official or unofficial, and see it implemented.

The final crisis

This had been a bad week for Robert. On Monday Tom Stewart had done another early morning inspection and two machines had been pulled up on grounds of poor cigarette shape. Two further machines had been pulled up with timing problems by the machine operators themselves. Two other machines were idle, pulled up by their operators after seeing that a quality defect had been recorded against them by Annie. The quality defect was a minor cosmetic one but the operators had decided that it was not worth risking another black mark and they were *de facto* working to rule.

The telephone rang. It was Tom Stewart for Robert. Tom indicated that he had just received a telex from Leicester saying that the unions in Leicester had agreed to the incentive bonus scheme in the Cigarette Making Department based on a formula linked to quality and production assessments. Both management and the union had advised all branches to accept the working of the agreement and recommended ratification locally. Perth management was instructed to initiate negotiations to secure this ratification. Tom wanted to see George and Robert to discuss tactics for negotiation with the men.

Robert saw this as an opportunity to bring to a head his grievance with Annie over the interpretation of quality standards as the administration of any bonus scheme would certainly be stoutly contested by members of his shift. He was, however, concerned over how he should attempt to influence Tom, with his dominant and overbearing personality.

Problems for analysis

1. What were the symptoms of the quality problem?
2. What was the real cause?
3. Was Annie a suitable quality supervisor?
4. What future would you see for Annie?
5. What role and future would one expect of George Callaghan?
6. What role does Jim Ross, the Quality Manager, play? What should he be doing?
7. What quality objectives would be reasonable for Impgalgo?
8. What do you think of Tom Stewart as a manager? How could his management skills be developed and by whom?
9. How should Robert Kennedy handle his position of discomfiture?
10. What could be done about Robert's suggestions on saving £16,800 per week without further disrupting relationships?

For feedback on this exercise see Appendix 1, p. 514.

References

Drucker, P. (1954), *The Practice of Management*, Harper.
Hertzberg, F. (1966), *Work and the Nature of Man*, Staples Press.
McGregor, D. (1960), *The Human Side of Enterprise*, McGraw-Hill.

Chapter 8

Decision-making

Overview

Clearly, decision-making is an activity that managers frequently need to do, either by themselves or in participation with others. In this chapter an attempt is made to sketch out a basic decision-making framework, which is then put to the test.

The reader should become conversant with the decision-making process and be able to recognise this process in both simple and complex environments. The reader should understand the use and limitations of some common decision-making techniques and be aware of the influences of organisational politics that may distort the process of rational decision-making. It should also be possible to distinguish between manifestations of the rational decision-making process and the intuitive approach.

Definitions of decision-making

1. 'A decision is a choice between alternatives' (Mescon *et al.*, 1985).

This sounds nice and simple, but other definitions are more complex.

2. 'Decision-making in management is complicated as it involves all the other functions of planning, organising, motivating and controlling. There is an embarrassment of riches when it comes to identifying alternatives and making choices in all such areas' (Mescon *et al.*, 1985).

This suggests that decision-making is a pervasive part of the management process. However, Mescon goes on to develop some useful steps in a rational decision-making process; he suggests the need to screen and filter data to reduce the time taken to review the alternatives, and he warns us of the need to take account of a few key behavioural constants. He thus equips us with a coping approach to the practice of decision-making.

3. 'A *programmed decision* is reached by going through a specific sequence of

steps or actions, similar to what one does in solving an equation. Usually, the possible alternatives are limited in number, and the choice must fall within guidelines established by the organisation' (Mescon *et al.*, 1985).

In the literature the programmed decision is generally regarded as the province of the lower-level decision-maker, generally making decisions at the operating level in the organisation. This is perhaps the epitome of the rational approach.

4. '*Non-programmed decisions* are unique and non-recurring. The decision-maker must develop the procedure for making the decision. Non-programmed decisions are required for situations that are somewhat novel, inherently unstructured, or involve unknown facts' (Mescon *et al.*, 1985).

Non-programmed decisions are generally regarded as the ones about business policy. However, the increasing influence of computers is likely to have a major impact on the development of policy decisions (see chapters 17 and 22).

5. 'Decision-making can be defined as the process of choosing one alternative from among a set of rational alternatives. (Of course, what is rational for one person may not be rational for another)' (Griffin, 1987).

The key word here is *rational*. The dilemma is that this word may mean different things to different people. In this chapter both rational and non-rational approaches will be examined.

6. 'Decision-making is complicated for managers as it involves selection of choices, in an environment in which there are multiple criteria of satisfaction, many intangibles, risk and uncertainty, long-term implications, inputs from different specialists and disciplines, group influences and value judgements' (Kreitner, 1986).

This framework might well help in conducting a constructive de-briefing on the decisions made in the many action research studies of this text.

7. 'Decisions may be made in three different conditions — the condition of certainty; the condition of risk; the condition of uncertainty' (Kreitner, 1986).

'A condition of certainty exists when there is no doubt about the factual basis of a particular decision and its outcome can be predicted accurately' (Kreitner, 1986).

'A condition of risk is said to exist when a decision must be made on incomplete but reliable factual information. Incomplete but reliable information helps managers cope with risk by allowing them to calculate the probability that a given event will occur and then to select a decision alternative with favourable odds' (Kreitner, 1986).

'A condition of uncertainty exists when little or no reliable factual information is available' (Kreitner, 1986).

This model is generally useful and is adopted by many of the writers on decision-making. Managers may sometimes take decisions on the basis of uncertainty, when they should have organised themselves to get the appropriate information.

8. 'It is the lack of, or unsatisfactory nature of the tools available, together with the complexity of the environment, that make *intuition* the key to strategic planning and decision-making. This decision-maker prefers experience, gut feeling, reflective thinking, and instinct, using the unconscious mental processes. These processes can be stimulated by brainstorming, creative orientation, and creative confrontation and, therefore, involve a number of people in the organisation. Intuitive decision-makers consider a number of alternatives and options simultaneously, jumping from one step of the analysis or search to another and back again' (Jauch and Glueck, 1988).

Jauch and Glueck undervalue the effectiveness and power of modern corporate planning models as an aid to rational decision-making. They will generally take precedence over intuitive methods, though in some instances there are such wide areas of uncertainty that the intuitive approach is also acceptable.

The rational decision-making process

A useful and simple rational model of the decision-making process comes from Platt (1976). The steps he outlines are as follows:

1. Define the aim.
2. Collect facts.
3. List choices.
4. Predict outcomes.
5. Make the decision.

Added to these steps are two important links. Firstly, there is a *feedback loop* from the final decision-maker to the initial problem-solver. This is to ensure that the decision made does in fact relate to the initial problem. Secondly, there is a forward link connecting the *criteria* for the decision, from the aim of the initial problem-solver to the objectives of the final decision-maker. This is to ensure that the decision criteria have been kept and that a good quality decision is made.

Platt (1976) then offers a training package bringing the process to life with examples. Some highlights of his package are listed below.

1. For *listing choices*. Platt offers a brainstorming technique to help a group of managers be creative in the consideration of alternatives.
2. For *predicting outcomes*. Platt offers *decision trees*. These are depicted as a network of events in a whole decision process, each of which has a series of outcomes and an associated probability and expected value. The expected value is a product of the outcome and probability.

   Decision trees are a useful and disciplined way of forcing managers to consider a wide range of possible outcomes. They also permit a variety of different decision criteria to be applied and assessed by a risk-taker. Although, normally, it may be expected that the manager will opt for alternatives that maximise the expected value, it may be preferable in practice to adopt a less risky approach with lower expected value, which cannot threaten bankruptcy if the project fails. When a decision-maker is influenced by the bureaucratic environment he or she is most likely to take *sound* decisions backed up by precedent, which are not threatening rather than innovative risky decisions, which may offer much better value, but also threaten the job holder. It is not always safe to perform in an exceptional way! For an example of a decision tree, the reader is referred to Figure 8.1.

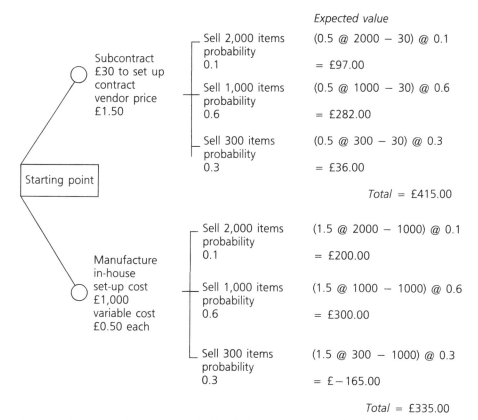

Interpretation: A manufacturer has to decide whether to invest £1,000 in his own facility, or whether to negotiate a subcontract with an established vendor for a starting cost of only £30 and a vendor price of £1.50. His own selling price will be £2.00. There are three scenarios about volume sales — high sales, medium sales and low sales — and each scenario is given a probability. To determine which choice to take, it is normal to calculate and then sum the expected values for each scenario for each choice. In the worked example it would look to be a better choice to go for subcontracting, with an expected value of £415, than manufacturing in-house at a value of £335, providing there are no other significant factors.

The decision diagram helps the decision-maker to identify events and probabilities and evaluate outcomes.

Figure 8.1 *A decision diagram for assessing whether to subcontract or manufacture in-house*

Options	(A) Self-employed small business	(B) High-tech industry	(C) Low-tech manufacturing industry	(D) City	(E) Missionary work

Criteria
(A) Vocational
    appeal
    30 points
	7	7	4	2	10

(B) Prospects
    of salary
    after three
    years
    24 points
	6	6	4	8	0

(C) Starting
    salary
    16 points
	0	5	3	7	1

(D) Prospects of
    travel/
    adventure
    15 points
	1	3	2	3	6

(E) Prospects of
    gaining
    professional
    status
    10 points
	0	4	2	4	0

(F) Low risk of
    failure
    5 points
	0	2	0	1	2

Totals	14	27	15	25	19

Comments
In making up a decision list it is necessary for the decision-maker to identify the options open in the top colums, in this case five possibilities for a graduate choosing a career.

Next, the criteria are selected for the rows, in this case six elements are given (A–F). A notional 100 points of value are then allocated to each row, reflecting the weighting preference of the decision-maker.

Next the matrix so created forms the basis of allocating the limited number of value points to each cell. This forces a decision-maker to reflect on relative positions in preference.

Finally, the matrix values are summed and the total line reflects preference in an order of merit based on the criteria given.

Interpretation: In the case illustrated a career in high-tech industry is seen as having a marginal lead over a career in the City, but there is also a fairly strong fallback position for a career in missionary work.

Figure 8.2 *A decision list for a graduate selecting a career*

3. For assisting in the *articulation of decision criteria*. Platt offers *decision lists*. The structure of a decision list is a matrix with two dimensions. Commonly, the columns represent different alternatives, e.g. for the decision to buy a car there may be model A, model B or model C. The rows represent different criteria. For a car purchase, this might mean price, engine capacity, seating capacity, fifth gear. For examples of decision lists, see Figure 8.2.

The decision list helps the decision-maker by getting value judgement points allocated to each element of the criterion and then simple addition of these in the matrix suggests a selection of the alternative with the highest value points. This approach is also useful in that it suggests an order of priority of choice. In budget bidding situations, particularly in the public sector, decision lists may be especially useful for this reason.

The decision list can be refined by establishing *essential* and *non-essential criteria*. The impact of failing on an essential element effectively removes that option altogether. This is a useful device for decision-making in the recruitment and selection process. A short-list of candidates may be drawn up by this method.

A recent example of the use of decision lists in the field of business policy, was offered by Mathewson (1989). He related how the Royal Bank of Scotland had developed its acquisition strategy in the search for a US bank to provide the necessary consolidation point for the extension of the Royal Bank operations into the United States. There were ten essential criteria involved in the search and each element of the criteria was weighted. The decision list technique helped the decision-makers bring a short-list of acquisition partners for the final decision.

A review of decision-making, in the cases and exercises of this text

It would be helpful to comment in particular on the decision-making qualities of characters in some of the cases and surmise the extent to which the rational decision-making model applied. However, as chapter 8 is not the last chapter of the book it would be churlish to comment too deeply on exercise and case material that has not already been read. Appendix 2 has thus been created at the end of the text and contains a review of decision-making dynamics in chapters 9–22. The reader is strongly recommended to read Appendix 2 at the conclusion of studies.

Case Studies 3.1, 3.2 and 3.3

In all three instances the cases illustrated various crises and a decision-maker was needed to move in and make vital decisions to keep the companies going. A corporate planning appreciation was carried out using the logical and rational business policy model outlined by Glueck (1976).

Glueck's framework, which is not all that dissimilar from the Platt process outlined above, involved a critical SWOT and PEST analysis and from the basic business pictures revealed, various priorities were suggested for decision and action.

In the case of Sykes a further knowledge of company law and the law of succession was required to develop a natural future programme of likely actions and decisions.

Britcan's previous decision-making was much criticised, as the corporate planning and forecasting system did not work efficiently. The Managing Director simply failed to interpret the information he already had, so the cutting back on production was done far too late and he ended up with a most uncomfortable over-stocking situation and consequent financial crisis. He would have benefited from a more rigorous application of the rational decision-making model!

Case Study 4.1

In chapter 4 a financial appreciation was offered in the M and N case study. The use and application of financial ratios and contribution analysis in a logical and rational approach to decision-making was an essential precondition for any serious decisions about the future of M and N. Without the hard financial analysis, the company members were set on doing the impossible!

However, financial analysis alone was still not enough to get the company out of its crisis. Some further creative thinking was necessary to mount expansion without huge injections of capital, and the solution was a novel one. The company was encouraged to be more creative on the purchasing front and get a volume contract at a discount from a new supplier of raw material, i.e. to use someone else's capital! Once that thinking barrier had been assaulted it was possible to take decisions to secure the future of what otherwise looked like a company moving rapidly into liquidation. So, decision-making in M and N was a mixture of the rational and inspirational.

Case Studies 5.1, 6.1 and 6.2

Decisions were made about objectives in Case Study 5.1, 'On Target'. The Chairman appeared to set objectives on the basis of instinct and what he thought would please a meeting of shareholders, and this had a dreadful effect throughout the business. A £1 million investment was nearly lost in a rash of labour relations hiccups and stoppages. The Depot Manager, Bullock, made ill-informed decisions about increasing productivity, since he had difficulty in communicating options and choices with the managers around him. With the flow of information failing, and the opportunity to consult eluding him, he could not make the decisions necessary to recover the situation. However, the MbO approach, rationally applied, would have pre-empted these decision-making difficulties!

In Case Study 6.1 some decisions on three executives were contemplated by Peter Drucker, acting as consultant to Hudson-Lansing. The decisions turned on the basis of the application of sound management development theory and Peter Drucker was severely criticised for his judgement of Mathis, Director of Research and Development and Quality Control. The quality of the judgement, rather than the decision-making process, was the issue under such lively discussion!

In Case Study 6.2, 'The Service Manual', Paul McKay was severely criticised for his decision to recommend Marshall for promotion. This case hinged on the definition of criteria of good performance. On the basis of Marshall's results he was an unmitigated disaster, but he was friendly with his manager, who indulged him in escaping from the job position and role of National Service Manager. McKay thus adopted an intuitive approach to decision-making, but with disastrous consequences. The solution suggested was to establish a 'good practice' appraisal process using MbO theory including a third party, and then to coach Marshall into basic effectiveness. Through that approach the promotion decisions would have been much better informed.

Case Studies 7.1 and 7.2

In Case Study 7.1 there are several decisions concerning the supervisor, Miss Clark. This case also relates to decisions about introducing new technology. In the literature this tends to be regarded as a situation of decision-making in conditions of *uncertainty*. The uncertainty arises as managers are expected to have only partial knowledge about the new technology and the implications of its introduction. However, it often becomes an excuse to make decisions in an entirely intuitive manner and with much more risk than if they attempted to follow more deliberately the rational approach.

In the case study, the Administrative Manager, Mrs Cook, makes a decision to purchase new machinery for the typing pool. Miss Clark is the recently promoted supervisor and feels slighted. Her attitude to the suppliers becomes hostile and she indulges in attempts to sabotage the implementation of the new equipment and training of her staff. Mrs Cook then has to decide on Miss Clark's future as a supervisor, as the productivity of the typing pool plummets along with the morale of the staff. This sad episode could have been prevented had the original purchase decision of the new machinery been better handled by Mrs Cook. As it is we end up with totally unnecessary morale, motivation and supervision problems.

It seems that the rational approach to decision-making is sometimes extremely difficult to implement sensitively. Purchase decisions of expensive capital equipment are very vulnerable to personnel difficulties. Effectively, the equipment is likely to be used by several stakeholders, all of whom will have different attitudes and preferences, many of which will be unknown to the one with the authority to make the purchase decision. In theory a process of active consultation should precede the purchase decision to reduce the uncertainty, but this is not always possible.

In Case Study 7.2, 'The Foreman's Dilemma', a major issue involved the decisions necessary to secure quality. This gave rise to a crisis over information-gathering and interpretation. On the basis of external quality control figures, the foreman's department was the best in the whole company, with one defective cigarette in 800 million produced. However, on the internal figures as interpreted by the Quality Supervisor, the department was in the quality doghouse and threatened with closure!

The Quality Supervisor had been aided and abetted by a zealous and authoritarian Factory Manager, Stewart, who usurped company standards by pulling up machines if the cigarette was not perfectly round. It had not been possible to get a consensus about the criteria for good quality among the decision-makers at the Perth plant and this problem then gave rise to many other problems, especially when there was a suggestion of linking pay to quality, a move in the circumstances quite unacceptable to a disenchanted and suspicious labour force.

This case illustrates rather well how the impact of organisation structure, management style and factors of personality can impede the application of the rational decision-making approach.

Case Study 8.1
The course admission decision

(This case is based on original material and was developed from action research done in an English college.)

The case illustrates how fragile the rational decision-making model is when applied to selection decisions. The decision to offer a place on a management course to a member of the non-academic staff of the host college was exposed to some internal political pressures.

Issues for discussion

1. What should the admission decision have been in Barry's case?
2. In the incident that follows, where were the examples of breakdown in the rational decision-making model?

Outline and materials

1. The College Council pass resolution on 'Equal Opportunity'. 1 March, Notice Board minute, Exhibit 8.1.
2. Note about admission tutor's terms of reference. 1 April, Exhibit 8.2.
3. Application is received from a senior technician, an internal candidate, selection interview, and outcome, 20 June. Letter from Admissions Tutor, Richard, to Barry, the candidate. Internal memo 1.
4. The applicant's Head of Department supports him, 30 June. Letter from Gerald to Barry. Internal memo 2.
5. The applicant's Head of Department makes a staffing case to the Assistant Director for another technician in the light of a recent spend decision for a new computer lab, 5 July. Letter from Gerald to Kenneth. Internal memo 3.
6. The Assistant Director stalls on funding for both the applicant and the technician post, 1 August. Letter from Kenneth to Gerald. Internal memo 4.
7. The Assistant Director, Kenneth, makes enquiries by telephone to the

Department providing the course on 3 August, and speaks to Simon, Senior Lecturer, who is not involved in course admissions. Simon advises the Assistant Director incorrectly of the situation and likely outcome. Simon copies Walter on the outcome. Telephone conversation 1.

8. The Head of Department gets in touch with the Admissions Tutor, on holiday, 6 August. Walter to Richard. Telephone conversation 2

9. The applicant's Head of Department withdraws support for his place after his request to Assistant Director for more technician support is questioned, 15 August. Letter Gerald to Barry. Internal memo 5.

10. The applicant resigns, 1 September. Letter Barry to Personnel. Internal memo 6.

Exhibit 8.1

Notice to all Members of Staff
from the Secretary of the Governing Council
Resolution on 'Equal Opportunity'

Date: 1 March

I would wish to draw your attention to the resolution passed by the Governing Council on 15 February. I would point out that this College now adopts this resolution as policy in all decisions affecting employment and promotion in this institution, and in all matters affecting staff development, both for academic and non-academic staff. The resolution also applies to members of the public applying for courses at this College.

The words 'Equal Opportunity' will appear in future in advertisements for staff vacancies.

If there are any queries on the interpretation of this policy please refer to me.

Yours sincerely,
Andrew
Secretary to Governing Council

Exhibit 8.2

Admissions Tutor's Terms of Reference
Minute from Management Course Board

Date: 1 April

The target for the first year of the part-time management course will be sixty and the Admissions Tutor should recruit to within plus or minus 10 per cent of this target, selecting the candidates who are most likely to benefit from the course and achieve a pass.

As the course is likely to be oversubscribed, on the basis of previous experience, there will inevitably be a competitive element in the selection process.

The admissions tutor will process course applications and make offers to well-qualified candidates, up to the recruitment target. He/she should call a panel of tutors to interview and review the admission decisions in marginal cases. The key elements in the selection criteria are as follows:

1. Relevant academic qualifications.
2. Relevant management and work experience.
3. Sponsor's support in course funding (£600 per year), and provision of time off for attendance and study.

As the recruitment season gets under way the Admissions Tutor will give the Head of Department regular reports on recruiting status, and indicate needs for further advertisement or publicity for the course.

The Admissions Tutor will give the Course Board a report on admissions at the end of the recruitment period for inclusion in the annual course board report.

Internal memo 1

From: Richard, Admissions Tutor
To: Barry, Senior Technician, Department of Business
cc: Gerald, HOD, Business
June 20

Dear Barry,

Application for part-time management course
Offer of place

You will be pleased to hear that I have agreed with my tutor colleagues after the recent interview with you to offer you a place on the part-time management course.

We found that you were well-qualified academically and we were impressed by the previous experience which you showed from your cv, particularly that of you managing those six laboratories in a US university.

We noted from your interview that you have support for this course from your own HOD. I am sending him a copy of this offer letter. I will see that joining instructions are sent to you.

The management course is ideally suited for a senior technician like yourself, who now wishes to enhance his prospects. The College has several precedents of its own staff taking this course and doing well. Good luck!

Yours sincerely,
Richard
Admissions Tutor

Internal memo 2

From: Gerald, HOD, Business
To: Barry, Senior Technician
30 June

Dear Barry,

Part-time management course

I am pleased to hear that you have been given an offer for the above course by the Department of Management. As I have previously indicated to you, your application has my support and I am prepared to fund the cost of the course from my department's staff development budget. In addition, I will allow you to have time off to attend the course, but as we are short of technician support, I may look to you to do some overtime.

Yours sincerely,
Gerald

Internal memo 3

From: Gerald, HOD, Business
To: Kenneth, Assistant Director
5 July

Dear Kenneth,

Case for another technician post

I am sorry to be bothering you as the holidays start with a case for more staff! However, in June a major decision was made in Faculty to fund a new laboratory of microcomputers ready for September with a capital spend of some £60,000.

I do not see how these new machines can be installed and maintained in the new session without having another technician on our establishment. My Senior Technician, Barry, is currently overloaded and he has come near to breaking point. New courses are coming on stream in October and the new lab is already overbooked and not yet installed. Help! I urgently do need your approval for a further technician, otherwise much of the academic plan for my department for the coming session will be compromised.

Yours sincerely,
Gerald

Internal memo 4

From: Kenneth, Assistant Director
To: Gerald, HOD, Business
1 August

Dear Gerald,

Your staffing requests

Within a day of receiving your 'May-day' call for a further technician post in your department, I received an application from your Senior Technician, Barry, for £600 staff development money for him to attend the college management course, and have a day off a week to boot for the next two academic sessions!

  In the circumstances, I do not see how I can justify to the Staffing Advisory Committee your request for further staff at the same time as you are contemplating letting Barry off for one day a week for management! I would not have thought it were a high priority for a lab technician to go on a management course.

  However, I am concerned not to raise false expectations in the mind of Barry.

Yours sincerely,
Kenneth

Telephone conversation 1

Between: Kenneth, Assistant Director
and: Simon, Senior Lecturer, Department of Management
3 August

Kenneth: Hello Simon, I gather that your own Head of Department is away on holiday and that you are holding the fort for him in his absence. I am rather concerned about an application from Barry for a place on your department's management course. Perhaps you would confirm for me as soon as possible his eligibility for such a course. I am not keen to encourage technicians here to do management courses when we are so short-staffed. Doubtless you will have to hand the relevant course admission criteria.

  At the same time I do not wish to be seen to turn Barry down myself. It would help if your department would give an assurance that he is not eligible for the course.

Simon: Yes, Kenneth, I will look up the recent course validation document and be back to you within the hour.

Simon (30 minutes later): Kenneth, the Admissions Tutor is on holiday, but it would be most unlikely that he would have made an offer of a place. The management course is clearly for someone with a minimum of two years' experience of supervision, and it would seem that Barry would not meet the minimum admission requirement based on his employment here.

Kenneth: That is some relief to me!

    (Simon writes a note of this conversation to Walter, his Head of Department, before going on holiday himself.)

Telephone conversation 2

Between: Walter, HOD, Management
and: Richard, Admissions Tutor
6 August

Walter: Richard, sorry to interrupt you on holiday, but there is some flack this end over Barry, the senior laboratory technician, and his application for a place on the management course.

Richard: Really? That is strange. He had a place offered to him on 20 June.

Walter: How is that so? He could not be eligible for a place. I have a note from Simon, advising against us offering a place to a technician, and he has given this advice to the Assistant Director!

Richard: I have Barry's application form here, and he is eminently eligible . . . academic qualifications, experience from the cv . . . he is one of the better applicants we have had this summer! He was interviewed by the tutors and we were unanimous in our offer decision. We even had informal assurances from Gerald, his Head of Department, that he would have time off and funding. For years now we have had precedents of non-academic staff coming on our management course and doing well.

Walter: Well the fat is in the fire now! Gerald has withdrawn support for Barry, and the Assistant Director has called me to account for the way we offer places. He seemed to expect to have been consulted in the first instance, as an internal candidate was involved.

Richard: There is only so far an Admissions Tutor can go in securing sponsor support. There are some 150 applicants on file, some from organisations like the Health Boards, with up to five levels of management above the management candidate, and all those high-ups can veto funding and time off. If I were to pursue through all those levels we would never get any course offer posted before the course starts! In Barry's case the Head of School or Head of Faculty might also have vetoed the sponsor decision. Anyway, we are supposed to be an 'Equal Opportunity' employer, and it seems intolerable that it should be harder for our own staff to secure places than outsiders! There are many outsiders on file with good technical qualifications, who like Barry are now thirsty for a management qualification and a chance for advancement!

    You said Simon had advised the Assistant Director about the application. Simon could not have checked to see what stage the application process had reached or had a sight of Barry's cv! What an embarrassment for you!

Walter: Sorry, Richard, I over-reacted, not knowing the facts as you saw them. I will do my best to put things right with the Assistant Director, but I too am vulnerable. He is sitting over an application from me for more staff now that we have extended the management programme.

Richard: I am beginning to appreciate that course admission decisions have to be taken against a backcloth of deals and counter-deals and vetoes, which pop out unexpectedly from the various offices in the corridors of power. How I wish that we could get something really simple like admissions on merit, as per the Admission Tutor's terms of reference!

Internal memo 5

From: Gerald, HOD, Business
To: Barry, Senior Laboratory Technician
15 August

Dear Barry,

Staff development

I am sorry to disappoint you after all over the management course this session. While we are under establishment for lab technicians it will not be possible to allow you time off for attending a management course. My priorities this year must indeed be to get the new labs up and running for the beginning of this session. I will gladly review your position again next session, when maybe the situation is not so tight.

I trust that you will bear with this decision meantime.

Yours sincerely,
Gerald

Internal memo 6

From: Barry, Senior Laboratory Technician
To: Personnel Officer
1 September

Dear Sir,

I wish formally to resign with effect from 1 October my post as Senior Laboratory Technician in the College.

I feel badly let down by the refusal of the College to grant me support for a management course despite being well-qualified for one. I would rather work for another employer who has more progressive staff development policies than I see manifested here.

Yours sincerely,
Barry

For tasks see beginning of this case. For discussion of feedback see Appendix 1, p. 520.

Summary

This chapter began with an examination of various definitions of decision-making. It developed with a review of both *intuitive* and *rational* approaches and gave examples of decision-making techniques, and the context of the problems which they could be used to solve. Then these theories were put to the test in a critical analysis of the decision-making demonstrated in the case studies up to this chapter, ending with Case Study 8.1 concerning a qualitative decision about who to admit in a college course.

A reference was then made to Appendix 2, where a further analysis was done to the decision-making done in the case studies after chapter 8. The latter analysis was intended to offer the reader a discriminating view of decision-making in the topics of planning, chairmanship, systems design, purchasing, organisation structure and finally the selection and deployment of management systems. The material of Appendix 2 was intended to be read last in the text.

References

Glueck, W.F. (1976), *Business Policy and Strategic Management*, 3rd edition, McGraw-Hill.

Griffin, R. W. (1987), *Management*, 2nd edition, Houghton Mifflin.

Jauch, L. J. and Glueck, W.F. (1988), *Business Policy and Strategic Management*, 5th edition, McGraw-Hill.

Kreitner, R. (1986), *Management*, 3rd edition, Houghton Mifflin.

Mathewson, G., Strategic Planning Director, Royal Bank of Scotland (1989), Seminar paper to Long-range Planning Society of Great Britain, Edinburgh Branch, unpublished.

Mescon, M.H. *et al.* (1985), *Management*, 2nd edition, Harper & Row.

Platt, B. (1976) *Decision-Making Take-Away Guide*, Multimedia Publishing.

Further reading

(*Note*: These include those referred to in Appendix 2.)

Harrison, E. F. (1975), *Managerial Decision Making Process*, Houghton.

Johnson, G. (1988), 'Rethinking incrementalism', *Strategic Management Journal*, vol. 9, no. 1, pp. 77–91.

Stoner, J.A.F. and Freeman X. (1989), *Management*, 4th edition, Prentice Hall.

Chapter 9
Communication in organisations

Overview

This chapter takes a wide view of the overall management process and within this context an analysis is attempted of the complex process of communicating within organisations. A first learning objective is to identify what that process is.

The analysis begins by identifying what the process consists of and then discusses some common communication difficulties and attempts some rationalisation of their causes and possible remedy. Options in decision-making about communication media and channels are considered, taking account of advances in information technology.

Some of the main components of persuasive decision-making are the ability to present a proposal, orally, in writing and lobbying. An analysis of a committee in action will help to highlight good and bad practice in chairmanship and illustrate the principles that guide the effective management of meetings.

Finally, the problems of communication in large bureaucratic organisations are discussed, reaching towards an appreciation of the complex notion of organisational learning.

Learning objectives

Ideally, managers wish to improve their communication skills, but this requires exposure to both the theory and practice of communication. This chapter provides material relevant to both, but some skills, such as chairmanship, can be improved over a lifetime. The aim of this chapter is to stimulate an interest in communication decisions and skills and a desire to practise them.

A communication model

Figure 9.1 represents a communication model, showing some of the important components of communication. Its only simplicity is that it is contained on one page.

Definition of communication — A Behavioural Response from an Audience.

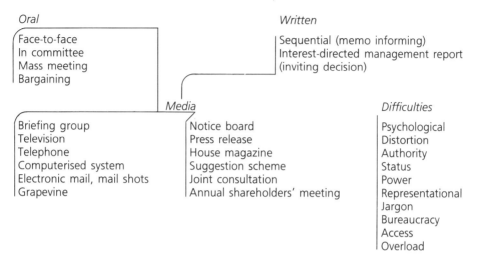

Oral

Face-to-face
In committee
Mass meeting
Bargaining

Written

Sequential (memo informing)
Interest-directed management report
(inviting decision)

Media

Briefing group
Television
Telephone
Computerised system
Electronic mail, mail shots
Grapevine

Notice board
Press release
House magazine
Suggestion scheme
Joint consultation
Annual shareholders' meeting

Difficulties

Psychological
Distortion
Authority
Status
Power
Representational
Jargon
Bureaucracy
Access
Overload

Process of communication

Sender→Message construction→Media choice→Transmission→Noise→Senses→Receiver—
Listening/feedback←Behavioural change←Interpretation/perceptions/listening

Message orientation

Up
Down
Lateral
Informing
Commanding
Problem-solving
Persuasive
Participative
Inspirational
Confidential

Complexity

Formal/informal

Appeal to senses

Sound
Sight
Smell
Emotion
Logic
Teamwork

Individual

Inter-group

Inter-organisation

Communication skills

Chairmanship

Constitutional process

Mutual interest
Access
Exchange
Sympatique
Alternatives
Evaluation
Commitment
Action
Result
Review
Experience
Learn

Figure 9.1 *Processes, decisions and barriers in communication*

The content is inevitably complex, because communication in organisations is a complex process.

The model starts with a definition of communication (Drucker, 1954). The model then suggests a nine-stage process of communication. From this process decision-making skills in the selection and choice of communication media may be developed; many options are available. However, these are also constrained by the need to overcome communication difficulties. Some of these difficulties are identified and possible responses discussed. The final section of the model relates to communication skills. One predominant communication skill is discussed — the skill of chairmanship.

The model offered is a useful framework from which to put into perspective decisions and options when considering the very complex process of communicating in organisations.

Definition of communication

The definition focuses on the audience, the receivers of information: 'Effective communication secures a behavioural response from an audience.'

The effect on the audience is the crucial aspect, and the term 'behavioural response' attempts to convey the notion of a change in behaviour, preferably in the intended direction. If the communication misfires in some way, it may generate hostility or, more commonly, indifference.

Drucker's business philosophy is directed towards the function of marketing; and indeed, marketing is the function that gets to customers, the 'audience' for goods and services. The more we think about the 'audience' the more we have acceptable goods and services, as well as a future for a business.

The opposite of being 'marketing-oriented' is being 'production-oriented', that is, more interested in products than how they are to be consumed — a very dangerous approach in competitive marketing conditions. Likewise, in communication, the ineffective communicator is inward-looking, thinking only of the message, not its articulation to secure the right impact on the audience.

However, this audience orientation is the very thing that makes effective communication so complex and difficult, because there is a long, tortuous process to go through between communicator and audience. The process is defined as a closed loop for two-way communication, though in reality much communication is also one-way and the feedback is non-existent or very weak.

The process of communication

There are at least nine distinct links or stages in the process chain for two-way communication These are as follows:

1. The sender of communication,
2. The message construction,
3. The choice of channels and media for the message,
4. Its transmission,
5. Noise,

6. Reception by the audience,
7. Decoding and interpretation by the audience, taking account of perceptions, listening,
8. Behavioural change,
9. Feedback to sender; listening to the feedback.

At each stage there are some complex options so choice is necessary. This is clearly a matter neither of science nor art but a subtle mix of each, together with the knowledge about the organisation's ethos and customs and the need to be imaginative in considering as fully as possible the various options.

The sender of communication

It is important to begin by considering who is the most appropriate person or persons to initiate the communication.

A conference organiser might wish to get authorisation from a Director, but knows that the letter may spend six weeks in the Director's in-tray before it secures attention. So, it might be better to write a draft note to a Head of Division and get that person to send the communication, knowing that a letter from a more senior source will get attention in a week. Politics is a hidden and ever-present influence in organisations.

The message construction

What the communicators say is influenced by aims and the orientation of the message. When we think of communication within the organisation there are many aspects to this orientation. These may include: up, down, lateral, informing, commanding, problem-solving, persuasive, participative, inspirational, confidential.

When we think a little more deeply about this issue of the orientation of the message, it is evident that a different set of options in choice of media comes into view, together with a different set of communication difficulties. It is a useful observation that communication is generally done within a 'framework of expectation'; the ethos of the organisation helps us to see what that expectation is.

Communicators often fail to think through the implications sufficiently. A problem-solving environment, for instance, needs a minimum of three people to get creative thinking stimulated enough to open minds and facilitate real change. Yet the world abounds with examples of ineffective procedures — ineffective because they need a problem-solving appraisal, yet they are structured by pairs of communicators.

A useful example lies in the promotion of good MbO practice, and the effective development of the appraisal process within this. Much of this process needs both a problem-solving and participative approach. That suggests a three-way set of participants and exchanges. A two-way set alone is likely to be no more than ritualistic, as it does not naturally generate the necessary problem-solving climate.

The choice of channels and media for the message

There are two basic channels of communication — oral communication and written communication — but signs, gestures and body movement also have a place in face-to-face situations. In all cases the communicator gets through to the targeted audience by successfully appealing to their senses.

The main distinction between oral and written communication relates to the immediacy of feedback, but even this distinction is becoming blurred in the environment of electronic mail, where the average turnaround time between sending and reply may be only a few moments or hours, rather than days as in the conventional mail system.

There are two main types of written communication. Although in physical form all written communication is sequential it may not be intended that the reader follows the author's sequence. Readers tend to read selectively on the basis of interest. The indexing, layout and sequence of written reports are vital for achieving impact.

Management consultants are particularly skilled at presenting the *interest-directed* consultancy report, which commonly begins with recommendations. The consultant usually tries to anticipate the management process, in which the report is circulated among various groups in the organisation as part of a decision-making process. Each group will review the report from its own departmental viewpoint and then provide contributions at the top management meeting called to decide the organisational response.

For important decisions top management might want to delve deeper into the implications of the report, and the consultant may be invited to a meeting for presentation, review and cross-examination. The whole gamut of communication methods and media may be considered to secure a major decision and ensure commitment to it.

There are many more options open for the selection of media than one might expect! Some explanation of the more unusual media and uses follow.

The briefing group

An organisation may wish to make an announcement to all its employees so that they are informed officially rather than by reading newspapers or listening to the radio. This is achieved by setting up a programme of meetings, generally in a single day, starting at the most senior level in the organisation and working down progressively to the shop floor. The purpose of the briefing group is to secure organisational goodwill, generally in the face of adversity, to a new development in company policy. There is generally a question-and-answer session to clarify the implications of the management announcement. Although two-way communication is facilitated through the opportunity to ask questions, briefing groups are not generally consultative. The core of the policy and the message itself will already have been decided.

Television and video

Some large organisations, such as warships, may have a television monitor in many different areas. The captain may make an announcement over the internal television to all hands without the crew having to leave their work-stations and come to a central theatre. This is one-way communication only, but it does appeal to both sight and sound and is appropriate for transmitting an inspirational-type message to all crew members at the same time.

This form of communication challenges the theory of constraints imposed by the 'span of control'. This principle, developed from the writings of Henri Fayol, suggests that a group of more than ten is difficult to coordinate and manage owing to communication difficulties. Electronic devices now play a significant role in making the organisation appear to be a much smaller entity.

Television may also offer an electronic version of an organisation's house magazine. This may promote organisational unity and goodwill, and offer senior management a natural platform for recognising achievement for the improvement of morale.

Television 'help' facilities may also assist an outsider or customer to get to the place or facility he is seeking. Transport organisations use this medium extensively to report arrivals, departures, delays, etc. Large department stores could with advantage use this technique to help customers identify whether items are in stock, where the items are displayed and the correct prices. The 'enquiry' facility in communication assumes a really active audience and the commitment that goes with it. The customer who perceives a bargain of his or her own making will return to the store. Store management may, however, find this a difficult idea to swallow. Stock control is for management, not customers, but creative communication and electronic devices have a wonderful potential for changing roles in a fundamental way.

Television can also be helpful in interactive learning for the transfer of skills.

In the 1980s Rockwell Glass's Scottish plant wanted to upgrade their bottling line with a new process to be imported from South America. The introduction of new technology posed a great variety of technical problems and associated training and morale problem. Effective communication was needed.

Firstly, the company produced a video of the process in action in South America, together with an encouraging message to its employees from the UK management stressing the many advantages of using the new technology. Next, a series of technologically-based interactive learning videos was provided by the Training Department, concentrating on the key occupational roles on the new bottling line and offering each operator a chance to become familiar with the new terms, procedures and skills required in the process. One instructor came from South America to introduce this package.

The company reported that the implementation date for the new process was achieved without any problem and that the new line was immediately effective — quite a feat considering the teething problems usually faced when a large group of workers is introduced to new methods.

The main disadvantage of this interactive, TV-based method of communicating the learning message is that it generally takes considerable time and expense to create the original learning material. If the material is good the delivery can be quick and successful, and complex technological know-how can be transmitted. Increasingly, developers of academic curricula are offering distance learning options; interactive TV-based material is a powerful channel in this approach.

The telephone

Excessive use of the telephone may reflect frustration in the organisation and, to the analytical observer, shows up possible weaknesses in its structure.

It is amazing how many companies have an annual telephone bill in excess of £1 million. In 1973 the author researched a UK company with an annual sales turnover of £30 million in which the telephone account was in excess of £1 million. The average bill which each employee with access to the network ran up was over £10,000 per annum!

Multidivision, multinational companies are commonplace and yet the customer may be many steps away from the group in the organisation who can give him even simple information, such as the status of his order. With manufacturing, marketing and research and development all possibly being conducted on different sites, communication difficulties are eventually manifested in long delivery dates and many deadlines missed.

One way of becoming aware of the nature and extent of this problem is to audit and analyse telephone traffic at each major site to reveal its pattern, then reinforce this with a reporting system on customer delivery performance. A common outcome of such an analysis is the acceptance of the need for a simpler organisation structure, a critical review of inventory policies and the realism in delivery schedules. The telephone system can change from being a simple communication device to being a useful tool of organisational analysis!

Teleconferencing

A further but expensive development of the telephone is the teleconference network. This is generally used for trouble-shooting conferences, in which a meeting can be held between executives from different sites without the need to be physically in one place. This approach is used mainly in high-tech international companies, where coordination is necessary among vendors in different countries.

In theory, the development of optical fibre telephone lines will soon reduce dramatically the cost of telephone communication, but tariffs are influenced by politics and very cheap lines may be a long time in coming!

Cheap, effective teleconferencing could have a profound effect on the location of offices away from expensive city centres to more salubrious suburbs. There is some evidence of this already happening in the financial services industry in the United Kingdom. Other possibilities which are opened up by extensive teleconferencing include that of executives working at home. However, the habit of going to the workplace with a social interaction and the current high telephone tariffs have both prevented the teleconference from becoming commonplace.

Another development of teleconferencing is in the field of distance learning, which is being pioneered in universities and colleges. The teleconference opens up the possibility of group tutorial sessions to be conducted on a remote basis.

The computerised system

Attention has already been given to computers and computer systems, but this discussion needs some further development. Two aspects are worth pursuing. The first is the use of databases for enquiry within the organisation, where the enquirer is the active, probing audience. The second is the pre-programmed computerised system which directs 'exception reports' to executives in the expectation of a response. In the latter mode the computer system takes on a role within the command structure of the organisation.

The database
A review of a few examples will highlight some of the possibilities. All open customer orders could be held on a database. Enquirers could have access and establish status directly from the screen. Airline booking systems are built on just such a principle.

Another example is the database set up as an archive of technical information. Rolls-Royce generates thousands of technical reports a year on overhauls of aero-engines, and from the database archive, engineers can scan these reports from remote computer terminals to detect fail patterns and possible causes. The archive becomes a means of storing meaningful experience and facilitating organisational learning. Much skill is required, however, in setting up the index and enquiry protocols so that the trouble-shooting engineer has ease of access. This requires an empathy between the database administrator, the designer of the archive and those who are potential users. This is in reality a very difficult task as user needs cannot usually be perceived without experience of using an archive, and with first time development there is, of course, no such experience. The database administrator is primarily a technical person who cannot see things the same way as the user.

Libraries in universities and colleges manifest, partially at least, the database archive. Increasingly, library information is being fed into communication networks so that the lecturer can check references and research reports, or even current orders for books, from his or her own room.

The database archive of customers and their records can also be of great use in market research and the development of a contact base for new products. A college might wish to promote a master's programme and direct attention, in the first instance, to its own past graduate students, those graduating with honours, who are at least 25 years old. Provided the student records are part of the archive, and in an appropriate format, it is a simple matter to get the computer to generate mailing labels for targeting such a group!

Similarly, a college, as part of its course monitoring procedures, might wish to highlight reasons why students withdraw during their course. This is a mini-research project in which data will probably be collected and analysed from questionnaires, sent using labels generated from the student record archives. Again this is a simple matter if the structure of the archive is planned for this type of access.

Pre-programmed computerised exception reporting
In the discussion of the database archive emphasis was laid on the activity of the enquirer, the receiver of the communication. However, organisations tend also to be directive. They wish norms and standards to be followed, and if anyone steps out of line attention must be directed quickly to the problem. Line management, in theory at least, develop and define policies and standards; these standards and policies can be embedded in the rules and processes of computerised systems. Such systems can be programmed to detect

deviations between actual performance and the expected standard, to assess the extent and importance of the variance, and if it is outside tolerable limits, to generate a report for a particular executive's attention, also possibly with a summary for higher-level management.

Early examples of the above exception principles may be taken from the field of inventory control. Buyers were frustrated with massive lists of inventory items. They needed just those which had come up that week for re-order. Hence the norms of the re-ordering cycle were programmed and only those items fitting re-order criteria were displayed for the buyer.

Gradually, much more elaborate business norms and standards yielded to the process of definition until it became possible to express the major parameters of the corporate plan as visible standards locked in to the computerised system. Once there, detection of deviation could become routine.

However, effective managers tend to have well-developed judgement for qualitative factors, but weaknesses in quantification, whereas computer systems excel in quantification, but are relatively weak and mechanistic when it comes to qualitative judgements. Also, norms and standards which seem reasonable on definition in the board room may look laughable and unrealistic when applied to a small branch. A key communication skill when dealing with computer exception reports is that of interpretation. It is also important not to underestimate the cost, time and skill required to develop and maintain computerised systems which do, in reality, reflect the norms and standards set by the organisation.

The grapevine

Whereas computerised systems represent a formalised communication approach, it is necessary also to consider informal channels and methods. In common parlance this is called the 'grapevine'. The key device of transmission is social and informal contact, outside the lines and channels of official company policy and organisation structure. The grapevine operates particularly in times of crisis, when groups of people at work perceive threats to their livelihood. Factory closures, takeover bids, rationalisations and redundancies are all events causing individuals to seek protection and a defence against the perceived threat in the group.

Management generally fears the effect of the grapevine, as by its very nature it cannot be controlled. Social contact is pervasive, but rumours can be particularly damaging to morale and company interests. The normal response by management is one of openness. Briefing groups, television, the house magazine and distribution of the annual report to employees are all counter-devices to ensure that official channels are predominant, and that there is no vacuum to be filled by the grapevine!

There is one interesting manifestation of the grapevine, often used by governments, but occasionally by the management of business organisations. This is the 'inspired leak'. There may be a situation where a new, controversial and risky policy is being considered and management is uncertain what the employee/customer reaction will be. They wish to keep some distance from association with the possible change until they are assured of sufficient support within the organisation. No management likes to lose face or authority, so the inspired leak becomes the testing ground. If the reaction is hostile, management can then categorically deny that the change was ever contemplated. If there is no adverse reaction, management can implement the change and feed confirmatory information about it through official channels.

It is not always easy to find a reliable channel through which to make the inspired leak! The company needs to find an assured listening device among employees, a 'mole', whose identity can be protected.

Transmission of communication

The next step in the communication process is the transmission of the desired message. It is necessary to reach the whole of the intended audience and to get the transmission timing right, and it may be necessary to retransmit several times to ensure validity and conviction in the minds of the audience in order to secure the expected behavioural change.

Reaching the whole audience

If a meeting is involved, it is necessary that all those expecting to contribute are invited in time to secure their attention. If the medium selected is a computerised system, it is necessary that the computer is programmed to prompt the executive intended to interpret and act on exception reports. If the medium is an interactive database and some of the audience is unidentified, then at least it will be necessary for the database designer to capture feedback from dissatisfied users so that the quality of future transmissions can be improved, and to ensure that there is a greater awareness of changing requirements. If the transmission medium is a mail shot, the mailing list needs to be kept up to date and comprehensive. This is really often just a matter of good housekeeping. For instance, in promoting management courses to personnel managers it makes sense to scan this year's recruitment list and feed the names of new employers into the list of next year's course promotion shots. Most managers have a poor appreciation of the value of information, particularly about customers, and how it should be actively managed for mutual advantage.

Timing the transmission

A variety of considerations will apply here. Firstly, there is organisational politics. There is no point in putting up a proposal for a large capital spend at times of great financial stringency, yet in the public sector, word sometimes gets through in the last two months of the financial year that there is money unspent in the budget and bids had better be put together quickly if the opportunity is not to be lost. With the right timing an appropriate proposal should not fail.

The timing of transmission of proposals in a bureaucracy will often depend on the cycle and programme of committee meetings which will need to approve and resource the proposal. It is also important to time any lobbying correctly, so that when the proposal reaches the committee it is supported by those with influence in the organisation. Primarily, it is a matter of taking the trouble to give these influential figures a full brief.

Retransmission of communication

Whenever there is a persuasive element in the intended message, generally to induce a buying decision (advertising) or to achieve a learning outcome (education), then some retransmission may be necessary before the full behavioural change is achieved in the audience. Each such transmission may have a limited objective and cover only one aspect of the message, but the programme of transmissions, taken together, will have a more ambitious objective to convey a possibly complex message. In any retransmission the timing is also important, as audiences forget as well as learn, and any communications programme should clearly be timed for a progressive increase in impact.

Retransmission of a message may also have a technical rationale related to achieving validity. With telecommunications devices it is always possible for corruption to take place during transmission, but if on retransmission the message returned does not match the outgoing message, then some invalidity is immediately recognisable.

Noise in communication

In radio transmission 'jamming' is the extreme situation where noise is predominant and the intended transmission is rendered unintelligible to the audience by technical intervention. 'Noise' can, however, be introduced by other more subtle methods, such as confronting the intended audience with an overload of information so that the importance and profile of the intended message is lost, or putting an item at the end of the agenda on a busy schedule, knowing that there will be no time for discussion. This effectively invites a higher-level group merely to rubber stamp the proposal rather than engage in a real consultative exchange. Lack of time can also be induced deliberately by talking out a previous agenda item, leaving no time for later items. This noise is a manipulation of the political process, a sort of anti-lobbying.

Noise can also come from another source, the messenger himself. The following example illustrates this point.

In the First World War, before the widespread use of radio, it was very difficult for generals at Headquarters to assess progress at the front line during major offensives. One general had the idea of using homing pigeons. An hour after the beginning of a battle he sent his ADC to retrieve a message attached to the bird's leg, expecting news about whether the objective had been taken or not. The label read, 'I have been carrying this filthy bird now for three days, and I am fed up!'

The motivation of the soldier was not exactly the same as that of the general. Yet often in transmitting messages we have to pass them through other people — a staff member, the boss's secretary, etc., and each time there is effectively a decoding and recoding sequence as the message reaches the next link in the chain, with an opportunity for noise at each point.

Reception by the audience

After transmission the message is received by the audience — through the senses. The senses develop in the brain an expectation of what is good, appealing and attractive, or threatening, urgent, needing attention. The senses are channels bringing stimulation into the human mind and leaving an impression on the memory. In this analysis the word senses has been used to include not only sound, sight and smell, but also emotion, logic and teamwork, all of which may have a part to play in securing the intended impression.

Decoding and interpretation by the audience, taking account of perceptions, listening

This step is often not recognised. The idea of coding and decoding messages is thought to be necessary only in the secret service or wartime environment of code-cracking. Yet all messages need to get through both technical transmission and a human perception system. That is what decoding is all about. The perception system should be regarded as a sort of 'window' through which the message is received, not received or received with some distortion.

For example, a communist and capitalist may be involved in exchanges, but as the ideology of each is so different many such exchanges will simply not be registered or heard. A businessman may be totally committed to a profit target of £1 million and when a customer pulls the plug on the order, this is so painful that it cannot be believed. Instead the salesman is given a 'come hell or high water' mission to recover an impossible situation, because the profit target seems to be carved in stone.

The author recalls being involved, as a data processing project manager, in attempting to secure the acceptance of some important system proposals from a manufacturing director. The director assembled his ten senior team members for the presentation. From internal intelligence reports it appeared that he was concerned with securing his own authority and perceived the system proposal as a threat and takeover bid by another group. He sat in the presentation for an hour, then got up to say what he wanted and criticised the proposal from start to finish. He then proceeded to say what he did want and formulated more or less the identical proposal he had just heard, but in his own words. Although the project manager had had much difficulty in finding the manufacturing director's perception window, the manufacturing director managed to find the perception window of the project manager. The outcome was that the project manager repackaged the proposal, adopting as far as possible the words of the manufacturing director and the overall proposal was then endorsed by the managing director, so that face was saved on all sides! The ownership of the proposal had moved from the design group to the using group — a very healthy development, but an outcome which observers at the end of the original presentation would not have expected.

It is often said of executives that they do not speak the same language or are on different wavelengths. What this really means is that they are having difficulty in finding one another's windows of perception in order to enable the hearing function to operate!

Interpretation of information can be much more difficult than many might expect. Indeed, whole professions are dedicated to the skill of interpretation. Lawyers spend their lives interpreting legal documents, statutes and rules, and making legal drafts, which can indeed pose a formidable challenge to others. The lawyer requires precise, technical language to ensure consistency in every interpretation, whereas non-lawyers are much more concerned with immediately recognising meaning. No wonder expert and non-expert often have difficulties in communicating with one another. The 'perception windows' of each may be very different.

Behavioural change

In our definition of communication the audience was the crucial target. When the communication process is successful — and this may be only after many exchanges through a variety of channels and appealing to a variety of senses — some new behaviour is expected. The outcome may be obedience to a brief or commands, a commitment to a new decision, a predisposition of goodwill, an improved knowledge and skill or a greater identification with a team and commitment to the organisation.

Where there is no behavioural change there may be a number of explanations. Perhaps the message was not transmitted to a member of the intended audience, perhaps it was muffled by noise, perhaps it was not 'heard', perhaps it was forgotten, perhaps it was resisted because it was not convincing enough or its articulation and orientation had something lacking.

Feedback to sender: listening to the feedback

This is the final step in this process. Those who send messages are generally keen to get feedback from the audience after transmission to confirm that the intended change has happened. It is for this reason that most communicators favour face-to-face exchanges, where feedback can be perceived immediately. However, in large groups feedback can still be weak, as many contributors will not have the opportunity to catch the eye of the chair; further, many people find it difficult to get up and speak in public. In small informal groups communication should be much easier.

Difficulties in communication

Figure 9.1 on p. 137 offers a useful framework for summarising difficulties of communication, some of which have already been discussed earlier in this chapter and are found within the many case studies in this text. However, a commentary on the summary may help to put the difficulties in perspective.

Psychological

The difficulty here is to transmit a message that is capable of being 'heard' by the audience. If the 'perception window' of the receiver of the message is very different from that of the transmitter, then it may not be heard at all. The capacity to hear seems to depend on a framework of expectancy. The human mind, as a protection mechanism, often filters out unpleasant messages. We may call this 'escapism' when the message is not heard at all.

Distortion

Whenever messages are passed through an organisation they go through various stages which are effectively decoded and recoded. This is done within the perceptual framework of each person in the link. Normally, some change occurs as decoding and recoding take place. If such a change occurs then we say that there is distortion. Distortion may also occur if there is noise during the transmission.

Authority, status, power

Particular barriers exist in communication between those in authority. The ego must be preserved and the right protocol observed if the 'perceptual window' is to be reached. Some skill is required in offering criticism in acceptable language.

You cannot say, 'My Lord Bishop, you are talking rubbish about these terms of reference. You simply do not understand what is involved in a college chaplaincy team.' More acceptable might be, 'My Lord Bishop, college chaplaincy is a new development in this diocese. Perhaps it might be appropriate to seek the views and opinions of those already in this field before terms of reference are defined for this ministry.' If they were written exchanges, then the first would not get an answer at all, but the second would certainly have the door kept open for further exchanges.

In communicating with authority, some things cannot be said at all, and for others the protocol is so complicated that we have to expect coded language and phrases and decode them if we wish to find meaning in an exchange.

Criticism of performance is another difficult topic. In this text this problem has been aired in the discussion of the appraisal process of the MbO approach to management. For the more sensitive discussions it was advocated that a 'third party' be present to facilitate the necessary problem-solving climate and to open up perceptual windows about management development which otherwise would be closed.

There is also a serious implication regarding top management's ability to be well-informed of what is happening at the lowest levels of an organisation. Top management knows what is going on through receiving reports which are transmitted up through the hierarchy of the organisation, and there may be distortion at each level. Bad news, or news of things happening which do not fit in with company policy, may be filtered out, so an over-optimistic picture reaches the board, unsupported by much realism!

A modern response to this probability of *filtering* is for top management to refer more to direct computer summaries of activity and variance. There may still be problems of interpretation in computer-generated reports, but there is less chance for distortion.

Representational

Those who represent others have a special power position within the organisation. There is always the implication that if they are ignored then sanctions may be forthcoming in loss of goodwill and possibly strike action, if the representation is from a recognised trade union. But the role of the representative is, as far as possible, to reflect the aspirations of the constituency behind the representation, and all the problems of 'face-saving' exist here as well. In addition the representative is expected to 'win' or to 'fight'. He or she cannot be seen to be a pushover, or there is the threat of failing to be re-elected.

The implication of this is that the representative cannot afford to be too creative and flexible. Management might offer the most superb proposals, well defended and conceived in logic, but if they are ahead of the expectations of the grass-roots membership, then opposition must be expected from the representative. Because by its very nature such opposition may be based on political or emotional reactions it tends to look most inarticulate and unreasonable. Once these reactions are formally minuted there is then the added difficulty that they are public knowledge and likely to lead to entrenchment.

There are two possible responses here for management. The first is to involve the representative in the very early discussions, so that there is time to refer back to the constituency before a decision is made and test reactions. There is no need to fight when persuasion and selling of new ideas is possible. The second response is to use a third party as a communication buffer and reduce to a minimum the problems of loss of 'face'. In the United Kingdom there is a Government agency, the Arbitration Conciliation and Advisory Service (ACAS), which will, on request, play the third-party role in industrial relations disputes.

Jargon

This difficulty relates to language. It must be a facile observation that language will only communicate ideas effectively if the words and expressions used have a shared meaning between speaker and listener. However, the growth and complexity of technologies, specialisation and professionalism means that there are frequent exchanges between the expert and layman. If the expert persists in talking in language which makes sense only to another expert, then the layman feels excluded, and is either resentful, confused or uninformed.

This begs the question of whether jargon is ever justified. For the expert it contains a summary code for complex ideas and facilitates communication with other like experts. The pressure of time enforces this approach, but any effective communicator will need to consider further who are the listeners and use language suitable to all. A common practice in written reports is to include glossaries to provide an explanation of the key terms used, which may be perceived as jargon by some readers.

Bureaucracy

Outsiders may have difficulty in communicating with a bureaucracy. They will be unfamiliar with the power structure, protocol, rules and processes which guide the bureaucrats. Proposals may need to be routed through several offices at different levels before an outcome is possible, and at each link in the chain there are the possibilities for distortion and delay. Any one bureaucratic official may have only limited authority, so the proposal from outside can just circulate and never emerge from the process.

A common response to this difficulty is to get an expert to guide the proposal through the bureaucracy. This may be a lawyer or tax expert, etc. With the rise of the European Community there are many large European funds, and cities and institutions which wish to get access to these may appoint experts whose sole function is communicating with the bureaucrats. The author attended an international conference in 1986, at which the principal of an Irish college claimed to have raised £30 million from the EC Social Fund for an educational project with the aid of experts dedicated to the role of dealing with EC bureaucrats!

People at work often wish to communicate within their own organisation to get things done and most organisations manifest some features of bureaucracy. Communication difficulties are not very different from those confronting the outsider. However, the insider should have much more information about the rules and processes and be in a better position for reducing and avoiding delays. There may still be a complex process involved, and this is summarised in the model of Figure 9.1 (p. 137) under the heading *constitutional process*. Possible stages and relevant verbs of activity are: mutual interest, access, exchange, sympatique, alternatives, evaluation, commitment, action, result, review, experience, learn.

Sympatique happens when the communicators can share situations fully and empathise with one another about causes of problems and possible courses of action. This leads the communicator to both the problem-solving and learning processes, which are clearly a part of sophisticated communication. From successful organisational learning organisational health and growth should flow. Examples were given earlier in this chapter of using computerised databases as a means of capturing, refining and extending existing technical knowledge, and knowledge about contacts and the customer base.

Access

Getting things done in an organisation requires support, authorisation of proposals and allocation of resources. The usual access will be through official channels up through the hierarchy. This is access through the normal executive structure. There are, however, two other possible channels. Firstly, a manager may access members of the representative structure, much in evidence in college or university environments, and from there recommendations can be passed to the executive structure. Secondly, the access can be done informally by direct face-to-face contact with a member of the executive. Which access route is chosen will depend on the timescale necessary for processing the proposal, the contact base of the proposer and the prevailing leadership style of those in authority. Whereas a formal approach to a senior executive may expose him to loss of face, the informal, 'off-line' contact may offer opportunities for compromises to be exchanged and accepted in private.

Overload

The difficulty caused by overload is simply one where the executive required to respond to another's communication has too much on his plate and, as a reader/listener, cannot give the item of communication the priority and attention it deserves. If the organisation structures or access procedures are not appropriately activated, bottlenecks and delays will occur. Appropriate responses to overload include refinement of organisation structure and improvement of delegation practice to reduce peak loads, a possible re-specification of the reporting system to reduce paperwork, and a practice of concentrating on exceptions alone. The technique of 'exception reporting' becomes a key principle in the design of computerised management information systems. The skills of interpretation of computerised exception reports are key skills for all management users, with particular importance for senior management.

Skills of chairmanship

These are summarised in Figure 9.2, where the principles of chairmanship are assumed to be within a small 'working party' environment, operating under normal committee rules. This model provides a useful framework of reference for analysis of the material contained in the Woodhouse Bronchial Unit exercise.

Some of the material in this model — the section highlighting the 'systematic approach' — was inspired by and adapted from the film *Meetings, Bloody Meetings*, starring John Cleese. The section of the model 'Features of bad chairmanship' was developed from exercises with students of management, and can easily be replicated by posing two questions and getting feedback. The questions are as follows:

1. Why do meetings/committees fail?
2. What are the preconditions for a meeting to be: (a) satisfying; (b) creative?

The skills of effective chairmanship are not learned quickly, and in working life, even in the environment of an academic community, it is amazing how few people demonstrate expertise in these skills. Often the minutes of a meeting as eventually published seem to be different from what actually happened. Inevitably, the minute secretary and the chairman have to decode and recode discussion points, resolutions, etc., and some distortion will occur. It seems to make sense just to publish the recommendations and resolutions that are essential for continuity between meetings.

A systematic approach — planning and managing meetings	The decision-making model — getting progress at meetings	Features of bad chairmanship
Purpose	Discuss and agree terms of reference for the assignment and its objectives.	No order, sub-meetings are permitted.

Preparation
  Time budget
  Order planning
	Gather data from those present and reports which are tabled.	No direction of discussion. Lots of wandering off agenda. Time-wasting.

Processing
  Proposition
  Evidence
  Interpretation
  Argument
  Resolution
	Consider alternative courses of action.
	
	Decision criteria for a good decision.
		Pressures of personalities and politics of members are stronger than the model of logic. 'Hidden agendas' are not recognised as such.

Putting it on record	Evaluate the alternatives.	Chairman will not face dilemmas with positive resolution, but postpones decision. Sets up endless sub-working parties to look further, but these are simply delaying tactics.
This systematic planning model is demonstrated in *Meetings, Bloody Meetings*. This training film is an excellent example of skills training material. From a re-run of some really chaotic situations in meetings, the systematic framework is superimposed.	Make the decision. Review the decision against the criteria. Communicate the decision for implementation. This model is a guide for a manager as chairman who has an assignment which requires a programme of meetings. The requirement is to get an objective assessment of the problem, options and solutions, which will be supportable in the organisation. A good chairman will continually make progress, maintain support from members and avoid time-wasting and duplication of activity.	Chairman insists on informal rules or unanimity. (Power manipulation.) Chairman leaves controversial items till last, so there is no time to deal with them and chairman gets away with unfettered 'chairman's action'. Chairman snubs members. Chairman fails to seek contributions or listen to them. Chairman offers *fait accompli* from decision of sub-group held elsewhere and will not permit further discussion. Committee becomes a rubber stamp.

(This list was generated and revised from live feedback from students of management.)

Figure 9.2 *Chairmanship skills*

Being over-economical with words can lead to being over-economical with the truth. Minutes can be challenged at the next meeting, when they have to be formally approved, but that may be too late.

There are particular difficulties in preparing minutes when two groups meet to discuss an assessment or deal involved affecting both parties, and there is some conflict between the groups. The official record may be a joint communiqué, with some difficulties conveniently glossed over. The stronger of the groups will tend to give greater emphasis to their point of view than that of the weaker group.

Summary

The chapter began with a review of a communication model, Figure 9.1. This was a representation of some of the important components of communication. Although contained on one page, the content was inevitably complex, because communication is in reality a complex process in organisations.

The chapter followed with a review of the principles of chairmanship and difficulties in managing meetings. This was developed from a model of chairmanship skills and difficulties (Figure 9.2).

Exercise 9.1
The Woodhouse Bronchial Unit

At the time of publication this exercise had been used for ten years among management students to allow them to experience the dynamics of behaviour in meetings. The exercise would be introduced as a practical workshop after discussion of the ideas involved in the chairmanship skills model of Figure 9.2. The situation portrayed is a fictitious one, based on contact with middle managers from the Health Service in Scotland.

The exercise material consists of the following items:

1. A background statement about a working party,
2. Today's agenda,
3. Nine participant roles.

The exercise can be run with as few as six members, some of whom may be asked to take on two role briefs. The individual reader may still get some benefit from the debriefing notes on the various decisions.

Running the exercise

1. Students should become familiar with the background statement and their individual role. Normally, roles are allocated at random, though it may be advisable to ask for volunteers for Role 6, the first convener of the working party. (Five minutes.)
2. Students should operate as a working party using the specified roles. (One hour.) Each student should only see a copy of his or her own role.
3. All participants should go through a debriefing process in a plenary session

with the tutor to review the outcomes of various decisions and obstacles, the chairmanship responses to each crisis and the behaviour of the members. (Thirty minutes.)

Background statement

A working party has been set up by the Scottish Health Board with a remit to advise on the most appropriate action to be taken in regard to the Woodhouse Bronchial and Chest Infection Unit. This is a unit in Glasgow which has been treating chest diseases for the last fifty years. The current premises must be vacated within six months owing to a demolition order affecting the whole street. The order has been approved by the Secretary of State.

The Woodhouse Bronchial Unit has some eighty beds, and a nursing staff of forty and £2.5 million of specialist equipment. The working party had its first meeting a week ago and is meeting for the second time at 10.00 a.m. today. Its members are as follows:

1. Mr(s) Barclay, of the Bartnavel General Hospital.
2. Mr(s) H. Ballantyne, member of the Scottish Health Board.
3. Dr Charles, a consultant specialist at the Woodhouse Bronchial Unit.
4. Mr(s) Erickson, of the Eastwood Royal Infirmary.
5. Dr Pasco, a general practitioner.
6. Mr(s) Scott-Henry, of the Scottish Health Board (Convener).
7. Mr(s) Woodburn, of the Woodhouse Bronchial Unit.
8. Mr(s) Western, of the Westwood Royal Infirmary.
9. Mr(s) Yale, a management consultant and expert in decision-making methods.

Each member has been appointed on the basis of the possible contribution he or she could make regarding the future of the Woodhouse Bronchial and Chest Infection Unit (WBU). The aim is to develop a practical plan of action for implementation within the next six months. Each member has a role specification. These should be used as a guide only for this morning's meeting. Each member may expected to ad lib with further facts and information regarding the interest being represented. This morning's agenda is given below. The meeting is expected to last for one hour.

Agenda

1. Minutes of last meeting (already circulated).
2. Matters arising.
3. Election of Vice-Convener.
4. Report from Mr(s) Scott-Henry regarding expected budget allocation for re-establishing the WBU.
5. Programme for working party for the next three months and method of working.

6. Any other business.
7. Date of next meeting.

Role specifications

Role specification 1: Mr(s) Barclay, of the Bartnavel General Hospital

Your hospital has only been established some five years as a general hospital and in your view is grossly underutilised. The accommodation and equipment is very modern, and the staff are enthusiastic about the possibility of absorbing the WBU. A recent and controversial decision was the removal of the Maternity Unit from your hospital. Many of the staff were unwilling to move with the unit. No redundancies were declared but such a possibility is not to be discounted. The hospital is sited about 15 miles from the centre of the city.

You wish to move a resolution under item 5 of the agenda that there will be a specific declaration from the Scottish Health Board that there should be no redundancies as a result of the demise of the WBU. Such a precedent would be most comforting for your own hospital.

Role specification 2: Mr(s) H. Ballantyne, member of the Scottish Health Board

You are a junior administrator of the Scottish Health Board and feel pleased to have been nominated for this working party.

You are keen to be elected as Vice-Convener (item 3 on the agenda) and are even prepared to nominate yourself.

You believe that avoiding redundancies is less important than maintaining a high standard in the care and treatment of bronchial diseases.

You believe that a new site should be found for the WBU and that it should retain its distinctive identity as a specialist unit.

Role specification 3: Dr Charles, a consultant specialist at the Woodhouse Bronchial Unit

You are a consultant specialist at the WBU and 90 per cent of your work is dedicated to that site. You are ambitious as a consultant and would now like to work in a much larger unit which would give you more scope to enhance your professional reputation. You regard the Eastwood Royal Infirmary as ideally situated in the city, only two miles from the present unit. It already has expertise in this field and is familiar with the specialist equipment required.

Role specification 4: Mr(s) Erickson of the Eastwood Royal Infirmary

Your general hospital already deals with bronchial and chest infections and has excellent relationships with consultants in this field. It is situated within 2 miles of the WBU.

The accommodation is somewhat old-fashioned and there are many unfilled vacancies on the staff at the hospital. You are unwilling to take the administrative strain which would be the outcome of absorbing the WBU.

You wish to move a resolution under item 5 of the agenda to the effect that a delegation of protest be made to the Secretary of State to challenge the demolition order passed on the WBU.

Role specification 5: Dr Pasco, a general practitioner

You are a general practitioner. You could never get on with the consultant specialists at the WBU and on more than one occasion were snubbed by the WBU administration.

You would like to see the WBU absorbed within the Bartnavel General Hospital. You have much respect for the administration there, know several of their consultants and have heard that since they lost the Maternity Unit they have ample space to absorb such an extra unit.

You are extremely tired of the schemes put up by the Scottish Health Board and think that they are too bureaucratic. You would like to see Mr(s) Barclay elected to the Vice-Convenership of this working party (item 3 on the agenda).

Role specification 6: Mr(s) Scott-Henry, of the Scottish Health Board, Convener

You are an administrator and want the whole matter of the WBU to be cleared up as quickly as possible with the least fuss. To you it seems obvious that the unit could be absorbed within the Westwood Royal Infirmary, achieving a staff saving.

Your budget for re-establishing the Unit has been set by the Scottish Health Board at £80,000. You are required to report on this under item 4 of today's agenda, and you regard the amount as generous.

You are anxious to maintain an air of impartiality from the chair.

Five minutes after introducing item 5 on the agenda you develop a migraine and decide to vacate the chair in favour of the newly elected Vice-Convener.

For the rest of the exercise you adopt the role of observer with the remit of reporting at the end of the exercise on the Chairmanship of the Vice-Convener and the behaviour of the members.

Role specification 7: Mr(s) Woodburn, of the Woodhouse Bronchial Unit

You represent the Woodhouse Bronchial and Chest Infection Unit. You are shattered that the demolition order for the WBU was approved by the Secretary of State. You are most anxious for your colleagues on the staff and their futures. You fear that if a large, impersonal general hospital absorbed the WBU it would never be able to maintain the current high standards of health care in the field of bronchial diseases.

You know that Mr(s) Ballantyne supports this viewpoint. You are prepared to propose his/her candidature for the Vice-Convenership of this working party (item 3 on the agenda).

Role specification 8: Mr(s) Western of the Westwood Royal Infirmary

Your hospital is 3 miles from the city centre and is a general hospital covering everything except bronchial and chest infections. There is plenty of spare accommodation but the size of the administration is such that it would burst at the seams if it had to absorb another major unit.

As soon as Mr(s) Scott-Henry makes the financial report (agenda item 4) you see fit to challenge it. Your grounds are that the budget remit is so small that the working party has no opportunity of viewing the WBU in any but a highly restricted way. You are prepared to resign from the working party unless you get an assurance from the Convener that a further approach will be made to the Scottish Health Board regarding the budget remit after the working party has reported.

Role specification 9: Mr(s) Yale, a management consultant and expert in decision-making practice

Your role is to help the committee by giving guidance on good decision-making practice. You see the necessity for a logical process as follows:

1. Gathering and interpreting information from the representatives present.
2. Identifying the criteria for a satisfactory solution to the problems of the WBU.
3. Building on the teamwork of the group to assess alternative solutions.

You get very irritated if the meeting becomes dominated by personalities rather than by the logic and facts of the situation, and are prepared to prompt the Convener to bring the discussion back on a logical course.

Exercise debriefing

Item 3

Who was elected Vice-Convener? Ballantyne or Barclay? How did the election take place? Was a vote taken?

Occasionally, a complete surprise occurs! Some personalities play their role really hard and are prepared to nominate themselves! A chairman can waste a lot of time on this decision.

Item 4

Did Mr(s) Western resign? How was he/she kept within the group?

Sometimes this role is played really hard. The group can be delighted when Western does resign and this allows progress at the meeting. If the role is not played hard the Convener will generally attempt to dissuade Western from resigning, as the unity of the working group would be compromised. Western might try other tactics to get the point made and, after getting support from other members, force a vote on the issue. The Convener might rule such a move out of order and prevent the vote.

Item 5

Was the resolution on redundancy moved by Mr(s) Barclay? Was it passed?

Was the idea of a delegation of protest to Secretary of State approved?

This is a 'hidden agenda'. Some Barclays do not attempt to get this debated at all, but others touch a sensitive chord and have the articulation skill to get the item put to the meeting.

Item 6

Was any real progress made?

The group are unlikely in one hour to get much further than gathering data and getting a feel for the options available for and the initial aspirations of the members. Some assessment might also have been made of the salient resource issues and constraints. They might have started homing in on the most promising of these by fixing a programme of visits and assignments for review at the next meeting.

General

What happened when the Chairman withdrew with a migraine?

The Convener's migraine can have a devastating effect on the continuity of the meeting and slow up progress for the Vice-Convener who takes over, unless the group has developed a practice of regular summing up at the end of each agenda item, with a secretary taking notes.

What points of discomfiture were experienced by the Chairman?

Most Conveners experience the discomfiture of 'overload' being confronted with both unknown personalities and considerable detail from the contributors, which needs interpreting and putting into perspective. The skills of listening are much in demand, as well as the skills of control to keep discussion orderly and relevant.

What irritation was felt by the members?

Was the Chairman aware of the many hidden agendas?

References

Drucker, P. (1954), *The Practice of Management*, Harper.
Meetings, Bloody Meetings, training film starring John Cleese, distributed by Audio Visual Arts.

Chapter 10

Planning processes at the operating level

Overview

On completing this chapter the reader should have an appreciation of the steps necessary to define and achieve tasks and sub-tasks which support relevant objectives and projects derived from the strategic planning process. The many common difficulties in the planning process include how to prioritise, coordinate, time, resource the elements and allocate appropriate management authority and responsibility. In an effective planning sequence it is an advantage to know how to involve participants in the planning process and stimulate the necessary motivation to make the plan happen.

The planning process also requires regular communication with top management to ensure continued support and the flexibility to respond quickly to a crisis such as a strike or a computer breakdown. A key objective of this chapter is to introduce the reader to planning techniques which meet these requirements. By the end of the chapter the reader should be able to set out and analyse a simple planning network.

The key technique of planning with networks was developed in the late 1950s, and the man most closely associated with its origins was MacNamara, chief executive of the Ford Motor Company, and later US Secretary of Defence. The technique was originally developed to speed up the launch of a new motor product. Later, it was used to coordinate the many thousand suppliers involved in the Polaris weapons project. Some observers were to claim that Polaris was ready two years earlier than would have been possible under conventional planning techniques! Since Polaris many authors have refined the approach, which is now generically referred to as networks.

It is probably easiest to see networks as an extension to the managing by objectives framework. MbO focuses on clarification of management job positions and getting a fit with corporate strategy. However, tasks and projects need rigour in clarification and definition as part of the process of programming, resourcing and allocation of assignments to groups. The networks are the links which facilitate the fit between the management group and the project or task.

Against the background of networks this chapter reviews the basic stages of planning at the operating and practical level of management. It then offers a list of criteria for judging the quality of any plan.

Two further developments are then briefly reviewed. Firstly, we consider whether mainframe and microcomputers can help in the process of making and manipulating networks and presenting results. Secondly, we consider the training and implementation difficulties associated with working with networks, and the 'natural' type of management planning problem which is most amenable to solution by network techniques.

Two points to remember

1. The world stands aside for the man with a plan because he has done his homework and carries strength at the conference table.
2. When timing is critical, plan backwards. This ensures realism at once and the problem is identified by the unfortunate realisation that 'today' should have been three weeks ago! Never mind — this does enable management by anticipation, which is less traumatic than missing critical ending dates.

The process of planning at the operating level

The seven steps in the planning process are as follows:

1. Define the goal.
2. Estimate the resources required.
3. Devise possible combination of resources.
4. Predict problems involved in each such combination.
5. Select the most economical combination and timescale.
6. Develop contingency plans to cover possible interruptions.
7. Expose the plan to all those involved and get them to validate it.

The seven steps of planning

Difficulty often arises over the level of detail needed for step 1 in defining the goal, and whether the definition should be as rigorous as the MbO statement that an objective is a result to be achieved at a cost not to exceed £x by [date].

Planning networks assist in the timing and coordination of projects. If the deadline is fixed as part of step 1, it may well be an outcome of the planning process that more resources are needed to achieve the date. It is at management's discretion to allocate these. It is impossible to start earlier, but at least the problem is obvious now when it may be managed, rather than later when there is the risk of reacting to events.

Management may visualise a fixed package of resources, while remaining flexible about the completion date of the project, and will accept the timing outcomes of the planning process. However, time does generally mean money as benefits are tied to the completion of a defined phase and delays may be linked to penalty clauses or missing a vital date for tender or for an event such as a national exhibition. In such cases the date of the project completion must be regarded as fixed and the resource package as variable. Companies may be much influenced by cash-flow considerations. A delay of one month of a £3 million payment could be crippling.

Step 6 covers contingency plans. It is true that some interruptions are unforeseeable, but on the other hand, events such as a strike, a project leader's illness or a supplier failure are all possible events and could severely undermine a project completion date. Whenever the completion date is vital and such interruptions are possibilities, it is worth making contingency plans with the aim of minimising the time for recovery.

Some organisations are particularly adept in the art of applying the concept of contingency planning. These include government departments and the armed services. Contingency planning in the private sector is often neglected, as indeed, it does cost time, money and attention. If contingency plans were made for every eventuality then we would never stop planning and actually start doing. Some priorities are needed to secure rapid responses to the most important threats of interruption to the planned project.

Step 7 of planning — validation by those involved — also gives rise to some difficulties. It assumes a background culture in which there is a wide participation in the planning process, and in authoritarian organisations this is not a valid assumption. In addition it might be seen as prohibitively expensive to get people together to activate a validation process. However, if this means that unsuitable plans are imposed there will be regrets that the validation was not attempted.

Achieving quality in planning

The criteria for the quality of a plan may be summarised as follows:

1. It will work.
2. It is comprehensive.
3. It is understandable to the participants as well as to the planner.
4. It is properly timed.
5. It is both stable and flexible.
6. It is compatible with the plans of other groups.
7. It is 'optimised'.
8. It is 'self-controlled' by a monitoring device which reports deviations in time for corrective action to be taken.
9. It is supported by both senior management and the participants, who through their involvement in the process are motivated to make the right thing happen.

The norms of stability and flexibility seem on first sight to be incompatible with one another! However, it is possible to achieve both flexibility and stability. The stability element suggests that the plan has been rigorously defined and expressed in an understandable format. The flexibility element suggests that the plan is easy to redefine and re-express in the light of changing circumstances and the use of contingency plans.

'Optimisation' may be hard to achieve. However, networks do enable a trade-off between time, resources and cost, and that is very useful contribution.

The effective monitoring of the plan is a vital activity and it is not difficult to set up. It is primarily a clerical activity, and once set up gives the plan a natural stability and continuity. With the aid of modern communication links it is possible to transmit the planning status of critical projects regularly to those involved via electronic mail. With the addition of graphics facilities it is possible in a simple and effective way to highlight any problem areas requiring attention.

Networks enable management by exception to be directed at the critical activities. When difficulties arise the networks should highlight the impact of such difficulty on the total plan.

Demonstrating networking techniques

The techniques are demonstrated by defining a typical planning situation, posing some management questions about timing and resourcing and then working through in a step-by-step sequence to a solution of these questions in Exercise 10.1.

Exercise 10.1 A new product introduction

(Material printed with permission of the National Computing Centre, Manchester.)

An established company has decided to add a new product to its line. It will buy the product from a manufacturing concern, package it and sell it to a number of distributors selected on a geographical basis. Market research has indicated the volume expected and the size of the sales force required. A planning network will be developed to assist management in taking decisions. The project planning group meets to decide what needs to be done and who will be made responsible for the achievement of tasks and sub-tasks. A full list is drawn up and screened by the planning team for comprehensiveness and clarity. The initial questions of interest to management are at the end of the list for analysis. The outcome of this part of the exercise is discrete tasks defined 'A−M' with estimated elapsed times for each in the following list:

A. *Organise the sales office* The first task is to hire the sales manager: 6 weeks.
B. *Hire salesmen* The sales manager will recruit and hire the salesmen needed: 4 weeks.
C. *Train salesmen* Training must be provided for the salesmen hired to sell the products to the distributors: 7 weeks.
D. *Select the advertising agency* The sales manager will select the agency best suited to promote the new product: 2 weeks.
E. *Plan the advertising campaign* The sales office and the advertising agency will jointly plan the advertising campaign to introduce the new product to the public: 4 weeks.

F. *Conduct advertising campaign* The advertising agency will conduct a 'watch for' campaign for potential customers to end at the time distribution receive their initial stocks: 10 weeks.

G. *Design package* On the basis of market research the company will design the package most likely to sell: 2 weeks.

H. *Set-up packaging facility* Prepare to package the products when they are received from the manufacturer: 10 weeks.

I. *Package initial stocks* Package the stocks received from the manufacturer: 6 weeks.

J. *Order stock from manufacturer* Order the stock needed from the manufacturer on the basis of the volume indicated by market research. The time taken includes the lead-time for delivery: 13 weeks.

K. *Select distributors* The sales manager will select the distributors whom the salesmen will contact to make sales: 9 weeks.

L. *Sell to the distributors* The salesmen will take initial orders for the new product from the distributors with delivery promised for the introduction date. If orders exceed stock, stock will be assigned on a quota basis: 1 week.

M. *Ship stock to distributors* Ship the packaged stock to the distributors as per their orders or quota. Note that the shipping will commence one week after the initial order taking, to take account of the order processing cycle: 5 weeks.

N. *Develop selling programme* Take orders for the new product for a further five weeks from the initial selling to distributors.

Questions that will influence management decisions

1. How quickly can we introduce the new product?
2. What are the critical activities?
3. If we hire trained salesmen and eliminate the training period of 7 weeks, can our product be introduced 7 weeks earlier?
4. How long can we delay the selection of our advertising agency?
5. What should the priorities be for the newly appointed sales manager in respect of the need to hire salesmen, select distributors, and select an advertising agency?
6. How could the overall programme be reduced (crashed), for completion in 20 weeks?

Developing the network

First of all, it is important to define what a planning network is. It is a diagram linking tasks and events, developed with a logic which takes account of real constraints. Every task will have a beginning point and ending point, and these are the events. Skill in networking involves getting a set of linkages in which there is as much concurrent activity as possible as this will give a shorter completion date for the project as a whole.

Figure 10.1 represents a first attempt at this exercise. The convention here is to represent a task as a line and an event as a circle, hence the name 'network'. Note

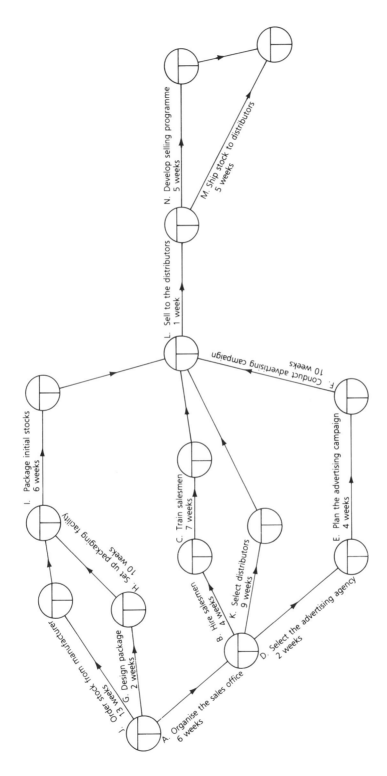

Figure 10.1 *Initial planning network*

that this figure is simply a business understanding of the problem of the new product introduction as defined in the original task list. As a network is a timed diagram, the natural logic is to draw from left to right, i.e. from beginning to end of the project.

The initial approach is to look at the original task list and to define a beginning event. We must assume a management organisation, so engineers are there to design the package (G), purchasing agents are capable of ordering stock (J) and a director can authorise the setting up of a sales office (A). Tasks A, G, J can thus begin at once, which is by convention day zero.

Once we have a sales office, a sales manager can hire salesmen (B); once the salesmen are there, they can be trained (C).

A sales manager may then select distributors (K) and select the advertising agency (D).

When the advertising agency is selected the campaign may be planned (E), and executed (F).

Now we can look at other branches of the network. Once the package is designed, we could set up the packaging facility (H). We cannot package the initial stock (I) until both the facility is set up and the stock is received from the manufacturer (J). The way we represent this practical difficulty is to make the starting event of packing contingent on both (J) and (H), by linking in both lines.

When we have the stock, the trained salesmen, the distributors and the advertising support we are ready to sell and ship the stock. Selling is thus contingent on four previous branches of the network, so the beginning event of selling has four constraint linkages attached. By convention when we have a logical constraint which does not in itself consume a time resource, we give it a task line with zero time. From the network in Figure 10.1 it will be seen that the estimated elapsed time is represented along each task line; in this case the scale is in weeks.

The network is a model of the business project, reflecting a clarification of what has to be done, a logical sequence of doing the work and an opportunity for developing a timescale for all activities.

Using the network

Timing

Now we can begin timing the network (see Figure 10.2). It will be seen that the circles, the event notation, have been divided into three segments. The left-hand segment represents the earliest possible event starting time; the top segment is a number which uniquely defines the event and is simply a label reference; the right segment represents the latest possible starting time for the event which would not make the overall project late. The significance of the left and right segments will be seen as the analysis proceeds. Differences in times between latest and earliest will suggest that there is some flexibility in doing some tasks; for other tasks there is no flexibility. This difference between earliest and latest event times is often referred to as 'slack'. When there is no difference in these times the 'slack' is zero and that part of the network is said to be 'critical'. Planning networks are sometimes called 'critical path networks' for that reason. The

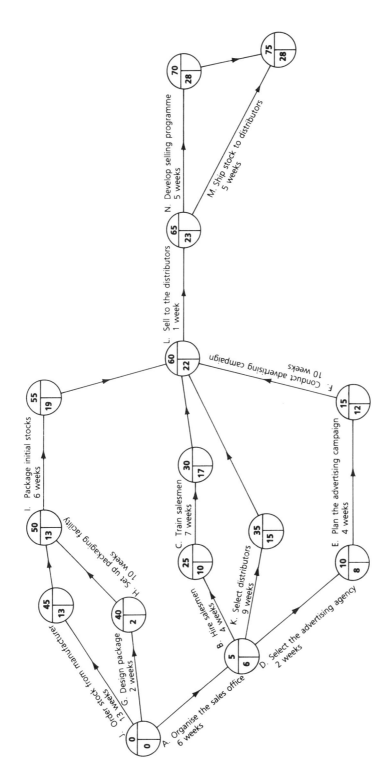

Figure 10.2 *Calculating earliest event times in the forward pass*

management significance is that a critical path is an exception condition requiring special attention and thus facilitates the great principle of 'managing by exception'.

The forward pass through the network

We now want to get an answer to management's first question concerning the earliest project completion date. In Figure 10.2 we have attached labels to the top of each event circle to facilitate identification. The convention is to number from left to right and increase label numbers in increments of 5. This enables additions to be inserted without completely upsetting the labelling system. In Figure 10.2 calculations have been done for the 'forward pass'. We begin with the event labelled 'start' and insert the earliest event times in each circle. 'Start' is rated zero. Now we move from left to right simply adding the duration times of each task. A is completed after week 6; B 4 weeks later, week 10; C after a further 7 weeks, week 17. We need, however, to develop one extra rule to cope with those events which have more than one preceding task. This is the situation for activity, I, at the top of the network. The path from J is $13 + 0 = 13$. The path from G and H is $2 + 10 = 12$. The logic is that we cannot commence I until *both* previous paths are completed, thus we always have to carry forward to the network the longest of the two conflicting times, in this case 13 weeks.

When we reach event 60 we find that there are no less than four preceding paths: 22 weeks from F, 15 from K, 17 from C, 19 from I. Clearly 22 is the greatest and is carried forward. We reach the end of the network (event 75) in week 28.

Twenty-eight weeks is the longest path through the network but also the shortest possible completion time given the constraints of existing logic and elapsed times.

The backward pass through the network

The reader is now referred to Figure 10.3. We need to calculate the latest event times from the end of the network working from right to left back to the beginning. We use the right-hand segments of the event circles and begin at event 75 with the figure 28. As we work to the left we subtract the activity duration times. Whereas in the forward pass when there is conflict from more than one incoming path we take the highest of any two figures, in the backward pass we take the lowest. Thus when we get to event 5 there are three incoming lines: from B, $15 - 4 = 11$; from K, $22 - 9 = 13$; from D, $8 - 2 = 6$. 6 is the lowest and becomes the approved latest event time. Figure 10.3 now has all three segments of the event circles completed.

Critical events

All events in the network have some slack (a difference between earliest event time and latest event time), except events 0, 5, 10, 15, 60, 65, 70 and 75. These events and the activities associated with them are known as the 'critical' activities. If there was any delay in these the whole project would be delayed unless further resources were provided.

Interpreting the network

Questions 3 and 4 in the list of management questions (p. 164) require some interpretation of the network. Would it save time to recruit trained salesmen? Event 30 shows a slack

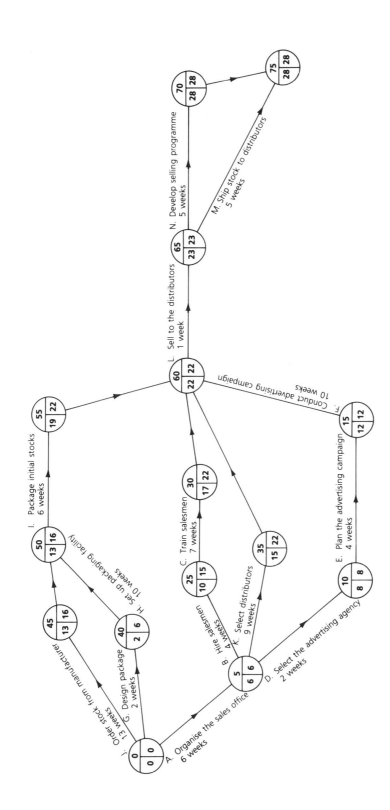

Figure 10.3 *Calculating latest event times in the backward pass*

of 22 − 17 = 5 weeks. The activity is not critical. It would make no impact on the ending date if they were recruited already trained. Recruitment could be delayed by 5 weeks without any problem. If, however, they were recruited on time but the training took 13 weeks activity 30 would have an earliest completion time of 23. This would become critical and the project would be a further week in completion, i.e. 29 weeks.

Management wants to know whether they could delay the selection of the advertising agency. A brief review of events 5 and 10 in the network reveals that there is no slack here. This is part of the critical path, and any delay would be immediately reflected in a later project completion date.

Management is also concerned about the sales manager's priorities (question 5). From the network we see that he is obliged to initiate activity B, hiring salesmen (slack 5 weeks); activity K selecting distributors (slack 7 weeks); activity D selecting the advertising agency (slack 0). He is most likely to concentrate initially on the advertising agency, then the salesmen and finally the distributors. The longer the slack, the lower the priority. The principle of management by exception is operating here once again.

Crashing the programme, question 6

When the plan is presented to management they may be most concerned about the 28 weeks required for completion. What if they have badly misjudged things and had intended this product to be ready for the National Motor Show, just 20 working weeks away from the current date? Staff planners cannot tell top management that a 20-week project is impossible. What they can do is to review the logic of the network and the resources and assumptions under which it was made. Luckily the network does provide a framework from which creative ideas may be tried out.

Attention will first be given to the critical path of the network to see whether any change of approach or sequencing may have a possible impact. When further thought is given to critical activity F, the conducting of the advertising campaign, one could argue that it is not necessary for the campaign to precede the shipping and selling of the product; it could indeed run in parallel. This requires the redefinition of the network, with event 15 now connected to event 75. This is illustrated in Figure 10.4. The network needs re-analysing by means of forward and backward passes. The change has several implications. Firstly, the completion date is now week 25, a saving of 3 of the necessary 8 weeks. Secondly, the critical path has changed to the top of the network, i.e. events 45, 50, 55, 60, 65, 70 and 75.

We still need to pare off a further 5 weeks, looking at the critical path. Let us take 1 week off the shipping timetable, a week off the packing of the initial stock (overtime would take account of that), 3 weeks off the lead-time for getting stock (activity J); with some bargaining between purchasing agent and supplier, it should be possible to arrange to receive two delivery batches, the first in week 10, the second in week 13. To get this concession we may have to forgo a price discount. Unfortunately, event 50 still has only 1 week saved, not 3, owing to the influence of event 40, and only 1 week of slack available. It would thus be necessary to install the packing line in 8 weeks instead of 10 but with overtime that would be tolerable.

Note that no attempt is made to reduce the design time of 2 weeks or the time needed to set up the sales office and hire a new sales manager. These are tasks involving meetings

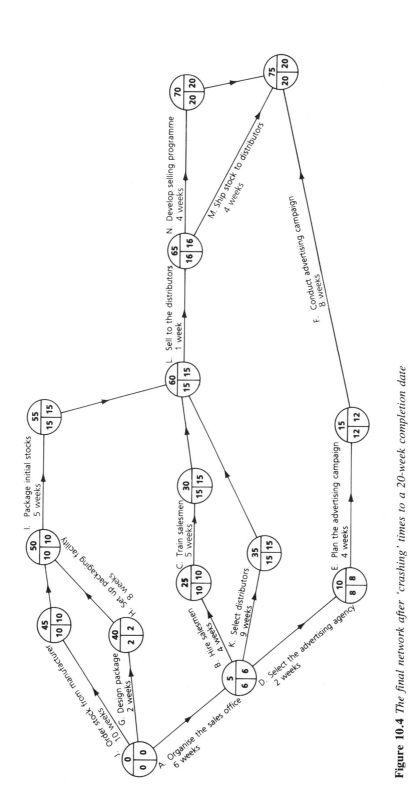

Figure 10.4 *The final network after 'crashing' times to a 20-week completion date*

and are particularly vulnerable to delays. A common failing in many network plans is to take insufficient account of the cycle of committees for management decision-making.

We need to scan the network for other adjustments as other paths will now become critical. A week's reduction in the training of the salesmen would be required (acceptable given suitable pressure) and 2 weeks' reduction in the advertising campaign (activity F). This hurts, but is inevitable and can be tolerated. The final network can now be seen in Figure 10.4 and the project completion date is that required by management, i.e. 20 weeks.

There are still some snags in this, however. There is very little slack time anywhere, so the plan is vulnerable to possible unforeseen slippage, and there is a need for extra overtime budgeting (activities H, I), a loss of discount (activity J), a reduction in the salesman training (activity C), and re-timing and a curtailment of the advertising campaign (activity F). All these are effectively the trade-off conditions between completion time and the necessary resource package. However, the staff planner's reputation is still intact, and management is likely to accept this revised plan and is pleased to have the opportunity to put its judgements into the planning model.

Developments of networking techniques

The technique illustrated in Exercise 10.1 can be made more sophisticated by today's information technology equipment. Since the 1960s computer programs have been available that aim at assisting in the definition and analysis of the network and automatically complete the forward and backward passes and highlight critical and sub-critical paths. Indeed, with a computer it is possible to analyse thousands of such activities. In the 1980s this capability reached the microcomputer, which makes it possible to do simulations easily without a lot of manual recalculating, but the computer does not do the thinking for the planner. He or she still has to apply rigour to the task definitions and the judgements about the programming sequence. Once the network is logically watertight, the computer can help with its analysis and even assist in the more detailed task of devising bar charts and resource schedules.

Simple computer programs require the user to define the network logic from a list on paper; more sophisticated application packages use graphics and offer the planner a skeleton pictorial representation of a network from which the logic can be developed. The pictorial representation offers a natural way of expressing the plan and giving a balanced and neat rendition of a solution. Ideally, the planner wishes to empathise directly and easily with senior line management, and any communication device that helps this process is to be commended.

Difficulty of estimating times

One assumption is that the length of time an activity will take is based on the normal probability distribution, and that a sound way of proceeding is to offer three time estimates. The first will be an optimistic estimate, assuming no snags. The second will be the most likely time. The third will be a pessimistic time, assuming some problems. The mathematician will then relate this to probability distributions and attempt the following rationalisation: add the optimistic estimate to the pessimistic estimate; then add four times the most likely time and divide the result by six; accept this figure as a best estimate. This approach is most unrealistic as it does not take account of the real considerations affecting providers of resources.

A much sounder approach is to begin by consulting the resource providers and asking for a minimum time estimate based on work study. This will assume a defined availability of resources and total dedication of these to the activity being estimated. From this raw figure the resource providers are asked to quote an elapsed time taking account of the week in the year when the commitment is expected and the likely availability of resources at that time taking account of other accepted priorities. When this second set of considerations is taken into account it is possible to allow for the impact of bank holidays, seasons and a full range of other commitments. When the resource providers do then declare an elapsed time from this basis, they can be made accountable for its achievement. When resource providers know that the project planner means business the estimating of times will become acceptable. This is another situation in which dialogue and communication are vastly superior in application than abstract rules of mathematics and probability theory! The only major snag with this approach is that the calendar date when the resource is required cannot be determined until the network has been analysed, and the analysis cannot begin until some times are quoted. Effectively, this means that networks are not provided at one analysis. Several iterations are required before resource providers can offer firm commitments. But the advantage is that once the firm commitments are given there is a high degree of motivation and momentum to make the plan a success.

Applications of planning networks

Some industries and exercises naturally lend themselves to treatment by network techniques. Building and construction are an obvious example. Architects and engineers start with well-defined blueprints, bills of quantity, etc., and from this naturally given logical framework the network structure can be put in place to regularise the construction timetable. Large, one-off projects such as commissioning a factory, building a ship to a delivery deadline or implementing a computerised information system are all typical projects to which the technique can be applied.

There can none the less be difficulties the first time a new type of large project is planned. The major difficulty is that the tasks and sub-tasks are not really known and the organisation brought into being to manage the project may be working for the first time together in which there are many uncertainties. Many of the participants may be new to the technique and method of critical path work, and may even have a desire to sabotage the technique or abuse its use to their own advantage. The very manifestation of a critical path network showing a 28-week completion date when a 20-week one is required may be enough to 'blow a management fuse', with the only possible response a resort to escapism. Suppose a chairman has made a public statement about a critical project completion date and he is about to retire, he simply cannot hear a voice of realism that says we need £2 million more in terms of resources to meet that date. The staff specialist likes to work in a world of logic and quantification, but senior management are often motivated by political considerations. The staff are there to support management; if realism does not suit the currently developing game-plan, then the staff may need to make way for others who can be more reassuring to the bosses!

It may be wishful thinking to expect the rigour of the network logic to be fully accepted and applied, replacing more familiar and informal methods and constraining a well-established and articulated leadership style.

Case Study 10.1
Implementing an advanced factory scheduling system

This case study shows how the effective application of behavioural science can assist in the successful introduction of modern quantitative management techniques. (It is based on the author's action research.)

The company had two main manufacturing divisions. Computer-assisted scheduling from a predefined application package was introduced in the first division after following an 18-month critical path network, getting it right and never losing control. A year after the completion of the first implementation the major benefits of the scheduling system were self-evident. The project manager was summoned by the divisional director of the second division, who by this time thought that it would be a good idea to get on the computer-assisted bandwagon. His division had no previous experience of computerised routines and the technology was more complex than that of the first division, so some significant amendments would be required to the application package. The project manager had done his homework before going to see the divisional director and had quite a good feel for what would be required in a possible second implementation plan.

At the meeting the divisional director summoned several of his senior staff to be present when the project manager arrived. The divisional director then made a formal presentation of his request for the full implementation within a 9-month period. The project manager knew that from his own critical path models a timescale of 18–23 months was realistic: 9 months was a non-starter for a combination of reasons connected with the need to learn the new techniques and apply resources to set up the database, to re-specify the scheduling rules which would fit the division's technology, and to test the revised package. However, this was not an appropriate time to confront the divisional director. The project manager suggested they set up a joint working group and give them a brief to set up a programme with the requested delivery timescale. The working group would meet the project manager the following week. This satisfied everyone and the meeting ended with goodwill preserved on all sides.

The following week the project group met. The project manager got the group to build up a network from first principles, using the previous network as a guide but being careful not to draw comparisons too obviously as the divisions had a great individual *esprit de corps* and did not like to be compared. This exercise was very healthy and the group identified all the key activities and resource requirements. The critical path was developed and, oh dear, it required 23 months! The project manager then led the group through a 'crashing' sequence (Exercise 10.1). At many points times could be reduced if further resources were provided and these became identified as items requiring extra budgetary authorisation. After the extensive 'crashing' sequence the group decided that the division could not live with or resource an implementation plan of less than 15 months.

The final and most difficult phase was then to get this revised plan adopted. The project manager contacted his superior, the data processing manager, and explained the predicament of the 15 months and the extra budget needed by the division for project viability. The data processing manager agreed to inform the divisional director informally of the situation. The divisional team also did some lobbying with their divisional chief accountant and prepared the outlines of a case for the extra budget. The divisional director was soon to see that the staff meant business and that there would be no loss of face in retreating from the original 9-month plan.

The outcome of this incident was successful. In 15 months the second division was savouring the fruits of computer-assisted scheduling. The management teams from the division and the data processing department were still on good terms with one another.

With two major projects in that field now perceived by the organisation as being successful, there was an added bonus. The networks giving the structure of the project planning and control could encapsulate this whole activity as a useful part of organisational experience. As other similar tasks were attempted, it was no longer necessary to start from scratch; a previous network could offer a very useful reference point. As improvements were discovered in methods used these too could be made available for others in the organisation for their benefit.

Summary

1. Planning networks are a means of quantifying and modelling business projects to assist in decisions about resourcing and timing.
2. The technique is no panacea. It can be used to significant advantage. Also, it can encourage the application of effective management practice. It is not robust enough to be immune from abuse.
3. The technique offers a logical and repeatable management process for planning and controlling projects, and the application of broader principles, such as managing by exception and managing by anticipation.

Summary of the networking process

1. The technique needs an organisation structure, the formation of a project team. This group needs first to develop a list clarifying the tasks and sub-tasks of the project and identifying who should be responsible for what.

2. Next the tasks and sub-tasks (known as activities) are developed into a logical and sequenced network in which as much parallel activity is done as possible.
3. Reference labels are assigned to each separate event.
4. The network is analysed. By a forward pass each earliest event time is established. The final event date gives the project completion time.
5. By a backward pass, from the ending date back to the beginning, the latest starting date for each event is established. The critical path is defined as a chain of events with no slack, i.e. the earliest and latest starting times are all equal.
6. Initial results are reviewed with management for approval of times and resources.
7. If the initial proposals are not acceptable, the participating project group will need to undertake a crashing sequence to get dates or resources into an acceptable state. This involves repeating items 4 to 6 to confirm timings. All final dates should be re-confirmed with resource providers to gain commitment and motivation.
8. Approval and support must be secured from top management.
9. The network must be monitored throughout the life of the project and corrective action taken whenever there are any threats to costs or completion dates.
10. Copies of all successfully completed networks should be incorporated into a library for the organisation so that the experience may be used again.

Further reading

Battersby, A. (1970), *Network Analysis for Planning and Scheduling*, Macmillan.
Price, D.A. (1982), *Critical Path Analysis — Basic techniques, a Programmed Text*, Longman.

Chapter 11
Control models and processes

Overview

Control was one of the action words listed by Fayol (1916) as part of the management process. Many references have already been made unobtrusively to control problems and techniques. These are embedded in other techniques, such as managing by objectives, corporate planning, planning networks and in the discussion on communication. The skills of chairmanship were found to be essential to controlling effectiveness in meetings; the computer exception reporting systems could be effective in alerting executives that something was wrong and needed management attention. This communication was inevitably part of a control system as well as a communication system. The objective of this chapter is to give the reader a useful framework for the *control* verb, from which a manager can develop a strategy for implementing simpler and more effective control systems and approaches.

Learning outcomes

The reader should be able to identify the separate elements in the control cycle and take an informed view about whether any control system under analysis has particular weaknesses in relation to these elements. The reader should be familiar with the structure of major organisational control systems and how they may be implemented. There should be some appreciation of techniques of control from within key functional areas of the firm financial control, profit control, quality control, and production control, for example.

Review of the universal control cycle

In effective control systems four distinct elements are generally present. These four elements interact with one another to form the control system. They are:

1. A sensing device,
2. A set of norms or standards,
3. A mechanism for generating a variance,
4. A management function capable of interpreting the variance and responding.

The universal control cycle is summarised in Figure 11.1.

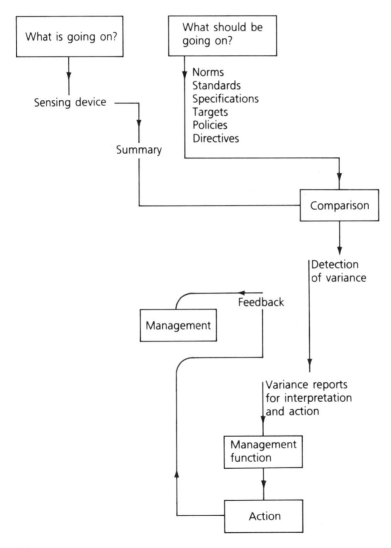

Figure 11.1 *The universal control cycle*

The sensing device

Without some awareness of what is going on, events cannot be perceived or controlled. The sensing device is the mechanism which collects data about the control subject. In mechanical systems this is often a device such as a temperature gauge to measure temperature or an electrometer to measure an electric current. In a clerical system the sensing device is likely to be a transaction such as a valid credit or debit to an account. In a management meeting the sensing device is the group of executives who can tell the chairman what has been going on in their plants, etc. A sensing device may also be the output reports, written or oral, from another control system. The only complicated aspect of a sensing device is that sensing can be conceptualised at different levels and definitions of detail.

If there is a weakness in the sensing device, and managers take action on insufficient information, then we are likely to get relatively bad, arbitrary decisions. Imagine a court sitting in which some key witnesses are absent or tell lies which are undetected, so that there is high chance that the wrong verdict will be reached. Yet courts exist to control behaviour in line with the norms of the law. Witnesses are the sensors that bring attention to judge and jury about what happened.

Much management activity is effectively an activity of sensing and then passing the information to a control system. The firm wishing to control the market-place will probably use data from its sales order processing system to detect and discern customers' product preferences. For new products it will probably engage in some external market research activity before the launch to reduce the business risk inherent in new products.

A set of norms or standards

Being aware of a situation does not mean controlling it. Managers need a meaningful picture, which is generally the sum of a series of readings or transactions, to give a gestalt picture of what the situation really is. Invoices, for example, may be summarised by customer, by area or by product. If we wish to control sales we need to know sales targets and the breakdowns of the targets and have some idea of sales policies. When we have these targets and policies then the summary picture of the totals from the invoices becomes meaningful, as it is *compared* with the standard or target.

Without standards and norms, action is likely to be arbitrary, and employees generally respond better when they know the standards expected than when they do not! This does, however, raise various questions about motivation and participation. If employees have had some say in the setting of the standards, and there is an *esprit de corps* in the organisation, this tradition will become manifested in individual responsibility and pride in the maintenance of such standards through strong internal forces, and will be reinforced by the culture, and possibly the official reward system of the organisation. The Japanese management style seems to be directed at the development of just this culture of individual responsibility of all employees, particularly for product quality. Drucker (1954), in his early advocacy of the principles of managing by objectives, averred that this approach offered the manager the opportunity of self-control through an active involvement in the setting of his or her own standards.

Managers and others often seem to be unaware that what they are doing is setting norms and standards. The budget is a schedule of standards regulating a programme of expenditure; an engineering drawing is a set of standards in a build specification; a railway timetable is a specification of when trains will run; a production schedule is a specification of the production rate; a critical path network is the specification of milestones for completion in an agreed timescale, with regular review and analysis built in to the process; a dismissals procedure is a specification of the *processes* to be followed before employment is terminated. When a systems analyst offers a specification of a reporting system he or she is specifying the norms and rules of processing, and the norms of the management reports. If this norm-setting activity is to achieve organisation-wide support, then it is necessary for the dialogue about such norms to include those who will be affected by their interpretation.

A mechanism for generating a variance

What is going right or wrong can be perceived when a comparison takes place between the data collected by the sensing device of the control system (and possibly summarised), and the norms or targets recognised by management. An accountant will be familiar with this process, which is called developing a variance.

If the variance is zero, there is no problem. If the variance is very negative then there is a crisis, and if it is very positive then this is a sign of excellence. Commonly, management has a limited but defined tolerance for both over- and under-performance, so variances of that nature will be screened away from management's attention, but what is left does require attention. This process of developing a variance and selecting out the important and sensitive elements is an aspect of managing by exception.

This process is easily discernible in many systems. The accountant develops costing and budget variances as a means of reporting what has gone wrong. Indeed, the capital budget is a major mechanism of control in organisations to prevent unauthorised expenditure and eliminate waste. In reality some managers, wary of losing out in next year's budget, have a tendency to spend this year's budget to the full towards the end of the financial year, even when some items are not strictly required.

Writers commonly use dictionaries to check spelling in their texts; indeed, in the era of the word processor and the electronic dictionary whole chapters can quickly be scrutinised. After loading into the computer's memory both the document and dictionary, the cursor on the monitor screen will highlight any word in the text which does not match a dictionary definition. Once this variance or mismatch is detected the author can *accept* the word, *edit* it (bringing it in line with the dictionary) or make the dictionary *learn* the new word, by incorporating this mismatched item directly into its own record. Thus over a period of time the dictionary as a set of norms will gradually improve and become able to cope with highly technical words.

In many processes that control dangerous machinery or traffic we often encounter *fail-safe* mechanisms. The driver of an electric train may have a heart attack, but as soon as he slumps, the drive handle is released and the train will automatically stop.

However, there are dangers in having controls that are pre-set and too automatic. In one passenger jetliner the pilot set the plane on autopilot, and he and the co-pilot temporarily left the flight deck for the passenger compartment. The doors between the two compartments automatically closed behind them! This was a procedure installed to defeat terrorism, but imagine the anguish among the passengers when they realised that the aeroplane was on autopilot and no one was on the flight deck! Seeing the pilot with an axe breaking down the door must have sent the odd shiver down some spines.

A management function capable of interpreting the variance and responding

A criticism of many poor control systems is that there is a weakness in the management function. Indeed, for effective control to be exercised decisions and actions need to be taken immediately the variance is detected. This implies that communication of the variance, its interpretation and the authority to respond should all be present in the management function. There are many possibilities for failure here.

The manager responsible may not be on the distribution list of the variance report and may be unaware of the need to respond. In theory this should be easily rectified, but there are always some politics involved in allowing another executive to become privy to an information report. The report might contain confidential items which he or she should not see; or there might be a power struggle going on among company executives — secrecy is a main weapon in the battle for supremacy.

The manager may not be trained in the art of interpreting the variance and as a result fail to understand or make the wrong response. In time this should be detected as a 'training need' and treated through the appraisal process (see chapter 6).

The variance may be reported too late once the problem highlighted has taken its course. This is a problem with many accounting systems, which are oriented towards historical book-keeping rather than immediate control.

Lastly, interpretation and response to the variance may be lacking in bureaucratic organisations, as any one official generally has limited authority. An effective response may require cooperation and coordination with other officials, for which time and motivation are necessary.

When things go wrong in organisations it is a common response for higher levels of management to attempt to retrieve control by getting the 'man on the ground' to refer exceptions to a higher level immediately. However, if the higher official is busy and not available, delay itself causes a further loss of control. This was the situation manifested in Case Study 5.1, p. 501. Furthermore, the 'man on the ground' is more likely to be better informed of the nuances of the situation (sensing device is sharper) than is possible in the manager's office, remote from the workplace.

A more positive approach is to examine in more depth the particular weakness in the management function of the control system and be prepared to change the organisation structure and the authority of the manager receiving the variance reports, and to simplify procedures for coordination.

Some implications of the universal control cycle

Now that we have examined the functions of each main element it should be evident that an outcome is a *feedback loop*. The management function which receives the variance may either correct it and bring the system back into line with previously defined control norms. Alternatively, it may do some re-tuning of the norms and standards themselves, or of the particular triggers which give variances enough significance to deserve attention. As long as the management function is aware of these norms and standards and has authority to change them, the control systems are flexible and responsive to current needs as perceived by managers in the organisation. A control system such as this may be regarded as a self-regulating one. However, often the norms and standards are set externally, and control effectively also becomes external.

Some further attention may be given to this notion of a feedback loop in a control system. In reality life is full of feedback loops, which are simply not recognised as such. Pain is a good example. It is nature's warning system that something is wrong. Without pain terrible damage may ensue. Who can remember going to a dentist for a filling, then afterwards crunching a barley sugar, only to find that you nearly bite off your own tongue? The local anaesthetic has the effect of removing the normal safety mechanism of feeling and pain.

Some devices are specially designed to facilitate control and feedback. The steering wheel is a good example of this! Where the driver wants to go, that is the norm. Where the car is actually going is sensed by driver's vision, and the driving wheel is the mechanism to make these two coincide. Accidents occur when the steering device fails, when the wheels skid (the car does not follow the direction of the wheels), when the driver's vision is defective or when he or another driver does not observe the codes of good driving practice — a further set of relevant norms of the control system.

For a deaf child the feedback device might be a hearing aid linked by radio to its mother, for a group of taxi drivers it may be a radio link to a controller within a network to get quickly to the next job, for the engineer on an oil rig it may be a robot on the sea-bed linked by television on the surface, or a bioscope connected to the inside of machinery, which can reveal wear in vital parts. The doctor may be alerted by a scanner to the presence of an abnormality in a patient in time for treatment. Telescopes help us to probe distances, microscopes help us to see minute particles, telephones keep us in touch over distances, radar helps us to see in the dark and fog. In all these situations the functions of accurate sensing and quick feedback are vital components to achieve control. The 'steering wheel' of the organisation is its range of control systems, manifested with control reports.

Examples of control systems in the functional areas of the organisation

In this section we briefly examine some control systems in finance, stock control, personnel management, safety and quality control, identifying in each case some of the main elements of the universal control cycle and common weaknesses of operation.

Financial control

If the organisation does not maintain its liquidity then it has to cease trading. Firms with a cash flow crisis may need to monitor hourly the flow of cash, and particular attention will be paid to transactions in the accounts receivable and payable and the identification of realisable assets. The control of key financial resources, such as cash, involves identifying variances from a few critical financial ratios, which serve as performance norms, relevant for the industry in which the firm operates. These are discussed and analysed in chapter 4, together with other financial control systems.

Capital and revenue budgets are the control mechanisms to confine activity and expenditure to predefined limits. Frequent reporting of variances enables management to discipline maverick spenders! However, the most powerful financial control system of all derives from the corporate plan. This is the annual profit target, which is commonly expressed as a monthly schedule of profit. Management will receive reports of monthly profit, as well as profit achieved by quarter and year-to-date. Attention will be directed to all major trends and variances and their causes, and there may be investigations into why the forecasts have not been achieved. This may be because the basis of the profit plan, volume of sales, prices and costs, have included some assumptions which are not substantiated. Vendors may be charging more than estimated; perhaps alternative vendors should be sought to achieve the profit targets. However, the control mechanism is only as good as the quality and accuracy of the profit plan and the precision and timeliness of the reporting of variances. A sound organisation will give appropriate attention to activities of market research and sales forecasting to improve the accuracy of the profit plan.

If the profit plan is not achieved then this has serious implications. Next year's capital budget is dependent on achievement of this year's profit, and stockholders lose confidence in companies and management that do not deliver what they say they will, so further financial resources will be more difficult to raise!

However, it is important not to underestimate the time, effort and cost involved in monitoring the profit plan. One commonly used device comes from organisation theory. Total profit must be a sum of contributions from products or divisions, so a large organisation is broken down into smaller 'profit centres', generally based on product families or divisions. A prime device of de-centralising control is to make the profit centre executives accountable, so that investment decisions are influenced by profit record, working with the corporate planning technique of portfolio planning (see chapter 3).

Financial systems are costly in setting up and the regular reporting and interpreting of variances are also costly. If all the company's energy is spent in accounting, measuring and self-analysis, then there may be no time or energy left for running the business and getting things done! The key to finding the right amount of time to devote to financial reporting lies in screening out the trivia from the variance reports, so management always gets a good overview of the few and important things which must be done. Financial reports should be digestible. If they induce 'overload' for executives, their main impact is lost.

Figure 11.2 gives an example of a system designed to control expenses.

Stock control

The computer is often perceived as ideal for checking stock and generating re-order notices, but it can also be devastatingly ineffective. In manual systems, the review of

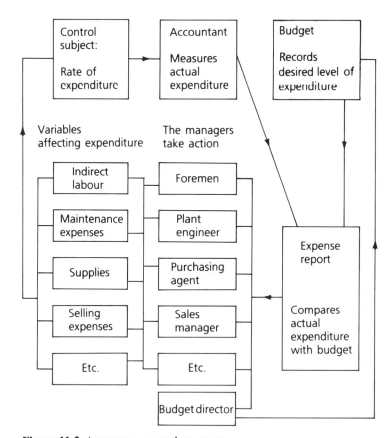

Figure 11.2 *A system to control expenses*

the possible re-order rules, together with local knowledge, generally operate to prevent the worst of abuses, but with automatic systems review of the rules is done much less frequently. In manufacturing environments, where finished devices require sub-assemblies and many bought-out parts, there can be particular abuse in computerised stock control. This may be manifested when a finished device is declared obsolete, yet the system continues to generate re-order notices for the parts. The fundamental difficulty is that the norms and standards that activate this type of system are based on a principle of historical usage, and the expectation that history will repeat itself in constant usage. The obsolescence declaration cuts that whole assumption at its core and the norms of the control system are no longer valid.

Fortunately, there are proper responses to this problem of automatic stock control. An effective computerised system will continuously re-calculate expected demand from current product forecasts, so the declaration of obsolescence should immediately highlight the amount of surplus stock, and indeed the anticipation of this will affect the timing of the obsolescence decision itself. This type of anticipatory and fast-responding stock control is called 'material requirements planning', and analysis of this is given in chapters 16 and 17. The response is, however, not a simple one, but one requiring some sophistication in using computerised packages and a proper link-up with forecasting data. Once we have such forecasting data the norms driving the control system are current, dynamic expectations of demand, vastly better than historical past usage.

Personnel management

There are many possibilities for control systems in this field. However, most attention is generally directed to recruitment, promotion and the control of various behaviours, such as time-keeping or alcohol abuse at work. In such systems as this the norms relating to the process are as important as those that relate to the data as they are processed through the universal control cycle. We have already discussed good practice in promotion systems, based on the appraisal process (chapter 6). The assumption is that appraisal is done frequently and records are made. When these data are sensed and summarised, and interpreted in the presence of a third party, it is possible to trigger promotion recommendations based on valid data. From recommendations summarised over time, actual promotion decisions can be made which are supported by data validated within the organisation. The appraisal system itself is activated by generating and analysing variances between what is done and what was expected to be done. Position descriptions and targets provide the norms of expectations, and management have to judge by progress report and face-to-face interviews what was achieved.

In the absence of well-developed appraisal schemes, promotion becomes somewhat arbitrary and more dependent on luck and contacts than on merit. In bureaucratic organisations formal paper qualifications, which are easy to identify, tend to have a greater weight in influencing promotion decisions than a sound work record, as without developed appraisal this is considered to be very subjective.

Recruitment systems have some similarities with promotion systems in that both are dependent on the norms of sound position descriptions, which provide a basis of valid expectations. In recruiting systems, however, the applicant's record will be based on external data, the cv and referees' reports or references. Management need to assess these data and prudence suggests that they look for corroboration in referees' reports. A control system, like a chain, is only as strong as its weakest part. Effective control will as far as possible be preventative, as in a recruiting system. If there are weaknesses in this checking, dishonest or utterly unsuitable people may be recruited. For sensitive government posts this checking can be a very sophisticated process, leading to what is called positive vetting, yet despite these safeguards an embarrassing number of diplomats defected from the British Diplomatic Service in the 1960s.

The exit interview

Elaborate control checks at the recruiting stage are natural as recruitment offers entry to the organisation and management has real discretion in the admission decision. Once an appointment is made it may be costly and difficult to terminate employment, due to union agreements, implications of tenure in the employment contact or redundancy laws. Many organisations also have a personnel control process at the conclusion of employment. This is called the 'exit interview' and is designed to develop a bank of summary data which reveals the reasons why employees are leaving. This puts many aspects of the organisation's employment policies under scrutiny for possible revision and can give feedback to those managers who recruited employees who did not stay.

Another natural control point in personnel systems tends to be the conclusion of any probationary period, the time immediately before the full contract is validated. The control process in personnel systems is thus seen as a set of check points and reviews to ensure that policies and standards of good employment practice have been maintained. In each case data have to be collected and interpreted, decisions made and feedback given to employees and management.

Control of behaviour

Systems that are designed to control the behaviour of people at work have many ingredients. Good behaviour may be encouraged by effective leadership and rewards. Positive motivation of those at work, through *esprit de corps* and by keeping them well informed of what is going on is preferable to setting up a system of sanctions to operate against those who transgress. This is motivation by fear of detection and punishment. The way work is organised can also have an effect on the control of security and prevention of crime. In the Inland Revenue the functions of tax assessment and tax collections are kept separate. Likewise in Data Processing it is preferable to separate the roles of systems analysis, programming and computer operating, to reduce the opportunity for computer fraud.

Effective sensing devices generally have a significant part to play in crime detection. The eye of the television camera is ever-present to detect the shoplifter. The effective supervisor will detect operatives who are ignoring standards of safety. However, the pressure to produce, and the fact that promotion to management positions is linked primarily to good productivity records, can lead even supervisors to compromise themselves in applying safety standards. For a fuller discussion of this see Case Study 19.3, 'The Tap'. In this case assembly-line foremen actually connive in passing aircraft, whose wings have a structural weakness and could drop off!

Reporting systems will throw some light on the incidence and pattern of absenteeism and identify those departments and people who are the main culprits. Management have the opportunity to seek the underlying reasons. Maybe the weakness is in the recruiting, or maybe the absence is induced by the design of a job which is perceived to be onerous or boring. Detection of the poor performer should be thrown up in variance reports of production or quality and may then be discussed more fully in the personnel appraisal system. A common way of detecting poor production is to compare 'standard hours' of what is made on the production line with 'actual hours' for the same period from the payroll system. The theory is that timing and material standards can be computed for the engineering process and material specifications to form the basis of standard hours. However, although this is an effective approach for direct production line workers, it is very difficult to produce the necessary standards for those in 'indirect' occupations, such as stores or security.

When poor performance is detected by such reporting system, the poor performer may, under pressure, admit alcohol abuse as the underlying cause. Most industrial organisations do not have the expertise to treat such a condition directly, but it should be possible to make a referral to an expert counsellor, internal or external.

Quality control

The purpose of quality control is to ensure that products are built to specification. Marketing and Engineering should ensure that the specification is high enough to diffuse customer ill-will, to avoid actions for product liability and to avoid excessive warranty claims, but not so high as to make for waste in the factory. Product quality and reliability are the sum total of quality in each and every part of the components and processes relating to the product, its packaging and after-sales servicing. There are many natural points of control in the overall process. Buyers will vet the quality of vendors. When raw material and bought-in parts enter the organisation they are normally subjected to quality checks before being passed to the stores and having the invoice authorised. Data generated at this point may be summarised to form the basis of a vendor rating system, with some useful feedback to the buyers. As the product moves through the manufacturing process there will be quality checks, some activated by automatic electronic devices, some activated by people checks, some operated by samples and *destructive testing*. In film manufacture, destructive testing may be the only way of knowing whether the product is satisfactory. Lastly, there may be a final inspection before the goods are dispatched. At each stage in the manufacturing process time and cost will be accumulating on the product and rejects will be more and more expensive. It is generally wise to have the most stringent quality checks early in the process before high costs have accumulated.

Figure 11.3 shows a simple quality control system.

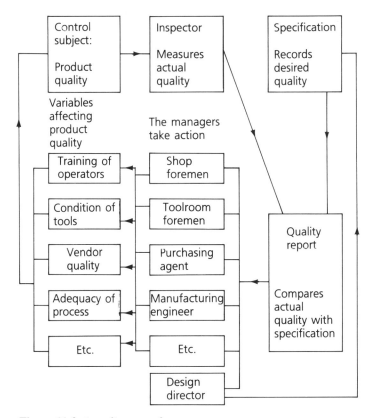

Figure 11.3 *A quality control system*

Options in organising quality control

Case Study 7.2 presented a problem relating to quality control in a tobacco factory. Much contemporary interest is devoted to the issue of who should be responsible for quality control in an organisation — the manufacturing people themselves or an independent quality department. The case study illustrated an incident in which a recently set-up independent quality control department became a counter-productive irrelevance, giving rise to over-zealous inspection attitudes, devastating loss of production and poor labour relations, and all for very little reason.

As a product becomes more and more sophisticated quality control and testing also need to be sophisticated. Ideally, employees like to do jobs that are enriched, where they feel that they can produce a finished product. Their pride in their craft extends to production and quality. The focus of this 'whole activity' may be the autonomous working group. Volvo adopted this approach in the manufacture of cars, and teams became responsible for assembly and quality in a car. The powerful norms of group conformity and teamwork were reported to be an effective, self-administered quality control system.

This was a major change from traditional car manufacture, with the boredom of the assembly-line, and the job very limited and specialised, requiring independent quality control to enforce standards. However, the testing of products such as computer chips is so complicated, requiring separate dedicated equipment, that it would not be practicable to dispense with a separate quality control department.

In international companies branded products may be manufactured and marketed world-wide. Clearly, consistency of quality is desirable. A central quality control department may act as guarantor of this, laying down quality control procedures and checks and regularly testing samples from each plant. Control will then be by means of reporting systems showing the incidence of failure from the random samples and summaries of customer complaints and warranty payments. These useful data provide feedback to plants and designers, and should provide a more informed view of the particular level of quality necessary for the market, no higher, no lower.

Quality circles

It seems self-evident that high quality in a product or service is dependent on good cooperation of employees throughout the whole chain of material purchase, manufacture, distribution and after-sales service. Traditional organisational structure, however, is generally based on specialisation of work and skill, and this can give rise to the problem of boundaries and lack of cooperation and sympatique among those of different fields. A way round this difficulty is to take advantage of the influence of the social norms of working groups and encourage the setting up a network of these with a remit to discuss quality and improvements across the formal organisational boundaries. Such units are called quality circles. The members of a unit represent a cross-disciplinary team who can bring a variety of different perspectives to a quality problem. The leadership of the circle is generally decided by an election held among the membership. The meetings are semi-official. Management will normally grant time in the working week for such meetings and may actively encourage quality circle leaders to go on courses to develop expertise in running quality circles. Line management generally adopt only this supportive role rather than an executive role, on the basis that grass-roots thinking and innovation from those at the workface of an organisation will be responsive to informal leadership in addition to that provided in the formal organisational structure.

Japan is generally credited with pioneering the concept and technique of quality circles, and the United States and United Kingdom have followed this development and with some successful implementations. For many, the quality circle idea is an extension of the 'suggestion box', further developed by techniques from the behavioural sciences, which focus on the norms of groupwork and people's natural desire to be a member of a successful and independent team. Firms with much expertise in project teams and systems teams already have the advantage of using multidisciplinary work at an official level, and would find it relatively easy to adopt the quality circles approach. It would appear that this technique can be adopted in cultures which are paternalistic or democratic, and have the effect of making the culture of the firm even more democratic! But quality circles are much more difficult to get going in authoritarian or bureaucratic cultures. No matter what the cultural environment is, a mechanism will be needed to reconcile possible conflicts between executive line management and the network of quality circles.

There is a similarity between the philosophy of quality circles and that of the more democratic versions of the technique of managing by objectives, particularly the versions which emphasise the role of the group in objective setting and appraisal. A great benefit of quality circles lies in the development of group problem-solving skills and skills in communication, as well as the building of team sprit in the organisation. Marketing too can make some capital out of emphasising the culture of quality generated by quality circles.

Use of organisational control systems to achieve strategic control

It has already been argued that the very core of a control system lies in the appreciation of major variances from established norms and standards and a rapid response in treating such difficulties. It is easy to visualise what tactical functional control systems can do — preventing waste, detecting stock-outs, identifying poor quality, etc. It is more difficult to get an overview of a whole set of control systems which are compatible with one another working to achieve organisational impact. Yet firms in a capitalistic economy need to make a profit, achieve excellence in products and markets and demonstrate high productivity. The very definition of this excellence is in terms of targets, schedules, ratios, performance levels, and policies of good practice. Once they are defined control systems can be fashioned around this profile of excellence to detect variances. The joy of using schedules and targets as the core of the normative structure of the control system lies in the fact that the orientation of the control can be to the future. A well-managed organisation should set out its plan for the future and then monitor itself against that plan. In this sense it is possible to say that a firm can — at least in part — make the future happen.

We were to find that at its highest conceptual level the profit plan and its monitoring were the most important aspects of financial control systems. Companies acquire excellence because, for some part of their operation, the core of their business, they are operationally superior to their rivals. In the running of an airline a very crucial area of performance lies in achieving high 'seat utilisation'. This will create pressures to set up a computerised booking system, as without such a strategic system the airline could have difficulty in competing. In the manufacture of high-tech products the production control and quality control systems may be crucial, as may be the communication network to reduce the timescale of engineering design.

Strategic control is primarily the recognition of areas of excellence relevant to the particular business, leading to the construction of the set of systems and sub-systems which will enable this excellence to be developed and monitored.

Another aspect of control, not covered in this chapter, concerns the concept of the *controlling interest*. Ownership of equity shares gives voting rights and the power to appoint a chairman and board of directors. Control in this sense equates with power and the ability to change the structure of the organisation through divestment and merger. These topics are considered further in chapters 3 and 18 on business policy.

A further aspect of control relates to the selection, implementation and monitoring of the firm's organisation structure, for without an appropriate structure the energies of executives and their ability to coordinate their activities would not reach the full potential. The behavioural science aspects of this are developed further in chapters 20−24. The most difficult process of all to control is that of the change process itself, and there is a distinct management approach to this called *organisation development*. This has some sophistication involving consultancies, change agents, interventions, also considered in chapters 20−24.

Exercise 11.1   Seminar topics on control

Discuss the following propositions:

1. Control without plans and standards is simply arbitrary action.
2. Critical path networks reflect good practice in both planning and control and are simply a good example of the principle of managing by exception.
3. The main difficulty with control systems is that the output of one system is often the input to another, the boundaries between one system and another are hard to draw and some systems are influenced by external factors which are beyond control.
4. Electronic sensing devices are more efficient and more effective in control than human ones. Robots can work under remote control to operate in dangerous environments.
5. The control of a profit plan exercises a much higher degree of real control than the mere setting of budgets.
6. It is just as important to control deviations from policy as it to exercise control from quantified targets.
7. Control by means of motivation and self-control is much more effective than systems which depend on detection and sanctions.
8. The major weakness in bureaucratic controls is that the rules become an end in themselves and are imposed from remote places. If the rules themselves were easily revised in the light of changing circumstances, the bureaucracy would be tolerable.
9. Automatic stock control systems can be open to serious abuse.
10. Identification of the elements of the *universal control cycle* should help a manager to detect a weak link in a control system.
11. An airline seat booking system should make a strategic impact on the operation of the airline as a whole.

12. Various financial ratios relating to return on investment, liquidity and earnings are the natural norms from which real trouble can quickly be spotted as far as a company's financial controls are concerned.
13. Quality circles are a way of making quality control the concern of everyone in the company, and integrating both formal and informal channels of communication.
14. Independent quality control from head office is essential in international companies to secure the uniformity of product standards in all global markets.
15. The most important feature of quality control is achieving quality standards which are congruent with customer expectations. To attempt to make a perfect product may seem attractive, but can render the product uneconomic in manufacture.

References

Drucker, P. (1954), *The Practice of Management*, Harper.
Fayol, H. (1916), *General and Industrial Management*, translated from the French by C. Storrs, Pitman.

Further reading

Dale, B.G. and Lees, J. (1986), *Quality Circle Programme Development : Some key issues*, Manpower Services Commission, Dept PP2CW, ISCO5, The Paddock, Fritzinghall, Bradford BD9 4HD.

Part 4

The information society

Introduction

Part 4 of this book, on the principles of management, is devoted to recognising manifestations of the *information society*, then exploring selectively applications and techniques associated with this society. The approach is to find success and then, and only then, probing the why and the how to get the techniques and processes to work. Thus the entry to the topics is always from the viewpoint of the business manager, using information technology as a tool. Certainly, there will be experts capable of applying expertise with computers, but let us be sure that they can work to the briefs of the business managers and not succeed in blinding the readers with mystique! Not forgotten, however, is the enormous costs involved in putting computer systems to use in new fields, and the need to be most discriminating in the approval of computer projects.

Chapter 12

The user and the computer in the information society

Overview

The objective of this chapter is to give the reader some compelling insights into various manifestations of the information society. It will include a discussion of some of the issues which arise from using or misusing computer-assisted systems. The material consists primarily of an analysis of established applications.

Background

During the 1980s the computer terminal or microcomputer had invaded the desk of many executives, and it was no longer credible to leave computing and computing techniques to the specialist. Managers were increasingly obliged to use computers directly and to have some computer literacy and familiarity with computer techniques.

Some companies went so far down this road of computer literacy that they took their systems out of the back office into the front office, and even redesigned their products and services around exploitations of these techniques. Reuters, the news-gathering company, is an example of fundamental re-orientation of its organisation and products. The company developed electronic reporting systems for the tracking of commodity prices, and vastly increased the scope and size of its services to those working in the financial services industry. There was enormous commercial value in having this commodity price information organised in a computerised database for instant retrieval. Reuters grew over one hundred times larger over the ten years since adopting computerised databases.

The high street banks supplemented their branch networks with cash dispensing terminals offering a seven-day, twenty-four-hour service. These terminals did not even need to be located in a bank branch: they could be located at a railway terminal, within a department store, social club or college union. Apart from simply dispensing cash they became the window into all sorts of new financial services. And as more sophisticated means of conducting fluent computer dialogue were being developed we could think quite seriously of the cash dispenser being enhanced from the 'hole in the wall' to becoming the 'manager in the wall'. By strategic positioning of these terminals the banks could court customers from a much wider social background and break down the class barriers associated with banks.

At the same time computer networks were having other fundamental impacts on business. The airlines were the first to realise the potential benefits of computerised booking systems — a small increase in 'seat utilisation' makes a significant difference to profit margins. If computerised systems can schedule passengers into aircraft, they can also accomplish the logistic tricks of scheduling the aircraft fleet into the routes, scheduling maintenance programmes for the aircraft and assigning crews. The logistics involved in running an international airline can be enhanced and improved with computer methods. In addition, the large pioneering airlines can turn their computer services into separate profit centres as computer bureaux and sell their software to other airlines.

What the airlines could do so too could the railways. Seat reservations on many inter-city services in the United Kingdom in the 1980s were controlled by computer networks. This again was intended to improve seat utilisation as well as passenger service.

When networks and databases were developed for use by the package holiday industry, the impact was quickly felt on industry profits and the customer got more choice as the market for packaged holidays increased.

However, seats and places are not all that different. Universities and colleges set up computer-assisted systems for the 'offer, reject, waiting list' communication situations, which require fast response for high 'place utilisation'. In this field even the small microcomputer in the hands of an admissions tutor can make a significant impact.

Command and control mode of operation

Computers in the police force — two applications

The basic principle here is that the computer is constantly kept up to date with the deployment of operational resources, generally the location of the patrol car. As incidents are reported through the 999 system the operational controller will stack those requiring attention on to the computer file. Once he or she knows the map reference for the incident a check will be made on the screen to see which cars are available in that area and the incident radioed to the nearest. The operator will then enter the feedback information and the system will regularly prompt him or her until the incident is 'closed'. The police soon acquire the discipline of reporting their position regularly when they are on patrol and of course other resources may be part of the system too. By capturing these operational data and storing them on history files it is possible to profile the pattern of incidents by time and place. On the assumption that the pattern is repeatable the resources can be pre-positioned in the areas most likely to generate incidents.

There are many other modern examples of computer applications in the command and control mode. One of these is another police application, a database for controlling crime. Information on this is taken from the report *Police Computers and the Metropolitan Police* (1984).

A database is a large set of files, generally held on a computer random access device (i.e. disk or drum), to which a range of enquiries may be directed. The data are held in a 'tree' structure so that the user may draw together whole classes of items. A good example of such a database is that supported on the Police National Computer at Hendon. This system has been available since 1968, and has eight indices which are as follows:

1. Stolen and suspect vehicles,
2. Vehicle owners,
3. Stolen chassis/engine numbers,
4. Fingerprints,
5. Criminal names,
6. Wanted/missing persons,
7. Disqualified drivers,
8. Cross-reference.

The volume of enquiries to PNC has steadily grown. The figure quoted for 1982 was 31 million.

A policeman on duty in a patrol car may radio base to check a car number, which he may suspect as being stolen. Local HQ will have a terminal linked to Hendon. Within 5 seconds the enquiry will have been processed. It will then be relayed to the policeman on duty. The whole transaction may be completed within 1 minute.

Another application using this system is based on a device set up on the motorway which automatically reads the car number plate. This is then checked automatically against the stolen car index, and if a 'hit' is made then the number and car description is radioed a mile up the road to alert a police car waiting to intercept. There is a link between the Police National Computer (PNC) and the Driver Licensing Centre (DVLC) in Swansea, so as addresses of drivers are altered so too will be the records on PNC.

A further look into the categories of stolen and suspect vehicles reveals the following breakdown of information:

1. Lost or stolen,
2. Obtained by deception,
3. Found or abandoned vehicle,
4. Vehicle repossessed by finance company,
5. Suspected of being used in a crime or other incident,
6. Of long-term interest to the police,
7. Removed to the police pound,
8. Removed by police to another street,
9. A vehicle used for police purposes,
10. Blocked (information available only over secure channels),
11. Seen or checked in noteworthy circumstances.

Although control of crime by more efficient use of resources and their deployment may be a laudable aim, the means used may well be perceived as an intrusion to privacy. It would be possible, for instance, to put electronic bleepers or tags on all vehicles, and have sensing devices throughout a motorway system to detect and control speeding. What a useful tool to combat the phenomenon of motorway madness! In the late 1970s the tachograph was introduced in the United Kingdom compulsorily for heavy goods vehicles to leave a trace of vehicle speed on a graph, and initially there was much opposition to this legislation, but it had become accepted with no fuss by the late 1980s.

Electronic tags, however, are likely to generate strong emotions. If you can tag a vehicle, then you can tag a bird and study its behaviour. Indeed naturalists already do just that. The conventional method of controlling the criminal is to shut him or her up in an institution. But with electronic tagging of prisoners, it would be possible to control their movements in the community; perhaps there would be much less need for prisons at all, except for the most violent offenders. The use of such tagging might be considered radical and progressive, and not necessarily oppressive. It would be particularly appropriate for the control of prisoners on remand awaiting trial. The key question is that of how far it is possible to go with political consensus in exploiting such computerised methods in a society with a democratic tradition.

Computer use in the gas industry and fire service

There are statutory levels of service laid down for responding to gas leaks owing to the inherent danger arising from non-treatment. There are a limited number of engineers working in the field and the business purpose is to utilise each engineer in the best way. The engineer is obliged to report his location over the radio, where it is entered on the computer file. Incidents are reported, classified for priority rating, then queued for the nearest resource available. For very high priority jobs, engineers working in adjacent areas may be called in and those already committed to a non-priority job requested to leave and move on to the emergency one. The components of this system are similar to those used in the deployment of the police described above. The key elements are as follows:

1. A computer file tracking where the engineer is.
2. An incident file for jobs as they are reported.
3. A controller capable of classifying the jobs on the basis of urgency, a function requiring discretion.
4. An information retrieval system on line to the controller so that he or she may direct the appropriate available resource to attend to the incident.
5. A feedback system to ensure completion of the process and provision of history profile data to help understand why such incidents occur and to point the best way to respond. Where the incident profile shows particular black spots then renewal of equipment, such as plastic pipe to replace metal pipe, may be considered.

In the fire service some units are adopting computers to assist in the initial stages of firefighting, before arrival at the scene of the fire. As the incident is reported, maps and descriptions of the premises and potential fire hazards are put on to a television screen for the benefit of the firefighting section, and from these a prediction can be made of the equipment and resources required which can be matched to the resource available. Useful intelligence such as the location of fire hydrants may be also displayed on screen.

In the commercial world there are many situations requiring rapid deployment of resources to meet clients' needs, in which computer-assisted systems could be beneficial, yet progress is still slow. People are reluctant to abandon conventional methods in favour of the learning required and the complexity of the new technology.

Point-of-sale systems

In the 1970s the larger retail stores were quick to reap the advantages of computerising the cash till, and because this was, as far as the customer was concerned, 'at the point of sale', these systems were named POS. POS had its strength with the links it made possible with other systems in the retail organisation. These were as follows:

1. It could directly link with stock control and warehousing. As the product codes and quantities of purchases were logged, the shelf stock could be reduced and provide data to trigger replenishment to the shelf and possibly replenishment to the warehouse itself.
2. POS could make a link with the accounts system and, for credit purchases, check that amounts were within authorised limits.
3. POS could make links with credit card companies and have purchases authorised so as to eliminate the risk of defaulting.
4. Sales management could work really fast during seasonal sales, repricing articles on the basis of the product code, eliminating the need for relabelling all the goods.
5. By tracking the activity at terminals by day of the week and time of day it would be possible, from interpreting the pattern, to make better judgements about staffing deployment.
6. Once the retail group had a national network, it could offer store credit cards and move unobtrusively into the financial services sector.

Viewdata, Ceefax and Oracle

An interesting development in the 1980s was the integration of the television with the microcomputer to offer the electronic newspaper. The television has attached to it a teletext device and the user may activate this with a simple handset. On tuning in to text mode the viewer is offered an index with page references, and by keying in the page number required, the desired page is called on to the screen. The BBC version of this is called Ceefax, the ITV version is called Oracle. The pages come from a news database, which is updated continuously.

However, databases can be interrogated for even more specialist purposes, and Prestel, a commercial database, offers literally thousands of pages of information for commercial enquiries. It can also be the vehicle for recording transactions from the home. Home shopping and home banking are both technically possible with this technology. Its relatively slow acceptance is noteworthy. Firstly, this technology does represent a culture shock. Secondly, it was expensive, particularly in the early days, although prices have dropped considerably.

Institutions also gradually became aware of this 'viewdata' technology. The institutional house magazine or bulletin board could be televised for all to see to attract clients and promote business. Railways and airlines already use this approach for the announcement of arrivals and departures.

Case Study 12.1
Data processing applications: integrated use of mainframes, minis and micros

Head Office in Bristol has a mainframe computer which has links with the key manufacturing facilities and these also support mainframe computers. The United Kingdom is organised into several sales regions. Each region supports a minicomputer and a warehouse for distribution. The company salesmen are organised by sales region and each equipped with a microcomputer, a portable computer known as a 'laptop'. This is very compact and fits comfortably into a briefcase. The monitor is a flat screen and is simply the lid of the case. The power source is provided by rechargeable batteries. Every evening the salesman unclasps the cassette from his microcomputer, attaches it to the acoustic coupler of his own telephone and dials the minicomputer at the region. While he is eating his tea the orders he took that day are transmitted from his cassette directly into the minicomputer's memory, and then the information flows back from the minicomputer to his own cassette — messages from the boss, statements of account for tomorrow's sales journey, sales promotion information, and so on.

Meanwhile the mini in the region starts the leg work. Orders just received over the telephone are converted into 'picking lists' for the night shift and delivery notes for loading first thing in the morning onto the delivery fleet. By midday the customer can expect delivery of the order.

Meanwhile the mini has done a check of warehouse stock and transmitted to head office its replenishment requirements. Head office collates these and arranges replenishment deliveries from the factories to the regional warehouses. The mainframes in the factories then schedule production taking account of the latest sales demand.

Each salesman used to spend many hours on statistics and book-keeping. Now he or she has just the microcomputer and the cassette. When he or she is with the customer it may be that the shopkeeper is busy and cannot remember what is normally ordered. The cassette has a skeleton order form based on a summary of the last three months'

Head Office
|
Mainframe computer

Factories
|
Mainframe computers

Regions and warehouses
|
Minicomputers

Salesmen
|
Microcomputers
Acoustic couplers

Figure 12.1 *Use of computers in Imperial Tobacco*

business as a guide. Using this system, the salesman can devote the whole time and attention to the trader. If the trader prevails on him or her for a really urgent order then that is no problem either. With the use of the acoustic coupler and then the cassette, the order information can be passed immediately to the regional warehouse, and in favourable circumstances delivery may be made that very day.

The system suits the regional sales manager. A salesman may be off to attend jury service and a relief is briefed to take his or her place. He or she connects the acoustic coupler to the telephone and the cassette is filled with the information that the absent colleague would have had, and in addition, local information for each call — who the proprietor is, how you find the site, where to park the car, what day is early closing, where the nearest bank is, and so on.

The essence of this approach is to put information technology right into the front line — that is where the sales and delivery battles are won. Yet to achieve this effect it is necessary to use a whole variety of software and hardware. The information technology strategy should become an integral part of corporate strategy.

Figure 12.1 summarises the use of computers in this company which produces consumer goods.

The principles behind successful applications of information technology

It may be helpful to reflect briefly on some of the applications developed in this chapter. There is always the major consideration of commercial reality. Customers want quick and accurate information about orders and delivery status. Managers want high utilisation of their resources, both of people and facilities, and communication links are vital in coordinating these. They may be intrigued by the appeal of computers and computer technology, and want to keep abreast of the competition, but it can be very dangerous if this is the only reason. The case study literature is full of examples of purchases of equipment which then gathers dust, the motivation for its use having strangely evaporated.

The proposed application must be accepted by those who are reaching for commercial objectives. They must be willing to rethink their methods and procedures. Information technology often offers new ways of working and new options, which are there to be exploited if managers are willing to look. Adoption of computer methods is often encouraged particularly strongly in organisations which support management development programmes and open communications.

It is essential to be realistic about the pace of progress in adopting computer methods. If the organisation has substantial resources it may be practicable to pioneer in new fields. If there is a lack of resources, it may be better to pursue a policy of digesting the successful applications of others, then importing and adapting the know-how to the home environment. The means of making such organisational improvements is an approach called organisation development, which is further discussed in Part 5. Another expression for this type of activity is 'intrapreneurship'. This is an adaption of entrepreneurship, and comes from the same idea of innovation, but from within rather than outside an organisation.

Concept of leverage

There is a need to justify computer applications, to evaluate them and prioritise them; otherwise authorisation is simply a random act, conditioned by organisational politics and carried out by senior managers who are relatively poorly informed about the new technology and its capability. The main concept of justification can be described in terms of 'leverage'. There are two sides to any discussion, the *benefit* of the proposed application and its likely *cost*, and when this is turned into a ratio it can be called 'leverage'. Authorisation is then a matter of scanning several applications and going ahead only with those of high leverage.

A simple example will suffice. A college has £2,000 to spend on information technology. At any point in time there is a variety of ways in which such a sum could be spent; the choice lies with management. If it were used to computerise accommodation bookings (a very scarce resource) and raised room utilisation by just 5 per cent, that would yield a capital benefit of 5 per cent of a £3 million resource, say £150,000, i.e. a leverage of 75. If the same microcomputer expenditure were allocated to preparation of payroll records, then benefit might be a modest one of £1,000 a year and a payoff in two years.

Naturally the main difficulty in getting this concept to work lies in attempting to quantify many factors, many of which seem to have a host of intangibles. Furthermore, many applications are most useful only after they are connected with other applications, which have an accumulative impact of benefit. And the time factors are also complicated. Some major impacts may not be obvious for several years. Unfortunately too, many of the projected costs of information technology equipment and the costs of introduction of systems have many variables and intangibles. All that can be done is to prepare estimated cash flows for the years ahead and then judge leverage on the basis of payoff periods and the rate of internal return of investment, which should give the longer-term projects a favourable viewing.

Any debate on the leverage of a proposed application, even though not conclusive, must be a healthy development, as it will focus particularly on the benefit. It is the creative thinking and commitment of managers to the technology which will achieve results. It is important too that the organisation learns about and is fully aware of its successes and failures in the use of information technology. The reality seems to be that when we look back with hindsight many inappropriate projects were authorised, even with negative leverage, which never had any chance of making impact. Yet no organisation can afford in the long term consistently to back losers! It needs to develop a decision-making structure which favours winners. In chapter 16 a further examination of the concept of leverage will be attempted, in the context of the stages of design, of a project on a mainframe computer.

Summary

In this chapter a brief review was given of the 'information society' theme of this book. Then attention was directed to some common applications of information technology, generally at the command and control level in an organisation. This is where operators and executives are obliged to make decisions at the very workface of the business. Looking at some applications in more depth, it was possible to discuss the commercial implications and the expectations of change once information technology was adopted. It was recognised that management play a vital role in decision-making when it comes to authorising applications and a few guiding principles were set out.

Issues for discussion in seminar

1. Would the technology described in Case Study 12.1 tend to enrich the job of the salesman or to dehumanise it? What are the factors which might affect the outcome?
2. Would the customers really get commercial benefits from this system? If so, what would they be?
3. In the commercial world there are many situations requiring rapid deployment of resources to meet clients' needs, in which computer-assisted systems could be beneficial. What are the factors inhibiting the adoption of such systems?

References

Police Computers and the Metropolitan Police (1984), commissioned by GLC Police Committee, then presented in seminar.

Chapter 13
Development of a management information system

Overview

In this chapter the reader will be introduced to the idea that by combining data from developed applications, it can be useful as a part of the organisation's management information system (MIS). MIS becomes such an important concept that it may be the prime justification behind the selection and implementation of a group of computer applications. Yet seldom does a computer provide all of what is necessary. In the real world of business and commerce, information has sources both internal to the organisation, which can usually be controlled, and external, which generally cannot. Furthermore, information may be of a quantitative nature, which can easily be represented in a computer, and also of a qualitative, judgemental nature, which cannot, without some prior process of interpretation and then quantification.

Learning objectives

The object of this chapter is to help the reader become familiar with how an MIS may further the business strategy of an organisation and recognise some of the principles behind good practice in computer-assisted MIS design. Through the study of some successful applications of MIS techniques the reader may learn to be more discriminating in assessing MIS proposals and seeking out opportunities for developing MIS.

The key elements of a computer application

When a computer application is proposed, there are usually three distinct aspects which attract attention. Firstly, it must do a commercial function successfully. Secondly, it should develop a trail of transactions which can comprise a business pattern. Thirdly, it should offer the opportunity to management to interpret these patterns, and on combination with rules and policies, to assist them in decision-making, planning and controlling the business.

An example is the airline seat reservation system already mentioned in chapter 12. The expensive resource offered is the seat and the customer clearly wants confirmation of that seat and also tickets. The airline wants to run the service fully booked, but not over-booked. Integrity of data is essential, as is a unique record for each seat. Access to that record, from any part of the world, allows transactions to be done until just a few moments before take-off.

A key element of this process lies in the offering decisions taken by the airline operator or agent and booking decisions taken by the passenger. Many commercial documents can be produced from this process. Tickets can be printed, passenger lists compiled, payment transactions initiated, and so on.

Notice how we naturally arrive at the notion of *transactions*. These transactions feed into other systems and so the flow of information passes through the corporation at electronic speed, and generally at much lower costs than paperwork. Computers store the information so the pattern of transactions may be revealed when they are summarised. Such a summary provides operating management, with status reports. After analysis and interpretation the status reports reveal crises and triumphs.

Summary data, particularly in demand situations, suggest a pattern of provision and resources, and thus becomes an input into planning the logistics of the operation. This is the function of top management, who have the entrepreneurial flair to see market openings and the resource management skills and authority to offer the product or service.

The more experienced middle management becomes in analysis of the patterns, the more confident managers may become in laying down *standards* and *policies* about provision. Predictions can be made about future performance and utilisation of resources. Eventually, by giving the computer system the predictions and the norms, it will, if programmed, automatically develop 'exception reports' to highlight trends and variances.

These are the rudiments of a management information system. Every computer application should be capable of generating transactions which can then evolve into the building blocks of exception reporting systems and aids for planning and control.

We can now conceptualise better what a computerised management information system can offer managers at different levels in the organisation. Anthony (1984), a leading theorist on management information systems, suggests that these levels may be classified as the strategic level, the level of supervision and middle management, and finally, the immediate level of the customer or operator. Readers may recognise this conceptualisation from a similar discussion on the theme of objective-setting. There is great advantage in management in relating as closely as possible the systems of objective-setting and MIS. Both have needs for planning and feedback phases and can mutually support and enrich one another. More will be said on this theme in Part 6 of this text.

Yet the paradox is that, when systems analysts approach managers, commonly they have considerable difficulty in articulating their own reporting or information requirements. The manager seems to see his decision-making work as an elusive, complicated and intuitive process. Leading research studies have been done to illustrate this observation. Perhaps the best known is Mintzberg's (1973). Equally, managers often perceive systems analysts as boffins, who know a lot about machines but nothing about people and management.

However, when we look at examples of good finished and working information systems from the literature, these do give us a chance to seek out the features of finished design, which fit the needs of managers at the different levels in an organisation. If we then 'walk through' these decision features with managers and ask to what extent it fits their actual requirements, they are likely to be able to state clearly the differences. This 'walking through' by the analyst allows him or her to communicate with the executive. Once we have the analyst and the manager sharing a common perceptual framework of design, then the barriers about the intuition of the management process, as well as the false assumptions about the boffin, may be breached. Managers can then feel more comfortable in coming to terms with the need to be part of the specification process of their own information systems.

It is also important to be able to recognise bad practice in the development of MIS. There are several easy clues to watch out for. The first is when a lot of expensive equipment is very poorly utilised. It may even have dust covers on it, never having been commissioned. The second is where the system is over-used in terms of print-outs or other reports. This is the negation of the principle of exception reporting. Recognition of this condition is generally easy — managers may be observed hiding behind a mountain of paper. There may be big problems experienced in storing thick tabulations, none of which seems to be regularly read, and which cost a fortune in preparation, distribution, storing and as fire risks.

Other clues are very high telephone bills which indicate that no one seems to be getting what they want from the information provided. In such cases the information is there but not easily accessed. There is a massive overhead under this condition too, the overhead caused by information 'overload' where the recipient is so over-exposed to the bulk of massive detail that the decision-making process becomes more, not less, difficult. The author can recall the horror of reporting that one department of ten people in a production planning and control unit was being fed with 50,000 pages of computer tabulations per month, yet their company telephone bill had risen to a horrific £750,000 per annum, more than the whole company profit!

However, although it is easy to joke about other people's mountains of paper it is not so easy to express clearly the principles that promote better exception reporting. Some guidelines were initially developed in chapter 11 and these will now be developed further.

The basic structure of exceptions

Gradually designers of MIS grasped the principles required to overcome the *mountain of paper syndrome*. They started perceiving useful information as that relating to exceptions, i.e. those special conditions which needed managerial attention. In the field of inventory control instead of remorselessly printing the status of every record it became the practice just to look at the 're-order' list, highlighting only those items which needed replenishment. The media for presenting information changed from the written report to a report on a VDU screen. This is particularly useful in cases where a further manual review might be necessary and the reviewer can use extra 'local' or intuitive intelligence to confirm the re-order recommendation. The final purchase requisition would probably still be printed.

The only problem is that the exception reporting which triggered the re-order notice would require some detailed business analysis, specification of the rules of logic, agreement of these by the user department, and programming — a rather bureaucratic process. Surprisingly, this process, generally called systems analysis, is as similar to a legislative process as it is to a mathematical process. But just as by-passing the legislative process and guillotining a bill usually gives rise to lack of consensus and bad law, so too shortcuts in the design process of MIS applications give rise to weak MIS systems. The bureaucratic process is a 'grin and bear it' situation in development and use of computer systems.

Further work then shed light on more sophisticated methods of defining exception conditions, and this was facilitated as managers became more familiar with the approach to management known as managing by objectives. Exceptions could then be defined in a much more pragmatic way and specific responses developed at management meetings. The following gives a few examples:

1. *Objectives*: 'The sum of the monthly billing plan was down by £1 million. The year to date total was under target by £2 million.'

   'The board meeting spent two hours in responding to this business situation, seeking out the areas of shortfall, and looking at further variance reports to understand the underlying reasons.'

2. *Policies*: 'Over 20 per cent of product sales were delivered outside lead times agreed and published in company catalogues.'

   This information can be gained by defining delivery norms or policies for every product sold, then tracking customers' orders, from entry point to invoicing, and capturing the delivery date as achieved. Then a simple statistical report determines delivery performance and trends, and with a definition of the norms, exceptions can then be detected.

   'This month marketing and manufacturing will need to take measures to improve this adverse trend. Exception reports suggest that the main production problem is confined to one product line at one factory. However, for another product in trouble, we believe that the delivery norms were set optimistically, and delivery promises for these will now be extended by two weeks in company bulletins, till we can get more production capacity on stream.'

3. *Standards*: 'Exactly 10 per cent of the factory output in May exceeded the costing standards by more than 5 per cent.'

This is the well-known financial variance report. However, notice that only significant variances were reported, i.e. those greater than 5 per cent, and the extent of the problem was also significant, 10 per cent of the output. If the limits are set too narrowly, then there would be too much to analyse and managers would suffer from overload. There is some skill and judgement required in the specification of significance for the triggering of such variance reports.

'Better control of labour and machines is required this month to ensure that variances from these standards are reduced.'

Design response

This was a major leap forward in the understanding of MIS design. Instead of focusing on what data existed in the organisation, one could start by searching out the policies, targets and standards of the organisation, and identifying which ones were causing problems and therefore needed more attention in order to bring them back into control. The information system would then have a natural focus and provide exception data for decision-makers so that their efforts could be concentrated where the real problems were.

The cartoon in Figure 13.1 encapsulates three management situations. The man on

Figure 13.1 *Managing by exception*
(Source: reproduced with permission of *Computer Weekly*)

the left needs to make decisions, but there is not enough information. He has to respond intuitively and is unhappy at the thought of being ill-informed. The man on the right also has a frown on his face. He is overwhelmed by a mountain of paper and cannot see the wood for the trees. He is exposed to a bad management information system. The third cartoon portrays the relaxed and cheerful manager picking up the exception report from a computer printer. The system is helping him in the quality of his decision-making. Now the computer is working for him.

The line manager needs a specialist systems designer to help him or her master the principles of exception reporting, as it is a very powerful technique. Both look for the policies, targets and standards of the organisation and then define them rigorously for computer recognition. The system designer then seeks to specify and arrange for programming the information flow of transactions to the computer for summarisation, and the computer system generates variance reports for interpretation and action. The information designer then has to see to it that the variance reports are available in tabulation form or on screen for the responsible manager for attention, interpretation, decision and action. By this time we should be out of the mountains of paper syndrome.

Exception reporting in material requirements planning

A brief review of the theory

In the early 1960s, Honeywell, a computer manufacturer, decided that the fundamental objective-setting areas of a manufacturing company, which naturally could lead to quantification, were the market plan and the manufacturing plan, and in any company it was essential that such plans were compatible (see Figure 13.2).

The market plan could be represented by a set of twelve monthly forecast figures for every product in the catalogue. In Honeywell's Residential Division there were 8,000 such items (so a computer was a help in recording their forecast judgements). Likewise, a high-level manufacturing plan could be expressed quantitatively by declaring twelve monthly capacities by assembly-line for groups of common thermostats (some 100 only assembly lines to plan). They then had the ingenious idea of getting the computer with these two high-level plans lying in its central memory to schedule the factory for every week for one year in the future. They then added engineering data to offer component breakdowns and timing standards for plant and labour and summarised the results. Thus the computer would generate directly the following 'resource profiles', or 'logistic profiles', for one year ahead:

1. Net purchase requirements: A year's snapshot of the future would give possibilities for bulk purchase, and all the leverage that volume can generate to enable bulk buying strategy to operate.
2. Labour requirements summarised by grade or skill, by man/hour and by week: This would indicate many months ahead when overtime should be authorised or a new shift should be started, and would help with deciding the timing of a recruitment or lay-off programme. It would also show the extent to which it

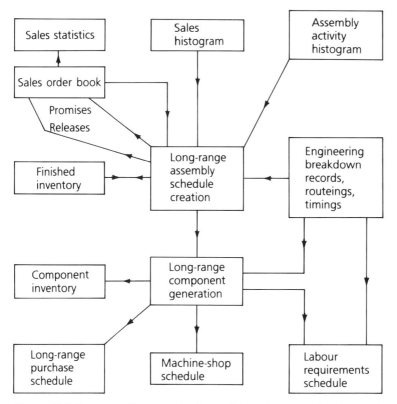

Figure 13.2 *Structure of computerised material requirements planning routines*

would be advantageous to develop flexibility in the workforce and what
particular training would offer the greatest potential from flexible working.
3. Plant utilisation by item by week: This would highlight both surplus and short
   capacities. The short capacities would either invite investment decisions or
   decisions to subcontract some of the total workload. The surplus capacities
   would suggest subcontracting to someone else's business, or the possibility of
   selling off or leasing surplus plant to generate cash flow. All assets are
   expected to contribute.
4. Cash flow and profit projection by month for a year in the future: This could
   be obtained by attaching prices to projected sales figures, and costs to the
   projected net production. This projection could be matched with high-level
   expected return on investment figures for comparison. (Note the emphasis
   placed in earlier chapters on the calculation and significance of ROI.) Although
   capital budgets and tax are not generally part of this computerised model, they
   can be superimposed on the revenue projections as a major tool in profit
   planning.

5. Projections for a year ahead of finished and component inventory figures: This may help to determine the need for working capital.

The harvest of 'managing by exception'

Any business needs realism in the planning, coordination and unification of its manufacturing and marketing. If there is a mismatch here this will result in late deliveries and lost business, poor labour or plant utilisation and an unbalanced inventory. The weekly generated logistic profiles may be compared with the existing planned provision and differences highlighted (see Figure 13.4 below). Management will thus have exceptions brought to their attention many months before the hurting starts and this allows for management by anticipation. Furthermore, there are many points within the scheduling process where the computer can be sensitised to policies and standards, so that variances from these may be highlighted for managerial treatment. This approach gives a practical way of implementing the generalised guidelines stated above about managing by exception.

The impact of this approach on the Residential Division of Honeywell in the late 1960s was effectively to make them the 'cash cow' of the company, giving the division a long period of growth. Turnover rose from $0.5 billion to $2 billion, with appropriate profit growth and market consolidation. Inventory turns increased from seven times a year to an incredible twenty-eight times a year as a result of better scheduling and planning and management by exception with computer aids.

This was an approach adopted by other divisions of the company and, gradually, by manufacturing industry as a whole. By the 1980s many proprietary packages replicated this approach to planning, controlling and scheduling factories in sympathy with market plans.

How the approach was put into practice

Scheduling the factory was a weekly computerised routine. A diagram of the model may be found in Figure 13.2. The main features were as follows.

The computer reads in the sales order book, which has already been ordered in a queuing sequence on to a disc, and releases all those sales orders, which are both ready for packing and for which there is available finished inventory. It then combines the order book with the sales histogram (forecast and plan) to accumulate a gross demand schedule for the finished product. From this gross demand any further inventory in stock is deducted, and the net inventory remaining needs to be made. Manufacturing capacity will now be allocated in the computer from the planned capacity, using the assembly activity histogram. The intention here will be to utilise as much capacity as is available so long as other defined business policies are not compromised.

Two exception situations are common and are reported on at the time of scheduling. In the first situation, demand exceeds capacity. The response here is to shift demand to a position of extended delivery until such capacity becomes available; this is highlighted on an exception report for marketing as scheduling outwith delivery policy. The second situation is where capacity exceeds demand; for this the computer allocates capacity, prorating in accordance with the safety stock level for each finished product on the line. Hence the schedule achieves a balance for all items. This prorating and balancing up of stocks will be permitted till the surplus inventory reaches a defined maximum set by management policy in order to avoid financing excess stock. After that point the computer schedules for the remaining weeks. The computer then repeats this process until completion of every period defined in the assembly activity histogram, commonly 50 weeks ahead.

At this point the computer has processed all new sales orders coming into the system and developed a long-range assembly schedule in accordance with the constraints of a capacity plan and defined management policies. However, there is a lot still to be done. The long-range assembly schedule is then matched in the computer with a file giving comprehensive engineering data and standards and *exploded* to pick up parts lists, routeings and timings for plant and labour.

The parts lists, when summarised, represent a gross demand schedule and once matched against a file of component inventory they are combined into batches to construct a net requirements schedule. The computer will normally respond to policies influenced by economic batch quantity theory in defining the lot size of the net requirements. The fundamental reason for batching is to minimise the impact of expensive set-up costs when a process is changed to deal with a new part or product.

However, batching theory is becoming less important now that computer-aided design and computer-aided manufacture systems (CAD/CAM) are reducing set-up times for an operation to an insignificant amount of total processing times.

Complex products have a parts structure, so this process of grossing then netting the demand needs to continue down the structure until all that is left is the bought-out parts, which become the long-range purchasing schedule.

At each stage in this explosion process, the timings for plant are accumulated by machine centre to determine requirements for plant and by labour category to determine labour requirements. Not all components will be made in-house; some will be purchased from outside, and for these the computer will generate a long-range purchase schedule, also in lots of economic batch size, to attract discounts, etc. At the end of this routine the computer system will have offered detailed short-term schedules and long-term 'logistic profiles', which then become the basis for forward trouble-shooting.

From this description it might appear that the computer does rather a lot. In reality, management does all the hard work involved in defining the policies and plans and agreeing the forecasts within the main top management team and relegates to the computer the leg-work involved in the calculations, projections and generation of the variance reports. The planning is effectively corporate planning, but with assistance from the computer. Because of the emphasis on policy-making and planning, there are clearly difficulties in implementing advanced systems such as this in manufacturing companies, where traditional culture is a matter of reacting quickly to the crises of the shopfloor and order book.

This computerised application is now known in the literature as material requirements planning and is often regarded as a natural pillar of MIS in manufacturing companies. In 1985, Hamilton published an article in *Purchasing and Supply* relating to MRP routines developed and running on a microcomputer. By 1987 some lecturers from Glasgow University were offering customised versions of MRP, developed using a powerful microcomputer package, Lotus 1-2-3. However, with the very wide product range (8,000 items) of Honeywell's Residential Division, it is very hard to see how MRP could be developed and implemented there except on a powerful mainframe computer.

In the 1980s MRP principles have been developed to act as an aid to corporate planning simulations, and the principles of managing by exception which it offered have been manifested and reinterpreted in many other non-manufacturing environments. However, it must be emphasised that companies do not find MRP routines easy to implement. Although there has been considerable development in this field, there are relatively few research studies showing successful implementations. Many organisations simply cannot get together the managerial teamwork to define the policies and standards which are preconditions for success. Nor can they easily perceive how to fit the MRP approach around the particular technology of their own firm. Policies, objectives and standards can still be very contentious and difficult to articulate, but when they are articulated they do provide a sensible starting point for serious MIS design.

Most advanced applications of MIS cannot be implemented unless there is a sound base of normative data. For that we need to use a database. In the case of a manufacturing company, probably the most significant database is the collection of engineering records. Figure 13.3 gives a typical example of an engineering database record.

The engineering database

Figure 13.3 shows a typical engineering database record and is printed with permission of Honeywell Limited. The main elements are as follows:

1. A record of product structure. This relates an item to its parts list. The example shows a sub-assembly, LS 50072, with the parts that go into it. With this list a storeman would know what to issue to an assembly-line, or a purchasing agent what parts to buy.
2. A process record. This defines the sequence of operations needed to be done on the item and lists the work stations through which it moves.
3. Records relating to the timing of labour for setting up a process and operating it (by skill category) and to the designated plant at each work station.
4. A tooling record listing the jigs, fixtures and tools necessary for manufacture.

This database of records defines the engineering specifications and standards for manufacture; on to this engineering structure a cost base may be superimposed. If labour

Production routeing sheet

L.C.	Part Number of Catalogue Listing	C V.	H. Pin.	Sik.	Description	Div. Prod.	Prod. Code	Issue No.	Issue Date	Eng. Ref. No.	P/D Issue	R.S. Type	Special Code	Order Quantity	Tool Number	Works Order Number	Total Quantity	Total Time
133	LS 50072	4 0	02		LEVER SW ACTUA	25		C14	21/10/74	CN 40338 B	008			2099		LN 081		

L.C.	Line No.	C. L.	Work Station	O.P. No.	Material Number Or	O.P. Ref. No.	Alt.	Description	Comp	Sik. Unit	Quantity.M Hour/M	Mail LF%	Noise	T. C.	Set up Time. Hrs.	Tool Number	Total Time
134	001			LS	50249			PLUNGER		24	10.00.0	0					
134	002			LS	50200			SCREW SPECIAL		24	1000.0	0					
136	003		2412Z01	010		02364		ASS SCR TO PLUNGER			2.720			S	0.0	M1704	5.709
134	004			LS	50248			PLUNGER		24	1000.0	0					
134	005			LS	10012			SPRING		24	1000.0	0					
134	006			LS	10016			WASHER		24	1000.0	0					
134	007			75	50224			MS 048 66			0.0	0	N				
136	008		2412P02	020		02691		ASS SPRING WASH TO PLU			4.916			S	0.0	M1455	10.319
137	009							SPIN & LUB									
134	010			LS	30242			BUSH		24	1000.0	0					
134	011			LS	50166			LEVERI SW ACTUA		24	1000.0	0	S				
134	012			LS	50226			BUSHING		24	1000.0	0					
134	013			75	50224			MS 048 66			0.0	0	N				
136	014		2412P02	030		02689		ASS LEVER PLUNGER & WA			5.468			S	0.0	M1788	11.477
137	015							TO BUSH LUB & SPIN									
134	016			LS	30084			SEAL		24	1000.0	0					
136	017		2412Z01	040		02367		ASS SEAL TO LEVEL ASS			6.880			S	0.0	M1259	14.441
134	018			LS	50076			LK RING		24	1000.0	0					

Form No. 3053.3   Total Times/Thousand   Operation   Set Up   PAGE

Figure 13.3 *Production routeing sheet*

and overhead rates are defined, and the bought-out parts have their prices attached, it is easily possible for the computer to summarise these cost elements to calculate the appropriate cost standards for every item — finished goods, assemblies, sub-assemblies, machined components and raw material. Thus, with a computer assist, the very standards that are vital for variance analysis may themselves be developed and defined.

Planning simulations

The MRP system outlined above is primarily used for scheduling the factory every week, firming up the short-term schedules, which become committed to 'work-in-process'. For periods outwith that short term, the schedules have the status of simulations, which may be expected to come about provided none of the planning assumptions changes. Naturally, as customer orders enter the system there is likely to be some difference from forecast. The computer system needs to accommodate these, highlighting forecasting variances in the process. The longer-term simulations are necessary as a factory has to undertake forward provisioning of components and labour requirements for which these schedules are excellent guides. The MRP system can also go fully into long-range corporate planning mode and generate logistic profiles for any plan offered. In this mode it will help senior managers discriminate between planning options and MRP becomes a major corporate planning tool in its own right providing an analysis of high level 'what-if' questions.

The logistic profile approach, illustrated in Figure 13.4, gives a picture of possible options and likely consequences.

Other manifestations of managing by exception

Tracking performance in a railway network

A good example of this technique is taken from the assessment of the performance of trains in a railway network. A train timetable is a schedule of targets and standards. The computer is given the timetable specification listing times and places each day of the week where trains are expected to be. The trains are coded with numbers that are recognisable to a computer, and a series of sensors placed on the track pass information through a communication system to a central computer. As the trains run, pulses may be directed to the computer at each sensor. A variance analysis can be developed which is triggered by the difference between the time on the timetable and the actual time.

Management likes information in summary form in order to track the trends against expected effectiveness standards, but with the above data summaries can be done hourly, weekly, monthly, by train, by locomotive type, by route, by region, by period in the day or week. In effect this is the key to the answer to almost any question about current performance in the train network. As better understanding is gained of the variables that cause poor performance, the system can be directed to focus on that particular

Definition: A logistic profile is a graph which indicates to management three possible conditions which relate with any defined resource, generally labour-hours for a special category of skilled labour, or machine-hours, for scarce and expensive machine-time. The profile relates with a convenient time unit, typically 1,000 hours/working month. The graph plots:

Capacity available @@@@@@@@@@@@@@

Capacity available with authorised overtime + + + + + + + + + + +

Requirements calculated as needed nnnnnnnnnnnnnn

The graph highlights situations of *under-utilisation* — response reassign labour out of that area. Shaded areas with 'U'.

The graph highlights situations requiring *overtime*. Areas shaded and marked 'O'.

The graph highlights situations where the requirement is even over the overtime limit. Response here is to either reschedule to within the limits or invest in further resources. Otherwise the product will be delivered late, or not at all. Areas shaded and marked with 'C'.

Logistic profile for labour-hours for skilled turners

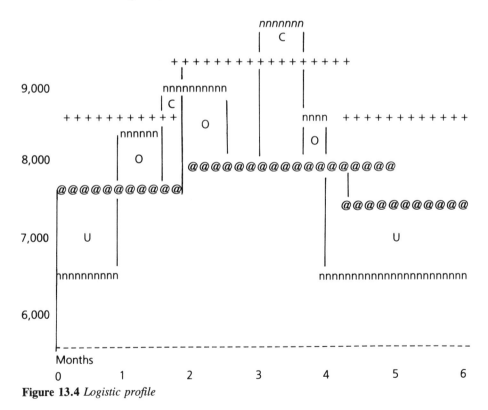

Figure 13.4 *Logistic profile*

aspect; alternatively managers can redirect resources to where they will make the greatest impact on performance.

Framework for computerised management information systems

'A management information system exists to get the *right* information at the *right* time at the *right* level to enable decision-makers to make better decisions for planning the future of the business and controlling existing projects' (Lucey, 1981).

This simple definition has some far-reaching implications. 'The right information' implies the right amount of relevant information. If the quantity is too much the manager will be subjected to information overload. 'Relevant' suggests that there is a screening process used to relate information needs to particular management positions and criteria which suggest information priorities. This information is directed at decision-makers. Decision-making in itself is a complex process of perceiving problems, putting them into perspective, searching out alternative courses of action, evaluating such courses, choosing a particular course and computing the logistic consequences of adoption, communicating the decision and monitoring its implementation.

The decision-maker is 'planning the future'. This implies that he is taking account of probabilistic information of a qualitative nature about the environment and integrating it with more quantified information from both external and internal sources. However, internal sources ultimately derive from people, who are not perfect communicators and who offer or withhold information depending on their motivation and strategy in the power game of the organisation.

'The decision-maker controls existing projects.' The effective decision-maker needs to be fully conversant with existing projects as well as with future needs. He or she must be able to spot deviations to assess their significance, search for detailed data to throw light on the causes of the deviations and provide remedies. In order to do this the decision-maker needs information. Mandell (1985), along with other modern writers, refers to computerised decision support systems for accomplishing this.

A primary means of implementing successful management information systems is through the application of management by exception (MBE). MBE can operate only if policies, objectives, programmes and standards are visible, i.e. known to everyone and clearly understood. This visibility, together with an effective method of data collection, allows comparison to be made between what is going on and what should be going on. Exceptions to the norm — deviations from objectives, policies or standards — can be identified and remedied when good exception reports are available for managers exercising the role of planning and control. Material requirements planning systems in manufacturing companies are a good example of the implementation of the principles of MBE.

Advantages and disadvantages of using an MRP-style MIS

Advantages

1. Better control can be exercised throughout the business.
2. An effective MIS is generally the result of integrated thinking and teamwork by the senior management of the corporation.
3. An effective MIS should provide a deeper understanding of achievement against target in a wide area of business functions.
4. An MIS should be able to point the way to better utilisation of the resources of the firm or organisation and the opportunity for anticipatory management.
5. An MIS will force the organisation to concentrate on the management disciplines of forecasting and planning. It should enable these functions to be done frequently and allow simulations to widen the options open to management.
6. An MIS provides a dynamic unified base of operating data.
7. An effective MIS can transform the organisation into a much more responsive one, in which market opportunities are more readily turned into realisation.
8. Many of the modern management techniques in operations research and inventory control would be purely academic without an MIS approach.

Disadvantages

1. Many organisations cannot afford the expense of adopting an MIS approach, though with reductions on the cost of hardware and greater availability of packages, this disadvantage is diminishing.
2. An MIS requires much time and education throughout the organisation before design and implementation is possible.
3. Poorly designed MIS can lead to inflexibility in the running of the business. In fact MIS only projects business concepts. If the business concept of design is weak then MIS will only quicken the date of disaster.
4. An effective MIS which works well in one business environment will not necessarily be easily transplanted to another without considerable retuning and restructuring.
5. A company fully committed to MIS is vulnerable in the event of stoppage to its computer facility through:
   (a) labour trouble;
   (b) physical disaster such as fire;

(c) the supplier of hardware ceases trading;

(d) falling victim to malicious or fraudulent use of data.

Features of good information systems design

The features of good information systems design may be summarised as follows:

1. The information system specified reflects the *real needs* of those who are using it. This implies that there was a real user involvement during the design phase, with the user taking an active role in the process of *validation*.

2. *Access*. The user can gain access to data which helps him or her take effective operating decisions based on accurate, relevant and timely information.

3. *Planning, control, coordination*. An effective information system helps managers do all these three critical activities and quality systems achieve in addition the principles of managing by exception.

4. *Future orientation*. Planning systems may also use data to simulate options for the future, and help managers take action in *anticipation* of the development of problems. This is particularly valuable for *resource* planning. In manufacturing environments the engineering data are the basis of resourcing standards, and when a computer is programmed to do scheduling, it can generate a time-bounded profile of resource requirements. When this is superimposed on current resource availability any *deficiency* is highlighted. This suggests appropriate timings for recruiting more labour, authorising overtime, investing in new plant or subcontracting work out. The technique for identifying this need is an analysis and interpretation of logistic profiles illustrated in Figure 13.4.

5. *Outside orientation*. Information systems should not only help managers manage internal resources better, they should also improve and enhance contact with outside stakeholders, particularly customers and vendors. When this is done imaginatively the very use of computing systems may fundamentally change the nature of the product and service and the method of distribution to customers. Thus information systems may enhance the product portfolio of the organisation. Many examples of this can be given in the field of developing financial services and marketing them to customers through terminals.

6. *Leverage*. Use of computer systems tends to be very expensive, particularly in applications developed for the first time. A company needs to develop a *value-for-money policy* for its computing systems. The experts call this leverage. This means that for a given unit of input of money spent on computing, there will be a high corresponding benefit. If an investment of £1,000 generated a benefit of £1 million then there would be a leverage of 1,000. When organisations are thinking well strategically they will have a good feel for where there is leverage in applying computer systems to further the objectives of the corporate

plan. There will be healthy contact between the computer steering group and the corporate planning group.

Exercise 13.1
Some questions for a seminar

1. When people use computer systems they generate transactions. Why is there a commercial significance in attempting to analyse such transactions into recognisable patterns of activity?
2. 'Objectives, policies and standards are the foundations on which exception reporting is built.' Explain this idea.
3. What are the problems associated with 'information overload'?
4. 'The emergence of VDUs has taken away the temptation to print vast quantities of reports.' Do you agree?
5. Policies may be expressed in statements of rules and quantification for computer recognition. Give some examples.
6. 'Logistic profiles are simply a means of identifying surpluses and shortfalls in resources in time for corrective action to be taken.' Is this the main justification for advising a factory to adopt a material requirements planning package?
7. 'The engineering database is probably the most significant of all databases for the company involved in manufacturing.' Explain a typical structure. In what way may its records be regarded as standards?
8. 'Principles of management by exception may be applied whenever performance attainment is an issue.' Do you agree? Give examples to prove or disprove this assertion.
9. 'Managers appear to find it difficult to be articulate when discussing their information needs.' Why is this so? Is there a way of overcoming this difficulty?
10. 'Many organisations simply cannot afford the expense of implementing a computer assisted management information system.' Would this be true of your own organisation? Why? Could you suggest priority areas for the development of MIS techniques within your organisation?

References

Anthony, R.L. *et al.* (1984), *Management Control in Non-profit Organisations*, 3rd edition, Dorsey.
Hamilton, T. (1985), 'MRP on microcomputer', *Purchasing and Supply Magazine*, March.

Lucey, T. (1981), *Management Information Systems*, Smiths.
Mandell, S.L. (1985), *Computers and Data Processing*, West.
Mintzberg, H. (1973), *The Nature of Managerial Work*, Harper & Row.

Further reading

Murdick, R.G. (1977), 'MIS for MbO', *Journal of Systems Management*, March,
   pp. 34–40
Orlicky, J. (1975), *Material Requirements Planning*, McGraw-Hill.

Chapter 14

The developing role of microcomputers

Overview

The aim of this chapter is to familiarise the reader with an understanding of how a professional may apply three main microcomputer packages, showing how this may enrich the job of such a professional, and provide many of the trappings of an electronic office.

The text is an adaption of a series of live demonstrations conducted by the author for management and professional students on college courses, which were originally presented with the aid of an electronic blackboard to groups of some thirty students and staff.

To replicate the atmosphere of demonstration and interaction the text is presented as a dialogue between expert and student. The expert is the tutor presenting material; the student is depicted as one who is sceptical about computers, but determined to master the principles behind the use of packages and appreciate advantages and disadvantages of using them.

The dialogue is illustrated as far as possible with figures which replicate the images projected from a television monitor on to a six-foot screen using a proprietary device called an 'Electrohone'. This simulates an electronic blackboard. Later versions from another manufacturer look like simple attachments to the top of an overhead projector and are also connected to the microcomputer under demonstration. In time, perhaps a majority of classrooms may be provided with such aids, as microcomputer packages are introduced to enhance teaching in all the main academic disciplines.

A primary aim in this approach is to overcome *computerphobia*, a tendency of managers to run a mile as soon as they are put in front of a computer keyboard. After a series of demonstrations and discussions the class group would normally be taken to a workroom with microcomputers installed for 'hands-on' experience allowing them to develop computer literacy.

As computer packages are inherently complicated — and it is the easiest thing in the world to blind people with science in their use — it is important to illustrate the management and business concepts behind their use. Only after this has been achieved should one worry about *how* to activate the package. There are many proprietary versions of each of the main types of packages — word processing, database and spreadsheet — and literacy and fluency in one such package does not immediately transfer to fluency with another proprietary version. A textbook cannot possibly cover every such version, so the inevitable compromise which has been adopted here is to concentrate on one version of each of the three types of packages. These are chosen much for the inherent simplicity in use and possibilities for their integration. The exhibits used in the demonstrations are:

14.1   Superscript cribsheet.
14.2   Sponsor list.
14.3   Application form for sponsorship (edit).
14.4   Application form for sponsorship (merged).
14.5   Mail order format.
14.6   Database menus.
14.7   Selection of 'men'.
14.8   Sum record.
14.9   Spreadsheet menu.
14.10 Spreadsheet key summary.
14.11 Balance sheet and formulas on spreadsheet.
14.12 Simulations on balance sheet.
14.13 Cash flow on spreadsheet.
14.14 Investment appraisal (NPV) model.
14.15 Graphics, a home-made Christmas card.

The business concept of three packages

Word processing

Word processing enables text to be processed on the computer. Text is the foundation of research literature, correspondence files and special reports. Indeed, text is a dominant feature in the life of nearly every professional, and particularly so in the life of a college lecturer. We may see too how the manipulation of text can help in applications done for pleasure in the family too.

Text is basically unstructured in nature. A word processor is superior to a typewriter in the manipulation of text owing to the ease with which documents may be edited, proof-read and corrected, stored and retrieved. An author with a word processor can commit ideas directly to disk, re-order and edit them at will, respond to reviewers' reports, maintain the integrity of the manuscript and have back-ups as a security against loss. When correspondence and research files are properly organised and sorted for ease of reference and retrieval, they become indeed the basis of the electronic office.

Database

Database is a package which deals with structured data. Normally, it is designed and developed for use around a particular application in which the fields of data are anticipated. The example developed in this demonstration is a course admissions system for management students. The business objectives here were to ensure achievement of recruitment targets, to provide management reports for course assessment procedures and to develop sponsorship lists for course publicity.

Spreadsheets

A *spreadsheet package* enables quantitative data to be summarised and manipulated using formulas. It is particularly useful for doing simulations of business situations and in the application of the techniques of management accounting. Examples are developed of the analysis of critical ratios from profit and loss and balance sheet data, cash-flow models and models dealing with investment appraisal.

Student: 'Can all these packages exist on a small microcomputer?'

Expert: 'Yes, they are manifested in this demonstration on a Commodore 64 microcomputer, using Superscript as the word processor package, Superbase as the database package and Mini Office II as the spreadsheet package. There are other popular packages available on Amstrad and the Applemac micro-computers, and several IBM or IBM compatible computers.'

Word processing

Getting started

Turn on the system; monitor first, then the disk drive, then the microcomputer.

Explanation of computer keyboard

This is like a typewriter with a few extra keys. Function keys F1−F8 command the computer package to execute a pre-programmed routine. Then there is a CTRL button, which is used in combination with another key to execute a further set of pre-programmed routines, and a run/stop key, which is used preceding any other key to activate a further set of routines pre-programmed by the user. The meaning of these function keys, CTRL routines and run/stop routines are defined in the 'Customised word processor crib-sheet' with these demo notes (see Exhibit 14.1). They are a single-page summary edited from the package manual.

Student: 'This all looks rather formidable. How long will it take me to master the manual? It looks as if it is several hundred pages long.'

Expert: 'The implication of what you say is that manuals are often very poorly written and seem to be more for the convenience of the software writer than

Exhibit 14.1 *Word processing*

Superscript function keys, fixed by software writer

F1 — Menu.
F2 — Get document from directory.
F3 — Previous command.
F4 — Spelling check.
F5 — View document.
F6 — Resume preview of document.
F7 — Tab.
F8 — Help screen.

Superscript control keys, fixed by software writer

(Hit simultaneously with CNTRL Key and another.)

Q — Quit (returns you to edit mode from menu).
R — Repeat previous command.

For rapid cursor movement

H — Cursor 1 cht left.
I — Cursor to tab position.
J — Cursor to next line.
K — Cursor to previous line.
B — Beginning of text.
G — End of text.
E — Go to next word.
W — Go to previous word.
P — Go to next paragraph.
O — Go to previous paragraph.
Y — Go to last column of previous line.
= — Back tab.
U — Cursor 1 cht right.

For text manipulation

S — Creates space at cursor.
H — Cursor 1 cht left.
F — Change case word.
C — Clears word.
D — Delete word.
L — Layout character.
V — Insert mode switch.
A — Copy defined block to cursor position.
M — Return.
N — New line, retains text.
T — New line, destroys text to right.
X — Reformat whole document (takes time).
Z — Reformat paragraph (quickly).

Superscript run/stop keys

(Hit run/stop key then another,

customised by user from experience.)

0 (prevent underline split)
1 (search and find)
2 (delete cht to right)
3 (link doc code)
4 (place current document on disc)
5 (begin enhancement)
6 (finish enhancement)
7 (generate footing code)
8 (delete current cht)
9 (letter interchange)
a (load doc from cursor)
A (remove merger markers and reset)
B (mark block and erase)
b (generate bottom margin param)
c (begin centring text)
C (centre text framework)
d (finish centring text)
e (erase line)
E (envelope framework)
f (change case word)
F (Yours sincerely, etc.)
G (column printing template)
g (define block)
h (change case of block)
i (insert doc from cursor)
I (end condense mode, rm73)
J (begin condense mode with rm137)
j (move stored block)
K (for mm code)
k (for variable mm block name)
l (move cursor to left of screen)
L (Cliftonwood letterhead)
m (margin release with np check)
M (memo skeleton)
n (view from page number)
N (name document)
o (print spec)
p (force new page)
P (label print parameters)
q (change case first word)
r (restore margin without indentation)
s (screen document)
S (generate spacing code)
t (indent text)
T (initialise tabs)
U (begin underlining)
V (file block as new doc)
v (view spec)
u (end underlining)
w (cursor to beginning current word)
x (remove current word or word to left)
y (cursor to end of para)

Exhibit 14.1 (cont.)

Z (cursor to line 7 for address copy)
z (cursor to tab position on return
   symbol)
+ (next screen)
! for table of figures
— (previous screen)
= (reformat and go to end of para)
@ (paragraph indent and end of page
   check)
£ (start bold)
* (end bold)
; (cursor end of current word)
: (underline framework after
   centring framework)
) (C112–rm92)
. (clear counter then add)
((C110–rm73)
& (multiply register by)
% (put result at cursor)
^ (margin release but no np check)
. (reformat and go to end
   paragraph)

Useful cribs from operating system

Dolphin DOS function keys

F1   List
F2   Monitor
F3   Run
F4   Verify
F5   Load "0:*,B,1 Return, printer
     on
F6   Save "@:progname return
F7   Display directory
@S: progname scratches progname
@V: validates disk
@N: name,id formats disk

To sort disk directory

FL   "ASDD-SORT, Follow menu

To recover deleted file

FL   "ASDD-SORT.

DLD to display directory to confirm
that there is a file to recover.

FR to recover.

the user. In the case of Superscript the original manual is rather long, but it is very well structured with an index, which allows immediate reference to any point of difficulty. It is not necessary to read three chapters to recover from a nasty predicament! However, the crib sheet, a one-page summary, is all the user needs after gaining some experience with the package.

'If a new user has the crib-sheet at the beginning, then the process of mastering the package would be much quicker, and might just take an hour a day for a week, perhaps with some tutorial help.'

Writing a letter

A crisis situation has arisen. Expert's Barclaycard has gone missing; he has telephoned through to report the loss, but decides to write to make arrangements for a speedy replacement to his new address.

Expert refers to the 'Superscript' crib sheet, on Exhibit 14.1, as he activates the system.

He loads the letterhead by pressing run/stop L. On screen is now Expert's home address, centred, and with today's date underneath.

He names the document created, run/stop N Barclaycard-8131. When this document is filed in the correspondence file it can quickly be retrieved from the disk by looking for Barclaycard. The last four references are ymdd, calendar format, so that correspondence is naturally filed oldest first, for convenience.

He selects the address from his address disk, and keys F1 D I. (F1 gets the command mode of the package, D is the option in the menu for document, I activates insertion from the disk.) The address disk which is loaded is like an electronic address book.

Each name is contained in a separate small document. Expert moves the cursor down the directory till it rests on Barclaycard. On pressing return the address is incorporated into the current letter. The electronic address book has 250 entries and is very convenient.

Expert inserts a few lines of text then closes the letter with a yours sincerely and name (run/stop F). This is a standard clause permanently held in customised memory, for convenience.

To create the envelope record Expert presses run/stop Z to take the cursor to the Barclaycard address at the head of the letter and run/stop g to store the text block. Run/stop E is a little sub-program, which moves the cursor to the foot of the document, generates the editing coding on a template for the envelope, with address centred and folding marks in position, and duplicates the text stored, but now in the envelope position. F5 is pressed for preview on screen and possible editing. The first page is the letter; the second page is the envelope. All OKAY. F1 P P ensures that the printer prints the two pages on continuous stationery.

To store the letter on disk expert keys run/stop 4, checks the document name and hits return. The letter is now committed to the correspondence file.

Student: 'It looks easy, but how is this quicker than just using a typewriter?'

Expert: 'Once you have set up the electronic address book and customised letterheads and phrases, just a few keystrokes generate whole chunks of text, so the author of the letter writes much less and it is much quicker to retrieve correspondence from a box of well-classified disks than rummaging around in a metal filing cabinet.'

Changing a letter

To do this Expert mounts the address disk in the drive, keys F2 to load from the directory and presses return on 'rbr', a standard letter to a bank requesting credit of a cheque to a customer's account, which also has an envelope record embedded in the second page. He wants to pay £100 into his bank. He moves the cursor down to the part of letter with space for the date. Run/stop D inserts today's date. He moves the cursor to part of the standard letter requesting posting of credit and inserts the amount, £100. He prints the document. With this 'proforma style' letter only two things needed changing, the date and amount, and the transaction is completed in seconds!

To record this transaction it will be necessary to rename the document before storing it by doing run/stop N. However, this transaction can quickly be verified on next month's bank statement, so the document is unlikely to be filed. If, however, it contained instructions about a share portfolio, it is likely that the record would be filed on disk, as there is no other natural back-up.

Student: 'It might be convenient for you doing this, but what about the bank? They expect you to fill in a standard credit counterfoil and a sealed envelope.'

Expert: 'Yes, but the bank work to my convenience and my proforma letters. I do not see why *they* should have a monopoly of proforma letters for business transactions. Anyway, they have never complained yet about mine!'

Writing to a vendor

Expert copes with another crisis. He goes out in the garden to use his strimmer, but it won't start. Something is badly wrong with the carburettor, even though it is still within the guarantee period, but he cannot remember the name or telephone number of the supplier, only that he filed this information in the electronic vendor's file at the time of purchase. He mounts the address disk and loads the file named 'vendors'. This is a document with 200 vendors in alphabetical order and accompanied by notes with each record about what they supply. There is a quick method of scanning the file to select the correct record. To activate the search facility, Expert keys in run/stop 1, then 'strimmer' and hits return. In one second the cursor rests by vendor Klondyke. He selects this address separately by run/stop g to mark the block, then run/stop V to store as separate document if he has decided to write, or alternatively takes off the screen the telephone number and rings Klondyke.

Completing the tax return

This year's collection of tax information and briefing notes for the accountant follows closely from last year's briefing, with a few amendments only. The solution is to retrieve the last year's records and process just the amendments. Expert loads document taxcor1-89 to see the process; two letters to banks requesting vouchers are called up. Other letters may be retrieved to continue the briefing of accountants, etc.

The first time this is done it takes about a day to do the correspondence, but in later years just one hour is sufficient and represents a significant productivity improvement. Indeed, commercial computer packages are often dubbed 'productivity packages', for good reason. Time is money and convenience. The electronic correspondence file becomes more than a proforma document. It has the potential to become a proforma system.

Student: 'Tax is surely a special case. Most business transactions are not repeatable.'

Expert: 'Well, that is disputable. When November comes you may need to think about Christmas cards, and one year's list is approximately 90 per cent the same as the list of the next. If you are dealing with a base of 200 you can generate address labels from the computer, which gives a considerable time saving.'

Authoring a textbook

A textbook requires careful organisation of materials, proof-reading and references. Word processors can help enormously in the preparation and editing of a large work. It is much more compact to hold material on disk than on paper.

In the original draft the author may fail to achieve the maximum impact, simply because certain ideas come in the wrong sequence or there is a failure to signpost and then summarise to capture the reader's understanding. However, word processors give opportunities to check spelling, 'cut and paste', duplicate material and emphasise certain facets through underlining, centring, italics and other editorial tools.

A point of logical quality in writing is that conclusions are based on valid facts and arguments. When writing conclusions with a word-processed document, it is easy to proof-read electronically to ensure that indeed the conclusions are directly supportable from the text. With such power at the fingertips it should be possible to develop a richer quality and conviction in writing style! For writers and researchers bibliographies always seem to be difficult to compile and maintain, yet with a word processor it is very easy to put them into an ordered list, alphabetically by name, and then when the name is indented on a print-out, the list acquires a proper structure.

Student: 'A book must be far too big for your computer memory. How do you cope with such a large document?'

Expert: 'No problem really! My computer will not make documents with more than 500 lines of text from a 40 character screen. But each document can be stored with a code linking to the next document in the sequence on the disk, thus a whole book is simply a collection of 200 or so linked documents. As part of the pagination for a chapter a reference will normally be given to the chapter and number within that chapter, so in proof-reading the editor can immediately relate printed text to a particular document on the disk. The author never needs to be concerned about pagination or reformatting of text as this is done automatically when the linked documents come to be printed. Proof-reading can be done away from the computer and corrections quickly applied later to the disk.'

Student: 'Surely the author is wasting a lot of time as he or she has taken over the secretary's role and you are *imposing* a new writing style on the author. How does he or she find time and the inclination to do this directly with the word processor?'

Expert: 'Yes, you are right. A lot of authors have a cultural hangover at the thought of abandoning pen and pencil in the writing and planning of text.

'Yet others, particularly those who had acquired the rudiments of keyboarding skills for the manual or electric typewriter, suddenly find such skills are readily transferable, and the word processor is much more tolerant of the typing error or the dyslexic operator. The good word processing package is designed to enable mistakes to be corrected really quickly by fast cursor movement with easy deletion or insertion of new text.

'Doing the secretary's job? Well, there are ways and ways of preparing text. The author can do it all direct himself or herself and have no rough pen or pencil manuscript, or he or she may pass the original pen draft to a secretary and receive back hard copy and a disk. The author would then limit keyboarding activity to editing the disk version, until it was deemed to be satisfactory for a further hard copy to be made.

'Obviously there are other combinations as well. The author might dictate the draft directly to a secretary taking shorthand, or to a dictaphone tape for transcribing to a disk and printing. When the disk comes back the author can take it home and edit it there.

'Then of course there are the possibilities of the author acquiring or developing his or her own keyboarding skills. There are good computer aids for this too. The BBC microcomputer has a proprietary programme, *TYPING*, which offers the learner a screen, and puts him or her through touch typing drills and tests, so that it is possible to assess progress. However, there are also manual methods. You can acquire an audio-tape and instruction book, which again offers the essential drills of touch typing, and with half an hour daily for a month the basic skills are acquired.

'What we are seeing, however, is that the secretary is still in a support role, but doing rather different things for the author. Snags do, however, arise if the secretary's and author's word processors are not compatible with one another. Also, early in such a relationship agreement has to be reached as to whether the author or the secretary keeps the master disk with the manuscript, and of course there are security implications in this.'

Mail merge

All powerful word processors are capable of personalising letters, so that one basic message is communicated to a group, with some customisation. This facility can have a dramatic impact on the marketing activity of course promotion within a college, as well as many other activities. The procedure is as follows:

1. The core message is constructed, identifying all variables, such as names, addresses, designation, greetings, personalised endings and comments, and stored on a document.
2. A list is made of all those who are to receive the mailshot, and the variables filled in according to the predefined template. The variable information is stored.
3. The core message is reloaded, and it is possible to view or print the merged results.

Applications

This is very useful for applications such as family letters to keep the whole family in touch when they grow up and leave home, as well as major applications in business and commerce for promotion of goods, services, education programmes, etc.

Glasgow College promoted its management courses with 300 mailshots yearly to employers in the West of Scotland giving course and promotion literature, and applications increased by 80 per cent for the course.

Demonstration of mail merge

Scenario: Alexander is desperate to get sponsorship to enable him to pursue a university course in engineering. Dad suggests putting mail merge to the test in this sponsorship exercise. Alexander goes to the careers office at school to get a list of companies offering sponsorships. The list includes 100 companies.

Alexander selects twenty-seven companies from the list on the basis of his criteria for the type of engineering course he wishes to pursue. Alexander then writes a cv. His school careers master coaches him in the style and content of the cv and offers him some trial interviews. Dad is expected to commit the cv to the disk.

Dad makes the mailmerge template for the cv, so that it may include sponsorship details. Alexander, who has acquired enough keyboarding skills to do homework on the family word processor, enters the list of twenty-seven potential sponsors on to the disk. Dad prints the twenty-seven personalised applications.

Twenty-three replies were returned and Alexander then replied to six.

Action

Load the document 'spon-list-9928'; this is the target list of sponsors, (Exhibit 14.2).

Load the document 'mm-eng-spon-9927', the cv and application form (Exhibit 14.3). This is the document as for editing. The first line contains a list of codes, starting *nm, which identify fields for the incoming merge list. The second line contains codes which control the printing of the document, margins, etc. In the body of the letter ⟨ ⟩ symbols define where the merged fields will be put for personalising the document. Key F1 (for menu), P M V, and each personalised cv to the sponsor is on the screen. (See Exhibit 14.4.)

Exhibit 14.2 *Engineering sponsors*

Mr R. Cook,
Personnel Department,
Alcan International Limited,
Southam Road,
Banbury,
Oxford OX16 7SP

Mr Cook

Graduate and Student Recruitment Department,
Austin Rover Group,
Canley Road,
Canley,
Coventry CV5 6QX

Sir

The Group Training Manager,
Baker Perkins Holdings PLC
Westfield Road,
Peterborough PE3 6TA

Sir

Mr P.A. Gilbert,
Senior Recruitment Officer,
BBC,
Broadcasting House,
London W1A 1AA

Mr Gilbert

Training Officer (Recruitment),
British Aerospace PLC
Space and Communications Division,
Argyle Way,
Stevenage, Herts SG1 2AS

Sir

Company Recruitment Manager,
British Nuclear Fuels PLC
Risley,
Warrington WA3 6AS

Sir

Exhibit 14.3 *Mailmerge sponsorship letter framework*

```
*nm:ad1,ad2,coy,ad3,ad4,ad5,who,m1
*lm7:rm73:ju1:sp0:tm0:bm10:of0:eo0:p170

*cy;CLIFTONWOOD, NEWBRIDGE,
MIDLOTHIAN, EH28 8LQ
031-333-2758
30 September 1987
*cn

⟨ad1⟩
⟨ad2⟩
⟨coy⟩
⟨ad3⟩
⟨ad4⟩
⟨ad5⟩

Dear ⟨who⟩,
```

ENGINEERING SPONSORSHIP

APPLICATION OF ALEXANDER W.I.M. ERSKINE

I have seen your company's name in the booklet prepared by the Manpower Services Commission, 'Sponsorships', and have much pleasure in making my application to you.

C V

I was born on 14 March 1970.

In June 1986 I sat ten subjects at 'O' Level of the Oxford & Cambridge Joint Board with the following results and grades:

SUBJECT	GRADE	SUBJECT	GRADE
Maths	A	Physics	A

(etc.)

At the same time I also sat the Scottish 'O' Grade in French and secured Grade 2.

I am currently in second year sixth, on an 'A' Level course, studying Maths, Further Maths and Physics, and intend to pursue an Engineering Course at university beginning in October 1989.

I would wish to have a university course with General Engineering in first year, followed by specialisation in the later years. I have applied through UCCA for the following universities:

Cambridge, Durham, Liverpool, Surrey, Reading.

HOBBIES AND OTHER ACTIVITIES

From my first year at secondary school I was in the rifle shooting team and represented the school . . .

SPONSORSHIP EXPECTED

I am expecting to secure three good grades at 'A' Level in June 1988, at least A, A and B. I would then hope to have a year's work experience (sponsored if possible), before commencing a university course in Engineering in October 1989.

REFEREE

Housemaster of my House at school . . .

CONCLUSION

I would be most grateful if you would give this application for sponsorship your kind consideration and send me an application form if you need more information.

Yours faithfully,
Alexander Erskine

Student: 'This looks good news! Someone playing the job market could apply for literally hundreds of jobs every week!'

Expert: 'Yes, indeed! There is no reason why just the credit card companies should be able to bombard you with propositions. You too can address yourself to the whole job market, but be careful to take one sector at a time! A cv directed at getting interviews for a job in the City would not be much good for seeking out jobs in publishing. There would, perhaps, be some common core, but style would have to be different, and the section detailing hobbies and experience would be customised to bring out particular points of interest and contact for the industry.'

Commercial documents requiring some computation

A good word processor should have a limited capability for doing simple calculations and creating structured documents such as orders or invoices. Superscript does have such a capability and it can be very useful in commercial applications. A short sequence is demonstrated below, showing Expert raising an order on a mail order house to purchase Christmas presents for forty friends and members of the family.

Exhibit 14.4 *Completed mail merge sponsorship letter*

CLIFTONWOOD, NEWBRIDGE,
MIDLOTHIAN, EH28 8LQ
031-333-2758
30 September 1987

Mr R. Cook,
Personnel Department,
Alcan International Limited,
Banbury, Southam Road,
Oxford, OX16 7SP

Dear Mr Cook,

ENGINEERING SPONSORSHIP

APPLICATION OF ALEXANDER W.I.M. ERSKINE

I have seen your company's name in the booklet prepared by the Manpower Services Commission, 'Sponsorships', and have much pleasure in making my application to you.

C V

I was born on 14 March 1970.

In June 1986 I sat ten subjects at 'O' Level of the Oxford & Cambridge Joint Board with the following results and grades:

SUBJECT	GRADE	SUBJECT	GRADE
Maths	A	Physics	A

(etc.)

At the same time I also sat the Scottish 'O' Grade in French and secured Grade 2.

I am currently in second year sixth, on an 'A' Level course, studying Maths, Further Maths and Physics, and intend to pursue an Engineering Course at university beginning in October 1989.

I would wish to have a university course with General Engineering in first year, followed by specialisation in the later years. I have applied through UCCA for the following universities:

Cambridge, Durham, Liverpool, Surrey, Reading.

HOBBIES AND OTHER ACTIVITIES

From my first year at secondary school I was in the rifle shooting team and represented the school . . .

SPONSORSHIP EXPECTED

I am expecting to secure three good grades at 'A' Level in June 1988, at least A, A and B. I would then hope to have a year's work experience (sponsored if possible), before commencing a university course in Engineering in October 1989.

REFEREE

Housemaster of my House at school . . .

CONCLUSION

I would be most grateful if you would give this application for sponsorship your kind consideration and send me an application form if you need more information.

Yours faithfully,
Alexander Erskine

Demonstration of Christmas order

Expert resets screen size to 136 to give a column width adequate for an order and sets print to condense mode, then loads document 'webb-ivory-89'

The sequence starts with searching out last year's list of names on the present list from a document on disk and checking what they were given. Then Expert adds new names and takes off some old names as well.

Next, Expert and his wife sit down together with the mail order catalogue, identifying items thought to be suitable. As a gift is selected the present list is manually updated and an order line created on disk for the items concerned, until all forty people have presents assigned. For convenience a comment line is retained under each line item, so that when eventually the consignment arrives it will be easy to unpack and repack the presents for individuals without any need to consult another list.

The reader might wonder how an order line could be retained within the confines of a 40-character screen. Superscript allows you to create a screen of any size and then lets you scroll. Only 40 characters are visible at any one moment, but that does not stop one using the whole of a 136-character record. The figure 136 is significant as it is the definition of a print format in condensed letters which fits in to the standard A4 stationery. Most commercial documents will fit happily into that screen size. For the finished document, refer to Exhibit 14.5.

The final stage is to copy the order for the mail order house, remove the comment lines, add all the line extensions on the order (F1 C C) and see that the total is within the budget. Lastly, the order is printed for the supplier and filed with the copy, on which the comment lines for allocating gifts are retained.

Now, labels have to be made, for extending good wishes to the recipients, and address labels printed. But that is no problem as they were generated last year from the electronic address book, so all we have to do this year is process some six amendments and print the labels.

Exhibit 14.5 *An order on a mail order house*

Webb Ivory Fundraising Service,
Queens House,
Wood Street,
Burton-on-Trent, DE14 3BD

Order from Robert Erskine,
passed to Val Lawrie.

Item	How many	Catalogue number	Description	Page number	Price each £	Total Value £
1	1	34-02-86	The indispensable pen	91 E	4.99	4.99
2	3	29-33-42	Calendars for plant lovers	31 B	0.99	2.97
3	3	29-32-10	Calendars jam-packed with fun	31 D	1.65	4.95
4	2	29-33-69	Calendars for puppy lovers	30 B	0.99	1.98
5	7	25-44-36	Hippo bathtime fun	79 E	2.99	20.93
6	1	49-83-19	7-in-1 tool	93 B	4.99	4.99
7	3	33-40-73	Mini-briefcase	142 A	3.99	11.97
8	2	33-91-21	Complete personal organiser	142 B	2.99	5.98
9	1	25-62-93	Six brass-framed bird studies	149 C	6.50	6.50
10	3	21-18-50	12 gold-plated mocca spoons	149 A	5.99	17.97
11	1	31-10-65	4 pretty plates of cats	150 A	5.99	5.99
12	4	32-42-05	1,000 recipe book	184 E	2.50	10
13	1	26-87-47	3 division frying pan	185 F	4.99	4.99
14	2	20-22-07	Multi-purpose rack for cassettes	163 H	2.50	5
15	2	32-90-10	Snake draught excluder	165 E	2.99	5.98
16	4	28-93-88	Digital lock	160 D	2.99	11.96
17	5	34-10-53	Pull-n-light	160 H	2.99	14.95
18	1	20-76-75	Panda pencil box	138 B	1.95	1.95
Total						144.05

The packing-up process takes just one more evening after the consignment arrives. Two evenings are thus devoted to choosing Christmas presents for the whole family — the computer aid is crucial for such productivity.

Student: 'It all sounds quite fun, but it must be an expensive way of dealing with Christmas, when you have to start off buying a computer to get the productivity. My wife would hate the thought of computer labels on Christmas presents — a complete dehumanisation of the event!'

Expert: 'Yes, computer methods can cause upset. However, my aim was to show what is possible in generating commercial documents and labels. Similar principles can be adopted in a commercial environment of production control to generate order lists, picking lists and allocation lists where the population of items is much more than the forty considered in the demo, and control of information is crucial for commercial viability.'

Student: 'You have rather upset my world today with the word processor. Could you just summarise why it is so much more powerful than the typewriter?'

Expert: 'Yes, life is full of the need to organise information. Each professional will have different needs, but a basic common need is to organise text in correspondence files, research in research files, etc., and the disk is a very convenient medium. Computers are very useful in allowing quick access to relevant data, they enable editing manipulations to be done very easily and they provide proforma-style documents and systems so that routine work is repeated very easily and quickly. Speed of response gives a businessman an edge over one who has to wait a week for documents. The ability to deal with groups via *Mailmerge* applications can have a profound effect on marketing and management style within an organisation'.

Database

There are various definitions of the term 'database'. In layman's language it represents a recording system in which files of information are structured and then coded on a computer device, usually a disk. The advantage for the user is that he or she may get very rapid access to retrieve a particular record for making a decision. Furthermore, a database can be the basis for retrieving lists of information, sorted in the order specified by the user, and such records can then, under user control, be rolled up into management reports and summaries.

The database is a package dealing with structured data. In contrast, word processing packages deal with free-form data, with some exceptions like the Christmas mail order form, demonstrated above.

Normally, database design is developed for use around a particular application in which the fields of data are anticipated. The example developed in this demonstration is a course admissions system for management students. The business objectives here were as follows:

1. To ensure the achievement of recruitment targets.
2. To provide management reports for course assessment procedures.
3. To trigger the paperwork involved in acknowledging, interviewing, offering, waitlisting and expediting candidates, and providing a variety of class lists for course administration.
4. To develop sponsorship lists for use in mail shots for course publicity.

Student: 'Database packages seem to be very complicated — the province of the computer expert not the layman. How would we ever get the time to master the skills of the programmer?'

Expert: 'Yes, you are right, database packages and techniques can be very complicated and in the early days they cost a fortune in development. Airline booking with database packages took years to get going, but since then packages, and menus which go with them, have been developed specially for the layman. The whole idea of menus is that they immediately offer the user a choice to which he or she may respond. With good package design it should be no more difficult to operate a database than it is for a bank customer to withdraw money from a cash terminal, and you cannot say that only programmers can have that privilege!

'In today's demonstration no use is made at all of programming routines, and the Superbase package does not require such skills. However, if you are a "computer buff", it is possible to use the package in this way, but I do not wish to blind you with science!

'The documentation which goes with any database package is crucial for letting the layman grasp the essentials and initially it is a bit difficult to appreciate the structure of the menus. A well-indexed manual, a good crib sheet and some well-thought-out and simple demonstration sequences are the way to painless learning! However, it must be stated that a database package is inherently more difficult to comprehend than a word processor package.'

Starting up

Expert mounts the database software program in the disk drive (it is contained on the demo disk) and hits F4 to load the program. The computer loads the first program on the disk and the database program is deliberately put in the first position.

On completion of loading, a software menu appears requesting the user to key in the name of the database for today's demonstration. If you have forgotten the database name, hit 'Control Q' and it is possible to access from the menu the disk directory.

Today, we assume we do know what database is wanted, and key in 'mbaadmissions'.

The computer directs this database into its memory, and the screen offers a menu (see Exhibit 14.6).

A menu is a list of options for the user to activate. In this starting up sequence we need an alternative menu to access a file.

Expert hits return to get the alternative menu and then we see F1 is for file. He hits F1 and what appears is a list of all files associated with this database. There are two available, 'applic', which has application records, and 'sum-record', which contains records of summaries of transactions. The sum-record is useful to define the pattern of demand and offers an admissions tutor a firm foundation for tracking the number of places available at any time during the recruiting season.

To get a view of the application records, expert keys in 'applic'. The computer now has in its memory both the right database (collection of records) and the right file for access.

Exhibit 14.6 *Superbase menus*

```
MODE : MENU 1      SUPERBASE 64
  V 2.02

FILE SELECTED  =  APPLIC

F1   ENTER
F2   SELECT
F3   FIND
F4   OUTPUT
F5   CALC
F6   REPORT
F7   EXECUTE
F8   HELP


MODE: MENU 2      SUPERBASE 64
  V 2.02

FILE SELECTED  =  APPLIC

F1   FILE
F2   FORMAT
F3   BATCH
F4   SORT
F5   PROG
F6   MAINTAIN
F7   MEMO
F8   HELP
```

Student: 'I understood that database always meant a collection of records related to one another. Why is only one file in memory at a time?'

Expert: 'This is just a simple package running on a 64K microcomputer. Other packages will do cleverer things, but they are more difficult to learn. This package can still cope with a sizeable commercial application, bringing in different files as required.'

Browsing

To browse through the file or select a particular record hit F2; this calls up a sub-menu. At the top of the screen there is a further menu of letters inviting the enquirer to decide which particular record to retrieve. The expert will now run over some of these decision options (see top of Exhibit 14.8 on p. 244): N, L, P, F, C, M, O, A, R, D. These letters mean: next record, last record, previous record, first record, current record, matched record, output record to printer, add new record, replace record, delete record.

This database has been set up alphabetically by a 'keyname', which includes the combinations of surname and initials (to ensure uniqueness).

Enquiring

If any telephone *enquirer* wants to know the status of his or her application, this may be answered either by referring to a summary printout of keynames or by hitting 'k' and then typing in the enquirer's name; the record will be retrieved in about five seconds. If the definition of the key is not correct, then a record will be retrieved which is the nearest to an alphabetical match.

Student: 'If I had applied for your course, how long would it take to know whether I had got a place?'

Expert: 'We do not normally interview until mid-May, so if you applied early, you would just get an acknowledgement, probably posted to you within three days of receipt by the admissions tutor. Later in the recruiting season, the admissions tutor would be able to tell you instantly from the screen what the application status is (like airline booking). If the admissions tutor were not at his desk, then the secretary of the department would be able to consult a daily printout. However, during the summer vacation a slightly longer delay may be expected. Once a week the admissions mail is sent to the tutor on holiday and is then processed within another two days, so there might be as much as a ten-day delay for the enquirer. Setting up a modem link between college and home to get a daily service would help, but lack of resources, both of equipment and staff, is a problem in the public sector colleges.'

Entering a new data record

This is easy. F1 produces an empty screen for a new record and on completion of all fields, press return.

Selecting a population of records

It might be necessary to send the course members on a residential study weekend. The curriculum specifies two such periods each year. The hotel manager will require lists of staff and students by sex, as rooms are shared.

The selection of such lists is easily achieved with a database package. Menu 'Find' is activated by F3 and the screen shows a template of the application record (see Exhibit 14.7). The user is then invited to key in the profile required for the selection.

Initially we would generate the list of men.

In the 'sex' field we key m, but that is not all. Possibly there are names on the file of people who have withdrawn or been waitlisted. So we need to move the cursor down to field 'processing-status' and key in the acceptable criteria. Two possibilities are acceptable — those who have had offers or given acceptances. The coding is thus acc*/offe*. Note the * means that anything after that point is eligible and the / sign means 'either, or'. The selection criteria are now complete, so we hit return.

The computer will now examine every record in the file for compatibility with the

Exhibit 14.7 *Defining a match criteria*

```
MODE: SELECT MATCH DATA         :£ 15 T


KEY [               ]
DESIG[          ]
S-N[               ]
INIT-FN [                ]
HOME-AD1[
  ] HOME-AD2[
    ] HOME-AD3[
      ] H-TEL [                       ] SEX[M]
AGE [  ] AC-QUAL [

              ] EMPLOYER [

                                    ]

JOB-TIT [
              ] YRS-WRK-EXP [
                          ] PROC-STAT [
OFFER*/ACC*             ] MD-O-AT [   ]
COMMENTS [

                   ]
OF-CRIT [                           ]
DT-LS-TRAN [      ] CODE [     ]
```

matching template and display matching items on the screen or printer to complete our list. Furthermore, the computer stores the references to such matching items in a special list 'hlist', so that this list may be further processed by being sorted, transferred to another file or transmitted to a word processor for making address labels, etc.

Once the art of selecting is mastered it is possible to make every kind of different list from the databases — lists of the whole class with qualifications, lists of half-day and evening students only, lists of morning students, lists of those on the waiting list pending decision by the group of selectors, attendance lists and mark lists.

Sorting

In course promotion it is important to identify the sponsoring employers and establish promotion links with the appropriate personnel officers. However, if the file is ordered by applicant it is quite a chore to compile reports by sponsor. All we need to do with a database package is to *sort* the file in a new sequence and display an ordered list of sponsors and any other reference data, which management might require. The sort sequence is activated by keying F4.

Student: 'Could you see if there were any comparison between entry qualifications and success on the course? That might be an interesting one.'

Expert: 'Yes, indeed. One year after the first year examination results we added up all the assessments, put the total figure in the database, sorted on descending order of merit, and printed the record along with the entry qualifications. The expectation was that the best qualified would be at the top of the list, but as you suggested the actual results were interesting!'

Management reports

At the end of a session of processing application forms and making decisions, it is sensible to enter a summary record of admission status for management review. If the pattern is different from a previous year at the same time in the recruiting season, it will be readily obvious, and if a trend is detected early enough there may well be time to respond with further publicity or other measures.

This is done by keying in F1 to change file in the database and entering 'sum-record'. Select the last record, then amend this one to create a new one for the current week (see Exhibit 14.8).

For easy use with word processing, and the extended editing facilities, we can now 'export' the sum-records into a list. This is done by keying F6 to get maintenance menu and then F4 in the sub-menu. All that is required now is to name the list. Records that are 'exported' are sequential and in the normal format of a document.

The same technique of 'exporting' is done with all admission records, which require a letter, and as the name and address is within a record, the word processor will be able to generate and print envelope labels to go on the decision letters.

Student: 'Did you suggest that the computer has any say in the admission decision?'

Expert: 'No, of course not! The computer just helps with group decision-making. The admissions tutor can get details of the waiting list and make copies of this for a review group of three lecturers. By sharing the comparable data, qualitative judgements may be made and agreed of the order of merit within the group, for a final set of offers. In manual systems there is a greater

Exhibit 14.8 *A Superbase summary report*

MODE SELECT N,L,P,F,K,C,M,O,A,R,D, + −

```
KEYDAY ⟨7821⟩
APPLIC          ⟨133⟩
OFFERS          ⟨91 ⟩
PEND-INTVW      ⟨0  ⟩
W/LST           ⟨16 ⟩
DECLINE         ⟨13 ⟩
WITHDRAW        ⟨16 ⟩
REJECT          ⟨10 ⟩
ACCEPT          ⟨60 ⟩
COMMENT ⟨

                  ⟩
MAX-UPTAKE ⟨76⟩
```

likelihood of an arbitrary decision by one person, owing to the difficulty of reviewing candidates together.'

Designing the database record

We can enter this part of the package by entering the file option, F1, and offering the name of a file not previously known to the database. A blank screen is offered the user. Fields of data will then be specified till the record's design is complete. The field which determines the file's sequence is called the 'key' field, otherwise the field is 'text', 'numeric' or 'result'. The 'result' field allows the field to be determined in relation to a formula linking the field with other fields. For instance, in a database record containing stock share valuations, the stock-value could be defined as [units-held] * [unit-price]. Any time any change should be processed to either [units-held] or [unit-price] and the computer would automatically recalculate stock-value.

On completion of the file design it will be saved by keying F1 run/stop. The computer will ask whether duplicate key records will be permitted. It is usual practice to insist on uniqueness of the key, otherwise there can be confusion when records are retrieved or deleted.

Student: 'What happens if you misjudge the record design, and later want to add more fields to the database records? Can you make amendments to the design?'
Expert: 'The ease of recovery depends on the facilities in the particular package. In Superbase it is easy to add new fields to the end of the design up to a maximum of twenty fields, but resequencing would require the recreation of the database, which is a longer task. You need to get as much of the design right first time as you can.'
Student: 'Could you summarise why you advocate a database to help administer admission records for your courses in preference to a manual system? Could you not have used the word processing package as an alternative? And in any case, why do most of your colleagues who are admission tutors continue to use manual methods?'
Expert: 'Three interesting questions! There is a great convenience in having a disk-based record. Over 140 applications in a manual system would take up an enormous amount of room and telephone enquiries about status would be much more difficult. Secondly, as much of the admissions work involves colleagues, in a manual system you can never be sure where all the application forms are, so if one goes missing, you have a problem.

'Once one has integrity of data one can be much more confident about the exact numbers in the system and recruiting to the target number of places is much easier. Thirdly, as the paper generation is done so quickly, applicants get a faster service and there is no need to prepare labels by hand each time a communication is sent out.

'The management reports for course assessment and course board monitoring are done in minutes with the computer's aid, rather than in hours if done manually.

'The word processing package could have been used and is better than nothing as a computer aid. Indeed, for one year that was the only aid we used for admissions, but many of the lists and management reports still took ages to develop without the structuring that the database package offered.

'Why do most of my colleagues not follow this lead? Well, that is a good question! The majority of them are simply not computer-minded at all and new techniques do take time to be learned and adopted.

'The college does not have a policy in this matter, so an admissions tutor would have to make his case to get and use the equipment, which is what I did. And there is no policy about equipment compatibility, so decisions here are fraught with confusion and difficulty as a back-up system in event of corruption or other failure is essential.

'Finally, administrative policy dictates that full-time admissions are done centrally on a mainframe computer; only part-time courses are handled by departments and each course is so different that a central system would be difficult to design to suit all. The decentralised approach adopted for the part-time management course admissions was both flexible and useful.

'It would be nice if all admissions tutors were given compatible computers and then put on to a college-wide network. We would then have the best of both worlds and admissions tutors would be obliged to adopt database techniques. Individuals and the institution would gain in productivity together. However, the issue of networks and computing policy which links personal computers and mainframe ones is really a topic in its own right and discussion is postponed until chapter 17.'

Spreadsheet with Mini Office II

A *spreadsheet package* enables quantitative data to be summarised and manipulated using formulas. It is particularly useful for doing simulations of business situations and applying the techniques of management accounting. Examples are developed of the analysis of critical ratios from profit and loss and balance sheet data, cash-flow models and models dealing with investment appraisal.

History of spreadsheets

In 1982 the first microcomputer packages in this field became commercially available. Essentially, a spreadsheet is like an electronic blackboard, constructed with definitions of rows and columns to facilitate simple arithmetic.

This was an ingenious idea, as in so many financial applications there is a need to present rows and columns of financial data, most of which form a logical structure. Computers are very good when they are confronted with quantitative data and structured relationships.

The starting screen of a spreadsheet shows this structured layout. Across the top the columns are defined, beginning with AA, then AB, AC, etc., for some 200 columns. It is quite a wide blackboard, only part of which is visible at any one time. Down the spreadsheet we see the definition of the rows — in this spreadsheet 01—90. Again, not all the rows are visible at one time on the screen, but all rows and columns are accessible simply by touching the cursor on the keyboard and then by scrolling. Exhibit 14.11 on p. 250 illustrates this format.

Spreadsheet content

Within the rows and columns, we may go to specific cells. CCRR, Column Column Row Row, is our watchword. The top left-hand cell is AA01, the one below is AA02, and so on. A spreadsheet may contain several thousand such cells.

Each cell may have three different types of information entered. Firstly, it is helpful for the viewer to read titles or text, so that data are meaningful. Ordinary text may thus be entered. Secondly, for any arithmetic to be done we need values, so numeric data, with signs and decimal places, may be entered. Thirdly, we need to define logical relationships such as would be found in formulas, and the computer has a means of knowing whether it is indeed dealing with 'text' or a 'formula'.

Professional people have no difficulty in defining formulas, particularly in the accounting world of balance sheets and profit and loss accounts, nor any difficulty in capturing the necessary financial data and, being artists in presentation, they have no difficulty in writing the appropriate text to communicate with clients.

Demonstration of profit and loss and balance sheets of M and N Limited

First he enters the demo disk into the disk drive and keys F4 to load the first program on disk. That is where the spreadsheet program has been put. After loading he gets an initial menu which invites him to take decisions. He moves the cursor on to the part of the menu he wants and presses the return key. See Exhibit 14.9 for structure of the menu.

Exhibit 14.9 *Spreadsheet menu*

Mini Office II

Spreadsheet menu

Edit sheet
Alter sheet
Print sheet
List formulae
Load sheet
Save sheet
Save graphics data
Catalogue
Hardware options
Mini Office II main menu

Use ↑ and ↓ to choose, then return

To view the blank screen he puts the cursor on edit and presses return. The blank screen appears, defined with columns and rows. For manipulation of this screen he needs to look up the Mini Office cribsheet, which summarises how to give commands and organise data on the spreadsheet. Exhibit 14.10 gives this information.

Now we shall take an actual working model, that of the M and N Company. Expert hits the run/stop button to get to the menu again, then moves to catalogue to view the directory of this disk. Then, having decided that the model for selection is mandnfiv, he selects load and then, on request for a filename, keys in mandnfiv.

This model reflects the print-out in Exhibit 14.11 for 'M and N Limited'. Expert scrolls to highlight the titles, data values and formulas and demonstrates the sum function and the calculate function.

Electronic models are useful because they enable the user to accomplish advanced analysis of performance ratios with some ease. This model calculates some seven critical ratios which relate to performance and liquidity.

Financial analysis generally throws up problems and opportunities; the manager naturally wants to develop a strategy for coping with these. A common tactic is to play 'Mr Ten Percent' via a simulation. To do this one makes an assumption that it is possible to change some of the ingredients that influence profit, such as price and cost. In this model material is a predominant influence, as is the sales price.

Simulation logic is built in to the model via a parameter, 'simulator', initially set at 1.0, which can be varied according to requirements. The logic is then imposed in the formulas of the model, in this instance to increase revenue by the simulator factor, and at the same time decrease material costs by the same amount.

Exhibit 14.10 *Spreadsheet key summary*

Function keys:

F1 Delete cell	F2 Delete column
F3 Update	F4 Delete row
F5 Enter formulas	F6 Insert column
F7 Edit cell	F8 Insert row
HOME Move cursor to cell AA01	

Control in conjunction with:

1–7 Change screen colour	N Unlock column
A Auto cursor direction	O Copy column
B Lock row	P Copy row
C Enter text centred	Q Scroll mode
D Change column decimal places	R Enter text justified right
E Evaluate expression	S Enter string
G Goto cell	T Enter text
H Help screen	U Auto update on/off
I Instant save	V Lock column
J Change cell justification	W Change column width
K Lock/unlock cell	X Copy cell
L Enter text justified	Y Change column justification
M Unlock row	Z Zero numeric cells

Exhibit 14.11 *Accounts and financial ratios*

	AA	AB	AC	AD . . . . .
01	M & N Limited			
02	Profit and loss			
03	Account for Year 1			
04				
05				
06				
07	Sales		3100000	
08	Less expenses			
09	Wages	500000		
10	Materials	2000000		
11	Mat less sim	0		
12	Depreciation	100000		
13	Other production			
14	overheads	100000		
15	Selling	150000		
16	Administration	50000		
17	Loan interest	100000		
18			3000000	
19				
20	Profit before tax		100000	
21	Corporation tax		55000	
22	Net profit after tax		45000	
23				
24				
25	Balance sheet as at			
26	31 Dec year 1			
27	Fixed assets			
28	Property (at cost)		1500000	
29	Equipment (at cost)	1000000		
30	Less depreciation	400000	600000	
31				
32	Current assets			
33	Stocks	450000		
34	Debtors	500000		
35	Cash	50000		
36		————		
37		1000000		
38				
39	Less current			
40	Liabilities			
41	Corporation tax	55000		
42	Creditors	495000		
43	Overdraft	100000		
44		————		
45		650000		
46				
47	Net working capital		350000	
48				
49				
50				

Exhibit 14.11

	AA...............	AB.....	AC.....	AD.....
51	Total net assets		2450000	
52				
53	Financed by:			
54				
55	Issued share			
56	Capital		800000	
57	Revenue reserves		650000	
58	Loan capital secured			
59	on property		1000000	
60			————	
61			2450000	
62	Company ratios			
63				
64	(a) ROI			0.018
65	(b) % margin on sales			
66				0.015
67	(c) Stock turnover			
68	times			6.889
69	(d) Asset turnover			
70	times			1.265
71	(g) Current assets/			
72	current liabilities			1.538
73	(h) Current assets			
74	less stock/			
75	Total current			
76	liability			0.846
77	(i) Overdraft cover			5.000
78				
79	Simulator			
80		1.00		

List of formulas

AB11	=	(1-AA80)*AB10	AC51	=	SUM[AC28:AC48]
AC18	=	SUM[AB09:AB17]	AC61	=	SUM[AC56:AC59]
AC20	=	(AC07*AA80)-AC18	AD64	=	AC22/AC51
AC21	=	0.55*AC20.	AD66	=	AC22/AC07
AC22	=	AC20-AC21	AD68	=	AC07/AB33
AC30	=	AB29-AB30	AD70	=	AC07/AC51
AB37	=	SUM[AB33:AB35]	AD72	=	AB37/AB45
AB45	=	SUM[AB41:AB43]	AD76	=	(AB37-AB33)/AB45
AC48	=	AB37-AB45	AD77	=	(AC28-AC59)/AB43

We may now see the impact on the company ratios. At 0 per cent simulation, the ROI and margin on sales are awful. No one would want to lend money to this company. However, with a 10 per cent simulation an immediate improvement is evident, and with 15 per cent there will be a mad rush of investors (see Exhibit 14.12).

A creative analyst may look into other features of these data and play 'Mr Ten Percent' elsewhere to determine where high impact is possible, and he or she will need to take account of business practicalities before specific recommendations are made.

Exhibit 14.12 *Ratios and simulations*

	AA	AB	AC	AD . . . . .
62	Company ratios			
63				
64	(a) ROI			0.112
65	(b) % margin on			
66	sales			0.089
67	(c) Stock turnover			
68	times			6.889
69	(d) Asset turnover			
70	times			1.265
71	(g) Current assets/			
72	current liabilities			1.538
73	(h) Current assets			
74	less stock/			
75	total current			
76	liability			0.846
77	(i) Overdraft cover			5.000
78				
79	Simulator			
80		1.10		

	AA	AB	AC	AD . . . . .
62	Company ratios			
63				
64	(a) ROI			0.159
65	(b) % margin on			
66	sales			0.126
67	(c) Stock turnover			
68	times			6.889
69	(d) Asset turnover			
70	times			1.265
71	(g) Current assets/			
72	current liabilities			1.538
73	(h) Current assets			
74	less stock/			
75	total current			
76	liability			0.846
77	(i) Overdraft cover			5.000
78				
79	Simulator			
80		1.15		

Exhibit 14.11 is a print-out of the basic M and N Company model, with no simulation effect operating. In the lower half of Exhibit 14.11 there is a list of the formulas of the model. This needs to be rigorously checked by the user for accuracy, before presenting results to management. The model is only as good as its representation of the real-life business situation.

Exhibit 14.13 *Cash-flow model on spreadsheet*

AA . . . . AB . . . . . AC . . . . . AD . . . . . AE . . . . . AF . . . . . AG . . . . . AH							
01 Sample cash flow							
02 Project							
03 Potblack model							
04	Oct	Nov	Dec	Jan	Feb	Totals	%
05							
06							
07 Income							
08							
09 Sales	11786	10944	10944	15946	20944	70564	
10							
11							
12 Revenue expenditure							
13 Purchases	500	500	1000	1000	2250	5250	11.59
14 Advertising	500	1000	1000	1000	1000	4500	9.93
15 Director's salary	1596	1596	1596	1596	1596	7890	17.61
16 Salaries	2216	2216	2216	2216	2216	11080	24.46
17 Rent			375			375	0.83
18 Telephone		300			300	600	1.32
19 Insurance		200				200	0.44
20 Printing/stationery		400		200		600	1.32
21							
22 Repairs and renewals				250		250	0.55
23 Hire of equipment	60	60	60	60	60	300	0.66
24 Motor and travel	500	500	500	500	500	2500	5.52
25 Sundry	200	200	100			500	1.10
26 Accountancy	250	425				675	1.49
27 Finance charges			250			250	0.55
28 Commission			250			250	0.55
29 Contingency	100	100	100	100	100	500	1.10
30							
31 Capital expenditure							
32 Fixed assets	100	500	500	1000	1000	3100	6.84
33 VAT			2293		4104	6397	14.12
34							
35							
36 Total expenditure	6022	7997	10240	7922	13126	45307	
37							
38							
39 Net inflow/outflow	5764	2947	704	8024	7818		100.00
40							
41							
42 Balance B/fwd	−4715	1049	3996	4700	12724		
43							
44 Balance C/fwd	1049	3996	4700	12724	20542		
45							

Exhibit 14.12 gives two snapshots of the model with 10 per cent simulation and 15 per cent respectively.

Exhibit 14.13 offers a cash-flow model, 'Potblack'.

Exhibit 14.14 offers some manipulations using discounted cash flow, 'NPV Model'. From this model investment proposals may be easily evaluated against criteria of 'pay-off period', 'internal rate of return', 'net present value'.

Exhibit 14.14 *Discounted cash-flow model*

AA	AB	AC	AD	AE	AF	AG	AH
01	NPV Model						
02	Interest 1.1110						
03							
04		Year	D/F	Spending	Saving	NCF	D/Net	NPV
05								
06		0	1.0000	−80000		−80000	−80000	−80000
07		1	0.9001		10000	10000	9001	−70999
08		2	0.8102		12000	12000	9722	−61277
09		3	0.7292		15000	15000	10938	−50339
10		4	0.6564		15000	15000	9845	−40493
11		5	0.5908		15000	15000	8862	−31632
12		6	0.5318		12000	12000	6381	−25251
13		7	0.4786		12000	12000	5744	−19507
14		8	0.4308		10000	10000	4308	−15199
15		9	0.3878		10000	10000	3878	−11321
16		10	0.3490		10000	10000	3490	−7831
17		11	0.3142		10000	10000	3142	−4689
18		12	0.2828		8000	8000	2262	−2427
19		13	0.2545		5000	5000	1273	−1155
20	Interest	14	0.2291		4000	4000	916	−238
21	1.111	15	0.2062		2000	2000	412	174

AA	AB	AC	AD	AE	AF	AG	AH
01	NPV Model						
02	Interest 1.1500						
03							
04		Year	D/F	Spending	Saving	NCF	D/Net	NPV
05								
06		0	1.0000	−80000		−80000	−80000	−80000
07		1	0.8696		10000	10000	8696	−71304
08		2	0.7561		12000	12000	9074	−62231
09		3	0.6575		15000	15000	9863	−52368
10		4	0.5718		15000	15000	8576	−43792
11		5	0.4972		15000	15000	7458	−36334
12		6	0.4323		12000	12000	5188	−31146
13		7	0.3759		12000	12000	4511	−26635
14		8	0.3269		10000	10000	3269	−23366
15		9	0.2843		10000	10000	2843	−20523
16		10	0.2472		10000	10000	2472	−18051
17		11	0.2149		10000	10000	2149	−15902
18		12	0.1869		8000	8000	1495	−14407
19		13	0.1625		5000	5000	813	−13594
20	Interest	14	0.1413		4000	4000	565	−13029
21	1.150	15	0.1229		2000	2000	246	−12783

Student: 'The problems which we have in commerce will have different figures from the ones shown in your models. Would we be able to use your models as proforma models like those shown in the word processor models in the first demo, when you were writing letters to a bank?'

Expert: 'Yes, that is one reason why teachers are so keen to develop models with the fundamental management accounting logic built in. Once you are conversant with it, any problem of that type can, with a little bit of trouble, be re-fashioned and solved. The long bit is getting in the models the formulas which are logically correct. Anyone can key in a new set of values for costs, savings, rates of interest, etc. The models themselves greatly assist in the general understanding of these management accounting techniques themselves.'

Graphics

Student: 'When you began the demo you said what fun a word processor was! Can you do cards and graphics?'

Expert: 'Yes, indeed. I have a separate graphics package, *Printshop*, and with that I can do customised cards. See Exhibit 14.15 of a Christmas card. All that is required is to fold it. The graphic symbols come from a graphics library. The text is generated simply by keying in on a screen and selecting font types and borders from a menu in the package. The card enclosed was designed and made in half an hour.'

Review of security with floppy disks

An important consideration is the degree of security which can be achieved in the electronic office. When there is a wide range of minicomputers and microcomputers in an organisation, which are operated and run by the non-expert, this raises particular issues concerning the security and integrity of the data in the system. Whereas with mainframe computers a professional operations manager will make sound provision for back-ups, when the user is in charge he or she has to be a professional operations manager and follow rigorously the norms of good practice about back-up. These may be summarised as follows:

1. When working with a floppy disk, save your work at least every half an hour. If a computer error or power failure occurs the worst that can happen is that the last half hour's data are lost! As printers often suffer from errors and may cause a system to 'freeze', it is good tactics to save work to disk before printing; in event of trouble, recovery is much more simple.
2. On completion of a whole session it makes sense to take a full copy of the work just completed on another disk, then store the backed-up copy in a different building. If a whole disk is corrupted, vandalised or stolen the loss may be significant.
3. When copying the original master disk, this should be done on a new disk. Do not overwrite the back-up immediately. If you do and an error occurs during the copying process both master and copy are lost. This means that there is always a minimum of three disks in a securely backed-up cycle.
4. Take care with the labels used on $5\frac{1}{4}$ inch floppies. Large sticky labels may

Exhibit 14.15 *Cards printed using Printshop*

tend to expand and contract under changing conditions of moisture and warp the disk, making it impossible to load into the disk drive.

5. Clean the disk drive heads at least once a month, using a special fluid soaked on to a cleaning floppy disk, which is inserted in the drive and run briefly. If cleaning is not done frequently, there is a tendency to create disk read errors.

6. If your system has a hard disk, be sure to back it up on a floppy disk, or another hard disk. Ideally, the personal computer will have dual drives, but this is expensive so back-up from hard disk to floppy is essential. However, back-up from hard disk to floppy may take a long time and many floppy disks. This suggests that hard disks are mainly used for software, floppies for data, so the hard disk only needs backing up when new software is introduced. Normal back-up for the floppies should be fairly quick. The more vital the data, the more vital is the back-up and its frequency.

7. Be sure that your hardware and software are covered by insurance to minimise potential loss, but do not forget that insurance will not generally be much good alone if the precious working data are not backed-up and duplicated in separate sites.

8. A further provision in an application such as course admissions is to leave an easy summary audit trail, so that it would be painless to revert, perhaps temporarily, to the manual system. All that is required here is the discipline of printing out an application status list after processing transactions and filing the original forms alphabetically.

Exercise 14.1
Computers in your own organisation

In your own organisation, identify good and bad use of microcomputer packages.

Suggest how greater productivity could be obtained by individuals and the organisation as a whole from their more creative deployment.

Suggest the outlines of a microcomputer policy which your organisation should adopt to get the best advantages from their use.

Further reading

Note: The texts below offer demo sequences for the more sophisticated versions of the basic packages, illustrated in this chapter.

Ingalsbe, L. (1987), *Business Applications Software for the IBM PC*, 2nd edition, Merrill.
Ingalsbe, L. (1987), *DBase III and DBASE III Plus for the IBM PC*, Merrill.
Long, L. (1987), *Computers in Business*, Prentice Hall.

Chapter 15

Applications of management information systems

Overview

This chapter assumes that some of the major routines within the manufacturing environment have already been computerised and that the reader's interest lies in recognising the main commercial benefits of this. The question of how these applications are specified, designed and implemented will be discussed in chapter 16. The main aim of this chapter is to show how computer systems can be used to give the organisation a competitive advantage in mainstream activity.

The spinal industrial process

In manufacturing there is an essential *spinal* activity involved in the making and managing of products. Database and other computer techniques can play a crucial role in this process. Once we have recognised this process it makes sense to discuss the organisational framework in which the computerised systems can flourish (see Table 15.1).

Each application of Table 15.1 is supported by relevant database structures — see Table 15.2.

Having identified these core database structures, we need to find out about the source of each main database — whether it is soft, external, qualitative data or hard, structured data.

Identification of core database structures

Research and development intelligence

This is both internal and external, and gained through networks. These data are primarily qualitative, but do need to circulate. Electronic mail and electronic retrieval of research reports and journals may help here.

Table 15.1   *A synopsis of the spinal industrial process*

1. Research
    Market Research; Research and Development; Interpretation
2. Creative design
3. Process control
4. Manufacturing
5. Assembly
6. Planning and provisioning
    Sales order processing, sales forecasting, provision of plant, labour, bought-out material
7. Warehousing
8. Distribution
9. Maintenance and after-sales service

Table 15.2   *Identification of core database structures*

1. Research and development intelligence
2. Market research intelligence
3. Product drawings and specifications
4. Process control tapes for machine tools, robots, plant and assembly processing
5. Manufacturing times and standards for all processes
6. Current sales order book
7. Sales history
8. Current long-term sales forecast by product
9. Current long-term capacity in plant, labour and flexibility
10. Current long-term purchasing schedule, calculated
11. Current long-term manufacturing and assembly schedule, calculated
12. Status of inventory and work-in-process, warehouse stock
13. Current and historical records of failure and after-sales maintenance

Market research intelligence

This is both internal and external. It is gained through networks. It is primarily qualitative data and may not be very structured. The internal sales force, marketing executives, reports from market research agencies and press reports are all valid sources. Considerable skill is required in collating and interpreting the data.

Product drawings and specifications

These can either be made manually or stored on computer for easy reproduction and amendment. They can be fully structured and if made using computer-aided design (CAD) packages, many of the calculations relating to stresses and strains may have been verified under program control with the appropriate engineering formulas.

Process control tapes for machine tools, robots, plant and assembly processing

These can either be made manually or with some computer assistance and come from CAD/CAM processes. There are many examples of computer-controlled machine tools that follow instructions on a punched paper tape or other computer readable medium to complete a long and complicated machining process.

One main advantage of this approach is that the tape only needs mounting and there is no need for spending a lengthy period setting up the machine. This offers great flexibility in manufacture, makes small short runs economical and has a major impact in reducing batch sizes of the product and amounts of components held in stock and in work-in-process.

Since the early 1970s this technology has been appearing in commercial applications. Other specialised and customised assembly controlled processes are now evolving and as a greater understanding of robotics is achieved, whole industrial processes are becoming amenable to structured computer-control techniques. In the motor industry in the late 1970s, Fiat led the field in developing robot-controlled painting and welding techniques. The data and rules needed to do this can be incorporated into a database.

The Japanese have a philosophy of having very low stocks on the shop floor, the 'just-in-time' (JIT) approach, and make machines which have very low set-up times, regardless of whether they are operated by computer tapes or manually.

Manufacturing times and standards for all processes

The drawings of a product reveal its structure in terms of assemblies and components. However, management needs to plan the logistics of the manufacturing process. This requires information about plant required, set-up times (if these are relevant, but now we have so many machine-controlled tools, set-up time may not be significant), tooling requirements and the timing standards for both labour and plant. Work study engineers will provide much of the information on standards. Finally, what is required is the routeing records to define what happens at each stage in the processing. Manufacturing engineers will provide the information for this. All these data are structured and may be committed to a comprehensive *engineering database*.

Current sales order book

These are very dynamic data and are active from the time a sales order is taken until it has been invoiced and shipped. After that point it is added to the sales history.

Sales history

This is a file of structured information and is a database of completed sales orders. It is used to review past patterns of demand by product, market or customer and other meaningful categorisations.

Current long-term sales forecast by product

This is a database containing the judgements of a specialist forecasting manager. It records expected sales, generally over a future period of some eighteen months, by month by product. The data in this database are the result of top-level planning, simulation and projections done in the corporate planning group of the organisation. The forecasting manager will use many inputs to this process, of which the sales history is one. He or she will also take account of the decisions of marketing and the many environmental factors interpreted by the corporate planners.

Current long-term capacity in plant, labour and flexibility

These data are structured, but their source is the manufacturing planners and it reflects their decisions on resource allocation. Commonly, each such key resource is given availabilities by week or month for the next eighteen months in a relevant unit of capacity — generally, hours or units. Data here are usually firmed up from the corporate planning group in light of the sales forecast data and possible planning simulations. Commonly, too, the data distinguish between normal capacity and capacity extended by overtime or extra shift working, hence the possibility of visualising how and where to use flexibility in balancing loads. When significant resource deficiencies are recognised in planning simulations, then either the forecast may be reduced (miss out on the possible business), subcontracting may be planned on others' plant or further investment must be made in own plant. Hence the comment that this database reflects management allocation decisions.

Current long-term purchasing schedule, calculated

This is a database derived from direct calculations and projections resulting from material requirements planning routines. The short-term orders will probably already be confirmed in the purchase records, and the longer-term ones are a simulation, but do provide a very good guide to possible long-term contracts and discounts based on the long-term volume. In the interest of maintaining low stocks (this is the influence of the Japanese JIT philosophy), it is likely that vendors are encouraged to make frequent deliveries of small consignments.

Current long-term manufacturing and assembly schedule, calculated

This is a database which is recalculated possibly as frequently as once a week. The short-term schedules are firm and comprise the immediate work of the plant; the longer-term schedules are a simulation of what is likely to happen given projections of existing demand and capacity and the rules of scheduling built into the system. The longer-term simulation is there to provide the basis of resource planning, particularly for the provisioning of sub-assemblies and components.

Status of inventory and work-in-process, warehouse stock

This is a database (or collection of separate databases) which reflects the dynamics of component stock, work-in-process and finished inventory.

Current and historical records of failure and after-sales maintenance

This database holds data, generally by customer and by product, reflecting after-sales activity. Analysis of such a database should reveal patterns of product weakness. Management may use this information as a basis for improving the quality control of the product, the quality control and specification of the bought-out components and the general engineering design of the product. In high-tech industries such as aero-engines, the database may contain the trouble-shooting reports of the maintenance engineers and exist on a network for access via a terminal for other engineers. This reduces duplication of diagnostic work being done on the more obscure faults.

Dynamics

Now we need to build up a picture of the dynamics between database and applications (see Figure 15.1).

Does any actual organisation have the exact structure shown in the model?

No, the model is a conceptual one, reflecting the experiences of many advanced users of computers in a great variety of business situations.

Much of the early inspiration for this came from the computerisation of the material

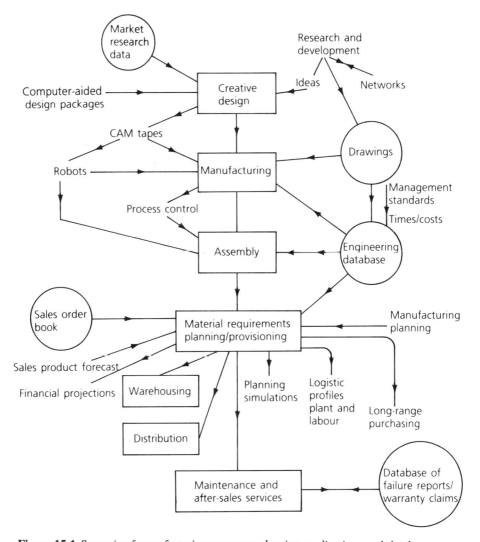

Figure 15.1 *Synopsis of manufacturing processes showing applications and databases*

requirements planning routines of Honeywell's Residential Division in the United States, which was later adapted for several factories in Europe. The business background of this unit was one of large volume, high variety (8,000) different thermostats, and complex manufacture (a maximum of seven distinct product levels from raw material, to machined parts, to sub-assemblies, to finished product).

The CAD/CAM part of the model was inspired by Caterpilla, manufacturer of large earth moving tractors, which found that much higher precision was possible with computer-controlled tools and that there was a great advantage in reducing the set-up times for the many machined parts which went into the product.

The process control was inspired by Fiat. Painting and welding in volume on the production lines was greatly speeded up with the use of robots. Other examples of how computer-assisted process control can have a dramatic impact on an industry is the printing industry. The journalist's story can now go directly on to computer disk for sub-editing into pages with electronic help, leading to the direct production of the printing plates. The advantage here is one of time. News quickly becomes outdated, and automation of this process naturally gives a competitive advantage.

In the printing industry there is also a natural link between the actual printing and the distribution of the papers. Once pages are ready and edited, they may be transmitted electronically to presses situated near the market.

The warehousing routines were inspired by a BBC television programme, *The Chips are Down*. This programme showed an automated warehouse, where a robot kept track of space and stock, and could stack consignments coming in from vendors and pick orders going out to customers. This may be ideal in the mail order business, where volumes would justify the investment of such an automated system.

The database of failed engines was inspired by Rolls-Royce. Aero engines are returned periodically for overhaul during their working lives and may be sent to more than one centre. However, it is of great help if engineers make available to one another the overhaul reports, so that common problems may be diagnosed quickly and experiences exchanged. To achieve this all that is required is a communications network, with VDUs at all overhaul sites and sufficient structure in the overhaul records for summaries and patterns to emerge and be recognisable by engineers and management. Furthermore, if a potentially dangerous situation is recognised, then it may be essential to recall all affected engines. Quite an elaborate information system is required to facilitate this.

Why are so many routines shown to be interconnected in Figure 15.1, when they were developed independently in a variety of companies and industries?

Computer applications, in the first instance, tend to grow adaptively through the force of local pressures and local innovations. However, when these have been put together they reveal a natural structure and it may be seen that common data then link one application to another. If we consciously look for the link we may avoid duplication in getting data into the organisation's total base of company data.

Database applications

A large engineering database

When the Residential Division of Honeywell introduced computer-assisted material requirements planning, they needed to create a database of over one million engineering records. Initially, this was done by keying in by hand the manual records on to the computer and then auditing them. When the computer scheduled the factory on the basis of these, many errors occurred because of inaccurate engineering records, but with this painful feedback, pressure was applied to get these records right.

Engineering integrated with design

It is much easier, however, if the database of engineering records is created directly from the engineering design stage, as a by-product of CAD/CAM. If this integration exists it should be possible to get an accurate engineering database first time and avoid the hiccups associated with the early factory schedules. When there is integration of the data used in designing and scheduling of the product it will be much easier to control engineering changes without leaving a large stock of components made under old designs.

Further integration to get profit simulation

Another example is of great financial significance. Gross profit is basically the difference between revenue based on selling prices and costs which accumulate from labour, raw material, processing costs and overheads. The engineering database is the 'natural' point for collecting the elements of the standard cost. The greater the integration of the engineering database with the CAD/CAM data the more accurate definitions there are of processes and times.

The material requirements planning routines are also capable of combining market volumes with factory capacities to generate medium-term (18 months), simulated schedules of factory activity. In this simulation we only need to point the computer to the roll-up of costs from manufacture and the roll-up of revenue from sales and it will calculate the gross profit forecast! It is useful to know the likely impact on profit of using managerial choice on prices and volumes of business and how these relate to the provision of different resourcing levels.

Looking for a strategic mix of applications

Although there are advantages in integrating data flows across routines — primarily those of accuracy and consistency — there are some disadvantages. Firstly, there is a limit to the amount of change that an organisation can absorb at any one time, so there is a need to prioritise in computerisation. Secondly, for many parts of the spinal process of manufacture, there are simply insufficient volumes of scale to justify computerisation except in a few crucial areas. The inevitable result in any organisation is a mix of computer-assisted and manually run applications. The real skill of effective computer experts is the identification of areas in which a relatively small amount of computerisation can have an impact that is so great that it immediately gives the organisation a strategic advantage over its competitors.

Where would any company start in computerising applications? Is there any optimal sequence?

A company is successful because it 'knows what business it is in' (Drucker, 1954). A business is specialised and owes its success to exceptionally good performance in some critical but limited areas. In the parlance of MbO, these are the *key result areas* (KRAs).

Understanding the KRAs is a great help as they indicate where computerisation may be expected to make the greatest long-term impact. However, experience suggests that two business areas stand out more prominently than others in getting priority for computerisation.

The customer order book

The first relates to managing the customer ordering process and generating data which tell the organisation much about the demand pattern for its products. This is a minimum requirement for any serious attempt at forecasting and corporate planning. Analysis of the order book will reveal levels of customer satisfaction related to achieving delivery dates. The customer order book is likely to be linked to routines for accounts receivable and thus gives assistance in controlling cash flow.

The engineering database

The second business area relates to the control of costs; the natural database for that is the engineering database. Data here specify product structure, routeing, times, tooling records, etc. — the basic fabric of control standards.

Other areas

Beyond this we cannot do much more than identify where there is a performance problem in the spinal processes of the business and develop a strategy to bring on-stream the applications which are most likely to relieve it.

A service industry example

In the banking industry, for example, we do not have to control physical stock, but there will be an active distribution opportunity for financial services. In the 1970s and 1980s this was enhanced by the provision of automatic teller machines (ATMs). With developments in the sophistication of electronic dialogue between customer and bank, a whole new and innovative range of financial services could be pioneered. ATMs were initially perceived as just electronic cash dispensers, which would save labour and reduce queues. Now they may be used to transact loan applications, house mortgage, share dealings, etc. With this mode of deployment of the computer system, the very structure and nature of the service provided is affected, a movement of use from the back office to the front office and beyond, giving computer systems a strategic role and impact on the business.

An example in high-tech manufacturing

In a high-tech industry, design has to be extremely quick. A firm that can complete design of a new circuit in three weeks will clearly have an advantage over another firm which takes three months to produce a similar design. This suggests that initial emphasis on the CAD/CAM part of the product cycle will be crucial. The packages that will be used will probably be very specialised. Indeed, in the late 1980s specialist companies appeared offering sophisticated CAD/CAM consultancy, backed up by hardware and software.

CAD/CAM systems may also be backed up by a system of electronic mail, so that specialist engineers working at different locations may be in constant touch as the design evolves.

The optimal sequence

The difficulty in facing this issue is of being able to recognise and evaluate the knock-on effects which result from computerisation. Many human factors are often at work too. An engineering department may see little advantage in committing its records to a database, whereas the production control people may see this as a vital part of their control of costs and their ability to generate factory schedules.

It is thus necessary to prioritise the programme of computerisation in the light of business objectives in the corporate plan. In addition, account needs to be taken of the necessary facilitating projects to enable database data to flow through the business without the need to recreate it from manual records.

All this requires well-informed decision-making and an organisation structure capable of evaluating and managing computer projects with some objectivity (see chapter 16). Organisational politics may often serve to frustrate this logical development. The reason is simple to understand. Information in a business is such a vital resource in its own right that it confers power and influence on those who control it or withhold it.

If you are using hardware and software packages from different vendors, is this a disadvantage?

Much depends on the scope of the applications which are earmarked for computerisation. The richer the portfolio of applications, the greater the chance that the organisation will have adopted a multi-vendor policy, with the extra complications that this implies. Then the answer is rather unfavourable as essentially it is important to look for compatibility and standardisation of equipment and software. Yet computer applications did not grow from master plans, they grew from *ad hoc* adaptations and developments.

Compatibility

In an ideal world all computer systems and packages would be 100 per cent compatible. Mainframe computers, minicomputers and microcomputers would have compatible operating systems and file structures. Interconnections through networks would follow internationally agreed standards. There are some projects trying to achieve this. Two deserve a special mention. Open Systems Interconnections (OSI) has made some progress, particularly in communication network protocols, and has published many agreed standards, but these are not comprehensive and it takes years for new standards to be defined, approved and adopted. Manufacturing Applications Protocol (MAP) is another set of standards being developed primarily in the CAD/CAM area so that there is better communication with and between robots. For further information see Morgan (1987).

In the market-place many of the competitive battles among computer suppliers are waged on the basis of product ranges that have a wide degree of compatibility, but when the mix of equipment used ranges between eight-bit microcomputers, sixteen-bit micros and thirty-two-bit mainframe computers, it is easy to visualise the difficulties in the achievement of compatibility. Even within the same supplier compatibility can be a problem.

As technology has progressed so rapidly in the 1980s, some experts have predicted that even desk-top computers will exist with thirty-two-bit microprocessors and that compatibility will be achieved through standardisation 'up market'. However, this would cause problems for the pricing structures of mainframes and the current customer base of early models of microcomputer.

Meanwhile, the reality is that we have to live in a world of non-standardisation, with multiple vendors and the need to get systems to interconnect. The response to this is to make 'black boxes' which provide emulators and translators so that software and data designed for one computer can be processed on another. The main disadvantage is that black boxes complicate the system, are expensive, are liable to have bugs, and slow up the processing. And the black boxes can be as expensive as the computer itself.

How long would it take a company to progress with computerisation right through the model?

The simple answer is that it would take far too long. However, normally a company is highly selective in approving the applications that seem to have the greatest business potential, and then buying and customising packages that are already proven. There may be no intention of moving right through the model. Many of the existing manual systems may be perfectly adequate.

To move into a new field of application it may take several hundred man/years of original design to get a working system. This was the situation with the early airline booking systems (400 man/years at British European Airways) and early material requirements planning systems (100 man/years). However, to adopt and customise a proven package running on a mainframe computer, even as complicated as MRP, might only take 10–20 man/years for implementation. However, if the business is very simple then it may be possible to use microcomputer packages and customise from an innovative use of spreadsheets.

As the technology gets smarter and cheaper, and the next generation of managers are educated in computer literacy, it is increasingly believed that computerisation is a creative tool to develop the business. It can be used to improve internal communications, to reduce costs and inventories, to enhance the product/service delivery mechanisms to the customer; it can be the mechanism for changing the shape and structure of the organisation. As long as the business is there and thriving, executives will constantly want to change to take account of opportunities. But in doing this they will not want computerisation to be a 'black hole', sucking up masses of costs. What they will want is a programme of computerisation focused on the long-term business and completely compatible with the objectives of the corporate plan. It may make sense to subject the computing policies to a hard, critical review every year, with developments projected for the next five years. With this longer-term framework it is more likely that hardware/software equipment purchases and applications will be made which achieve compatibility in the flow of data throughout the organisation.

It is most important that computerisation takes place at a pace which the organisation can absorb and that new applications are developed and consolidated. If the pace is forced too fast and control of the business is lost, irreparable damage may be done. Ambitious programmes of computerisation tend to have some risk associated with them.

How do material requirements planning applications tie up with corporate planning?

This is best demonstrated by use of an example. The natural example is the Residential Division of Honeywell in the United States and its manufacturing of the 8,000 different finished thermostats. Another example is Honeywell's Micro-Switch Division of the United Kingdom. The product range of that was only 4,000 different finished micro-switches. The main point of interest is that the system and approach were transplanted from the one host organisation to another and run effectively in both.

The key to the operational link between corporate planning and material requirements planning lies in the role and activity of the corporate forecaster. Figures 15.2 and 15.3 reveal the essence of this role.

The forecaster's role

The forecaster stands at the centre of an information-gathering and interpretation system and he must try to be objective. Thus he will not report to a marketing director or to a manufacturing director, but to a neutral executive or simply to the chairman of the corporate planning group. For a very large organisation such as Residential Division he is likely to be part of a team effort of forecasters in which each team member looks after a share of the product range. Experience seems to be that one person can cover as many as 2,000 discrete product numbers! This seems to be a very large population, and indeed each forecaster will rely on computer assistance to help in the analysis and interpretation of the data. Experience in Micro-Switch Division was similar, with one person looking after 2,000 product listings and just two forecasters looking after the Division.

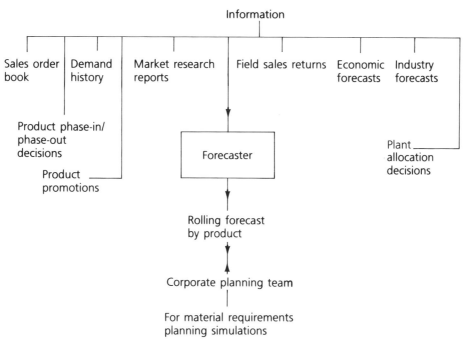

Figure 15.2 *The corporate planning forecaster in action*

The forecaster's aim

The forecaster's aim is to get the best *prediction* of future product business from existing relevant data, both internal to the organisation and external. The forecaster predicts this demand for a particular factory unit. If a good job is done then there will be a good balance of figures by a certain time period, generally for each of the next eighteen months, both for the totals of product families and for the individual products, i.e. the mix is right. If there are a lot of common parts between one item in a product family and another, then accuracy in the product total is more important than accuracy in the mix. If a forecast is inaccurate either business will be lost through quoting long delivery dates or some inventory will be built up which is not immediately saleable. If the industry is one in which the customer is prepared to wait for the whole provisioning cycle, then it would not matter if there was no forecast, but in that case we would still miss out on data which help the calculation of total plant and labour requirements.

The input data for interpretation

Phase-in/phase-out decisions
These are decisions of marketing management. The forecaster simply needs to know what these decisions are and the effective dates. No further predictions are required,

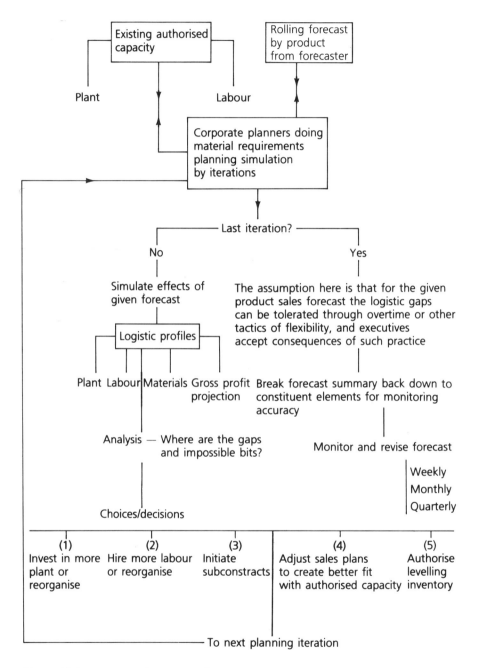

Figure 15.3 *Corporate planning simulations*

but there is a need for good company communications so the forecaster may be aware of what is happening on this front and use this intelligence in the rolling forecast.

Product promotions
Marketing should provide intelligence on promotions and give the forecaster information of the likely impact of price changes and product improvements. Some qualitative interpretation is required to reflect this into the growth/decline figures in the rolling forecast.

Sales order book/demand history
This will show recent movements of business and totals by product for business actually booked. It will link demand for products with particular customers and this may reveal some risk in stocking at the finished product level. These data will often be used in combination with the demand history over the past few years and to provide a basis for identifying demand patterns and seasonal patterns. The current period may be compared with a previous year to indicate areas where there is an underlying trend from a previous pattern of demand.

Projections
Where the forecaster finds products that service a wide range of customers, then it may make sense to get computer programs to do some curve fitting and offer *projections*. These are justified on the basis that with a large population, behaviour is inherently repeatable.

Predictions
However, with 8,000 products in the catalogue list many must be dedicated to a narrow range of customers. By a working rule of thumb, when one customer takes more than 30 per cent of the total product demand then that customer is flagged as a 'major' customer for that identified product, and projection as a technique of forecasting is not attempted. The forecaster will instead look to the salesmen for a direct field forecast return. The salesmen will be in touch with buyers who should know their own 'phase-in/phase-outs' and that direct intelligence is far better than inspired guesswork.

Field sales returns
This data source, mentioned above, needs some management. Salesmen like selling, but often hate doing paperwork. The forecaster highlights to them, from a computer exception report, cases where he needs this return for major customers and has a tracking system for feedback to assess, and in time improve on, the quality of data returned. Sales management agreed that one of the factors used for salesmen in their job appraisals would relate to the quality of these intelligence data, so that its importance was appropriately emphasised.

Market research reports
These may come from both internal and external sources and will particularly influence forecasts for new products, which do not have any history.

Economic forecasts and industry forecasts
These will affect the forecaster when he or she is considering the aggregation of totals by industry and for the company as a whole. The forecaster might well be able to use leading indicators which will guide predictions of future demand for thermostats from an analysis of current house-building starts.

Plant allocation decisions
These decisions are made internally by management and have a particular significance when a company has several plants and operates internationally. We noticed above that a forecaster provides a prediction of product demand to a factory unit, as that is where machinery and labour are provisioned. However efficient a factory might become in manufacturing, if it is working from a bad forecast it will simply make the wrong things! The forecaster will need to be privy to all such plant allocation decisions and their effective dates.

The forecaster's output
The above sections have summarised the forecaster's main information sources and the methods of analysis. The resulting judgements and interpretations are then quantified and put into a database containing a rolling forecast by product for the next eighteen months. These data will also be aggregated so that a dialogue may proceed concerning the data sources, analysis and final quantified figures. This dialogue takes place with the senior executives of the corporate planning committee.

The forecaster and corporate planning team in action
When they have agreed the forecast then it achieves the status of a sales plan, but one supported by the whole executive team under the principle of collective responsibility. However, this agreement does not come easily. A business has finite resources and might not match with market demand, so before agreement is secured the corporate planning committee will conduct some simulations. This part of the process is illustrated in Figure 15.3.

The simulation sequences
In chapter 13 we explored the principles of managing by exception and illustrated these with an explanation of material requirements planning routines (Figure 13.2). However, it was pointed out that the process may be used for looking ahead for the whole year and determine aggregate resource requirements for plant and labour for each week in the future. This may then be plotted as a logistic profile (see Figure 13.4).

We thus have two main inputs to the simulation and one output. The inputs are, firstly, the resource data reflected as currently authorised plant and labour capacity; and secondly, the rolling forecast by product, prepared by the forecaster. The main output consists of the tabulations or screen displays of the logistic profiles. The areas of where there is a discrepancy then become objects of analysis and problem-solving by the corporate planning committee working as an integrated executive group.

Preliminary decisions are made to secure a more realistic fit between expected market demand and authorised resources. After an interval for processing updates to the database, which reflect these decisions, the simulation is repeated. This iterative process continues (generally through three passes done over a working week) until there is sufficient executive support for the adoption of a revised rolling forecast and a revised package of authorised resources. At the end of this process, marketing and the resource providers should be on the same wavelength, and if the principal line departments are in harmony, there should not be much conflict elsewhere.

For small adjustments to resources management would probably assume some overtime and load the pricing mechanism for affected products to maintain profitability. For the larger mismatches there is really no alternative but to invest in more resources or to subcontract. Why not let the vendors take some of the shock of the peak loads, so that the company's own labour force has a natural stability?

If the problem condition is caused by seasonality of demand management must either consider flexible use of plant and labour and dynamic reallocation or the authorisation of some levelling inventory to take the shock out of the system. Stockpiling will always hurt a bit — it needs financing, the inventory might be perishable or bulky or both, or the inventory might become obsolete. If management does decide to indulge in some stockpiling then the MRP programmes will require some easily accessible rules built in, so that there is a firm upper limit set on this compromise.

However, an executive team gains in experience for its own business in exercising discretion and choice under the five basic headings of the model in Figure 15.3. Once they have passed over an initial learning curve, some good judgements may be expected.

Inaccuracy of forecast

The further the forecaster looks into the future the greater its inaccuracy. The response to this dilemma is to review all forecasts very frequently and look out for any signals to indicate a problem. Hence in Figure 15.3 there is a path to be followed after the last simulation cycle. The forecaster's philosophy is: 'If you cannot forecast well, then forecast frequently.'

This means that it is important to break down the finally accepted forecast as far as possible back to the constituent elements which can be related back to the sources of information and judgements made, so that in time forecast accuracy should improve.

However, even if the cause of inaccuracy is known it is still necessary to respond to it, hence the critical review cycles, weekly, monthly and quarterly. At each critical review the forecaster will interpret what is happening and decide whether marginal changes alone should be processed, or whether it is necessary to start again with a clean slate and call in the corporate planning committee to reactivate the planning simulations.

When a forecasting group looks ahead for eighteen months there are several underlying scenarios which form the basis of the forecasting assumptions. Once these scenarios are seen to be false then the forecaster must respond to the changing environment by reactivating the simulations.

It is perfectly possible too that one of the assumptions about authorised resources might have been inaccurate. For instance, an extension to a plant might be contingent on getting planning permission, which in the event is refused. The simulations from the logistic profiles will need an immediate analysis to see what can be done to minimise the ill-effects of a postponed plant investment.

Flexibility

Some people in business shudder at the thought of working with a forecast, as they perceive that all flexibility is lost once the eighteen-month figures have been agreed. But once the frequent critical review cycles are built into the process, management immediately regains its flexibility and can replan far faster than other organisations, which are simply reacting. The early experiences of Residential Division, when they first adopted MRP, was that when the market did expand unexpectedly, they were quicker to respond than their competitors and this led to a long period of achieving an increased market share — a very significant bonus indeed for a large producer.

However, flexibility in a manufacturing plant is also dependent on lead times throughout the cycle for assembly, sub-assembly, machined parts and bought-in materials. The shorter the lead-times, the less work-in-process is likely to be on the shop floor and the easier it is to change direction in the plan. It should be management policy to take measures to reduce lead-times whenever possible in order to make for a slimmer and slicker production system.

The Japanese JIT philosophy of manufacture is based on very short set-up times, small manufacturing lots and zero inventory. The MRP approach of this chapter could reflect exactly the JIT philosophy and work on very low inventories, but it may be preferable to let stock and plant take some shock when the plan runs into problems, rather than the labour force or the customer.

Future development of forecasting

Much of this discussion has emphasised the role of the forecaster in the corporate planning committee, yet this role is not developed in the literature and there are as yet no professional societies which come to mind in supporting such a discipline. Effective product forecasting is clearly vital in the implementation of any MRP system. As soon as top management is committed to this approach, it has little choice but to appoint a forecaster or group and get them to develop a procedure and role which really does fit the industry and organisation. Innovation of all new roles and procedures causes problems, but responding to the techniques of MRP is no more difficult than responding to other new techniques of high technology. As more people do this type of work, there may eventually be a professional society to support it.

Top management too will take some time to get used to the planning simulations from the MRP routines and become comfortable with the interpretations from the logistic profiles. It would seem sensible for much thought to be given to selecting the corporate planning committee, so that it is sufficiently multidisciplinary for good judgements to emerge from the six possibilities of choice outlined in Figure 15.3. The committee also needs authority to confirm the decisions that are made. If the corporate planning committee has only weak advisory powers, it will just be another layer of bureaucracy and will slow up the decision making process and compromise the organisation's flexibility to act.

Summary

In this chapter the reader was taken briefly through the life cycle of the manufacturing process, called the 'spinal process', to identify the main stages from design to after sales-service. From this broad review, groupings of possible computer applications and databases associated with each were derived. This is in line with developments in the contemporary information society.

Next, an attempt was made to suggest policies for introducing computer applications where they would be most likely to secure a strategic impact for the organisation. Some difficulties were encountered owing to incompatibility of equipment. Particular emphasis was then placed on finding useful starting points for computer applications; the sales order book was one and the engineering database another. These would help the organisation to make good use of marketing intelligence; and the application of costing and timing standards.

Examples of applications were considered. Fast design of chips through use of CAD/CAM was looked at, as were enhanced financial services through ATMs. Finally, the discussion turned to MRP routines and their activation within a corporate planning committee, with assistance from a forecaster and using simulations. The underlying aim was to demonstrate how computer systems could facilitate a more flexible and pro-active business.

Exercise 15.1
Possible seminar or project topics

1. Select an organisation of your own choice and from the spinal process of its operations suggest priorities for computer applications.
2. CAD/CAM and MRP have some common elements in the databases which link their applications. What are these? What are the advantages to be had when the linkages are achieved through compatible computer systems?
3. What sets of choices and decisions are expected when a manager is interpreting print-outs or visual displays on screen from the simulations provided by logistic profiles? In what ways may use of this technique give an organisation a strategic advantage over one not using the technique?

4. If interactive dialogue through computers is further developed, what could this do to enhance financial services through automatic teller machines?

References

Drucker, P. (1954), *The Practice of Management*, Harper.
Morgan, E. (1987), *Through MAP to CIM*, Department of Trade and Industry.

Further reading

Hordeski, M.F. (1986), *CAD/CAM Techniques*, Prentice Hall. See particularly chapters 1, 9 and 10.
Laudon, K.C. and Laudon, J.P. (1988), *Management Information Systems, A Contemporary Perspective*, Macmillan.
Medland, A.J. and Burnett, P. (1986), *CAD/CAM in Practice: A Manager's Guide to understanding and using CAD/CAM*, Kogan Page. See particularly chapters 3 and 7.
Orlichy, J. (1975), *Material Requirements Planning*, McGraw-Hill.
Schonberger, R.J. (1982), *Japanese Manufacturing Techniques*, Macmillan.

Chapter 16

Design and implementation of advanced management information systems

Overview

In this chapter attention is directed to organisational and behavioural issues which must be faced if implementation of computerised systems is to be achieved in an orderly and systematic manner. However, two separate themes are involved. The traditional approach is based on mainframe computers located within data processing departments with data processing specialists prominent as a centralised influence in the organisation. The modern approach is based on minicomputers, microcomputers and dedicated computers located throughout the organisation and run chiefly by the end-user. In this latter approach the end-user seeks self-sufficiency and adopts much of the computing skill right into the line management process. If help is required, consultancy is provided by experts, but the prime influence lies with the end-users themselves.

Real organisations generally use a mixture of approaches. Mainframe computers have such a strong position, with a tradition going back some thirty years, so some design and implementation is done with the traditional centralised, specialist approach, some with modern decentralised approaches, and the result is a rather awkward relationship in some end-user situations.

The purpose of this chapter is to give the reader an outline of the organisation of a central data processing department and a synopsis of the stages in the design of information systems, and to review teamwork which must be developed between systems designers and the users of the information system. This review will concentrate on how line managers may develop a more purposeful rapport with systems design experts so that further participation may be achieved in the difficult process of systems implementation.

The discussion will turn to modern methods and how they put the user into the forefront of systems design decisions. An environment is assumed in which both mainframe computer systems and microcomputers, both as stand-alone machines and in networks, coexist.

The chapter begins with a critical review of the relationships between a parent organisation and its specialist data processing department, going back in time to when the first mainframe computer was an innovation in a business. The main points of conflict and differing expectations are examined. The chapter then proceeds to develop various models of good practice responses to such difficulties and offers discussion and comparisons of these.

A main outcome is a preferred model of organisation for the data processing function and a definition of the stages of design, which facilitate the necessary specification, validation, implementation and maintenance of information systems. Within this model it is shown how policy decisions may be developed for the effective deployment of information technology resources, policies which are congruent with the strategic objectives and strategies emanating from the corporate plan.

Account is then taken of the variations from this general model in the light of the availability of much pre-packaged application software and the growth of software houses, which may undertake much of the systems development process.

A critical view is also taken of the security implications of reliance on computerised systems. Some good practice responses, which are necessary to minimise the threat posed to the continuity of the business through failure of the data processing facility, are also examined.

Two cases are then included for the reader to analyse using the models of good practice to draw out the salient points of weak practice.

Introduction

The purpose of this section is to describe some organisation structures appropriate for the data processing function and comment on a good practice approach and the forces behind its evolution.

Data processing as a major functional department has a relatively short history. Initially, in the earlier 1960s, computing was not considered more than a narrow specialist activity, which simply supported accounting and payroll processing, but with little impact on the organisation of the company as a whole. In these early days it was common practice to locate the data processing department under the accountancy function, often with an accountant as the first manager. Initially, the design of computerised systems was not much of a problem within this narrow field. The usual strategy was simply to mirror the manual system in computerised procedures; the benefits tended to be that the systems were more accurate and ran faster. There were improvements in efficiency, but not in organisational effectiveness.

However, in the late 1960s other applications were developed using the power of the computer to deal with numbers and also organise data so that they could flow across the functional departments and play a major role in the operational decisions of the organisation. The problem with this development was that the computerised systems that emerged were often radically different from the previous manual systems which they replaced. They offered the expert a powerful computing tool to extend his expertise and provided new methods of planning and control for much of the organisation. Some imaginative companies saw the potential offered by computing and used computer techniques to extend the very heart of their product range and delivery strategies. An example of this is Reuters, the news-gathering organisation. They realised the market value of collecting and disseminating information on movements of commodity prices and specialised in this, building on the computerised database set up for the gathering of news. The impact was to increase the asset value of the company a hundredfold. Computers were being taken out of the 'back office' of the organisation and used at the sharp end in marketing, engineering, manufacturing and many other vital areas of the company in addition to the traditional areas such as accounting. The banks too followed these principles and used computer-based automatic teller machines to offer a new style of service.

'When you buy a computer it is a more complicated decision than buying a lawnmower.' This is a celebrated quotation from Professor Roy Wilkie of Strathclyde University. He makes the point that computers are major organisational tools and that they will affect the way things are done. Managers and experts will need to revise radically their styles and expertise to take advantage of the potential enhancements offered. Departments of data processing needed to adjust to their new role as a major force for change in the organisation. What could be done in data processing could generate shock-waves through the entire organisation. The rechanelling of information could upset the delicate internal political power structure of the organisation and bring about changes in the occupational roles of many administrators and experts.

David Allner

In his indictment of data processing departments, 'The lamentable isolationism of data processing' (1974), David Allner accuses them of deliberately taking an isolationist stand and of consequently failing to make a creative contribution to the development of control and decision-making mechanisms within the organisation structure. Extracts from David Allner's article are published with permission of *Computing Magazine*.

The problems — Allner's perspective

Data processing continues to be an intellectual island in the sea of practical business reality. DP management in general has expressed a desire to become more associated with the business, but still persists in its isolationist behaviour.

From management's point of view data processing often seems pointless and confusing — pointless, because after all the shouting the company is no more efficient; confusing because DP staff often seem to be saying one thing and doing another.

DP's propensity for conceit knows no bounds. This conceit stems from patting itself on the back for working solely for the user, while continuing to be organised in such a way that it isolates itself from the organisation and the potential user.

DP fails to respond to the needs of the organisation because of its incestuous nature. This is demonstrated by DP management's concern with the internal structuring and politics of the DP department, but rarely with thinking out a changed approach to DP which will better satisfy the organisation's needs.

DP management is often caught between two stools. It does not have the confidence to specify to the organisation the limitations of computing and to determine realistic plans. On the other hand, it does not know how to deal with being used by the organisation as a short-term prop to shore them up. The result is that DP often does unproductive work which engenders suspicion and mistrust within the organisation's management structure.

Organisations have their own mechanisms and very few DP departments see it as a priority to define these. The process of developing organisations must in time lead to the more effective application of computer systems to the control and decision-making mechanisms in the organisation. This is because computers are organisational tools, not the tools of individual people. This means that the practice of DP in time will have to be modified to concern itself primarily with the motivation and participation of the people within the organisation. This will not be an easy process.

Allner views the solution as follows:

1. Decentralise as much computing as possible to divisional teams which will be nearer to the real problems.
2. Alter the process of systems analysis so that techniques can be developed which enable organisations to define their own systems problems, using the systems analyst as an adviser and coordinator.
3. Develop techniques that enable people in organisations to become more aware about systems in general and about the status of their own systems. Capitalise on this consciousness to motivate them and gain their participation and commitment.
4. Structure DP as part of an overall function including multidisciplinary teams of line and staff specialists, but with a much sharper perception of the underlying business perspectives.
5. Accept that systems once implemented are rarely more, initially, than an embryo, a target for further enhancement and integration with other company systems.

Evaluation

Allner's problem diagnosis has much to commend it, as there are still some communication problems between DP specialists and line management and systems often fail to meet their full potential. At the same time there is now a much greater awareness of computers and their capabilities than in 1974. The development of the personal computer and the wide use of work-stations, word processing and spreadsheet applications, together with much attention from the media, has ensured this greater awareness, but Allner's solution does require refinement and development to reflect current good practice. This chapter attempts to take us to that position of good practice.

The trap of expectations

The following is a further explanation of bad relationships between DP and line management. A crucial question is that of why DP often designs the wrong or hopelessly inadequate systems. Is this solely because of bad will or is there an aspect of organisation structure which plays a part?

There is much evidence to suggest the latter. Consider the following chain of events which may happen in a large organisation:

1. Top management authorises the purchase of an expensive computer system, maybe for a vague objective relating to public pressures to be seen to be up-to-date and innovative. However, there is a high degree of expectation for the DP manager to make an immediate impact on a variety of organisational problems.
2. The data processing team are formed. They go out to senior members of the organisation seeking involvement and participation and find to their disquiet that the managers are very busy, cannot easily articulate their information needs and find it difficult to conceptualise their own decision-making process (see Mintzberg, 1973). As a result, involvement and participation becomes really sticky. There is, however, still a high degree of pressure on DP to deliver systems on time to justify the initial investment.
3. DP specialists return to their own home department. At best they have partial commitment from the line departments and a patchy picture of the line environment, as line managers were not too willing to reveal very much and succumb to pressure for increased competence, yet the need to deliver working systems still exists. DP specialists tend to be well-qualified and have a strong instinct for survival, so they withdraw to their ivory tower (there is nowhere else to go) and design the systems which they perceive reflect line management needs. What a blissful escape this turns out to be. Months can go by in systems development and it can be so much faster without the constant involvement of other people and the stupid snags which they keep coming up with to frustrate progress.
4. There are high expectations for successful systems delivery and when systems are delivered there are cries of pain from the client managers. The business strategic concepts were totally misread. There were many informal practices in the running of the line department operation and these have been ignored, so the computerised systems simply will not run!
5. As a result of this chaotic and expensive waste there is no alternative but to go back to the drawing-board and start the proper process of systems development from a firm foundation.
6. The first thing to think about is the question of system ownership. Is the system finally a DP system or a line management system with DP providing the resources? Who should take the decisions on priorities for computer application in design and development? How should policy rules be articulated,

interpreted and later possibly amended? These are fundamentally questions stemming from principles of managerial responsibility and accountability.

Credible systems design

This section should be read in conjunction with the organisation charts given in Figures 16.1, 16.2 and 16.3. The aim is to find a structure which allows credible systems design and leaves ownership in the hands of line management.

The policy unit

The first component of structure is clearly the policy unit; this is generally called the computer steering committee. This group consists of senior managers who should also be members of the organisation's corporate planning group. It is their experience with the corporate planning group which gives them a first-hand picture of the organisation's basic mission, objectives, values and ethos. If the steering committee does a good job, it will ensure that data processing priorities and projects are those that further the corporate strategy of the organisation. This is a critical role fitting computer systems and capability directly to corporate strategy. If the company is chaotic and does not use corporate planning it is likely to have major problems in operating any computing applications other than rudimentary book-keeping. The clear articulation of corporate strategy is an essential input to any advanced data processing strategy.

The executive unit

Leadership

The data processing manager needs a place on the computer steering committee and a reporting relationship which enables him or her to offer computing widely throughout the organisation. In the United Kingdom the function generally associated with this neutral position within the company is that of Director of Management Services. In the United States the position might be called Manager, Director or Vice-President of Information Services. Note that it is most unlikely to be one of the functional managers, from marketing, finance, manufacturing or engineering, as if that were the situation then the principle of organisational neutrality would be broken. Management services is often a happy choice as there are likely to be other corporate sections under the same umbrella. These may be specialist groups such as work study, operations research and an organisations and methods group. These other sections may well contribute on an *ad hoc* basis to data processing projects, adding their special expertise during appropriate stages in the systems design process. The data processing department can thus gather considerable resources of a multidisciplinary nature from internal staffing of management services.

Internal organisation of the data processing department

There are many alternatives here. The main options will be outlined. Firstly, in nearly all organisations there will be an operations group. This is responsible for scheduling the workload of the computer, crewing the computer, staffing the tape and disk library, setting up communications terminals and dealing with the vendors of computing equipment. In summary, the operations group run the logistics of the current operation. They are like a factory production unit except that the output is a service giving information instead of goods.

In organisations that are highly dependent on running mature information systems without hiccups, some importance and prestige attaches to the function of computer operations management and the measures of service and satisfaction that this vital unit requires. A modern approach is for users and the operations manager to develop a service agreement and review this frequently, so that priorities and difficulties are well understood and managed.

Secondly, there will be a group responsible for creating new systems. Here there is likely to be more deviation in practice. The grouping as a whole is generally referred to as a systems and programming group (see Figure 16.1). The main occupational roles

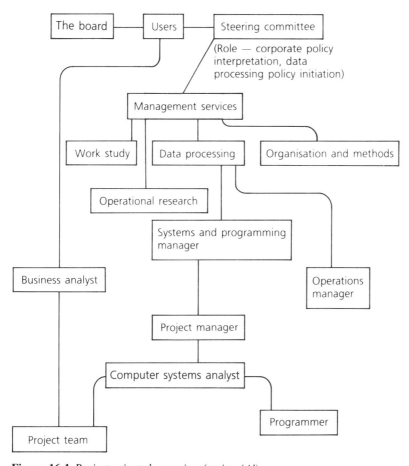

Figure 16.1 *Project-oriented grouping (option 'A')*

of those who work in this area are those of systems analysts, who design systems and work with the user groups; programmers, who program computers starting with specifications written by systems analysts; and analyst/programmers, who design systems from contact with the user groups and also program them, generally from someone else's specifications.

Project-oriented organisational grouping — option 'A'   Under this option the key manager is called the systems and programming manager. The group is then split under various project groupings each under a project group manager. Each project is then headed by a project manager or a senior systems analyst. The emphasis here is on project management and in each team there will be the number of analysts and programmers for the current workload of the project. The project team will have an involvement over the whole of the project's life. Note that in this organisation structure, career development is an on-going activity and it is absolutely normal for staff to progress from programming work to systems work, followed by project management. The work environment within the project team is stimulating and staff development policy can be operated creatively since there is the opportunity to offer a wide range of project assignments to each team member; as a result, he or she should grow in experience through such close contact with other team specialists.

Functionally-oriented organisational grouping — option 'B'   Under this option, illustrated in Figure 16.2, the group is split into two main sub-groups. The systems analysts are grouped under a systems manager; the programmers are grouped under a programming manager. There will be no one in the role of analyst/programmer. The emphasis is on specialisation in the separate roles. The user departments need to maintain contact with both managers to ensure progress of the computer systems application. In terms of career development it is difficult to progress from programming to systems work in this structure without leaving and re-entering the organisation.

Further variations   As very large organisations are using computer systems, and a wider range of equipment is adopted, it is possible that specialisation may reflect the organisation of the parent company, i.e. divisional groups or groups from a certain company location, or may reflect the main components of hardware, i.e. groups for mainframe computer, groups for minicomputers, groups for personal computers.

Comments on option 'A' and option 'B' grouping   In the early days of computing the basic structure of option 'A' tended to be the natural informal organisation structure and was widely adopted. Two major difficulties emerged.

Firstly, the contact base in the project team was too narrow, and it needed much more forceful involvement from the user department to ensure reality of the system and to transfer ownership of the system to the user. This required the creation of a new occupational category, the business analyst, appointed by the user department to represent their interests and working as a key member of an expanded project team. (More will be said about this concept later.)

Secondly, working in this informal structure meant that documentation was often patchy or wholly neglected. Computer systems are very complex and if the rules and

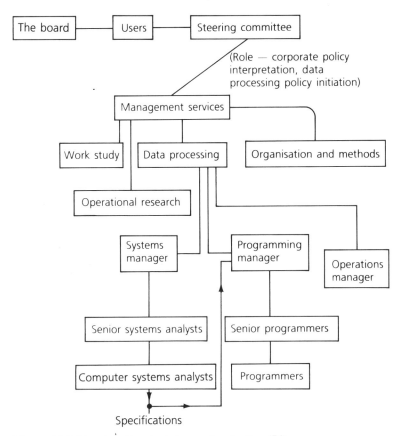

Figure 16.2 *Functionally-oriented grouping (option 'B')*

policies are not visible then the system becomes the master rather than the malleable slave of the user. Although it is easy to have good intentions of documenting after the event, in reality project groups are under such pressures to produce results that staff are often reassigned to other groups before this is completed. It is well-nigh impossible to get technical people to give the documentation the emphasis that it requires. If they are the only ones to know what the computer is doing then they have the opportunity to use this unique knowledge as a lever to 'hijack' the company.

As the failure of major computer systems can be devastating to cash flow and other vital company areas the 'hijack' can be a serious threat. In the interests of developing 'robust' systems many companies adopted option 'B' in preference to option 'A'

Under option 'B' the mode of operation is to generate specifications, then pass these through the bureaucracy from the systems group to the programming group. The latter will not respond until the specification is regarded as interpretable without any loose ends. In reality the specifications generally need some editing before they are good enough for the programming stage to take place. The programming is closely supervised with high standards enforced and sometimes structured programming techniques are used to ensure that one programmer can follow the work of another. Maintenance demands are also initiated by formal maintenance requests and preceded by specifications. The specification (pre-documented) approach is the pillar of stability for the systems design process and offers a permanent visibility of the policies and rules written into the system. With that visibility the system is the user's slave rather than its master! There is, of course, a snag — an enormous amount of time is spent in running the bureaucracy of contact between systems manager and programming manager and the users become frustrated at the rigmarole to reflect priorities. In systems design and development there are many points of interdependence and the managers have no chance of grasping all such points so the development process is painfully slow. Users become frustrated. Their projects need a much more integrated treatment for the implementation stage to be achieved.

Users are now requiring more sophisticated applications so there is intense pressure to revert to the project organisation — option 'A' — but to run this with sufficient ground-rules to overcome the lack of documentation or 'hijack' problem. This may be done by adopting a rigorous role segregation within the project team. The ground-rule becomes that a person never does both the systems work and programming on the same part of the system. This preserves the *specification* basis of the documentation. The project manager has to be a 'policeman' to enforce this rule rigorously.

The key roles of computer systems analyst and business analyst

This is a further discussion about option 'A' — the project approach. Earlier discussion focused on the issue of system ownership and the need to lock in user participation. Traditionally, textbooks and courses have concentrated their attention on the activity of the 'systems man', given the role the label of computer systems analyst, and assumed that this activity is done by a single group of staff all reporting to data processing management. Allner pointed out the need for the DP department to be aware of the organisation's business needs, but the reality is that the computer systems analyst, initially anyway, has great difficulty in empathising with this. His or her training and expertise is primarily with computers rather than with business and in reality the fields are very different. Equally, one cannot expect the high-level managers of the computer steering committee to have the time or to have sufficient grasp of operational detail of current systems to play an effective user-representative role. Large organisations tend to have many levels in the hierarchy and the operating perspective is very easily lost. A solution (post-Allner) has been to divide the systems role into two distinctive but complementary roles, hence the role and classification of business analyst. And it is essential to provide an enriched and active role for this occupant. The business analyst is appointed for his or her in-depth knowledge of current working practices, objectives and ethos in the user area. Note that the reporting relationship is directly to user management and appointment is also by them. In systems design there are several major functions and phases (in this analysis we concentrate on eleven), and we must be clear where the business analyst has major involvement and examine how the teamwork relationship with the computer systems analyst should develop. A brief general list follows, which is also discussed more fully later in this chapter:

1. Feasibility study:
   (a) investigation,
   (b) systems proposal,
   (c) economic evaluation.
2. Proposal validation.
3. Detailed systems specification.
4. Specification validation.
5. Program specification.
6. Program validation.
7. Program writing and testing.
8. Data collection.
9. Systems testing.
10. Implementation:
    (a) management and clerical training,
    (b) issue of implementation manual,
    (c) pilot runs,
    (d) 'go live' decision.
11. System maintenance and post-system audit.

From the above activities it will be noted that the activity of *validation* is given equal prominence to that of proposal and investigation. In reality it is comparatively easy for a bright systems analyst to think through a business problem and to offer a solution. The real skill comes in steering such a solution through the process of validation to win the support of the organisation for the changes implied. User groups can have internal organisational politics, which are barely visible to the outsider, but may be manifested by resistance to change. For effective systems design we need both the expertise to undertake the design and the ability to manage the change process. The two processes are inextricably dependent on one another. The role of the business analyst is crucial for activating the validation process and the management of change. The major involvements of the business analyst are discussed below.

Economic evaluation is essential because, unless the user is committed to achieving the real benefits outlined and can vouch for the positive cash flows involved, their realism and the projected pay-off period, there is no case to proceed.

Under the proposal validation the user must be convinced that the system fits its formal and informal environment and reflects its ethos and values. If the validation is competently done it is much more difficult later for the user to abort the system, for the validation represents commitment.

Under specification validation, the business analyst must take all colleague managers and section leaders through the proposed system and to get them to validate it at their own level in order to consolidate user support.

Under data collection, the business analyst must ensure that the files from his user colleagues are comprehensive, accurate and audited. When data are computerised, ownership is still the ownership of the user department.

Under systems testing, the business analyst should not only have the common transactions tested, but also all conceivable error conditions, to ensure that the system is robust enough to cope with even unusual situations. During this stage he or she will work closely with the computer systems analyst as systems testing is a joint task.

Under implementation, the business analyst will have a major role in training managers and others in the new system before it goes live. This task is done jointly with the computer systems analyst, and one useful outcome of this stage is the preparation of an *implementation* manual, which captures the spirit and detail of the training sessions and provides a working 'cook-book' for guidance of users during and after implementation, when the new system is at its most vulnerable.

Under maintenance, it is the business analyst who is the most likely to initiate and justify maintenance requests. If the systems design process has been competently done these should not be significant in the early life of the system, but environments are hostile and in the end the system must respond to the changing environment if it is to retain any usefulness and credibility.

The business analyst will also play a supportive role in stage 1, the investigation. All interviews by the computer systems analyst will be organised through the business analyst, so that the whole business picture of the user environment is communicated to the computer systems analyst, and responsibility for informing the designer is put squarely in the hands of the user group. This is in contrast to what is taught in many conventional texts on systems development, where the computer systems analyst is expected to do the whole investigation, but for an organisation determined to resist computerisation it is easy to hoodwink the technical person coming from the systems department. In contrast, once entry to the organisation is through the business analyst as an organisational gate-keeper, we should start getting realistic data to form the basis of systems design.

In essence the key to robust systems design is empathy throughout the project between the computer systems analyst, who reports to data processing management, and the business analyst, who reports to the user department. This is nurtured within the management structure of a multidisciplinary project group. In time, with a good working relationship, some element of bilingualism will emerge. The business analyst, the expert on the user environment and ethos, will develop an appreciation of computing concepts. The computer systems analyst, the expert on computing concepts, will develop an appreciation of the user's business environment. In some design situations, for instance, advanced scheduling of a factory, it might be necessary to call on further expertise, such as that of the operational researcher. In this situation this expert should join the project design team for the period of his or her contribution. With the appropriate experts in the design team and some goodwill it should be possible to develop a positive problem-solving posture for the effective deployment of computerised systems. The key management norm for driving the empathetic project team is collaboration rather than competition among the members. With a well-run project the project leadership will also be flexible. At some stages in the project it may be appropriate for the computer systems analyst to be leader, at others it may be far more appropriate for the business analyst to be leader. In no circumstances should the user feel that he is merely tolerated to make way for data processing to usurp the line management function by manipulating the flow of information, preventing line management from doing their basic job.

The social skills of both the computer systems analyst and business analyst will be significant. Many computer projects have ramifications across several departments, and thus the territories of different business analysts, and it may be a considerable diplomatic job to define business policies which are sufficiently precise for computer interpretation in the specified system and which command support from all the user departments concerned. Often there may be conflict and resistance to the whole notion of computerisation. In this instance the computer systems analyst will need to know how to activate interest at a higher organisational level to resolve conflict and clash of priorities, before it is possible to work more fluently with his colleagues, the business analysts.

Some organisations have been so impressed with the notion and concept of the business analyst that they have enriched the role, so that there are no computer systems analysts at all in the data processing department and all design activity is done from a user perspective (see Figure 16.3, option 'C'). In reported instances of this approach being adopted, severe strains and problems were also reported as the business analysts were so user-oriented they did not have the computer expertise to communicate effectively with programmers.

Prototyping

The major snag in conventional design/validation sequences is the time taken. In the 1980s the personal computer came into its own and with it a wide range of computer packages. Packages do not normally require respecification for every user, but every user needs to select options and possible adjustments to the specified system. The process of proposing a solution and getting it validated (see above) is often done through the process of prototyping. The computer systems analyst will sit alongside the business analyst and the two will unpack the package and jointly walk through possible options until they can make positive recommendations. This is a very useful development as it enables an end-user to get a real feel for the final product during the design process, rather than being pressured into validating a specification some of whose inputs, reports, screens, etc., can only with difficulty be visualised as a complete working system from the specification.

Prototyping is particularly useful when the new system is different in nature from the old system, as it allows the user to visualise what the changes will be before he or she has the experience of it. However, prototyping is only possible when the back-up software is sophisticated and the designer can activate options quickly and easily without significant redesign time. In the 1980s very significant advances were made to put this flexibility and choice into software packages and improve dramatically the level and quality of communication between designer and user.

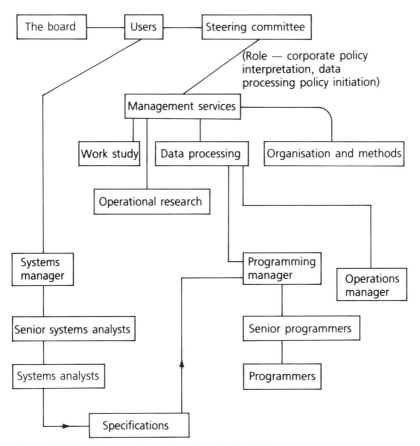

Figure 16.3 *Business analyst orientation (option 'C')*

Conclusion

Current good practice in DP organisation is on balance reflected more in option 'A' (Figure 16.1), the project-oriented approach, than in any of the other models, but to achieve the advantages of this structure great care must be taken in the competent management of the project teams. When the project team method is really working fluently the result should be 'integrated bilingualism', where the team as a whole can appreciate all the problem-solving/organisational political issues as a whole to implement supported and robust systems. This is a major advance on the tentative solution suggested by Allner (1974).

Stages in the design of computerised systems

Stage 1   Feasibility study

The feasibility study includes the investigation, the systems proposal and the economic evaluation. It is the first stage in any computer application and provides the basis of management decisions for the whole project life. The outcome of the feasibility study is a recommendation to proceed or otherwise on a computer solution to a defined application area. Normally, there are three distinct aspects of feasibility.

Technical Feasibility

Under this heading the practicalities of getting the computer to do what is required and apply the rules to the situation under review is being looked at. Why would a manual solution still not be more practical? What particular advantages would accrue from a computer solution — short- and long-term?

Economic Feasibility

Under this heading the project is considered as though it were an economic proposition to be judged by financial criteria such as pay-off period or internal rate of return (IRR). The cash flow of benefit should be constructed, with user commitment to attain such a benefit if they get the system. The computer people will normally give outlines of time and cost to complete the cash flow projection. On the basis of the long-term economic health IRR is a useful indicator of relative priority for judging one project against another. Difficulties arise in assessing intangibles such as better control, better planning or better customer service. One would normally expect a pay-off period of less than five years and in excess of 30 per cent IRR. A much shorter period would be expected for the dedicated project, which did not have some overall place in the computer implementation strategy. Accountants often place too much emphasis on the length of the pay-off period, but ambitious projects such as CAD/CAM applications or material requirements planning may well take a number of years for the impact to be felt, but will then offer very high rates of IRR and possibly a major competitive advantage.

Business Feasibility

Under this heading a wider look is taken at feasibility in general. An organisation needs to be able to *adopt* a computerised solution. The new methods to be applied may be alien to the existing staff, and some retraining or restaffing may be necessary. The timing of this may be difficult. The unions may have a strong presence and influence to retain the status quo. There may be many other considerations. It is important to establish to what extent this particular proposal reflects the soundness of computing strategy and some sense of positive leverage. Leverage is positive when for a low input of computer resources a high benefit is obtained.

Overall feasibility

The feasibility proposal fails unless there is a green light of approval from all three aspects of feasibility. If one area is overlooked there is increasing risk that the project will not be sufficiently supported for the eventual benefit to be obtained. Commonly, the outcome is positive on all three counts of feasibility but the priority is not sufficiently high to do more than get the project into the queue for later development.

Stage 2   Proposal validation

The proposal contained in the feasibility study is destined for user management. They need to give formal approval to proceed. They are expected to verify all the policies written into the proposal, plus the aims and objectives of the system, and state that they are compatible with corporate objectives. They are expected to be aware of the logistics and resources required in outline to complete the project. If the go-ahead is given, they are committed to the resource provisions in the proposal. The business analyst has a major role here in providing recommendations to senior management. For complex systems, embracing more than one part of the organisation, it may be necessary for the data processing project team to make oral presentations to management to supplement the written proposal in the feasibility study.

Stage 3   Detailed systems specification

The proposal validation gives the project team terms of reference to continue the design phase to the next level of detail. All operating aspects of the system — its logic, detailed report layouts, screen layouts, and its main operating procedures, as they affect the operating management and support staff in the user areas — will be specified, as well as links with other computerised systems. The specification will be directed at the user and couched in user style language. The business system specified in detail will be expected to provide operating procedures which are practical for the user and which will enable users to do their jobs. When a database is part of the specification, care will be taken that its design takes account of other users.

The common unit of the systems specification is a grouping called a computer run. This may be identified by a run number or a job number, so that after the design stage the user can apply to the computer operations manager to schedule that job number. Each run will thus cover a particular and distinctive part of the business operation. The computer systems analyst also has to produce the technical part of the specification and for each run this is a 'suite' of program specifications, written at the level of detail which will enable a programmer to program without further contact with the analyst. The program specification is the prime piece of documentation for each program. The programmer will supplement this with details of how he or she has accomplished the task in such a way that another programmer would have no difficulty in following the logic.

In principle the specification of an information system is akin to the specification of an engineering structure. No one in his right mind would think of designing the Forth Bridge on the back of an envelope. In reality the design would be manifested in a series of blueprints, each offering an ever-increasing level of detail for review and approval by clients and other design specialists, to ensure the compatibility and robustness of the whole design. An information system is similar, as the flow of information does indeed have a structure and many points of interdependence, and if compatibility is not achieved, overall performance will be poor. Furthermore, the later improvement of a poorly specified system will be very difficult. You can only change what is visible and understandable, and computer staff are mobile, moving from project to project, company to company, taking their experience with them. The design specifications become the permanent record of design to insulate the system from any threat to continuity.

Stage 4   Specification validation

The business analyst will formally take the specified design and walk through it with any colleagues who will be affected and seek their approval. The conclusion of this process of validation is a signal that the project team can proceed.

Stage 5   Program specification

This activity is done after the computer systems analyst has completed the design of the computer runs in suites of programs.

Stage 6   Profram validation

Before programming can begin the programmer will want to be convinced that the specification is complete and understandable, both in business terms and in technical terms. The programmer has the right to refuse to start until all the loose ends have been tidied up and notes of interpretation added to cover any problem areas. Some contact may be permitted between the computer systems analyst who specified the program and the programmer, but this should not be a frequent dialogue, as that would indicate a lack of completeness in the specification. Inevitably some design changes may be imposed by user influence during design, but this may be very expensive in terms of redesign time and should be logged. Ideally, after the system specification has been validated, a freeze is put in operation for the programming phase and alterations will be dealt with later as a maintenance request.

Stage 7   Program writing and testing

This can be a difficult scheduling problem. Those in the project management team should have a good feel for when the programs are needed. This may influence the phase of data capture and training, so analysts should have considerable influence in the management of this activity. However, programs also have to be tested both individually and as a group, and testing may take as long as the original coding. The philosophy in testing should be one of 'destructive' testing. The key test is whether the program will be able to respond to hostile conditions as well as being able to cope with normal ones. The programmer should open and maintain a documentation file for each program under development, which should contain the design specification, design techniques, samples of input and output, a checklist of the test data and test results, a maintenance section to reveal authorised maintenance requests and details of release to operations as a working program.

Stage 8   Data collection

This phase may affect both the business analyst, representing the users, and the computer systems analysts. Original data may need collecting in the user area and this could be a major sub-project in its own right, with a need to audit the data on collection. The data collected may already be on computer file in other systems and simply need re-formatting, which the computer systems analyst can organise.

Stage 9   Systems testing

This is an activity for the whole project team. The object is to test the application as a whole. Programmers have already fully tested individual programs and now testing needs to be done on a group basis, first for each suite of programs and then finally linking the suites to form the application as a whole. A successful systems test is a precondition for the final activity, 10, implementation.

Stage 10   Implementation

Implementation includes the following aspects:

1. Management and clerical training,
2. Issue of the implementation manual,
3. Pilot runs,
4. 'Go live' decision.

Implementing a new system can hold major risks for the continuity of the business if it fails in the critical first few weeks of operation. Hence there is a need for staff and managers to have a working confidence in the new system. Managers do not relish the prospect of losing control and it is essential that they have a first-hand familiarity with its operation, as they have a line responsibility for seeing that all other staff affected will be competent in the system. Commonly this phase is organised by the business analyst, but as the computer systems analyst is so familiar with the computer logic it is likely that he or she will assist in training and helping users to interpret possible unexpected results.

The *implementation manual* will be created during this phase to reflect the training and be edited into a 'cook-book' for instant reference by users as a self-help for them. If no implementation manual is available to spread the know-how of system operation there will be an unacceptably high degree of pressure on the project team during the critical implementation days. The implementation manual will reflect ideas in the system specification, but will be a more selective, concise, self-help document.

Pilot runs may be possible when the new computer system mirrors much of the old system, but they are not always possible as the new system may be entirely different in nature from the old. Pilot running, where applicable, reduces the risk of failure during implementation, but costs a lot in terms of delay.

The 'go-live' decision should be the result of a joint recommendation for the project team and top user management. User management have line responsibility and will not want to expose their business to unnecessary risk. They may well insist on having contingency plans ready. The business analyst will play a major role here as the user's representative on the project team.

Stage 11   System maintenance and post-system audit

Once a system has been implemented and accepted as a production running system it must be backed up with the appropriate maintenance requests, which are usually triggered by the business analyst. These will normally be costed and prioritised before being accepted and scheduled. When a program change is involved an audit trail reflecting the change will appear in the program file.

Usually some six months after system implementation a post-system audit is conducted to review the performance of the system. Error rates are scrutinised, the volume and pattern of maintenance requests are inspected, the time and cost of systems design and implementation are compared to the budget and an assessment is made of the benefit derived as expected from the original feasibility study proposal. The pay-off period or IRR rates are looked at to review the economic aspects of the system.

Essentially this represents management accountability in the systems development process. Users are responsible for getting the system benefit and the audit should throw up variances. From these variances and appreciation of the underlying reasons for them the organisation should learn how better to use and manage the resource of data processing. When full management accountability has arrived for the DP function that should mark the end of Allner's problem of isolationism of DP.

Use of computer bureaux

An alternative to having an in-house data processing department is to use a bureau on a contract basis; indeed, many DP installations were only established after they got too big for a bureau to handle. Bureaux exist in a variety of forms: some just apply a narrow range of application packages run on a bureau machine; some supply a dedicated service for one part of the DP activity such as data preparation; while some apply a 'turn-key' operation, in which they assume responsibility for the systems work, programming and running of the whole system. The organisation employing the bureau does, however, need to have some system for commissioning and validating the work of the bureau; at a minimum they need a computer steering committee and a business analyst to provide the design link with the 'turn-key' operators.

A positive feature of this type of relationship is that it gives realistic costs for the service supplied, and this in itself helps management to be more aware of the true costs of computerisation. In-house DP installations, in contrast, are usually set up as cost centres and this creates pressures to computerise routines to get utilisation of the computer, but with poor justification. Some two or three years later when the machine is fully committed to marginal applications, the more important ones are rejected for lack of capacity, but it is politically difficult to convert computerised applications to manual ones again so one is left with an embarrassing overhead! Some mature installations are deliberately reorganised as 'profit centres' so they can be treated as a bureau with a more visible cost-effectiveness.

Organisations with mature installations such as the clearing banks may well wish to use their computing facility to develop computer-based products in the banking industry, perhaps payroll or portfolio valuation services. British Airways have marketed their airline booking systems to other airlines to recover the high costs of development. The portability of such services is obviously better developed from 'profit centre' organisation than from 'cost centre' organisation.

Adoption of computerised packages

The eleven stages of design described above seem to represent a formidable bureaucracy for activating computerisation. Surely there is a simpler way? If a user decides that he or she is only going to have the minimum viable number of data processing staff, and maximise use of the finished industry products already available in the form of packages, then some savings and short-cuts must be expected through the eleven stages of design. But beware, if the cuts are too short we could well get the disadvantage of adopting an unusable system and falling right back to the difficulties experienced by David Allner and described earlier in this chapter.

The safe thing to do is to re-examine carefully those eleven stages of design, to see where cutting corners is viable.

Stage 1   Feasibility study

Much of the investigation work will still be required to be sure that the problems and objectives of the user groups for this package fit what the package is supposed to do. Interpretation of the package specification by the computer systems analyst will be important. Full interpretation of user needs from the business analyst will still be required, but communication between the two should be easier as there is a finished product forming the basis of a proposal. The cost of the package should be easy to determine (purchase price plus implementation), but the business analyst will need to determine the benefit just as much as would be required with in-house design. If we forget benefit estimation, there is a risk that the package will be bought and then gather dust. The buyer must really want it. There is no short-cut on that part. The three green lights of feasibility are still required for an informed judgement to be made.

Stage 2   Proposal validation

This phase is probably subsumed by stage 1, so there is a saving.

Stage 3   Detailed systems specification

There is a big saving here, provided the package documentation is comprehensive.

Stage 4   Specification validation

There is some saving here, but there will be problems if the user refuses to adopt the package solution. Some shoe-horning might then be necessary. Two options are open. The first is to change the package to fit the exact user requirements. The second is to change the user procedures so that they fit the current package specification. Both of these options hurt. Changing the package may require intervention by the package supplier and/or access to original code and some technical expertise. Changing user procedures may require some considerable persuasion to achieve this. If this phase is not even considered, however, then users might be in a dreadful spot, having purchased a package that is totally unusable.

Stage 5   Program specification

Hopefully this phase will not be required, unless lots of changes have been authorised.

Stage 6 Program validation
As for stage 5.

Stage 7 Program writing and testing
As for stage 5.

Stage 6 Data collection
There is no saving here from that required in original design. The only advantage is that the user has all the package programs immediately available and thus has more flexibility in planning the phases of data collection than would be the case in original design.

Stage 9 Systems testing
There are no savings here. In fact the testing of the system will be more difficult, as in original design the designers have a familiarity with the client environment, but packages are made for general environments, and some depth of interpretation of the package specification will be required to determine what is possible and what is not.

Stage 10 Implementation
There is not much saving here. The better the quality of the package, however, the fewer problems will be encountered in implementation. The danger is that as the package is bought, management does not initially see the need for special training. If this stage is bypassed the danger is that the package will fail after implementation and control is lost, with a high risk to business continuity.

Stage 11 System maintenance and post-system audit
There is not much change here, except that normally the package vendor provides continued support. Vendors can, however, be maverick and withdraw support from an old product to force users to buy a new and better version. The user will be prudent to look carefully at the fine print in the clauses concerning support and maintenance.

As far as post-systems audit is concerned there is no change. All package purchase decisions should be seen to be sound as well as systems designed in-house or there will be waste.

Computer security

Finally, we need to look at the broader picture of security both of the systems and the physical facility. Information systems are so vital in the information society. Two inputs are offered. The first is a checklist taken from *Management Today* with a few original comments added. The second is a research report from the *Financial Times*, showing what scant attention many organisations give to security considerations.

Sixteen questions to test security of computer facilities
(From *Management Today*, December 1984, reprinted with permission.)

No one has a monopoly of wisdom or possesses a unique insight into the problem of crime. Here, however, is a checklist for managers in their consideration of computer security. As a first step, find out the answers to the following questions:

1. In your organisation, who is responsible for computer security?
2. Have the risks of a breakdown in computer security been quantified and assessed?
3. Is there a disaster recovery plan and do you have adequate insurance?

Comment

Normally, an assessment is made of the consequences of a possible breakdown for different lengths of time — an hour, a day, a week, a month. For each length of breakdown a priority list of applications and hours of resources for maintaining viability is developed, followed by a strategy for getting stand-by coverage.

Generally, the computer manufacturer will provide back-up and time according to contract, or this may be done by another user with a similar configuration of computer. Now, the vital bit. Every three months managers should try out the stand-by coverage as though it were a fire drill. If the testing is not done regularly, there is every possibility that it will not work. Over time configurations change and any change may mean that the back-up facility is no longer compatible. The pattern of workload also changes, so the free, undedicated time on the back-up facility set aside for your purpose might not be available when your disaster happens.

The logistics of stand-by need to be very carefully pre-planned. If you were to move to a new site would you use your own operators or contract ones? If the latter, it is essential that all house operating instructions are of sufficiently high standard for contract operators to follow, without the need for a special training programme.

The threat to the hardware of a DP facility is not, however, the greatest threat. The threat to data in terms of master files on tape and disk is much greater, as they are irreplaceable without back-up, and that means copies kept in a different building. This topic of back-up was discussed in chapter 14.

In very large organisations disruption to cash flow, even for a few days, could cause major problems. In response to this threat one Scottish organisation has developed a full contingency plan for alternative service. This includes the takeover of the headquarters car park, the construction of an air-pressure balloon for instant erection as a new computer room and well-rehearsed activation of billing programs on an alternative minicomputer.

4. How good is the liaison between the data processing manager, the auditors and the security manager?
5. How thorough is the personnel department in screening job applicants, taking up references, etc.?
6. Are the organisation's objectives clearly stated and successfully communicated to staff? Does this include a stated position on business ethics, on crime and punishment?

7. Are staff performances regularly reviewed and the results communicated? What provision is there for staff counselling? Is there a staff development and manpower plan?

Comment
Questions 5–7 reflect some norms of good career planning and personnel management practice and in many respects follow the principles of managing by objectives. The underlying theme behind these questions is the desire to pre-empt possible disaffection by data processing staff. In reality very exceptional security measures need to be set up to forestall a really determined attempt by a malicious employee to disrupt the system.

8. Are there adequate access controls? To the computer equipment? Round the site as a whole?

Comment
Controls are needed also around any terminals which give access to the mainframe computer and logging-off disciplines must be enforced or unauthorised users could move in on an unattended terminal recently left by an authorised user.

Controls must also be applied to the disposal of old, sensitive, computer-printed documents. They should be slit before being committed to refuse. This policy will need to be enforced wherever there are users with sensitive tabulations — a wide population. Tapes and disks with sensitive data will not normally be physically destroyed, but scratched and then recirculated into the security of a library.

9. Is there proper segregation of duties in the processing of financial transactions among the computer staff?

Comment
Segregation of roles would mean that only via a group conspiracy could malicious fraud be perpetrated. For instance, in the Inland Revenue a group which makes a tax assessment is organisationally separated from another group responsible for tax collection; this makes collusion very difficult. Many organisations insist that computer operators never work alone, but always in pairs or larger groups, and programmers are not normally given unsupervised access to the computer room.

10. Do management targets for the computer centre make specific time allowance for the development of security controls?
11. How good is the computer documentation? Are the external auditors satisfied with it?
12. How good are your auditors? Are their staff fully conversant with computer technology?
13. What happens when systems controls reject a transaction? Is there an

investigation by a senior manager or are the controls merely bypassed? Does anyone really take any notice of the computer log?

14. Who controls the purchase of small business computers?
15. Where a discrepancy exists between stock and the computer record, is this merely written off as a 'physical shrinkage' or are the computer records also scrutinised?
16. Do any staff never seem to take their holiday entitlement?

Comment

The implication here is that the dishonest staff member never wants to have a substitute doing the job, in case a fiddle will come to light. In any case, if people are not taking holidays there is a staffing shortage and the organisation is getting into a situation where disaffection can rapidly develop.

Companies cite computer failure threat

(Article by Michael Skapinker in the *Financial Times*, 1 October 1987. Reprinted with permission.)

European companies have no effective protection against a breakdown in their computer systems, although many believe substantial disruption and financial loss would be caused, according to a survey conducted in Britain, France, the Netherlands, West Germany and Italy.

The survey carried out by accountants Arthur Young and co-funded by the European Commission found that 20 per cent of the 490 companies questioned said that they would not be able to function effectively without their computer systems for more than a few days.

Even so, 42 per cent of the companies did not have a written contingency plan to deal with computer failure. Of those with such a plan, only 27 per cent had tested it in the last 12 months.

The companies also conceded that they could suffer considerable financial loss from employee error or fraud on their computer systems. 54 per cent said that their potential financial loss could be more than £50,000 and 24 per cent estimated the potential damage at more than £500,000.

Asked, however, whether they investigated the past history of data processing staff and computer users, 57 per cent of the companies said, 'Not at all.' Fewer than half said they conducted a full review of new computer applications to ensure that there were adequate safeguards against fraud and error.

While the companies said they thought their employees were generally honest, most agreed that up to a quarter of their workforce might behave dishonestly if they were under sufficient pressure or if the rewards were great enough.

Comment
This report is a devastating picture of complacency. A lot needs to be done to come to terms with the information society.

Summary

This chapter began with an expression of concern about the development of relationships between potential users of computerised systems and the designers. An analytical process in which the user has a real influence in the design and an involvement in the validation of systems proposals produced a way to pass ownership of design directly to the user. The finished process could be defined as eleven distinct stages of design.

This led to some propositions about effective organisation structures for data processing departments and the roles of those working on teams to develop information systems. The role of the systems analyst may be split into two separate roles — the business analyst, who is a user representative, and the computer systems analyst, who reports to the data processing function — and follows the more conventional approach of the literature. The secret of robust systems design and implementation lies in the setting up of mechanisms where team members occupying such roles can communicate fluently with one another. The process of validation of systems proposals is just as important as the proposals themselves! We found three basic models of organisation and could make distinctions and preferences about these.

Two further variations of systems design were then considered. The first was when the organisation did not have its own in-house data processing department, but used a bureau. The second variation considered the acquisition of a complete software package instead of original design, and in this variation we were to find that it was not quite as staightforward as might have been expected. There were some savings as against following the eleven stages of design but many stages still required to be done, otherwise the company could run the risk of purchasing an unusable package.

Design with minicomputers or microcomputers, primarily by end-users with limited support from specialists, was by implication very similar to the package acquisition problem approach and contained dangers if there were too many short-cuts taken in the stages of design and security not given sufficient attention.

Finally, some security aspects were examined and this chapter concentrated on the disaster recovery plan, necessary to cope with a major threat to a data processing facility.

The chapter aimed to shed light and understanding for the line manager wishing to know enough about the disciplines of systems design and development, so that a more meaningful dialogue could be developed with specialists and a better understanding be given of how to assess proposals for information systems.

Finally, two case studies were offered. The first illustrated the need for sound organisation and design disciplines to help data processing to make an impact first time with useable information systems. The second illustrated the issues of security and the possibility of hijack by data processing staff, if they are working with weak organisation structures and without the disciplines of the 11 stages of design.

Exercises

1. Read Case Study 16.1, 'Desert Oil Company', answer the questions posed in the case brief and compare your answers with the tutorial guide notes. (This will take approximately 2 hours.)
2. Read Case Study 16.2, 'Hijack in XYZ Company', answer the questions posed in the case brief and compare your answers with the tutorial guide notes. (This will take approximately 3 hours, but the narrative and incident sequence is very useful for reinforcing an understanding of concepts of design and security.)
3. Complete Exercise 16.1 — review questions. Run down the review questions 1–18 below. If you have difficulty in answering the questions, then refer back in the text of this chapter to where the issue is discussed, or come back to this assignment after tackling the questions in the two case studies above.

Exercise 16.1

1. Why does the data processing function often manifest a tendency to isolationism?
2. Why is the purchase of a computer more complicated than buying a lawnmower?
3. What is the role of the computer steering committee?
4. Why does the writer disagree with the idea that the data processing department should report to a chief accountant?
5. What are the essential distinctions between a computer systems analyst and a business analyst?
6. What are the main distinctions between a data processing department run on project management principles and one organised with separate functional specialists headed up by a programming group and a systems group?
7. Why are there likely to be difficulties in communication if the systems group is taken altogether out of data processing and reports only to users?
8. The writer develops the concept of integrated bilingualism. What does this imply for project management?
9. The writer alludes to threats of hijack by computer staff. How can such a situation arise?
10. Why are specifications so important in the design of computerised systems?
11. The writer is concerned about the measures of economic evaluation of systems. What should the financial criteria of viability be?

12. The writer suggests a way of ensuring user commitment to the system at the stage of the feasibility study. What is this?
13. What is involved in the techniques of prototyping?
14. The writer suggests three aspects of feasibility. What are they?
15. The writer suggests a way of ensuring management accountability for systems design. What is this?
16. What are the differences between cost centre organisation and profit centre organisation of DP?
17. What can be bypassed in the stages of design when an organisation decides to buy an industry standard computer package in preference to designing its own tailor-made system?
18. What is involved in disaster planning for a data processing facility?

Case Study 16.1
The Desert Oil Company

(Published with permission of G. Penny, editor of the National Computing Centre.)

This case is a demonstration of a typical instance of the introduction of a mainframe computer, when such commercial systems were not well understood by general management. What went wrong and why?

Synopsis

The Desert Oil Company has introduced a mainframe computer from an existing base of punch-card equipment dominated by the requirements of an accounting group. The introduction was not as easy as might have been expected. Subsequently, the company has realised that a great deal of money could be saved by using the computer for engineering calculations. They consider replacing the newly installed computer for a larger and faster one. But when they find out that the new computer building would need to be replaced as well, they realise that they will have to stay as they are. In the meantime, existing work has suffered; the original project is completed late and overspent.

Little anticipation had been made of the necessary organisational machinery for the introduction of such a change or of the likely outcomes and consequences of introducing such an instrument of organisational change. The technology of the mainframe computer was unfamiliar to general management and they did not know the potential of this device.

Twenty years later it may seem incredible that such difficulties were encountered. However, now there are many more components available within the framework of information technology, many of which are also currently unfamiliar to general management. Yet the lack of a relevant organisational machinery to assess and introduce the new technology often leads to its poor utilisation in the first few applications. It seems exceptional to get it right first time! Yet the most progressive organisations seem to be able to cope with risk and uncertain technology better than others. A precondition for this progressiveness is probably the ability to activate the necessary consultative machinery of organisation at very early stages.

The company

The Desert Oil Company (DOC) has been operating in various territories for thirty years and has become a major employer of labour, not only locally but from most parts of the world. Accordingly, like other oil companies it maintains a number of oil towns in its operating territories. In these towns the employees work, live in company houses, buy from company shops and relax in company-owned clubs and cinemas. Employees' children attend company schools until the age of eleven when they normally return to their home country for secondary education, with financial assistance from the company.

In these circumstances DOC has to act both as a normal employer responsible for internal company organisation and as a local authority with responsibility for housing, education, medical care, recreation, and so on.

The company is headed locally by a general manager (GM) who is an oil man and has spent all his thirty years working in the oil industry. He is a sound administrator and is well versed in the technical aspects of the oil industry. Reporting to him are three assistant general managers (AGMs) responsible for Finance, Administration and Production. The organisation chart, Figure 16.4, shows the various relationships.

Most of the managerial positions are held by European staff but the majority of DOC staff are Asians, with the exception of the production division, where more European specialists are employed than anywhere else in the company.

Salaries are directly affected by employment and earning potential in the countries from which the staff come. This means that the European managers are paid considerably more than their Asian supporting staff. However, the Europeans are paid twice what they would be paid in Europe as compared to the Asians who may be paid five times as much as at home.

Figure 16.4 *Desert Oil Company organisation chart*

Data processing

The company has used punch-card equipment for data processing for the last ten years. The data processing manager (DPM) is a qualified accountant who has been in punch-card processing for twelve years. He has been in his present post for five years. He is well regarded in the company and runs an efficient department. Normally reports are produced on time, but occasionally problems arise due to the advancing age of the present tabulators which are engaged for two full shifts and any breakdown causes major reshuffling of schedules. The incidence of breakdown is increasing and the DPM feels that unless some replacements are available within two years the entire data processing operations of the company will be endangered. He has formally reported his concern to the AGM Finance.

Supporting the DPM are two European staff who are responsible for the overall design of systems, the punch room supervisor and the senior operator. The other departmental staff number thirty-five, of whom twelve are punch operators, twelve are machine operators and the remainder are engaged on planning and plugging new and revised systems. The machine maintenance staff are employed by the hardware supplier on contract.

Currently five major systems are operated — payroll, salaries, stores, personnel and supplies.

The DPM submitted a strong case to the AGM Finance for the installation of a mainframe computer to replace all the present punch-card equipment. He had calculated that the rental of a suitable machine would be slightly less than the rental on the present equipment. In reply, the AGM stated that the DPM should undertake an investigation of the subject and make a report detailing all the relevant facts. (A copy of his memo is included below.)

Memo

To: DP Manager
From: AGM Finance

I have considered your report on the mainframe computerisation and it seems that there is a cause for concern in the frequency with which our data processing equipment is unable to deal with the normal daily workload due to mechanical breakdown. In the circumstances I think that it would be wise for you to investigate the economic soundness of installing a mainframe computer to do the work currently on punch cards.

Can you let me have by the end of next month a detailed report showing the following information:

1. The approximate annual cost of a suitable mainframe.
2. The present annual cost of the existing equipment.
3. The implications on your staff. Would a mainframe call for more or less staff?
4. The timescale needed for the changeover.
5. The total cost of the changeover.

Within a month the DPM had completed his investigations and had submitted the detailed report. This proposed that five major systems be transferred to the mainframe. The machine would have a small central processor and magnetic tapes and disks, a fast line printer to cope with the numerous reports and punch-card input to assist compatibility with the present systems and therefore simplify changeover.

The cost of replacing the present punch-card processing equipment would be £25,000, whereas a computer would cost £40,000. The staffing could be reduced and the best of the present staff retained as computer programmers. It was expected that staff reductions would quickly provide the savings necessary to justify the extra capital expenditure of £15,000.

The one-time total cost of the project, including change-overs of systems, would be £100,000 and could be completed within eighteen months. The costs quoted included the conversion of the existing machine room to a computer room. The size of the room was adequate for the computer specification in mind.

After studying the recommendations, the AGM Finance reported to the GM that he was proposing to install a computer. The expenditure involved, being within the AGM's authority, did not require higher authority.

The new system

Tenders from computer manufacturers were invited and an order was subsequently placed for a machine comprising the following: 16k words of memory store; 2 tape decks; 1 disk drive; 1 printer; 1 card reader.

Within six months of signing the contract the computer was delivered and installed. Commissioning trials were conducted and the machine handed over within five days.

During that year the staff selected as programmers had been trained by the computer manufacturer's staff. Prior to the delivery of the computer some fifty programs had been written and tested remotely.

After the delivery of the computer, program writing and testing became easier. In all some 200 separate programs were to be written and there were twenty major files to be created and maintained.

Although the DPM had attended a manufacturer's appreciation course he had no experience of mainframe computer systems and programs. He requested a one-year secondment of an experienced programmer/analyst from the machine supplier and this man was now acting as project leader reporting to the DPM.

After the first year the payroll and salaries systems had been completed and tested and both were due to go live on 1 January.

At about this time a number of the senior employees were becoming increasingly aware of the application of a computer and were expressing curiosity about it. Although no secret had been made of the use of the computer, no deliberate attempt had been made to keep the staff informed. The suggestion was made that a series of courses be held to familiarise the company staff with the computer and how it was being used.

These courses were designed by the manufacturer's project leader and in January of that year he began the first of a series of two-day courses. They were open to anyone who wished to apply and a good cross-representation was achieved.

Other possible uses of the computer

Among those who attended were representatives of the production research department. These were mainly engineers whose work involved analysis of oil-well production and measurement of unused oil resources. They realised that the availability of a computer would enable them to carry out more complex calculations, improve their predictive reports and thereby optimise the company's drilling activities, the most expensive operation in the whole of the company production process.

A request was made by the Head of Research for a course in mathematical programming for six of the Reservoir engineers to enable them to assess the potential use of the computer.

In March that year the Head of Research reported to the AGM Production that he considered that use of the computer on an experimental basis would enable him to decide whether his department should have permanent access to computer facilities. AGM Production requested the cooperation of AGM Finance in conducting the experiment.

A conflict of interests

The programming of the stores and supply systems had fallen behind schedule due to unforeseen complications and the DPM was doubtful whether the target of changeover within twelve months was still feasible. This fact had just been reported to AGM Finance and he refused AGM Production's request for facilities as it would hold up the planned process even further.

AGM Production appealed to the GM who, being sympathetic to the technicians, instructed the AGM Finance to make two hours a day available to the Head of Research. Naturally, this caused some bad feeling between the parties involved, but the instruction was carried out.

After two months of using the computing facility the Head of Research reported that, by virtue of calculations he had been able to program, he estimated that the company had been prevented from spending £10,000 unnecessarily on test drilling and other research activities. He also reported that he estimated that the annual savings potential resulting from full-scale computerisation would yield savings from £75,000 to £100,000 annually, with additional benefits to company sites in other territories. However, he warned that this was not feasible on the present computer because of the small and relatively slow memory which it had. Enhancement by replacing it with a large, fast processor would be necessary.

The AGM Production submitted his report to the GM and asked for modifications to the computer to be put to hand to meet the engineers' requirements. The AGM Finance raised a number of objections to the proposal but was firmly overruled and instructed to contact the manufacturers.

The DPM prepared the necessary specification for the manufacturer and requested a visit from a technical specialist.

Wise too late

The specialist conducted his investigation and reported to DOC that although the enhancement necessary was technically possible, the existing processor would need to be replaced as the requirement was beyond the capacity of the present model. He also pointed out that because the larger processor required twice the floor area it would not be possible to site it in the present computer room.

Faced with the prospect of constructing a completely new computer room and replacing the processor the GM decided that the expense could not be justified and ruled that the research department must use an external computer bureau. However, because of the geographic remoteness of the company, use of the bureau proved to be expensive and presented practical difficulties, so that the engineers ceased to have access to a computer. Unfortunately, the indecision had caused the data processing staff to relax and the throughput of tested programs had fallen off, resulting in even greater delays in completing the changeover. The period of secondment of the programmer/analyst ended in June that year and no attempt had been made to recruit a replacement. A request was made for him to remain for a longer period but, by this time, he had been committed to another project which was critical and he could not be spared.

Eventually, a replacement was found and he joined the company in November; but by this time the original project was well behind and was eventually completed one year late and was overspent.

Tasks for discussion

1. To what extent were the processes relating to good practice for selecting a computer system for an organisation ignored?
2. By what criteria should computer applications be justified and approved?
3. Did DOC develop a good or bad strategy for introducing computer systems?

For feedback see Appendix 1, p. 522.

Case Study 16.2
Avoiding a potential hijack

(Material developed from action research by Robert Erskine.)

The background statement explains the company's environment and its concern over the evolution of viable data processing standards for the protection and promotion of robust business systems.

This is followed by an outline of assignments which might be used for the purposes of class discussion; and a file of company correspondence which illustrates conflicting attitudes towards the crises as they develop and the role of DP standards in the resolution of these issues.

Company background statement

XYZ Limited operates in the United Kingdom as the manufacturing plant of a large United States-based multinational company making sophisticated industrial robots. The UK plant does part only of the manufacturing process, but owing to the advantageous trading conditions in the United Kingdom it exports the product world-wide. The British plant concentrates on the assembly of components to form a sophisticated end-product range, together with some sub-assembly work and a little machining. The company relies heavily on purchasing semi-finished components from its US parent and pays customs duty on this at the UK port of entry. When the finished goods are subsequently exported they claim back the duty paid on the imported content.

The company decides to install a mainframe computer to assist the complex production planning and control routines and some financial routines. The manual system for claiming duty drawback is hopelessly inefficient and the company estimates that if this were computerised to the satisfaction of HM Customs, a saving of over £1 million a year would be achieved.

Much of the case study relates to the project to computerise the duty drawback claims. The company gets into a vulnerable position when the systems analyst leading the project is hospitalised and the thought passes through his mind of the possibility of hijacking the company to the tune of £1 million. He alone holds the key to the project completion.

Good sense prevails and the hijack never occurs. The project is, however, seriously delayed and the data processing manager is replaced by a professional who introduces some demanding data processing standards intended to prevent a threat of hijack in the future. These standards are not, however, without their own problems in implementation.

Assignments for discussion

Case discussion is likely to hinge on the issue of definition of viable data processing standards and getting them revised and adopted with appropriate support from user management and data processing staff. Specific questions are given and the possible solutions discussed in Appendix 1, p. 523.

1. What are the minimum guidelines necessary to prevent line management being hijacked by their own data processing department or by an individual working there?
2. In the complex environment of mainframe computers working together with microcomputers in a distributed data processing set-up, what provisions in the way of design standards should be made in order to develop viable company systems?

3. Highlight within the case material instances in which the pressures of organisational politics influenced information systems design decisions.
4. Would it be supportable to assert that an effective data processing manager needs to adopt a particular management style? If so what would that style be?
5. Assess whether potential data processing hijacks are more or less likely within a project-oriented or a functionally-oriented DP facility.
6. What is the secret of achieving the project team empathy described in Memo 15?
7. How would you react as a programmer if you were obliged to adopt a modular or structured programming approach?

List of memoranda

1. From Graham, Managing Director, to George, Personnel Director. New appointment, Data Processing Manager.
2. From George, Personnel Director, to Graham, Managing Director. Confirmation of Fred's appointment as DP Manager.
3. From Fred, Data Processing Manager, to Graham, Managing Director. Data processing strategy.
4. From Arnold, Purchasing Director, to Fred, Data Processing Manager. Computerisation of duty drawback recovery routines.
5. From Keith, Systems Analyst, to Fred, Data Processing Manager. Outline of proposal for computerising duty drawback procedures.
6. From Lionel, Customs Surveyor, to Arnold, Purchasing Director. Options open for computerising duty recovery procedures.
7. From Keith, Systems Analyst, to Fred, Data Processing Manager. Resource estimates for drawback project.
8. From Fred, Data Processing Manager, to Arnold, Purchasing Director. Duty recovery project. Complex approach promised for January, Year 2.
9. From Arnold, Purchasing Director, to Fred, Data Processing Manager. Status of duty drawback project. The crisis begins.
10. From Keith, Systems Analyst, to Fred, Data Processing Manager. Duty drawback crisis and some data audit problems.
11. From Keith, Systems Analyst, to Fred, Data Processing Manager. Progress report, duty recovery. One year later.
12. From Keith, Systems Analyst, to Philip, Keith's brother. A fantasised hijack from his hospital bed.
13. From Fred, Data Processing Manager, to Mary, Fred's wife. Despair.
14. From Doreen, Data Processing Manager (just appointed), to Graham, Managing Director, cc other Directors. The checklist approach to information system design.
15. From Keith, Systems Analyst, to Charles, ex-colleague. Two years later. The new design environment.

16. From Barry, Finance Director, to Doreen, Data Processing Manager. Problems of validating specifications. Threat to adopt distributed data processing approach.
17. From Dick, Consultant, International Division, to Doreen, Data Processing Manager. Package for computerised material requirements planning. Rewrite decision criticised.
18. From Doreen, Data Processing Manager, to Dick, Consultant, International Division. Stands firm on rewrite decision.

Memo 1

From: Graham, Managing Director
To: George, Personnel Director
January, Year 1

New appointment, Data Processing Manager

You will be aware of the importance I attach to the appointment of a first-rate person to the position of Data Processing Manager. I see this as a major strategic step for this company and I am keen to get someone who will earn real credibility. In my view we should appoint someone really knowledgeable about company systems in the target user areas. The top person can then surround him- or herself with appropriate data processing technical expertise, but such specialists would naturally be at a lower level. I will rely heavily on your judgement in making up a short-list for the appointment. However, in this instance, I would prefer we as a company promoted internally rather than by recruitment.

Regards,
Graham

Memo 2

From: George, Personnel Director
To: Graham, Managing Director
January Year 1

Confirmation of Fred's appointment as DP Manager

I hope that you had a quiet trip back yesterday from Hong Kong. I am pleased to say that we were able to make an appointment, while you were away, of Fred, to the position of DP Manager. He showed up as the outstanding man on our short-list. He is a real dynamo of energy and is particularly well thought of in his present post of Manager, Production Planning and Control Department. The factory manager had been delighted with his innovation in his job these last two years. He has a reputation as a real doer and is not afraid to tackle new things. I feel we can have high expectations for the function of data processing in this company with Fred at the helm. We have already put in hand a programme for recruiting the specialists in the data processing group. I will keep you informed of developments.

Regards,
George

Memo 3
From: Fred, Data Processing Manager
To: Graham, Managing Director
February Year 1

Data Processing Strategy

I have made myself well aware of the relevant sections of the company's corporate plan and attempted to identify particular data processing projects which I believe should have priority on the basis that they most obviously support the key result areas in the corporate plan. For a company such as ours I believe the first priority should be for stock control as there are many millions of pounds tied up here and only a marginal improvement would have significant impact on company profit. Our second priority should be the setting up of the engineering data so that we can establish timing and cost standards, and from this eventually do factory scheduling. My suggested third priority (having discussed this with Arnold in purchasing) will be to computerise the duty drawback routines. He tells me he believes that we are losing over £1 million a year in the existing manual system. The quantity and volume of transactions of parts and the constant change in product structure make an acceptable audit trail impossible in a manual system for HM Customs. I am hoping that I can rely on your support for these priorities when you discuss them at the new computer steering committee next month.

Regards,
Fred

Memo 4
From: Arnold, Purchasing Director
To: Fred, Data Processing Manager
March Year 1

Computerisation of duty drawback recovery routines

I am delighted to hear that you are one of my allies in the moves to establish a project to computerise the duty recovery routines. In anticipation of this happening we have established our own clerical section which is recording by part number all the customs entries on forms called miscellaneous cash deposits. In the manual system we have struggled to recover no more than some £50,000 a year but I know on the basis of 'rule of thumb' that there is over £1 million a year for recovery on the current trading figures and breakdown of home/export sales. We are in a growth business and this figure could become £2 million within five years. For the last two years we have had on site a resident customs officer, but it looks as though there is no way with the manual system that we can provide sufficient concrete audit trails to get more money recovered. The customs are traditionally a bureaucracy and protection of the revenue is their guiding norm. However, I have made it my business to get to know the local surveyor, Lionel, who oversees the customs in this district. Lionel is a young and very ambitious man determined to introduce computerised routines within the customs. Great things await him in London if he introduces computerised methods in this area. He has made overtures to me to the effect that we could be a guinea-pig for the pioneering of such routines. For such a pilot scheme he would endeavour to exercise the maximum amount of discretionary power in the interpretation of the regulations to offer us the real opportunity of making the full recovery of money due.

I would ask you, Fred, to allocate a capable team to this project and give it a really high priority. Substantial resources could be justified for a net gain of £1 million a year. The sooner this gets moving the better and I am fully prepared to be involved in discussions with your staff.

Regards,
Arnold

Memo 5

From: Keith, Systems Analyst
To: Fred, Data Processing Manager
June, Year 1

Outline of proposal for computerising duty drawback procedures

I have now completed a preliminary survey for the duty drawback project and got a system outline for possible solutions. I wish to keep you posted of my thoughts as eventually Arnold will need to take a decision on one of the alternatives or we will have to go back to the drawing board and think again. I predict that there are considerable differences in resource requirements and complexity involved in the two alternatives and I feel that if Arnold opts for the more complex one you may be expected to allocate more people to this project for a reasonable completion date.

In the first alternative, a diagram of the system is contained in Figure 16.5. The routine starts with taking the file of monthly receivables. This contains all invoices issued in that month and by the coding on the invoice we can select the export invoices only. From these we extract the finished products sold abroad. To get the imported parts content we need to mount an engineering file, the bill of material, to break down the finished product into its component parts. We call that the 'parts explosion'. From the parts thus exploded we select those which according to

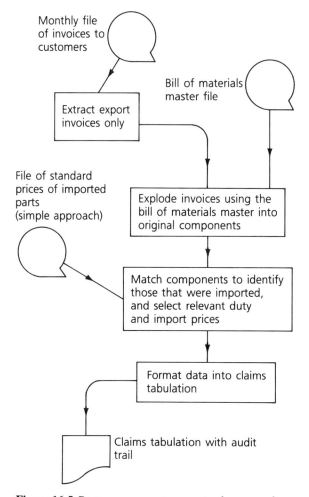

Figure 16.5 *Duty recovery system — simple approach*

our company files were originally imported. Our simple proposal is to incorporate in our standard costing file a code which indicates that the part was imported; the amount of duty claimed would relate with the purchasing price as per the established standard. With that data it should be straightforward to format tabulations under duty rates and tariff headings to whatever specification HM Customs lay down. The only assumption in this approach is that the purchasing standard so entered is realistic; if the prices change during the year this could not be reflected in the duty claimed. Where prices are falling that would be to our advantage, but if they were rising we would lose on the amount claimed.

Arnold, however, seems determined to claim the very maximum, regardless of cost. In the second alternative the above routine is identical, except for the price extraction from a standard cost file. Arnold, instead, wants us to take all the imported documents (some 70,000 transactions in current backlog) and set them up on a database of imported parts. Customs have indicated that they would permit a processing logic which would allow the computer to pick off the database the parts in descending order of value for the export invoices, but would then insist that the database is then reduced by each such claims run and reduced by home invoices concurrently, but these on the basis of lowest price first. A diagram of this system is shown in Figure 16.6.

The proposition sounds attractive on paper, but would require us to process without error some 20,000 transactions a month to feed the database as a bank

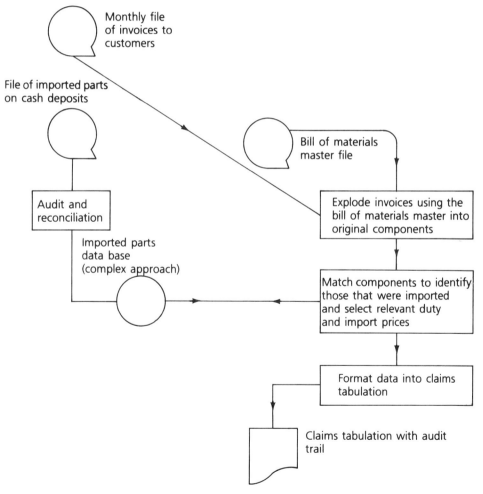

Figure 16.6 *Duty recovery system — complex approach*

so that there will be matches when we re-export. I also suspect that a large and complex suite of programs will be necessary to set up, audit and maintain the database, with much computer time expended. In contrast I do not foresee any real difficulties in the simple approach with a standard cost file which would have new standards posted only say twice a year, and it should be straightforward to audit and maintain this type of file. I cannot anticipate the amount of resources you may wish to allocate to this project but I would suspect that the delivery date for the complex version of the project could be as much as six months later than the simple version and accompanied with much greater risk.

I would urge you to resist pressure from Arnold to adopt the complex version outlined here.

Regards,
Keith

Memo 6

From: Lionel, Customs Surveyor
To: Arnold, Purchasing Director
July, Year 1

Options open for computerising duty recovery procedures

I am most encouraged at the progress which is being made in the forming of a computerised procedure in XYZ Co. Limited and have been busy in London explaining what you are up to and the very real advantages which we may expect from adopting computerisation in drawback routines. I can confirm that we will permit traders like yourselves with very significant export business to select parts for claims on the basis of the highest prices from what you call the 'data bank' of imported components and then process the home claims on the basis of the lowest prices. The advantage of processing both home and export business is that we should achieve total accountability leading back to the miscellaneous cash deposits which are the prime record at time of component import.

I understand that your Systems Analyst, Keith, has reservations about this approach, but he did assure me that it was technically feasible to go for the big advantage of the data bank. Now that I have had backing from London for the data bank approach it would be disappointing to return to the approach of having a static standard cost file as the basis of the computations, though I do have authority to allow you to continue either approach.

I feel that you are the experts as computer users and I wish you well in completing this project as soon as possible.

Yours sincerely,
Lionel,
Customs Surveyor

P.S. I find it most stimulating to be working with you on such an innovative project.

Memo 7

From: Keith, Systems Analyst
To: Fred, Data Processing Manager
August, Year 1

Resource estimates for drawback project

Now that the main options forward on this project have been all but settled I wish to offer briefly the resource estimates for the detailed systems work and programming necessary for the project to be completed:

1. For the basic system using a static cost file as the basis for computing the claim, design would take some nine man/months of work.
2. For the same system with a data bank the estimate will be eighteen man/months of work.

   Naturally I am hoping for an allocation of team members adequate to meet Arnold's deadlines.
   Incidentally I am most concerned at the lack of proper filing cabinets in the systems department for filing documentation about systems as they are developed. I anticipate as many as sixty computer programs in the suite for duty recovery and cabinets are essential for development and maintenance. Already I am finding that the work environment is too slipshod. We are being obliged to move on to new work before the previous work has been consolidated by documentation. This leaves any system fragile in event of a change of people. I do appreciate that you are under very considerable organisational pressures to get systems designed and working, but I feel we must as a group learn to walk before we run!

Regards,
Keith

Memo 8

From: Fred, Data Processing Manager
To: Arnold, Purchasing Director
September, Year 1

Duty recovery project

I have decided to allocate two programmers to Keith for the above project. I agree with you that we should adopt what is known as the data bank approach and maximise return for the company. I know Keith is concerned about the complexity of this approach, but I think he is a bit of a fuddyduddy in his outlook. He keeps asking for things like cabinets to file programs in. I tell him to get more in the sharp end and have high productivity and early delivery of the system. We can always put in other programmers later to tidy up if necessary. I am prepared to offer you a working system by January Year 2. I would not wish to promise you an earlier date. I have many other projects to resource as well. Keith will be rather upset as he seemed to want twice that in resources and some elaborate 'Feasibility

Study' report, but I think that is just so much more paper! As long as we have a good mutual understanding between us then I have every confidence that this project will be a success. My success in management in Production Planning and Control was much to do with shaking the bag and getting things done. I am endeavouring to do the same here.

Regards,
Fred

Memo 9

From: Arnold, Purchasing Director
To: Fred , Data Processing Manager
March, Year 2

Status drawback project

I am really concerned about this project. We are already two months late for a full working system and to my horror it looks as though we will be much later and the duty recovery expected in this year's financial returns will not be available. You can imagine that it has not been easy explaining this to the Financial Director. The wires have been humming also to Graham, our MD.

Furthermore, I understand that you have not even got the backlog of the 70,000 miscellaneous cash deposit entries into the data bank in any usable form. We were expecting a reconciliation of the data at some £4 million of purchase value and we are out to the tune of over £1.5 million! We face being a laughing stock for HM Customs unless we can get these data audited. I am amazed that your systems people did not foresee this type of difficulty. Please get Keith on to a computer assist to help to achieve the data audit as fast as possible.

Regards,
Arnold

Memo 10

From: Keith, Systems Analyst
To: Fred, Data Processing Manager
April, Year 2

Duty drawback crisis

As you are well aware this project has had its share of setbacks. Firstly, when I check over many of the records in an attempt to locate the main reason for the £1.5 million reconciliation error I find that there are many occasions when there was confusion from the punch bureau in the interpretation of certain figures. One clerk in the manual system out of the three in the group had a '4' almost identical with a '7'. This is a random error going over so many records that we have but little option but to go for a very thorough audit and reconcile individually every miscellaneous cash deposit with the entries made on the part number cards, which we had used as our source document. Furthermore, in attempting this audit on a small sample with the Section Supervisor, James, I had occasion to find him falsifying some records. You may be aware that he has steadfastly opposed the computerisation project as he sees it as a threat to his position, but now we are dealing with a sabotage attempt, playing fire with our prospects to recover the expected £1 million a year for the company. I trust that you will deal with this discreetly with Arnold, as after that incident I do not wish to work any more than I have to with James in his position as Section Supervisor.

I believe that we have a real can of worms in this data bank and we may need to deploy further programming staff to construct audit programs to check also under tariff headings, as it would not surprise me if Customs themselves in haste to clear the goods have referenced them under incorrect tariff categories. I have seen may such inconsistencies on tracing part numbers back from their cards to the original MCD.

Regards,
Keith

Memo 11

From: Keith, Systems Analyst
To: Fred, Data Processing Manager
April, Year 3

Progress report duty recovery

You will be pleased to hear at last that after a mammoth audit exercise taking over a year we are actually processing recovery claims and the customs officer is satisfied with the audit trail. We required fifty-four extra computer programs to complete the audit and get figures reconciled. So much for the complexity of dealing with a data bank of that size. The suite of programs which does the audit is very fragile. The documentation leaves much to be desired and Tom, a programmer on the project, has a unique style which is very difficult for anyone else to follow. All our computer programs contain tag names which represent the main routines and we normally try to give them meaningful names for ease of understanding. Tom, however, gives paragraph names which are meaningful to incidents in his personal life, for example I found the statement in the program 'Go to River-Julu'. Tom tells me that when he wrote that program he was mentally reconstructing a trip he did in his native Nigeria to claim his bride! Every special place became a paragraph name in the program. If Tom goes off sick these next few months we will be in real trouble.

For the last six nights we have been processing a month's worth of the original backlog each night. The claim value has been £35,000 a month. It is very exciting to look at the printer and find something near what we expect. However, Arnold is still not satisfied. There are two reasons for mismatches occurring, which of course reduce the amount claimed. The first is that our MCD records contain part number details from the supplier, and when the supplier is not our own parent in the United States but another supplier the part number definition is not recognised on XYZ's engineering files so the parts explosion does not work.

Another more ominous development which occurred after the first six months of claims were processed was the very real decline in amount of the claim, and this at a time when export business was increasing. My appreciation of this situation, after looking at the mismatch list, is that it is now of the utmost urgency to replenish the data bank with parts which have been imported during the last year. Up to now only the original 70,000 item entries were in the data bank, and 20,000 per month are lying waiting to undergo the massive audit exercise before the data bank is ready to provide an adequate base of claims for later exports. Arnold is going berserk at the delays. The Financial Director threatened with another missed profit target has Arnold over the barrel. There will be blood spilt soon.

Meanwhile, there is a problem with this project and the computer operations section. The duty drawback project has been very hungry of computing time. We will not be popular if we put in requests for computer rerun time, yet I feel it is pointless processing claims worth £40,000 a month and submitting to HM Customs tabulations with only £25,000.

I feel it is necessary for you to call a conference with the parties affected and get a set of priorities agreed and properly resourced within a time-scale that we have a chance of achieving. Sorry for bellyaching, but we are living in dangerous times. Our users seem to blame us for everything and will not accept ownership of the system, *their* system.

Regards,
Keith

Memo 12

From: Keith, Systems Analyst
To: Philip (Keith's brother)
Hospital
May, Year 3

Philip,
What agony to be landed in here with acute back trouble. No one seems to know why I collapsed in pain last week just as I was about to do a presentation at work. I cannot even sit up yet though the pain is less acute. The operations manager at work was not long in getting in touch with me, persuading the hospital to put the mobile telephone by the bed. Arnold is putting the pressure on to get at least a £1 million duty claim before the end of the month. It looks as though the data bank will not yield more than £1.5 million of duty claimed, and he does not really understand why. I do have rough specifications of the system in my desk but some

of the vital bits have gone missing since we moved office last month, and there are no production operating instructions to drive the project. My goodness, I do wish I had won the battle with Fred to get filing cabinets to secure the specifications, but you know what Fred was like, a production control manager to the last, dynamism, rush, rush, like a tornado always pressurising his group to move on to new work before the old was secured, no feasibility studies and then authorisation by the user, so we are in the ridiculous situation that Arnold has a system which he does not understand and the telephone and me are the only link he has with the missing £1.5 million. He will have no joy with Fred, who says he stands at the touch-line cheering the technical people on but admits that he cannot contribute anything to the computer or business logic of the system. Unfortunately, he has no rapport at all with any of the systems people and has left me on my own. Tom, who was helping program the system, left suddenly this month to join London Transport, and you will remember that many of his programs are completely unreadable owing to his unique programming style! Several of the programs written in haste to complete the data audit are still only in the advanced stages of testing and visibility of coding and style is essential if the remaining bugs are to be eliminated. I cannot remember the number of times I asked Fred to allocate more staff to this vital system to preserve the continuity in event of staff movement.

The hospital staff have been giving me lots of tests. They suspect TB, but I hope they are wrong. It would not be at all difficult for me to refuse to speak to the operations manager at work on medical grounds and bring the whole project to a grinding halt — damn their missing millions (and with the total backlog to bring everything up to date I reckon we are talking about £3 million in outstanding drawback claims). What a wonderful opportunity to do a hijack on them! Anyway I am quite prepared to make them sweat a bit to learn their lesson. I am sure that Fred will be dismissed in any event and I should be in a strong position with any successor of Fred as I alone hold the key to the missing millions! The cash-flow crisis alone caused by this project's late completion will mean Graham will need to get bailed out by Head Office in the United States. This is truly a company crisis.

I hope that my next letter will be more cheerful. I cannot help fantasising about the hijack.

Love to all,
Keith

Memo 13

From: Fred, Data Processing Manager
To:　　Mary (Fred's wife)
August, Year 3

Darling,
I do wish that I had come with you on holiday to Germany. This last week has been the most unpleasant one I have ever had in my whole career, and you know

that I am normally a fighter. Well, I have been sacked by Graham! He comes up to the plant on Monday from Head Office with a high-flying data processing consultant and he calls together all the key management in the plant to review the data processing projects. All my friends desert me. Arnold spills the beans about the duty recovery project and says that our department is a circus! We are threatening the recovery of £3 million of company profit. The Production Director joins the hunting pack and says our stock control routines are rubbish, the printouts are always late and he is fed up with his staff working for the computer. He thinks that the computer should work for them and do something useful like scheduling the factory. He does not trust us to keep the most elementary records. His punch line is: 'I would not put you in charge of the toilet roll stock.' The Finance Director complains that we were a month late in getting out the statements and worsening the already critical cash-flow situation. Arnold says we must complete the drawback claims 'come hell or high water' and he wants my head. The data processing consultant says that he has completed a brief review of our department and is appalled at the slap-happy way we manage the data processing facility. He says that if an insurance company came in to assess risk we would be crucified, with no fireproof cabinets for master files and documentation, and some 50 per cent of the computer run-time being devoted to reruns of aborts. Graham gave me a real rough time in a private exit interview. He says that my management style is like a tornado and utterly ineffective in the DP management situation, that I could not control the technical people, that I exposed the company to being held to ransom by letting them get too powerful, that I had not learned how to get support from line managers. Well, he could hardly say any more. I feel very bitter about this treatment. There were so many missed business targets it was inevitable that someone had to be a scapegoat and they got my scalp. Graham, wise bird, must have had a mole in the DP department who could prime him about all our difficulties. The data processing consultant did not appear to be conducting an impartial investigation, but a verification of someone else's preliminary work. A replacement for me has already been appointed!

Ever your devoted Fred

Memo 14

From: Doreen, Data Processing Manager (just appointed)
To: Graham, Managing Director
cc: other Directors
September, Year 3

The checklist approach to information system design

After some three weeks in my new post I feel that I must share with you my appreciation of the current state of play regarding data processing projects at XYZ and make a stab at establishing the ground-rules from which solid progress can be made. My first priority is to guarantee the vital existing systems, particularly the financial routines. The next is to establish two new posts held by real professionals, who I am expecting to hire from outside. These are the posts of operations manager and systems and programming manager. As the existing computer is fully loaded and is anyway most unsatisfactory for any form of three-year plan I would be proposing to initiate a full rewrite of all our systems ready for a new computer, which I would expect to be installed within one year. The existing base of systems is so weak I do not feel that we have any alternative but to start from scratch on the main application areas with a proper check-list design approach, i.e. commencing with feasibility studies, then leading to specifications at the appropriate level in the design process. I call this the check-list approach as the key idea is that I would wish to work in a disciplined way from a series of blueprints, which after being published are scrutinised by the user and if appropriate signed. The very signature would give us the authority to proceed. If the user department will not sign there will be no system until such time as it is possible to agree the specification. This might sound a bit formal but I might add that the opposite of this is an informal approach done on the nod and wink, and that has signally failed in XYZ. Under the check-list approach the system ownership is the client's. The business logic contained in it is his. The files created are the responsibility of the user for accuracy and maintenance. The calling of computer jobs would be the responsibility of the users requesting through the operations manager. When any system has passed testing procedures both to the satisfaction of user and the systems development team, it would be passed over to operations for routine running.

My belief is that the systems department is a staff department facilitating the design and implementation process on behalf of the line department users. There should never be any confusion over the logic in any system. It will be contained in black and white in the systems specification signed by the user. If he gives us crummy logic then he will get a crummy system and its design and running cost will be absorbed in his budget. In difficult design cases when there are many alternatives the feasibility study should throw light on the pros and cons of each such approach and there will be an economic justification prepared jointly by the user and data processing. We will be responsible for quoting the estimated cost and time for alternatives, and the user for expected benefits. The pay-off period will probably be the key concept in judging system priorities and these will be agreed by the computer steering committee. At the completion of any system there will be a short post-system audit to ensure both cost and time responsibility from ourselves and expected benefit from the user.

I feel that the above measures are essential if there is to be an integration of the data processing department within the overall organisation of XYZ. To reinforce this approach I am proposing to publish to all concerned the standards to which we will be adhering and I expect this to be done in a most professional way. I much hope that I can count on the support of all senior members of XYZ for this approach.

I could not conclude this memo without reference to the duty drawback project. I appreciate that this is of acute and immediate concern to this company. However, my preliminary conclusion is that the existing system with the elaborate data bank concept is not viable. The base of data is full of original error, some of which is not the fault of XYZ. Also the volume of monthly transactions at 20,000 cannot be maintained without very heavy staffing. We are wasting time dealing with this muddle. I understand that Arnold has appointed a new section leader for the duty drawback section in place of James. The new man is Bruce, an ex-Customs Officer, who is suggesting with our analyst, Keith, to use the simpler standard costing approach. Keith, thank goodness, is now out of hospital and working on the feasibility study for this project to find a way forward as quickly as possible.

I am putting into operation this revised approach immediately and anticipate a quick restoration of confidence in our department. We do have some very able members and if they are allowed to work under professional guidelines we will all be winners!

Regards,
Doreen

Memo 15

From: Keith, Systems Analyst
To: Charles, ex-colleague
October, Year 5

Dear Charles,
Great to hear you on the telephone today wondering whether it would be a good idea to recommence working here. During the last two years there have been very big changes, in fact you would hardly recognise that you were in the same company. Doreen has done a superb job in those two years and I am preparing to go to the United States with a group of six analysts — three from the European subsidiaries. We are going to study the material requirements handling system with a view to introducing it in all the European subsidiaries.

You might be wondering what happened to the duty drawback project! Well, I am happy to say that all the troubles there are now over. Doreen insisted on a rewrite preceded by a feasibility study and then virtually held a gun to the head of Arnold until he accepted a technological possibility. She then got Bruce from the user section virtually to move his office down here in the role of user business analyst and he and I sat together till the specifications were fully developed and agreed. He could bring to me the complete detail of HM Custom's requirements, which I could relate with a business specification and then break down for the programmer. Then the programmer was obliged to follow company standards introduced by Doreen to establish modular programs, which were then immediately visible to the systems man. Bruce then had a hot-line to Arnold to get the necessary resources and we were a united team communicating effectively with one another and properly resourced. It was Bruce's role to quantify the various benefits in the options and clear the way with Arnold. The whole project was then monitored on a critical path network and within six months we had recovered the outstanding £3 million! Once the system had been established Bruce moved back to his home department, fully understanding the logic and policy and able to request computer runs and check the print-outs. I am now off that project completely and any maintenance that may be requested will be initiated by the user, Bruce, and then done by a maintenance section without reference to me, only to the documentation, which needless to say lies in fireproof cabinets.

I feel that it is like being born again! The analyst can design, then move on in the confidence that work done on a solid base from agreed specifications can then be developed by a team and then handed over. Under the old regime of Fred the original designer would have the system as a millstone round his neck after development, with users not wanting one bit to get their fingers on the pulse, hence the 'ownership' issue. Now the ownership is clearly the user's and my role is simply as a catalyst at the critical problem-solving stage. We communicated so well within the project team latterly that we said we had invented a new term for systems development, 'integrated bilingualism'. Each team member was expert in one field and had enough understanding to listen to other experts. With a balanced team you get this near-perfect team empathy.

Doreen is very ambitious. Now that she has had several successes under her belt, and with very high morale among the Systems and Programming staff, we are all now itching to get into the hard planning and control systems of the company and make a really big impact on the company operations. She is very popular too with most of the line managers who have identified her with their own success. There is some friction sometimes over setting the development priorities, but the long-term plan is to offer major assistance in corporate planning routines.

I hope that this note is enough to persuade you to return here to work. We are all very happy here now thanks to Doreen's check-list approach.

Regards,
Keith

Memo 16

From: Barry, Finance Director
To: Doreen, Data Processing Manager
November, Year 5

Validating specifications

I am really aghast that I should have to sign the specification prepared by your staff for the new corporate financial projection model by Tuesday next. There are some 300 pages in the specification and with the best will in the world I shall be unable to pin my mast to the whole of that complicated logic. In any event you need to be a Philadelphia lawyer to undertake the task of interpretation. I have had my senior Management Accounting Supervisor playing the role of user business analyst during the development but even he and your own staff cannot fully visualise a dynamic computer-assisted business approach till we have had some experience of using it, and I expect that then we will want to mould it to our own style. We want an interactive approach with much more flexibility for the user to try new ways of analysis and not to be fixed in some stringent design straitjacket. Your so-called check-list approach might be good for the data processing bureaucrat and his routine allocation of staff but I need to respond to the crisis and the MD's demand that we rework the figures on different scenarios many times during the annual one-week corporate planning workshop.

If I cannot get a more flexible relationship I may be forced to adopt a self-sufficiency policy and buy dedicated microcomputers with software packages and run them with only nominal reference to the data processing manager. I understand the jargon for this approach is distributed data processing. The sad fact is that you in data processing have had it all your own way for too long now. We users want to be more in the driving seat in systems design for those systems which are dedicated to a single functional user and not have to wait helplessly in some queue squabbling about priorities.

I will sign your specification but only under protest and on the understanding that we may feel free to make radical change requests during the first year of use. During that time we would want one staff member assigned to support the package for our satisfaction.

I hope we can agree that standards in data processing and information technology must be seen to be to the advantage of all concerned and not just one group. I am going to suggest to Graham that we convene a group to look at the whole issue of design and development standards in the environment of distributed data processing users. I hope that as a company we can make a mature and useful contribution.

> Regards,
> Barry

Memo 17

From: Dick, Consultant, International Division
To: Doreen, Data Processing Manager
December, Year 5

Package for computerised material requirements planning

I am most disappointed by your recent report of the visit of the six analysts to the United States. You say that you want to accept the framework of the system but not the programs as they have not been written to a high enough standard and would be impossible to maintain. I must admit that they were written before we had established the standards on modular programming, but the system your analysts saw took some 100 man/years in development and encapsulates our experience over the past eight years of plant operation.

If it would help I am prepared to persuade the US data processing manager to release the chief programmer for six months with a view to guiding your staff over the more complex areas of the package, in order to avoid the rewrite decision and save the resources.

Regards,
Dick

Memo 18

From: Doreen, Data Processing Manager
To: Dick, Consultant International Division
January, Year 6

Rewrite decision

I have considered carefully the issue of whether to accept or rewrite the package for material requirements planning and I am sorry to say that I cannot see it being reversed. In Europe we have a variety of factory environments and for each there is a need to fit the package. Our staff have to be confident in planning each such fit and a precondition is that each program is visible to any competent programmer. We could not possibly go into this venture on the basis of a loan of the chief programmer from the US data processing department. We would be in the position of being held to ransom in event of any hiccup. Our staff estimate that the rewrite of the total package will take up some twenty man/years of resources, and then from a solid base a further five man/years to accomplish the necessary fitting for each of the six European plants. Our French and German colleagues have agreed to cooperate on this project. We have laid down the boundaries of the sub-systems and the project is under way. I have been involved in high-level presentations to all the subsidiary managers, the punch line being that the system offered is being customised to their requirements, European priorities, European technology and work methods, European factory economics of scale, with European user management in the driving seat. Otherwise the whole project would fall down on the basis of 'it's not invented here'. Our line management here is very suspicious of packages being forced down its throat. You may feel it is like reinventing the wheel, but the introduction of advanced computerised systems in the field of planning and control has a major organisational impact and line management here insists that it understands the system and its concepts well enough to drive the system, not get into a situation where the system drives management!

Thank you all the same for your very kind offer of help and I am sorry to decline.

Regards,
Doreen

For feedback on this case study see Appendix 1, p. 522.

References

Allner, D. (1974), 'The lamentable isolationism of DP', *Computing Europe*, 14 November, p. 11.

Mintzberg, H. (1973), *The Nature of Managerial Work*, Harper & Row. (Sheds light on the nature of decision-making and the manifestation of informal practice and organisation structures.)

Penny, G., (ed.) (1974), *Data Processing Case Histories*, NCC, pp. 13–21 for Case Study 'More than an Accounting Machine' (adapted in this chapter as 'The Desert Oil Company').

Skapinker, M. (1987), 'Companies cite computer failure threat', *Financial Times*, 11 October.

(Unattributed) (1984), 'Sixteen questions to test security of computer facilities', *Management Today*, December, p. 410.

Wilkie, R. (1980), Professor in Organisational Behaviour, University of Strathclyde, Address to the Chamber of Commerce at Erskine (unpublished).

Further reading

Earl, M. (1989), *Management Strategies for Information Technology*, Prentice Hall.

Meiklejohn, I. (1989), 'Not yet in top form', *Management Today*, April, pp. 143–6. (Gives an excellent review of Michael Earl's (1989) text. Good reading for all those trying to get executives to relate information technology strategy to business strategy.)

Mumford, E. and Henshall, D. (1979), *Participative Approach to Computer Systems Design: a case study of the introduction of a new computer system*, ABP. (An early work which recognised the real problem of getting active involvement from users.)

Sweet, P. (1988), 'Agreeing how to disagree', *Computing*, 13 March, p. 20. (About service level agreements for data processing operation managers.)

Thierauf, R.J. (1987), *Effective Management Information Systems*, 2nd edition, Merrill. (Refer particularly to chapters 7 and 9 for organisation and control in MIS projects. Chapter 11 looks at corporate planning and the MIS.)

Chapter 17

Developments in corporate planning

Overview

The objective of this chapter is to introduce the reader to developments in contemporary corporate planning processes. The narrative, analysis and case exercises are intended to develop familiarity with the concepts of strategic management and strategic choice and to concentrate on the main corporate planning techniques and models. Much of the review will concentrate on how modern corporate planning approaches can be implemented in organisations.

In this chapter both public and private sectors will be discussed. Much of the material used is based on direct action research by the author, supplemented by material digested from meetings and seminars organised by the Strategic Planning Society of Great Britain.

After working through this chapter the reader should have a sufficient grasp of the concepts behind corporate planning to be able to contribute to discussions about corporate planning issues in his or her own organisation, or to be able to go into another organisation and do an audit on their corporate planning expertise!

Simple corporate planning

In chapter 3 a very simple process of corporate planning was introduced. An analyst will need to:

1. *Interpret* what is going on by building up various business pictures of the organisation and its environment.
2. *Analyse* the business pictures to seek out possible new pathways and choices of corporate direction.
3. *Respond* to such choices by adopting a limited number of new strategies and planning for the necessary logistics, resources, changes to organisation and people to enable the plan to happen.

In addition, two simple techniques of corporate planning were introduced and then demonstrated in case studies. A PEST analysis was done to bring out the *political, economic, social* and *technological* aspects of the environment, so that the business organisation may be pro-active in the change process. A SWOT analysis was done to bring out *strengths, weaknesses, opportunities* and *threats* to the organisation.

From these techniques planners should be able to identify the winners and losers in the activities and business areas of the organisation. The business can then be managed to promote and consolidate the winners, rationalise in the middle ground and redeem the losers or consciously divest away from the losers and reallocate resources to the winners.

In chapter 3 it was recognised that corporate planning requires two distinct groups to develop good team working relationships. The board would have overall responsibility for the policy development and changes and a multidisciplinary corporate planning team would do the leg-work and analysis to inform the whole board. From the interaction of these groups the mission of the organisation would be much more visible.

Corporate planning developments

A main outcome of this process was the definition of key result areas for the organisation to enable realistic plans and compatible objectives to be defined and worked on throughout the ranks of management. The technique of MbO was demonstrated in chapters 5 and 6. It was stressed that objective-setting without a corporate framework of key result areas (KRAs) is not much use. In chapter 6 the emphasis was on assessments and feedbacks and these naturally are directed back to the planners for refinements of the KRAs, leading to greater realism in their content.

Key result areas have a variety of dimensions, an obvious one being the financial one. In chapter 4 the critical financial ratios were demonstrated to assist in the assessment and development of the crucial areas of financial performance.

Chapter 10 discussed techniques at the operating level of planning which assist in breaking down the KRAs into detailed projects. Activity networks coordinate the efforts of project groups and the timing and resource allocation.

In Part 4 the central assumption was made that we are living within an information society and that computerised systems have a major role to play in the collection, collation and dissemination of information. This in turn is a major influence on decision-makers, including corporate decision-makers, and thus may make a further crucial contribution to the corporate planning process.

Chapter 12 explored the ways in which computerised systems assist the operating manager to the extent that there could be a strategic impact on the organisation, given successful implementation of systems. Airline booking systems, for instance, increased the degree of choice which could be offered to the consumer. A computer-assisted booking system led on to computer-assisted fleet management and crew scheduling, making a decisive impact on the KRAs.

Such applications required the use of information networks, but once these were in place they could become a prime means of delivering intelligence and indeed consumer service, thus offering a new dimension to an organisation's product/market strategy.

Yet computer systems were horribly expensive to develop in new areas and management needed to be very selective in their investment decisions on computer applications. In that chapter the concept of 'leverage' was developed. Invest £1,000 on computing to gain a million! Seek out always the high leverage applications and make them natural priorities.

In chapter 13 attention was turned to manufacturing and the ability of the computer to do projections and simulations. The computer could generate various logistic profiles to visualise likely consequences of any change to the volume of activity or to the deployment of resources. This technique was an advanced manifestation of the principles of managing by exception.

In chapter 14 attention was directed to the decision-making processes that could enhance the role of the planner as a result of using microcomputers, for gathering, retrieving and analysing data.

In chapter 15 a further analysis was given to the manufacturing organisation. Speed in the development of new products is crucial in business strategy. The relevance of computer-aided design and computer-aided manufacture (CAD/CAM) to this strategy was considered. The role of corporate forecasters was discussed. Integrated within a corporate planning team, they develop simulations of commercial plans and logistic profiles to refine the short-term sector of the corporate plan (the first eighteen months).

Chapter 16 recognised that organisation structure is crucial in the deployment and management of advanced computer applications, those intended to make a strategic impact in the organisation. A 'good practice' approach to guide this strategic change puts the user management more in the driving seat, passes ownership to them and makes them more accountable for achieving high leverage on their investment in computing.

The Glueck model

The basic activities — interpret, analyse and respond — were a simplification and synthesis of the corporate planning process of the Glueck model, portrayed in Figure 3.1 (p. 27). In 1976 Glueck's model was seen as a major contribution to the process of corporate planning and a refinement of earlier work done in the 1960s by Ansoff. However, in the 1970s and 1980s some major criticisms became apparent and these have given rise to the need for a more comprehensive and dynamic form of corporate planning.

The following paragraphs give a brief criticism of aspects of Glueck's model.

Organisation structure

Glueck was good at defining verbs and activities, but there was little mention of the organisational process of actually getting this done.

The prime organisational machinery suggested by later writers is the formation of a distinct corporate planning group, working to the briefs of the organisation's directors. The corporate planning group do the leg-work involved in the corporate planning process and undertake special assignments, while the main board adopts policies and makes decisions on direction and resource allocation, prompted much by the staff work done in the corporate planning group.

An annual cycle

Glueck seemed to assume that the corporate planning process was done regularly once a year, and that between planning cycles there would not be enough change to require a radical rethink before the next annual planning cycle. However, in the 1970s and 1980s, the pace of change quickened dramatically and the application of information technology in networks and management information systems generated pressures for management to take account of change whenever the pressures of problems became evident or opportunities for entrepreneurial action were opened up. Management wanted to adopt a more pro-active posture (sometimes called strategic management) in place of the systematic management which was really the hallmark of the Glueck model. In the perception of many Glueck had simply offered a bureaucratic response to corporate planning.

Lack of technique and quantification

Glueck could tell us something about the corporate planning process, but could shed little light on how such a process should be carried out. Implementation of corporate planning procedures was still a problem area.

Three developments have provided a response to this criticism. Firstly, business consultants and marketeers, led by the Boston Consultancy Group, developed the concept of business portfolios, from which each strategic business unit (SBU) would be selectively managed. Secondly, computer simulation techniques were introduced to develop logistic profiles and unify the planning of production and marketing. This offered a much less confused picture of what would be going on during the next eighteen months and also provided a pro-active base from which some change could be immediately adopted without loss of control and profit. Thirdly, database techniques were being adopted to help in the quantification of many of the critical key result areas and this in turn suggested where the 'winners' and 'losers' were in the organisation. After aggregation of such figures it would be much clearer how and where to promote, rationalise and divest.

The dynamic open systems corporate planning model

This model (illustrated in Figure 17.1) assumes that corporate planning is a continuous process and is encapsulated within the principles of open systems theory. Exchanges

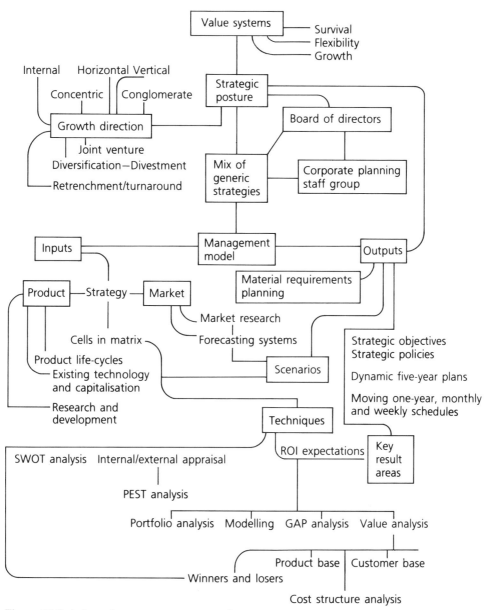

Figure 17.1 *A dynamic open systems approach*

within the model can occur at any time and as new opportunities or threats arise, they can be dealt with and evaluated against a backcloth of well-formulated strategic objectives and policies, to ensure that the response is both rapid and informed.

The basic model has inputs which, after analysis and processing, become outputs. The process is influenced by the driving force of the value systems and restrained by techniques which provide both quantitative and qualitative data. The outputs are expressed as updated strategies, policies, plans, objectives, tactics, scenarios and yearly schedules. The summary of the patterns of the inputs suggests changes in direction and from these changes revised policies can be developed.

Corporate planning does not happen in a vacuum. Line and staff management groups need to work together to develop plans through the exercise of good teamwork.

Two-pass analysis approach

There are really two initial passes or exercises involved in using the dynamic model of corporate planning. Firstly, there is the need to take top-level decisions about the direction of the organisation which come from a clear appreciation of aggregate pictures of the business. Secondly, there is the need to analyse critically each basic element of the business for its value and role in the corporate plan. From the second exercise the aggregate picture may be expected to emerge. That in turn should ensure that the first exercise has a basic credibility.

Competitive forces

Michael Porter (1985) identifies five key influences from which competitive pressures arise:

1. Current industry competitors,
2. Potential entrants,
3. Buyers,
4. Substitutes,
5. Suppliers.

Porter avers that there are three key strategic options open to counter these competitive forces. They are:

1. Least cost — the product or service is cheaper,
2. Differentiation — the product or service is different,
3. Focus — the product or service is the most visible.

Growth direction

The most important single concept in corporate planning is the notion of growth direction. This must take account of competitive forces and the threats and opportunities they bring. As an organisation grows, it absorbs further internal resources or combines with other units in a search for synergy. Synergy occurs when the sum value of combined units is greater than the sum of them as individual parts. The recognition of synergistic opportunities forms the bedrock of a successful policy on growth direction. Basic economics sheds light on the main choices of growth direction. These are as follows:

Internal growth

A healthy business can plough back profits to consolidate and evolve naturally.

Horizontal growth

An organisation can take over another organisation in the same industry to achieve economies of scale. This is generally adopted when the industry is doing well and there are more growth opportunities than can be accommodated by internal growth. This policy can be used to quicken the growth process. Synergy is often found through the manufacturing, marketing or research and development opportunities brought about by the combination of two organisations.

Vertical growth

An organisation can opt to control a longer supplier or customer chain for the business clout that this control will bring. A motor manufacturer may take over its distribution chain. That would be called forwards integration, i.e. nearer the customer. If the motor manufacturer took over the supplier of tyres, then that would be called backwards integration, i.e. nearer the supplier.

The major snag of vertical integration is that the more a business is stretched across different technologies, the more likely it is to lose its expertise and excellence and business performance. For example, the core technology of motor manufacture is assembly work and very different from the technology of making tyres.

Concentric growth

An organisation which has a mastery of a technology can exploit this further through being repositioned into other products. An engine-maker might wish to expand from making engines for lawnmowers to making engines for water pumps, gaining necessary economies of scale and thus synergy in the core activity of engine manufacture.

Partnership or joint venture

In this choice there is generally a common core of technology which at least two organisations wish to develop and thus gain economies of scale, particularly during the research and development stage. This sharing of costs by joint venture may be preferable to growth by full merger, particularly when the two organisations are from different countries. A variation on this theme is to license a product or process on a royalty basis to another party.

Divestment

In this choice a part of the business is sold off to another organisation and the capital realised is used to promote the remaining core part of the business. This might mean a shrinkage of the parent business, but with a realignment of financial resources it may still open the path to growth.

Diversification

This option may be attractive when the firm is very concentrated in a single technology in an industry which is in decline or under severe pressures. The diversification is done to spread the risk. Commonly the direction in which diversification is undertaken will reflect a direction which is compatible with the strengths of the firm whether in marketing, manufacturing, property, etc.

Imperial Tobacco, for instance, at one time diversified into printing and then into the food industry. Its skills in brand management were relevant in the food industry and its skills in printing and packaging were transferable outwith the core tobacco business, which had come under threat from reports connecting cancer with smoking. Eventually this diversification rather backfired as Imperial did not achieve the expected benefits and Hanson Trust took them over and then sold off the main non-tobacco interests with good profits.

In the financial services industry diversification has often been inspired by the forces of deregulation and the requirement to offer a wider portfolio of services in order to compete. In 1987 the Trustee Savings Bank, which had lots of cash deposits, took over Hill Samuel, which needed much more capital to back its merchant banking business. This diversification was also a consolidation of position in the financial services market.

Conglomerate growth

The word 'conglomerate' suggests that there is no natural similarity between the business of the parent and the business of the acquired organisation. The inspiration behind this growth is basically financial opportunism and the outcome of 'wheeler dealer'-type entrepreneurs. In times of economic boom this can be a successful form of growth, but in times of recession the conglomerate, with its lack of specialisation, tends to be vulnerable. The core expertise of the conglomerate is probably financial management, but because such an organisation is likely to be involved in many different technologies and businesses it is extremely difficult to achieve consistency in investment decisions.

Retrenchment or turnaround

This is almost the reverse of a growth direction. In the early 1980s in the United Kingdom, the credit squeeze imposed by the Thatcher Government to curb inflation put many businesses under strain, particularly in terms of liquidity. They were obliged to manage for cash rather than manage for profit in order to survive in the short term.

Successful turnaround management requires massive cost-cutting and generally a change in the executive team. As change in top executives represents a change in the power structure of the organisation, this is very difficult to secure until the crisis is developed sufficiently for some form of external intervention to be possible. Dr Slatter, of the London Business School, did many studies on turnaround situations in the United Kingdom in the early 1980s.

As a last resort a company may actively seek another company which is prepared to take it over. However, synergy does not develop when two weak units come together. This was a bitter lesson for Upper Clyde Shipbuilders in the 1970s. Unless the weak unit can be turned around it may become a black hole sucking in requirements for cash and bringing down its takeover patron.

A variation on this theme is the *management buy-out*, when the company is secured through finance raised by the existing executives, generally with help from a merchant bank, and perhaps also through loans or grants from a public authority such as the

Scottish Development Agency. The management buy-out will work if the business is basically a healthy one in terms of products and technology, but perceived as weak commercially by its existing proprietors as a member of a larger group. Once broken up to a more manageable size and with dedicated owner-executives, commercial performance may be restored.

The above analysis could give a business a set of broad strategic choices about growth direction, but the snag is that they are dependent on the visibility of aggregate business pictures. Gathering the organisation's data which go into making the aggregate pictures requires a further significant and disciplined analysis.

Building up aggregate pictures

The starting point under the dynamic model of corporate planning for this part of the exercise is a critical appraisal of each of the basic units of the business, i.e. each cell of the product/market matrix.

The assumption is that the business operates in more than one market and with more than one product, and that the combination of the concept of market and product gives several distinct cells for the business. These are defined as strategic business units. This focus on strategic business units is a refinement of the more traditional concept of divisions.

Many large companies for convenience of organisation structure break themselves down into decentralised and profit-centred divisions and run them as though there were separate independent businesses, each under a general manager. In reality it might not be practicable to set up a separate management structure at the level of the SBU as it would be expensive to staff each one as a separate unit. However, the concept of the SBU is a convenient one to adopt for the purpose of business analysis.

The analysis of strategic business units

Each SBU is carefully defined and scrutinised. Its past performance and future prospects are examined. A PEST analysis of the external environment is combined with a SWOT analysis to take account of both internal strengths and external competition. This gives a profile for each SBU cell.

Product life-cycles Next there is the process of summarising the groups of cells to build up a business picture which takes account of the product life-cycle and changing market conditions. Products and services are said to have a life-cycle of eight stages. These are as follows:

1. Research,
2. Pilot run or mock-up,
3. Production runs,
4. Launch on the market,
5. Acceptance and development within the market-place,
6. Consolidation in the market-place,
7. Decline,
8. Product obsolescence.

To achieve continuity, the business forecasting largely relates to analysis of product life-cycles and the need to fund research and development to produce new products at the right time. Add to this estimates of costs and prices and the engineering data related to manufacturing standards, then the logistics required to support a particular volume may be computed. The resulting business picture will reveal profiles by product, by product family, by major customer or market, by division, by country, etc., and these profiles may be permanently maintained on a database for continuous review. In chapter 13 of this text, the computerised routines for material requirements planning were illustrated, demonstrating this kind of analysis in action, and then chapter 15 illustrated a practical implementation of the ideas with the forecasters.

From these data and analysis it is possible to develop an aggregate view, so that the strategic posture of the firm may be continuously reviewed. From the strategic posture some ten generic strategies may be considered to reflect the future direction of the firm. These strategies are listed in Table 17.1.

In practice a firm will adopt some mix of these generic strategies. There will, however, be a shared perception throughout the ranks of management about what this mix is and how it relates to their own position. When new opportunities arise they will be related to the strategic posture and if a fit is achieved within this outline, they will then be evaluated using one or more of the techniques highlighted in the model. Techniques are used to screen proposals, to decide whether or not to pursue particular action or to attach a priority rating to such proposal. Many choices will be offered, not all will be approved and not all those approved will be funded.

Outputs

The model of corporate planning as defined in Figure 17.1 is essentially an input/output model. After the raw data have been analysed, management needs useful outputs. In

Table 17.1   *The ten generic strategies reflecting an organisation's strategic position*

1.   Maintenance of the status quo.
2.   Consolidation of the existing business.
3.   Liquidation of weak business units or underutilised assets.
4.   Strategic cost reductions or efficiency improvements in the existing business.
5.   Search for new markets.
6.   Search for new products within existing range.
7.   Search for new range of products.
8.   Search for new technology for products.
9.   Search for joint venture with other partner.
10.   Search for new partner for diversification and growth. Options: horizontal, vertical, concentric, conglomerate. Some element of synergy is expected to influence choice of option.

(Much of the above is developed from the work of Ansoff, 1965.)

this model they are a revised strategic posture, strategic objectives and policies, dynamic five-year plans, rolling one-year monthly and weekly schedules and finally key result areas. This mix of outputs attempts to blend the long- and short-term perspectives and give a realistic framework for planning. Because the plan is timeframed, quantified and detailed for the first eighteen months there is considerable reliance on effective forecasting for the short term backed up by computerised routines such as material requirements planning.

Flexibility is, however, maintained in the short term, as the MRP routines are designed to respond to changes authorised in the short-term forecasting or capacity provision. Regular monitoring of actual business against forecast throws up variances and when these become serious a full new review is triggered for the short-term section of the corporate planning process.

For the longer term, use is made of scenarios, i.e. the stating of assumptions about the future. Writers in the late 1970s were highly critical of companies producing just one corporate plan. The turbulence of the business environment can render one plan much too fragile. Contemporary wisdom suggests that companies really should have several corporate plans. Each one will be contingent on a set of significant assumptions about the future which would directly and significantly affect the company's future. Such significant pictures of the future are named scenarios.

The process

Some quantitative techniques of corporate planning may be grouped together and associated with the notion of satisfying expectations concerning the return on investment. The outcome of applying such techniques is the segregation of the products and services and their associated markets into winners and losers, which should make investment decisions more rational. These techniques include value analysis, cost structure analysis, gap analysis and portfolio analysis.

Corporate value analysis

This is a technique with its roots in engineering, sometimes called value engineering, and its purpose is to achieve simplicity and the best possible value in purchasing components and processing the product.

This technique may be applied for finished products and product groupings. There are generally two dimensions to the process. The first dimension is that of the product. Value analysis applied to the product identifies winners and losers by simply listing the total range in descending order of annual value (from invoices), annual profit, annual cost. Pareto has a rule which often applies to populations and is known as the 80/20 rule. In inventory situations it is common for 80 per cent of the value of items to lie in just 20 per cent of the items. This observation also often applies to profit distributions, so we may try it out on the annual usage figures for recognition of significant winners. The top 20 per cent of items may be expected to contribute 80 per cent of such profit. These top 20 per cent are highlighted for product improvement, the bottom 30 per cent of items are scanned for removal from the catalogues altogether and the middle 50 per cent are scanned for possible product rationalisation. This is essential for cutting out the dead wood in the product range and determining priorities for increasing resource effort, but it must be done using agreed protocols to prevent over-pruning and removing of low-cost, weak-profit items, which may support high-profit items. Items that come early in their product development cycle, and have not had a chance of reaching maturity, need special protection in this analysis.

Some marketeers might take exception to the above paragraph, as it seems to strike a blow at customer choice and product variety! If this wide choice is crucial to success in marketing, it is essential that pricing policy reflects this situation, so that unrationalised product structures still make the appropriate contribution to profit.

This exercise is generally done twice: firstly, using the annual value as a base, which reflects the gross activity of the business; secondly, the annual profit is used as a base. The two lists are then compared and significant differences in the order placings are carefully analysed. If the profit does not follow the business activity, then there is at least the suspicion that the business is busy but not effective.

British Leyland for some years seemed to fly in the face of this policy by their treatment of the smaller cars in their product range. The Mini, for instance, sold for over twenty years with a tiny profit margin, yet received a significant percentage of company resources. The argument seemed to be that customers would be drawn into the Leyland range from the smaller models, then gradually move up-market to the higher-margin larger models. Many critics were, however, very sceptical about this interpretation of consumer buying behaviour and suggested that consumers seek the best bargain available in a general price range, regardless of manufacturer.

The second dimension in a value analysis exercise is to the firm's customer base. Customers are listed in descending order of business volume and also of perceived profit, taking into account discounts and selling expenses. Again, the list is divided into bands and marketing policies are articulated for each different band to get maximum profit from each element within the customer base. Pruning and promotion of this base are carried out to gain maximum impact on profit. The only major difficulty in implementing this part of the analysis is in the collection and analysis of discount and cost information by customer.

Proposals for change, articulated as investment propositions are then related to cash flows and pay-off periods associated with risk, and the screening process can be completed. Following this analysis and screening process (leg-work done by the corporate planning team), the board may choose particular strategies for the formulation of the corporate plan. This value analysis approach can be a very powerful technique for developing the aggregate pictures of the business in terms of winners and losers, necessary for making sense on decisions about growth direction for the organisation.

Cost structure analysis

A firm operating with several profit centres will have to overcome the problem of allocating overheads fairly in the cost structure of the products. There is no one right way of doing this. Cost structure analysis is a technique for valuing the options available.

This will be particularly necessary in a competitive situation where the chief competitor has a different mix of profit centres and thus a different allocation of overheads, which may distort pricing decisions, offering competitors an advantage.

Dr Slatter (1984), of the London Business School, was to find this technique of much relevance in consultancies on 'turnaround' assignments of the early 1980s.

Gap analysis

Gap analysis was developed by Argenti (1968). He recognised that inertia killed most attempts at setting up a corporate planning capability. His technique was to start with the crude assumption that the organisation would undertake no new developments for the next five years. He would then analyse the firm by projecting cash-flow from existing product lines and product markets, taking account of expected return on investment on capital already invested in the business. The result of this projection would almost inevitably show a decline in the return on investment over the future five-year period. Many products, in the normal course of events, would in terms of their product life-cycles move from maturity to decline and from decline to obsolescence. He would then quantify the gap as the difference between normal return on investment and the projection. The gap would then quantify the minimum amount to be done to maintain the profit position. This amount would provide input to the decision-making process relating to new products and new markets. If these new products and markets could not be developed through the existing business structure then a strategy of diversification would have to be considered. Argenti builds on the foundations laid by Ansoff (1965) and Drucker (1954) from their discussion of product/market strategy.

Portfolio analysis

Hedley, of the Boston Consultancy Group, offers this refinement from Argenti's gap analysis. Hedley's view (1977) is that at any one time a large business may be operating in many product market segments, each of which is, in a sense, a separate business. Just as a farmer spreads his risk by having several crops, so a business may run a cluster of mini-businesses. Decisions have to be made; for example, in which mini-business should investments be made, from which mini-business should profits be transferred to other businesses and which mini-business should be liquidated? Each business segment is placed on this two-dimensional matrix. On the basis of the subsequent analysis, particular business policies are developed to maximise business success. This process is known as portfolio analysis. The word portfolio comes from stock exchange usage and the word analysis relates to those specific business policies which may be suggested by placing in this matrix. The businesses so defined are also called strategic business units, described above.

Example of product portfolio management

Product portfolio management, as developed by the Boston Consultancy Group, emphasises the assumed relationship between market share and per unit profitability. As market share increases, and as the total industry growth increases, the experience curve effect on production costs makes market share in a growth industry attractive

Market share
(indirectly correlated with funds source)

		High	Low
Industry/ product growth rate (indirectly correlated with funds use)	High	Star products	Question marks
	Low	Cash-cows	Dog products

Figure 17.2 *Growth-market share matrix*

through its relative profits. Product portfolio managers should analyse products by means of a growth and market share matrix, using a circle of proportional size for each single product's sales. As growth slows or market share declines, proceeds from declining products should be invested in products with increasing market shares or relative growth, unless reinvestment in slow growth and declining share is the only alternative. Underlying the movement of products over the matrix are the industry and company's decisions and the product life-cycle itself. The Boston Consultancy Group's work with Joseph E. Seagram and Sons Limited provides a useful example of product portfolio management. The growth-market share matrix is summarised in Figure 17.2.

The best portfolio strategy is to utilise funds from cash-cows to make star products from question marks.

After a product portfolio is completed for the firm and its competitors, the marketing strategist then assesses the company's own position versus the industry in general and competitors in particular, the balance of funds, the distribution of profits and the movement or trend of products over a period of several years.

Figure 17.3 shows the Seagram brands on a BCG matrix. Canadian Club is a dominant cash-cow with 7 per cent growth but 40 per cent market share. The circle size represents volume by cases. Vodka has a spectacular growth of 36 per cent, but only 11 per cent market share. It is currently a question mark, but a possibility for star status if greater market share can be expected from further investment. Gin, however, is in a dog position with a decline of 6 per cent, and only a market share of 8 per cent, so it is better to divest from here altogether.

Implementation of portfolio analysis
It is difficult to fault the concept of portfolio analysis from the perspective of profit, but it is not so easy to get management to apply this type of thinking and maintain an

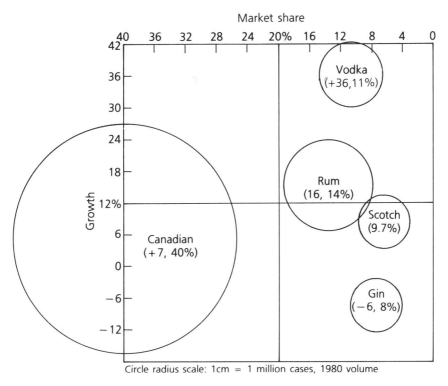

Figure 17.3 *Seagram brands on BGC matrix*
(Source: Justis, Judd and Stephens (1985), p. 197. Reprinted with permission of Professor John Barnett)

open management style. In many organisations it is difficult for an executive to move from one part of a business to another. It must be rather demoralising knowing that you work for a 'dog' strategic business unit and that you will be liquidated at the first opportunity. Furthermore, in most organisations, several of the leading executives have a long-established historical connection with and commitment to certain business deals or products and are most unhappy about the type of labels which portfolio analysis generates.

The existing organisation structure can also be a significant restraining force which frustrates the application of portfolio analysis. There tends to be much commitment to the power and other relationships which are built up over time from an existing structure and change is painful. Yet in order to develop effective and productive businesses it is not possible to ignore the techniques of the management accountant, including portfolio analysis, which can play a part in the processes of corporate planning. However, it is necessary to manage the change process so that implementation is possible. The behavioural sciences can provide assistance in doing this and getting a feel for what it takes to initiate interventions. This is covered in Part 5.

Summary of corporate planning concrete

1. The adoption of a long-range corporate planning approach gives a company a regular and systematic way of taking stock of its strategic posture and renewing this in the light of the changing environment.
2. Techniques of corporate planning help companies anticipate trouble in time for corrective action to be developed.
3. Techniques of corporate planning help to identify winners and losers both in the product catalogue and customer base and detect when a change in strategy is called for. The process of building up aggregate pictures of a business from the basic elements tends to stimulate an innovative and critical approach.
4. Evaluative techniques of corporate planning help in screening possible strategic changes to improve their prospects of viability.
5. The corporate planning approach encourages teamwork in staff work in groups working for the board and gives emphasis to the activities of forecasting and scenario development.
6. With careful implementation the corporate planning staff group should be able to clarify issues for the board without a functional bias. The group should assist the board in achieving unity in expressing corporate policy.
7. A credible output from the corporate planning process should provide a solid input for the transmission process — i.e. MbO can be used to translate and integrate activity throughout the business.

The model in action

The dynamic model developed above concentrates on corporate processes at the summit of the organisation and at the level of strategic business unit, where each such unit is considered as an integral entity. Unfortunately, large companies tend not to be organised in quite such a neat fashion. Typically, sales and manufacturing units are separated and then coordinated under regions. IBM UK may be regarded as an example of this. Barry Goodier, Strategy Management Manager at IBM's Greenock facility, gave a presentation to the Strategic Planning Society at the Glasgow Branch on 21 April 1988, which illustrated how these concepts of corporate planning may be applied in specific situations. The presentation was entitled 'Concepts of Strategy'. Barry Goodier formerly had been the Quality Manager for the IBM PCs at the plant. Extracts and comments are given below.

IBM could clear £14,000 net profit after tax per employee. What was the management practice behind such a formidable performance? What was the nature of strategic management away from Head Office?

Goodier began the presentation with the organisation chart of IBM at Greenock. The Plant Director has two main line managers under him, both with several layers of management. Attached directly to the Plant Director was the strategy management group, as a staff group, and Barry Goodier has three assistants working with him.

The strategy management group had been going for two years. The role of the group was a developing one and was unique to the Greenock plant, though its activities had attracted some favourable attention at the English sister plant in Havant and at the European Headquarters in Paris. The current high-level corporate planning was coordinated in an annual cycle at Paris, whose outcome was a set of strategic goals. The established input to the Paris annual planning cycle was representation by the main unit directors from the other plants and organisations within the European Community.

At the highest level strategy management is about winning in business. It is essential to compete in order to win and for that it is necessary to do the following:

1. Know your own goals.
2. Have interlocking strategies (many pieces here).
3. Have a winning structure.

The highest level goals of IBM are simple and can be summarised as follows:

1. Excellence of products,
2. Sustained growth of business and market share,
3. Products that fit the changing taste and demand of the market,
4. Excellence in quality.

Figure 17.4 suggests that it is possible to target in particular areas for specific objectives from the fragmentation of general goals. As a result it is possible to identify very specific projects, and these require action to be taken.

Goodier stated that strategy was the art of generalship and had:

- a long-term aspect — towards an idea,
- a short-term programme for action,
- maintenance to keep standards up.

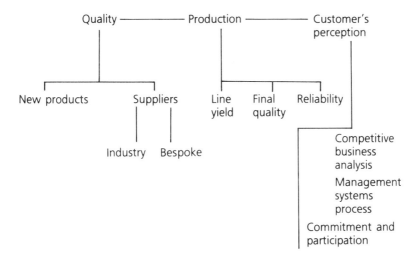

Figure 17.4 *Goal fragmentation at IBM Greenock*

The characteristics of effective management strategy had to be:

- consistent with plant goals,
- relevant to what had to be changed,
- achievable,
- offering viable alternatives.

When people are working on strategy management projects they need to play a coherent and constructive role based on collaboration. Three basic roles had been identified by IBM. The owner of the project assumed total responsibility; the sub-owner had a stake in the immediate outcome; the staffing groups contributed expertise or resource.

Two years after the formation of this strategy management group at Greenock there were some eighty projects in action. Initially, there was much opposition to the group. It was perceived as just another part of the bureaucracy, but as the Plant Director gave it much support it was seen as the relevant mechanism for getting vital performance improvements at the plant. Project review data helped again in the feedback to Regional Headquarters in Paris, and in the dialogue about the strategy and objectives for the Greenock plant. Two years on the strategy management group had achieved acceptability and credibility.

The most healthy aspect of Goodier's presentation was the emphasis on teamwork and getting things done in a collaborative and systematic way. IBM also embraces the techniques of managing by objectives and they use an executive appointment system, whereby every two to three years they are given a move. This tends to stimulate an innovative approach to business, to cross-fertilise, to widen the general management experience of the more senior executives.

The corporate planning model in the public sector

Three inputs are included in this section. The first is from a seminar contribution by the General Manager of Glasgow Greater Health Board, Lawrence Peterkin. This relates to the adoption of a strategic cost-cutting strategy in a large public authority. The second is based on a guidance note 'Corporate Planning in Non-Departmental Public Bodies (NDPBs)', issued by the Treasury and Civil Service College in February 1988. The third is an account of a corporate planning exercise done in a college in the public sector completed in 1988, which follows the general approach of the dynamic model (Figure 17.1 and some features of the guideline on NDPBs above).

Aspects of strategic planning in the health service

Lawrence Peterkin held the post of General Manager of the Glasgow Greater Health Board. He had previously been Controller of Operations of the Greater London Council, and this was after over twenty years in industry.

Peterkin stated that strategic planning was not a ten-year, look-ahead, book-work exercise. Planning must indicate a course of action over a reasonable time-scale. Managers need to know what they can and will execute, and that they have got the money to do this work within their resources. Planning is about change and managers must know how to finance change. When managers make proposals for a project they should be sure that they have the money to start it within a year.

He went on to describe his early days as General Manager at GGHB. The first three months were a honeymoon period in which he could ask questions, and indeed there were many questions in an organisation with a budget of £400 million a year. His obvious first interest was about priorities; after forty years of operation there should have been plenty of evidence of these from many reports, but he was in for a shock. There were no real priorities. The picture was as though there had been little management over the past forty years.

On pressing the point about priorities Peterkin wanted to know how the establishments of the forty-six hospitals in the area were arrived at. It seemed that this was done in response to random pressures. Generally, money was allocated to hi-tech projects regarded as exciting and prestigious, but at the cost of neglecting other areas, particularly the area of mental health. The situation at Lennoxtown Castle, with over 1,200 patients, showed up some real neglect.

Good strategic management is about establishing priorities, thinking through the rationale, getting the balance right and implementing projects to ensure a correct balance. In the past there had been some machinery to establish priorities at the Scottish level and the SHAPE report of 1980 had highlighted mental health as an area of top priority, but nothing had been done about it at lower levels. The reason was that funding was allocated on a formula based on population numbers and age profile and in eight years Glasgow population had reduced from one million to 700,000, putting a great strain on all existing establishments to reduce costs. There was not sufficient discretionary money left to reallocate to the perceived priority areas.

Strategic reviews and cost-cutting in mental health

One way of tackling the mental health problem was to do a concentrated strategic review in the particular area of mental health and to question radically existing methods and the provision of buildings, establishments and teams, in order to find a new way of getting better results. This strategic review might come up with rationalisations and possible savings as well as suggestions of better services and if there was still a gap in funding then costs somewhere else in GGHB might have to be cut to provide for mental health.

There was plenty of opportunity for new and radical thinking. Existing provision was dominated by large institutions set up in Victorian times on the periphery of the city, such as Lennoxtown Castle, with over 1,200 patients. Many patients had been there for twenty or thirty years with little prospects of ever returning to the community. The modern way was to set up mental care teams and give patients treatment and then support so that they would return to live in the community as soon as possible.

Strategic reviews and cost-cutting in maternity

There was some speculation that there was an over-provision of maternity beds in GGHB. Would it be possible to close a unit or achieve some other form of rationalisation?

To make judgements and decisions here it was necessary to have sound information and then apply some realistic assumptions to get to a policy. Details of the population numbers and trends for women of child-bearing age in the catchment area could be provided by the Registrar General for the next ten years.

Next, it was necessary to know what provision of resources would be required to satisfy the demand. This was more difficult, as changes in social attitudes and medical practice would affect how long beds would be occupied. Some years ago the average figure was ten days, now it was only 3.5 days; some women even went home the same day their baby was born. There was a big variation in the average figures from one maternity unit to another, sometimes with good reasons, but in some cases only because of local tradition. Changes in practice could bring these nearer the 3.5 day norm.

There was also a variation between units in the average time a bed was empty. This reflected differences in internal management information systems and admissions practice. Again, it was necessary to establish an attainable good practice norm and secure changes in the units which were currently operating below these norms.

This exercise led to the conclusion that there was an over-provision of some 100 maternity beds. With a rationalising of existing provision and an upgrade of current low performers to the norms a saving of over £1 million a year could be implemented without loss of service.

Finding money from administrative cost cuts

GGHB employs some 27,000 people. Of these, 60 per cent are direct staff — consultants, doctors, nurses, etc., 40 per cent are indirect staff — administrative, catering, etc. The aim was to attempt to shift the balance to two-thirds direct staff and one-third indirect, a shift of some 6 per cent overall. In 1987/8 this was achieved and 1,000 jobs were taken out of the indirect category, creating enough money to fund a further 500 direct staff. This should have improved significantly the level of care for patients. Now how are cuts achieved from the indirects?

An obvious area to scrutinise was catering. The average cost per meal in the different forty-six hospitals ranged from £1 to £2.50. Once you had a picture of these differences, then it was possible to establish acceptable norms and authorise programmes to bring maverick costs into line. The key to this process was the ability to work with data on relative efficiencies and apply the results.

Competitive tendering

For building programmes it was interesting to reflect the balance of costs between professional fees and the actual direct costs of bricks and mortar. It was found that the professional fees charged in GGHB amounted to a uniform 25 per cent of the contract price, so a new form of competitive bidding was introduced among the professionals. This achieved very big savings, but there was a howl of protest from the professional architects' association.

Peterkin's summary

Peterkin stated that realistic strategic planning involves the following factors:

1. Having a mechanism for determining priorities in health care provision.
2. Assessing demand for services.
3. Having an information system which delivers ratios on outputs.
4. Monitoring these.
5. Delivering supported management programmes to secure the actual cost-cutting opportunities.
6. Reallocating saved resources to fund improvements in priority areas of provision and improving staffing of direct labour.

Peterkin was asked how he secured these cost-cutting objectives against opposition from unions and others. He replied that after data on cost-cutting opportunities had been reviewed, management had to be very subtle in securing the change programme. A direct challenge to those with vested interests with open and quantified targets would not always produce the best results.

Comments

Much of Peterkin's address seemed to have its theoretical root in the writings of Frederick Taylor on scientific management. Nearly a century ago Taylor was to postulate the need for critical analysis, followed by setting standards for the one best way of doing the job, then training people to meet the standards and rewarding them with bonuses when the standards were exceeded.

Peterkin's initial observation was that for forty years there had been no visible management at all, save *ad hoc* reactions to pressures, and the Taylorite principles applied to GGHB were a lot better than the previous managerial vacuum. In particular it forced groups to confront the need for innovation and change in GGHB. Peterkin also stated that his own salary was influenced by bonus payments based on achieving financial targets agreed with the Board, hence the emphasis on cost-cutting strategies.

However, the feature which marks out Peterkin from those normally associated with 'Management Services' and Taylorism is that he, Peterkin, was the supremo line manager articulating these techniques, and with his undoubted subtlety and closeness to authority he was able to implement ideas and concepts which few staff-aligned people ever have a chance to do.

Taylorism was much criticised for its inhumanity in implementation. Only the fittest could achieve quantitative standards. Little effort was made to measure and achieve qualitative standards. Yet there seemed to be little real opposition to Peterkin in his implementation tactics.

Corporate planning in non-departmental public bodies (NDPBS)

This section gives a summary of some of the salient points made in the guidance note referred to above (p. 347).

What is a corporate plan?

A corporate plan is a strategic plan for the medium to long term which sets down fundamental aims and the means of progressing towards them. An effective corporate plan will be one which does the following:

1. Agrees a common set of aims and objectives for an organisation.
2. Considers those factors likely to affect their achievement.
3. Establishes comprehensive plans which will ensure that objectives are achieved.
4. Sets out, where necessary, alternative strategies.

What are main benefits of corporate planning?

It ensures that top management makes time to develop a coherent strategy. It can be used to forecast resources and it allows an organisation's existing resources to be allocated appropriately in line with policies and priorities agreed within government.

Many NDPBs and their sponsoring departments and the Treasury hold regular informal meetings throughout the corporate planning process, which can iron out difficulties as they arise.

What is involved in the corporate planning process?

The factors involved are as follows:

1. Setting organisational aims.
2. Deciding longer-term objectives.
3. Assessing the organisation's strengths and weaknesses.
4. Making explicit assumptions about the body's operational environment.
5. Identifying priorities among objectives and targets.
6. Identifying performance indicators and measures of output.

Summary of good corporate planning

Good corporate planning incorporates the following features:

1. *Integrative* — bringing together all parts of the organisation.
2. *Simple* — the underlying principles and structure should be easily stated and understood.
3. *Clear* — forecasting and other assumptions are explicit.
4. *Feasible* — it is realistic and anticipates possible barriers to its achievement.
5. *Flexible* — it is readily adjusted in the light of changes to the internal or external environment.

Comment

The guidance note inevitably has an emphasis on funding and getting value for money, particularly in a time when Government saw fit to impose cash limits with some rigour. However, it does provide the basis for realistic dialogue between the fund providers and users, and thus offers a useful contribution to accountability. Once one looks at particular NDPBs it is evident that they offer a portfolio of services, so the priority setting and determination of winners and losers may be done in a similar way as that adopted in the private sector and demonstrated in Figure 17.1. However, political considerations will probably play a more prominent part than in the private sector analysis.

A College corporate planning exercise

Background

In late 1987 the Scottish Education Department sent directives to the Colleges designated as 'Central Institutions' in Scotland requesting them to participate in a corporate planning exercise to cover the period 1988–92. The author participated directly in this exercise.

The Central Institutions of Scotland are those Colleges funded directly by the State. Some have many of the attributes of the English polytechnics. They offer a wide range of courses from Higher National Certificates to programmes leading to a master's award and research degrees. Unlike a university, which has authority to award degrees in its own name, the Central Institutions generally award degrees in the name of the Council for National Academic Awards (CNAA), the validating body.

The exercise considered here was done in a college with an establishment of 4,000 full-time students and a budget of £12 million recurrent grant.

Input guidelines

There were three main guidelines offered by the Scottish Education Department. The first, 'Corporate Planning in NDBPs', has already been discussed in this chapter. The second was contained in a memorandum giving detailed financial parameters and funding assumptions for the Central Institution Sector. The third was a seminar and papers giving government's view of expected student demand in the early 1990s.

Development process in the College

In December 1987 the Directorate, Heads of Departments and other senior officers attended a residential weekend to develop the outline College objectives and strategies and to carry out a critical review of organisation structures, which was necessary to make and implement a corporate plan. A note of this meeting was written and circulated throughout the College.

In January 1988, a small taskforce was set up to write and review the corporate plan and report to the 'Academic Policy Committee'. This was the senior committee of policy of the Academic Board of the College. At the same time a joint committee was set up with representation from the Academic Policy Committee and the College Governors, and some six sub-task groups were formed to develop specific aspects of the corporate plan.

In adopting this process the intention was to get a plan which had support and realism from the three college faculties, the directorate and the College governors.

By June the plan had been through five drafts and had been very widely discussed and was approved for sending to the Scottish Education Department by both the Academic Board and the College Governors.

Methodology

The central bedrock of the corporate plan was the academic plan. This was the statement on the portfolio of course provision and its rationale.

In the business private sector attention is normally focused on product/market strategy and the strategic business units which comprise meaningful groupings, for critical analysis and management. In the college environment the critical analysis started at the course unit. From some three years of annual course board reports, it was possible to develop aggregate pictures of groups of courses, their strengths and weaknesses.

In this instance the taskforce categorised courses as 'P', priority, and requiring more resources; 'S', standard, not requiring a change in funding, 'O', other, requiring a strict annual review either for priority funding or for phasing out owing to problems of student and/or employer demand, quality, etc.

Inevitably many issues were raised and discussed in the crucial development of the academic plan and the relative priorities which emerged from this exercise.

The main outcomes were declarations of priority in honours provision in some crucial areas, the possible shedding of some Higher National Certificate provision to make way for the honours developments and the development of more flexible course structures to reach out more effectively to part-time post-experience students, and those who required a different pattern of education from that currently available. This would enable the College to meet the challenge of the more diversified student population of the 1990s, when there would be fewer children coming through secondary schools for tertiary education.

Some innovation in seeking out new sources of funding was also expected. Collaboration with industry would give rise to more part-time courses, partially funded by employers.

The final document

This was structured as follows:

   Section 1 — The Institution Plan Narrative,
   Section 2 — The Academic Plan,
   Section 3 — Financial Projections.

In section 1 the main objectives, developments and priorities of the College were stated in the light of current government policy and the argument was put forward that funding should be increased over the first three years of the plan. The consequences of adopting a lower level of funding were explicitly stated.

Arguments for improvements in buildings, capital equipment and staffing for the priorities in the academic plan were made. Arguments for a more realistic establishment funding of part-time courses were put. Approval was sought for the more entrepreneurial posture of the College.

In section 3, financial projections were done using the guidelines of the Scottish Education Department and a College-generated guideline. These brought into a finer focus the case for an improvement in funding for three years. The use of computer spreadsheets was used extensively to develop the projections and options and show the consequences of alternative courses of action. Much of the information on resource utilisation (rooms and staff) was gathered and analysed from a computerised College database.

Benefits

Regardless of the final outcome there is no doubt that the development of the Corporate Plan helped much in harnessing together the combined talents of the senior management group of the Institution and providing a framework in which there would be a greater consistency in the allocation of staffing posts, capital equipment, etc. This should become a very useful contribution to ensuring value for money and quality in course provision, and form the relevant focus each year for revision and improvements. The dialogue generated should strengthen still further the relations between College management, Governing Body and the Scottish Education Department.

Summary

The reader may have found this chapter rather complex. The practice of corporate planning is evolving very rapidly in both public and private sectors, and indeed the information society has provided the means and techniques for more elaborate quantification, modelling and review. The dynamic open systems model (Figure 17.1) offered a means of analysing the multi-product company and the offering of many insights into possible directions of growth/divestment, the building up of aggregate pictures from the elements of the business and the managing of the total business in a general awareness of where winners and losers were. This suggested the nature of strategic objectives and policies. Figure 17.1 also suggested a process of analysis which would get the most out of corporate planning efforts and allow techniques of corporate planning to be absorbed within the organisation's culture.

Problems of implementing strategic management at the plant level were considered. The importance of collaboration in task teams working on programmes whose legitimacy derived from the corporate plan was stressed. Finally, attention was turned to the public sector and a brief review of guidelines required for achieving value for public money and setting priorities. This guideline was used to develop and apply a corporate plan for a college. The public sector is normally thought of in terms of a portfolio of services or courses, and a methodology and process for finding winners and losers in these and then managing scarce resources in light of this treatment, taking account of the major stakeholders: government, students, employers, staff. In all work on corporate planning the collaboration of teams and task groups with the main line management structure was seen to be essential.

Case Study 17.1
Mendip Jeeps

(Case published with permission of the Scottish Vocational Education Council.)

This is a simple case in business policy relating to the defence of company independence against a takeover bid and other threats.

Mendip Jeeps Limited was a manufacturer of vehicles designed to operate in extremely difficult terrain. The vehicles were amphibious but because of their unique wheel design could also be used on hilly and rocky ground. Exports accounted for 70 per cent of its sales and the British Government was a major customer. It had a good quality product, much respected for its ruggedness and reliability.

Despite the name, the factory was located in Dumfries, where it was a major employer. The location was the result of intensive lobbying by local politicians and sympathetic Ministers in government. The company had originally wished to set up in Glasgow. However, Government pressure had won the day.

In the fifteen years since its inception the company had become a very important part of the community. People were proud to work at Mendip Jeeps and were well rewarded. The industrial relations record was good, with only one strike (over a dismissal) in its history. During this time there had been no redundancies and the workforce had expanded to its present size of 700.

Because of the unique nature of the Mendip Jeep there had been no direct competition for thirteen years, when the Japanese company, the Mifune Corporation, had produced a jeep similar enough to present increasingly serious problems.

A year ago several large contracts which Mendip had expected to land went instead to the Mifune Corporation. The Mifune jeep was 14 per cent cheaper, of good quality and was being sold through aggressive marketing strategies abroad, especially in the developing countries. When the first Mifune jeeps came on to the British market they sold very well — the result of a sustained and imaginative advertising campaign.

The management of Mendip Jeeps were concerned about these developments but not unduly worried, as they had foreseen the entry of other firms into their market. They felt that a new marketing strategy incorporating a new advertising campaign and a special sales team for developing countries would help to regain lost ground.

Management, especially the Managing Director, Sir Ian Laidlaw, were more concerned about the rapidly rising costs and the liquidity position of the company. By the second quarter of this year the position of the company in liquidity terms was serious indeed — various sources for loans had been approached but none (banks especially) was keen to lend.

In late June thoughts of sales and liquidity were put into a new perspective by a bid for the company by the Columbia Corporation, a multinational firm specialising in the manufacture of heavy trucks and earth-moving equipment.

The management of Mendip Jeeps were keen to resist the bid from Columbia Corporation, but were now in a weak position to oppose it. The share price was low partly because of the competition from Mifune Jeeps and partly because of the rumours of the liquidity problem. However, it was decided to go ahead and oppose the bid. Advertisements placed in the newspapers declared 'Hands off Mendip Jeeps', and appeals were made to shareholder loyalty. At the same time, the Columbia Corporation commissioned a series of advertisements condemning Mendip's policies and results and indicating how much better off Mendip Jeeps would be in their hands.

As the campaign proceeded various interest groups combined to put pressure on the Government to keep Mendip Jeeps in British ownership. The Government declared, however, that this was for the market to decide and was nothing to do with them. Though the opposition tabled a motion condemning Government inactivity, the Government won, albeit with several MPs on the Government side voting against. Mendip Jeeps was on its own and would stand or fall by its own efforts.

Tasks for discussion

1. Develop an appraisal of the situation at Mendip using the corporate planning techniques of PEST and SWOT analysis.
2. Suggest what should be done to secure a sound future for Mendip and its stakeholders.

For discussion of possible feedback see Appendix 1, p. 527.

References

Ansoff, I. (1965), *Corporate Strategy*, McGraw-Hill.
Argenti, J. (1968), *A Practical Guide to Corporate Planning*, Allen & Unwin.
Drucker, P. (1954), *The Practice of Management*, Harper.
Glueck, W.F. (1976), *Business Policy*, McGraw-Hill.
Guidance Note (1988), *Corporate Planning in Non-Departmental Public Bodies (NDPBS)*, issued by the Treasury and Civil Service College, February.
Hedley, B. (1977), 'Strategy and the business portfolio', *Long-Range Planning Journal*, vol. 10, 10 February, pp. 7–15.
Justis, R.T., Judd, R.J. and Stephens, D.B. (1985), *Strategic Management and Policy*, Prentice Hall.
Porter, M.E. (1985), *Competitive Advantage: creating and sustaining superior performance*, Free Press.
Slatter, S. St. P. (1984), *Corporate Recovery: a guide to turnaround management*, Penguin Books.
Taylor F. W. (1911), *Principles of Scientific Management*, Harper.

Part 5

Management, organisation and change

Chapter 18

Schools of organisation and management

Overview

This chapter takes some of the ideas expressed in chapter 1 on the process of management and describes in more detail the theories of major groups of writers, attempting to see relationships between the different schools.

Ten schools of management thought will be outlined, beginning with the nineteenth century and ending in the 1980s. Each school represents a synopsis of a theory about management. A theory is intended to explain managerial behaviour, to predict possible outcomes to managerial situations and to outline and prescribe acceptable management practice. Each theory will relate to the managerial culture of the environment and period. The writers of each school influenced other writers as they responded to what they saw as inadequacies in existing theories until this reaction gradually became recognised as a new school of thought in its own right. Hence the evolution by the 1980s of some ten main schools of thought and the robust dismissal of the assumption that managers are born not made. Current wisdom suggests that managers can learn from exposure to managerial theory and grow in managerial knowledge, skill and competence as they put their real-life managerial experiences into a coherent framework of theory and sound practice.

Learning objectives

After working through this chapter readers may be expected to recognise the organisational climate and management style of their own and other organisations and whether such a style is appropriate. The chapter ends with exercises to reinforce this learning objective.

Figure 18.1 links together various schools and attempts to show the relationships and influences of schools on one another.

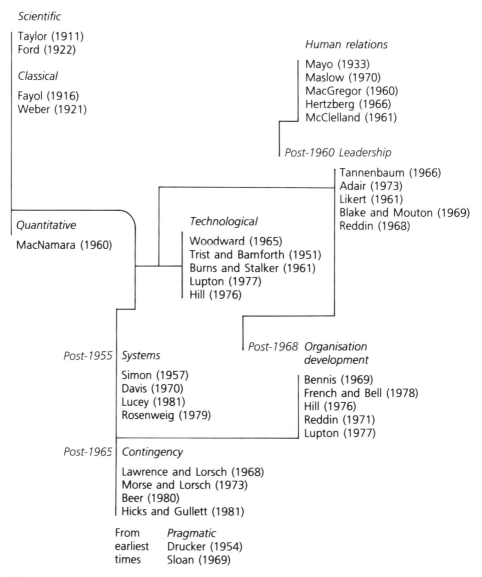

Figure 18.1 *Schools of organisation*

The scientific school

The roots of this school lay in the United States. Frederick Taylor experimented in the 1880s and published his results in 1911. Taylor was a production engineer and is acknowledged as the father of a discipline called Work Study. In the Bethlehem Steel Corporation he observed the unsystematic methods that labourers employed to move pig-iron from one part of the yard to another. On studying this job scientifically he found poor use of layouts, inappropriate tools, inappropriate transport buckets and far from optimised gang-working practices. From his laboratory, with the pig-iron worker Schmidt he experimented at length until he was satisfied that he had designed an optimum working method. This involved the minimum effort, the minimum resources and the optimum sequence of predetermined, specialised activities. Having designed this optimum method and tested it out in the laboratory his next task was to transfer the method to the other members of the workforce, who were only allowed to stay in his workforce if they achieved his rigorous standards of production. His main organisation norm was the norm of efficiency to which everything else was subservient. The employee was encouraged to look upon himself as an extension of the machinery and high bonus earnings were assumed to be the only reward necessary for efficient and boring work. Work study seemed to be the answer to all production management problems. The production workforce would be divided into two groups. The first group would be the experimenters and thinkers who developed current practice into scientific method, and the second group, the 'doers', who simply implemented the scientific practice developed by the 'thinker' group. The owner/stakeholder within this theory was the predominant stakeholder of the system. Taylor did, however, run into trouble when he was called before a Committee of Congressmen in 1910 and charged with exploitation of his labour force through setting unattainable and unreasonable standards of work.

Rigorously ordered activity and the possible exploitation resulting from scientific management methods can arouse strong emotions. In the 1980s factory farming methods (a manifestation of scientific management) were much criticised. Who cannot but sympathise with the lot of the battery hen? One can only hope that after some twenty generations the genes of the bird have conditioned it to tolerate boredom.

Taylor's success with developing scientific production methods was adopted by Henry Ford in the development of the car assembly-line. The idea of low-cost, high-volume mechanistic production methods was to dominate much of production industry well into the twentieth century. Another development from Taylor's work-study methods is the scientific critical method for office and paperwork procedures. Many contemporary large organisations base their establishments of clerical and office labour on the results of organisation and methods analyses. The methods and outcomes of this branch of scientific management theory are slightly different from work study, but the assumptions about implementation and the norms of efficiency and mechanisation are the same.

Writers such as Shaw (1952) developed analytical techniques with a view to balancing the movements of the human body and questioning the widely accepted cultural assumption that people are not ambidextrous. Much evidence suggests, in contrast, that with encouragement the majority of people are capable of sufficient ambidexterity to enable common DIY activities, such as painting a house or washing a car, to be done with two brushes in half the time! An ambidextrous squash player who can swop racquets can virtually double his or her reach and develop a game with a high order of play. To get the advantages of this approach it is necessary to be able to challenge creatively long-held assumptions about the way things are done.

The scientific school does not generate as much attention in management as it did earlier in the twentieth century. Yet it is still claimed by work-study practitioners that when they move in to investigate an operational process for the first time an improvement in utilisation of resources of some 30 per cent is not unusual!

An incident in a factory

The author can recall an incident in a factory in the early 1960s, when he was a trainee and was asked to complete a small work-study assignment in the department responsible for cutting pipe tobacco. The work group consisted of a line of ten cutting machines, each with an operator. The men were all long-service employees; tea breaks — a vital part of the day — were assigned on the basis of seniority, and the junior man in this group got the last tea break — he had only done 42 years with the company, all in the one job!

In analysing what the men did it soon became clear that the operation had three phases. Firstly, the man was busy preparing a tray of bars of tobacco and putting flavouring on them. Secondly, both man and machine were busy, while the bars were inserted in the machine for cutting and held during the cutting sequence. A wooden slat was held at the end of the tray, so his fingers would not get near the dreaded blade. Thirdly, the man alone would be busy, removing the cut tobacco and stacking the tray with others, ready for packing. It is easy to mime this sequence among managers and expose it to scientific management scrutiny. With a little coaxing, suggestions for improvement will come quickly. One such suggestion might be: 'Put an automatic device on the machine to free the man during the cutting sequence, when both man and machine are busy.' A more radical suggestion might be: 'Reposition the layouts of the machine, so that one operator can handle four machines from the centre of a circle.' Suffice it to conclude that in this instance the 30 per cent productivity improvement was easily achieved. The intriguing observation was that this group of ten operators had spent a lifetime at work without realising that these improvements were possible and trainee managers could spot these same improvements within half an hour. People seem to be so easily institutionalised by their own environment or their vested interest in the status quo.

The classical school

This school of thought has its roots before management as such was considered to be an academic discipline. By the nineteenth century large organisations were a familiar part of the economy. The theory of the state and of constitutional practice had been well developed within the United Kingdom through the development of constitutional law and practice. Much interest at that time was focused on balancing the power of the state in such a way as to ensure the liberty of the subject. Other large organisations included the ecclesiastical and the military. All such organisations are organised within the framework of a hierarchy of authority. Thus hierarchical structure exists to ensure the norm of conformity among the members. The authority itself tended to have its source in patronage exercised by the establishment.

In the 1870s there was a major outcry to remedy incompetence and move away from patronage in the public service. The Civil Service Commission was formed to select a meritocracy based on academic excellence which would supersede patronage. As soon as professional, academic, merit-oriented criteria form the basis for selection and promotion within organisations there is the beginning of systematic management, whose purpose it is to ensure managerial effectiveness. Norms of meritocracy and professionalism and the principles of impartiality were promoted at the expense of corrupt practice and patronage.

However, the individual finds that the organisation is viewed as a tool of its hierarchical head. This head is the predominant stakeholder and highly mechanistic rules ensure that power is exercised downwards throughout the organisation. This organisational type is appropriate when operating in a simple environment, which is not required to adapt rapidly, which has an inherent need for operational unity and which reflects the organisation's expectation of standardisation and conformity.

Some main contributors to classical management theory are Henri Fayol (1916) and Max Weber (1921). Fayol, whose background was as the head of a large industrial mining organisation within a stable environment and run on militaristic principles, is well known for his six verbs of the management process: command, control, coordinate, forecast, plan and organise; and his fourteen principles, which he believed had a universal application. His fourteen principles are as follow:

1. Division of work. The principle of specialisation of work in order to concentrate activities for more efficiency.
2. Authority and responsibility. Authority is the right to give orders and the power to exact obedience.
3. Discipline. Discipline is absolutely essential for the smooth running of the business, and without discipline no enterprise could prosper.
4. Unity of command. An employee should receive orders from one superior only.
5. Unity of direction. There should be only one head and one plan for a group of activities having the same objectives.
6. Subordination of individual interests to general interests. The interest of one employee or a group should not prevail over that of the organisation.
7. Remuneration of personnel. Compensation should be fair and, as far as possible, afford satisfaction to both personnel and the firm.
8. Centralisation. Centralisation is essential to the organisation and is a natural consequence of organising.
9. Scalar chain. The scalar chain is the chain of superiors ranging from the ultimate authority to the lowest rank.
10. Order. The organisation should provide an orderly place for every individual — a place for everyone and everyone in their place.
11. Equity. Equity and a sense of justice pervade the organisation.
12. Stability of tenure of personnel. Time is needed for employees to adapt to their work and to perform it effectively.

13. Initiative. At all levels of the organisational ladder, zeal and energy are augmented by initiative.
14. *Esprit de corps*. This principle emphasises the need for teamwork and the maintenance of interpersonal relationships.

Another writer of the classical school was Max Weber. He was a sociologist best known for the mechanistic principles which he developed to describe an organisational form which he called bureaucracy. Our contemporary interpretation of that term is one of abuse and red tape. In contrast, Weber used the term to denote an efficient organisation structure. The predominant stakeholder within Weber's bureaucracy was clearly management. This group desired predictability, standardisation, conformity and straightforward administration. Other stakeholders such as employees, customers, clients and suppliers were largely ignored. Management was seen as the prerogative of managers, developed in the interest of managers. Every other stakeholder was obliged to tolerate the predominant managerial interest.

The quantitative school

Writers of the quantitative school are significantly influenced by the groundwork of Taylor. The following disciplines were developed by this school and they are all manifestations of critical analysis and modelling.

1. Critical path analysis,
2. Operational research,
3. Organisation and methods techniques and principles,
4. Management accounting,
5. Decision theory,
6. Robotics.

The rationale behind these techniques is that it is possible to create an abstract mathematical model to simulate business conditions. Once such a model has been constructed, a declaration is made of an objective function and figures are entered to suggest managerial action towards the optimum and at the same time an analysis is provided of the sensitivity of the model and the consequences of adopting sub-optimal solutions.

There is a number of significant difficulties in this approach. Firstly, there might be a mismatch between the abstract model so constructed and the real world. Secondly, the model may be so complicated that users find interpretation of results impossible. Thirdly, some of the relationships assumed in the model are invalid. Fourthly, in real organisations objectives tend to be multiple and conflicting. The solutions coming out of the quantitative models assume a single optimum criterion. Thus, they are an aid to complicated decision-making, but only an aid. If implemented mechanistically, disastrous results can ensue.

The quantitative school is experiencing rapid growth, development and refinement in the 1970s and 1980s with the availability of cheap and plentiful computing resources. The delivery of meaningful organisational results using the ideas of the school depends on the numeracy skills of middle and senior management. Traditionally, numeracy has been a significant weak point among UK managers, but the development of management courses and the greater acceptance and credibility of management qualifications is helping to redress this lack of numeracy.

In this school of thought, resources within the organisation are the focal point of interest. The people, political and organisational variables take a poor second place. The weaknesses of Taylor's scientific approach are still evident in the development of his techniques by the quantitative school. Both schools assume a culture of economic rationality where order and certainty become ends in themselves, whereas humanistic, social-oriented mankind, with a desire for variety and stimulus, will reject the extreme implications of the quantitative school and its methods.

An interesting point does sometimes arise. To change a process, 'hi-tech' methods may be adopted to dehumanise an already boring job or robots can be deployed to do it altogether. If we let the robots move in, perhaps that will mean that all that is left will be interesting jobs.

The human relations school

During the late 1920s a reaction was setting in against the extreme implementations of the scientific management school. A particular trouble area was the real tedium and boredom of assembly-line work, which was giving rise to alienation among employees manifested in high absentee rates and high incidence of industrial disputes. Industrial psychologists came on the scene and research programmes were undertaken.

The best known of such programmes was developed under the leadership of Elton Mayo in assignments at the Hawthorn Electric Company in the early 1930s. Elton Mayo is generally acknowledged as being the father of the human relations school. He initially attempted to define scientifically the relationship between productivity from a work group and the quality of the working environment. His initial hypothesis was that improvements in the working environment would naturally lead to an increase in productivity. However, a surprise result was encountered when he put the experiment in reverse. Instead of productivity declining with a measured deterioration in the working environment, productivity continued to rise! Mayo then developed a dialogue with the research group to find the reason for this. The main conclusion from this dialogue was that people at work related to a social environment as well as a technical environment. The experimental group had, prior to the experiment, considered itself an unimportant group. However, during the experiment the members developed a feeling of cohesion and importance as a result of observation by top management and Elton Mayo's researchers. Elton Mayo concluded that high productivity was obtainable only if human social needs were taken into account in addition to task and job needs.

Mayo then moved to another part of the plant where management could not understand why they had encountered such difficulty in changing an output standard. After interviewing the people concerned he reported on the existence of an informal organisation at work. The essential element of this informal organisation was the influence exercised by a few key norm-setters. The norm-setters decided among themselves what their perception of a fair day's work was and anyone exceeding that standard would be labelled a 'rate-buster', while any member of the group significantly under-producing would be labelled a 'chiseller'. Chisellers and rate-busters would then be subjected to severe group pressures to ensure that they conformed to group norms. As rejection by the group is perceived as a very severe penalty, the norm-setters' standards would tend to be observed unanimously, even though in the light of changing business circumstances they might be perceived by management as being utterly unrealistic.

Many writers following Mayo have researched the informal organisation and even offered some guidelines on how it may be managed to the advantage of management. Informal organisations are founded primarily on the basis of friendship and bondage, and groups of people with similar interests will combine, particularly if their interest is threatened. Informal organisation structure often operates to distort and filter information, particularly information moving upwards in an organisation. To report events or happenings which are contrary to company policy to company management is clearly exposing oneself to threat, so the natural human reaction is to filter out such information and executives may thus be prevented from knowing about non-implementation of company policy. To manage organisations rationally and make well-informed decisions it is necessary to be particularly vigilant that filtering and corruption of data coming up are anticipated and prevented.

Writers following Mayo next attempted to articulate more clearly what it takes to create a more realistic social environment and thus increase productivity.

Maslow (1970) developed a pyramid model of human needs. The lowest level was physiological, the next level the need to love and belong, the next level the need to achieve and, finally, the top level, the ego needs of self-actualisation and discovery. Maslow postulated that once human beings were satisfied at one level in the model further satisfaction can only be achieved by directing attention to a higher level in the pyramid. As far as reward at work is concerned money was seen as a physiological factor and thus insufficient alone to enable higher levels of job satisfaction and human motivation.

Hertzberg (1966) offered a refinement to the theory of motivation — the motivation/hygiene theory. In his view the job context tended to be a hygiene factor but the motivators relating to achievement and responsibility depended on the structure of the job itself. Hertzberg offered an implementation strategy for his model through job enrichment programmes, which were marketed as management development packages focusing on strategies of delegation.

In 1960 Douglas MacGregor contributed further to the discussion on motivation. He declared that managers' expectations of subordinates were much influenced by their underlying assumptions regarding human nature. He contrasted these assumptions giving them labels: theory x and theory y.

Under theory x the assumption is: 'The average human being has an inherent dislike of work and will avoid it if he can. Thus management needs to stress productivity, incentive bonus schemes and a fair day's work; and to denounce restriction of output. Because of this human characteristic of dislike of work most people will have to be coerced, controlled, directed, threatened with punishment to get them to put forward adequate effort towards the achievement of organisational objectives. The average human being prefers to be directed, wishes to avoid responsibility, has relatively little ambition and wants security above all.'

Under theory y the assumption is: 'The expenditure of physical and mental effort in work is as natural as rest or play. The ordinary person does not inherently dislike work; according to the conditions it may be a source of satisfaction or punishment. External control is not the only means for obtaining effort. Man will exercise self-direction and self-control in the service of objectives to which he is committed. The most significant reward which can be offered in order to obtain commitment is the satisfaction of the individual's self-actualising needs. This can be a direct product of effort directed towards organisational objectives. The average human being learns, under proper conditions, not only to accept but to seek responsibility. Many more people are able to contribute creatively to the solution of organisational problems than do so. At present the potentialities of the average person are not being fully used.' MacGregor's aim is to confront classical organisation theory and to suggest a more human-centred approach.

Likert (1961), following MacGregor, postulates that there are four different management systems. In his view the most significant management problem is that of achieving participation within an organisation and it requires the effective development of lateral communication systems in addition to the vertical communication systems of a classical organisation structure.

McClelland (1961) develops motivation theory by concentrating on the factors that give rise to achievement, affiliation and power. He further stipulates that people's needs in these areas change according to their age, personality and environment. Motivation thus has several complex contingency factors related to it and thus is difficult to interpret and apply.

British industry has generally been very sceptical about the findings and approach of the behavioural scientists. A common view is that they are too expensive to contemplate, and a firm operating in an economic squeeze and competitive markets will prefer to fund projects with direct short-term savings than those with merely intangible benefits.

Example

The incident of a cleaner supervisor

This incident is part of the folklore of management lecturers in the West of Scotland, where there are many multinational companies operating through local Scottish subsidiary companies. There is a tendency for the parent company to encourage the transfer of respected techniques from HQ to Scotland, but the transfer is not always as simple as might be expected.

In the company where this incident took place there was an enthusiasm for the Hertzberg approach to job enrichment. The personnel department were encouraged to do a talent-trawl among employees with a view to helping them to improve their career prospects. Diane was a supervisor of the cleaners, with responsibility for staff and executive washrooms. She participated in the talent-spotting exercises set up by the personnel department and came through with flying colours. She was offered full staff status if she agreed to undertake training for office work and, after some persuasion, she accepted and gave up her job with the cleaners.

A month later the personnel manager was surprised to find that Diane was scheduled for an 'exit' interview with her. She soon learned that Diane had decided to resign and was currently working out her notice. The office traineeship had not been the expected career improvement.

Diane told her, 'I find all the accounting work is so dull. It is figures, figures, more figures, and posting, and handling disagreeable customers with complaints. I just cannot stick another month of the dreadful confinement in that office. I loved my previous job. I had real authority with the other girls, and it was a pride to keep the washrooms so spick and span. And I had such power too. When Mr M (the Managing Director) was there with all those high-ups from the States, I could so easily lose the keys to the executive washroom, what fun that was! There's never an opportunity like that in the boring accounts department, and the boss there is adamant that I cannot be transferred back to the washrooms.'

A motivational theory may put in context the interpretation of behaviour, but it can be wrong in predicting the actual behaviour, unless the persons concerned have been open about their beliefs, values, self-image, power needs and ego needs. Once a group leader knows these for each individual member of the team lots of things are possible, but if the bureaucrat is just working on generalisation then as Diane suggested, the ground is really shaky. The implementors of management theory need to know its limitations as well as its positive aspects.

The technological school

After the Second World War Britain's environment was becoming increasingly more complex, with new and fast-growing technologies. Management researchers wished to put to the test the universal themes of classical management regarding the number of levels, the structure and the guidelines regarding the span of control at each level. Joan Woodward (1965) completed a research study in 100 firms in south-east Essex in 1948. Her initial research design was based on a hypothesised link between profitability and organisation design. In the event the hypothesis was upturned. Woodward then reanalysed her data and, after she had reclassified the firms on the basis of the technological process, she found that there was a positive link between profitability and organisation design within each technological process.

The four industrial processes she identified were as follows:

1. Unit production,
2. Batch-oriented production,
3. Process production,
4. Mass production.

Firms that ignored the norms of organisation prescribed by the most profitable firms within each such category did so at their peril. Ignoring these norms meant much loss of profits. Her other conclusion was that the technological process significantly affected the structure of organisation design.

Many other researchers followed up Woodward's findings. A research group called the Tavistock Institute was formed and they attempted to use behavioural science findings to solve industrial problems. Trist and Bamforth (1951) are well known for the longwall coal-cutting case studies. Coal mining prior to the development of longwall methods was a manual task generally shared by groups of three miners who worked as a team with little direct personal supervision. With the longwall method a machine staffed by a group of some twenty employees would cut coal from a coal face. There were three stages in the work — preparing and breaking up the coal face, moving coal to the tubs, filling and advancing, and fixing pit props and moving forward to the next coal face. With the new method, each of three shifts would be responsible for one phase only in the operation. The implementation of the new methods was initially a disaster. Very low levels of productivity and high absenteeism were reported. When Trist and Bamforth critically examined the system they developed a method to re-establish team work for the whole process of every shift. Having re-established social systems at work the production achievement rose 78–95 per cent of target — a dramatic improvement. They demonstrated eloquently the need to integrate technical and social systems at work to establish productivity.

Burns and Stalker (1961) did a critical study to determine the rationale behind long-term profitability in a hi-tech industry, the electronics industry. Their findings were that the firms that survived were those best able to adapt and integrate the results from research and development departments. Firms with a rigid organisation structure were effective at making profits where high-volume business was the norm, but in an environment of rapid technological change a freer organic structure was more appropriate. Organic structures were related to project management techniques and with decision-making oriented towards expertise rather than rank and status. Burns and Stalker's findings are particularly appropriate in the 1970s and 1980s to the problems of relating creative facilities such as information processing to a parent organisation structure. When the whole environment is rigid and mechanistic, integration becomes very difficult.

Lupton *et al.* (1977) conceived the idea of 'socio-technical analysis' and used it to develop multidisciplinary project teams whose purpose it was to screen plant design from the social and technical viewpoints before commissioning. He demonstrated this technique in his proposals for a change at a glass-making plant commissioned in Australia for Pilkington Brothers of St Helens. However, the timing of his report to management was misjudged, the Australian management ignored his prediction that the plant would be unmanageable and the report was pigeonholed. Two years later, after considerable difficulty in operating the unit, the report was retrieved, its findings reassessed and implemented and the Lupton approach vindicated. However, the incident sequence does suggest that there are hazards in implementing the findings of behavioural science particularly when they are being introduced into an organisation which has a strong classical management culture.

Hill (1976) masterminded a project in Shell UK to achieve job restructuring in UK refineries. He developed and implemented a new company philosophy based on the principle of joint optimisation of social and technical systems to improve the meaningfulness of jobs within the refinery context, establish sufficient job enrichment at work and improve productivity. The programme was implemented company-wide and gave rise to productivity bargaining and a major improvement in the labour relations climate.

Writers of the technological school had made much impact on the integration of ideas and concepts both from the human relations school and also from the scientific school.

The leadership school

Since the 1960s considerable academic attention has been directed towards the definition and uses of leadership style. Theorists in this field believe that leadership style is a significant component of organisation effectiveness. Tannenbaum (1966) initially postulated a leadership continuum. One pole was boss-centred and the other subordinate-centred. Another way of looking at this continuum would be to label the poles 'autocratic' and 'democratic'. However, seven points were defined in this continuum and the majority of managers are able to relate to these distinctions. Tannenbaum postulated that sophisticated organisational structures such as matrix structures demanded the development of a consultative style of leadership, whereas in hierarchical structures a variety of styles would be effective, the success being determined by the particular criteria being used by the observer stakeholder.

John Adair (1973) developed a leadership model which reflected his experiences in officer selection in the army. Adair's model was called 'action-centred leadership'. His model postulated three main components — group needs, individual needs and task needs. This model has considerable credibility for the analysis of operating problems, particularly those with a short time-span for decision-making.

Blake and Mouton (1969) developed an elaborate leadership grid. One scale had nine points which rated the manager's ability to deal with tasks or production. The other dimension, also with nine points, dealt with the manager's ability in dealing with people and with group or relationship problems. Blake and Mouton postulated a leadership style of excellence. This was 9.9, i.e. a manager both articulate with people and efficient with tasks and production. By giving managers questionnaires their leadership position on a grid could be determined and this could form the basis of a management development programme designed to shift their style to the 9.9 position of excellence.

Two years after the early research findings of Blake and Mouton, Reddin (1968) developed the theory further by adding a third dimension to the grid, that of effectiveness. Reddin postulated that the effectiveness of a manager's style depended on a situation analysis of the organisation and that there were four style categories which could be labelled effective. In addition, he defined four style categories which he saw as ineffective. He further suggested that 'style flexibility' was a possible and worthwhile skill to nurture in management development programmes.

Both Blake and Mouton and Reddin were reputed to have become millionaires as a result of their theories. Expectations were high. Many organisations with managerial weaknesses looked to the grid theorists to deliver a panacea. There were enthusiasts for this approach in the United States, Canada and the United Kingdom. Many client companies used the language and concepts of the grids to structure their management development programmes, primarily by providing a language of leadership which could be understood and shared by practising executives.

In the mid-1970s some discordant findings regarding the grids were published. Davis exposed a group of twelve police cadets to the two grids to determine leadership style in the expectation that there should be considerable correlation in the two findings. To his disappointment correlation was weak. Two years later work records were matched with the leadership style prognosis and the Reddin tests proved to have some predictive power. However, the predictive power was not considered strong enough to be a reliable selection mechanism. They could only be used as a background to help the manager in self-diagnosis and self-awareness, but never as an absolute measure of his or her effectiveness.

In the late 1970s theorists began to question the importance attached to leadership style as a component of effective management. A study was conducted in an advertising agency where records were kept of accounts and account executives. The expectation was that the most profitable accounts would be those of executives with effective leadership style ratings. Significantly, no correlation was reported.

The systems school

In the late 1950s there was a rapid development of computerised systems. Theorists then perceived systems as a critical component of managerial effectiveness. Simon (1957), particularly, was interested in open systems. In an open system transactions are transmitted to and from an external environment and the organisation can thus adapt by changing the flows, the processor or the relationships of the system. Simon, a Nobel prize winner in economics, disputed the sanctity of the profit motive. Instead, he postulated that an organisation must have a multiplicity of objectives and a balance must be achieved. Each objective-setting area needed to be 'satisficed', not maximised.

The computer-oriented theorists looked upon the computer as a means of forcing flows of data through pre-programmed channels. They saw the critical component of an organisation as the decision-maker. Success would be related to the long-term quality of decision-making by executives. Executives would make good decisions if they were based on valid information and rational analysis. The systems school developed the notion of a credible management information system, with the computer assisting in quantifying and directing the flows of data. Furthermore, they looked to the computer to make projections and simulations where there was incomplete information, in order to give a better understanding of the dynamics of risk. The major difficulty in implementing the systems tended to be the organisation's demands on people to prescribe the relevant rules and policies and to offer banks of uncorrupted data. Systems theorists, therefore, looked to many other theorists to solve design and implementation problems. They looked to the behavioural scientists for ideas on developing the necessary teamwork for design and implementation. They looked to the quantitative school to provide useable mathematical business models. They looked to the technological school to relate systems both to people and to the complex technologies of business environments. Effective systems today aim at securing good resource utilisation, at enhancing the managerial job and offering possibilities of quantification of complex future plans by providing structured data for executive decision-makers.

Ineffective systems, however, create complex bureaucracies, paper mountains, job dehumanisation and alienation. Davis (1970) and Lucey (1981) contributed to the notion of computerised management information systems and the application of the principles of managing by exception, which is the foundation of design of management information systems. Rosenweig and Kast (1979) contributed to the theory of relationships and the behavioural science aspects of systems. Mumford and Ward (1968) developed strategies for achieving greater user participation in the design process and breaking down the barriers between line manager and computer specialist.

Current research effort is being directed to developing the boundaries and interfaces between the most significant systems of a company. The thinking here is that not only should the payroll system be working efficiently, but so too should the corporate planning system, the production planning and control system, and with computer assistance in the form of material requirements planning there is the opportunity of linking long- and short-range planning within the organisation. In this approach the highest level of control in a company is the tracking of deviations from the corporate plan, which requires a profit schedule month by month, quarterly and, of course, annually. The behavioural scientists and the pragmatists who have developed objective-setting systems, (MbO), Drucker (1954), Odiorne (1972) and Reddin (1971) then open up the opportunity to use MbO to break down the key result areas of the corporate plan into meaningful sub-objectives for all lower-level units in the organisation. Once there is a computerised MRP capability, this produces a useful feedback mechanism to reinforce the appraisal processes of the MbO approach. When a company has the three systems of long-range corporate planning, MbO and MRP firmly in place and interfaced, the results should be formidable.

The organisation development school

Bennis (1969) was concerned at the dysfunctions of bureaucracy. He perceived organisations as being people-oriented rather than authority-oriented. He was particularly interested in the need to promote democratic human values. He wished to fit the individual's needs more conveniently with the organisation's needs. The leadership grid theorists also reached towards the organisation development school. They primarily saw the organisation as a composite of effective units and sub-units connected by organisation structures. An organisation would need to develop clearly its mission, then its strategy and finally to fit its structure to the strategy. As organisations are inherently dynamic, structure would constantly be adjusted to take account of a hostile and turbulent environment and changes in mission and strategy. The grid theorists saw their leadership grids as providing the entry and unfreezing mechanism for consultants to make interventions as change agents within an organisation in order to locate and treat any organisational mismatch. These are very complex notions and research interest is still very active in clarifying and developing such notions.

Although there is much scepticism in the United Kingdom surrounding organisation development concepts, practitioners in this field do claim considerable success in helping organisations to adjust to rapid technological change. As technological and other organisational change develops in intensity and rapidity in the latter part of the twentieth century, more and more attention is likely to be devoted to these concepts. An organisation development capability is often regarded as a prerequisite for implementing advanced company systems such as managing by objectives, management information systems and long-range corporate planning. The organisation development capability provides the behavioural science underpinning to enable the necessary high level teamwork to implement these advanced systems. Other contributors in the field of organisation development are French and Bell (1978), Beckhard (1969) and Hill (1976), also mentioned above as a contributor to the technological school.

The contingency school

By the 1980s the theorists had developed a real harvest of organisation and management theory. The contingency theorists look upon the other schools as contributors to a complementary mosaic of managerial knowledge. Their position is that every theory has its strengths and weaknesses, but will generally apply well to a sub-set of organisational situations. The manager grappling with too much theory is expected to identify the key components of the situation which is a problem to him then scan the theory developed by the different schools to extract that which is most likely to illuminate the particular problem. The manager has to fit theory to situations. This is an open-ended approach and unfortunately very sophisticated. Writers in this field, sometimes called the composite approach, include Hicks and Gullett (1981), Lawrence and Lorsch (1968), Morse and Lorsch (1973) and Beer (1980). This school has a root in the mid-1960s and much research is active in this field.

The pragmatic school

There are two sources of management theory. The first is created initially in an ivory tower to describe, explain and predict managerial behaviour. It is generally based on a refinement of previously validated theory. The second comes in contrast directly from the industrial workface in the form of biographies written by successful executives who then attempt to rationalise on their success.

Peter Drucker is a pre-eminent example of this approach and has written up his very extensive, successful consultancy assignments. He is well known for his consultancy with General Motors and the resulting development of what is now known as the 'marketing concept' and the philosophy of 'managing by objectives'.

The management student needs to be particularly vigilant in assessing the theory developed by a pragmatist. Although the pragmatism was successful in the environment of its author, that does not mean that pragmatism will always work equally well in a different environment. Pragmatism may be elevated to accepted theory after many studies have been done in different environments and the rules of success have been validated. Crudely, the pragmatists believe that nothing succeeds like success. In the early days of an academic discipline that is better than nothing. However, academic discipline gets its credibility in the field of management when the theory applied yields consistently better results in organisations.

Summary

This chapter has made a wide-ranging survey of management thought and grouped writers into appropriate schools. Figure 18.1 groups the writers into schools and shows the main lines of influence between schools.

Most other texts in management tend to adopt a classification based on three schools — the classical or scientific, the human relations and the systems school. However, the division into ten schools may allow a deeper understanding of how the three major schools evolved and the likely direction of research activity in the closing stages of the twentieth century.

As it is common for managers to work for a variety of different organisations in a variety of different roles in the course of a career, it must make sense in management education to expose them to the full range of contemporary theories of management thought. It is an advantage to be able to analyse one's own organisation and interpret style and culture, as this may well give insights into which initiatives are possible and which are not.

Exercise 18.1
Fayol's principles

A popular and practical exercise is to review the fourteen principles of Fayol (1916) from the classical school and discuss the validity of each of them today. (See p. 363 for the list of principles.) This draws out the changes in managerial assumptions since Fayol formulated his list and also calls much into question the limitations of line management in an age when line and staff are popular forms of organisational structure along with task teams and project management methods.

For feedback on this exercise see Appendix 1, p. 530.

Case Study 18.1
Whithouse Fun Goods

(Material published with permission of Scottish Vocational Education Council, Glasgow.)

Whithouse Fun Goods was a medium-sized business making small toys and novelties which found a ready market, especially at times like Christmas. Consequently, there were times of the year when the company was extremely busy. At these times, part-time seasonal staff were employed. The staff, both full- and part-time, were recruited from the mining town of Whithouse. The factory was in fact the only sizeable employer in the town apart from the two pits and the indications were that the Coal Board was soon to announce their closure.

Some five years previously the company had been taken over by the national group, Scampton Toys. Despite the takeover, things had changed little. Old Matt Cullen stayed on as manager and continued to operate as before. In the busy period, for example, full-timers were paid a bonus for the extra responsibility of looking after the seasonal workers. Cullen also tended to turn a blind eye to the employees taking off-cuts for use at home. Many a pigeon loft was said to have been finished, if not wholly built, by Fun Goods. In other matters, Cullen was much stricter. For example, many highly inflammable materials were used in the factory and the no-smoking rule was strictly enforced. Over the years three employees had been dismissed and none of these had been defended in any way by their shop-floor colleagues.

After four years under Scampton, Matt Cullen died. Jim Cooper, his assistant, took over and all expected that he would be confirmed as manager. But after two months, Arthur Hallwell was appointed by Scampton Toys from the group's factory in Northampton, where eight years earlier he had started as a graduate trainee. Since then he had been in several different jobs throughout the group and had completed a one-year post-graduate business degree before returning to Northampton as manager.

In his first weeks at Whithouse in June Hallwell observed much and did little. But he was dismayed by what he considered the parochialism of the workforce, management and shop floor alike. Gradually, he brought in his own team. Jim Cooper was offered early retirement and was grateful to get out. Others followed. What had been almost a village community was gradually broken up. Then followed a big security operation to check what Hallwell called 'stealing' from the company. He had arranged for a local scrap dealer to buy off-cuts and other materials from the factory.

In October of that year, at a planning meeting, Hallwell heard for the first time of the Christmas responsibility bonus for the full-timers. He flatly refused to pay it unless output was shown to be improved at the same time. The shop stewards argued that the seasonal workers' productivity would be much lower without the full-timers' supervision, and that for the full-timers to continue to produce while taking on this extra task was the equivalent of extra production. But Hallwell was sceptical and refused to budge. A week later, the workers walked out, complaining that the heating in the factory was inadequate. This was the first action of its kind in the history of Whithouse Fun Goods.

Discussion questions

1 Comment on the possible advantages and disadvantages of the different approaches used by Cullen and Hallwell.
2 . Suggest theoretical approach(es) which would have been more appropriate to the situation in which Hallwell found himself.
3 . What can Hallwell do now to retrieve the situation?

For feedback on this case study see Appendix 1, p. 533.

References

Adair, J. (1973), *Action Centered Leadership*, McGraw-Hill.
Beckhard, R. (1969), *Organisational Development: Strategies and models*, Addison-Wesley.
Beer, M. (1980), *Organization Development — A systems view*, Goodyear.
Bennis, W.G. (1969), *Organisational Development: its nature, origin, prospects*, Addison-Wesley.
Blake, R.R. and Mouton, J.S. (1969), *Building a Dynamic Corporation through Grid Organisation Development*, Addison-Wesley.
Burns, T. and Stalker G.M. (1961), *The Management of Innovation*, Tavistock.
Davis, G.B. (1970), *Management Information Systems — Conceptual foundations, structure and development*, McGraw-Hill.
Drucker, P. (1954), *The Practice of Management*, Harper.
Fayol, H. (1916), *General and Industrial Management*, translated from the French by C. Storrs, Pitman.
Ford, H. (1922), *My Life and Work*.
French, W.L. and Bell, C.H. (1978), *Organisation Development. Behavioural science interventions for organisation improvement*, Prentice Hall.
Hertzberg, F. (1966), *Work and the Nature of Man*, Staples Press.
Hicks H.G. and Gullett, C.R. (1981), *Management*. McGraw-Hill.

Hill P. (1976), *Towards a New Philosophy of Management. The company development programme of Shell UK*, Teakfield.

Lawrence, P.R. and Lorsch, J.W. (1968), *Developing Organisations: Diagnosis and action*, Addison-Wesley.

Likert, R. (1961), *New Patterns of Management*, McGraw-Hill.

Lucey, T. (1981), *Management Information Systems*, Smiths.

Lupton T. *et al.* (1977), *Organisation Behaviour and Performance: An open systems approach to change*, Macmillan.

McClelland, D.C. (1961), *The Achieving Society*, The Free Press.

McGregor, D. (1960), *The Human Side of Enterprise*, McGraw-Hill.

MacNamara, R.S. (1966), Unpublished material on critical path analysis while Chief Executive of the Ford Motor Company, Inc.

Maslow, A.H. (1970), *Motivation and Personality*, Harper.

Mayo, E. (1933), *The Human Problems of an Industrial Civilisation*, Macmillan.

Morse, J.J. and Lorsch, J.W. (1973), 'Beyond Theory Y', *HBR*, May/June, pp. 46−9.

Mumford, E. and Henshall, D. (1979), *Participative Approach to Computer Systems Design: A case study of the introduction of a new computer system*, ABP.

Mumford, E. and Ward, T.B. (1968), *Computers: Planning for people*, Batsford.

Odiorne, G.S. (1972), *Management by Objectives: A system of managerial leadership*, Pitman.

Reddin, W.J. (1968), *Effective Management*, McGraw-Hill.

Reddin, W.J. (1971) *Effective MbO*, BIM.

Rosenweig, J.E. and Kast, F.E. (1979), *Organisation and Management — A systems and contingency approach*, 3rd edition, McGraw-Hill.

Shaw, A.G. (1952), *The Purpose and Practice of Motion Study*, Columbine Presses.

Simon, H.A. (1957), *Administrative Behaviour*, Collier-Macmillan.

Tannenbaum, A.S. (1966), *Social Psychology of the Work Organisation*, Tavistock.

Taylor, F.W. (1911), *Principles of Scientific Management*, Harper.

Trist, E.L. and Bamforth, K.W. (1951), 'Some social and psychological consequences of the longwall method of coal-getting', *Human Relations*, vol. 4, no. 1, pp. 3−38.

Weber, M. (1921), *Theory of Social and Economic Organisation*, translated from the German by A.M. Henderson and T. Parsons, Oxford University Press.

Woodward, J. (1965), *Industrial Organisation: Theory and practice*, Oxford University Press.

Chapter 19

Making decisions about organisation structures

Overview

In this chapter attention is directed to decisions about choice of organisation structure. Many options are offered of formal, consultative and informal structures.

The chapter begins with a wide-ranging classification of structures under a variety of different dimensions, then attention is concentrated on an analysis of a few of the most common and important structures. The dynamics of these structures are examined.

Learning objectives

By the end of the chapter the reader should have a good feel for the range of organisation structures which are manifested in his or her own organisation and an informed view of whether such structures are appropriate.

Classification of organisation structures

Chronological

Common forms of organisation structures have evolved over the centuries from simple structures to contemporary and complex ones. These are as follows:

Line organisation
Line organisation represents authority based on a hierarchy. Line organisation is prevalent in the State and most large organisations.

Line/staff organisation
Line/staff organisation reflects the need for the specialist staff member to advise or provide a resource so that line management can do their jobs. Staff members have status,

expertise and professionalism and contribute to teamwork in a management group. The term 'line/staff' comes originally from military usage, but has been adopted by industrial organisations with the rise of a wide range of professions.

In industrial organisations the functions of manufacturing and marketing are generally classified as the main 'line' groups and all others as 'staff' groups.

Project organisation

Project organisation is based on forming a multidisciplinary team to complete a defined task. Members are selected on the basis of expertise rather than rank and report to a project manager. Members normally disperse on completion of the project back to their own home departments. This form of organisation is often used to bring about rapid change in an organisation. It has evolved rapidly since the 1950s and is often associated with the management control technique of critical path analysis.

Matrix organisation

Matrix organisation is a development of project organisation and is a sophisticated structure in which each member relates to at least two strands of authority. When the environment is very sophisticated and the members in project teams move continually to other project teams then we have a matrix organisation. This developed in popularity from the late 1960s, but its use is selective.

Legal dimension to organisation structure

Legal form influences what can be done and establishes ground-rules for the stakeholders in an organisation. The following legal forms may be observed:

1. Sole trader,
2. Partner,
3. Private limited liability company,
4. Public limited liability company,
5. Non-departmental public bodies,
6. Local authority,
7. Armed forces,
8. Government,
9. Club,
10. Charity,
11. Church.

A full analysis is not attempted here, but a few comments follow on these forms of structure.

The small family business may evolve from partnership to limited liability and the incentive is the desire to raise capital. Shares are not publicly quoted in the private limited company, so it is safe from unwelcome takeover. The private limited liability company has fewer obligations to report its accounts than the public limited liability company. The public limited liability company has a share quotation. The prime stakeholders of companies are the shareholders, though there is an increasing recognition of the need to take account of the influence of other stakeholders — managers, employees, suppliers, customers, the public and trade unions. The main incentive of 'going public' is to gain access to the capital market to acquire financial backing.

Once the structure evolves into public liability status, there is an increasingly greater separation between the owners of the business and its managers, so informal and paternalistic relationships are replaced by management by professionals and generally more formalised structures.

In the public sector organisations the driving force tends to be the bureaucratic rules which define the structure and operation of policies. Commonly these operate within budgets, but are not usually profit-oriented. Many public sector organisations have elaborate committee structures with a mixture of officials and representatives in positions of power. This gives rise to *executive* groups, *representative* groups, *consultative* groups and *mixed* groups.

Managing change within the public sector can be exceptionally slow and difficult, simply because authority is so diverse and there is an expectation that consultation precedes change.

Technological dimension to structure

This dimension suggests that the organisation structure needs to follow and fit the demands imposed by what the organisation does in a technological sense. The wider the range of products, services or markets which are served, the richer the range of structures which may be adopted. Decisions are required about centralisation and decentralisation of the functions of the business.

A classification on this basis of organisation structures might be as follows:

1. Single product or service,
2. Single product or service, multiple market,
3. Multi-product or service, multiple market,
4. Multi-technology/multiple market.

The above list shows an increasing sophistication. There are greater difficulties in coordinating the necessary specialists. Once a business is dealing with multiple technologies it is more difficult to achieve economies of scale. The research and development function is commonly centralised until the organisation grows to take on multiple technologies.

To make matters more complicated, within the production field there is still a further classification of technology, as follow:

1. Mass production,
2. Process production,
3. One-off production,
4. Batch production.

This classification is due to Woodward (1965). She was a researcher who found that profit was correlated with forms of organisation structure, when this fitted the norms suggested by the production process.

Buchanan and Hucynski (1985) disagree with Woodward. In their view, new technology offers some influence in structure, but management still retains discretion in matters concerning its strategic deployment. They reject Woodward's view that technology alone determines structure. To back up the strategic choice approach they discuss research into the effects of introducing a word processing unit into a firm doing marine consultancy, employing a large number of authors. The results fell far short of the expectations of the authors and operators, owing to poor deployment strategy.

The interaction of technology with organisation structure is a complex issue, giving rise to what some writers term the 'contingency approach' to organisation.

Specialisation in organisation structure

There are three main aspects of specialisation. The first is by product or service. This leads to a divisionalised organisation structure, with most of the business functions split up and the groups led by general managers. Secondly, specialisation may be by functional process or professional discipline and this leaves a centralised structure. Thirdly, there may be a mix of the two, where specialists work for more than one division and authority is divided.

The most common split of functional process is between manufacturing and marketing. The siting of factories is influenced by the availability of suitable labour, materials and floor space. Marketing may be more influenced by the proximity of customers. Once these two functions are geographically separated product development policies are much more difficult to coordinate and warehousing is likely to be a problem area. The factory sees the warehouse as a means of taking shock out the varying demand patterns. Marketing sees the warehouse as a guarantor of acceptable levels of customer service. If manufacturing and marketing are split geographically then much more stock is likely to be needed, unless there are exceptionally good systems and communications.

Size in organisation structure

It may be convenient here to refer to a model of military organisation for purposes of classification before widening the discussion to the industrial set-up:

Section, up to 10 men under a corporal.
Platoon, up to 40 men under a second lieutenant.
Company, up to 130 men under a major.
Battalion, up to 1,000 men under a lieutenant-colonel.
Brigade, up to 4,000 men under a brigadier.
Division, up to 15,000 men under a major-general.

'Staff' members are also in the above structure. The platoon has the sergeant; the company, the captain, sergeant-major and quartermaster-sergeant; the battalion has the adjutant (captain); the brigade has a brigade major; the division has a brigadier-general staff. The officer is given experience in both line and staff roles and generally he gets a new appointment every two years to reinforce this. He is unlikely to rise above the rank of major in the British army until he is fully staff trained.

Optimum size of unit

There is much controversy over whether there is an optimum size for an industrial unit and further controversy over how many managers one senior manager can coordinate, when their work is interlocking. Fayol (1916) depicted the organisation as a hierarchy of authority in a structure of levels. He introduced the notion that each level was headed by a manager who had a direct span of control over subordinates. He suggested that the optimum size is between five and eight. If the manager has more than this he or she will tend to lose control, and if he or she has less than this figure there will be too many layers in the structure, with some role ambiguity and possible interference. Woodward's research did not, however, support the Fayol suggestions. In Woodward's findings the technology had an overriding influence in making decisions about structure.

It seems, however, that owner/founder managers can cope with an organisation on one site with as many as 500 employees and maintain a personal if informal contact with all to preserve a family paternalistic style. When the organisation gets beyond a size of 2,000, even with a professional management team, communication becomes difficult. Some organisations deliberately limit any one site to that number as a matter of policy. Policy might also be expressed in the number of levels in the structure, with anything above five levels discouraged. If the firm makes errors in configuring the size of its site units, then relationship and morale problems will be more prevalent and difficult to solve.

There are two main responses to problems of size. The first is to concentrate on the vital functions of the business and subcontract the less vital functions. This is also a strategy for coping with variations in trade activity. In effect the contractors take the shock out of the process, leaving a small but permanent set of employees in the parent organisation, but at the cost of some loss of control. Contractors cannot be quite as closely supervised and managed as a firm's own staff. The second response to size problems is to split the organisation into smaller units, but this will generally involve much greater cost and disruption.

Geography in organisation structure

A simple classification here would include the following possibilities:

1. Local single-site,
2. Local multiple-site,
3. Regional,
4. National,
5. International.

As we progress through the list there is a greater need for coordination and a stronger part is played by legal and cultural dimensions as well as by technology.

At the international level there is a wide range of options for strategic choice and the international company may appear to be even more powerful than a national government. By seeking out investment inducements from governments or regional authorities, and subtle use of transfer pricing to reflect profit in subsidiary companies located in countries with low corporation tax, the international company may gain a distinct advantage over companies with only a national base of operation. But this is at the expense of having much more elaborate and complex structures.

Decisions on site location for organisations thus may depend not only on physical size but also many other tactical and political factors.

Some irritation was experienced in the 1980s in the west of Scotland with the way some international companies in making site location decisions exploited the system of local grants. For instance, a plant would be opened up rent free and with capital allowances for a fixed period in one grant area, then closed at the end of that period, and opened up again a few miles down the road in a different grant area with all the same privileges.

In chapter 17 there was a discussion of strategic business units, sub-units of major divisions with individual profit management and investment. This classification does not always fit in well with a geographical classification. It depends on the degree of integration and interdependence of the unit under consideration. Discussion of a computer manufacturer's organisation structure may throw light on this dilemma.

Typically, research and development is located at HQ. Different plants are responsible for different parts of the process, reflecting specialist expertise. Disk drives may be made in a different plant from printers or processor units. Software packages may be developed at a further site. Marketing may be done internationally through subsidiary companies and agents and many of the plants may be in different countries. Yet when the buyer buys he buys a 'system', which is a unique combination of hardware, software and peripheral equipment, which is compatible and works when connected. The system has to be delivered in one working consignment. Plants are thus very interdependent and an efficient information network is essential to coordinate the shipments which will make up the finished consignments.

If one specialist plant fails this might mean that cash flow from customers would cease altogether. This question prompts the need to consider dual sourcing of very specialised items to reduce risk of a strike, a fire or transport failure. This may be by duplication of plant or by subcontracting, but in every event some loss of economy of scale occurs and the more complex the product becomes (technological dimension), the greater the risk of compromising the delivery date.

Choice of organisation structure

One of the most difficult decisions of management is that of knowing when to reorganise, particularly when this implies adopting a different structure. The major force that influences a decision to reorganise is a change in the corporate plan and adoption of a new business strategy. Organisation structure should fit the needs and demands of business strategy. Usually only minor incremental changes are required to achieve this fit as a structural reorganisation causes a major upheaval and if undertaken must be fully justified. Many businesses are large and complex and in reality represent several different organisational patterns attached to what is perceived as the predominant structure.

Initially, we shall review choices in structure evolving from the classification given above under the heading *Chronology*.

Paternalistic structure

This is the family business unit in which the owner/founder knows all the employees and can control the business and its products with little delegation of authority to other managers. There is generally much goodwill from the staff and warm and informal relationships exist throughout the group. Major problems arise through lack of continuity when the owner/founder retires or dies. There are also problems when the business unit reaches a size of over 300 employees and the simple flexible structure cannot cope with the complexity of the business. It is often difficult to attract capital until shareholding is widened. Marketing problems are also significant in the growing family business.

A mature family business often runs with very low return on investment. There is a tendency for complacency in product development and product improvement. The family business finds new technology is difficult to finance and it is difficult to cope with the new skills and management styles required for its implementation. Promotion for management is usually based on patronage dispensed by the owner/founder and continuity depends on succeeding family generations having the same drive and businesslike qualities as the founder. It is generally competition from larger firms or a succession crisis which forces a change in structure.

An intermediate structure

In this structure the owner/founder influence is no longer evident, unless careful succession planning was undertaken. A management team exists but may only be reacting to the environment. Decisions may be made arbitrarily and communication breaks down with lower levels of management. The business is likely to die unless a more professional management team and a more formalised organisation structure are established. This is likely to take the form of a line organisation or a line/staff organisation to bring the necessary order to the business.

Line organisation

This is the pyramid type of organisation based on the formal delegation of authority to managers at successively lower levels in the organisation, a scalar chain. Fayol (1916) was an advocate of this type of organisation. This structure is intended to provide role clarification for all members and order and discipline for the organisation. A cardinal feature of pure line organisation is that each worker has only one boss, so there can be no confusion or problems over priorities.

It must be noted, however, that the adoption of line organisation is not the only way to achieve role clarification. This can also be done using the technique of managing by objectives.

Line organisation is not appropriate when there are a lot of specialists and professionals. They tend to want to be guided by the expertise of their specialisation rather than by the formal authority of their superior, and it might be uneconomic to attempt to employ a specialist with one manager serving just one area of a business. To get mileage out of the specialist he or she may need to develop several working areas, hence the need for a more elaborate structure, probably line/staff.

Line/staff organisation

The staff are incorporated into the structure on the basis that they provide service, advice and control systems to enable the line managers to do a better job. Staff are appointed for their professional and specialist expertise. Their main difficulty is that they are obliged to serve in two conflicting authority systems. The branch accountant (staff), for instance, will be trying to help the branch manager (client authority) with a financial service at the same time as satisfying head office (professional authority) that the branch is adopting company policies. This dual relationship often gives rise to conflict.

Line/staff organisation enables a much wider range of specialists to be utilised to take the pressure off the main line managers in manufacturing and marketing. This organisation type is adequate if the organisation is changing slowly, but it is still too inflexible to cope with major change.

See Case Study 19.1 for an example of the development of a line/staff structure at the end of this chapter.

Staff/line conflict

Before looking at the further evolution of line and staff organisation structures, it may be appropriate to recognise another common phenomenon in organisations, that of line and staff conflict. An example of this was given in Case Study 7.2, p. 112.

In theory line managers see themselves as the main groups responsible for the operating profit of the firm, for making the goods and marketing them. All other functions are supportive and staff-oriented. But line managers often see staff managers as irrelevant and impractical, as getting in the way and preventing them from doing their legitimate job.

Staff managers often see line managers as out-of-date and resistant to new technology and new methods. Staff managers see themselves as highly qualified professionals and specialists with superior status to line managers who, certainly in the United Kingdom, tend not to be so well qualified.

Often, too, staff managers see themselves as representing Head Office, ensuring that the company's policies are implemented locally. At the local level, the staff person may be perceived as the Head Office spy and not the supportive resource which staff are supposed to be.

Salaries depend partly on the extent to which the manager is qualified, so staff managers are often paid more than their line management colleagues. Yet the staff role is facilitative and supportive of the line management role.

There is also a loyalty dimension in staff/line management relationships. The staff person tends to be loyal first and foremost to the profession and will seek a career structure in which he or she moves within the profession, possibly to different employers. In contrast, the line manager tends to see his or her future and loyalty as much more closely integrated with the success of the employer; promotion will be based to some extent on time and services rendered.

With these differences in perceptions no wonder there is potential friction between the two groups of line and staff. There is no easy answer to this problem. Managers must be aware of its possible manifestation, and good judgement and communication must be exercised to ensure that any developing conflict does not become unhealthy. As a matter of good career and management development it makes a lot of sense to reassign managers frequently, so that they can gain experience from exposures both to line management and staff management situations. This wider experience provides a basis from which line and staff managers can deal with one another from a position of empathy and mutual respect.

Bureaucracy

Line organisation also has its counterpart in the public sector. That type of structure is normally termed a bureaucracy. In this structure much emphasis is placed on the hierarchy of authority and chain of command in the structure. Promotion is on the basis of formal qualifications. The organisation depends on the employees knowing and interpreting many rules with impartiality. The sources of such rules will be statutes, by-laws, committee minutes, terms of reference and a plethora of case law.

The main criticism of a bureaucracy is that it is slow to respond to changes in the environment, is frustrating for both employees and customers as the rules are all-embracing, and is not easily kept up-to-date (see Fayol, 1916 and Weber, 1921).

Background to bureaucracy

In the United Kingdom major reforms during the 1880s made the Civil Service more professional, when the Civil Service Commission established an examination system for entry to the service, based largely on academic attainment. Merit, impartiality, consistency, loyalty to the State — these were the norms of the reformed Civil Service.

Bureaucratic structure is suitable when there is a high need for uniformity. It would be intolerable if social security benefits paid in Birmingham were significantly different from those paid in Glasgow.

Mass production units tend to be run on bureaucratic principles, producing efficiently in high volumes and resisting change. There is little job satisfaction in such an organisation for employees who enjoy social contact and the variety of creative work. Many large business organisations tend to become bureaucratic as they increase in size. Managers are often more concerned with the size of their budgets and establishment than with the attainment of a profit objective.

Managers often wish to exercise tighter control and they may establish bureaucratic procedures and structures to achieve this. They may even introduce computerised information systems to apply the principles of bureaucracy. Yet the skill of the computer people may overcome some of the bad effects of bureaucracy by applying the principles of managing by exception, and setting up their systems so that it is easy to change objectives, standards and policies, and thus retrieve some flexibility.

Although 'bureaucratic' is often a term of ridicule, nothing can be more frustrating than being in a country where the bureaucracy is not soundly established. In some developing countries, for instance, it is not unknown when crossing frontiers to be confronted with demands for a 'stopping tax', levied at the discretion of the officials, or for soldiers to raid a train demanding protection money when their government has not paid them. At least bureaucracy is an antidote to chaos, corruption and generally arbitrary behaviour.

Bureaucratic structure also has its variations.

Bureaucratic/consultative structure

The main features are an executive system running alongside a representative system, where members are elected. There are checks and balances aimed at achieving a high degree of acceptability among all employees. This is the model of universities and polytechnics in which a maturity of behaviour and judgement is expected. Committees operate with a network of sub-committees and these each have a status in the hierarchy.

An advantage is that this relatively democratic structure offers many opportunities for the individual to contribute, but the disadvantage is that the structure has a tendency to be unwieldy and the pace of change is relatively slow.

Most business organisations could not afford the cost and time needed for an elaborate consultative structure, though the private business will nearly always have some consultative structure to handle the labour relations function.

Project organisation

When an organisation has to undertake a major change quickly it will often set up a taskforce to manage the change. This is organised around a project, hence the term 'project organisation'. Members are selected primarily because of their expertise and this is more important than their seniority or status. A project manager takes overall responsibility for the change and the group disbands on completion of the task.

Individual members of the taskforce have a divided loyalty, firstly, to the project manager, and secondly, to their home department. To add to the difficulties, it may be that one person is working in more than one taskforce at one time and there will be problems in deciding priorities.

The leadership of a project team or taskforce may also be flexible. The leadership role may move to the individual with the most expertise relating to that particular phase of the project. Project management is excellent for managing complex change to tight time-scales, often with the aid of critical path networks, and is good for job enrichment, but it is somewhat stressful. A good example of a working project group was given in Exercise 10.1, p. 163.

Matrix structure

When an organisation is involved in a hi-tech environment then the project organisation becomes a permanent feature and may be called 'matrix'. The word 'matrix' implies a latticework of authority. One manager thus has to report both to a regional group and a specialist group. He or she has to reconcile conflicting demands on his or her time. Examples of matrix structures are found in advertising agencies, the sales forces of computer manufacturers, management consultancies and defence contractors.

Major problems arise in adopting a matrix structure from a more traditional structure owing to its complexity.

Elements of the matrix structure
The elements of the matrix structure are as follows:

1. Customer demands are sophisticated and require a team response.
2. There are many and complex variables in the business environment.
3. There are complex internal resources which must be coordinated to meet customer requirements, and experience and precedence provides little guide to the pattern of coordination needed.
4. The technology is complex and undergoing change.

Features of the matrix structure
The features of the matrix structure include the following:

1. Each manager (except the managing director) is likely to have more than one boss.
2. Line departments will be involved as well as staff departments.
3. Profit or potential profitability, and the visibility of this, significantly influence resource allocation and conflict resolution.

Setting up the matrix and examples
Before setting up a matrix organisation from a previous line organisation, the following must be done:

1. Lines of authority must be set out absolutely clearly. These lines will be criss-crossing and any fuzziness will result in ambiguities and chaos.

2. A major education effort is needed. Managers must fully understand the new rules of the game. Some may find that their authority is threatened. Similarly, rank and file must be taught how to function with two or more bosses.
3. Extra book-keeping may be in order to reconcile the lines of authority on a cost-centre basis.
4. The grid is brought in to handle unhealthy conflict.
5. Decision-making may be slowed down a bit. The crossed lines of authority mean that a horizontal manager should not commit resources to a project before clearing this with his vertical counterpart. Improved quality in decision-making makes up for any decrease in speed.

The advertising agency
The key role of the account executive   The account executive has to go to the client organisation and relate to an executive group there under a brand manager. The brand manager of the client group runs a team which deals with the many variables of the marketing mix, which will be relevant in a promotion campaign. Equally, the account executive needs to coordinate a team of specialists from the agency, who are capable of coping with the demands of the promotion campaign. We thus have two teams which have to work together. One line of authority will be to the brand manager or account executive, the second line of authority will be to the resource-providing specialists. Media men will report to a media manager, copy people to a copy manager, etc. The specialists will be working with several account executives in the structure. Assignment to accounts will become a matter for negotiation between account executives and resource-providing specialists, and the guiding principle is the expectation of profit from the account.

The management consultancy
The role of the management consultant   This example is very similar to the one of the advertising agency as far as the need to coordinate two sophisticated teams is concerned, though naturally the management consultant may have a variety of entry points into the client organisation.

Management consultancies may also be very specialised and one consultant may be able to do everything without help from his consultancy. When that is true, there is *choice* in matters of organisation structure. A simple line organisation might be more appropriate than a matrix. The key contingency factor is the nature and complexity of the consultancy service offered and the extent to which coordination of the consultancy resource is required.

The sales force of a computer manufacturer
The key role and interaction of the industry specialist and the regional account executive   From the chapters on the information society it will be evident that the selling and installing of a computerised system is a complex operation involving many people and a prolonged period of time. The client or buyer will normally be a committee and the seller will need not only to bring in selling expertise but also a team to train users

and do installation and maintenance. Computer manufacturers gain market share generally on the basis of their expertise in particular application areas, and customers will expect this expertise. The manufacturer will need to reflect this requirement in the organisation of the sales operation. The national head office will build up teams of industry application experts, experts in finance and banking, experts in manufacturing, experts in local authority work, experts in retail, etc.

The client company also has a geographical location, so the computer manufacturer also needs to maintain a regional organisation of account executives, who then coordinate the industry and other specialists who are brought into the sales team to meet the requirements of the client at any particular stage. This is another common manifestation of a matrix organisation, with the dual authority chain linking the regional account executives to the Head Office-based experts.

Contract management for defence
The role of the project managers   Any visitor to Ferranti plants will soon be struck by the absence of job titles such as factory manager, and for good reason. Much of the company work is tied up in defence contracts, which are complicated and authorised by a team of civil servants. At the supply end the company needs to coordinate design, production and testing of a wide variety of equipment and systems, and the natural vehicle for this is the 'contract' manager, who requisitions resources from the various specialists on site. The dual authority of contract managers and resource providers is similar to that described above in connection with the advertising agency.

The electronics and aerospace industry
A major example is Dow Corning, where a change from the previous organisational structure became the subject of an article by Goggin, published in the *Harvard Business Review* (May/June 1974).

The company previously had a line/staff organisation and while it produced a relatively unsophisticated aircraft in volume the structure was satisfactory. But with a more sophisticated product and a more demanding customer, delivery dates and quality were both being compromised, so the company reorganised into a matrix structure, similar in concept to that described above in connection with Ferranti.

Goggin was to report many advantages in adopting the new matrix structure, but this reorganisation took some time. Attitudes needed changing and executives needed to get used to lower-level managers having to set priorities which previously had been set higher up. Executives required to get used to constantly renegotiating resources from others in the light of fast-changing commercial priorities.

The advantages and disadvantages of the matrix structure
The literature was rather slow in responding to the evolution of matrix organisations, but in 1978 there is another contribution in the *Harvard Business Review* by Davis and Lawrence, which has become well known for its criticisms of matrix. The article is summarised below in eight points, with additional comment. The disadvantages of the matrix structure are as follows:

1. A tendency towards anarchy,
2. Power struggles,
3. Severe 'groupitis'.

Each of these three points reflects difficulties which arise whenever authority is divided. It was not without good reason that Fayol suggested that one employee should have one boss and that the scalar chain should be in operation to order the organisation. Human nature is often competitive and hence power struggles will arise unless senior managers can intervene and mitigate the consequences or provide simple ground-rules for their resolution.

'Groupitis' can be a terrible affliction, with no one taking decisions until the whole group is present, unless managers learn that many decisions only affect a limited number of other executives and can be handled informally or over the telephone. With suitable training and the development of trust and goodwill, this problem can be overcome. Matrix as a structure does not mean that committee management replaces executive management.

4. Collapse during economic crunch,
5. Excessive overhead.

These two points suggest that a matrix structure is complex and unwieldy, and a threat to the profitability of the organisation in times of economic slump. Clearly an organisation is built around assumptions of volume of business, and if that volume does not exist, some cuts in staff may be necessary. Firms in a cash-flow crisis will be managed for cash, and survival creates particular pressures and the need for quick, decisive executive action.

However, there would be little point in reorganising an advertising agency into a line structure, which would be wholly inappropriate to the task, simply because there were a slump. Staff shedding could be done, if necessary, within the existing matrix structure.

6. Matrix established at inappropriate level in organisation,
7. Decision strangulation,
8. Navel-gazing.

The matrix part of an organisational structure can begin at company level, divisional level or even at the functional level. In the discussion above of the computer manufacturer's sales organisation, which used regional account managers and industry specialists, the matrix appeared at the functional level. It might have been nonsense to set up a matrix structure at a higher level.

Decision strangulation is a further possible manifestation of severe 'groupitis'. Again, with good training and goodwill only the important decisions will be discussed in depth in meetings. With an appropriate group of decision-makers the quality of decision-making should improve.

The point about 'navel-gazing' suggests that matrix organisations are inward-looking and so concerned about internal power politics that the world outside is ignored. It is possible for this to happen, but if sales, marketing and market research people are involved in the structure then some healthy outside influence should still be apparent. Membership of groups is just as important in matrix structures as in others if benefits are to be won.

An example of the practical dynamics of matrix organisation is illustrated in Case Study 19.2 below.

Informal organisation

The last form of structure examined in this chapter is the informal organisation, a structure to which references have briefly been made in several case studies.

One of Mayo's principal observations in the Hawthorn studies of the 1930s was the existence of an informal organisation and communication method which existed independently of the formal structure as recognised by organisation charts and company policy. Furthermore, the informal organisation often exerted critical influence over getting things done or alternatively in frustrating initiatives.

Hawthorn Electric Company

In one part of the Hawthorn Electric Company plant management perceived the possibility of an increase in output standards, yet the workforce steadfastly refused to consider this improvement. Results of interviews indicated that the driving force in the work situation was the norms set by the informal group through their leader. The increase in output was perceived by the group as a threat; those who attempted it would be labelled 'rate-busters'. Those who produced significantly less than group norms were given the label 'chisellers' and threatened with ostracism.

Management's response to this situation might be as follows:

1. Identify the informal group leader and establish a dialogue.
2. Use the dialogue to ameliorate the situation.
3. If this fails, reassign or promote the informal leader and then try once again to change standards.

Senior civil servants

A group at any level in an organisation may feel threatened and may close ranks and respond through the informal organisation. Chapman (1978) describes how senior civil servants were accused of sabotaging the efforts of Chapman's cost-cutting initiatives through survey teams, as the work exposed complacency and, by reducing size of budget and staff establishment, directly threatened status and promotion prospects.

This senior management group was seen as sabotaging Chapman's efforts in the following ways:

1. They adopted delaying tactics in forming and deploying survey teams.
2. They appointed low status members to do the survey work and gave them unreasonable time-scales for completion.
3. They gave the work a low priority.

4. When reporting back to the minister they filtered out the true picture of progress to get him off their backs.
5. They exploited the lack of continuity as ministers changed office.

People at work tend to be motivated by their desire to avoid pain and sanctions. The influence of the peer group (often the focus of the informal group) may be immediate. No one likes to be sent to Coventry, whereas the threat of sanction from official sources may be remote and thus less effective.

Consumer company sales force

This example is based on action research carried out in a large UK consumer company in the summer of 1961.

A new branded product was being launched and the company wished to increase the size of its sales promotion teams during the first six weeks of the campaign. For two training weeks the management trainees were coached by the regular promotion men in the arts of promoting new brands by cold-calling on the smaller traders, who were not large enough to have direct accounts with the company. In the third and fourth weeks the management trainees were let loose in the south of England.

Relationships were initially good between the regular men and the management trainees, but this was to be short-lived. The standards under which the regular men worked were an average of twenty-five calls a day of promotion work; if the regular man was conscientious in the varying conditions of territory, weather and trading, this standard could be maintained, but it was still regarded as a stiff standard.

Under summer conditions, with a massive television promotion campaign and a successful projection of this new brand, the management trainees soon found their feet. Success was sweet; they were regularly turning in forty calls a day and a very high percentage of these were backed up with orders.

Management was delighted with these results, but the attitude of the regular salesmen changed quickly to one of outright hostility. They felt humiliated and threatened by the work of their recent pupils and did their best to discourage the breaking of the twenty-five calls a day standard. Tyres of the cars of the management trainees were mysteriously let down, record cards for guidance of the management trainees disappeared and every kind of subtle pressure was exerted to restrain them.

Fitting structure and strategy

This section reviews IBM's change to the organisation structure on the launch of the personal computer range of products.

It would be helpful to develop some underlying principles to guide managers in making decisions about organisation structure. From the analysis of this chapter we have been able to explore a wide range of choice of structure. In some cases we have been able to talk about 'natural' structures in which there was little freedom for manoeuvre. Matrix was discussed in this context.

Changing structure is only one option which can be adopted to get a solution to problems; other strategies can also be applied to an existing structure to achieve a solution. Changing structure is one strategy among others for management problem-solving. Other possibilities would seem to be to change management style, managerial appointments or technology. However, it would be nice to feel that management regarded change in organisation structure as part of pro-active management practice and not just as an afterthought.

The application of this principle would suggest that effective organisation structure fits and enhances the prevailing business policy for the organisation. This principle was applied by IBM.

In the early 1980s IBM decided to enter the personal computer market. From their long experience of making and marketing mainframe systems it seemed to be a simple technological change to get into the new market for PCs, just some concentric growth. However, an early issue which arose concerned the organisation structure necessary to market PCs. With mainframes each sale is worth a large amount and a dedicated sales team operates on the basis of direct contact with customers. But PCs are much cheaper. It was no longer viable to think in terms of a dedicated sales team calling directly on all customers for the PC. IBM would have difficulty in staffing such an expanded organisation. A change in organisation structure had to be contemplated and it was to be the incorporation of agents to provide the necessary coverage.

Yet computers have both hardware and software and there is a need for provision of technical advice to potential users. Would it be possible to get agents to do this as well as selling, particularly in the early days, when the agents might not have sufficient know-how about the IBM product line to be effective in every aspect of technical advice?

The IBM solution was to set up a telephone network of technical advisers, situated in plants and branch offices, who answered questions direct from customers. One function of the operation was thus centralised into a direct telephone help network, another function was subcontracted. The new marketing organisation had been configured around the newly perceived needs of both the technology and the customer and took account of the economics of distribution.

IBM had been clever enough to introduce the new product line and organisation structure pro-actively and quickly became the dominant market force for PCs.

Summary

This chapter has described many of the common models of organisation structure. Managers may have a wide range of choice when they are making decisions about structure. Inevitably the analysis and demonstrations of structure have had to be selective. The case illustrations at the end of this chapter are intended to force the reader into creative criticism and thought about structure, as it appeared along with other business problems. Some principles for guidance in decisions of choice are also available in Appendix 1. Figures 19.1 and 19.2 offer a summary of structures.

Figure 19.1 contains a brief representation of the main organisational forms. The dotted line appearing under 'line/staff' represents the dual relationship between the authority of the staff manager to the professional boss (generally at head office) and to the client manager locally, i.e. the manager to whom he or she provides the staff service. It must be noted that as the staff member is generally relating to both of these authority figures he or she rarely has the luxury of one 'boss'. Some ambiguity is thus naturally built in to the staff position and role.

Project management is depicted by a critical path network, as network techniques are the most common management approach for bringing order and control to that type of organisation.

Matrix organisation is depicted by following just two dimensions of a latticework of relationships, the commonest two dimensions, linking specialist resources and regions.

Bureaucratic/consultative structure is represented by circles for 'executive', 'legislative' and 'representative'. The model is an adaptation from Brown (1960). This

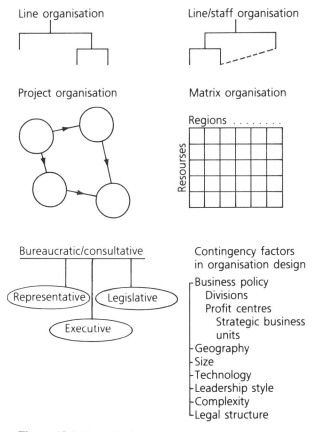

Figure 19.1 *Organisation structures*

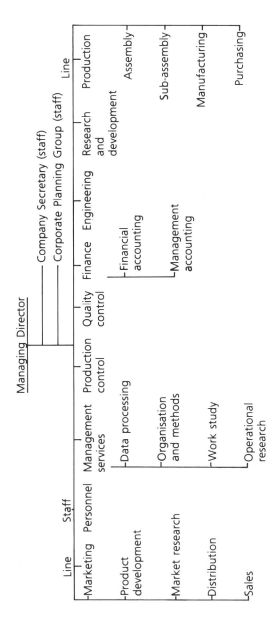

Figure 19.2 *Functional organisation in manufacturing*

was inspired by much earlier work by Montesquiez, a nineteenth-century constitutional lawyer, who developed the theory of the democratic 'separation of powers' in the State.

The list of contingency factors at the right-hand side of Figure 19.1 is a summary of key influences affecting decisions of design structure in organisations.

Figure 19.2 identifies, in simple outline, a line and staff functional organisation in a producing company. Marketing and manufacturing are the line groups; all others are staff.

Again, there can be much variation in practice from this general model. Purchasing, for instance, in this model is a sub-section of manufacturing, yet for some companies purchasing is a major function reporting directly to the managing director, but in a staff role, rather than as depicted here as a line role. In a multidivision company, where the different divisions bought similar materials, it would make sense to centralise purchasing as a staff role, whereas if the purchasing for each division were unique then it would be better for purchasing to be decentralised as a line role under production.

Case Study 19.1
Pender and Quaille, Ironfounders

(The case material was edited by Robert Erskine from original material written by Mr N.G.D. Black and is published with permission.)

This is a case of a small family firm which experiences some discomfiture in getting its organisation structure to adapt to the contemporary business pressures on the firm. It illustrates a sequence of conflict developing between line management and staff specialists and raises some interesting issues of delegation tactics, leadership style and management development. The narrative relates to the early period of the firm though is discussed with the benefit of hindsight and contemporary theory.

Issues for discussion

1. How did Major Quaille set about setting up and strengthening the line and staff organisation in the company? Was his approach appropriate for the company?
2. To what extent would you support the consultant's suggestion of a divisionalised structure? (See Figure 19.5.)

The reputation enjoyed by the firm of Pender and Quaille, Ironfounders, was based on the quality of goods it offered for sale and on the tradition of integrity built up by the partners over a period of many years.

Mr Quaille, the technical expert, had always felt that the future success of the business rested on maintaining a high standard of technology. He had often expressed this view to his son, Edward, and had been rather disappointed when Edward insisted that he was not interested in the business.

In 1932, however, Edward joined the company. He had recently graduated in law but in a time of economic recession had found it impossible to obtain a post in his chosen profession. In agreeing to accept a job in the company he had been influenced by his father's promise that when the Sales Manager retired, the job would be his. As Assistant Sales Manager he acquitted himself to the satisfaction of both partners, and in 1936, at the age of 27, he became Sales Manager.

Mr Pender, the commercial expert, found this arrangement satisfactory. He was pleased to see his friend's son taking a place in the organisation and, as a man of 66, saw this move resulting in an opportunity to retire in the not too distant future.

Mr Quaille's death in 1937, at the age of 54, was quite unexpected. The problem of finding a suitable successor was discussed by Pender and Edward at some length and, to Pender's way of thinking, an uneasy solution was found when Edward suggested: 'At least for the meantime, I can look after that side of the business; we can keep a look out for a suitable man and until then we can appoint an assistant to give me the necessary technical advice'. He added that he was sure that his father would have wanted him to take this step. The partnership having been dissolved, a private limited company was formed. Pender styled himself General Manager.

The search for an assistant to Edward Quaille was not very difficult. The late Mr Quaille had mentioned frequently that the best technical man in the organisation was Keene, the General Maintenance Foreman. Thus, Edward adopted the title Works Manager and Keene became his assistant. A new Maintenance Foreman was appointed. Although the question had been discussed when the changes mentioned above were made, no decision was reached as to the appointment of another Sales Manager. The four travellers continued to report to Edward.

When the matter was raised again some weeks later, Edward said: 'The sales organisation pretty well runs itself: it doesn't need a full-time man at the head.' He suggested that no appointment be made. Again, rather reluctantly, because he felt that the burden of that work would also fall on him, Pender agreed. Edward, however, continued to supervise the travellers' work and although the frequency of visits to agents decreased, they did not cease altogether.

In late 1939 the company received its first war contract and, just as a decision had been reached some four months earlier to discontinue manufacture of domestic goods, Edward was called to the forces. Pender, now over 70, was left to run the business himself.

With considerable expansion to the machine shop necessary, Keene was promoted to Works Manager. In the year that followed he took increasing control of the organisation and Pender gradually withdrew from active participation. By 1946, when Edward was demobilised, Keene had assumed full control, although he deferred to Mr Pender before making any important decisions.

Major Quaille, as he now liked to be called, set about re-establishing himself. As a result of his discussion with Pender, it was agreed that Pender should continue as Chairman of the Board, but that Quaille take over the post of Managing Director. The 50-year-old Keene was given the title of Factory Manager and his salary was increased. The company reverted to the manufacture of domestic goods, and since Quaille felt that the machine shop would provide a very profitable addition to the company's facilities, he suggested that it be kept in operation and that enough subcontracting work should be sought to build up and expand that side of the business.

Keene was asked to concentrate his attention on manufacturing and on the machine shop in particular. He questioned the value of the suggestion that the machine shop should receive special attention, pointing out that the foundry needed even more building up if pre-war standards were to be achieved.

Quaille modified his suggestion in light of Keene's observations, saying, 'Until the foundry is on its feet again we can simply maintain the machine shop at its present level of activity.'

The two men then busied themselves with the problems of conversion. In the early stages, Quaille spent time re-establishing contact with the agents. He assured them that it was his company's intention to return to pre-war trading practices and to maintain the well-known P & Q quality. He sought out the original travellers and, although two of them were now fairly well on in years, put them back in their former posts, saying that they knew the work and were well-known and that the sales job would therefore be an easy one.

As a result of a wartime contact Edward was brought in touch with a number of management organisations within the district. He attended their meetings, read their publications and developed great interest and enthusiasm for management problems. He was heard to say: 'There is no reason why P & Q should not become one of the best-managed companies in the country.'

He set about reorganising the office and administrative arrangements and, while Keene was left to take care of the manufacturing departments, Quaille devoted the next two years of his modernisation plans to 'organisation development', as he called it.

He had a new office building constructed. He overhauled the office systems (buying, invoicing, wage payment, and so on), introduced a system of standard costing and had plans laid for the introduction of a budgetary control system. To assist him with his plans he appointed an accountant as Office Manager, placing him in charge of all office activities, with the exception of sales and production control.

He appointed a Personnel Manager and installed him in an office in the main block. The organisation chart displayed in Edward's office showed the Personnel Manager, the Office Manager and the Production Control Manager reporting directly to him.

In the course of these changes Quaille found it necessary to dismiss and replace four members of the office staff, none of whom was of a calibre suited to the type of progressive organisation he was trying to establish.

All seemed to go well during this time. Keene and Quaille established a satisfactory working arrangement, which was that while neither attempted to interfere with the other, each kept the other informed of what was going on. This was done at a daily conference which was instituted by Quaille in order that he could 'keep everyone in the picture'. It was attended by Quaille, Keene, the Office Manager, and the Personnel Manager.

The products of the company did not change very much during this time. Most of them were modernised versions of pre-war designs. The machine shop continued to function at almost full capacity.

Quaille gradually became aware of a general 'tightening' of the market. Increases in prices which he was forced to make resulted in a dropping off of orders, but as the situation generally re-established itself within a week or two, and the order book remained full, this did not cause Edward any real concern.

In January 1949, Major Quaille turned his attention to the machine shop. He pointed out that, as the foundry was now well established, he wanted to go ahead with his plan for the expansion of the machine shop. He asked Keene to submit a plan, outlining the steps which would be necessary to double the output in two years. As Keene was to spend considerable time on that project, Quaille suggested that a foundry manager be appointed. Keene resisted this suggestion saying that he could exert general supervision over the foundry. After some discussion, Quaille agreed not to go ahead with any new appointment.

Two weeks later Quaille sent for Keene. He asked how the plans for the machine shop were progressing. Then he said: 'There are one or two points which I want to take up with you.' He went on to say that he thought that something had to be done about the incentive plan used in the foundry. 'I want you to move a couple of the time study men from the machine shop into the foundry so that they can have a go at straightening out the rates.' His second point was that he was not very happy about conditions in the moulding shop. He gave Keene a list of items which he said needed attention and said: 'I have instructed the maintenance staff to drop everything else and and get on with these jobs as soon as you give the go-ahead.'

Finally, he said that he was concerned about a report from the Personnel Manager that it was becoming increasingly difficult to get trained moulders. 'I have asked him to prepare a draft training scheme, which I would like you to have a look at. We can start recruiting unskilled men whenever our training scheme is organised.'

Keene said nothing more than that he would study the proposals, but his expression was that of someone who was far from pleased with life. He left hurriedly, slamming the door as he went out. As Keene left, Edward said to himself: 'I wonder what can be upsetting him?'

Following the conference on the next day, during which Quaille had informed the Personnel Manager and the Office Manager of the proposals he had made to Keene on the previous day, Quaille had a series of interviews which surprised him.

Firstly, Keene came into his office and said, rather awkwardly, that he was sorry he had been rude the previous day, but he had had personal problems which were causing him some concern. Quaille said, 'Oh, that's all right. If there is anything I can do, let me know.'

Then the Personnel Manager came to see him and said that he was concerned by the fact that three of the foundry supervisory staff had handed in their resignations and that he had learned that quite a number of the older hands had been making enquiries in other foundries about the possibility of employment. Quaille said that he would have a word with Keene and find out what was happening.

Some time later, the Office Manager came along. He had two points to make. The first was that he sensed some unrest among the office staff on the factory side and that the production control staff and the dispatch clerks had had some sort of meeting that morning before work started. He did not know what it was about, but at times it had been rather heated. His second was that he had just received the weekly statements of losses in the moulding shop. 'The last two weeks', he said, 'show an increase in our loss figures. I thought that it was a temporary business, but this week's position is even worse.' Quaille said he would have a word with Keene about it.

Just before he left for lunch, one of the travellers paid him a visit. He said to Quaille: 'Up to now, we have had no difficulty in selling everything we made, the fact that we made no domestic goods during the war was responsible for that. The same applies to our competitors. Now things are beginning to change. I have just had a word with some of our oldest agents. They tell me that they are beginning to find it difficult to sell our products. The price is not the problem so much as the quality. Our competitors have been putting out better stuff and if we do not watch out, we will be losing orders.' Quaille said that he would talk to Keene about it and see what could be done to improve quality.

Quaille left the office a worried man. 'I must think seriously about this,' he reflected. 'I wonder what can be going wrong?'

In 1952 a business consultant looked at the facts of this case from the company records of Pender and Quaille and noted the organisation structures shown in Figures 19.3 and 19.4. With the benefit of hindsight he developed the organisation chart of Figure 19.5. It may be regarded as a partial divisionalised structure offering a separation of the foundry from the machine shop and with the functions of purchasing, production control and

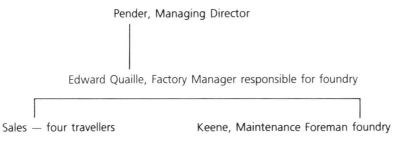

Figure 19.3 *Organisation structure in 1937*

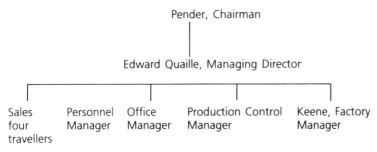

Figure 19.4 *Organisation structure in 1949 for foundry and machine shop*

Figure 19.5 *Possible divisional structure*

quality control under the two division managers. He recommended that Keene should be appointed as one divisional manager and a new appointment should be made for the other post.

Issues for discussion

See the beginning of this case study (p. 397) and Appendix 1, p. 534 for feedback.

Case Study 19.2
A matter of priorities

(This case is taken from unpublished material, whose source is unknown. The commentary is the author's.)

This case illustrates some of the practical difficulties of working in an environment of multiple projects. It may be regarded as representing a situation often encountered in organisations where project work is so commonplace that the result is effectively a simulation of a typical matrix organisation structure in action. Figure 19.6 gives an organisation chart.

Issues for discussion

1. If a manager like Ted Michod has more than one boss, how should he go about reconciling the conflict of priorities?

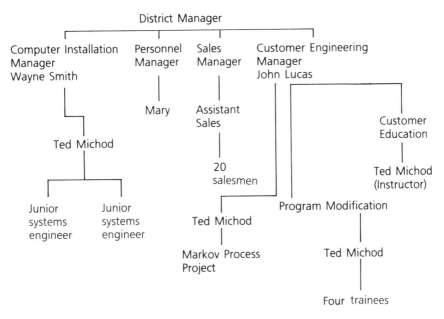

Figure 19.6 *Midwestern marketing region partial organisation chart*

2. What are the preconditions for establishing successful matrix structures among the senior managers of a company?

Ted Michod graduated from the Newark College of Technology as an electrical engineer and went to work for a small but growing computer manufacturing firm in Philadelphia which employed about 10,000 people. His first position with the company was that of junior engineer in the data processing systems division. He worked with twenty other junior engineers designing primary computer circuits and electro-mechanical linkages. Basically, Ted's job consisted of fitting various electrical and mechanical components into a package which would perform logical and arithmetical operations with the greatest reliability at the least cost. Most of the time he worked out designs on paper, although on occasion Ted tried out his ideas in the lab.

After two years, Ted received a promotion which, along with an increase in pay and status, provided him with an opportunity to expand his knowledge of the industry. As an associate engineer in the programming systems division, he served as liaison between his old design group and a systems engineering team which was responsible for the creation of new programming languages. Ted's duties were to make sure that the programming languages being developed were consistent with the design capabilities which were being incorporated into new computer systems by his old work group. Thus, he was able to relate his previous experience with hardware (circuits) to the creation and design of software (program languages) and round out his technical education.

After a year in his new position, Ted began to realise that while he was mastering the technical end of the computer business, he was unprepared for the managerial responsibilities it entailed. Furthermore, it seemed to him that a graduate degree in business administration would greatly improve his chances of promotion in the future. After giving the problem considerable thought, Ted decided to take a two-year educational leave of absence to study for an MBA degree. His decision was based on the fact that in addition to his need for managerial development, his interests had gradually shifted from the technical to the managerial aspects of the industry.

Ted Michod graduated from the local university, finishing in the top 20 per cent of his MBA class. Within two weeks of graduation, he was married and he decided to return to work with his old company. This time, at his request, he was assigned to the Midwestern marketing regional office in Chicago as a customer engineer. Ted felt that experience in the field of customer relations together with his previous technical work would greatly increase his worth to the firm and thus his chances of success.

Once settled in Chicago, Ted reported to the Customer Engineering Manager, John Lucas. Lucas assigned Ted to the customer education section as an instructor. The section's purpose was to train customer employees in the installation and use of computer systems. Since this was not considered to be a full-time assignment, Ted was given additional duties as the supervisor of a program modification team. This second job consisted of giving technical assistance and direction to a group, consisting of four programmer trainees, which was modifying existing computer programs written by the manufacturer for the customers to keep them consistent with improved methodology and technology. Both positions required that he report directly to Lucas. On average Ted taught about 30 hours a week and he devoted 15 hours a week to the second job.

As a result of the group's work in modifying a set of market forecasting programs, Ted hit upon the idea of using a form of the Markov Process to predict growth in sales of new industrial products. (The Markov Process is a statistical approach which basically views life as a series of possibilities that an event will or will not occur given that it has or has not taken place in the past.) Ted had learned about this technique in his MBA program. He studied the problem at home in the evenings and in mid-October submitted his ideas to Lucas in the form of a well-researched documented proposal. Lucas seemed interested in the project but told Ted that it would have to be shelved until the necessary manpower and finances became available.

About two months later, however, Ted's program modification team completed its assigned projects and the group was disbanded. When he reported to Lucas to be reassigned, Michod was instructed to see Wayne Smith, the head of the computer installation department. Smith, like Lucas, was the head of a staff department. Smith and Lucas enjoyed equal rank within the firm and reported to the same district manager.

Smith outlined Ted's next assignment as follows. Ted would supervise two junior systems engineers in the installation of small computers and he would have complete responsibility for each installation project. The job, at first, would require about 20 hours a week of his time. In addition Ted would continue to serve in his present capacity of instructor until the middle of the year. At this time, an additional instructor would be transferred to the Midwestern region and Ted would be relieved of his teaching responsibilities to devote his entire efforts to the installation department. Until then, however, he would report to Smith concerning installation problems and to Lucas for matters involving the education program.

The following day Ted received a note from Lucas to see him as soon as possible. Upon entering Lucas' office, Ted found himself engaged in the following conversation.

Ted: You wanted to see me Mr Lucas?

Lucas: Yes, Ted. Sit down. You know, I liked the proposal you submitted for forecasting with the Markov Process. I'd like you to work up some programs and make it operational. Do you think that you could wrap up the job in two months?

Ted: Well, if I had the time, but as you know I'm still working as an instructor and I've just taken over an installation team for Wayne Smith.

Lucas: Yes, I know about that. You'll have some free time on Wayne's project though. I don't see why you won't be able to fit my project around your other work. It won't take long, will it?

Ted: I just don't know. I can make a wild guess at 120 man hours. I don't think I'll have the time to tackle it.

Lucas: Sure you will, Ted. Smith's project won't take all your time. Besides, 120 hours isn't very much. Why, it's not even 2 weeks' work.

After leaving Mr Lucas' office, Ted stopped in to see Wayne Smith.

Ted: Hi. I was wondering when I should start working for you?

Smith (jokingly): Today! Now!

Ted: Well, what I mean is, will it be full-time at first or will I have some time on my hands?

Smith: No it should be a full 20 hours a week right from the start. Why did you ask? Any special reason?

Michod told Smith about his conversation with Lucas and explained that he didn't think that he would be able to handle all three projects. Wayne Smith agreed but felt that there had been some misunderstanding. He told Ted that he would talk to Lucas that afternoon and that Ted should let the matter ride till it had been discussed further.

Ted: Good. I hope that this gets cleared up soon.

Smith: Don't worry, Ted, we just have our wires crossed. Stop and see me first thing in the morning.

The next day the following conversation took place between Ted and Mr Smith.

Smith: Ted, I saw John Lucas yesterday and I'm not sure that I've solved your problem. He said that the project he had in mind wasn't very big and that you would have plenty of time to get it done.

Ted: But I told him that it would take 120 hours. Since then I have been worried that my estimate would be way too low if the work is done over an extended period, with lots of stops and starts.

Smith: Well, you'd better talk with him again. I understood that I was to have you for 20 hours a week and believe me I need you for every bit of that time!

Ted saw Lucas a few hours later and explained again his commitments and lack of available time. He went on to suggest that he could instruct a new man to carry out the project if that was acceptable to Lucas.

Lucas: I don't know who else would be available to do this type of work . . .
   Look, Ted, just fit it in around your other work. You'll have time to do it . . .
   Oh, before I forget, see Mary in Personnel on your way out. They need some information for their records. And tell my secretary to come in, will you? I have a stack of letters to get out.

Ted walked down to Personnel wondering how he wound up in the middle of all this. Furthermore, he wondered what he should do next.

For discussion issues see p. 402. For feedback on these issues see Appendix 1, p. 536.

Case Study 19.3
The tap

(Material adapted from Bensman and Gerver (1963), 'Crime and punishment in the factory'. Published with permission of the *American Sociological Review*.

Issues for discussion

1. Identify in the case material following the distinct different work groups in the factory.
2. What is the formal response to the use of the tap by each identified group?
3. What are the informal responses to the use of the tap?
4. Why do the formal and informal responses differ so widely?

The research base

The research was carried out in an airplane factory employing 26,000 people in the New York metropolitan area. One of the authors was a participant observer from September 1953 to September 1954. He gathered his data daily while working as an assembler on the aileron crew of the final wing line. No special research instruments were used; the ordinary activities of workers along the line were observed, noted as they occurred and recorded daily. All aspects involved in the use of the tap were discussed in the context of the work situation when they are relevant and salient to the personnel involved, and without their realising that they were objects of study.

The tap and its functions

The tap is an extremely hard steel screw, whose threads are slotted to allow for the disposal of the waste metal which it cuts away. It is so hard that, when it is inserted into a nut, it can cut new threads over the original threads of the nut.

In wing assembly work, bolts or screws must be inserted in recessed nuts which are anchored to the wing in earlier processes of assembly. The bolt or screw must pass through a wing plate before reaching the nut. In the nature of the mass production process alignments between nuts and plate-openings become distorted. Original allowable tolerances become magnified in later stages of assembly as the number of alignments which must be coordinated with each other increase with the increasing complexity of the assemblage. When the nut is not aligned with the hole, the tap can be used to cut, at a new angle, new threads in the nut to bring the nut into a new but not true alignment. If the tap is not used and the bolt is forced, the wing plate itself may be bent. Such new alignments, however, deviate from the specifications of the blueprint which is based on true alignments at every stage of the assembly process. On the basis of engineering standards true alignments are necessary at every stage in order to achieve maximum strength and a proper equilibrium of strains and stresses.

The use of the tap is the most serious crime of workmanship conceivable in the plant. A worker can be summarily fired for merely possessing a tap. Nevertheless, at least half the workforce in a position to use a tap owns at least one. And every well-equipped senior mechanic owns four or five of different sizes. Every mechanic has access to them and, if need be, uses them. In fact, the mass use of the tap represents a widespread violation of this most serious rule of workmanship.

The tap is defined as a criminal instrument, primarily because it destroys the effectiveness of stop nuts. Aviation nuts are specifically designed so that, once tightened, a screw or bolt cannot back out of the the nut under the impact of vibration in flight. Once a nut is tapped, however, it loses its holding power and at any time, after sufficient vibration, the screw or bolt can fall out and weaken the part it holds to the wing and the wing itself.

In addition, the use of a tap is an illegal method of concealing a structural defect. If the holes, for example, were properly drilled and the nuts were properly installed, the use of the tap would be unnecessary. Deviations make subsequent maintenance of the airplane difficult since maintenance mechanics have no records of such illegal deviations from specifications. Taps can be used in certain cases by special mechanics when such usage is authorised by engineers and when proper paperwork supports its use. But such authorisation usually takes one to three days.

The tap, then, is an illegal tool, the use or possession of which carries extreme sanctions in private organisational law, but which is simultaneously widely possessed and used despite its illegal status. The problem is to account for the wide acceptance of a crime as a means of fulfilling work requirements within a private organisation, the aircraft plant.

The socialisation of the worker

To most workers entering an aircraft plant the tap is an unknown instrument. Dies which thread bolts, i.e. the process opposite to tapping, are relatively well-known and are standard equipment in the plumbing trade. The new worker does not come into contact with the tap until he finds it impossible to align the holes in two skins. In desperation, and guilt in case he has made a mistake, he turns to his partner (a more experienced worker) and confides his problem. The experienced worker will try every legitimate technique of lining up the holes, but if none of these succeeds, he resorts to the tap. He taps the new thread himself, not permitting the novice to use the tap. While tapping it he gives the novice a lecture on the dangers of getting caught and of breaking a tap in the hole, thereby leaving evidence of its use.

For several weeks the older worker will not permit his inexperienced partner to use a tap. He leaves his own work in order to do the required tapping and finishes the job before returning to his own work. If the novice demonstrates sufficient ability and care in other aspects of his work, he will be allowed to tap the hole under supervision of a veteran worker. When the veteran partner is absent and the now initiated worker can use the tap at his own discretion he feels a sense of pride. In order to enjoy his new found facility, he frequently uses the tap when it is not necessary. He may be careless in properly aligning perfectly good components and then compensate for his own carelessness by using the tap.

He may forgo the easier illegal methods (which are viewed as less serious crimes) of greasing and waxing bolts or enlarging the misaligned holes and indulge himself in the more pleasurable, challenging and dangerous use of the tap. Sooner or later he inevitably runs into difficulties which he is technically unprepared to cope with. When his partner and mentor is not available, he is forced to call on the assistant foreman. If the situation requires it, the foreman will recommend the tap. If he has doubts about the worker's abilities, he may even tap the hole himself. In doing this, he risks the censure of the union, because as a foreman he is not permitted to handle tools.

At the time the research was conducted, there were four levels of foremen. These were: assistant foremen (one star); foremen (two stars); assistant general foremen (three stars); and general foremen (four stars). The stars are on the foremen's badges and are their insignia of rank. The assistant foreman is the immediate supervisor of a work crew. The four star general foreman is the shop supervisor. The two and three star foremen have authority over increasingly larger sections of the assembly line. In the following discussion 'foreman' refers to the one star, assistant foreman, unless otherwise stated.

While the foreman taps the hole, he also lectures on proper and technically workmanlike ways of using the tap: 'The tap is only turned in quarter turns. Never force the tap. If it snaps, your ass is in a sling and I won't be able to get you out of it.'

The foreman warns the worker: 'Make sure not to get caught, to see that the coast is clear, to keep the tap well hidden when not in use, and to watch out for inspectors while using it.' He always ends by cautioning the worker: 'It's your own ass if you're caught.'

When the worker feels that he can use the tap with complete confidence, he usually buys his own, frequently displaying it to other workers and magnanimously lending it to those in need of it. He feels himself fully arrived when a two star foreman or even an assistant general foreman borrows his tap or asks him to perform the tapping. The worker has now established his identity and is known as an individual by the higher-ups.

Once the right to use the tap is thus established, its indiscriminate use is frowned upon. A worker who uses a tap too often is considered to be careless. A worker who can get his work done without frequently using the tap is a 'mechanic', but one who does not use the tap when it is necessary does not get his own work done on time. Proper use of the tap requires judgement and etiquette. The tap addict is likely to become the object of jokes and to get a bad reputation among workers, foremen and inspectors.

Agencies of law enforcement

The enforcement of the plant's rules of workmanship devolves upon three groups: foremen, plant quality control, and Air Force quality control. The ultimate and supreme authority resides in the latter group. The Air Force not only sets the blueprint specifications, but also and more importantly, can reject a finished airplane as not meeting specifications.

Furthermore, the Air Force inspectors reinspect installations which have previously been 'bought' by plant quality control. If these installations do not meet Air Force standards they are 'crabbed', i.e. rejected. When this happens, the plant inspectors who bought the installations are 'written up', i.e. disciplinary action is taken for unintentional negligence, and this may lead to suspension, demotion, or in extreme cases, loss of job. The Air Force Inspector has the absolute right to demand that any man be fired for violating the rules.

There were only two Air Force inspectors to a shop at the time of these observations, so that it was almost impossible for the Air Force inspectors to police an entire shop of over 2,000 men. As an Air Force inspector walks up the line, it is a standard procedure for workers to nudge other workers to inform them of the approach of the 'Gestapo'. When tapping is essential and when it is known that the Air Force inspectors are too near, guards of workers are posted to convey advance notice of the approach to anyone who is actively tapping. This is especially true when there are plant drives against the use of the tap.

In all instances, when the Air Force inspector is in the vicinity, workers who have a reputation for open or promiscuous use of the tap are instructed by the assistant foreman to disappear. Such types can return to work when the coast is clear.

Despite the Air Force inspectors' high authority and the severity of their standards, they are not sufficiently numerous to be considered as the major policing agency for detecting and apprehending violators of the rules of workmanship. Plant quality control is the actual law enforcement agency in terms of the daily operation of surveillance. There are approximately 150 plant inspectors in the 2,000-man shop. They work along the assembly-line with the workers. In some cases a panel of inspectors is assigned to inspect the work done by a number of crews who are supervised by a two star foreman. In this system a call-book is kept which guarantees the equal rotation of tasks. When a worker has completed a job and requests an inspection, he enters his wing number and the requested inspection in the book. The inspector, after completing an inspection, marks the job as completed and takes the next open inspection in the call-book.

A result of either type of inspection set-up is the free and intimate intermingling of inspectors and workers. In off moments, inspectors and workers gather together to 'shoot the breeze and kill time'. Inspectors, unlike workers, may have long waiting periods before their next assignment. During such periods, out of boredom and monotony, they tend to fraternise with workers. This causes conflict with their role of policemen. A major cause of leniency on the part of inspectors is the nature of the relationship between them and the mechanics in circumstances not involving the tap. There is a considerable amount of mechanical work which is not easily and immediately accessible to inspectors. This is particularly true if the inspector does not want to spend several hours on a fairly simple inspection. In order for the inspector to complete his work and make sure that the work he 'buys' will be acceptable to later inspectors, he must rely on the workmanship of the mechanic. In brief he must have faith not only in the mechanic's workmanship but also in his willingness not to 'louse him up'. If the inspector gets the reputation of being a bastard, the mechanic is under no obligation to do a good job and thus protect the inspector. Since the penalties for the use of the tap are so severe, no inspector feels comfortable about reporting a violation. A number of subterfuges are resorted to in an effort to diminish the potential conflict.

There is a general understanding that workers are not supposed to use the tap in the presence of plant inspectors. At various times this understanding is made explicit. The inspector frequently tells the workers of his crew: 'Now fellas, there's a big drive now on taps. The Air Force just issued a special memo. For God's sake, don't use a tap when I am around. If someone sees it when I am in the area, it'll be my ass. Look around first. Make sure that I'm gone.'

At other times the verbalisation comes from the worker. If a worker has to use a tap and the inspector is present, he will usually wait until the inspector leaves. If the inspector shows no sign of leaving, the worker will tell him to 'Get the hell outa here. I got work to do and can't do it while you're around.'

If the worker knows the inspector he may take out the tap, permitting the inspector to see it. The wise inspector responds to the gesture by leaving. Of course, the worker has already sized up the inspector and knows whether or not he can rely upon him to respond as desired.

When there is an Air Force drive against the tap, the inspectors will make the rounds and 'lay the law down': 'I want no more tapping around here. The next guy caught gets turned in. I can't cover you guys any more. I'm not kidding you bastards. If you can't do a decent job, don't do it at all. If that s.o.b. foreman of yours insists on you doing it, tell him to do it himself. He can't make you do it. If you're caught, it's your ass not his. When the chips are down, he's got to cover himself and he'll leave you holding the bag!'

For about three or four days thereafter, taps disappear from public view. The work slows down and ultimately the inspectors forget to be zealous. A normal state of haphazard equilibrium is restored.

Other types of social relations and situations between workers and inspectors help maintain this state of equilibrium. An inspector will often see a tap on the top of a worker's tool box. He will pick it up and drop it in the bottom of the box where it cannot be seen easily. Perhaps he will tell the worker that he is a 'damned fool for being so careless'. The inspector thus hopes to establish his dependability for the worker, and creates a supply of goodwill, which the worker must repay by protecting the inspector.

Another typical worker—inspector situation occurs when a mechanic is caught in the act of tapping and the inspector does not look away. The inspector severely reprimands the mechanic, 'throws the fear of God into him', holds him in suspense as to whether he will turn him in, and then lets him go with a warning. This, generally, only happens to new workers. Occasionally when a worker has a new inspector and no previously established trust relationship, the same situation may arise. In both cases they are an integral part of the socialisation of the worker to the plant or, rather, to a specific phase of its operation.

The role of the foreman

Another type of ceremonial escape from law enforcement through pseudo-law enforcement involves the foreman. In rare cases an inspector will catch a worker using the tap, reprimand him and turn him over to his foreman. The foreman then is forced to go through the procedure of reprimanding the errant worker. The foreman becomes serious and indignant, primarily because the worker let himself get caught. He gives the worker a genuine tongue-lashing, and he reminds him once again that he, as foreman, has to save the worker's neck. He stresses that it is only because of his intervention that the worker will not lose his job. He states: 'Next time, be careful. I won't stick my neck out for you again. For God's sake don't use a tap, *unless it's absolutely necessary.*'

The worker is obliged to accept the reprimand and to assume the countenance of true penitent, even to the extent of promising that it won't happen again. He will say: 'Awright, awright. So I got caught this time. Next time I won't get caught.' Both foreman and worker play these roles even though the worker tapped the hole at the specific request of the foreman. The most blatant violation of the mores in such a situation is when the worker grins and treats the whole thing as a comic interlude. When this happens, the foreman becomes truly enraged: 'That's the trouble with you. You do not take your job seriously. You don't give a damn about nothing. How long do I have to put up with your not giving a damn!'

The public ritual, therefore, conceals an entirely different dimension in social functions involved in the use of the tap. It is inconceivable that the tap could be used without the active or passive collusion of the foreman. As noted, the foreman instructs the worker in its use, indicates when he wants it used, assists the worker in evading the plant rules, and when the worker is caught, goes through a ritual of punishment. These role contradictions are intrinsic to the position of foreman. His major responsibility is to keep production going. At the same time he is a representative of supervision and is supposed to encourage respect for company law. He is not primarily responsible for quality since this is the province of plant quality control, i.e. inspection. He resolves the various conflicts in terms of the strongest and most peristent forms of pressures and rewards.

The work requirements of a particular foreman and his crew are determined by the production analysis section, another staff organisation. Workers call it 'time study' although it is only one part of its function. Production analysis determines, on the basis of time studies, the number of men to be assigned to a specific crew, the locations of the crew on the line and the cutting-off points for work controlled by a particular foreman. Having done this, they determine the workload required of a foreman and keep production charts on completed work. These charts are the foreman's report cards. At a moment's glance, top supervision can single out foremen who are not pulling their weight. In aviation assembly, since the work cycle for a particular team is relatively long (4—8 hours) and since a foreman has relatively few teams (usually three) all doing the same job, anything which delays one team damages the foreman's production record in the immediate terms of the report card. Moreover, delay caused by the inability of one crew to complete its task prevents other crews from working on that wing. The foremen of these crews will complain to the two or three star foremen that they are being held up and that their production records will suffer because of another foreman's incompetence.

As a result of these considerations, the pressures 'to get work out' are paramount for the foreman. There is relatively high turnover among foremen, even at the two star level. In the last analysis, production records are the major consideration in supervisory mobility. All other considerations — sociability, work knowledge, personality, etc. — are assumed to be measured by the chart.

In this context the foreman, *vis-à-vis* the ticklish question of the tap, is compelled to violate some of the most important laws of the company and the Air Force. Crucial instances occur at times when the Air Force institutes stringent anti-tap measures. When key holes do not line up it may be necessary, as an alternative to using the tap, to disassemble previous installations. The disassembling and reassembling may take a full 8 hours before the previous stage is again reached. The production chart for that 8-hour period will indicate that no work has been done. In such a situation a worker may refuse to tap a hole since he risks endangering his job. The foreman also may be reluctant to request directly the worker to tap a hole. To get the work done he therefore employs a whole rhetoric of veiled requests such as: 'Hell, that's easy . . . you know what to do . . . you've done it before.' 'Maybe you can clean out the threads.' Or, 'Well, see what you can do.'

If the worker is adamant, the foreman will practically beg him to do the right thing. He will remind him of past favours, he will complain about his chart rating and of how 'Top brass doesn't give a damn about anything but what's on the chart.' He ends his plea with: 'Once you get this done, you can take it easy. You know that I don't work you guys too hard most of the time.'

If the veiled requests and pitiful pleadings don't produce results, the foreman may take the ultimate step of tapping the hole himself. He compounds the felony, because he not only violates the rules of workmanship but also violates union rules which specifically state that no foreman can use a tool. To add insult to injury, the foreman furthermore has to borrow the tap in the midst of an anti-tap drive when taps are scarce.

From the viewpoint of production the use of the tap is imperative to the functioning of the production organisation, even though it is one of the most serious work crimes. This is recognised even at official levels, although only in indirect ways.

Taps, being made of hard steel, have the disadvantage of being brittle. If not handled carefully, they may break within the nut. This not only makes further work impossible, but makes for easier detection of the crime. To cope with such a problem, the tool crib is well equipped with tap extractors. Any worker can draw an appropriately sized tap extractor from the tool crib. All these are official company property. He can do this even amidst the most severe anti-tap drives without fear or danger of punishment.

For discussion of tasks

See the beginning of the case study, p. 406. For discussion of feedback see Appendix 1, p. 538.

References

Bensman, J. and Gerver, I. (1963) 'Crime and punishment in the factory: The function of deviancy in maintaining the social system', *American Sociological Review*, vol 28, no. 4, pp. 588–598.

Brown, W. (1960), *Exploration in Management*, Heinemann.

Buchanan, D.A. and Hucynski, A.A. (1985), *Organisational Behaviour*, Prentice Hall.

Chapman, L. (1978), *Your Disobedient Servant*, Chatto & Windus.

Davis, S.M. and Lawrence, P.R. (1978), 'Problems of matrix organisations', *Harvard Business Review*, May/June, pp. 131–42.

Fayol, H. (1916, 1949), *General and Industrial Management*, translated from the French by C. Storrs, Pitman.

Goggin, W.C. (1974), 'How the multidimensional structure works in Dow Corning', *Harvard Business Review*, May/June, pp. 54–63.

Mayo, E. (1933), *The Human Problems of an Industrial Civilisation*, Macmillan.

Weber, M. (1921), *Theory of Social and Economic Organisation*, translated from the German by A.M. Henderson and T. Parsons, Oxford University Press.

Woodward, J. (1965), *Industrial Organisation: Theory and practice*, Oxford University Press.

Chapter 20

Leadership

Overview

In most modern management syllabuses there is a section on leadership or leadership styles. Research has focused on this topic with an increasing intensity since the early 1960s.

In this chapter the reader is taken through a brief review of the main approaches to leadership from very early times, and then recent developments growing out of the behavioural sciences are reviewed.

Learning objectives

By the end of this chapter the reader should understand the main concepts of leadership and be able to analyse business situations in which leadership has become an issue. The adoption of a particular leadership style will be one among many choices open to the manager who wished to introduce change and innovation into the business situation. The chapter will also consider how leadership styles may be nurtured through management development programmes.

Reasons for studying leadership

It is natural that people should strive for success and wish to recognise its features and principles. If these principles turn out to be based on innate factors it will be rather a sterile exercise, for the natural desire is to grow in leadership expertise, so the focus must be on those principles which can be learned. The study of leadership can become one more dimension in which the manager is constantly aware of possible alternatives and can gradually enrich his or her leadership style repertoire.

Early contributors to leadership problems and solutions

Leadership is not a new topic and indeed is embedded in even some of the most ancient literature. Whenever we read biography we find descriptions of leadership dilemmas and sometimes some vivid coaching sequences. Moses, in Exodus 18: 13, is having trouble in leading the Israelites out from Egypt; and dealing with large numbers of people gives rise to a problem of *delegation*. His father-in-law offers some advice in eleven well-known verses, which are a remarkable passage from the Bible. It gives us a picture of organisation structure and the notion of delegation of authority, as without delegation it is not possible to set and adhere to priorities.

In real life it is sheer agony to work for a manager who is a poor delegator, yet this situation is common and often the manager is completely unaware of this black spot. The real difficulty is creating this awareness in the superior without offering direct criticism. The appraisal process of MbO does provide this mechanism (see chapter 6); further guidelines are given in chapter 7.

Leadership in Roman times: Gaius Petronius AD66

'We trained hard; but it seemed that every time we were beginning to form teams we would be reorganised. I was to learn later in life that we tend to meet any new situation by reorganising, and a wonderful method it can be for creating the illusion of progress while producing confusion, inefficiency and demoralisation.'

Leadership seems to depend on organisation structure, but the new leader needs to establish dominance, so a high profile is required. Reorganisation is probably the easiest way to get that attention as it affects so many people.

Leadership in the First World War

The mass recruitment of young men in 1914 and the need for young leaders created a real need for theory and practice. Young officers needed commissioning and sending to the front, and no longer could commissions in the British Army be purchased as part of a system of patronage, based primarily on land-ownership and wealth. The solution seemed to be to select officers on the basis of academic criteria, record at team sports and qualities of honesty, loyalty, *esprit de corps* and reliability, so the leaders came from the officer cadet forces of the British public schools and to a lesser extent the grammar schools.

However, this simplistic approach to selection for leadership was much under pressure as there were simply not enough young men with the required leadership background. Promotion in the field, based on effectiveness in lower ranks, meant that many leaders emerged who did not have the set of attributes and qualities of the men from the public schools, so other, less traditional selection methods were sorely needed.

So far we have only looked at the young officers. The senior leaders had been staff trained, given rotation of both command jobs and staff jobs and promoted on the basis of annual reports and supposed merit. The sheer scale of modern war required not only an effective organisation and command structure, but also rapid and effective communications, so that decisions in headquarters could take into account the realities of the front line. Without this congruence of thought and action between commanders and staff there was to be an appalling loss of life, the agony of a war of attrition and criticism of the generals' leadership. A less severe view is that the generals could not win in that situation of poor communications and that a harsh and unfavourable environment could defeat even the most brilliant examples of fortitude, courage and leadership.

Churchill's view

Even the greatest leaders sometimes slip up badly; there seems to be no consistency in leadership success. The following is a passage concerning a First World War campaign, referred to by Winston Churchill (1955) in his account of the Second World War. His role in the incident described was as First Lord of the Admiralty, with membership of the War Cabinet, but its outcome was a temporary removal from the world of politics, and transfer to France as an army colonel.

> *On Being Number One*
>
> In any sphere of action there can be no comparison between the positions of number one and numbers two, three and four. The duties and problems of all persons are quite different and in many ways more difficult. It is always a misfortune when number two or three has to initiate a dominant plan or policy. He has to consider not only the merits of the policy, but the mind of his chief; not only what to advise, but what it is proper in his station to advise; not only what to do, but how to get it agreed, and how to get it done. Moreover, number two or three will have to reckon with numbers four or five or six, or maybe some bright outsider, number twenty. Ambition, not so much for vulgar ends, but for fame, glints in every mind. There are always several points of view which may be right, and many which are plausible. I was ruined for the time being in 1915 over the Dardanelles, and a supreme enterprise was cast away, through my trying to carry out a major and cardinal operation of war from a subordinate position. Men are ill-advised to try such ventures. This lesson had sunk deep into my nature.
>
> At the top there are great simplifications. An accepted leader has only to be sure of what it is best to do, or at least to have made up his mind about it. The loyalties which centre upon number one are enormous. If he trips he must be sustained. If he makes mistakes they must be covered. If he sleeps he must not be wantonly disturbed. If he is no good he must be pole-axed.

Churchill's grand strategy had been to develop a second front through the Dardanelles, the back passage of Europe, and bring the war to a quick end in 1915, but military chiefs were not particularly disposed to divert sufficient resources to this naval operation to guarantee success, and when stout resistance occurred, the operation was abandoned.

Leadership practice in the Second World War

The inter-war years saw the birth of behavioural science, the evolution of motivation theory, the beginnings of credible personnel management theory and practice and a natural concentration on more reliable methods of selection and training. When conscription came to Britain and young officers needed selecting for leadership a new, more sophisticated procedure was adopted. It became known as the War Office Selection Board Interview, WOSBI.

The philosophy here was to simulate a good cross-section of typical leadership/team exercises, in which the junior officer would be critically observed by experienced senior officers over a three-day period. They would then share their assessments and decide whether the standard had been attained. The earlier tradition of looking for prowess in teamwork and good academic grades was continued, but there was also assessment of reactions to a range of problems and the benefit of group wisdom from respected mentors.

The WOSBI approach is now an established part of the selection culture for the British army officer and has been adapted for use by many other public and private organisations as the basis of leadership selection and leadership training.

The military men have also adapted their leadership approaches to the world of business and commerce. Major John Adair, ex-Scots Guards, now Professor of Leadership in the University of Surrey, conceptualised a theory of leadership from the WOSBI process, which became known as action-centred leadership (Adair, 1973). It was backed by the British Industrial Society and incorporated into many courses and seminars for industrial supervisors. The conceptualisation of ACL is that the leader needs to satisfy three conflicting influences simultaneously. These are the task needs, the group's needs to contribute and the needs of individual group members. A well-balanced leader would be sensitive to the forces of each such influence and develop the self-confidence and judgement to balance the forces and adopt a strategy to achieve a group performance acceptable to superiors.

This leadership model had a major advantage, that of simplicity. Trainers could relatively easily customise it by constructing typical group exercises reflecting the common problems of their own environment. People tended to become much more aware of how others saw them through role-playing in leadership situations and better able to assess their own strengths and weaknesses.

Major Nicholas McLean-Bristol, Director of Project Trust, an organisation devoted to sending young persons out for one year's service in developing countries in the gap between school and university, also adapted a WOSBI/ACL-type process to test for resilience and leadership those preparing to be sent overseas. The exercises were customised to replicate, in the tough climate and environment of the Hebrides, a set of tasks which might be typical for a volunteer abroad. This approach certainly stood the test of time, and twenty years on from the organisation's foundation, it is still the bedrock of selection and training.

Post-Second World War leadership developments

Churchill and Attlee

Churchill was the charismatic war leader, brilliant orator and writer and much admired statesman, dominant in the House of Commons, surrounded by a Cabinet of well-known and striking personalities in their own right; yet in May 1945 there was a landslide against him in the general election, which he had failed to anticipate. The war-time coalition dissolved and Attlee, previously deputy prime minister, headed a newly elected Labour Government. He was much less well-known, few would describe him as charismatic, yet he could dominate a Cabinet with precise chairmanship, never suffering fools gladly. Attlee presided over the setting up of the welfare state. Many would regard his administration as one of the most innovative of this century in Britain, yet there was very little resemblance in terms of personality with Churchill. The crucial forces in leadership success may be situational — personality factors may, contrary to the common-sense view, be of relatively minor importance.

North American contributions

Peter Drucker

Drucker makes an important contribution to the theory of leadership. Two main theories emerge. Firstly, the manager/leader needs to take account of all the stakeholders in the situation. This leads to the approach of managing by objectives. This is regarded by Drucker as a philosophy of leadership, a linking of managers and groups at each level with each higher level. To develop the coaching aspect he suggests that managers send a letter to their superiors suggesting appropriate objectives for the superior to adopt! All this is intended to increase a general follower/leader empathy, the environment of working in mutual expectancy.

In *The Effective Executive* (1971), he suggests that leadership can be learned by adopting effective executive habits, which have nothing to do with personality. He suggests that executives should rigorously manage their time, set objectives and priorities regularly, develop skills of delegation, open up good upward communication and feedback to their own managers and adopt simple organisation structures, with just a few organisational levels. He sees a need for the senior executive to get out of the ivory tower and be able to relate directly with customers, to understand their irritation with bureaucracy. He suggests that managers should know themselves and their strengths and use management development programmes to develop these. He is much less concerned with weaknesses, but this does leave some dilemmas. What of the narrow specialist with a blindspot about teamwork? If that blindspot is not recognised and treated, then the specialist may never achieve full potential.

Fred Fiedler

Fiedler (1974) is a prominent US authority on leadership theory. He conceptualised a contingency theory of leadership, which seems to have had much influence in later research. He refers to Couch and Carter (1952) who developed three major categories of leadership behaviour:

1. Group goal facilitation,
2. Individual prominence,
3. Group sociability.

There is a striking similarity between this categorisation to the one developed by Adair (1973). The development of these approaches seemed to have been going on at the same time on both sides of the Atlantic.

Next, Fiedler refers to Cattell (1951) in a search for a definition of leadership: 'The leader is the one who creates the most effective change in group performance.' A further development of this definition is taken from Homans (1950): 'The leader is the one who comes closest to realising the norms the group values highest; this conformity gives high rank, which attracts people and implies the right to assume control of the group.'

Fiedler then refers to Stogdill (1948), on the credibility of *leadership traits*: 'There is much activity in early research but very little agreement pattern.' One main conclusion is as follows:

> The qualities, characteristics, and skills required in a leader are determined to a large extent by the demands of the situation in which he is to function as a leader. A person does not become a leader by virtue of the possession of some combination of traits, but by the pattern of personal characteristics, activities, and goals of the followers. Thus, leadership must be conceived in terms of the interaction of variables, which are in constant flux and change. The factor of change is particularly characteristic of the situation, which may be radically altered by the addition or loss of members, changes in interpersonal relationships, changes in goals, competition of extra-group influences, and the like. The personal characteristics of the leader and the followers are, in comparison, highly stable. The persistence of individual patterns of human behaviour in the face of constant situational change appears to be a primary obstacle encountered not only in the practice of leadership, but in the selection and placement of leaders. It becomes clear that an adequate analysis of leadership involves not only a study of leaders, but also situations.

Next, Fiedler refers to his own research and begins to develop and define his contingency theory. The aim of Fiedler, in 'The Belgian Navy Study' (1966), was to determine if there was any consistency in leadership effectiveness in undertaking different leadership tasks.

Ninety-six three-man teams were assembled and each given four identical tasks, in the expectation that a success pattern for one task would carry over to other tasks. These were as follows:

Task 1 Write a letter urging men to join the Belgian Navy.
Tasks 2 and 3 Route a ship convoy through ten and then through twelve different ports in the most efficient manner.
Task 4 Assemble and disassemble an automatic pistol.

No significant correlation was reported of success across the four different tasks.

Fiedler then suggested that there were three significant components in situations which would influence group performance and offer some predictability of outcome. This evolved into a contingency theory of leadership. These three factors were:

1. Leader/member relationships (popularity),
2. Task nature (structured or unstructured),
3. Position power (the right to reward, punish, evaluate).

Through a combination of these three components the leader's situation is favourable or unfavourable for performance.

However, Fiedler needed one more variable to experiment with in order to test this theory and here he took a personality characteristic which later writers were to call 'relationships orientation'. Although Fiedler distrusted personality factors in leadership studies, he did find one which retained a consistency over long periods of time and continual retesting. He developed a questionnaire which described a leader's feeling towards the 'least preferred co-worker' with whom he or she could identify in work experience. This questionnaire would yield an index, which he called an LPC score.

The philosophy behind this seemed to be that leaders experience two basic pressures. The first is the pressure to complete an assigned task within a prescribed timescale. The second is to keep the goodwill and unity of the group, as an investment in future assignments. An autocratic bully (low LPC score) may force completion by driving the team one day, only to find that next day there is so much absenteeism that production plummets. It may have been better to keep goodwill and achieve 90 per cent of target two days running.

If the leader is master of all the variables in the task then it is possible to be directive and insist on established methods. This is what an autocratic leader (low LPC) would do to maintain production. However, with many group tasks the leader does not have mastery of all the variables; indeed, that might be the very reason why a team of experts has been set up, to achieve integration of available expertise. An authoritarian leader will feel most uncomfortable in such a situation, as he or she has no capacity to direct, only an opportunity to persuade and reward the relevant contributors.

Fiedler suggested that, when the task was unstructured and unprecedented, the relationships-oriented leader (high LPC score) would perform better, as in the more democratic atmosphere it would be easier for experts to contribute to a leader who was not obviously uncomfortable.

Fiedler then put this 'contingency theory' to the test and reported a consistent correlation between the two variables of 'situation favourableness continuum' and 'LPC' score, in several studies (Fiedler and Chemers, 1974, p. 80). The impact of this was that many other researchers were soon on the scene adding flesh to this basic theory.

A positive outcome would be that coaching could be directed towards variables which would make the situation more favourable for the leader, and thus make him or her more powerful.

The theory did, however, give rise to a dilemma, the specification of effective leadership training in anticipation of promotion. Typically, senior management jobs are progressively less structured and require more relationships orientation once general management problems are tackled, yet in middle or junior management positions the manager is probably dealing with tasks that are structured and require a more task-oriented behaviour. When promotion comes then the 'magnet has to change its poles' and a new set of behaviours becomes necessary. But Fiedler's LPC score is consistent and unchangeable, so this is really a problem situation. One way out of the dilemma is to disavow the assumption that 'relationship orientation' is anything other than one more fluid and dynamic situational variable.

Other North American leadership style models

Tannenbaum and Schmidt (1958) offer a 'leadership continuum'. One pole is boss-centred (autocratic), the other is subordinate-centred (democratic). Six points are defined on the scale giving slight variations in typical leader behaviour. The model seems to assume that a leader is consistent in style and is assigned the job that fits that style, which is fine for the job with a narrow role requirement, but not so good if a wide range of roles are expected.

The points on the Tannenbaum continuum are defined as follows:

1. *Telling style*   Boss-centred point. A problem is referred to the manager. He or she decides the objective and the solution. He or she gets the staff to implement the solution.
2. *Selling style*   A problem is referred to the manager. He or she decides the objective and the solution. He or she sells the solution to the staff.
3. *Consulting style*   A problem is referred to the manager. He or she decides the objective. The solution is subject to change on the suggestions of the staff and they implement the solution.
4. *Participating style*   A problem is referred to the manager. He or she decides the objective and seeks suggestions from the staff. He or she decides the solution and gets staff to implement the solution.
5. *Joining style*   A problem is referred to the manager. He or she decides the objective. Staff decide the solution. Staff implement the solution.
6. *Abdicating style — extreme subordinate-centred point*   A problem is referred to the manager. He or she refers to subordinates, who decide the objective and the solution and who implement the solution.

This is a relatively simple model and an advantage is that people can readily identify the predominant style of their own manager. A researcher can get quite consistent leadership profiles, as perceived by subordinates, simply by gathering information using questionnaires. An interesting observation among Scottish managers is that, commonly, they would prefer to be exposed to a more subordinate-centred style than is the current style of their manager.

However, if one assumes that one has just been promoted into the boss's job and asked to indicate what style one would adopt, a more boss-centred style is the likely choice. The interpretation of this is that managers, when they are first promoted, wish to establish their authority in the new post, which means an emphasis on control and power, hence its influence on preferred leadership style.

Later on the leader will have a better feel for the abilities of the subordinate and pressures may be building for delegation, so the preferred style is likely to move towards the subordinate-centred end of the continuum. In reality the style seems to change to suit the situation, so we are back to the contingency view of leadership, but the difference is that both situation and choice of style are dynamic variables.

Choice of leadership style is influenced by the predominant organisation culture. In banks, for instance, there is often a lot of bureaucracy surrounding the lending decision. This is incorporated in policy manuals, standing instructions and formal job descriptions and is a given and almost unchangeable factor, which limits the discretion to delegate and thus prescribes a boss-centred style for lending decisions. Of course, not all of a particular manager's decisions will be lending decisions, so the choice of style will depend on the nature of the decision to be taken. Once more we are adopting a contingency approach. Organisation structures in banks tend to be rather stable, but the rules of the game may change dramatically when there is a change in ownership. This may even change the authority to delegate in the lending situation, but again this is a part of the current predominant organisation culture.

Rensis Likert

Another authority on leadership styles, well-respected in the literature, but of a similar orientation to Tannenbaum and Schmidt, is Likert (1967). He conceptualised four leadership styles, as follows:

System 1 Exploitative autocratic.
System 2 Benevolent autocratic.
System 3 Participative.
System 4 Democratic.

And these were defined with three leadership variables, as follows:

1. Confidence and trust in subordinates,
2. Subordinates feeling of freedom,
3. Superiors seeking involvement with subordinates.

Likert's model is then developed as a matrix with cells across the two dimensions, each cell describing typical behaviour. Like Tannenbaum's model, people can readily relate to these definitions. However, it would be a trap to expect that participative or democratic styles are necessarily always the best. A main advantage of familiarity with the definitions and language of leadership seems to be that more open communication is then possible between leaders and followers, so that informed choices may be made.

R.R. Blake and J.S. Mouton

Blake and Mouton (1969) developed a managerial grid. It has two nine-point dimensions for definitions of leadership style. The horizontal dimension is 'concern for production'; the vertical dimension is 'concern for people'. Note that all the authorities on leadership style mentioned in this chapter have, to some extent, developed definitions of leadership style which encompass the inherent conflict between 'task' and 'people', though the terminology does vary — boss-centred/subordinate-centred; autocratic/democratic; exploitative/participative; task needs/group needs.

Blake and Mouton then make some rationalisations and offer definitions at five points on their grid. They get managers to determine their position on the grid by filling in questionnaires. These points are as follows:

Point 1.1 Management (low in both concern for production and concern for people) Minimum effort is exerted to get the required work done, which is appropriate to sustain organisation membership. This is sometimes referred by critics as the 'abdication style'.

Point 9.1 Management (high in concern for production and low in concern for people) Efficiency in operations results from arranging conditions of work in such a way that human elements interfere to a minimum degree.

Point 5.5 Management (mid-point in both concern for production and concern for people) Adequate organisation performance is possible through balancing the necessity to produce work with maintaining the morale of people at a satisfactory level. This is a style where the manager is resting on his or her laurels, rather than striving for excellence.

Point 1.9 Management (low in concern for production and high in concern for people) Thoughtful attention is given to the needs of people for satisfying relationships, which leads to a comfortable friendly work organisation and work tempo. This is sometimes called by critics as the 'country club style' of leadership.

Point 9.9 Management (high in both concern for production and concern for people) Work is accomplished by committed people; interdependence through a 'common stake' in organisation purpose leads to relationships of trust and respect. The basis of point 9.9 is one of *excellence* and all managers are expected to aspire to this!

Blake and Mouton had a remarkable consultancy record in the late 1960s and early 1970s in which the managerial grid was a key instrument. The philosophy seems to be that many organisations are 'sick' and that the root of the sickness lies in poor organisation structure and inappropriate leadership styles among executives. Once their styles are 'plotted' on the grid map, and a profile by group and department developed, etc., the deviation from the norms of excellence, i.e. 9.9 styles, is shown up. This leads on to diagnostic data, interpretation, sharing, remedial action and programmes of organisation development. The logic is inexorable! The expected outcome is corporate excellence founded on the universal adoption of 9.9 leadership styles. The Blake and Mouton managerial grid is one route to organisation development (see chapter 21 for further discussion).

Bill Reddin

The Canadian researcher Bill Reddin (1968, 1987) goes along with a minor variation of the Blake and Mouton dimensions of leadership. 'Concern for people' becomes 'relationships orientation' and 'concern for production' becomes 'task orientation'. However, Reddin rejects emphatically the notion of a style of 'universal excellence'. He re-establishes the Fiedler (1966) notion of contingency theory, stating that leadership style should vary according to the situation. Reddin's contribution is to develop a third dimension to the grid, a dimension of *effectiveness*. This extension complicates the definitions of leadership style, which now becomes a twelve-set framework. Four styles are basic, then there are four effective versions and four ineffective versions. This is shown in Figure 20.1 and the leadership styles are explained more fully below.

Basic styles

Separated   A low score on both x and y axes. The manager attempts to get distance from the problem and activity, wanting to avoid involvement with the task and/or the people.

Related   A high score on the y axis and low on x axis, indicating a full involvement and relationship with the people elements in the situation.

Integrated   A high score on both axes, indicating a fully integrated approach.

Dedicated   A high score on the x axis, indicating dedication to the task or technology and little concern for people.

Effective styles

Bureaucrat   The manager deliberately sets up policy manuals or procedures to cope with the situation and it is legitimate for him or her to become uninvolved. The effective version of separated style.

Developer   The manager makes an impact in his or her relationships (a personnel manager, for instance) and succeeds in developing people. The effective version of related style.

Executive   The manager strikes a good balance between the people and task influences and makes sound decisions. The effective version of the integrated style.

Benevolent autocrat   The manager gives appropriate emphasis to task and technology without alienating people. The effective version of the dedicated style.

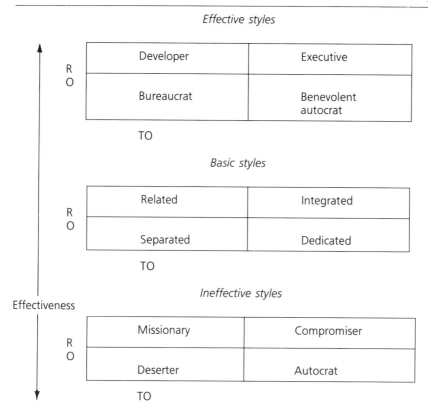

Effective styles

| Developer | Executive |
| Bureaucrat | Benevolent autocrat |

Basic styles

| Related | Integrated |
| Separated | Dedicated |

Ineffective styles

| Missionary | Compromiser |
| Deserter | Autocrat |

RO = Relationships orientation
TO = Task orientation

Leadership style explanations

Basic styles

The model shows the two dimensions of 'Task orientation' on the x-axis, and 'Relationships orientation' on the y-axis.

Figure 20.1 *Reddin's leadership style definitions*
(Reproduced with permission)

Ineffective styles

Deserter   The manager runs away/abdicates from the situation and it deteriorates. The ineffective version of the separated style.

Missionary   The manager relates to people, but somehow does not cut ice, and the situation deteriorates. The ineffective version of the related style.

Compromiser   The manager fails to reconcile task and people pressures and the situation deteriorates. The ineffective version of the integrated style.

Autocrat   The manager fails to achieve goals and tasks and disrupts the people relationships and expectations. The ineffective version of the dedicated style.

Style Diagnosis

Reddin also adopts a questionnaire to determine leadership style and, like Blake and Mouton, can generate leadership profiles in divisions and departments in organisations. The interpretation and action phases which follow are based on developing managers towards any one of the four effective styles, rather than a single style of *excellence*.

Reddin then goes on to suggest that fundamental leadership skills are *situation sensitivity* and *style flexibility*. The manager's job has much variation and the manager should adapt and adjust once a new situation has been correctly appraised. Reddin uses further management techniques to underpin the leadership style diagnostic data, by adopting Drucker's framework of managing by objectives. The effectiveness part of Reddin's scheme relates to objective-setting, and the coaching and management development aspects use the MbO staff appraisal process as the platform which ensures that leadership styles are naturally on the agenda of management.

Reddin promotes the skill of *situation sensitivity* by getting managers to assess carefully what decisions are to be made in a given time-scale, taking account of the following people influences: superiors, subordinates, clients, co-workers, representatives and the philosophy of the organisation.

When the time-scale is very short, as would be usual at the operational level, there would not be time to consult, nor would subordinates expect this. On the other hand, decisions on budgets, with more time for taking account of inputs and bids, would normally be the subject for consultation, and indeed if this were not done there might be lots of bad feelings.

Reddin promotes the skill of *style flexibility* by actively advocating career development through job rotation as an addition to thorough and analytical staff appraisal processes.

The major outcome of Reddin's work is a more credible, contingency-oriented theory of leadership styles and an opportunity for this diagnosis to be readily used. He enhances the development of the technique of MbO, which many organisations had welcomed, but then found difficult to implement.

As can be seen from the analysis of this chapter, there is a very large number of variables in leadership situations, many of which are difficult to isolate for the purpose of rigorous research. The models that eventually emerge tend to be rather crude rationalisations and leave open questions of validity and consistency. In the Reddin model there is a reasonably high level of satisfaction recorded for the measures of both relationships orientation and task orientation, but on the effectiveness dimension the satisfaction is decidedly less! Naturally, managers are somewhat upset when they find themselves with unfavourable leadership labels such as 'deserter'. The questionnaire which does the style diagnosis and the way it is administered is open to error. Anyone filling in the questionnaire must, in a disciplined way, concentrate the mind on one particular job and be consistent in replying. That might sound easy, but for senior managers the job has a wide range of projects, assignments and responsibilities, and it is unrealistic to expect to be able to identify just the core of the job and mask out all the interesting variables. Yet without some masking out of the unusual bits, there will simply be 'noise' in the questionnaire results and a retest will reveal a different leadership profile, when perhaps other more recent job incidents influence the answers.

Perhaps people were expecting too much from the Reddin leadership-style diagnostic tests, even wanting to use them in isolation as a device for selecting effective leaders without the expense of the three-day WOSBI-style selection process. But it was not to be. A cool evaluation of the Reddin instrumentation of leadership-style tests showed that they could be very efficient at breaking the ice in difficult relationship problems between managers and subordinates, but interpretation of the data and their validity did require much care and an active face-to-face session with the people involved before any sound conclusions could be made. The tests are simply a tool and a technique, not a panacea, for finding and promoting leadership.

Developments of contingency theory

In the 1970s and 1980s other researchers attempted to extend current leadership theory. Mintzberg (1973) rationalised the behaviour of chief executives, defining ten roles (see p. 11). The interest of Mintzberg's approach is that group behaviour is indeed very dependent on the role adopted and that even leadership roles come in a variety of different guises, each with a slightly different level of expectation of participation and each with different natural decision-making time-scales. Disturbance-handling is essentially short-term, whereas resource allocation is essentially long-term. In one day an executive might do disturbance-handling as a 'benevolent autocrat', then attend a budget meeting in the early planning phases and adopt a 'developer' style, then attend another product launch meeting and adopt an 'executive' style to finalise the launch, and in the evening preside over the annual social gathering, once more as the 'benevolent autocrat'.

Reddin emphasises *situation sensitivity*, Mintzberg emphasises role clarification and identification, and the two concepts used together can be very useful in weighing up leadership situations.

United Kingdom research

R.M. Belbin

Belbin's research focused on the leadership of project teams. He suggested that much executive work in the exciting areas of product innovation and the introduction of new technology was done within the environment of a multidisciplinary project team; the secret of success was to have a balanced team competent to get through all stages of the project. Belbin identified eight distinct but useful roles for people to adopt in successful project teams — company worker, chairman, shaper, plant, resource investigator, monitor/evaluator, teamworker, completer/finisher.

There are many similarities between the Belbin team roles and the Mintzberg process roles. Belbin's model, however, constantly reminds the leader of the need to balance the team and make relevant role assignments, recognising in people the skills which could fit the available assignments. Where the team was lacking in skills, outside recruitment of the missing talent, or a management development programme to promote the needed talent from within the team, would be necessary, and the really successful leader would be a naturally good team coach. There is clearly some evidence of the internalisation of the Reddin concepts of *situation sensitivity* and *style flexibility* in this research.

Belbin's research was tested by observing executive teams under training, which involved playing a competitive computer business game offering a profit profile over periods of trading. It does have some validity in the particular circumstances of that type of competitive business game, in so far as profit equates with effectiveness. Unfortunately, real world situations have a much richer variety and complexity, so further work will be needed to develop a fully-fledged leadership model. But Belbin does make considerable progress.

A final refinement of leadership

Frederick Mumma

There seems to be a need now to reconcile the twin ideas of *process* and *role* in a leadership model. Mumma (1984) does just this. The process is: initiation, ideation, elaboration, completion. The roles are: leader, moderator, creator, innovator, manager, organiser, evaluator, finisher.

Mumma's works contain self-administered questionnaires which enable managers to find out where their strong and weak points are for both role and process aspects.

The reader may notice some similarity in the approaches of Mumma and Belbin.

Summary

This chapter has given a brief review of leadership as traditionally perceived. Next, some main twentieth-century authors were examined. The crisis for military leadership of the First and Second World Wars was examined and the topic of leader selection discussed. Much progress was made in the development of the War Office Selection Board Interview (WOSBI) technique used in the Second World War and then adapted for business by Professor Adair.

Next the review was done of the works of Fiedler, a US researcher, who gave credibility to a contingency theory of leadership and made some progress in predicting leadership outcomes and developing situation management techniques. The chapter continued with developments and refinements of this approach through different models. Observations were made on the implementation of these theories and techniques, and some comments made on their limitations.

Exercise 20.1
A group exercise on the Tannenbaum continuum

Objective

The objective is to gain familiarity with leadership style definitions and the dynamism of real-life preferences.

Task

Form a group of managers, and pose the following questions:

1. Refer to the definition of the Tannenbaum continuum (p. 421), and state what in your view is the predominant leadership style of the manager for whom you currently work.
2. Indicate to which style you would prefer to be exposed in your present job as a subordinate of the same manager.
3. Now focus on yourself as manager of your own subordinates. Which leadership style do you feel most comfortable in adopting for your own subordinates in your current position?

Data collection

It may be advisable to get those who are participating in this research to make written responses to all three questions above, then summarise the answers.

Analysis

If there are differences — and they may be expected — attempt to get explanations directly from the participants.

Exercise 20.2
The improvised drama

Objective

The aim is to analyse leadership behaviour in a newly-formed group set up to complete an unstructured task.

Method

This may be considered as an ambitious leadership exercise; the *timings* are vital. Group competition is important. A group of 30 students is ideal who may be broken down into sub-groups of 6–8.

Two roles are picked by lot — the leader role and the group observer role. Each sub-group must give a ten-minute improvised drama before the other sub-groups after no more than three hours' work — preparation, brainstorming, rehearsal and production. The role of the observer will be to keep a diary of events providing a record of data for the final debriefing session (session 4).

First session — two hours
The group must make two decisions. The first is the *context* or *theme* of the drama. The second is about the *problem* or *message* of the drama. Next the group must develop the necessary script and roles. For example, the theme may be an editorial room of a newspaper; the problem may be one of sex discrimination against a female sub-editor.

Second session — one hour
Rehearse the drama, with props, etc., so that the theme will be recognisable to the audience.

Third session
Each drama is performed before the other groups. (This facet generates a pressure to produce. No group wants to feel that it has failed before other groups.)

Fourth session — one hour
The tutor and group observer do a thorough debriefing session with each sub-group. Topics covered may include the following: How did the group form? How were decisions made? What leadership style was in evidence at the beginning of the project, at the decision-making points, and at the production phases? Did leadership style change as urgency put pressure on the team? Did members contribute all the time, some of the time or not at all? Did the leader make good use of the resources of the group? How? Was everyone involved some of the time or all of the time? How did the group maintain its cohesiveness? Did other leaders emerge during the session? Get the group to relate their behaviour to Mumma's model, or one of the other models of this chapter.

For feedback on the exercise see Appendix 1, p. 541. A brief review is given of two occasions where this exercise was done. Generally it is most enjoyable, but there are usually some initial tensions.

Variations

The model of the improvised drama provides many other role-playing opportunities, relating to topics other than leadership. Often, for instance, relationships between a research and development department and a production department may be a cause of concern, so a role-play here may help participants better to understand the reasons for this. Naturally, an exercise like this would be more meaningful in consolidating learning once the group had become familiar with the basic issues.

References

Adair, J. (1973), *Action Centered Leadership*, McGraw-Hill.
Belbin, R.M. (1981), *Management Teams — Why they Succeed or Fail*, Heinemann.
Blake, R.R. and Mouton, J.S. (1969), *Building a Dynamic Corporation through Grid Organisation Development*, Addison-Wesley.
Cattell, R.B. (1951), 'New concepts for measuring leadership in terms of group syntality', *Human Relations*, vol. 4, pp. 161–84.
Couch, A.S. and Carter, L. (1952) 'A factional study of the rated behavior of group members'. Paper presented at meeting of the Eastern Psychological Association, Atlantic City, NJ, April.
Churchill, W.S. (1955), *The Second World War*, Chartwell.
Drucker, P. (1954), *The Practice of Management*, Harper.
Drucker, P. (1971), *The Effective Executive*, Pan.
Fiedler, F.E. (1966), 'The effect of leadership and cultural heterogeneity on group performance: a test of the contingency model', *Journal of Experimental Social Psychology*, vol. 2, pp. 237–64. (Referred in the text as 'The Belgian Navy Study'.)
Fiedler, F.E. and Chemers, M.M. (1974), *Leadership and Effective Management*, Scott, Foresman.
Homans, G.C. (1950), *The Human Group*, Harcourt Brace Jovanovich.
Likert, R. (1967), *The Human Organisation*, McGraw-Hill.
Mintzberg, H. (1973), *The Nature of Managerial Work*, Harper & Row.
Mumma, F.S. (1984), *What Makes Your Team Tick?*, Organization and Design Inc.
Reddin, W.J. (1968), *Effective Management*, McGraw-Hill.
Reddin, W. J. (1987), *How to Make your Management Style More Effective*, McGraw-Hill.
Stogdill, R. M. (1948), 'Personal factors associated with leadership: a survey of the literature', *Journal of Psychology*, vol. 25, pp. 35–71.
Tannenbaum, R. and Schmidt, W.H. (1958), 'How to choose a leadership pattern', *Harvard Business Review*, March/April, pp. 95–101.
Tuckman, B.W. (1985), 'Developmental sequence in small groups', *Psychological Bulletin*, vol. 63, pp. 384–99.

Chapter 21

Managing change

Overview

A topic of major interest to the manager and the consultant is the management of change. In the literature this topic is generally referred to as organisation development (OD). In this chapter the aim is to offer the reader a set of approaches to this difficult topic, building on research findings from the behavioural sciences. A generalised model is developed of this process and the techniques needed to organise and apply it. Some criticism is offered of current practice as reported in the literature. This provides a focus for further exploration. The reader is also exposed to a practical example of interventions to secure change in order to develop a familiarity with both theory and practice.

Theoretical framework

Any competent management consultant will wish to ensure that his or her ideas and recommendations are turned into action. The implication is that he or she will have to influence individuals and groups to manage the process of organisational change in order to get the full harvest of the work. A review of the relevant areas of academic thought leads the researcher to look at the area known in the literature as 'organisation development'.

Although there is some debate about the origin of the term 'organisation development' (OD), it seems clear that the discipline has its roots in the behavioural sciences. French and Bell (1978) state that the two basic origins of OD are laboratory training and survey feedback. The laboratory training aspect has its origin in 1949 in workshops held at the State Teachers College in New Britain, Connecticut, assisted by people such as Kurt Lewin, Kenneth Benne, Leland Bradford and Ronald Lippitt (see Thakur, 1974). From these workshops emerged an organisation called The National Training Laboratory for Group Development and T-Group Training. It was found that within the laboratory it was possible to induce substantial behavioural changes in individuals and small groups. Getting to know oneself and how others perceived one could have a profound impact on behaviour. However, the transfer of such learning to a participant's home organisation raised considerable problems (Schein 1965). Meanwhile McGregor (1960) was looking at this problem in his own organisation, Union Carbide, and was later joined by Herbert Shepard and Robert Blake (see Thakur, 1974).

In 1957 assignments in Union Carbide and Esso, Blake changed the focus of OD to emphasise group activity. He concentrated on teaching people the elements of effective group dynamics, and on methods of securing collaboration with both external staff departments and also consultants. About that time the term 'organisation development' was first used in publications. Later, Blake joined forces with Mouton and they developed the managerial grid (1969). Their intention was to devise a framework of ideal behaviour and then invite groups to measure their actual behaviour against the ideal model. This experience would provide the basis for leadership training based on the group (see chapter 20).

The second root of OD — survey feedback — was developed in 1946, when Rensis Likert founded the Survey Research Center in the University of Michigan. His basic data came from groups who completed attitudinal questionnaires. Results were fed back to the groups who were positively encouraged to develop and interpret the data. He found that positive behavioural change took place after managers and groups *shared* data results. Earlier in the Hawthorn Studies, Mayo (1933) had found that there was a highly therapeutic outcome when employees suffering from workplace frustration had a chance to speak freely to a consulting agent trained in the skills of empathetic listening. The body of knowledge developed from survey feedback methods was further enhanced by Lawrence and Lorsch (1968) who gave more structure to the particular surveys. The method they used, called systems analysis, directed their survey questionnaires at specific organisational interfaces. A key outcome of this *sharing* of survey data was to *unfreeze* client groups, in readiness for an active and supported change process.

They also postulated that organisations must establish an essential fit with their environment. Different parts of the organisation have different relationships with the external environment and different needs. Consequently, integrating mechanisms have to be developed at all hierarchical levels. Lawrence and Lorsch had no notion of an ideal managerial style but instead examined managerial interrelationships at organisational boundaries and interfaces. Their approach is particularly suitable to the fast-developing organisation in which relationships are highly complex and dynamic.

The leadership and behavioural elements from laboratory training combined with the relationship analysis from survey feedback form the basic methodology of current organisation development.

Definitions of organisation development

Bennis (1969), an eminent authority in this field, defined OD as:

a process of planned organisational change which centres around a change agent, who in collaboration with the client's system, attempts to apply valid knowledge from the behavioural sciences to the client's problem.

Lawrence and Lorsch (1968) offered the following more detailed definition:

Ways to change the organisation from its current state to a better developed state ... involving systems analysis and the development of interfaces between organisation−environment, group−group, individual−organisation, and person−person ... outside consultants can provide new approaches and tools from time to time, but in the final analysis the capacity for OD must reside inside the organisation.

Beckhard (1969) emphasised the need for OD throughout the organisational hierarchy:

OD is a planned change effort involving the total system managed from the top to increase organisational effectiveness through planned interventions, using behavioural science knowledge.

Blake and Mouton (1969) identified five essential aspects of OD:

A systematic way of inducing change:
(a) Based on a structural model for thinking. (The idea versus the actual.)
(b) Progressing in a programmatic sequence of steps from individual learning to organisational application.
(c) Focused upon those silent and often negative attributes of culture which dictate actions that so frequently contradict business logic.
(d) With emphasis on confronting and resolving conflict as a prerequisite to valid problem-solving.
(e) And employing a variety of techniques of organisational study and self learning to bring about needed change.

Vaill (1971) defined OD as:

An evolving collection of philosophies, concepts and techniques which aim at the improvement of organisation performance by changing the social systems men use to collaborate with one another. Change may be directed at individuals, dyads, groups, inter-groups, formal structure or cultures.

Thakur (1974), sponsored by the Institute of Personnel Management, surveyed sixteen companies to find out if there was any consensus as to the meaning of the term 'organisation development'. There was none. This was hardly surprising in view of the wide variety of definitions in the literature.

Several criticisms of accepted definitions may be made. First of all, problems arise when the definition insists on 'involving the total system from the top'. General support and approval of an OD programme is highly desirable, but the transfer of organisational know-how cannot be programmed from the top precisely because the knowledge base of such know-how may rest with particular specialist groups and is resisted by other client groups within the organisation many levels below. Resistance to change adopted by such client groups may often be articulated through the informal structure, with informal methods. For many decades now the existence of the informal structure has been recognised by management theorists, and this informal system and informal organisation operates outside the formal control of top management.

Secondly, criticisms were made of those who emphasise the organisation-wide nature of an organisation development programme. This contradicts the notion of management by exception. An OD programme must have a focus, and it must gather a record of success in particular consultations in order to achieve an organisational credibility. Organisation-wide programmes can be very clumsy and costly in their operation. The organisation-wide focus of OD supported by behavioural scientists, such as Blake and Mouton (1969) and Reddin (1968), manifest themselves in whole packaged programmes.

Research results based on Reddin's 3D programme were reported by Hill (1973). The industrial company John Player expended fifteen man/years in seminars to make its managers more effective.

> In March last year Player directors, meeting as a board, assessed progress under seven headings after the programme had been running for twenty months. Their conclusions were:
> Improved objective setting: little progress.
> Increased commitment to manager's objectives: little progress.
> Increased commitment to team objectives: some progress.
> Increased acceptance of a readiness to change: much progress.
> Increased identification of the need for more appropriate change: much progress.
> Increased implementation of changes needed: some progress.
> Improved inter-functional co-operation: much progress.
> Increased use of participation in decision-making when this improves the decisions or obtains necessary commitment: some progress.
> Increased job satisfaction: little progress.
> Increased candour: much progress.
> Increased trust: little progress.

The evidence would suggest that organisation-wide OD programmes need a very special focus before the harvest can be gathered from a substantial outlay of resources.

A rationalisation of the literature and of good practice leads to the following definition of OD. Organisation development consists of an evolving collection of techniques and concepts which are directed to the critical analysis of the dynamic problems of organisational mis-performance. Such diagnosis leads to consultancy intervention directed at the planned change of organisational culture. This includes the development of more acceptable constitutional processes for the achievement of a better fit between the demands of a hostile environment, the needs and aspirations of groups within the organisation and the norms of effective organisational performance. Such interventions are primarily directed at the unfreezing of groups that are in conflict with one another and providing data from which they themselves may re-establish better empathy and self-help. The interventions rely heavily on the application of behavioural science knowledge. The interventions are directed to confront the real issues between such groups to achieve a problem-solving climate and avoid escapism. Interventions are often aimed at achieving organisational self-learning and are frequently required to facilitate the portability of technological know-how from one part of the organisation to another.

The term 'constitutional processes' is used deliberately with a wide meaning. Constitutional processes focus on power and organisational structure, and the patterns of etiquette required to establish meaningful and trustful relationships.

Many industrial disputes are particularly intractable because the parties have not established the channels and processes necessary to achieve a meaningful dialogue. Conflict within organisations can manifest itself in a wide variety of guises. Commonly, conflict arises between departments. For example, if the marketing programme is not properly synchronised with the production programme there is often a failure to develop efficient interacting mechanisms in the production control department and also with the corporate planning group to avoid friction between the two line groups. Conflict may also exist between line and staff. A data processing department, for example, cannot easily collaborate with a user department when the user department fears a takeover by DP, or a very reduced influence in the power structure after the introduction of computerised systems.

In the field of data processing there are particular difficulties of fluent communication between designers and users of management information systems, as problems and ideas and their consequences need to be shared by those who are sensitive to the sophistication of modern data processing facilities. One solution to this dilemma is to establish multidisciplinary teams and procedures for working following the principles of 'integrated bilingualism'; and splitting the role for systems design into that played by the business analyst from the line department and computer systems analyst from the computing department. This idea was developed and illustrated in chapter 16.

There is a need to emphasise the notion of 'fit' in OD programmes. This comes from Morse and Lorsch (1973). They postulated that organisational effectiveness depended on establishing a better fit between three variables. These they identified as organisation structure, task structure and competence motivation. It would appear that the factors of fit will vary widely in different organisational settings. Notions of fit in public sector environments will vary widely from those in the private sector. But even within these broadly different environments many similarities may persist. A key role of the organisation development interventionist is to foster self-help among his clients. One of his tasks is, therefore, to get them to discuss the particular factors of fit which are relevant in their environment.

A complication of this is that there is both an internal environment and an external one. Market researchers, financiers, buyers, etc., should know a lot about the external environment; everyone should be expected to know how they fit in the internal environment. The corporate planners each time they go through a planning cycle should be attempting to analyse critically PEST factors and SWOT factors (see chapter 3), so there should be plenty of relevant data around for interpretation.

Purposes of organisation development

If there is some confusion in the definition of OD then there is little wonder that the literature identifies many different purposes of OD programmes. An analysis of the literature suggests that there are fourteen basic purposes. The first three identified by Thakur (1974) are as follows:

• Change employee attitudes.
• Deal with technological change/transfer.
• React to market changes.

The fourth purpose is to facilitate the introduction of other management programmes, i.e. managing by objectives, long-range corporate planning, management information systems, job enrichment, management development programmes and leadership grid programmes. It would seem that OD programmes are particularly useful in the facilitation of these other programmes.

The fifth purpose, defined by Blake and Mouton (1969), is to turn striving into action.

The sixth purpose is to develop models of corporate excellence from which gap analysis and realistic goal setting may proceed. Blake and Mouton (1969) expand their ideas in a framework called the 'Rubric of corporate excellence'. This has no less than seventy-two windows through which the consultant or observer may view critically the company. A comment which may be in order here is that it is laudable to reach for excellence with Blake and Mouton, but there are quite a lot of different pictures of excellence in the management literature and a practitioner needs one which is both credible and simple.

The seventh purpose is to facilitate a management reorganisation. This is allied to the eighth purpose which is to assist a new department in being accepted and integrated into its parent organisation. Burns and Stalker (1961) consider this problem in their studies of the light engineering industry in the late 1950s. The particular issue they looked at was the integration of a research and development department with manufacturing units. They were to report that organisations tended to have both cultures and sub-cultures within them. A production group, for instance, could be typically a large unit run on classical management lines to produce efficiently, with a *mechanistic* management style. In contrast the research and development unit had the ideas men, the boffins, who established close-knit, *organic* project groupings, with much less structure and with more democratic leadership styles. The difficulty perceived by Burns and Stalker was to find collaborative mechanisms so that when these two sub-cultures met one another they worked together rather than resisted one another. In the context of the fast-moving electronics industry, if they found this collaborative approach, the companies tended to stay and prosper in the market; and if they could not integrate these different sub-cultures, then the company was likely to go out of business. A favoured collaborative mechanism was to assign a few key people from the research and development group to follow the projects into pilot run and production and only to leave the scene to the *mechanistic* management people after it had fully settled down as a new viable product.

Twiss (1983) extends this idea further with the introduction of the notion of a 'project champion' to manage the change process. His research suggests that the key lies with giving the research and development group a continuing and predominant influence in the organisation structure and a voice in the implementation of corporate strategies. To reinforce this credibility, the project champion needs to establish effective project and review procedures.

Pettigrew (1973) follows a similar theme of organisation conflict in his research. He studied in depth the purchase decision for a new computer configuration. His analysis is directed at the relationships between two occupational groups — a programming group and a systems analysis group. His study highlights the very complex problems of integrating the efforts of these two competing groups with the needs of the parent organisation and retaining managerial authority and power over the specialist programming group after they had successfully held the rest of the organisation to ransom (see Case Study 16.2).

The ninth purpose relates to trouble-shooting within the complex environment of organisational conflict.

In the tenth, OD is concerned to overcome the filtration process of management reporting and to ensure that top management are more aware of reality throughout the organisation structure. Gardner (1968) supports this notion. Behavioural scientists are aware of the existence of both the formal and informal information systems in organisations. A common observation of the impact of informal organisations is that senior management are told only what they expect to hear, i.e. about actions within prescribed policies and plans. The informal organisation often conspires to suppress bad news.

The eleventh purpose of an OD programme is to foster the entrepreneurial spirit in organisations which would otherwise be complacent, institutionalising their behaviour patterns. This is Bennis's target (1969). Large organisations have a tendency to bureaucracy and rigidity. Yet large organisations have just as great a need to keep on their toes and continuously develop a relevant and effective product/market strategy.

The twelfth purpose of OD is designed to ensure a better fit between the organisation's personnel policies and the social expectations of employees within their local culture. This is another target of Bennis. He argues that in the twentieth century, with better education and more affluence, people bring to work expectations far beyond the need to earn a living. Nineteenth-century paternalistic or authoritarian management practice may tend to alienate employees. OD programmes, with an orientation towards the building of trust and the democratisation of the decision-making process, are intended to counteract this tendency to alienation.

The thirteenth purpose is to facilitate the work of multidisciplinary task groups. Warmington *et al.* (1977), who developed socio-technical analysis, are the leading theorists for this OD purpose. Increasingly, large organisations are responding to the complexity of their environment through the development of project-oriented or matrix-type organisations. Difficulty is often encountered in getting technically-oriented specialists to integrate their activities within economic or social constraints.

Finally, the fourteenth purpose of OD is to focus attention on the processes of organisation behaviour to avoid overemphasis on task achievement.

The fourteen purposes of OD programmes represent the aspirations of OD practitioners and theorists. OD still has many weaknesses and little guarantee may be offered that a particular OD programme will accomplish its stated purpose. The major problem seems to be to change the culture of an organisation. The OD values of the interventionists may conflict with the established cultural values and, in any power struggle, neither external consultant nor a staff group is likely to win. The classical bureaucratic organisational culture is particularly dominant in UK industrial organisations. This is often reinforced by payment schemes and by promotion and selection practice. These can only be changed gradually. Although OD programmes may shorten this process there appears to be a severe limit to the pace at which organisations can absorb change peacefully. Furthermore, change is much harder to introduce in times of recession or stagnation than in times of growth. In times of recession, when change does come, it tends to be very drastic, involving closure of unprofitable divisions, new owners, new managing directors, etc. This is known as a 'turnaround management' (see Slatter, 1984; and chapter 17).

Other constraints to change

In the UK economy, and particularly in Scotland, mobility of labour is constrained by the lack of housing in a new district, so change becomes threatening. OD programmes require the nurturing of an environment in which change is acceptable, followed by the change itself. This first phase may never be achieved in the face of entrenched attitudes based primarily on the fear of job loss.

Definitions of the stages of an OD project

Further definition of the stages of an OD project has been the subject of recent research. Burke *et al*. (1984) offer a seven-stage model. Blake's interest was in distinguishing between successful and unsuccessful OD projects and he reported that 245 completed questionnaires were received in his study using this model, inferring that the sample of OD practitioners could readily relate to his definition of stages. He concludes his article as follows:

1. Entry
Three conditions for success are critical at this stage: the readiness of the client system for change, the power of the primary person with whom the practitioner will work to implement change, and the client's willingness to assume responsibility for the effort and its outcome.

2. Contracting
Clarity is critical; it is better to err on the side of too much detail. Assuming agreements on specifics without making them explicit is a clear road to failure.

External consultants routinely pay attention to the details of contracting; internal practitioners should do the same.

3. Diagnosis

Using either a 'homegrown' model or one from the literature is important. One factor in an OD project's success is the degree of access the client has to the organisational resources, i.e. people and information. Accessibility should be tested and considered during the contracting phase.

4. Feedback

The consultant's confidence in the diagnosis is a critical success factor, as is the client's affirmation that the data and diagnosis are valid. Effective intervention must be based on valid information.

5. Planning change

It is critical to conduct such planning, but the first plan is not likely to be the one implemented, at least for successful OD efforts. It pays to test plans and to remain flexible regarding which plan to adopt.

6. Intervention

Successful OD projects use multiple interventions. But beware of introducing structural changes; they are fraught with risk, and the risk probably increases when a structural intervention is used alone. Without other interventions to support it, e.g. some change in the reward system or in management style, the effort is likely to fail.

7. Evaluation

Except for the fact that OD practitioners reporting successful projects were more likely to conduct evaluations and were more satisfied with their evaluation phases than were those reporting unsuccessful projects, no significant differences were found for this phase. One interesting finding was the reported purpose of evaluation for most OD practitioners: to determine more clearly the change effort's next steps.

Figure 21.1 offers a model of the organisation development resource as adapted in light of interpretations from the management literature.

The top box is a reference to excellence in organisation; if all the fourteen purposes of OD discussed above have been achieved, then the result must be some form of excellence.

The next box, 'key components of organisation', attempts to isolate five main factors and four further sub-factors for attention. Five are rather easier to handle than the seventy-two rubrics of corporate excellence suggested by Blake and Mouton (1969).

Next, the box 'organisation development processes and techniques' shows the roots of this topic from the literature; the traditional approach is on the left. Further developments from this text are outlined under 'other roots'.

The box labelled 'process' is an adaptation and extension of the processes from Burke *et al.* (1984). This adds the key word *unfreeze* as a stage between entry and contracting.

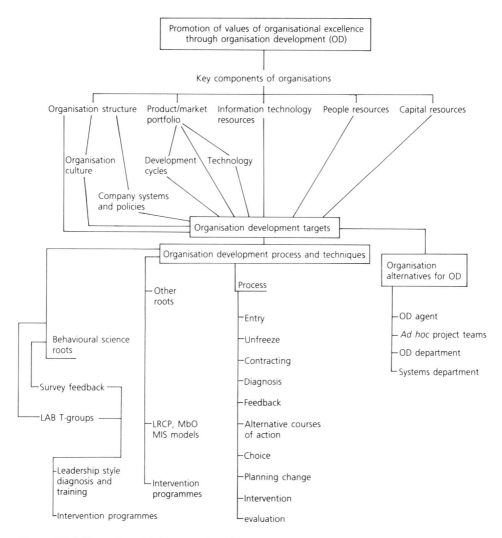

Figure 21.1 *General model for managing change*

It seems that the 1970s and 1980s were significant for the formulation of a rich variety of techniques to secure this unfreezing action, without which a programme of change would probably be stillborn. The processes of change also have a root in the common process of decision-making, where there is a consideration of 'alternative courses of action'. In an OD programme these will probably be *shared* between change agents and clients to improve the level of understanding and commitment.

A final box on the generalised model relates to alternatives for organising the OD project.

The OD agent

Researchers such as Blake and Mouton (1969) and Reddin (1968) seemed to assume that OD was the province of the external consultant, who could bring into the organisation that essential objective external view. Such a consultant was called the OD agent, and tended to be a specialist in the behavioural sciences.

The ad hoc project team

Later, with the merger fever of the 1980s we find many instances of predator companies moving in on their acquisitions, getting the victim to accept the 'excellence' of the predator. The technique here tends to be the setting up of *ad hoc* project teams in a limited number of key areas, where there is joint representation of the two groups, although real power is wielded by the new owner. Typically, the *ad hoc* project teams work to a demanding programme of analysis and reporting back, top management oversee this action, and the outcome is a new corporate plan for the victim and authorisation of the necessary projects to secure implementation. This was the basic strategy adopted by Australia National Bank when they absorbed Clydesdale, the Scottish subsidiary of Midland Bank, in 1988.

In the *ad hoc* project group, members are picked on the basis of relevant expertise. The behavioural scientist might be there to advise on the process of change, but line and staff managers, who are experienced in the theory and practice of corporate planning, are likely to be more prominent in the groups.

The OD department

This was the option adopted by the UK company researched by Warmington *et al.* (1977). The company was so impressed with the potential beneficial change effects from working with behavioural scientists that they set up their own in-house OD department and made it report to the Head of Personnel. They established links with academics from the Manchester Business School, who were experienced in the theory and practice of OD.

Erskine (1985) followed in Warmington's path and found that the OD programme had some problems. The perceptions of this OD programme by the academic members of the Manchester Business School were at variance with the perceptions of the senior company member of the team. The key sequences of this analysis are included in this chapter to give the reader a better idea of what can happen when there is a clash of cultures and the Personnel Director assumes a powerful position as company catalyst.

The systems department

This option arises as commonly a data processing department has to develop company information systems, which require analysis and evaluation, and are likely to involve the implementation of change. People from the systems department may become comfortable in working with multidisciplinary project teams and, as they develop the skills of managing change, they become the natural change agents for spearheading company change outside the specialised environment of information technology.

Research sequence at West Midlands manufacturer

This material is based on research done by Erskine (1985), when he followed in the path of Warmington *et al.* (1977) to appreciate the operation of an OD programme in a large manufacturer in the West Midlands. Interviews were conducted with Professor Tom Lupton and Dr Alan Warmington, both of the Manchester Business School, who were the OD consultants for this company. Interviews were also held with Mr Wieldon, a senior manager in the company, who was a founder member of the company OD team. He had previously held the position of corporate planner for one of the divisions and prior to that had been responsible for the production planning and control functions. Wieldon could explain the company's reasons for setting up the original group of company members and academics, the attitudes of senior management and the benefits and limitations of OD in a company from his perspective.

Warmington's analysis

A main interest in the Warmington book lies in the analysis of three case studies described in depth which illustrate the organisation development team in action in the environment of the West Midlands manufacturer. Three cases were chosen to illustrate the open systems approach to planned change and these were based on the approach of socio-technical analysis. The main thrust of this technique is to activate the change process from the bottom up in an organisation through a deeper understanding of the many variables at the workface which require an informed and integrated approach for their management.

The theoretical framework of the authors is logically and interestingly presented. Each case in the book begins with a phase of diagnosis followed by a phase called 'strategy for planned change'. After developing a high expectation for results and success in the reader, the authors describe what actually happened, and here one gets a feeling of disappointment. Every one of the three cases fails to achieve implementation. Top management either withholds resources at the vital point of implementation or deliberately announces a revised policy wrecking the projects. An explanation for this perceived failure of OD needs to be found. This sequence relates to both aspects. Firstly, let us examine the explanation in the published book (Warmington *et al.*, 1977).

The first OD case of the company programmes described was called 'The finishing shop'. The problem diagnosis highlighted many variables which would need adjustment to ameliorate the situation. The incentive bonus schemes operating had become very complex and had distorted the even flow of work through the shop. A change strategy had been outlined and the shop-floor members invited to be involved in the development of the changes. The timing of the invitation to participate had seemed right and the involvement gave rise to some positive thinking which was adopted by the OD team. However, the planned change solution required some capital expenditure, and when this approval was delayed line management imposed a 'short-cut', which was unplanned and which caused many problems with the production scheduling manager. He opposed the change because of his lack of previous involvement in the project. The change proposals were finally put forward for the shop men in the expectation of starting pay negotiations for implementation, then management clumsily put a freeze on recruitment of labour. This caused a long-drawn-out bargaining exercise and the overall improvements were then minor and much below the expectations of the OD group.

This case indicates the pitfalls an organisation can encounter in not getting sufficient support in depth from middle management groups in the early stages to generate the momentum to overcome an operational hiccup in a programme of planned change. Yet it is difficult to anticipate such varied aspects of the work environment and the ways in which other managers might subsequently be affected. If one casts the net of involvement very widely in the early stages then the group is likely to become too large for creative work and those invited will be reluctant to give of their scarce time until the project has more form and substance. Twiss (1983) hypothesised that successful change programmes tend to be identified with a 'project champion' and a key facet of the role is the generating of organisational support throughout the ranks of management. In the process he or she will often use the informal network of contacts.

The second and biggest case described in the book was called 'The lower foundry'. This illustrated the approach of socio-technical analysis: 'The lower foundry was a rather complex system with a dominant and difficult technology, also working in difficult market situations, and in which it was difficult to achieve a good fit between technological requirements, market requirements, social requirements and the control systems within which the men had to work.'

This was part of a factory making a product for a declining market. Profit margins were tight; there were great fluctuations in the rate of activity in the plant and the change team putting up a change strategy proposed widening the product range in order to extend the life and stability of the plant. Independently, top management did a marketing appreciation of the plant and decided to close it. No representation was permitted from the OD change team after the close decision was taken. There was thus no visible impact of the OD team in convincing the company that their methodology was worthwhile but the project did give the team good experience in conducting an OD enquiry. Members of the OD team were particularly upset as word got round the foundry that the closure decision was taken as a direct result of the work of the OD team, and this gave them a reputation which inhibited them when operating on other sites. As an outside observer it is difficult to decide whether this outcome was simply bad luck and a response to an unanticipated change in the market situation, or whether alternatively the investigation never had even a sporting chance without a little more enlightened political lobbying. However, it seems surprising that management should not attempt to coordinate what were in effect two separate investigations at the one site and permit normal communication between the two investigating groups.

The third case study analysed in the book is called 'The pressroom'. In this case study a works manager has already authorised a project in the area of the pressroom. It has been set up with his terms of reference, his control scheme and his deadline. He welcomed the assistance of members of the OD team when they offered themselves. They clearly strengthened the project effort and some success was reported. In the reports of the project little acknowledgement was given for the socio-technical analysis methods that had been applied; the reports mentioned only the orthodox engineering methods contributing to the project's success. There was some kudos which rubbed off on the OD team, but existing behaviour patterns had already been reinforced and the OD team were to admit that there had been no outcome of organisational learning. The difficulty arising is one of how a consultancy group can get credit for change when the line department are responsible for implementation and are reluctant to forgo recognition themselves; yet if no credit is claimed by the OD group its overall existence and funding is at risk.

Dialogue with Warmington and others

In this section of the research, direct interviews were arranged with Dr Alan Warmington and Professor Lupton of the Manchester Business School. These two eminent academics had played consultant roles in the organisation development programmes at the West Midlands manufacturer. Professor Lupton had initiated the programme, but day-to-day direct involvement on the company team was the role of Dr Warmington, who occupied the post of Senior Research Fellow at the Manchester Business School.

Professor Lupton offered information on the initiation and development of the OD programme. Originally, the company had approached him with a request for consultancy advice for simplifying the tangle of incentive bonus schemes, which had grown up over thirty years during a period of much technological development and growth. His initial brief was to advise on methods of improving productivity at the plant in the wake of tidying up these complicated incentive bonus schemes. He proposed to found a joint team with Warmington, an expert in the skills of social science, using the technique of socio-technical analysis. He felt that a multidisciplinary team was essential to unravel the many and varied influences brought to bear in understanding shop-floor and management behaviour and the many hidden barriers to adequate productivity. From this initial base the team developed a full OD role capable of tackling a wide range of difficult organisational and technical projects. There were many successes and failures in these assignments, but enough credibility was generated to legitimise the activity and presence of an OD team in the company and for it to survive major company cuts in the recession of the mid-1970s. The academic partners remained members of this OD programme over a period of some seven years.

Professor Lupton outlined his perception of the overall aims of the West Midlands manufacturing company's organisation development programme as follows:

1. The induction of real and lasting change within the organisation giving organisational improvement and building on effective learning within the organisation.
2. Induction on a company-wide basis of genuine multidisciplinary thinking both at the diagnostic phases of problem-solving and in the implementation of business solutions.
3. The introduction and ready acceptance of genuine participation in management through bottom-up working, to capture man's creative resources.
4. Develop genuine organisational structures that favour decentralisation into profit centres for the job enrichment of middle management.
5. To provide an alternative to the dominant existing culture within the organisation to stimulate innovation and overcome the overriding impression that management at the top knows best.

The centrepiece of the technique of socio-technical analysis using a multidisciplinary project team was then illustrated in a working study undertaken by Lupton and Warmington. They had been given a brief to offer a critical examination of the company's plans to set up in the Australian subsidiary a new plant which incorporated the latest technology of the industry. The multidisciplinary team looked at this plan through the following seven perspectives:

1. Job enrichment. Was the layout, plant and process conducive to rewarding teamwork from the operatives?
2. Technical expertise. Did the plant and layout incorporate the best of modern experience and expertise required to achieve technical innovation in the product?
3. Payment schemes. Did the plans incorporate realistic proposals for payment schemes?
4. Management structure. Was the organisation structure designed with the technological process in mind?
5. Culture. Was the overall mode of operation compatible with the accepted Australian culture for management and workers?
6. Flexibility. Was the layout and organisation structure compatible with the market pressures for a changing product mix?
7. Innovation. Was the technical and management structure such as to encourage innovation both technically and managerially?

Indeed this study initially stalled through the late involvement of the multidisciplinary team. After they had analysed the above plans they reported to management their significant reservations concerning this plant, but to their annoyance top management merely pigeon-holed the report saying that contracts for the plant construction had already been signed and key management appointments for the venture had been announced. However, Professor Lupton recounted that some two years later UK management expressed their concern that the plant in Australia had fared badly in achievement of operational targets and requested another look at the pigeon-holed reports. A taskforce was subsequently dispatched to Australia and were to find that the multidisciplinary team had been correct in their predictions. The recommendations in the original report were subsequently adopted.

It was clear that both Lupton and the company felt some irritation. Next the mode of operation of this multidisciplinary team and its authority and reporting relationship with senior management were discussed. Lupton related that the reporting relationship was to a board member, the Personnel Director, a member of the owning family, who had a brief to listen sympathetically to all reports coming from the OD group, but to delay implementation until approval had been obtained from the board. At a crucial period in the programme the company experienced a seven-week strike, the first major strike in the company's history, and an event which shook to the core management's confidence in their predominantly paternalistic style. At the end of the strike company members of the OD team were hastily returned to the departments from which they had been loaned in order to help line management recover from the immediate effects of the strike. Meanwhile those projects which had been authorised for implementation were handed over to a new group of senior managers with a brief to implement the changes quickly. Unfortunately the newly appointed group knew nothing about the socio-technical approach adopted by the OD group with the help of the academics and was thoroughly resentful at having to implement proposals with which it had little sympathy. After this set-back the academics then re-established an OD team, but managed to negotiate terms of reference whereby they would have both diagnostic and implementation responsibility for projects subject to the approval of the Personnel Director acting in a line management capacity. Group members, however, had no individually agreed job descriptions and the group had no designated manager. Lupton had insisted on this freedom to establish the norms of multidisciplinary teamwork, the very essence of which was to encourage members to break out of the straitjackets often associated with teams of specialists. Furthermore, the leadership role was in Lupton's view one of flexibility. Different members could be expected to lead at different stages in a project according to the expertise they could offer in managing the issues of difficulty at that stage. This follows the concepts developed by Burns and Stalker (1961). It was at variance with existing culture and practice for all other groups in the company. The OD team as described by Lupton orally and in writing had many set-backs and it may be reasonable to assume that top management had not fully accepted this new organisational device imported by the Personnel Director and might delay or sabotage attempts at change which were perceived as a threat to existing culture.

Discussions with Lupton then turned to another early OD project, 'The lower foundry'. For this case the OD team had been given a wide remit to investigate the causes and circumstances which contributed to a position of declining profit. They had no remit to change anything. At a very early stage in the project the factory manager offered to join the team as a full member and ensure that they had access to all relevant data and people, and he fully supported Lupton's mode of operation. The OD team thought this a generous offer; in effect the whole factory could be the target of their OD methods and for a time this large unit would be perceived as an OD laboratory. Later it seemed to Lupton that the factory manager had an ulterior motive in his enthusiasm. He had felt very oppressed by the straitjacket of his line management position and saw no way of rescuing the situation within such terms of reference. Membership of the OD team, however, was the means by which he could perceive himself wriggling out of the straitjacket!

It may be recalled that this unit was eventually closed down by top management, supposedly ignoring the reports from the OD team. The decision was a complex one. Owing to technological change it was necessary to replace quickly much of the product range, but there was a shortage of marketing talent to specify viable replacement products. Meanwhile top management redefined its strategic markets and products and the role of the lower foundry with a revised product range did not fit within these newly declared priorities. Meanwhile the 'cooperative' factory manager could share the problems of the lower foundry with the OD team and escape individual line responsibility for the closure and the impact which such a decision would have on his career. Lupton was clearly bitter at the way the OD team was 'used' on this project. An interpretation of the communication problem highlighted is that the terms of reference and power relationship of the OD team were not adequate. A personnel director may not have enough standing in discussions of corporate strategy. It may well have been a different story if the OD team had reported to a corporate planning team and had assimilated within it proper representation from the marketing function. It would have been much more likely that there would have been one integrated investigation into the lower foundry, not two.

Discussion then turned to the nature of the working role academic members of the OD team. Warmington related his experiences. He saw himself primarily as a 'process' consultant. He would offer a behavioural science framework to help team members interpret their own behaviour within the team and the complex behavioural relationships between those who were the target of the investigations. Company members, in contrast, tended to see their role in terms of task and concrete result, primarily for the short term, as this represented the culture they knew. Warmington himself remembered agonising over his own role in a situation where the company members wished to take short-term action which in his professional opinion would prejudice the long-term and lasting effects which he expected OD to achieve. He was, however, able to play a team 'coach' role when it came to interpreting results and then writing them up for the benefit of management.

He was, however, critical of top management for not being more empathetic to such reports couched in the terms and concepts of the social sciences. When a factory manager on loan to the OD team found to his surprise that many foremen's attitudes were significantly different from company policy, making senior management look very out of touch, he could easily refer to many such manifestations of the 'informal' organisation apparent in the writings of the social science literature. Warmington also alluded to worry and concern of company members over how their performance was being assessed at times when the OD team specifically did not have the authority to do more than investigate. This situation was so different from the performance guidelines in the established line management structure of the company.

The company perspective

In this part of the research direct discussions were held with Mr Wieldon, who had been a founder company member of the organisation development team. At the time of the interview he had some seven years of continuous experience within the group.

The initial formation of the OD team was on the initiative of the Personnel Director, who had developed links with the Manchester Business School. He wanted to improve productivity within a manufacturing environment which had become the victim of ever more complex bonus payment schemes. The MBS offered expertise in clarification and management of payment schemes, but acknowledged openly that a multidisciplinary team approach was essential for an understanding of the complex interrelationships to be found within social and technical systems. A new approach and new thinking were advocated and the company authorised the formation of the team. Founder members were as follows:

> One works manager,
> One specialist from work study,
> One accountant,
> One engineer,
> One man from production planning and control,
> Two members from the personnel department,
> Two academic members from the Manchester Business School.

The team's initial objective was to develop a method of working together as a multidisciplinary team and to launch a major investigation but with no authority to change anything. The academic members were to introduce the concepts of systems thinking and the technique of socio-technical analysis. The team took some three months to develop a multidisciplinary mode of communication and the company members were amazed at the wealth of informal practices which came to light as a result of observation and surveys. The initial targets of the study were at shop-floor level. The supposition of the academic members was that once a true picture emerged of shop-floor practices it would be a simple matter to induce change by inviting the appropriate involvement at shop-floor level and exerting subtle pressures to remove the obstacles to productivity improvement. This early optimism was misplaced. For implementation of any scheme, management needed to read and understand the team's findings, and the personnel department needed to succeed in pay negotiations. Levels of middle management resented their own lack of involvement and withheld the necessary support to achieve benefit through the pay bargaining. An unexpected seven-week strike was a blessing in disguise as it brought into question existing management style and developed an expectation of change. The OD team was in abeyance for some six months and was then reformed with terms of reference which enabled it to do both diagnostic and implementation work. Approval had, however, to be sought before the implementation could proceed. The target group was no longer only the shop-floor target with the emphasis on bottom-up change; in contrast the targets for change were all perceived 'stakeholders' in the situations requiring productivity improvements. The team now had freedom to engage with all those affected. This wider remit enabled the team to work on other organisational problems, not only those with a predominant payment issue, hence the legitimised title of organisation development group.

The reformed team had an appointed leader with a normal job description and a formal line reporting relationship with the Personnel Director, who held responsibility for implementation decisions, a significant extension of the obligation to offer no more than sympathetic listening. The team then divided into groups of three and became involved on five sites with an emphasis on getting middle management involvement in any projects undertaken. They had now established their multidisciplinary orientation and mode of communication and had a record of completed organisational projects to give them credibility.

Discussion then turned to how the decentralised OD team initiated its assignments on the five sites. Wieldon explained two approaches. Firstly, a team would become aware that a line manager had initiated a development project and would welcome assistance from the OD team if they offered their services. Many projects were expedited in this way and much goodwill was generated. However, line management would often attribute project success to orthodox methods and the expected acknowledgement of socio-technical analysis was not made. The underlying intention of achieving organisational learning was not perceived.

The second method of initiating a site project was for the OD team to follow their perception of organisational concern after making contact with site executives and then propose an OD project to the site manager. Before the project could proceed beyond a preliminary stage it was necessary to get the site manager's backing. Although the methodology of the team and the terms of reference would be then completed by the OD team there was often difficulty in obtaining the necessary commitment of the site manager and small setbacks could leave the project very vulnerable.

Discussions then turned to the type of assignments which had recently been completed. If, for instance, a new division had been created or a major new facility established it was most unlikely that the OD team would be directly involved at the formative planning stage. It was disappointing that relatively parochial, departmental issues seemed to be the commonest ones undertaken. Major decisions of strategy or organisation structure tended not to be referred to the OD team. Only problems with a major personnel management aspect tended to be directed to the OD team. Top management seemed to be very wary of adopting Lupton's aim of changing organisational culture. Indeed, the ruling family adopted a subtle method of getting membership of key policy-making groups to ensure that they were well informed of what was going on in the organisation and could perpetuate their influence. Company members of the OD team wished to go out of their way to emphasise that in their reformed mode of operation they now had a recognised leader, formal job descriptions and in many respects conformed to the predominant company culture. They wanted to shed the group identity as a fifth column and become a supportive group using multidisciplinary techniques to offer higher management more options.

The methodology of deploying teams of three on a site was to be further reformed.

A recession affecting the industry caused management to impose a general 10 per cent cut for all staff groups and in the case of the OD team a 15 per cent cut was imposed. The team was then split into two separate sections. One section was classified as 'agents' who would work on a site as individuals, but would be capable of forming a team as the project developed. The second section, consisting of three people, assumed a staff role, whose aim it was to formalise concepts of organisational improvement and to attempt to put into practice throughout the company any good principles that they had established through the large number of site investigations. This latter section had assumed a strategic training role.

Wieldon reflected on a recent questionnaire to line managers seeking to determine the perceived value of the OD team's work. This questionnaire had reported favourably: 50 per cent of the work accomplished by OD agents was regarded as essential (i.e. it would have otherwise been assigned to another staff group had they not been available); 40 per cent was 'useful' though not essential, but perceived as cost-effective; and only 10 per cent was not appreciated.

The interview then turned on the question of relationships which the OD team had cultivated with other specialist staff groups and how Wieldon would see their role in the organisation developing further. He felt that they had much in common with colleagues in other sections of the management services function, which also reported to the Personnel Director. In particular he thought further links should be developed with those in the Data Processing Department, who were engaged in systems development.

Differences in perspective between company and academic members

As a result of the action research in this sequence it was clear that the aims and roles of company members of the OD team were significantly different from those of the academic members. The role of the academics seemed to be primarily a process one. They reflected back to the others what was happening in their relationships among themselves and with line departments and assisted in the writing up of project results within a social science framework. Their aims were primarily for the long-term improvement of the sites in the company and they had an underlying value system which encouraged further delegation of authority from management and relied significantly on goodwill from the workers at the workface. The academic members were open in their disenchantment at the paternalistic management style of the company and stated that this should be changed in the interests of organisational health. They were averse to working within written job descriptions as they felt this would inhibit creative thought.

Company members, in contrast, accepted the predominant task-oriented company culture and felt the need for short-term benefit and recognition of results. They were positively relieved when the OD team was reformed after the seven-week strike to find themselves working in a more structured environment with an appointed leader, clear terms of reference and a clear reporting relationship with management. They rejected the idea that permanent change could only be induced from very high shop-floor participation. They stated the perceived need for getting in-depth support from all interested stakeholders of the organisation, paying particular attention to needs and constraints imposed by middle management. They were wary of the plug being pulled on OD projects at the implementation stage and advocated an adequate dialogue with top management throughout site investigations to reduce the chances of subsequent abandonment. They were supportive of the view that an OD team should have authority both for the investigation and implementation stages of a project, though they admitted that the composition of the team might need to change at any phase of a project to enable more expertise to be added or to redeploy expertise no longer required. They were irritated that top management did not involve the OD team early enough in major strategic work, though they got satisfaction from the many completed studies done at the site or departmental level of the organisation.

Conclusions

Based on the evidence presented in the interviews and in Warmington *et al.* (1977), both productivity improvement and organisational learning generally required more than fully-developed shop-floor participation from the bottom of the organisation and fluent process consultation. Successful change in company projects in reality seemed to be *most elusive*. The change agents needed to have more than just process skills. They needed in addition a network of contacts in middle management and a sense of timing to introduce the involvement of those with power. They were particularly vulnerable at the point where an implementation decision was needed for a project. A separate implementation group without significant membership from the diagnostic group tended to fail badly. Without a commitment to and full understanding of the techniques of the multidisciplinary project team an implementation group would not possess the know-how to complete the implementation phase.

If, however, the project group was kept together as a team for the implementation phase (revised mode of operation), then the group would still be vulnerable if they were dependent on getting a further allocation of company resources and had not gone out of their way to keep top management informed of their thinking. Top management was not amused to be taken for granted and was capable of pulling the plug on a project at late stages of development. Top management was also capable of authorising two different studies at once into the same site and then putting barriers up to frustrate normal communication between the two groups.

Top management seemed to have a lot to learn about how best to use its OD group. Calling in the OD group is sometimes a mere company ritual and there is no real expectation that they can contribute. Higher management consists of personalites with opposing policies and objectives, and an OD team might provide just the ammunition one protagonist may need. He may need to play for time or divert attention away from his own areas of vulnerability, and the OD team with suitable terms of reference may do just that. For the OD team to succeed, it requires leadership and good judgement to know when the authorised assignment is part of some 'hidden agenda' and when it is a genuine one for organisational improvement with a reasonable chance of eventual success. They need a reporting relationship to the very summit of the corporation to prevent this waste of time and resources. If the OD team report to a functional executive, such as the Personnel Director, then they may be perceived as a fifth column working primarily for the advancement of the Personnel Director, but at the expense of other directors.

The academic members of the OD team did not like formal terms of reference for the team, but without these the team would naturally attract suspicion from members of line management. The evidence suggests that the OD team should have reported to a corporate planning staff group with open terms of reference shared between that staff group and the managers of the sites where the work was accomplished. This would have prevented much of the friction and frustration in evidence in this study and could possibly have allowed the involvement of the multidisciplinary team at the inception of major strategic projects, instead of later when things had gone wrong.

The findings of this study are congruent with other findings of writers on OD. Burke's model (1984) of OD processes and stages offered many useful insights into success in OD projects, and evidence suggests that these insights were not anticipated by Warmington *et al.* (1977). Twiss (1983) required a 'project champion' for success in innovative projects, and McLean *et al.* (1982) required for successful consultation both process skills and expert skills relevant to perceived areas of concern. They also were cynical about models of planned change unless these were underpinned by consultants who were prepared to play an active role in organisational politics.

Summary

The reader was warned that the topic of managing change as developed in the literature on organisation development would be a tough one! There are many pieces to this jigsaw and some risk attached to intervention programmes as we know them from current research. Yet there are some research results on the management of change which do report success. Like most management techniques, management itself has strategic choices in the activation and deployment of OD.

In this chapter a generalised model of organisation development — its origins, processes, targets and choices for *modus operandi* — was presented and emphasis was given to the traditional approach with heavy reliance on the findings of the behavioural sciences. However, when we look deeper into the topic and attempt a synthesis, there are other possible approaches, which are not so reliant on the behavioural sciences. OD is about achieving excellence in an organisation. Yet we cannot really conceive of excellence unless we have a clear perception of the norms of good practice and a means of aggregation, so that significant deviations from this are visible and interventions for change can be better focused.

When we looked at data processing applications in chapter 16 we talked about the principle of managing by exception as a basis of spearheading the design of information systems and we talked about the concept of leverage as a guide to choosing between relevant applications. Ideally, we would spend £1,000 and get back £1 million. Yet when we examined the research of Warmington *et al.* (1977), we found the OD programme had little leverage and not much focus. The perceptions of excellence of the academic members of the team were at variance with the company perceptions of excellence and there was no natural solution to this clash of cultures.

Perhaps company and academic members both lost their way in a search for excellence. Certainly, the team never seemed to get any integration with the power system of the company. With hindsight, the attachment of an OD department to a director of personnel looked ridiculous. The company seemed to operate with a fifth column in its midst, and in the end only relatively non-significant problems and sites were selected as OD targets.

The good news is that the dilemmas and crisis experienced in this chapter do offer a strong challenge to establish the norms of excellence. When we realise this, there is a natural route to interventions which are more likely to succeed in achieving improvements.

References

Beckhard, R. (1969), *Organisational Development: Strategies and Models*, Addison-Wesley.

Bennis, W.G. (1969), *Organisational Development: its nature, origin, prospects*, Addison-Wesley.

Blake, R.R. and Mouton, J.S. (1969), *Building a Dynamic Corporation through Grid Organisation Development*, Addison-Wesley.

Burke, W. *et al.* (1984), 'Improve your OD project's chances for success', *Training and Development Journal*, September, pp. 62–8.

Burns, T. and Stalker G.M. (1961), *The Management of Innovation*, Tavistock.

Erskine, R.K. (1985), 'Effective Management', M.Litt. thesis, Glasgow University, unpublished.

French, W.L. and Bell, C.H. (1978), *Organisation Development. Behavioural science interventions for organisation improvement*, Prentice Hall.

Gardner, J. (1968), 'We the People', Millikon Award Address, California Institute of Technology, unpublished.

Hill, R. (1973), 'Unfreezing the cigarette giant', *International Management*, July, pp. 46–9.

Lawrence, P.R. and Lorsch, J.W. (1968), *Developing Organisations: Diagnosis and action*, Addison-Wesley.

Mayo, E. (1983), *The Human Problems of an Industrial Civilisation*, Macmillan.

McGregor, D. (1960), *The Human Side of Enterprise*, McGraw-Hill.

McLean A.J. *et al.* (1982), *Organisation Development in Transition. Evidence of an evolving profession*, John Wiley.

Morse, J.J. and Lorsch, J.W. (1973), 'Beyond theory Y', *Harvard Business Review*, May/June, pp. 46–9.

Pettigrew, A.M. (1973), *The Politics of Organisation Decision-Making*, Tavistock.

Reddin, W.J. (1968), *Effective Management*, McGraw-Hill.
Schein, E.H. (1965), *Organisation Psychology*, Prentice Hall.
Slatter S. St. P. (1984), *Corporate Recovery: A guide to turnaround management*, Penguin Books.
Thakur, M. (1974), *O.D.: The search for identity*, IPM Information Report 16.
Twiss, B. (1983), *The Management of Technological Innovation*, Longman.
Vaill, P.B. (1971), *The Practice of Organisation Development*, American Society of Training and Development.
Warmington, A., Lupton, T. and Gribbin, C. (1977), *Organisation Behaviour and Performance: An open systems approach to change*, Macmillan.

Further reading

Reddin W. J. (1985), *The Best of Bill Reddin*, Institute of Personnel Management, esp. Ch. 15, 'Confessions of an Organization Change Agent'.

Part 6

An integrated view of management systems in a reach for excellence

Chapter 22

Reaching towards excellence through integration of management systems

Overview

For the persistent reader who has battled with all the topics of this text it must be self-evident that management is a very complex subject. There has been a massive amount of theory, some conflicting, since the nineteenth century, and every school of management thought postulates that it has given the whole picture, and that by managing according to the edicts of that school, effective management will naturally be achieved.

In this final part of the text, an attempt will be made to reach for excellence in management. This will be hedged with words such as 'contingency', indicating that there is never really a single final route, but that as we enter the era of the information society, we are entering a world of systems, a world where details can quickly be aggregated and interpreted, where the picture of the organisation's strengths and weaknesses may be seen, where big and important deviations from excellence are evident, where the business consultant needs not to be myopic but can attempt to be far-sighted and confident in sharing sequences of diagnosis and action to bring health and vigour to organisations. You might well ask, who is that consultant? The astonishing reply is that it is you, the reader, who is hungry to grapple with aggregate business pictures and eager to join in reaching for improvements.

Learning objectives

By the end of this chapter the reader should be able to relate to and cope with the key concepts of the contingency approach to major management systems and their implementation.

Contemporary views on effective management

Fortunately for the writer, management has but a short history as an academic discipline. As we review the main currents of management thought it is possible to depict, in broad terms, what readers and laymen have sought from management writings at different times.

1850–1930

The focus is on classical management, being efficient in the deployment of capital and labour, and mechanistic in organisation structures. Work study and bureaucracy are two main points of attention. Organisation efficiency is perceived as an aggregation of very efficient labour and capital elements, and management style tends to be directive.

1930–54

This is the era of the behavioural sciences and the recognition of the variables which influence individual and group motivation. This theory eventually develops into good practice personnel management and leads to recognition of leadership styles and tactics for the management of change. The people resources of the organisation are regarded as essential for effectiveness.

1955–64

This is the era of the business policy theorists. Managing by objectives and corporate planning are defined and refined and attention is given to the composition, planning and control of large, diverse and decentralised units, comprising a portfolio. The emphasis is on synergy; the whole is greater than the sum of the parts. At last the elements and activities of entrepreneurship receive attention, and are no longer perceived as outcomes either of intuition or ideal, rational man.

1965–74

This is the beginning of the era of the computer theorists and practitioners. This is very slow at first to make impact. The business manager and computer specialist boffin cannot easily communicate with one another and expectations are not met.

1975–80

The computer theorist has developed more business knowledge and in this era we find a growing repartee between the business policy theorist and the information technology strategist, who has discovered the concept of being 'user friendly'. When they work well together many organisational improvements are possible.

1981—5

Readers are bored with theorists — they want to rationalise on success and excellence as perceived in the real world. The attention of writers switches to mass readership and an understanding of how 'excellent' companies operate. Peters and Waterman (1982) concentrate their research on US companies with a long track-record of performance in growth and profits, and attempt a rationalisation of useful management guidelines, so that this excellence can be recognised and replicated. Goldsmith and Clutterbuck (1983) follow this line of research but they pick mainly European companies in their search for the winners and find significant cultural differences from Peters and Waterman.

In truth this 'excellence' movement has an earlier root in the writings of business consultants. Drucker, for instance, based many of his observations on managing by objectives and the marketing concept on his real-life consultations with Alfred G. Sloan, the General Manager of General Motors. Also in the early 1970s we find Townsend (1970) explaining how he turned around Avis Car-Hire using rules of management which could be generalised. He emphasised the importance of getting the Chief Executive out of the ivory tower and relating to real issues and real people. Peters and Waterman rewrite this with the advice to manage by walking around (MBWA).

Post-1985

The emphasis swings away from recognition of the characteristics of excellence towards a deeper understanding of the processes and systems of management which provide the infrastructure for successful organisations. Under this approach the emphasis is on attaining an enduring excellence by incorporating the guidelines of others into a flexible but useable approach to effective management. This is the final approach advocated in this text.

Peters and Waterman — in search of excellence

Attributes of excellence

In this summary eight attributes are identified by Peters and Waterman, a rationalisation from their extensive interviews with senior executives from excellent companies. As each principle is developed, comments and criticisms are also made. The criticism tends to dispute some of the interpretations made by Peters and Waterman.

A bias for action
A company must not be paralysed by analysis. The best is the enemy of the good.

In essence this is a criticism of excessive bureaucratic processes, which prevent innovation, and constantly delay moves which are in any way perceived as risky.

We do have to be careful, though, not to dismiss analysis altogether. With many of the processes developed in this text on corporate planning there is the opportunity to get aggregate business pictures quickly, particularly with computer aids, and as long as the speed and relevance of these pictures is appropriate there need be no paralysis by analysis! In the era of the information society managers need to be fluent in the principles of managing by exception, then computers can track key result areas, develop logistic profiles and produce a realism with figures. We do need some relevant analysis combined with good qualitative judgement.

Get close to the customer

Excellent companies learn from their customers. They provide unparalleled quality, service and reliability as a matter of course.

This idea makes a lot of sense. Drucker (1954) made a similar suggestion, and incorporated market standing as one of the pillars of the managing by objectives philosophy. Service, quality and reliability can, however, cause problems. Unless appropriate organisation and a sound feedback mechanism of incidents and performance trends are available it is likely that an organisation will slip. A company needs to secure enduring excellence here. Policies and intentions alone are not enough. But with management information systems pointing directly at the effectiveness standards of service, quality, etc., excellence can be attained.

Autonomy and entrepreneurship

Innovative companies foster many leaders and many innovators throughout the organisation. They are a hive of what we have come to call 'champions'. They encourage practical risk-taking and support good attempts.

This is a sensible ideal to work for and it reinforces the views of other writers such as Burns and Stalker (1961), who emphasised the need for excellence in communications between the two different cultures prevailing in production departments and R & D. Twiss (1983) recognised the need for innovation and project 'champions'. The literature on organisation development and the management of technological change gives some credible further guidelines.

Entrepreneurship needs the sobering influence of corporate planning disciplines to prevent the development of hunches, hobbies and waste and in extreme cases bankruptcy. This principle of Peters and Waterman does need particularly careful interpretation.

The 'autonomy' aspect also provokes some thought. It generally makes sense to decentralise control as much as possible through divisions and profit centres. This leads to the corporate planning technique of portfolio management, but major funding decisions still need referring to central management. That must compromise autonomy.

Productivity through people

The excellent companies treat the rank and file as the root source of quality and productivity gain.

This guideline tends to be supported by writers on Japanese management and those who believe in job enrichment at all levels of management. Current wisdom suggests that higher levels of quality are attained in teams where groups are responsible for both production and quality and where there is active use of quality circles. These aim to recognise and reward those who are nearest to problems and most likely to recognise innovations. However, rank and file members may also fear productivity gains for the possible impact on their job or on promotion opportunities. The literature is full of examples of informal practice designed to prevent production exceeding standards. This is very much at the mercy of the local organisation culture and is certainly not a universally acceptable guideline, easy to adopt and implement.

Hands-on, value-driven

The basic philosophy of an organisation has far more to do with its achievements than do technological or economic resources, organisational structure, innovation and timing.

Few would deny that achievements are important, but equally they do not generally come about by luck; they are dependent on resources, innovation, organisation, timing and the clever articulation of all these to make up entrepreneurship. To say that achievements may happen without these factors is wishful thinking!

The second idea is the popular one of managing by walking around, and some of this is laudable. Indeed it is highly desirable that a chief executive gets a feel for the workface and is well informed. Organisations have a horrible tendency to 'filter' information on its way upwards and report only on things that are going on within company policy.

However, managing by walking around can be overdone. If all the senior executives overindulge in walking around then they can be perceived lower down the organisation as interfering and undermining middle management and supervision. Consequently the practice of good delegation, development of trust and sound and strong decentralisation, is lost.

Stick to the knitting

Never acquire a business you don't know how to run. Proctor and Gamble has never left its base. It seeks to be anything but a conglomerate, yet innovates within its core skills and core markets.

This guideline is very controversial. The early works of Drucker stress the need to have specialisation in business to achieve simplicity and excellence in products and markets. However, difficulties arise when a firm is in an industry which is in decline and needs to diversify. Ansoff (1965) built an early corporate planning model to suggest directions of diversification, and this was elaborated later by the Boston Consultancy Group into the technique of portfolio analysis (see chapter 17). To stick to the knitting for an industry in decline would be a sure recipe for bankruptcy! Indeed, in the United Kingdom many companies have broken away from the knitting and achieved remarkable growth; Hanson Trust is an example. A much more positive guideline on growth is to seek out points of synergy on the basis of products, markets or technology. The Royal Bank of Scotland did a brilliant job in this respect in the late 1980s to achieve an international standing for the provision of financial services.

Simple form, lean staff

The underlying structural forms and systems in the excellent companies are elegantly simple. Top-level staff are lean; it is not uncommon to find a corporate staff of less than 100 people running multi-billion dollar enterprises. Toyota has only five tiers of management in its structure.

Most writers would agree with the philosophy of simple form and lean staff, but there are exceptions, particularly in the 'hi-tech' companies. A visitor to IBM's plant at Greenock, Scotland would indeed find evidence of such exceptions. Progressively over the years, with the automation of many of the production processes, the bulk of the people have moved off the production lines and into administrative work with much computer assistance. Production planning and control, materials control, etc., have a lot of staff dedicated to coordinating the making and delivery of complete systems for customers which work first time. A sophisticated organisation structure reflects the sophisticated technological environment.

This principle of simple form and lean staff is inevitably bound up with contingency factors, which cannot be ignored. It might be legitimate to have lean staff at HQ, but more staff will be in depth down in the divisions and profit centres. An overall principle is that *structure* should reflect *strategy*, and strategy is increasingly developed around profit centres.

Simultaneous loose—tight properties

The excellent companies are both centralised and decentralised. For the most part they have pushed autonomy down to the shop floor or product development team. On the other hand, they are frantic centralists around the few core values they hold dear.

On the surface the above guideline looks as though it makes sense, but it is not easy to interpret and apply in a real environment. There is a nice passage in Goldsmith and Clutterbuck (1983) about variations in delegation of authority for capital expenditure, and contrasts are made between Hanson Trust and Bulmers, both excellent companies by UK standards: 'At Hanson Trust the standing joke is that any manager who asks to buy a new typewriter will receive a note from the group chairman telling him to check first whether there is a spare machine at Whetstone ... every request for unbudgeted capital expenditure in excess of £500 is routed through group headquarters.'

'At Bulmers once they have a budget, managers have almost total discretion on how they spend it. Nelson can authorise capital expenditure of up to £250,000 without reference to the Board.'

Lorenz, writing in the *Financial Times* (1984), has produced another criticism of Peters and Waterman:

> At the very moment when that American publishing phenomenon, *In Search of Excellence*, has begun to spawn a shoal of pale European imitations, a more ambitious activity is bursting into life in the US: excellence knocking!
>
> The very success and the loose Californian style in which the book was written, could prove its undoing. Authors, Peters and Waterman, admit, 'We

didn't know we'd been taken so seriously. If we had we would have been more careful in the way we had written it but then it would have been very dull.'

What the duo did was to compress into a racy volume some lessons from America's best-run companies. They distilled these to eight key attributes of successful management: such eminently worthwhile things as sticking close to your customer, motivating your staff by wandering around among them, encouraging internal entrepreneurship, and so forth.

But they did themselves a disservice in three key respects: they failed adequately to make clear that these were not the only attributes necessary for success; they failed to issue a warning that even excellent companies can have problems and let their standards slip; and they neglected to point out with crystal clarity that virtually none of the dozen companies was excellent across the board. As Waterman explains now: 'It was a composite view.'

The *Business Week* investigation into the performance of the 'excellent companies' makes stimulating reading: fourteen of them have, to say the least, stumbled!

The above review looks a bit hard on Peters and Waterman, yet their book is very widely read. Why does their summary look so thin when carefully analysed?

Peters' research is built on the assumption that successful people can explain easily why and how they made their success and that it is easy to generalise from one environment to another. But the path from interview, anecdote and biography to sound management theory is not that easy.

When people started introducing computerised systems to business it was thought that analysts could easily go to line managers and get them to articulate their information needs, but they could not conceptualise what they were doing. If managers cannot easily articulate their information needs, why should they be any more articulate in defining their business success, in any other terms than those of personal experience? Mintzberg (1973) also found that managers had great difficulty in conceptualising what they actually did. Their combination of intuition, experience and some sound theory was complex to interpret. Mintzberg's research rather overtook the previous assumptions about what managers did and recast their activity into ten distinct roles of management (see chapter 1).

It is also hard to conceptualise leadership skills (see chapter 20). Research results point away from a trait theory of leadership and towards a contingency approach. This is a helpful approach, although a long way from a final theory. Peters and Waterman are, however, reaching beyond a trait theory for individuals; they are attempting a trait theory for successful organisations. But what is missing is the hard analysis of the relevant contingency factors. Their mass of anecdotal data does not add up to the necessary consistency and coherence which one would seek in any blueprint for effective management or organisational excellence.

However, it would be churlish to be defeatist in this search for excellence. Perhaps a way can be found to consolidate the approach. The key to the way forward is to look in a very discriminating way at established good practice approaches, then concentrate selectively on these and define the various contingency factors.

The contingency approach to systems

In this text every chapter attempts a review of management theory and practice and seeks out good practice. Management is, after all, a combination of art, science and technique. There are four main themes in the text. These are represented in Figure 22.1 and summarised below.

Theme 1   Corporate planning

This theme is crucial, as it is the main inspiration behind any coherent attempt at entrepreneurship. The organisation must have a core of excellence and added value to get started, survive and grow. It needs a regular review of its competitive position and a constant stimulation of its product/market portfolio. It needs a clear appreciation of all the main stakeholders and their interests, as well as how they may be balanced. Its senior executives need a sound appreciation of the synergistic combinations that will stimulate strength and growth and the teamwork to build a continuity in business philosophy that is strong enough to outlive the talents of any one dominant personality.

The organisation needs a board whose members are well versed in good corporate planning practice and who are assisted by a staff group to do the creative leg-work involved in seeking out new directions and in providing the logistics and implementation strategies to forge ahead in new directions.

Two main attempts have been made in this text to establish the logic and credibility of corporate planning. In chapter 3 the Glueck model (1976) was described and used to help analyse some simple case situations. This was described as a simple basic model.

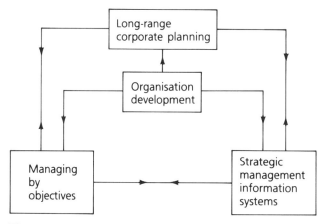

Figure 22.1 *Crucial systems of management*

The second attempt was made in chapter 17, at the end of a wide-ranging review of the information society, and a more elaborate model (p. 333) was developed in Figure 17.1. This model outlined how a business could be conceptualised as a cluster of mini-businesses whose performances could be aggregated into sound profiles of winners and losers and into sound business policies of improvement, growth, consolidation and divestment, based on synergy. The model then suggested an approach to quantification of resources required to cope with new ventures, so that management could be pro-active in the short term, and in the long term anticipate the major changes in direction necessary to maintain growth and strength.

Figure 17.1 incorporated the main techniques and themes established by several leading authorities on corporate planning. The only originality claimed in the model was the way of presenting these techniques in a coherent and integrated manner. However, it was recognised in chapter 17 that there are some significant differences between private sector organisations and their public sector counterparts. Some guidelines on the public sector organisations were also discussed and illustrated.

These models were certainly not the last word on corporate planning. The management literature is growing very rapidly in this field. However, the models do offer a viable guideline to allow organisations to get started, to think about corporate direction and to get moving in new directions without loss of control and a high risk of bankruptcy. If any organisation adopted these models it would be reasonable to expect an improvement in morale and performance and a more informed and committed team of senior management.

A summary has already been offered in this text on corporate planning (see p. 354).

Goldsmith and Clutterbuck (1983) make the following observations on strategic planning:

> Strategic planning at STC starts with a top-level committee on which sit both directors and corporate planners. 'We take planning and action to shape the future very seriously. We try to be as realistic as possible.'

> Sir John Clark of Plessey sees planning systems as crucial to his company's survival and growth ... 'We started with financial planning systems which weren't really planning at all. Then we got into Boston Consultancy Analysis ... the theory can be overdone, but it is a good starting point.'

> GrandMet uses strategic planning as the basic starting point for turning around any loss-making company it acquires ... Within three months of acquisition Grinstead visits them and they have to give a thirty-six hour presentation about their company ... at the end of the exercise he feels comfortable or [uncomfortable] about the management and what they are doing.

Theme 2 Managing by objectives

Chapters 5 and 6 were devoted to this theme and principles of good practice were summarised in Figure 5.1 (p. 63) and in the summary of chapter 6. This set of principles was originally conceived by Peter Drucker, and then later developed and refined. The principles were based on the notion that teamwork and collaboration between managers would be enhanced when a firm framework of expectancy was constructed and managers encouraged frequently to redefine their job positions and priorities.

Attached to sound-objective setting was a thorough feedback mechanism, defined in the model of this text as the appraisal process. On this foundation the *coaching* process between managers and superiors or mentors could naturally take place, a reinforcement of norms of merit and competence. A summary of MbO is given on p. 98.

Goldsmith and Clutterbuck (1983) make the following observations:

> Summers of Booz Allen suggests that the lack of top management involvement in innovation, especially in technology, is that R&D and marketing set themselves different goals.

> MacGregor, in addition to giving the British Steel top management the freedom to get on and manage, put heavy emphasis on setting clear goals, something he immediately diagnosed as absent when he assumed control.

> The STC management board almost never makes decisions. Decisions are taken all over the place by groups given the responsibility. It means spending an immense amount of time giving people a wide understanding of company objectives.

Theme 3   Management information systems

Chapters 12–17 were devoted to the tactical and strategic use of information technology in organisations. Now that we are operating in the environment of an information society it is clearly important that we relate to the opportunities that emerge and the enhancements that this new technology brings to the management process.

Several themes were developed in those six chapters, but probably the most significant was the contribution of computing to the corporate planning process in manufacturing companies. The development and implementation of the principles of managing by exception (MBE) make it possible to summarise and simplify and build up aggregate pictures of the business. MBE requires the triggering and interpretation of variances, establishing business norms and manipulating these. This simple idea can have a massive impact. When the norms are the engineering norms of product structure, product processes and labour times, and when they lie in a database, it is possible to introduce a market schedule of activity; then the computer can generate logistic profiles through all the main dimensions of resources, labour, plant utilisation, stock and delivery date expectations.

This can be a major aid to the timing of investment decisions on plant, to the recruitment of labour for new and existing projects under turbulent market conditions and to obtaining discounts from vendors for bulk-buy contracts and for simulating different possible profit plans. If the computer-assisted scheduling works really well, then the customer can expect much greater reliability in knowing the progress of orders and in getting deliveries on time. Used consistently over time, this capability is likely to achieve growth in market share. However, all the main stakeholders of the business can benefit from precision scheduling.

The particular application within which this set of principles may be adopted is illustrated in Figures 13.1 and 13.2 (pp. 210, 212) as computerised material requirements planning and the text suggests that this model is one manifestation of the Japanese JIT approach for manufacturing companies.

This approach will not get off the ground unless management is prepared to plan well, and to think in terms of schedules, targets and policy rules about performance standards. These are the outputs of corporate planning routines and MbO approaches. But once this environment exists and there is a will to manage well, these computerised models will enhance that process. The exception reports may be tuned to give rapid and accurate feedback on key result areas and the logistic profiles of the future will fundamentally affect the planning process itself.

The teamwork associated with computers in corporate planning is illustrated in Figure 15.3 (p. 270) and there is discussion in chapter 15 on the crucial role of the forecaster as a member of the corporate planning staff group.

There are now some twenty years' experience of using these techniques, originally developed by the computer manufacturing companies themselves, and from an original complexity they are now emerging with an increasing degree of simplicity and flexibility for users.

Chapters 12−17 on the information society reviewed many other creative uses of computerised systems for design, manufacture and distribution via networks and a range of possibilities for getting productivity improvements and better quality decision-making by individuals using microcomputers. But for integration and support of the corporate planning process it is the material requirements planning model that has the greatest potential as an aid to planning.

In the extract below Mill (1989) makes a plea for the information technology strategist to join the board as a full member of the business strategy team. Midland Bank were the trailblazers in the United Kingdom:

> Things are looking up for information technology directors who are starting to be seen as vital enough to firms to merit a seat on the Board.
>
> The idea of a computer professional as business whizz-kid is a relatively new one outside the world of consultancies ... but as companies start to realise how dependent they are on information technology, this attitude is changing. At the forefront of these changes is Gene Lockhart, who in May was promoted from being chief executive of IT to head of all Midland's banking operations.
>
> Lockhart joined Midland at board level in March 1987. He was unusual in the upper echelons of the banking world for two reasons. He was only thirty-seven, and he came from a computing rather than a banking background. A few years ago, the idea of someone getting to such a key position in the banking world from IT would have been unthinkable ... but this is a sign of the times.

Caulkin (1988) makes the following observations on JIT manufacture:

The most influential computer aid is JIT. Its overriding value lies in its simplicity and a powerfully self-reinforcing nature. By removing buffer stocks between work positions JIT exposes obstacles to smoother and smoother flows of production. As each problem is solved another presents itself. Thus do problems magically become opportunities. By turning every workstation into a customer or supplier of another, JIT mandates instant feedback on quality or quantity problems; otherwise the line stops. Quality gains automatically become productivity gains, and both knit together in a project of continuous improvement ... JIT aims at nothing less than the elimination of all business waste — no wasted time, no wasted quantity.

JIT does have remarkable one-off effects on inventory levels with equally striking effects on the balance sheet. Yet the knock-on implications are cumulatively even greater. Less inventory means less space for stores, fewer storemen, fewer fork-lift trucks. It means shorter production lines (no buffer stocks) and fewer simpler conveyors. It releases space for manufacturing.

At the same time JIT is a potent vehicle for organisational redesign. JIT demands simplification of physical layout with simplified management structures to match. Instead of traditional machine shops and tortuous product routes through the factory, five of these plants have straight-through cells or factories within factories.

People motivated by quality, rigorous organisation and a drive towards JIT, supported by the appropriate technology, these are the constituents of Britain's best manufacturing plants.

Lee (1989) discusses the inexorable march of the information society:

Buyers and suppliers are using electronic data interchange systems to exchange a range of business documents, including orders, goods received messages, invoices, payments etc., over direct computer to computer links. These links are typically provided by private network operators such as International Network Services, Istel, and IBM.

Electronic data interchange 1988 conference speaker and former ICI Chairman, Sir John Harvey-Jones, picked up the strategic theme, arguing that too many boardrooms were still unaware of the implications of electronic trading. 'There has never been a time when we've needed more to apply this technique aggressively. The single European market and 1992 will mean a fundamental change in the way we do business. We're still not accustomed to thinking of information technology in strategic terms. For example, just-in-time technology is much more than savings in stockholding; it's giving all the advantages of integration without being in one company. So it's a mistake to think of electronic data interchange as just saving on clerical effort and paperwork. In future it's the company that is *closest* to its trading partners that is going to survive.'

Of greatest benefit to Tallent Engineering has been access to its customers' production schedules, allowing it to run a just-in-time supply operation. Make no mistake about it, JIT manufacture and purchase can only really be implemented with fast information flows. JIT cannot be stand-alone; it has to be supported by fast and accurate means of communication. And electronic data interchange (EDI) is about flying information.

It won't be long before EDI will be a mandatory requirement imposed on suppliers by the bigger companies. For Tallent, the set-up costs were minimal; Ford meets all the installation cost for its suppliers.

Theme 4   The management of change through organisation development

Every lively organisation has constantly to adjust and adapt to its environment and respond to changing business strategies by introducing new business systems, yet people in organisations often resist change. If we want to reach for excellence then the organisation must be open to strategies of change, and these we find, crude though they may be, in the processes of organisation development.

This theme was developed in chapters 20 and 21 and became a focus for the application of knowledge from the behavioural sciences. From a review of the variations in leadership styles we moved to the topic of managing change, beginning with client and sponsor and ending with interventions aimed at improving the organisational climate and solving organisational problems. Figure 21.1 (p. 441) offers a model to reveal the targets and processes of this technique.

The reader was warned that the topic of managing change as developed in the literature on organisation development would be a tough one. There are many pieces to this jigsaw and some risk attached to intervention programmes. Yet there are some research results on the management of change which do report success. Like most management techniques, management itself has strategic choices in the activation and deployment of OD.

In chapter 21 a generalised model of organisation development — its origins, processes, targets and the choices of approach — was presented (see p. 441). Emphasis was given to the traditional approach, with heavy reliance on the findings of the behavioural sciences. However, when we look deeper into the topic and attempt a synthesis, other possible approaches emerge which are not so reliant on the behavioural sciences. Organisation development is about achieving excellence in an organisation. Yet we cannot really conceive of excellence unless we have a clear perception of norms of good practice and a means of aggregation, so that significant deviations from this are visible. Then interventions for change can be better focused.

A consultancy model

The four themes highlighted in this chapter are each systems of management which evolved over time and as a result of much research and refinement. They represent norms of good practice in process and structure. As they are norms in such a vital area of company activity they provide a most useful instrument of consultancy. A 'sick' company is sick to the extent that it is operating against the norms of good practice and clearly the most important norms of good practice to get right are the ones represented by the long-range corporate planning models.

Now we can make sense of Figure 22.2. This assumes a consultancy sequence between sponsor and consultant. Initially, the sponsor is simply aware of trouble or concern. Once the consultant agrees his or her terms of reference he or she then observes the organisation's planning activity. He or she then attempts to relate the trouble or concern to any bad practice in corporate planning and goes on to look at the transmission process of objective-setting, good MbO. Any deviations from good practice are put into some perspective. Similarly, the consultant will follow the norms of strategic computing and the material requirements planning type routines. He or she then looks at the three dimensions of deviant practice as they relate to the original trouble or concern.

This process in real life throws up a mass of data for interpreting and sharing with the sponsor and, as a result, the original trouble or concern gets a much finer definition. The emphasis is often replacing bad practice in management systems with improved practice. A set of priorities emerges, a step-by-step plan is agreed with the sponsor and an appropriate intervention programme constructed and implemented.

We now have a credible and useful method of consultancy, which gets to the root cause of the trouble or concern and not just the symptoms. This approach constantly provokes a dialogue between consultant and sponsor over the aggregate pictures of the business, so that change can take on a natural momentum and secure improvements under all three dimensions.

Notice that it is important always to seek sponsor approval before the intervention is done. This secures the sponsor's culture and suggests that the consultant does not impose his or her culture on sponsors. No fifth columns here! This is a difference in approach from most of the previous exponents of organisation development such as Blake and Mouton (1969), who constantly attempted to create healthy organisations based on ideal leadership styles.

There is a natural advantage, too, in homing in on the corporate planning process as the central norm of good practice as it is less personalised and less likely to create resistance from individuals. If the early 'unfreezing' action of a consultancy focuses on leadership style, then senior management may feel threatened and a future positive dialogue may be impossible.

A tactical model to implement effective management systems

It may appear that the three systems of management — long-range corporate planning, managing by objectives and strategic management information systems, all with guidelines of good practice — are impossible to introduce in a coherent way to an organisation. Naturally, a step-by-step approach is necessary. Figure 22.3 suggests a credible way forward. It is constructed with reference to a manufacturing company.

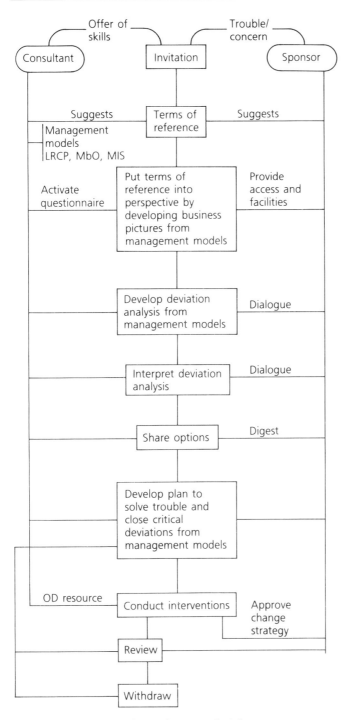

Figure 22.2 *Overview of consultancy methodology*

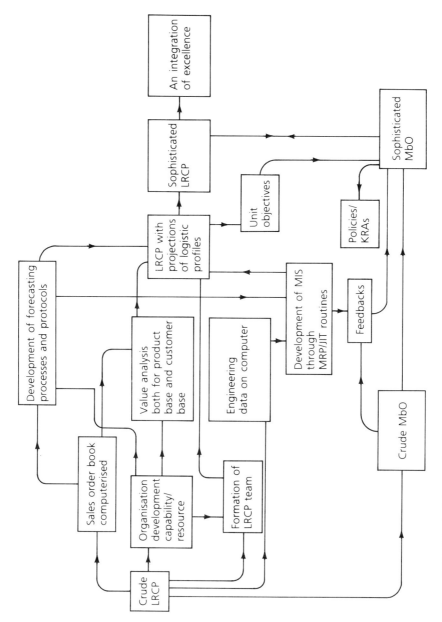

Figure 22.3 *Principal interactions between system components*

It follows just what was done for a computer manufacturer, so it is feasible and it is not so very difficult to replicate. Indeed, it was replicated within the computer manufacturer in several subsidiaries and divisions whose products had nothing to do with computing.

The sequence starts with an assumption that some crude process of corporate planning is in operation. This means that the principles behind the Glueck model, illustrated in Figure 3.1 (p. 27), are operating. Note that this model has very little in the way of quantitative data and was regarded as a simple but effective starting point for corporate planning.

The next sequences naturally follow on from this point. A team of people is set up that can articulate change processes (the core of the organisation development theme), and there is a formation of a corporate planning team set up to do the corporate planning leg-work (boards of directors do not have the time to do the detail), and there is the beginnings of computer assistance, a computerised sales order processing system. This is a natural starting point for computerisation as it is the link from inside the organisation out to the customer, not only to provide service but also to gather essential aggregate data about demand patterns and their changes.

We can then commence another phase and engage the basics of MbO. Note that in the text it was suggested that MbO only starts when there is some knowledge and coherence resulting from the corporate plan. If we tried to implement MbO in isolation lower down the organisation, then executives would tend to do their own 'empire-building' and there would be no natural coordination of objectives from different functional areas. Marketing and R&D might easily go their own way, which would be very expensive. However, once even a crude form of corporate planning is in position then we do have enough definition of key result areas from a base of collective responsibility to go about breaking them down and transmitting them vertically and laterally — the prime role of an MbO management system.

In the next phase, some further new elements can be added. Once we have a computerised sales order processing function it can provide one important data source for the forecasting people to work with, and they can then join the corporate planning team with some credibility. Their role and process was described in chapter 15. Now a lot more things are possible. The corporate planners can analyse the forecast data and historical data and attempt a value analysis both for the product and the customer base. What we are likely to be getting is aggregate pictures of activity and profit by every product and product family and by any other grouping which is meaningful for the business. The aim of this is to seek out the winners and losers of the business. Glueck suggested doing a SWOT analysis, looking out for strengths, weaknesses, opportunities and threats. This value analysis takes us a long way down that route.

At the same time the engineering data are being collected into a normative database to reveal the standards of structure, process and timings. When that is rolled up we have a comprehensive base of standard costs for every product. When we analyse invoices and deduct standard cost we get gross profit, and the aggregate picture for the whole business tells us immediately where the profit profiles lie and where the high-activity, low-profit blackspots are too. When we have an appreciation of these pictures then further intervention and action can improve the organisation.

With forecast information and an engineering database on line, we have the ability to put the computer to work once more and introduce material requirements planning or JIT routines. These give the corporate planners the vital logistic profiles for the business, pictures of the future resource requirements in terms of labour, plant, stock and profit. The corporate planning team has a corporate planning simulator. As market conditions or assumptions change, and this is manifested in changes to the agreed product forecast, we can track the logistic profiles to see the consequences. If we follow the prospects of market growth, that will probably mean more investment so that need and capacity match one another to take on board new opportunities. Likewise, where the logistic profiles reveal poor utilisation of people or plant then we can reallocate labour or divest and convert unused plant into money for fuelling investment of the winners.

This gives the opportunity for very active management of the organisation's product/market portfolio. This process gives finer definitions of targets and effectiveness standards, so we can put these norms into the computer and trigger exception reports on these vital areas, showing trends.

In the final phase of this sequence unit objectives become much clearer from the enhanced corporate planning action and this gives enhanced input to the MbO system. The key result areas still need further breaking down, but we can be much more confident that what is being broken down are worthwhile organisational KRAs, not someone's hobbyhorse. MbO, it may be recalled, has two phases. The first relates to the breaking down of KRAs, and the second to the feedback process or the appraisal process. Chapter 6 advocated using groups of three at any one time to review activity and enter, if necessary, a coaching sequence. It was recognised that it was essential to avoid escaping, particularly from uncomfortable problem areas in the organisation, yet with only subjective judgements available, even with three people present some escaping would be possible. Once we have put the computer to work on the exception reports and the aggregate pictures are readily available as an added dimension to these groups of three, then a much more objective approach can be made. The vital coaching should be that much more realistic and effective. Furthermore, the computerised exception reports should make it much easier for managers to be self-sufficient in getting feedback and managing better their own environments.

Now, at the end of the sequence of Figure 22.3, we have arrived at sophisticated long-range corporate planning, as represented in Figure 17.1 (p. 333). This is backed by the infrastructure of the other management systems.

Notice that there are double arrows in Figure 22.3 at the right-hand side of the model, linking the sophisticated MbO box with sophisticated corporate planning. This reflects the constant feedback process within the different layers of the organisation structure, so that good ideas and innovations can become visible by healthy upward communication. With this healthy flow top management and the corporate planners should not become isolated, but remain constantly in touch with the dynamics of the business. If this dynamic communication flows well, we really do have a form of managing by walking around, but without undermining middle and lower levels of management.

Summary

At the beginning of this chapter it was noted that many others had tried to conceptualise the essential ingredients of effective management, or the components of excellence in organisations. Writers have attempted to home in on a few fundamental but universal guidelines to attaining this worthy ideal.

A review was then done of the major attempts to develop this framework of effective management from the literature. All these approaches were criticised for their shortcomings. Finally an attempt was made to draw together the major themes of this text to see if it was possible to conceptualise an infrastructure which would nurture effective management practice. Such a model was defined in terms of four main themes, three of which were visualised as systems of management built on the solid groundings of good practice. The fourth theme was the resource of organisation development, a necessary approach to achieve interventions and organisational change. The corporate planning system tended to be the core of this approach and from that basic core the other management systems would join in reinforcing the corporate planning processes.

There were two main outcomes of this thinking. Firstly, the integration of good practice norms provides a powerful consultancy tool to diagnose organisational problems and look beyond their mere symptoms to the more fundamental causes. This approach was portrayed in Figure 22.2.

Secondly, we found that there was a credible and not too complex route to establishing in a step-by-step fashion this very powerful set of management systems. These would combine the best known management practice with the techniques and capabilities emerging from the information society. It was possible to overcome the 'paralysis by analysis' syndrome and offer a dynamic and realistic capability of corporate planning. This was represented in the logic of Figure 22.3.

Case Study 22.1
The problem of the warehouse

(Written from action research by the author in 1987.)

Exercise objective

In this final exercise the reader is invited to grapple with the dynamics of a company wishing to use systems for better integration, but there are snags in the implementation process as revealed through a file of company memoranda. The reader should become more conversant with the use and integration of management systems, particularly with the need for adopting a sound corporate planning posture, without which other management systems become relatively ineffective. As usual organisational politics have some influence on the various developments.

Study assignment

Carefully assess the case for and against relocating the finished goods inventory warehouse from Glasgow to Crawley. If you propose a relocation indicate the particular business problems which such a relocation would solve. If you reject the proposal to relocate, suggest other ways of mitigating the existing company problems.

In carrying out this analysis it will be helpful to view the company data against the following norms of good practice:

1. Corporate planning and forecasting,
2. Financial analysis,
3. Computer-assisted material requirements planning,
4. MbO,
5. Choice in organisation structure.

In working on a response to the issues and problems of the company it will be helpful to suggest the components of a possible organisation development programme to get things right.

This case study is intended to illustrate how the use of information and information systems directed at key decision-makers can influence the structure of a manufacturing company. The material in the case study relates to the important management decision of whether to relocate a warehouse function away from the manufacturing facility. It is based on a real incident, although the names of the characters, the name of the company and some of the operating statistics quoted in the text have been changed. Students may be expected to grapple with issues of business policy arising in the fields of data processing, marketing, production control and internal company communications.

The case study material is presented through a statement of background facts about the company and its problems and then illustrated by a file of internal company memoranda.

Background statement

International Electronics and Electric Motor Company was founded in 1920 in the United States and began its international operations in the 1930s. In 1985 it had manufacturing plants in ten countries outside the United States and had marketing operations in fifty countries world-wide. The company had two main product divisions. Firstly, there was the computer peripherals division; secondly, there was the electric motor division. The company initiated its operations in the United Kingdom in 1936 by setting up a wholly-owned marketing subsidiary company located at Crawley, near Gatwick Airport. In 1936 the company was a single-product operation manufacturing electric motors. In 1948 the company rented government factories and set up a manufacturing base near Glasgow, Scotland.

In 1963 the company set up its computer peripherals division and from mid-1965 had been manufacturing both the electric motors and the computer peripherals at its Scottish base. In 1955 the marketing operation at Crawley relinquished the warehouse function for finished goods and the processing of all customer sales orders. This finished goods inventory control and order processing role was assumed from that date by the Glasgow operation. At the time of the case study the manufacturing operation at Glasgow had some 5,000 employees, approximately half in each product division. Many of the company's prestigious customers were located within 100 miles of the Crawley marketing subsidiary.

The Glasgow operation was headed up by a General Factory Manager Scotland, Kevin Ogilvy. An outline organisation chart (Figure 22.4) shows the functions and key executives

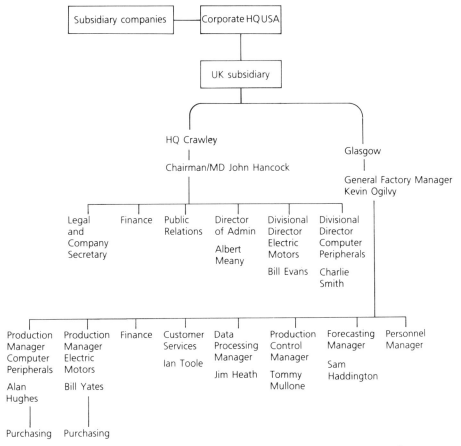

Figure 22.4 *International electronics and electric motor company organisation chart*

reporting to him. The southern operation at Crawley was headed up by the UK Managing Director and Chairman, John Hancock, and employed 150 staff housed in a prestige modern building. The southern operation was the centre of all marketing activity, and the Headquarters from which the national sales force was deployed. The southern office also had responsibility for public relations, field service back-up, customer training, legal services, financial and corporate planning. Divisional Operating Statements, one for each Division, are included below.

Divisional operating statement Electric Motors Division as at year 3

1. *Annual billing*: £6 million.

2. *Net profit*: 2 per cent of annual billing, dropping (3 per cent in last year, 5 per cent two years ago).

3. *Product range*: 1,000 items (100 new this year).

   800 items traded on a 'make' basis. (£1 million billing, 4—6 week delivery promise from receipt of order.)

   200 items served on 'stock' basis, 100 of which are quoted for immediate delivery and 100 are quoted for 1—3 week delivery promise. Stock items accounted for £5 million billing.

4. *Stockholding*

Finished goods inventory	£150,000
Obsolete inventory written off	£ 50,000
Component and raw material inventory	£800,000
Obsolete inventory written off	£ 30,000
Work-in-process inventory	£500,000
Inventory turn:	4.14 times/annum

5. *Actual delivery performance*

Within delivery policy	£1 million
1—2 weeks outside policy	£2 million
2—4 weeks outside policy	£2 million
Greater than 4 weeks outside policy	£1 million

6. *Market outlook*

   The Electric Motors Division is facing increasingly competitive conditions in its market, manifested particularly in better delivery performance from competitors and keener prices.

7. *Factory productivity*

   Labour utilisation at factory reported as 60 per cent effective standard hours. This low figure accounted for by the very wide product range, small batches of production, relatively high set-up costs and low inventory buffer stocks.

8. *Return on investment*

   ROI 10 per cent in last year, dropping from 14 per cent two years ago.

Divisional operating statement Computer Peripherals Division as at year 3

1. *Annual billing*: £9 million.

2. *Net profit*: 5 per cent of annual billing, steady for the last two years.

3. *Product range*

   600 items, all on a 'make' basis.
   500 items on delivery policy 1–6 weeks.
   100 items on delivery policy 6–25 weeks.
   150 items new this year.

4. *Stockholding*

Finished goods inventory	£50,000
(This stock represents items manufactured for orders which were subsequently cancelled.)	
Component inventory and raw material	£1 million
Spares inventory	£100,000
Work-in-process inventory	£800,000
Obsolete inventory written off	£100,000
Inventory turn	4.62 times/annum

5. *Actual delivery performance*

Within delivery policy	£3 million
1–3 weeks outside policy	£3 million
3–5 weeks outside policy	£1 million
5–25 weeks outside policy	£1 million
25–60 weeks outside policy	£1 million

6. *Market outlook*

   A rapidly changing market in which delivery and price are critical and there is a need to customise for new designs very rapidly. Market share has remained static for the last two years.

7. *Factory productivity*

   Labour utilisation at factory reported as 70 per cent effective standard hours. This relatively low figure represents rework owing to initial faults in customised design and queuing times and delays at a variety of places in the factory process.

8. *Return on investment*: 7 per cent, steady for last two years.

The approach to material requirements planning (MRP)

The company has considerable expertise in the computerisation of its production planning and control routines. The project to computerise these was undertaken over a period of nine years, and was completed in its present form just three years before the memos of year 1 were written. The system was based largely on the proven systems developed by the US parent company and then adapted to the UK environment. The overall computerised system is depicted in Figure 22.5.

The data processing department at the Glasgow site has twenty analysts and programmers and the company has carried out a massive thirty man/year design programme to implement a system which would be responsive to the demanding and turbulent environment of each division. The main features of the system included daily processing of incoming customer orders and generation of the ordering paperwork, acknowledgement of customer orders, delivery quotations, release notes for the warehouse, invoices and statistics. Weekly, the system would reschedule the factory for all stages of inventory, responding to a twelve-month sales forecast, the current sales order book and a factory capacity plan for the next twelve months. The first three weeks of the finished product schedule would be 'frozen', consisting of work-in-process actually committed and purchase orders already placed would be respected, otherwise the remainder of the year's activity would merely be simulated to generate accurate projected requirements for plant, labour and standard hours for the full year ahead. One observer from a firm of consultants remarked that the system represented the fine tuning of a corporate plan every week! Monthly, the sales forecast would be updated to take account of recent trends and this would be reviewed together with a revision of the factory capacity plan. Quarterly, this exercise would be done in depth when the production and the sales plans would be united with a planned figure for finished goods inventory, and then the plans tuned to achieve such a figure. Inventory holding would be related to the parameter 'safety stock'. All components would carry a safety stock expressed in a number of weeks' usage. Finished goods serviced on a 'make' basis would have an entry on the sales forecast and no actual safety stock; the sales forecast entry would generate requirements, so that component provisioning and plant requisition would be accounted for. Finished goods serviced on a 'stock' basis would have appropriate safety stock to achieve a laid down delivery policy without stock-out.

Incoming customer orders would be promised automatically by the computer system by being processed in a queue and allocated against actual finished stock and the computer-generated twelve-month production schedule.

Owing to the general sophistication of the computerised system there was a diversity of opinion among company executives over its development and control, and the formulation within it of the policy rules and parameters which were intended to reflect a credible commercial response to market conditions and requirements for profitability.

The memoranda following illustrate some of the issues involved leading up to the whole question of where the finished goods inventory control function should be located — at Glasgow at the end of the assembly line, or at Crawley with the Headquarters and marketing staff.

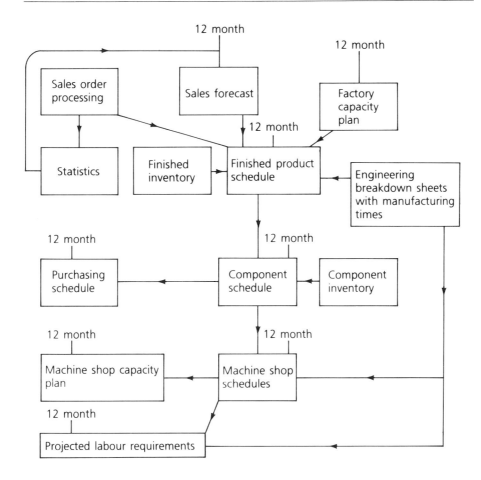

Figure 22.5 *Integration between production and marketing as reflected in Glasgow computer system*

List of memoranda

Memo no.	From	To	Topic
1	Jan de Vries	Bill Evans	Deliveries to Belgian sales subsidiary
2	Bill Evans	Ian Toole cc Jim Heath	Deliveries to EC subsidiaries
3	Jim Heath	Bill Evans	Subsidiaries delivery problem

4	Bill Evans	John Hancock, MD	FGIC
5	John Hancock	Kevin Ogilvy	FGIC
6	Kevin Ogilvy	List of Glasgow executives	FGIC
7	Albert Meany	Kevin Ogilvy	Telephone bill — £750,000
8	Tommy Mullone	Kevin Ogilvy	FGIC
9	Jim Heath	Kevin Ogilvy	FGIC
10	Sam Haddington	Kevin Ogilvy	FGIC — forecasting implications
11	John Halliday	Charlie Smith	Spares problem
12	Charlie Peters	Jim Heath	In-house equipment

Memo 1

From: Director, International Electronics and Electric Motor, Belgium SA, Brussels
To: Director, Electric Motor Division, UK, Bill Evans, Crawley
Date: September, Year 1

Deliveries to Belgian sales subsidiary

I am most concerned at the service we have been getting from the UK company. In Belgium the market for electric motors is booming, yet our salesmen are exasperated at the unreliable supply from the United Kingdom. I would ask you to give this matter your urgent attention for we are seriously considering buying our supplies direct from the United States. We cannot understand why we sometimes have to wait six weeks for shipments of stock which is quoted in company bulletins as one-week delivery, particularly when we send you orders some two months before the request date. I appreciate that you are not sited at the Scottish factory but I trust that you will make your influence felt in appropriate quarters. Incidentally, the United Kingdom is unique in not separating the finished goods inventory control function away from the factory. All other marketing subsidiary companies in the European Community control their own FGIC, and this gives us a chance to put the customer first. It makes no commercial sense to allow production-oriented engineers to make and interpret marketing policy when the industry is as competitive as that for electric motors.

Regards,
Jan de Vries

Memo 2

From: Bill Evans, Director, Electric Motor Division, Crawley
To: Ian Toole, Customer Services Manager, Glasgow
cc: Jim Heath, Data Processing Manager, Glasgow
Date: January, Year 2

Deliveries to subsidiary companies in the European Community

We have received some serious complaints from our subs over the unreliability of deliveries for stock items from United Kingdom in Electric Motor Division. It would appear to me that your computer system is giving customers much too optimistic promises and that they are greatly disappointed when deliveries go late, despite an earlier firm factory promise within our agreed delivery policy period. I would like you to discuss the matter with Jim Heath and see if you can jointly suggest how we can improve our supply record to subs. I have never really understood the weird and wonderful rules you adopt in your computer system and hope that you will not blind me with science and artificial constraints, which as a marketing man I would find really hard to accept.

Regards,
Bill Evans

P.S. Our salesmen are most disenchanted with the figures on your published booking report for last month. I spent a full day trying to sort out the mess. They were most indignant that three major orders taken at the end of the month were not reflected in the totals. If it is a matter of cut-off dates then you simply must get your cut-off dates to reflect the salesmen's working month, rather than your computer operation manager's convenience.

Memo 3

From: Jim Heath, Data Processing Manager, Glasgow
To: Bill Evans, Divisional Director, Electric Motor Division, Crawley
Date: April,Year 2

Subsidiary delivery problem

I have just had a joint meeting with Ian Toole to review the rules about promising customers' orders which are programmed into our computer system. A brief outline of the rules follows.

Customers' orders are queued onto the computer on the basis of a number of parameters. These parameters are: the date of entry of the order; the customer's request date for delivery; the delivery policy for the item concerned; the type of order (domestic or export). The system currently distinguishes between domestic and export orders as margins for domestic are some 10 per cent higher than for export. Domestic orders are queued ahead of export orders regardless of the date of entry. This rule was suggested by yourself some three years ago to maximise profit potential in the United Kingdom, and defended on the grounds that as we were supplying domestic customers direct, they should get the first crack at available stock, whereas export trade was with a subsidiary, who held a buffer stock to cushion delivery problems with customers. The effect of the current rule is that a three-month-old order on the Belgium Sub might have its stock reallocated instead to a UK customer with an order of only one day's standing! Note, however, that in Computer Peripherals Division we have always queued the orders on the basis of entry date in the interests of maintaining delivery reliability, and this 'first come, first served' rule has had the adamant support of the Divisional Director, Charlie Smith.

I feel embarrassed that the two divisions should adopt such inconsistent practice and that this anomaly should be officially recognised in our computerised system. The subsidiaries cannot understand us, and I believe that a firm ruling in favour of the 'first come, first served' approach should be made by John Hancock.

Regards,
Jim Heath

P.S. Ian Toole has just had sight of profit figures for the first quarter for Electric Motor Division and we are 10 per cent below target. Tommy Mullone, in production control, says that he is being starved of finished stock to take the shock out of the system. He cannot understand why we emasculate the levelling effect that long-term schedules should produce on a computerised system by running stocks so low. He says that we are now reacting and expediting as much as we were ten years ago under a manual system! Factory productivity has been steadily getting worse as lack of stock takes away our flexibility.

Memo 4

From: Bill Evans, Divisional Director, Electric Motor Division, Crawley
To: John Hancock, Managing Director, Crawley
Date: December, Year 2

Finished goods inventory control

I am feeling the discomfiture of the profit squeeze that Electric Motor Division has been exposed to over these last three years, and believe that we in marketing are not really in charge of our own house. As long as the finished goods inventory control system is operated from Glasgow our performance is controlled by the factory-oriented voices in Glasgow and the computer people who are trying to take the show over, and blind us with the elegant rules that they only understand, but which take no account of the commercial reality to which our salesmen are exposed. They have recently written to me to authorise another £200,000 of inventory to make their *factory* more efficient!

I feel completely impotent to act the referee between de Vries in Belgium and our own domestic customers in squabbles over who should get priority for our stock items.

We would be much happier to revert to the former practice when FGIC was done here, and we in marketing could concentrate on achieving sales goals independently from the factory. At that time Crawley had responsibility for UK sales only. The European subsidiaries developed their own relationship with the Glasgow factory, and we had no desire or opportunity to interfere. All other subsidiaries in the EC control directly their own FGIC, and I believe that now is the time to make the strategic decision to relocate the warehouse from Glasgow to Crawley.

I have had informal discussions with Albert Meany, our Director of Administration, and he is in full agreement over the feasibility of such a change. Indeed he recalled the ten-week strike just five years ago, when we temporarily conducted the FGIC function on our small Crawley computer, to keep our customers going in the face of closure at Glasgow. In my view it was a great pity that we did not then establish the emergency set-up as a permanent feature of our organisation structure.

Regards,
Bill Evans

Memo 5

From: John Hancock, Managing Director, Crawley
To: Kevin Ogilvy, General Factory Manager, Glasgow
Date: February, Year 3

Finished goods inventory control

A source of much friction in our UK organisation over the last two years has been the operation of our finished stock warehouse in Glasgow, and I propose its possible relocation to Crawley next year; the decision is to be made at the corporate planning conference next month. I would be grateful if you would brief those most affected by such a move and prepare papers shedding light on the business policy implications of such a reorganisation.

I would emphasise that I have an open mind on the issue and intend to make a decision on the objective business case presented at the planning conference. I regard the matter as of sufficient importance to allocate two days of conference time to this policy decision.

Regards,
John Hancock

Memo 6

From: Kevin Ogilvy, General Factory Manager, Glasgow
To: Jim Heath, Data Processing Manager
        Tommy Mullone, Production Control Manager
        Ian Toole, Customer Services Manager

Bili Yates, Production Manager Electric Motor Division
Alan Hughes, Production Manager Computer Peripherals Division
Sam Haddington, Forecasting Manager, Glasgow
Date: February, Year 3

Finished goods inventory control

Please refer to memo 5 from John Hancock. Please send me in writing your ideas within the next two weeks and attend a preliminary meeting in my office on 15 February to decide our response.

I am keen that Scottish factories help the Managing Director to make an informed decision and that the interest of the company as a whole remains uppermost in your minds. John does not suffer fools gladly, and with his management science enthusiasm and background he will expect a well-articulated presentation of business policy.

Regards,
Kevin Ogilvy

Memo 7

From: Albert Meany, Director of Administration, Crawley
To: Kevin Ogilvy, General Factory Manager, and list
Date: February, Year 3

Telephone bill Scottish factories £750,000

Bearing in mind that only 150 of your staff have authorised access to outside telephone lines the telephone account needs an in-depth investigation. I simply cannot understand how members of staff spend on average £5,000 a year each on company business. If we are indulging in that amount of inter-office conversation then something is sick about the entire organisation structure and the business policies which we operate. I have highlighted to John Hancock that we will devote at least a full morning at the corporate planning meeting next month to the problems of company communications, of which the telephone bill is merely a symptom.

I have always believed in a simple administrative structure and feel that much of our problem lies in the finished goods inventory control function being done at the factory instead of in its rightful place at the sales subsidiary. My colleagues in Brussels never stop saying that we British are out of line!

Furthermore, I am proposing to unite the two purchasing sections in the Glasgow factories under one office at Crawley. They will be much nearer most of our suppliers and if they operate as a single unit under a new manager our whole purchasing effort will have a greater impact.

Kind regards,
Albert Meany

P.S. We have booked the hotel in Crawley for our corporate planning conference, which was the site of the murders of John George Haig, the acid bath murderer of 1946. I hope that my decision does not have an unfortunate omen!

Memo 8
From: Tommy Mullone, Production Control Manager, Glasgow
To: Kevin Ogilvy, General Factory Manager
Date: February, Year 3

Finished goods inventory control

The idea of relocating the FGIC function to Crawley is absurd, and merely pandering to the empire-building twins, Bill Evans and Albert Meany. In no way does this proposition solve any of the business problems which we face as a company. In any event we shall still have to process export orders here and replenishment orders from Crawley. Instead of having one finished goods stock, we would have two. The finished goods stock left in the factory for the EC and for the levelling activity would be even less, so the factory would have to react even more than now. It really runs against the grain to consider that we spent thirty man/years setting up a highly-responsive computerised production control system only to find that through the influence of remote and naive marketing policy the system is run as though it were a shabby manual system. You are aware that all of Computer Peripheral Division business and 80 per cent of the line items of Electric Motor Division are traded on a 'make' basis, i.e. the assembly-line is only committed on receipt of order, owing to the risk involved in building stock when the item is unique to a particular customer. At the moment 'make' orders of course come to us direct from customers, whereas if FGIC were relocated at Crawley, 'make' orders would be further delayed in the Crawley mailing system, without any value being added before receipt by ourselves. We are concerned here about profit, but profit is influenced by cost, and if cost cannot be reduced by scheduling the factory with suitable commercial policies, then the profit squeeze is going to get tighter.

I appreciate that interest rates have increased substantially since the Thatcher Government took office, and that simply underlines that we cannot have stock controlled by other than experienced hands assisted by proven and powerful computerised systems. In the United States the manufacturing and sales operations are under the same roof, and this yields a considerable saving of overheads. No problems there with £750,000 telephone bills. Also I understand that the US experience of using the MRP routines was that they achieved a stock turnover ratio of twenty-eight times, two years after implementation; what a comparison with ourselves! My solution to our UK problems would be to close down Crawley as soon as possible and relocate their operations near us in Glasgow.

Kind regards,
Tommy Mullone

P.S. Jim Heath has read my draft and he will be writing to you supporting the strength of management feeling on this issue in Glasgow.

Memo 9

From: Jim Heath, Data Processing Manager, Glasgow
To: Kevin Ogilvy, General Factory Manager, Glasgow
Date: February, Year 3

FGIC preliminary discussions

This FGIC relocation issue is a really hot potato. Tommy Mullone's note to you was shared with me and although he writes good sense and with some good humour I would dearly love to see the reactions of Bill Evans and Albert Meany to his suggestion that they be relocated to Glasgow.

The real problem is that the relocation issue has become one of political ego and nothing whatever to do with the merits of its business policy background. The crucial facets are profitability and good customer service. Both of these objectives can only be achieved by directing and articulating objective information to impartial decision-makers, and the provision of an environment in which better business decisions are consistently made and implemented. The physical location of the warehouse is a red herring. It can operate satisfactorily either at Crawley or at Glasgow, providing that the policy rules of the processing system reflect good judgement and policy. I am only too willing to open all the rules locked in our computerised system and adjust them and reprogram them to incorporate the marketing orientation of Bill Evans and Charlie Smith. My only problem is to get those gentlemen to develop a meaningful dialogue about the relevant policy rules, and to persuade them that once they control these rules then they control the system. If that dialogue is achieved, and the system rules reflect their influence, allbeit exercised from a remote location, we have an answer to our dilemma.

I suggest that we save the £800,000 which it has been estimated would be involved in a relocation of FGIC to Crawley and in its place have monthly integrated workshop sessions to review FGIC policy rules. The workshops could rotate, one month in Glasgow, the following in Crawley. I am convinced that a regular exposure face-to-face of the marketing executives to factory executives would lift us out of the current atmosphere of mistrust. Indeed this would be the proper implementation of what some would call the corporate planning approach, working through the aegis of a corporate planning group.

Regards
Jim Heath

Memo 10

From: Sam Haddington, Forecasting Manager, Glasgow
To: Kevin Ogilvy, General Factory Manager
Date: February, Year 3

FGIC relocation

I am not impressed at the current state of play *vis-à-vis* the FGIC relocation issue. As Forecasting Manager I have much contact with both the subsidiary companies and also our UK marketing group at Crawley, and as such hope that I may be permitted to project a 'company' view. Every month on the computer system we track the forecast variance with actual sales. Consistently over the last three years the subs have been improving the quality of forecast data, but our UK colleagues have made no progress whatever. Much of our UK business is 'make', i.e. only a few customers order this particular line, and for this business I require the salesman to submit a field sales forecast. He is the only one who can possibly predict the ups and downs of this individualised customer business, yet I am fighting a losing battle in getting these forms filled in and submitted on time.

I believe that we should introduce a discount to customers whenever they give us firm orders with delivery dates outside our published lead-times. This should force salesmen to get to grips with the future ordering policy of their customers, and take much of the pressure off the factory in having to react so much. Without so many 'at once' orders much of the £750,000 telephone bill resulting from frustrating expediting activity and other unnecessary overheads would evaporate. On this suggestion I am not 'kite flying'. In the United States I noted that the Forecasting Manager had persuaded marketing to introduce a category in their appraisal system for salesmen of accuracy in completing field sales returns, and this had an immediate impact on forecast accuracy.

I cannot see that relocation of FGIC from Glasgow will improve the profitability situation in the United Kingdom. At the moment the business game is like a complicated game of chess, but many of the players are naive in their play. Our Chairman went on record when he was appointed as saying that we get the pencils in the right place, but we get the concrete in the wrong place. FGIC at Crawley would be a white elephant. We could much more profitably initiate what some academics label an organisation development programme to raise the level of our existing game.

Regards,
Sam Haddington

Memo 11

From: John Halliday, Manchester Sales Office
To: Charlie Smith, Divisional Director, Computer Peripherals Division, Crawley
Date: February, Year 3

Spares problem

I wish to highlight to you a recent rejection by a Manchester customer of £100,000 worth of equipment. We experienced failure of one of the standard packages on the day before the acceptance trials, and neither Crawley nor the factory could supply a replacement for ten days. I feel particularly sore about losing this order, which took no less than twenty calls over a six-month period, and gave the possibility of a further £200,000 worth of business, for lack of a package whose list price is £25. To add insult to injury, I discovered that the factory did have this package in stock but the production controller had allocated it to an Australian production shipment which was not due for delivery for a further two weeks.

Please help to make sure this never happens to me again!

Regards,
John Halliday

Memo 12

From: Charlie Peters, Scottish Area Sales Manager, Computer Peripherals Division, Glasgow Sales Office
To: Jim Heath, Data Processing Manager
Date: February, Year 3

In-house equipment for next year's budget

I am happy to serve you as an internal account! I am pleased that you should have taken me into your confidence about possible data processing strategies for the manufacturing facility in Scotland, and how these relate to decisions on the location of the finished inventory warehouse.

I feel that now is the time to explore creatively with you and your staff some equipment options in our current catalogue which are the most up-to-date technologically and which are selling well in the Scottish Region.

I appreciate that your group was a pioneer in developing the advanced planning and control system within the plant, and has a fine reputation in this respect, but being a pioneer is also a disadvantage as it may lock the user into out-of-date technology! Today's marketing thrust is directed at giving systems a retrieval capability in seconds for critical operating data, using real-time devices such as disks, communication networks and visual display units, i.e. a conversion from traditional data processing to a full use of information technology, and leading on to applications like electronic mail. This approach can bring together groups in an organisation that are physically many hundreds of miles apart. Effectively it gives the sales office a window into the plant; there is no need to send executives on aeroplanes on trouble-shooting missions or suffer the traumas of relocating warehouse sites! I feel that a constructive way forward this year would be to graft on to your existing systems points from which VDU access may be obtained, both for use within the plant facility and also in the sales offices. The cost of lines must be far cheaper than high telephone bills, and possible loss of business. The cost of a VDU network would be in the region of £30,000.

I will look forward to having further discussions with you on possible enhancements of your equipment for the coming year before the end of this month.

Regards,
Charlie

For feedback on this case study see Appendix 1, p. 543.

References

Ansoff, H.I. (1968), *Corporate Strategy*, Pelican Books.

Blake, R.R. and Mouton, J.S. (1969), *Building a Dynamic Corporation through Grid Organisation Development*, Addison-Wesley.

Burns, T. and Stalker, G.M. (1961), *The Management of Innovation*, Tavistock Books.

Caulkin, S. (1988), 'Britain's best factories', *Management Today*, September, pp. 58–80.

Drucker, P. (1954), *The Practice of Management*, Harper.

Goldsmith, W. and Clutterbuck, D. (1983), *The Winning Streak*, Penguin Books.

Lee, A. (1989), 'Paperless purchasing moves closer to reality', *Purchasing and Supply Management*, January, pp. 28–30.

Lorenz, C. (1984), 'Excellence takes a knock', *Financial Times*, 1 November.

Mill, J. (1989), 'Room at the top', *Computing*, 5 January, pp. 8–9.

Mintzberg, H. (1973) *The Nature of Managerial Work*, Harper & Row.

Peters, T.J. and Waterman, R.H. (1982), *In Search of Excellence. Lessons from America's best-run companies*, Harper & Row.

Townsend, R. (1970), *Up the Organisation*, Michael Joseph.

Twiss, B. (1983), *The Management of Technological Innovation*, Longman.

Appendix 1

Exercise and case study feedbacks

Exercise 1.1

1. The verbs are as follows:
   (a) From Fayol (1916): command, control, coordinate, forecast, plan, organise.
   (b) From Mayo (1933): motivate.
   (c) From Gullick (1939): staff, report, budget.
   (d) From Drucker (1954): delegate with objectives, innovate, market.
   (e) From Reddin (1968): lead, communicate, participate.
   (f) From Simon (1957), Lucey, (1981) and Davies (1970): systematise the flow of information, make decisions.
   Many management textbooks make individual management verbs the subject of chapters or major parts of the work.
2. The broad division is between 'line' and 'staff' functions. 'Line' functions are the core parts of the business directly responsible for activity and profit. In industrial companies these are normally production and marketing. 'Staff' are all other groups which support the 'line' groups. Prominent among these are: personnel, accounting, engineering, research and development, quality control, systems and legal.
   Many management textbooks follow this structure, concentrating on a single management function or sub-part of a function.
3. Management is an integration of the following disciplines: business policy, economics, accounting, behavioural science, organisation structures, personnel management, marketing management, statistics, business law, systems (or information technology).
   Many management textbooks follow this structure, often concentrating on a single academic discipline. The exception is business policy, which copes with a broader view and attempts integration itself. Business policy homes in on the

References cited in Appendix 1 are given in full at the end of the relevant chapter.

corporate planning process and the overall options of an organisation for policy and growth, and the difficult process of implementation.

4. Management is a study of how to develop useful skills, roles and techniques. What are they?

   (a) Mintzberg (1973) defines ten roles of the Chief Executive: figurehead, leader, liaison, monitor, disseminator, entrepreneur, spokesman, disturbance handler, resource allocator, negotiator.

   (b) Drucker (1954) defines the technique of managing by objectives.

   (c) Reddin (1968) defines leadership styles and offers organisation development programmes to improve organisations.

   (d) Belbin (1981) offers techniques of team selection and team development within the project team environment.

   (e) Lucey (1981) and others offer techniques for 'managing by exception' using computer aids.

   (f) Glueck (1976) outlines the corporate planning process.

Exercise 1.2

Possible responses to heresy 1

Sir John Toothill, Chief Executive, Ferranti 1974: 'Management development is a waste of time. Let managers be self-selecting.'

The statement was made at a time when training and development in the United Kingdom was mandatory through a levy grant system administered by Industrial Training Boards. It was possible to make a 'profit' from this activity by getting grants that exceeded the levy, and this gave rise to some abuse and waste, particularly where training needs had not been properly established. Ferranti had a grudge about the level of the levy and was satisfied with its 'home-grown' management development.

Ferranti is an atypical business organisation. Firstly, it employs a very high percentage of graduate engineers, so that there is a pool of talent from which its managers may grow. Secondly, its business is primarily 'high-tech' and typically managers are grouped in project teams organised around main contracts, often centred on defence. This tends to be a very exhilarating learning environment, in which one expert naturally learns from the others as they work closely together. Furthermore, the management style required in a project team tends to follow the expertise of the expert, allowing the leadership of the group to change according to the stage reached in the project. Leadership skills are thus highly visible and leadership selection is not a big problem as leadership opportunity is so readily available.

This is very different from that of a large 'line' organisation with many different levels in the hierarchy where 'status' and the command structure are more significant and the aspiring leader may find much more difficulty in obtaining a leadership opportunity.

In the project environment much management development will naturally take place on the job, and this is much to be commended. However, it does beg the question of whether Ferranti would have benefited from off-the-job conventional management development as well. Observers have criticised, for instance, financial management in the company — crises over excess profit-taking leading to repayments and a later cash-flow problem leading to government intervention. Defence contracts with a 'cost-plus' basis of development provide a privileged financial environment. Engineers are traditionally more interested in things than people and profit and that observation seems appropriate in the case of Ferranti.

The general sentiment expressed by Toothill is, however, completely contrary to the position of Peter Drucker (1954). Drucker states that management is a scarce resource, needing nurturing and nourishment. His view is that management is a set of knowledge areas, good habits and principles which can be learned. He rejects the notion that a manager or leader must be born into a particular class or have a particular set of personality traits. It is difficult now to reject the findings of several decades of developing management thought and the influence of the business schools. Clearly current wisdom is to encourage the further development of management courses in the West.

What is true, however, is that there is a wide variation in the management ambitions of different managers and that there is choice for deciding which talents or knowledge areas it would be most appropriate to develop. Which of Mintzberg's ten roles need to be strengthened for each manager in his or her current post? Could they be developed by on-the-job coaching, by career planning and job rotation, by external courses or by self-development and reading?

Possible response to heresy 2

Alistair Mant, *The Rise and Fall of the British Manager* (1978): 'The prime role of business is business at the sharp end. Management is incidental to this process; if emphasised it creates barriers, class systems and privileges, "us and them" attitudes with a vengeance.'

Alistair Mant is an erstwhile teacher of management development and this experience was a disappointment to him. The view he had of British industry was one of class barriers, manifested in different canteens for different levels of management, much abuse of 'fringe benefits' and 'slush funds' for senior management, different hours of work, holidays and pensions, and bonus earnings. His view was that this caused resentment and confrontation and led to industrial decline in Britain.

The ideal he put up in its place was Japanese style management, with the emphasis on sharing the problems of management at the sharp end. He described a Japanese manager arriving in the morning at the same time as the workforce and with his office in the middle of the shop-floor and a philosophy of 'open access' at all times. Under this style managers could develop a direct involvement and empathy with all in the plant, and constructive use could be made of the informal contact between managers and workers.

Other extensions of this approach are the development of quality circles to widen the involvement of all levels of staff in the improvements of product quality and customer service.

In view of this the question arises whether Mant's opinion was in fact a heresy.

Firstly, his statement about class in Britain is a generalisation. In some industries and localities it is true, but to suggest that the whole of British industry is like this does many companies an injustice.

Secondly, he assumes that a 'class'-oriented business culture is necessarily always wrong and rejected by others in the industry. It is arguable that the morality of 'class' is wrong, but there are still many firms, particularly in the financial world, with signal success over long periods, in which class divisions are integral to the company culture and are accepted as such by the employees.

When observing an organisation it is necessary to be aware of the culture of that organisation, as this is a hidden force which induces in people a state of expectancy of acceptable behaviour. People may be uncomfortable at attempts to change that culture, perceiving this as an attack on their values. This calls to mind the earlier discussion of the management components of the 'amateur gardener', whose motive was not profit, but pleasure.

In thinking through Alistair Mant's 'heresy' a sensible conclusion seems to be that management values and the management process do not exist in a pure form with universal application. They are inevitably conditional upon the environment, culture and ethos of the nation and of the organisation.

Case Study 3.2   Sykes Industries

Building business pictures

1. Sykes is the owner/founder of the firm. What about succession?
2. Fifty years of growth from engineering base into construction, demolition, transport and toy-making.
3. Two transport sections — one operating in the United Kingdom, the other operating trans-Europe.
4. Engineering interests closely connected with defence industry.
5. Paternalistic management style. Sykes group run by five general managers. Not much evidence of in-depth staffing at the top of the organisation, even though it is diversified.
6. Management resentment at frequent unannounced visits to plants by Sykes to 'keep them on their toes'.
7. Business ventures being done on whims of Sykes without formal business justification (toys).
8. Corporate planning undertaken independently by general managers, with no legitimate coordination from the centre.
9. Sykes' personal staff keep him in the dark about developments.

10. Sykes has well-developed relationship with the ex-head of a nationalised firm and is making overtures to him about becoming his successor.
11. Sykes is 73 and soon to retire in any event.
12. Four immediate problems are:
    (a) Death of Sykes, the owner/founder, before succession plans had been completed.
    (b) Sykes Trucks denied permits through Austria and Germany. Future viability of this operation is in question.
    (c) Construction company's bridge collapses. Questions arise about contract damages, insurance cover, damage to commercial reputation, potential cash-flow crisis.
    (d) Threatened strike in UK transport depots. Has the company the financial reserves to ride this out? Is management ready to cope with this situation?

Analysis
1. Starting from the four recognised problems develop a PEST analysis and SWOT analysis.
2. As the owner/founder's death is a watershed, there will be a need to think through possible future structures and objectives.

Succession crisis problem

Short-term action on the other pressing problems in the case study will not be effective in an environment of anarchy and clearly any long-term objectives or strategy for Sykes must depend on the proper solution of the succession crisis.

The key to this analysis is to take account of *shareholder power*. Who owns the majority shareholding? A look at the company share register and at Sykes' will are the essential starting points. It may be expected that Sykes himself has the majority shareholding but estate duty will be levied and the liquidation process needed to raise money to pay the estate duty will probably mean that the company has to 'go public', i.e. seek a quotation on the London Stock Exchange.

Meanwhile, whatever status the company has it should be possible for leading shareholders to call an extraordinary general meeting to elect a chairman to oversee this process.

The general managers of the company and the friend of Sykes who was head of a nationalised industry will not get a look in unless they can gain the support of majority shareholders. The existing board may elect an interim chairman, but that choice will soon be overtaken by the outcome of an extraordinary general meeting.

What vision for the future?

If the firm goes public then the following main options regarding structure arise:

1. Set up as a consolidated holding company in which the units are separate legal entities wholly owned from the centre.

2. Set up as a single company structure. It is more difficult to liquidate separate units should some liquidation be necessary.
3. Liquidate altogether and raise money for reinvestment and satisfaction of tax demands.

The most likely option is 1. The separate units may be managed as separate business portfolios, with the strong businesses supported and the weak ones sold off.

The following programme of events may be expected
1. Interim chairman elected by existing board.
2. *Ad hoc* action on three of the immediate problems above.
3. Get Sykes' will and the company share register.
4. Notice for extraordinary general meeting to elect new chairman from new shareholders.
5. Set up corporate planning group to decide and develop company business.
6. Develop policy and legal structure for the group as a whole and prepare if necessary to go public or sell off part of the business to satisfy estate duty demands.
7. Get corporate planning team to gather data from which the group can be run as a business portfolio and set up divisional planning groups.
8. Recruit or promote managers to develop competent management teams.
9. Direct attention back over the three problems highlighted earlier and develop long-term responses using PEST analysis and SWOT analysis to bring issues into a fine relief.
10. Adjust overall company organisation to fit new legal structure and revised set of business policies moulded by the corporate planning teams.

Note: a more detailed analysis could be done under 9, but more information is really required.

Case Study 3.3   Peter Dunn Tyres

Business pictures

1. Peter Dunn has stockpile of 700,000 tyres. These are finished goods and represent seven months' supply.
2. An immediate lay-off for two weeks of all 500 employees of four-shift working.
3. Other component manufacturers had planned for short-time working for next six months.
4. The major customer (British Leyland) has announced it is cutting UK-sourced supplies by 8 per cent because of availability of cheaper foreign components; prices are up to 33 per cent lower.
5. Other Peter Dunn plants in Ireland and England are similarly affected by weak market.

6. Major feature of motor trade is high seasonal peak in the month of August coinciding with new registration letter.
7. Major customer (BL) is utterly indifferent to long-standing vendors, e.g. the brake drum manufacturer of twenty years' relationship.
8. Peter Dunn's own forecasting system is now regarded as optimistic, yet only a few weeks before the Director of Tyres stated that production and demand were in step.
9. Peter Dunn has three plants dedicated to the supply of BL. Have they no other customers?

PEST analysis

Political factors

BL, the major customer, is publicly owned by the Government and thus some of its business policies may be affected by short-term pressures to attain particular profit figures in preparation for being privatised. After privatisation, policies towards vendors may change.

There are no tariffs with EC countries and the impact of recession may mean that foreign component manufacturers effectively dump their surplus on the UK market, undercutting UK component suppliers.

Economic factors

Finance of seven months' finished stock could be crippling for Peter Dunn and there is a severe threat of erosion of margins. With short-time working overheads will contribute to increasing cost.

Social factors

Unanticipated short-time working is very unsettling for a labour force which does expect a continuity of employment. This could give rise to a loss of employee goodwill and possible strike action.

Technological factors

New technology may reduce the costs of tyre manufacture but this is only likely in the long term and is dependent on a strong research and development presence in Peter Dunn. No data are given here.

SWOT analysis

Strengths

PD has an established position as a volume producer for a sophisticated product.

PD has a flexible labour position with four continuously operating shifts.

Labour shedding is possible without redundancy payments where less than one year's continuous service is completed.

Weaknesses

Finance: Cash flow is likely to be under severe threat owing to excess stock position and poor demand for the next few months.

Marketing: The immediate threat is to market share and to sales margins. There is a great need to develop alternative markets and reduce dependence on the single customer (BL).

Systems: Sales forecasting seems to be deplorable in an industry in which a lead/lag relationship is possible which should give at least a month's warning. Production planning and stock control are significantly affected by the poor forecasting system. PD's corporate planning appears weak.

Opportunities

The company could use the modern production facilities as a basis for producing for new markets and possibly new products. What about becoming a vendor to Japanese manufacturers who are planning a UK manufacturing base? What about trying to develop the replacement market (through such chains as Kwikfit)?

The present cash-flow crisis position could be used to justify severe pruning of overheads (generally a healthy exercise after a period of producing at high volumes).

Threats

The main threats are to financial viability over the next six months until the stock position is brought under control, and also loss of the main BL market and market share. Labour could also be a threat unless cutbacks are sensitively handled.

Case Study 5.1 On target

Responses to the questions are as follows:

1. From the text it looks as though the Chairman 'plucked out of the air' the original target of 100 tons per man per week. He was committed through and through to its substance as he had made statements to shareholders promising his company that level of productivity in justification of the £1 million expansion scheme. There is the possibility that the figure was gleaned from a passage within a feasibility study report giving an informed view, but the impression given is that he is not a bit concerned about the practicalities of the implementation of this target. He is prepared to pick an enthusiastic young manager, Bullock, and brief him without the presence of the line manager responsible for this depot, the Regional Manager.

   This management style looks much as though it is simply management by instruction, with no account given of expectancy or consultation.

2. The text suggests that Hooker has been a supervisor since the war, for over twenty years. As the incident in this case develops there are conflicting ideas

over his competence as a supervisor, but his immediate manager, the Regional Manager, does not seem to want to remove him from supervision. The impression given by the AGM is that his opinion of Hooker is a subjective one, not substantiated by regular appraisal reports from the Regional Manager. Under MbO principles people expect to be judged by the extent to which they achieve expected results. Under this regime it looks as though supervisors are judged by whether they are liked or not, and grudges are allowed to influence the situation — a most unhealthy procedure. Under MbO principles, using the 'appraisal process', Hooker should at least have been exposed over twenty years to twenty snapshots on his promotability, some eighty snapshots (quarterly) focusing on management development issues, and 240 monthly progress reviews! It is amazing, if he is incompetent, that nothing has been done on all these occasions to remedy the problem.

3. This raises the question of whether Hooker's competence is an issue of prime interest to the AGM or to the Regional Manager. Under principles of delegation and line management Hooker's situation is of concern to his immediate manager, Bullock, and as Bullock is a new appointee, to the Regional Manager. Hence, the AGM's attention should be confined to company reports about the depot and direct reports from the Regional Manager. The AGM should not have a direct role with Hooker at all. Senior managers such as the AGM will need to see that objective-setting sessions and the appraisal process is properly conducted and resourced. If, for instance, a supervisor is performing poorly, and his own manager wishes him to undergo a remedial programme, then that should be reported and resources made available to implement such a programme. Under MbO principles, problems of competence will still arise but they should be resolved much more quickly.

4. The text suggests that the Regional Manager thought that 100 tons per man per week was unrealistic and that 80 tons was possible. However, the expectation is that he should resolve the conflict as soon as he is aware that conflict exists. He might well complain to Head Office for not being involved in Bullock's briefing session, and it is up to him to make every attempt to get the conflict resolved by better communication or new thinking. For instance, some of the assumptions behind the productivity target might relate to contingency factors such as the volume of trade, and revision might be appropriate in the light of current developments. Policy about the size of the labouring establishment at the depot might be influenced by many other considerations apart from short-term productivity figures. Otherwise it looks as though the Regional Manager is being used as an expensive doormat and there is no role for him. If management really thinks that the position of Regional Manager is superfluous then a reorganisation should take place and the structure should be simplified.

The present situation for Bullock is unacceptable. On the one hand, he has a brief to do all in his power to get 100 tons or fear displeasure from the AGM and GM; at the same time, if he exceeds 80 tons, he is likely to put himself in an embarrassing light with his immediate superior, the Regional Manager. The conflict above him puts him into a lose/lose situation.

5. The first contacts in people relationships are often the most important. Bullock made no early communication with Hooker about objectives. Perhaps he had been influenced by the AGM's comments that it would be a good idea to get rid of Hooker as soon as possible. Hooker was left to interpret his own objectives by reading the events. Men left and were not replaced, and Hooker, right in the front line, had had no say at all in the targets, hence he felt some resentment. Yet in MbO we are always looking for this mutual framework of *expectations* coming from discussing and sharing of objectives. From this basis sound relationships of leadership and good teamwork can develop, but if resentment is allowed to fester there will be bad relationships and a lowering of morale.

6. This is really a trick question! How will Hooker's perception of the overall objectives be articulated? By experience he will be aware of effectiveness standards concerning requirements to make timely deliveries and he will know how to meet the needs and expectations of his crew of twelve men. As far as productivity figures for his immediate manager are concerned, he is simply kept in the dark. He could well believe that he is taking proper account of the stakeholders as he sees and understands them.

7. Certainly the situation regarding productivity did not improve, even after a change of supervisor, so the squeeze evidently did fail. However, it showed every prospect of failure in its inception. Productivity figures were not being achieved because there was some lack of resource at the lowest level in the depot. Yet an important resource is always the conceptual one of 'authority' to deal with the situation and with any exceptions and difficulties as they arise. That is why supervisors are appointed. Yet we see Hooker's authority greatly restricted under squeeze conditions. He must refer every difficulty to Bullock for a ruling, but Bullock often cannot be found so difficulties fester and productivity worsens. Hooker loses face with the men, who will be aware of his need to refer up decisions he previously took himself. This MbO principle about the need to balance authority and responsibility is a very real one. Hooker needs authority and expertise if he is to succeed in improving productivity.

8. Without some new thinking in this situation any progress is unlikely. Both Supervisor and Depot Manager have entrenched positions. There is, however, always the possibility that a new and creative approach could yield a movement. We might with benefit call in an outside expert or group, possibly with work-study experience, to examine afresh the group work at the depot and the new equipment installed with the £1 million investment programme. This should activate a real problem-solving environment in which new ways could be tried out and evaluated, and possible improvements implemented. At least

such a step should repair worsening labour relations, for if these are not repaired there is a serious threat to the continuity of the whole depot and its investment.

Summary

The case study reflects a simple company situation, but throws up the real difficulties of securing improvements in a non-MbO environment.

1. The line management structure is by-passed and weakened.
2. A £1 million improvement and expansion programme is authorised before realistic productivity improvements have been assessed and validated by those with implementation responsibility.
3. Performance data about a supervisor are most unreliable despite his having been promoted twenty years previously. The organisation does not seem to know how to recognise and manage systematically problems of competence.
4. The communication system between head office and depot became so distorted that a serious labour relations problem arose, which should have been avoided.
5. Managerial control is tightened, but at the wrong level, so actual control is weakened.

In an MbO environment none of the above five problems could have gathered any serious momentum. However, the reader may appreciate that MbO principles may not be easy to implement if they are distinctly different to the style and culture of the existing management team.

Case Study 6.1   Interview 1

Job role of the sales manager — was there a mutual agreement on what this role was?

From the text one really wonders what contact there had ever been between Lansing and Fisher. They each see the job in an entirely different perspective and had never tested one another out to ensure that they were on the same wavelength! Lansing is ultra-conservative. He wants the sales management job done in exactly the same way as it had been previously done, cultivating the customers who were his personal friends. When these buddies get on to him to complain about his Sales Manager, and he does not even know about the change in calling sequence, he loses face and that is very painful!

Fisher is the new broom who wants to change everything. He has utter contempt for Lansing. He analyses the sales work and finds that the growth business is in new areas with big new accounts, which have developed with new products. But he has never communicated this business appreciation to Lansing; he simply implements new methods on his own.

Some form of mutual objective-setting could hardly have failed to have brought out this difference in orientation, and from that openness it should have been possible to get a movement in the policies of the job. But objective-setting and feedback should take place regularly, at least once a month on the operating figures and performance trends!

Fisher's perceptions of his authority — did this match Lansing's?

Fisher's view is clear. He thinks that he has full authority and responsibility for the *whole* job of Sales Manager. Lansing's view is that he has authority and responsibility for the operational aspects of the job, but no licence to change the style and structure of the job without consultation — this includes the sales policies, calling sequences, identification of priorities and overall allocation of resources to the sales function.

The key aspect of the phase of *job clarification* involves breaking down the work into functions (spheres of activity) and defining the authority level for each main responsibility area. Job clarification is an utterly meaningless exercise unless the 'C' levels of authority, the policy areas, are recognised and mutually discussed and agreed. In the absence of discussion and agreement particularly on the sensitive 'C' level points, a bad relationship is almost bound to develop. In this case the relationship was so bad it was broken altogether, and Lansing set to seek out a new Sales Manager.

Salesmen who left after expenses were disqualified — was this Fisher's fault?

In the text Fisher complained that his salesmen were encouraged to join the competition, after the Controller, Evans, had disqualified their expenses. Under the normal principles of line management it might have been expected that the Controller would have drawn Fisher's attention to this problem and it would have been up to Fisher to take the appropriate action. It is unusual for the Controller, a staff manager, to assume a line management role with another manager's staff. It looks as though in this company Evans is 'well in' with Lansing, a life-long friend, and is prepared to use his special influence. However, if Fisher has any communication skill whatever, he should be sensitive to what is happening and be prepared to make a case for more generous treatment of his salesforce, if indeed salary compensation and expenses are worse than what the competition offer. He could make such a case to the Controller, Evans, or if need be direct to Lansing. But Fisher does not manage this policy issue at all. He just accepts the situation and bears a grudge against Evans. As a manager Fisher has no idea about the recognition of policy issues or how to manage them.

Lansing, however, does not realise that it is his responsibility too to secure sound terms of reference for his key subordinates. Once he is out of the dominant owner/founder situation, the new president will need to get mileage out of his management team. Lansing should be prepared to rethink policies in the light of change and opportunity. He should be encouraging Fisher to bring new thinking and new proposals to him, although in important policy matters he will naturally want to reserve the right to approve. However, the temperature in a relationship is much hotter if there is a *fait accompli* presented by a junior manager than would have been the case if there was a disagreement in consultation over a policy issue. The junior manager might have another chance to be persuasive and get his way!

Case Study 6.1   Interview 2

How does Mathis see his managerial role and discharge it?

Certainly he does not enjoy the management role. He hardly ever gets home. The dog barks at him as though he were a stranger! He has no time. Drucker chides him for wanting a special calendar. This implies that he finds delegation a real difficulty. From the beginning of the case study it was obvious that he has great problems with quantifying the resources needed and then making a case to get them. Like Fisher, he is not particularly good at making a case to higher-level management, but without resources a department can become ineffective. Perhaps this is partly due to the influence of Evans, the Controller.

However the boffin orientation is very strong in Mathis. He came from the research bench, where he was remarkably successful, and still hankers over four research projects that he now no longer has time to get to. Instead, he is double promoted with responsibility for both research and quality control, two entirely different business functions. One would need an exceptional manager to be able to cope with both. Yet here he is managing quality control for which he has no background and it is this part of the job which is a real headache to him. At the end of the sequence he is considering his future position; the implication is that he will leave Hudson-Lansing.

However, the company can hardly be satisfied with Mathis. The quality control is under-resourced and poorly organised, and initiatives in research have not been followed up. Something does need to change!

What are his training needs? How should they have been detected?

Mathis lacks some rather basic management skills. His ability to communicate needs much improvement. He needs to know how to quantify resources for his department and communicate a case to secure such resources. He needs to build up a management team so that much of the work can then be delegated. He needs to develop skills in objective-setting and reviewing progress so that he can get mileage out of the research scientists. At the moment he does not know how to tell them what to do, because he is so used to doing research himself and experimenting until he comes up with a lead, etc. He needs to know how to recognise priorities and build a programme of action to put them into effect.

All these management weaknesses are very easy to recognise given a dialogue with Mathis. The MbO appraisal process provides opportunities at three distinct stages: monthly reporting on assignments, quarterly in management development discussions and annually in determining a promotion decision. In the text much of the information on training needs came from Mathis's own self-appraisal. If the process is properly managed these training needs cannot fail to emerge.

If Hudson-Lansing had any MbO principles in operation, and had been able to interpret data coming from the appraisals, it is most unlikely that they would have taken the risk of giving Mathis a double promotion to head up both the research and quality control functions.

If the job is too big for Mathis how could it be redesigned?
The obvious option is to split it into two functions each under a separate manager. One for research, the other for quality control. Both functions seem big enough and important enough to be viable on their own.

Should Mathis be a target for management development?
When we look at Mathis's training needs there is a question mark over whether he wants to manage at all. Yet if we think through the skills needed for a super boffin in the research lab it is difficult not to conclude that teamwork is an essential ingredient of effective research. If we demoted Mathis to the bench without some exposure to training in teamwork and communication we would not get the full potential out of him and, as he is reputed to be the best bench scientist in the industry, it would be most annoying if he joined the competition. Hudson-Lansing has an interest in retaining him and getting the best from his boffinry! Most observers suggest that the type of training needs which we have identified for Mathis are treatable. If he is given a supervisory role in research and a management development programme there is every likelihood that appraisal results in a year's time may indicate that Mathis is ready to take on full managerial responsibility for the Research function. At the moment he is not comfortable in that role and cannot continue as manager. It would seem that Mathis at the moment is still much more of a boffin than a manager. But nearly everyone has the potential of management skill. In a few years' time and given some management success Mathis will want to manage well. It still seems unlikely that he would want to be a general manager, but there is no reason why he could not become a competent head of department.

Case Study 6.1   Interview 3

What are the key roles of a financial controller?
The full answer will be found by examining the syllabuses of courses in finance and accountancy. However, a simple answer would be as follows:

1. A book-keeping, controlling role in which all the financial records are kept straight.
2. An advisory role in relation to major management decisions and the application

of good practice financial techniques, such as discounted cash flow, use of spreadsheets with relevant financial information, development of costing and budgeting systems and interpretation of results.

3. A specialist advisory role on matters such as tax.
4. A management role in relation to the company cash-flow, financial capital structure and financial resources.

Does Evans do well in all or some of these roles?

On the evidence from the text he seems to excel at both the specialist tax role and the book-keeping control role, but he does not exactly distinguish himself on the other two main roles. He is so over-zealous in the book-keeping role, it is clear that he would be a nuisance in any new venture requiring large expenditure. His attitude to people, particularly young people, is hardly objective, and this must diminish the value of any form of financial advice he gives to senior management.

He has been with the company some thirty-four years, and it is amazing that he has been in such high office for so long with such significant role weaknesses.

Evans's role competence — when and how is it assessed? How should deviations be managed?

There is no reason why Evans should not be subject to the normal appraisal process defined in this chapter. That gives a maximum of seventeen snapshots per annum, and some 587 in a thirty-four-year career! When deviations are detected then it is up to those conducting the review to work at remedial action and be prepared to resource it or move the executive to a less demanding position. If, however, the appraisal process data is carefully interpreted, the two blind spots, which Evans himself identified, would probably have disqualified him from ever reaching the top position in the first place. But to survive all those years with these two gaping holes and no serious attempt at treatment is incredible!

Would the appraisal process be appropriate?

The more senior the executive the more important it is that the appraisal process is operated, as the consequences of incompetence in high places is devastating.

Who would play the third party role?

Evans's superior, Lansing, does not have another colleague of his own status to play a third party role in the annual promotion decision or the quarterly management development sessions, so the choice is likely to narrow down to a third party from Evans's own peer group, i.e. Mathis or Fisher. This indeed would be a very healthy development as both Mathis and Fisher would probably bring up the important business issues resulting from Evans's blind spots and not rest easily until there were some treatment!

Who did play the third party role?

In the text it looks as though there was no on-going appraisal process of any kind in Hudson-Lansing. That is a key reason why they have such people problems which fester and then get right out of control! However, Drucker himself, as the External Consultant, does a quick and effective assessment of Evans and the outcome is inevitable. Evans must leave.

If there had been an appraisal scheme working in Hudson-Lansing, it would have had no effect whatever without a third party present to create the necessary problem-solving environment for the resolution of the difficult issues of these two key blind spots. Lansing and Evans had known one another for so long as close friends, two-party appraisal would have been no more than a ritual, a mutual admiration session. The blind-spot issues would not have come out in the open and they would not have been treated.

Case Study 6.2   The *Service Manual*

Responses to the issues for discussion are as follows:

1. There is generally a wide variety of opinions expressed on this question, with a tendency to indulge the non-performance in year 1 through interference from McKay, and some confusion over the priority that the *Service Manual* was given. If this is your own view, then you have fallen nicely into the trap set up for you!

Jim Marshall has been appointed National Service Manager precisely because the rules and policies concerning service are poorly understood and are certainly not being implemented. With the benefit of hindsight it can be seen that the absence of an implemented *Service Manual* has seriously compromised the viability of the service organisation and the inference is that the profitability of the unit must have been much eroded, with a serious knock-on effect on the parent organisation.

Jim Marshall is a senior manager and thus decisions on priorities for completion must lie primarily with him. He is in the hot seat and should know what the implications are far more clearly than McKay, so the 'law of the situation' suggests strongly that the *Service Manual* project cannot have any other than first priority till it is completed.

But Marshall has a background in the branches in a line management capacity. An assumption is that he has had no previous experience in a staff role and that it is a really painful transposition to get that staff perspective. As this is such a difficult perspective to develop it is convenient to indulge himself with some escapism and to continue to do his old job, conveniently ignoring his new job, with some encouragement from McKay.

The cardinal mistake is to perceive the *Service Manual* as a personal *doing* job. If Marshall called all the shots himself, and from Head Office imposed an elaborate manual on the branches, it is most likely that there would be a very adverse reaction. The integrity of the manual, its comprehensiveness and the prospects of its implementation, would all have been much in doubt. The manual is in fact a policy document.

In the text there were offers of help from the branches, but Marshall was much too slow to follow up this line and he never conceived himself in an editorial role. Given a much more mature, 'systems' approach, there is every prospect that the *Service Manual* assignment would have been completed in the first year. A possible programme might have been as follows:

First quarter: Construct the structure of the manual in terms of the headings, which reflect the effectiveness standards of acceptable service. Circulate to all service branches and other staff managers, including the Accounting Manager, a copy of the outlines with an accompanying questionnaire designed to seek out ideas on good practice in all the areas of concern in branches and request *help*. These should include measures of activity, of customer waiting time for service and profitability measures.

Second quarter: Edit the material coming from branches and other staff managers, reconcile differences wherever possible by face-to-face discussion or negotiation, to get a good first draft document.

Third quarter: Call a conference of Service Managers and other interested staff managers and invite them to approve the document. If there are any problems or impractical points, these are likely to be highlighted. It becomes the document of Service Managers for Service Managers, and this act of validation will clear the way to its acceptance and implementation.

Fourth quarter: Distribute the validated policy manual with implementation guidelines and a monitoring process. Visit branches to get a first-hand view of the manual in action. Set up a revision process to take account of service developments and any changes to company policy.

2. Some discussion of this will have been included in a response to Question 1. However, if in that response the argument was for year 1, together with a plan of action for getting there, we must still look into the text material for other reasons for the delay. The predominant reason was because Marshall, in conjunction with McKay, never saw fit to give the project an appropriately high priority, and Marshall, not having a staff management background, did not know how to tackle such an assignment. In an ideal situation he might have expected more advice and support from McKay, instead of misdirection and interference. There is no reason whatever for getting Marshall involved with the negotiation of a union contract. Although Marshall may have the line management background of the branches and a familiarity with that sort of work, why doesn't the Personnel Director keep with that assignment? If Marshall becomes a prop for Carr, then Carr will never get on top of union negotiations.

If we examine further the objectives and extra assignments Marshall undertakes, one really wonders whether he has actually assumed the responsibilities of the National Service Manager. He certainly has difficulty in keeping his eye on the ball; he and McKay could go over a job clarification process, but this does not seem to happen. There is very little conscious mutual planning done between the two. The impression is that Marshall simply accepts a list of instructions passed on to him by memo by McKay. Where are the vital face-to-face discussions relating to both objective setting and appraisal?

3. Many people initially think that much of the appraisal was fair to Marshall, in the circumstances, but readers who really think that the appraisal process, in this sequence, was effective have fallen headlong into another trap!

Firstly, there was no evidence of interaction between Marshall and McKay, save two written reports which are then filed. This is purely ritualistic. At the end of the first year there was no problem-solving posture adopted to ensure the completion of the *Service Manual*, or to probe around the fundamental reasons for failure. There was no real recognition of the existence of a serious training problem with Marshall and no attempt to get on top of this. A complete whitewash was followed a year later by another whitewash, and recommendations for Marshall's promotion to bigger things! Yet the main role he was to accomplish was still nowhere near completion, and there was much anguish expressed throughout the organisation about non-delivery of the manual.

We are dealing with a very half-hearted attempt at implementing MbO principles, a manifestation of which is a weak and ritualistic two-party process performed just once a year. What we need is a much more frequent interaction and the insertion of a third party to get to a problem-solving posture and shake Marshall out of his complacency. McKay, who may be expected to have appointed Marshall, perhaps finds it very difficult to adopt this problem-solving posture on his own, as if he finds fault with Marshall he is by implication criticising his own judgement for the appointment. Furthermore, we find that much of Marshall's difficulty is accounted for by McKay's own interference. Is he going to admit that one easily? Yet if the Sales Director, White, is put in as third party in the appraisal process for Marshall, the real problems and possibilities for their solution will be most readily on the agenda. White even volunteered himself in this role, but it looks as though the offer was not accepted.

It is most unlikely that Marshall is ready for better things, certainly not in a staff capacity, without full staff training and coaching in a junior staff job. If he aspires to go to better things, then he should be moved back to a line management position where his existing talents can be developed, but not to senior management. Senior managers need a better achievement record both in line and staff positions.

4. Paul McKay seems to have an organisation on charts only! As soon as he has any problem he rings up his buddies and gets them on to the scene. But managers do need roles and must take accountability for fulfilling them. If others come in and work outside their own roles, on the basis of contact and goodwill, interfering in the work of other colleague managers, they might succeed in a crisis-holding operation, but long-term solutions are much less likely. Paul McKay's style might work in a small family business, where contact and goodwill are at a premium, but once an organisation grows then it is much more important to appoint and develop a strong executive team. The very ingredients of this are the framing of organisation structures around the key result areas of the business, and the appointment of executives who can contribute to these key result areas from these structures, and accept accountability regularly through the appraisal process. Where difficulties arise extra resources or training processes need

putting into place. It is no good accepting non-performance indefinitely unless you want to go out of business.

There was also much confusion over the interpretation of priority ratings in this case. You cannot really express importance by the method adopted here. It is much better to control priority by attaching completion dates to assignments and then revising these regularly in light of current circumstances. This is much more flexible.

Case Study 7.1   Miss Clark

Responses to the issues for discussion are as follows:

Miss Clark

1. Miss Clark seems to have been very upset by the manner in which Mrs Cook made the purchase decision of the new machinery, supposedly over her head. She had not long been a supervisor, and was clearly sensitive about the level of trust and authority she could expect to have placed in her own judgement. She already exercised unfettered authority for purchase of consumable materials, and assumed that authority to purchase capital equipment would also be hers. However, in the purchase of capital equipment many areas of policy are inevitably involved — compatibility of equipment within the organisation, service and maintenance contracts, training and installation programmes, bulk buying and budgeting policy.

It looks as though there were serious misunderstandings between Miss Clark and Mrs Cook over the role of supervisor, and this should have been clarified by giving greater attention to the definition of all 'C' (policy) areas of authority as she grew into the new promoted job.

Mrs Cook failed to interpret the behaviour of Miss Clark, when she showed lack of interest in the discussions with Holmes. With some sensitivity at that time she may have been able to retrieve the deteriorating personal relationship with her.

2. Miss Clark adopted the view that as the machines were supposedly so good there would be no need for much training. She also wished to distance herself from the purchasing decision of Mrs Cook, and with some rationalisation she decided that she would play down the importance of this particular machinery and the work of installing it to acceptable standards of quality and productivity. She thus delegated the task of attending the demonstration and training to her assistant, Mrs Reilly, but in such a manner as to suggest a lack of commitment and enthusiasm. The signal received by Mrs Reilly was that she should not waste her time on this.

Miss Clark misjudged the likely implications of adopting new machinery, thinking that there were only technical implications. This implies that she was not really on top of new developments in this field — a training need of her own.

She seemed also to be suffering from time pressures and some stress, a typical problem with a newly-promoted supervisor. Perhaps she was genuinely understaffed and had previously had conflict with Mrs Cook over this issue, and was now keen to prove her point, as indeed attending demonstrations and training can be very trying when a group is already fully committed in its workload.

However, this lack of enthusiasm for the new machinery, and the manner of transmission (delegation), is reflected at all lower levels in the organisation, with devastating effect. From Mrs Reilly's viewpoint, if the machinery fails Miss Clark will be delighted, though she will still receive some complaints from the typing pool customers. If the new machinery is a success then by implication Miss Clark, her own superior, will still not be pleased owing to her prophecy of doom, although in this case the customers will be happy. For Mrs Reilly to be comfortable, both her own superior and the customers need to be satisfied, and she also needs to maintain the morale of the group of staff. But until the principles of delegation have been competently applied Mrs Reilly will be in a 'catch-22' situation.

3. We have already referred to the motivational problems of Miss Clark. Vetti has installed the machinery and given instructions about the settings of it, and this training has not been enforced by the typing pool. Such an act of omission has caused problems of quality, turnaround time and morale, and Miss Clark is the line manager responsible. Her action was clearly effective in sabotaging the efforts of Holmes and Yates, and the manifestation of her instructions could be construed as a deliberate attempt to work off her grudge against Mrs Cook.

The staff

The customers want the machines to work to specification. Mrs Reilly wants the machines to fail to please Miss Clark, who never wanted new machines at all. The staff cannot at the same time satisfy both their customers and their own immediate supervisor, Mrs Reilly.

Mrs Cook

1. We have already suggested that Mrs Cook should have been aware of the sensitive nature of the issue of authority, particularly 'C' level policy items for a newly-promoted supervisor, and she should have communicated much more fluently with Miss Clark before the machine purchase decision became such a hot issue. With better face-to-face contact with her at that stage, she could have coaxed her into a more positive role before the decision to purchase Vetti equipment had been finalised. In developing her own delegation strategy Mrs Cook failed to read the clues in the responses coming from Miss Clark and to take action quickly enough. She does not seem to have ever discussed with Miss Clark her own delegation style and the tactics which she should use with her own subordinates. If Mrs Cook had had an effective dialogue with Miss Clark on this issue then it would have been much easier to interpret and deal with the rapidly deteriorating situation with the machines.

2. Mrs Cook ends up in the typical dilemma of needing to reconcile 'task' demands and 'people' demands at the same time. Under the 'task' requirements, she would like to protect the investment in the new Vetti equipment. Public money has been spent for which she is accountable; she would like to get productivity, turnaround service times and other customer service good practice norms quickly established.

Under people demands she would want to see a way of re-establishing morale in the typing pool, and consolidating the experience and service of Miss Clark and her continued future as a supervisor.

One solution would be to write off the new machines, and return to the previous familiar work pattern in the typing pool. With such a solution the investment becomes expendable, but some people problems remain:

(a) unless there is a change in supervision style the morale of the typing pool staff is going to be low. They have got used to reducing standards;

(b) can we really tolerate being lumbered in the long term with a supervisor who cannot delegate, and who finds innovation difficult to handle, without some remedial training and attitude change.

The second alternative would seem to be to tackle directly the people problems with Miss Clark. This would require Mrs Cook to have an interview with her. When this has previously been done with Mrs Cook on her own it has not been effective, so we need a third party to be present (probably a colleague of Mrs Cook), and some levelling attempted, as one would have in the appraisal process during a promotion review. In this session we would need to get a positive commitment from Miss Clark to acknowledge the whole of the supervisor's role in this situation and get assurances that she wants to and is able to complete the task requirements of her responsibilities in the typing pool with the new equipment. She might ask for help for some aspects of this, and some sympathy should be extended.

If the help requested is not reasonably available or likely to be effective quickly enough, or if the assurances asked for are not given, then Miss Clark cannot continue in her present position. There is a clear question mark over her future as a supervisor at all. After some management development and training it is possible that she could gain competence for a supervisory position in another area of the organisation. Alternatively she could perhaps be reassigned to another section at a lower level, where at least her technical knowledge could be retained.

The approach of a 'levelling' interview does offer the chance of a long-term solution, though in a bureaucracy there may be some constraints to Mrs Cook in her action, and she too has something to learn about developing her delegation skills.

Case Study 7.2   The foreman's dilemma

Answers to the issues for discussion are as follows:

1. The main symptom was the concern expressed over quality at Perth as reflected in the official reporting system to top management in Leicester. This is backed up with a threat by Head Office not to develop the Perth facility.

2. There is a strong supposition that the quality standards as interpreted by Annie Martin have in some way been distorted giving Head Office a false picture. How otherwise can be explained the quality standards as reflected in customer complaints, which put Perth defects as 1 in 800 million, the best in the company?

   Annie takes her cue from Tom Stewart, the factory manager, who insists on perfect quality, perfectly round cigarettes — and standards beyond those laid down by the company. She sees him on the shop floor pulling up machines on quality pretexts, so she manages to rationalise on her own zeal in quality detection. She has considerable influence over the workforce too, as company management are attempting to integrate quality assessments (hers, not the customer's) into the bonus payment scheme. She also has Robert Kennedy, the foreman, potentially over a barrel, for his promotion prospects are likely to be affected by the quality assessments which she makes and she knows the importance that Tom Stewart attaches to this measurement.

   Annie's influence becomes so strong that she effectively controls both quality and production levels. Her own superior, Jim Ross, backs her to the hilt, so there seems to be no appeal against her power to interpret the standards. This is a classic example of a staff group dominating a line management group.

3. The most important attribute in a quality supervisor is that of objectivity and the strength of character to stand by such objectivity. In this feature Annie fails badly. She wants to give the crews a 'run for their money', as she believes that they are overpaid. She resists any attempt to get her interpretations checked by other quality supervisors and simply secures support of a political nature from her own superior.

4. Ideally Annie should be moved to another supervisory post that was not so demanding of the requirement for impartial and objective judgement. However, she will expect some independent checks which provide the justification for the move, and in the present organisational climate it will not be easy to achieve this justification. The quality control system has only recently been introduced by consultants. Those involved in it will naturally feel defensive about its operation, and these pressures make it particularly difficult to deal with criticisms of the system.

5. We find that George Callaghan is experienced and knows what pressures are building up on the shop-floor, but he is exceptionally cautious. He does not want to 'rock the boat' in his relationship with Tom Stewart and perceives the dangers of crossing him. Neither will he take up the issue of interpretation of standards with Jim Ross, the Quality Manager, who holds the same management rank as him. The only advice he gives to his own foreman, Robert Kennedy, is to humour Annie. For him the informal approach is the only feasible one, and when that does not work he abdicates any further interest in solving the problems relating to interpretation of quality. In the delegation checklist this type of behaviour is labelled 'escapism' — a refusal to accept a key component of the management job.

Kennedy is a young graduate of 25, and probably George Callaghan sees him as a threat. We notice that Kennedy developed an unpopular productivity suggestion and progressed it through the company suggestion scheme after seeking support from Callaghan, but it was met only with indifference.

However, Kennedy's problems are also Callaghan's problems, as he has line responsibility over his foreman. He must take a more active role if he is not to see the Cigarette Making Department fall apart. Kennedy's humiliation at Tom Stewart's constant interventions also represents humiliation for Callaghan. Unless he has authority restored to him he can hardly contribute constructively in the organisation at all.

6. Jim Ross, like his colleague George Callaghan, has no intention of crossing Tom Stewart on an issue which is perceived as a losing case. 'Don't rock the boat' is a safe power response; in the circumstances it is easy to support Annie Martin in both a group and political sense. Even the foreman's own manager, Callaghan, has not put him under pressure to check the interpretation of Annie's standards. Unless there is a much more forceful intervention it is safer to do nothing. Yet the very reason we do have a quality manager is to ensure objective interpretation of company standards, so it should be incumbent on him periodically to play the watch-dog on his own watch-dogs. As it is, he merely plays a ritual, non-problem-solving role and one wonders what his position contributes to the organisation. Why doesn't he have a stronger link with the quality people at head office and try harder to explain the major differences between the internal and external quality reporting systems?

7. This is perhaps the most fundamental and relevant question in this case. We know that as far as customers are concerned only 1 in 800 million cigarettes is considered faulty enough to return. It would be interesting to analyse which were the faults perceived as returnable but the population of faults is very small — only about nine from this factory are returned a year. Perhaps the quality standard is set too high! How high the standard should be set correlates to the tolerance for something sub-standard. Unless we reach that level of intolerance there can be no significant impact on marketing, i.e. the saleability of the product. But if the standard is unnecessarily high there is clearly a cost — the cost of stopping machines — and thus getting poor utilisation and poor return on capital employed. The case material suggests that when Stewart has one of his drives on quality, or Annie has her field-days with fault scoring, as much as 40 per cent of potential production is lost — a very high proportion. Furthermore, rejects are sent for remanufacture and in this process much of the product is lost as waste. The raw material is a very high percentage of the product, so remanufacture is expensive.

We must also be mindful that in the cigarette industry manufacturers' profit margins are very narrow: some 3 per cent of turnover as a gross margin is regarded as typical. But in the case of the manufacturing practices of Perth, the increase in overheads owing to a loss of 40 per cent capacity utilisation can easily erode the 3 per cent gross margin and turn it into a loss of 3 per cent or more.

Stewart and his ideas on roundness, and Annie with her zeal in rejecting the most minor cosmetic faults, thus have the power to turn a potentially profitable operation into one which is a devastating operational failure — the difference between a £6 million annual gross profit and a £6 million annual loss.

Perhaps the real villains were the consultants who introduced this scheme of quality fault scoring with the independent supervisor. This was to be done in addition to the previous practice where quality was the responsibility of the production crews alone.

Much modern management theory on the issue of motivation suggests that jobs should be enlarged to make them more meaningful and rewarding for employees. Hertzberg (1966) calls this technique 'job enrichment' and he typically cites production and quality as being the twin responsibilities for one single group. McGregor (1960) also makes a case for the responsible worker, who adopts Theory 'Y' attitudes and is exceptionally well self-motivated. The consultants, in contrast, offered a scheme whose organisation and people assumptions were distinctly nineteenth century!

We also know that the new procedure was introduced at the same time as a new generation of electronically controlled cigarette-making machines was introduced. These had sensing mechanisms which could detect the major functional faults of wrong weight and 'no gum on seam' and halt automatically. In view of the already very adequate electronic control mechanisms, and the proven good sense of production crews over many generations, the independent quality system looks like a hideous and expensive irrelevance.

8. The Perth factory is in a really bad state. Production figures are weak, further development of the site is threatened owing to the poor reported quality and an industrial relations problem is blowing up, of which Tom Stewart seems to be unaware. He is so used to intervening directly on the shop-floor that he destroys the foreman's authority. He usurps the company's standards with an obsession for 'roundness' and seems to be unaware of the consequences of his managerial behaviour. Effectively, he terrifies both George Callaghan and Jim Ross so that they have no scope to fulfil the creative roles of their job positions. This prevalent 'don't rock the boat' attitude is a cancer in the management team and leaves little room for any improvements.

He does not seem to be able to cope with evaluating ideas for improving productivity from his own foreman. One wonders what is happening about his role in managing the factory. He has over 500 employees and insists on managing them all as a one-man band. He is heading for a succession crisis when the time comes for him to move on.

There are real problems in finding an appropriate organisational machinery for improving Tom Stewart's management skills. Firstly, he does not seem to be aware of his shortcomings and, as he is not a good listener, that awareness will be difficult to acquire. The delegation checklist would be very useful to him, but he is unlikely to accept this from those who are junior to him in management, while those who are senior to him in Leicester may not have a sufficiently clear diagnosis of his training needs to be able to give him the opportunity to use the checklist and other much needed managerial training.

It is possible to look to the appraisal process for some help, but owing to his seniority this could only be activated by head office management, some 400 miles away. They will be much influenced in any assessments by the company reporting systems, which we already surmise have major distortions. They will also be influenced by events such as industrial stoppages, and by concern if company schemes and proposals are not implemented. But head office gets no forewarning of things like this, except from Stewart himself, so anticipatory action with Stewart is not likely.

The case illustrates the crucial role the internal company reporting system has in its effect on a remote branch, particularly when there is a major distortion in its information.

The case also illustrates the very special care a company needs to take when promoting a manager to a remote branch as unit manager. He needs as a minimum a long record of clean appraisals particularly on that vital management skill, the skill of *effective delegation*.

9. Kennedy is the 'meat in the sandwich'. There is pressure below him from the labour force, with deteriorating morale, and threats coming from the shop steward. His immediate superior, Callaghan has abdicated; Stewart, the factory manager, bullies him about an ill-conceived and ill-understood quality problem. And now Stewart thinks that the workforce will soon adopt a bonus scheme linking pay and quality. Kennedy at last has access to Stewart and an opening. He knows what the shop-floor feeling is and must warn his manager that there is *no chance* of entering negotiations with any expectation of success until there is confidence in the quality checking scheme, and the shop steward has real power of veto. Even Stewart cannot ignore power!

However, Kennedy must try to get proof of Annie's bias. He could suggest that she does a swop with the quality supervisor of the other shift and monitor changes in the reported fault pattern.

10. The problem with Robert's suggestion is that it is a direct threat to Stewart's perception of his own competence, and as long as Stewart is a part of the evaluation process of the suggestion scheme, and has the power to veto it, Kennedy has no chance of getting it reviewed on its merits. He might be very tempted to follow the behaviour pattern of Callaghan, i.e. not to rock the boat and to forgo the satisfaction of getting the productivity improvement implemented, instead simply withdrawing the suggestion.

He could appeal to Head Office over Stewart's head, but that would be dangerous in the light of his current vulnerable position. He must either repackage the idea in such a way that it is no longer unacceptable to Stewart and a direct threat to his ego or find another way of lobbying through other colleagues to get the ideas accepted. He should work harder to get Callaghan's support, and if he is a really skilled communicator he could get support from the Personnel Department and Finance, or with some deviousness plant the idea in the mind of the shop steward. After all, it would be in the interests of his members to have another whole department included within the ambit of overtime arrangements, but it could be embarrassing if the reasoning pointed to Kennedy's leak and disloyalty to his factory manager. Innovation from a junior position can be a very dangerous occupation and disloyalty is a much more severe crime in organisations than incompetence.

If there were an MbO scheme in operation there would be much more opportunity for Kennedy to highlight suggestions on management and organisation through the line structure when discussing his objectives with his own manager.

In this case it is amazing what communication problems existed because of the barriers which were erected by an authoritarian manager such as Stewart.

What happened next

1. Tom Stewart reluctantly agreed to transfer Annie on to the other shift for a trial period of two months at the behest of both Kennedy and the shop steward.
2. The problems of high fault assessment followed Annie and the other shift got near to breaking point.
3. Tom Stewart refused to acknowledge that the quality figures showed a significant difference after the trial period and posted Annie back to Kennedy's shift and back came the quality problems.
4. Kennedy applied for a transfer back to Leicester, which was granted, but he had such bad confidential reports from Stewart that he soon realised that it was in his interests to leave the company.
5. Industrial action broke out at the Perth factory when Head Office proposed to impose the incentive scheme tied to quality control.
6. Callaghan retired. (He had conceptually retired three years earlier!)
7. Stewart, under the pressure from the strike, had a heart attack and died. The one-man band behaviour over the years had taken its toll.
8. A senior manager at Head Office admitted that Leicester had found Stewart very hard to deal with. He had been a war-time promotion and was dispatched to Scotland to get him out of the way; it was assumed that with his dominant personality he would be good at getting a green-field site established. The appointment of Stewart had been a matter of convenience, not an appointment on merit. (Where were the necessary and effective appraisal processes which should have preceded the appointment?)
9. The independent quality control system was dismantled after yet another consultant's review, some five years after the case incident reported here.
10. The Perth factory survived some ten years further, but when the industry contracted it was closed, despite having very high productivity through shift

work and eventually also high quality. Being a small unit it was eventually expendable. The factory never overcame the damage done to its reputation and standing by Stewart's time as factory manager.

Case Study 8.1   The course admission decision

Responses to the tasks for discussion are as follows:

1. Some of the main factors in the incident include the following:
   (a) The College operated an Equal Opportunity policy approved at the highest level by the Governing Council. We do not have the full text of this policy resolution, but the spirit of the policy is clear enough. An interpretation would be that non-academic staff have a reasonable opportunity to undertake staff development to improve their prospects. In any event they should not be less eligible for a management place than an outsider, provided they are as well qualified.
   (b) The College has previously accepted non-academic staff on management courses, and they have done well. The risk of Barry failing the course is thus no worse than for others.
   (c) Barry has been subjected to the full and legitimised selection process by a group of tutors. They have unanimously found him to be a competent and well-qualified candidate fulfilling all the selection criteria, even in a competitive situation. The only minor point of uncertainty related to the question of Barry's funding, but informal assurances were offered at the time of the selection interview and subsequently this was backed up in writing by his immediate superior, Gerald. The selectors could not know that Gerald's formal power to approve the funding was limited.
   (d) Barry expected to take advantage of the Equal Opportunity policy and when this was denied him he resigned with some ill-will. The College had to replace him at a time of crucial shortage of technicians. We may assume that the commissioning of the new laboratory was delayed and that this compromised the academic plan.

Conclusion

It might be expected that there would be some difficulty in making Barry a priority for staff development funding; we do not know what other competing claims there were against that budget, but no indication is given that funds were not available. Based on a rational decision-making model Barry should have had the offer of a place on the management course and secured the necessary funding. Also, this conclusion must naturally be derived on the basis of enlightened self-interest of the College, otherwise they lose a useful senior technician.

2. The main features of breakdown in the rational decision-making process were examples of where expediency and power were brought to bear to corrupt the rational process. Examples in the incident follow:

   (a) Kenneth, the Assistant Director, is annoyed at being confronted with a request for more technician staff in the light of the £50,000 capital release for the new microcomputer laboratory. We do not know how tight his staffing budget is. Perhaps he cannot balance his books. He attempts to throw out the request for a new technician post on the grounds of the provisional approval from Gerald of day-release for Barry. This must mean that he is overstaffed. This becomes a useful tactic of expediency.

   (b) The Assistant Director is uneasy about explaining this to Barry, so he looks for someone in the management department to do his dirty work for him! Simon is a willing horse and is easily framed. With no knowledge of the actual application status or of Barry's cv, he is gratuitous in his ill-informed advice to the Assistant Director, who is delighted to be told what he wants to hear.

   (c) Walter, HOD Management, is embarrassed. He receives a note of the ill-informed advice from Simon, yet has confirmed from Richard, the Admissions Tutor, that a legitimate offer has already been made to Barry. Walter's embarrassment is that he too has a request for increased staffing in the in-tray of the Assistant Director and that is also most vulnerable.

   (d) Walter's priority is to get a new member of academic staff on the establishment. The admission tutor's credibility is expendable. Out of expediency there will be no confrontation with the Assistant Director. Barry is also expendable. After all he comes from another department and the course place can easily be reallocated to another fee-paying candidate from outside.

   (e) Gerald's priority is to get a new technician on his establishment, otherwise his new £50,000 laboratory will not be commissioned and his part in the academic plan will be compromised. Barry can be fobbed off temporarily. He may get the day-release granted next year. That is seen to be the inevitable compromise in an otherwise impossible situation.

A rationalisation? What about the equal opportunity policy?

Barry's management place and the Equal Opportunity policy both seem to be expendable. When resources are tight the authorities in power will develop priorities as they see them and the resource decisions which follow may well ride roughshod over other good policies or good causes, which for whatever reason are not backed up by real power. Do the College Governors not mind being usurped? With a concentration on policy and meetings just once every two months, what match could they be against a vigilant executive like the Assistant Director, who is making the day-to-day resource allocation decisions?

Case Study 16.1   The Desert Oil Company

Responses to the questions for discussion are as follows:

1. Under principles of good practice we would expect a corporate policy group to be in action to develop computing policy. Such a group is often called a computer steering committee. Its overall role is to interpret the company's corporate plan, to offer possible target areas for computer application and to oversee the major computer hardware purchase decisions and the authorisation of the major applications. In a mature organisation they will initiate the process of authorisation of applications and review reports from feasibility studies. Authorisation for further application development will depend on the results of the feasibility studies; those which predict high leverage in terms of expected benefit will more likely be approved than those whose leverage or pay-off is weak.

In DOC there was no group in existence with any remit to look at computing policy. The DPM got authorisation to spend within delegated financial powers from AGM Finance, and the replacement of punch-card equipment was considered an end in itself. The GM was a collaborator in this initial decision, but at that time had no concept of the possible impact of computers on engineering. If a computer steering committee had been operating it is much more likely that an engineering need for computing would have surfaced much earlier and a larger and faster memory could have been built in to the original specification.

Under good practice it is most unusual for a data processing manager to report to a functional executive, such as AGM Finance. Current wisdom suggests that data processing and other providers of major information technology equipment should report to a head of management services or a director of information, and the remit is to provide a service for the whole corporate organisation, prioritised on the basis of expected impact.

In DOC there seemed to be no idea of how to set up a proper feasibility study and there was no mechanism to develop any form of prioritisation.

2. When we have the organisational machinery of a computer steering committee in place and the process of feasibility studies operating it should be a simple matter of interpreting the feasibility study reports to get to an informed and deliberate authorisation.

The criteria will be developed from norms suggested under the three headings of *technical feasibility, economic feasibility* and *business feasibility*. Technical feasibility clearly requires sound technical judgement. Economic feasibility is normally worked out by generating expected cash flows following a cost/benefit projection. Where some of the benefits are strictly qualitative some attempt will be made to quantify these in terms of value. Authorisation is then done by applying cut-off criteria, e.g. the project must have a pay-off period of less than two years, the project must have an internal rate of return of not less than 25 per cent. Both criteria should be carefully used, as ambitious projects often have a long development period and therefore could not have a short pay-off period. However, long-term projects which are authorised should expect at the end of the project term a very large internal rate of return.

In DOC the financial applications never paid for themselves, nor did they have any chance of doing so. The computer was significantly more expensive in terms of capital than replacement punch-card equipment, and it had a one-time conversion cost of £100,000, which would never be recouped. The overall cash flow would have been negative all the way.

Business feasibility, the third criterion, relates to qualitative judgement. It is necessary to consider such subjective questions since if a computer system were deployed in this application area, could we get the staff to absorb and adapt to the new systems without recruitment and training? How much training and recruitment should there be? Could we bear the organisational pain and effort needed to see this project through?

In DOC it was found that considerable training was required before the engineers could take advantage of computerisation, and thus much of the expected benefit was uncertain. The computer room was too small for a computer large enough to do engineering work. Could DOC bear the pain of commissioning a new building? There seems to have been a lack of resolve here!

3. They made about every mistake that it was possible to make! This was largely due to their lack of experience and a systematic approach. Furthermore, DOC left themselves in a vulnerable position. The computer systems analyst in DOC was only seconded and on a short-term contract. Without proper systems specifications and back-up of people for this vital activity DOC is running the risk that no one understands how to service and develop the six financial systems after he leaves. As it is, he leaves before they are even working and DOC has no replacement. A scenario must be that DOC is offered systems which it cannot understand and maintain until it goes through an expensive rewrite with possibly another £100,000 set-up cost.

Instead, DOC invests in programmers, whose work is much influenced by the quality of the systems specifications. It would have been much more realistic to hire and develop analysts on permanent contracts and programmers on short-term contracts.

How should one rationalise the DOC computing decisions? It might be unwise not to risk some loss of financial resources in the short term for expected long-term benefit. The sum of £100,000 is but a small sum for an international oil company, and in the long term its competitiveness may fundamentally be related to its skill in using the techniques of information technology. Perhaps the first experience should be written off as an organisational learning exposure, but next time through the sequence DOC should get it right! Most people and companies can learn from their own mistakes, but bright people and progressive companies can learn from the experiences of others and from the literature.

Case Study 16.2   Hijack

Responses to the issues for discussion are as follows:

1. The most important simple principle is that detailed design must *follow* specification. The practice of documenting computer programs after they have been made to run is

a work heresy. Under good practice the systems analyst develops program specifications which are detailed enough to be virtually stand-alone documents for the programmer. When the programmer does the programming he or she also follows the programming standards laid down by the installation. The planning structure is done first and standards are closely kept. If the programmer is off sick for a day another programmer should be able to move on to the design and take it forward. Work at all levels should be transparent to other specialists so that assignment transfer should be easy. A well-structured program is easy to maintain, and the extra time needed to give it visibility and robustness is a worthwhile investment in time.

Secondly, a great clarity in roles must be maintained within the group and no one person on one assignment should do more than one role. A systems analyst must never program on the program he or she has specified. The temptation to by-pass the rigour of the specification and to cut corners is too great. An analyst who does his or her own programming can hijack the organisation. Likewise, a programmer should never be given the duties of a computer operator with access to computer programs he or she has designed as there is the temptation to manipulate the system fraudulently. If the roles are kept separate then it is necessary for a minimum of two to conspire before a hijack can take place.

A fuller discussion of this question would also need to take account of the principles of good security and back-up of hardware/software systems and with fully tested stand-by provisions, should there be a threat of fire or flood to the main data processing facility.

2. First, we need to define what is meant by distributed data processing, a rather nasty piece of jargon. The main idea behind DDP is that a mainframe central computer may not necessarily be the driving force behind the use of computers. Commonly now we also have powerful microcomputers whose systems and intelligence is local, so that the computer may be used as a powerful stand-alone device. However, it might be nice to link such computer to another microcomputer or to a mainframe. Whenever this linking is done we have a network, which facilitates communication between users.

When the network connects the mainframe to the remote micro we have effectively distributed data processing. This opens up many possibilities. The user from the micro can make the mainframe view such a micro as though it were just another mainframe terminal and offer the user the facilities of the mainframe. Also the micro user can get a file of data or a computer program sent down the network to the micro to be absorbed into its own stand-alone capability, then the link may be broken and all further processing done locally on the micro. The great advantage of this is that the mainframe is relieved of much detailed computing work leaving a capacity to service more terminals. Equally, the remote user with the dedicated micro can do complicated operations and still get quick responses on the material downloaded from the mainframe, as there is no sharing with any other user on the micro. Everyone benefits from such arrangements.

However, the above links do not work unless there are specified protocols, standards and interfaces, so that the different computers can communicate efficiently with one another. Furthermore, the remote user, after he or she has processed programs or data, may want to pass the results back to the mainframe ('up-loading') and, if the standards and protocols are not compatible with those of the mainframe, there is the possibility of corrupting the integrity of the mainframe data.

The DDP environment is a complex one, but enormous benefits in inter-company communication are theoretically possible once standards of design, communication protocol and purchasing are developed and enforced company-wide. That is increasingly difficult in the wake of such very rapid technological progress and new product launches and a very large population of users.

In Memos 17 and 18 the question of standards arose to provoke Doreen. She was not convinced that the International Division had developed a package for material requirements planning robust enough to transfer to other areas without being rewritten to higher standards. The designers may not have realised that they were really operating within a distributed data processing environment, in which packages would be required to be transferred as a matter of course.

However, another interpretation is that Doreen was over-cautious and her group would find it difficult to adopt any house software package, simply because their standards and conventions were different from her own installation's, so Doreen could become a very expensive data processing manager.

3. It was very evident from the exchanges between Keith, Fred, Arnold and Lionel that there were organisational pressures which influenced the design process; furthermore, those articulating such pressures were not particularly good at listening to information requiring compromise. In Memo 5 Keith gives a warning about the complex approach to Fred, who either does not understand or takes no account of the suggestion, as Keith has little organisational status, whereas Arnold, a senior line manager, does have clout. Arnold wants maximum financial return from the project, regardless of the difficulties of getting that. In Memo 6 Lionel puts some pressure on Arnold to go for a proposition which will improve Lionel's promotion prospects, but this is done with some rationalisation to make it acceptable. Neither Lionel nor Arnold is really capable of evaluating Keith's points of concern about the complex approach. They look to Fred for this judgement but he does not have the technical competence to make an informed decision. Fred does, however, have ample opportunity as the two approaches require radically different resource packages (see Memo 7), but he does not seem to be able to assimilate such discussion of the basic logistics of the project, which would have an influence on the completion date. When we are considering expediting a cash flow of £1 million a year, delivery dates are rather important! When unpleasant news arrives on Fred's desk, i.e. that he needs to deploy further resources, he indulges in escapism. Human nature seems to militate against threatening technological change.

4. In the case we see many contrasts between the approaches of Fred and Doreen in their roles as data processing manager. The literature warns us against being enthusiastic about correlating effective management with personality traits, yet we do see very different behaviour patterns between Fred and Doreen. Fred tends to be more the political animal. He takes account of those with clout in the organisation and tends

to filter out technical advice from below. He is a dynamic go-getter, with a tornado management style, determined to get the quick result and completely unconcerned about the long-term effects. Orderliness, filing cabinets and standards are simply in his view obstructions to quick effective achievement. But then Fred does not deliver and lets the situation deteriorate, so that a hijack was almost inevitable.

Doreen, in contrast, is concerned about continuity, standards and long-term effectiveness. To her the computer design process is inevitably a long bureaucratic process involving a lot of consultation, analysis, planning and resourcing. Doreen knows how to deploy design teams and is prepared to resource them for major organisational objectives. The major influence guiding her is the force of professional practice, and this is much stronger for her than those with political impact in the organisation. It would be most unlikely that Doreen's regime would allow an environment in which a hijack attempt could be made.

It is a point of some interest whether Fred could ever be trained or coached to adopt Doreen's more effective approach. Fred after all had been a successful manager in the dynamic situation of production control manager with a manual system, but he does need more style flexibility if he is ever to come to terms with the situation in a systems department, and he needs to internalise much more professional practice. At the end of the case Fred would look a high risk to be allowed anywhere near data processing again without major reforms. He would be better employed in line management and at a lower level.

When we think of Fred's original appointment, major errors of judgement were made. It seems as though he were chosen because he knew at first hand the procedures involved in production control, a likely important application area for this company. But the real unperceived need of the company was to articulate a major corporate change and set up a systems facility; that required the skills and knowledge of an able staff manager, preferably one with professional knowledge of data processing. As the profession of management in this area is a new one it is understandable that the company made a mistake in picking a company man. However, if they did pick one then it would be up to such a company man or woman to balance up the team with professional knowledge at a lower level or to make better use of the professional knowledge already available. Keith had a good idea of professional practice, but this was not recognised by Fred.

5. This question takes us back to points of theory developed in chapter 16, in particular the discussion of the two organisation charts, Figure 16.1 project-oriented, option A, and Figure 16.2 functionally-oriented, option B approaches.

Under the functional alternative we have both a programming manager and a systems manager. Communication between the staffs of the two is predominantly via specifications from systems to programming and then assigned on the basis of who is available. Programmers may thus be doing work on several different application projects at any one time. The basis of the work, since it is founded on specification, is secure, but the user has difficulty in getting information on the status of applications. He or she has to develop contacts through two different sections in data processing and inevitably this becomes like introducing another level in the bureaucracy. If things go smoothly then there is no problem, but whoever heard of computing projects not hitting snags fairly frequently? If this extra level in the bureaucracy slows things up the consequences are increasing levels of backlog and the feeling that data processing is not responsive enough to the user's changing demands. A consequence is that safe, straightforward projects only are tackled, while the more demanding, creative ones are avoided, but at least we should avoid hijacks.

However, in the chapter 16 discussion, the author still preferred the project-oriented option A, as it offers better communication with users and better coordination of work, but the project manager *must* play a policeman role to ensure that the specification base of design is secure and that the standards discussed in question 1 of this case are fully implemented. Under such circumstances the risk of a hijack is minimal, but only if the project managers exercise sound professional practice.

6. Memo 15 explains the need of the analyst to get the design validated by an informed user, and then as design is completed the user assumes 'systems ownership'. The analyst can then move on to another project in the confidence that the user can request modifications by a maintenance group, based on a detailed understanding and knowledge of the system. In time the analyst should grow from a variety of design experiences.

The emphasis on validation between the analyst and the user representative is the basis from which an empathetic relationship developed — in this case between Keith and Bruce — and at the relevant level. Bruce thoroughly knew the formal and informal requirements both of HM Customs and the company's duty drawback section. Keith knew exactly what a computer could do in this well-defined business situation, but on his own he could not cope with the organisational problems which developed around Arnold, Lionel and Fred.

In many organisational situations management does not seem to realise the need to appoint someone in Bruce's role (called in chapter 16 'user representative' or 'business analyst'). Yet without someone to validate computer design against the reality of both formal and informal practice the computer design is not robust enough to survive the implementation process. Some manifestations of informal organisation practice are further developed in chapter 19. Case Study 19.3 (p. 406) gives an excellent manifestation of this.

7. Those who have experienced programming work generally find that there is much creative art and style involved; the building up of that style gives pleasure and ego satisfaction. Yet under a structured or modular approach the programmer is obliged to cast aside his previously developed methods and follow a precise methodology, often considered pedantic and time-consuming. It might be nice for the supervisor to transfer design to another programmer for organisational convenience, but human nature being what it is there is a reluctance to let go and share in creative work. Many people feel the need to be indispensable.

Yet programmers with highly individual styles can hijack their organisation with devastating effect — see the sequence of Tom in memo 12. Clearly, professional practice demands the introduction of the techniques of structured programming, but it is up to organisations to find acceptable methods of introduction and versions of 'structured programming' which still leave room for program reliability and pleasure in creation — an eternal tussle between the twin pressures of ergonomics and efficiency at work. An advantage of putting programmers into a project team environment is that they are exposed from their early days to discussion on systems problems as well, and this variety of exposure offers some job enrichment to make programming more tolerable.

Case Study 17.1   Mendip Jeeps

A response to question 1 might be as follows:

Building up the business pictures

1. Exports account for 70 per cent of the market and HMG is a major customer.
2. A major employer in Dumfries, guided to the site by political pressure.
3. A good industrial relations record over fifteen years' stability and growth in Dumfries to the current 700 employee level.
4. Held a monopoly position in this market till entry by Mifune in 1984; much competition since.
5. Competition gains strength in the United Kingdom in 1985 and in developing countries.
6. Mendip's Managing Director is concerned about rising costs and cash flow and the banks refuse to extend further credit in 1986.
7. A takeover bid is launched in June 1986 from Columbia, a multinational for Mendip.
8. Management oppose the bid, but Columbia increase the pressure; Mendip liquidity is weak.
9. The Government decide not to intervene.

PEST analysis
Political factors
Government pressure caused Mendip to go to Dumfries, fifteen years ago, and the government would be embarrassed by possible unemployment if the firm went bust in a period approaching the general election. Government is also a customer taking 30 per cent of company output, but might also relish changing vendor to Mifune if this resulted in a reduction in public expenditure. On the other hand, the Government would be embarrassed at the implications to the balance of payments if Mendip failed.

Economic factors
High costs and liquidity are serious threats. More volume is required to maintain low costs, so new markets need developing; meanwhile immediate cuts in labour are essential

to recover from the liquidity crisis. A review of stock levels of raw material and work in process from a balance sheet is essential to relieve liquidity pressure. Foreign markets take 70 per cent of Mendip output but these are in the developing countries, vulnerable to exchange rate fluctuations and with long debt collection periods, which adds to liquidity pressure.

Sociological factors

Mendip owes it to the community to maintain the continuity of employment if possible, as they are the major employer in Dumfries. Other component suppliers in Scotland would also be affected.

Technological factors

Until 1984 the product was unique, and although the technology is still appropriate there is a great need to simplify in order to reduce costs. Why was this product not continuously improved during its thirteen years of supremacy through market research and research and development? Is the unique wheel design a piece of technology that could be put to other uses?

SWOT analysis

Strengths

Developed home and export markets, a high quality product, loyal workforce and thirteen years' growth and stability in the industry of making jeeps are the company's main strengths.

Weaknesses

Weaknesses include: high costs, poor liquidity, refusal of the banks to extend credit, an unsympathetic, non-interventionist Government and a long period of monopoly position which probably stifled cost improvements and led to complacent management. Management still does little, even when it knows of the threats from competitors.

Opportunities

It may be possible to find a 'white knight' more acceptable as a takeover partner than Columbia, or a UK banking group prepared to give its blessing to a management buy-out. It is essential to get another bidder into the takeover situation, otherwise Mendip will fall at a knock-down price to Columbia. We need to get the share register to see where the holdings of Mendip shares are, so that an appeal to their loyalty can be made. We probably need a merchant banker to help prepare and fight the takeover battle. Meanwhile there is need to improve liquidity by reducing any excess stocks and disposing of any non-essential assets, perhaps selling and leasing back the factory facility.

Mifune, the arch-competitor, may also be interested. Some shareholders might be happy for a takeover to take place, but employees would be likely to have to respond to more change and redundancy if independence is lost. Some diversification may then be possible, but no information is given about R&D strength and therefore the possibility of concentric growth. It may be possible to refer the takeover to the Monopolies

Commission and plead that the merger is not in the public interest, but it would be difficult to succeed in this move without Government approval or some political lobbying, which is more likely to be effective in election year than at other times.

Threats
The receivers could be called in if the liquidity crisis is not quickly resolved, otherwise Columbia may succeed in their takeover bid.

Question 2
Possible responses are as follows:

The stakeholders are Mendip Management, Mendip employees, Mendip stockholders, suppliers and customers, the community around Dumfries, the UK Government and the trade unions.

Who has the power? Once the shareholders are organised they have positive power to enable changes to happen. Trade unions, employees and Government have veto power, i.e. they can prevent or hinder a course of action.

In developing a strategy the ideal would be to meet the objectives of as many stakeholders as possible, as business is an activity requiring cooperation.

The future has both a short term (3–6 months) and a long term. In the short term, survival against liquidation is the immediate threat. This can be met by activating asset liquidation, making stock reductions and authorising short-time working in the factory. Retrenchment in every sense is called for.

In the longer term, shareholder power will probably win, so if Columbia bids the highest in takeover terms, then ownership will move to Columbia. If a 'white knight' is also bidding then the existing shareholders will make a nice profit on their investments. With Columbia the unit may be expanded into new products and new markets and employment at Dumfries developed, but existing management would be replaced and some rationalisation might give rise to labour shedding.

The only defence against the takeover predators would be a referral to the Monopoly Commission, with some support in this from Government.

If the company does nothing but spend all resources on resisting the takeover, it will have nothing left to get back its threatened markets and develop an improved and more cost-effective product range.

Exercise 18.1   Fayol's fourteen principles

Discussion of contemporary relevance

1. Division of work. The principle of specialisation of work in order to concentrate activities for more efficiency.

   A good general principle, but highly qualified in the latter part of the twentieth century by people's expectations for rewarding occupations which have challenge, variety and discretion. The irony is that in a hi-tech society there are more and more specialists, for without knowledge in depth through competent specialists an organisation cannot compete.

2. Authority and responsibility. Authority is the right to give orders and the power to exact obedience.

   This principle still stands but not so securely, and with some difference in emphasis. It is generally agreed that job positions should define the manager's sphere of responsibility, and from this should flow the consequent authority level (this is a norm of good practice developed in the chapter on managing by objectives, with the aim of getting realistic jobs that are balanced). Today we look to effective delegation strategies rather than emphasising the power of management as in Fayol's time, simply because they are at the summit of the organisation. As the wellsprings of democracy embrace the industrial organisation people are very weary of being exposed to the abuse of power.

3. Discipline. Discipline is absolutely essential for the smooth running of the business. Without discipline no enterprise could prosper.

   The overall outcome is still difficult to dispute, but today the implementation technique would be very different. There is much unfair dismissal legislation now, as well as the expectation that disciplinary power is exercised by groups, sometimes even including trade union or staff association representation. The overall unity of the corporation is still important, but today this is achieved through articulating corporate planning processes, rather than in relying on the control of the chief executive, as in Fayol's time.

4. Unity of command. An employee should receive orders from one superior only.

   This seems appropriate for a simple organisation which has only got line management, but for those organisations with staff specialists this principle falls down badly. The staff specialist needs to feel the influence of both the professional head (often located at head office) and the client management to whom the service is provided (often a branch manager). If he also works in a project team some time will be dedicated to a project manager, some to the home functional manager. Such a person has to cope with instructions from several sources and he needs the skills and initiative to reconcile possible conflicts of priority.

5. Unity of direction. One head and one plan for a group of activities having the same objectives.

   There is the same problem here as with principle 4.

6. Subordination of individual interests to general interests. The interest of one employee or a group should not prevail over that of the organisation.

   This principle still holds, but in the latter part of the twentieth century there is the real expectation that the individual's needs and group needs are also taken into account. (See the discussion of Adair's 'Action-Centred Leadership' in chapter 20.)

7. Remuneration of personnel. Compensation should be fair and, as far as possible, afford satisfaction to both personnel and the firm.

   This is still true, but there is the expectation of some degree of peer and self-assessment of performance, combined with management assessment, as a valid input to compensation policy.

8. Centralisation. Centralisation is essential to the organisation and is a natural consequence of organising.

   This principle is currently under assault. With more developed communication systems — broadcast, telephone, teleconferencing and electronic mail — there are very high pressures to decentralise decision-making and control.

9. Scalar chain. The scalar chain is the chain of superiors ranging from the ultimate authority to the lowest rank.

   In hi-tech organisations authority tends to flow on the basis of expertise, rather than the basis of rank and status.

10. Order. The organisation should provide an orderly place for every individual. A place for everyone and everyone in their place.

    This principle tends to be rejected today. The majority tend to expect to have prospects and the opportunity to contribute and move upwards in society, based on their education and success and not be limited by class or lack of patronage. An order based on acceptance of democratic principles is expected.

11. Equity. Equity and a sense of justice pervade the organisation.
    Still acceptable today.

12. Stability of tenure of personnel. Time is needed for the employees to adapt to their work and to perform it effectively.

    Yes, time is needed and there are more sophisticated training methods available than at the beginning of the century. However, it is not generally accepted that incompetence is untreatable unless due cause is given, i.e. an act of misfeasance is carried out. Tenure does give independence and this may be commendable for judges and bishops, but what is the case for tenure for academics? In reality, it is particularly difficult to get objective criteria of acceptable performance for very high-level managers, which is not sullied by considerations of politics.

13. Initiative. At all levels of the organisational ladder, zeal and energy are augmented by initiative.

    Yes, this principle is valid, but Fayol must have had his tongue in his cheek when espousing this principle as those with bright ideas and the impertinence to threaten the existing order were not a bit popular with managers in his own time.

14. *Esprit de corps*. This principle emphasised the need for teamwork and the maintenance of interpersonal relationships.

This is still very relevant, but now we have much more opportunity to activate and promote good teamwork. The behavioural scientists have helped much in this field.

Case Study 18.1   Whithouse Fun Goods

Building up the business pictures

1. The toy industry has seasonal demand. This is a medium-sized firm, a large employer in a mining town (a close-knit community).
2. The other employer (NCB) is threatened with closure.
3. The unit is taken over by Scampton Toys. (Motive for merger?)
4. Existing management continue for four years. Cullen (probably owner/founder) has a paternalistic style. He is generous to full-timers, but strict to smokers. His authority is respected.

   New management takes over when Hallwell replaces Cullen's assistant.
5. This leads to different expectations of workers and management team.
6. Old management's 'village community' is broken up.
7. Previous informal practices regarding scrap cuts and the Christmas bonus are abolished unilaterally.
8. Industrial action is triggered on the pretext of lack of heating in mid-October, during the build-up of the busy period. This is the first strike in the firm's history.

Responses to questions

1. *Cullen's approach*: His basic style is paternalistic. He is well known, well liked and well respected. He is a member of the local community and well trusted over many years. He supports *esprit de corps* (like Fayol). He connives at waste and losses which are not considered important (we do not know the financial impact), but does give full-timers recognition at Christmas through the bonus. He uses the Hawthorn effect to improve morale. He does not provide for succession and management training. He is complacent about PEST factors, particularly new technology, which is vital for the toy market with competition from electronic-based toys.

   Hallwell's approach: Initially he observes a lot and does little. Then he adopts a 'new broom' approach in classical management style. He does not seem to be able to listen to those in the representative structure. He changes the perks unilaterally and introduces his men into the structure. This is perceived as a threat to existing shop floor/junior management. He gives high priority to financial cost-cutting objectives but is apparently unconcerned about employee expectations. He has a Taylorite outlook about production management. He is probably trying to impress Head Office on financial grounds. The main disadvantage is that goodwill has been severely compromised in the busy period. Can Whithouse survive a long strike? How will cash flow be affected? Would Scampton rescue them? The company does not seem to have much in the way of MIS. Hallwell does not seem to know the cost structure or details of overtime or bonus budgets, which should find a place in the computation of overheads. There is no evidence of MbO or corporate planning.

2. Hallwell needs to become acquainted with the products, the markets, profits, the workforce, and management talent and expectations as soon as possible.

   He should use the human relations approach to understand the management structure and workforce aspirations and feelings and group identity. He would need to relate directly to the personnel function and the representative labour structure.

   He would need to adopt a corporate planning approach to help weigh up marketing and financial aspects and possible opportunities for growth.

   He would need to adopt an MbO approach to get greater involvement in setting objectives and provide an opportunity for delegation and possible management and people development. This would also provide enough data to satisfy the stakeholders of the business. He needs to build on the know-how and goodwill of the existing group.

3. What can Hallwell do now to retrieve the situation?

   He must let Head Office know of the situation and establish his freedom in time and money to cope with the immediate business threat caused by the strike. He may also wish to use Head Office resources, particularly those in industrial relations, and be aware of the Head Office corporate plan for Whithouse.

   He will need to establish dialogue with shop stewards and union officials to know exactly what were the points of concern in addition to the heating.

   He will have to establish a machinery of consultation and a direct link with the workforce to re-establish Whithouse as a desirable place to work.

   For the longer term he will need to develop an appropriate business strategy and appoint or develop an executive team to implement this.

Case Study 19.1 P & Q Company

Possible responses to issues for discussion are as follows:

1. We should first perhaps consider the main problems facing the company as at the conclusion of the text, then build up an analysis from that recognition.

Firstly, on the marketing side we find a serious problem of quality. The product has not been re-engineered since before the war and now it is competing against better products. That is particularly serious as a full product development cycle from the research and development stage is needed to retrieve the situation and that would take time. But before R&D can cut much ice we need a market research input to determine better what market needs are, and there is no mention of any part of the organisation performing that function.

Secondly, there is evidence of unrest in the plant, triggered probably by feelings of insecurity in the knowledge that losses are being made and the firm is threatened.

Thirdly, we find a strained situation has developed between Quaille and Keene; the normal principles of delegation appear to have been flouted. Quaille seems to be running what is now a large organisation with daily meetings. He has become a one-man band, with the illusion that this style gives good control, but the reality is that the business and its future are far from secure.

When Major Quaille returned from the war he was determined to make the family business a paragon of good organisation and management and made many organisational moves to achieve this objective. Where were the fundamental errors?

Normally in organisations the line structure is first put into place and then the staff structure grafted on at the appropriate place and level to ensure that it can provide the necessary resources and information to improve decision-making. But in Pender and Quaille we do not even have a marketing organisation of any recognisable sort, just a few aged travellers who report to Quaille. There is no product development and no market research.

When we examine the production side of the business, the other main line function there are also gaps. There is no quality control, no research and development function, and a lack of role definition for Keene. He seems to find himself responsible for lots of things, but the authority has reverted to Quaille and much is left uncoordinated lower down. The staff function of production control has been created and there is a real job to be done there, but it is of little use having a production control section unless it works to solve the problems occurring at the lower level.

Quaille's cardinal error has been to reorganise the staff functions first, before thinking through what type of business and line organisation he needed, and then configuring more appropriate relationships for staff groups, so that they could be relevant and supportive.

2. Figure 19.5 reflects a much improved structure, with the line organisation much more in evidence. Both the machine shop and foundry elements should get an opportunity for development and growth, but it may just be too late to save the business! Keene would probably be appointed to one of the two division heads and the other would need to come from outside or a promotion, though there are no very obvious candidates. Keene too has not much longer to go before retirement, so there is still a potential succession problem with him.

Note that in the marketing function several new appointments may be necessary to get the strength and that production control sections now are split and report lower down in the organisation. Quaille still has rather too many executives reporting to him, but they are so structured in a team for more effective delegation to take place.

Even though Figure 19.5 suggests a divisional organisation, not all functions have been assigned to divisional level, so it is really a mixed organisation.

A criticism might be that the new organisation might be too expensive to introduce without a much greater volume of trade, so initially some of the positions outlined above may need to be integrated into the responsibilities of fewer executives. Major Quaille, with his propensity to want to manage as a one-man band, might resist the changes involved in such a reorganisation, and as the owner his resistance could block the changes.

Other business policy choices might also exist, for instance the divestment of one of the divisions and a consolidation of the one remaining. Financial pressures could force this action.

Case Study 19.2   A matter of priorities

The following are possible responses to the issues for discussion:

Issue 1

Firstly, we need to face problems of perception in this case. Michod certainly seems overloaded, but as soon as he approaches his superiors he gets the brush-off; they see him as trying to reduce commitment to them and they also are short-staffed and simply do not want to know about time difficulties. It appears that both John Lucas and Wayne Smith are typical line managers, who have been accustomed to having staff totally dedicated in a line relationship, with no need to share assignments.

Michod is basically a talented young man, growing from a technical competence to competence in a wider field of management, stimulated by his MBA programme, and wanting to spread his wings and put into practice some of the techniques learnt on the MBA programme. For him the MBA programme has offered him the opportunity for job enrichment and personal growth. But at his low level in the organisation he is clearly not in control of the pace of this growth and the operational control of assignments, which appear to land on his desk without any real quantification.

In our earlier analysis of planning techniques in chapter 10 we used critical path networks. This involved breaking down work and quantifying tasks and sub-tasks into times and resources, and attempting to programme activities within these constraints. To get any credibility in the definition of Michod's current predicament all he needs to do initially is to quantify his weekly load; such a quantification will force the issue on priorities.

This quantification could be as follows:

Commitment to Wayne Smith on
customer installation   20 hours

Commitment to John Lucas on
customer education   30 hours

Commitment to John Lucas on programme modification	0 (was 15)
Commitment to John Lucas on the Markov process	15 hours
Total commitment	65 hours

Brief appreciation of the assumptions

The commitment of time on the development of the Markov process is probably the most speculative. If it is taken on as a part-time assignment over a long period of time then the forgetting cycle will doubtless have an impact, and the 120 hours quoted could be a severe underestimation. Applying a rule of thumb to this figure we should perhaps replace the weekly average figure of 15 hours by 20 hours. This is a bit arbitrary, but it is often necessary to resort to a rule of thumb! The revised total commitment would then be 70 hours.

We do not know from the text what normal hours are, but it may be safe to assume a maximum of 50 with overtime, unless we are in a real sweat-shop! That gives us an overload of 20 hours a week.

Now that there is a hard quantification of the assignments this problem must be managed. Michod initially wonders if he could supervise someone else on the Markov process, i.e. his way out may be by delegation, but management will not wear that one. They will not hire or assign more staff, and there is a disbelief that anyone other than an MBA graduate would be able to do justice to the intellectual demands of that assignment.

It might be technically possible to bring other staff in to take on some of Michod's other assignments. If not we would need to retime the assignments and that implies back-scheduling. (This sounds a bit like a crashing sequence from the discussions of critical path networks in chapter 10.)

Now the facts are in place, we need to think of the necessary people strategies. Informal individual approaches to Wayne Smith and John Lucas have already failed; they did not want to know. Now Michod has a quantification of his problem he has more leverage with the two superiors to secure executive action. The next move is likely to be an attempt to see them together and jointly discuss his paper, inviting them to resolve the issue of priorities. This puts the responsibility squarely back in their court. He might also send a copy of his report to the District Manager, who is his superior's superior. That might cause resentment, but Michod must get this problem resolved. The only other avenue open to get some movement in this problem would be an informal approach to a manager of the same status as Lucas and Smith. There are two possibilities here: the Personnel Manager and the Sales Manager. They may be sympathetic in nudging Smith and Lucas to relate to Michod, but much depends on the personalities and culture in the organisation and the extent to which executives have opportunities for informal contact and are capable of adopting collaborative attitudes. Michod too must be prepared to stand his ground. If he accepts the brush-off too easily he will never win!

Issue 2

We should think briefly of a further perspective to this problem. What is likely to happen if Michod's problem of priorities is unresolved? The following are possibilities:

1. Michod will be utterly fed up and decide to leave the company. His know-how and the company investment in his training will go too. The current assignments will still need to be completed.
2. Michod will struggle on with all three assignments, but without full resources none will be done well. He will be very wary in future of pushing too hard to give effect to his MBA-style competence.
3. Michod will concentrate on what he can do well and the third assignment will simply not be done or will get done very late — that could compromise the company's business policy.

What this sequence seems to demonstrate is that a matrix-type organisation structure creates ambiguities for the lower-level manager. He or she as well as superiors need good sense in recognising priority clashes and the managerial and communication skills to have such issues resolved. This demands a high degree of motivation and professional competence even among relatively junior managers.

Senior managers need to be collaborative in style and sensitive to the need to deal quickly and objectively with clashes in priorities as they are perceived from below, above and laterally. They need to be able to activate formal and informal procedures to resolve such issues. This suggests almost an antithesis to classical or bureaucratic practice. No wonder organisations which have grown under classical or bureaucratic practice find matrix organisation hard to cope with in the implementation period.

However, we do see advantages when matrix organisation works well. Professionally-trained managers such as Michod can use much more fully their range of talents throughout the organisation. The ideal of job enrichment can become a reality. Much more complex teamwork becomes possible.

Peter Drucker suggested as long ago as 1954 that effective management was about successfully employing 'knowledge workers' and getting full contributions from them. Project and matrix organisation structures often provide the environment where this contribution may flourish.

Case Study 19.3   The tap

The following are possible responses to the issues for discussion:

Issue 1

Four main groups are identified in Figure A.1. Three are internal to the company, the fourth is an external group, the Air Force inspectors, of whom there are two. The internal

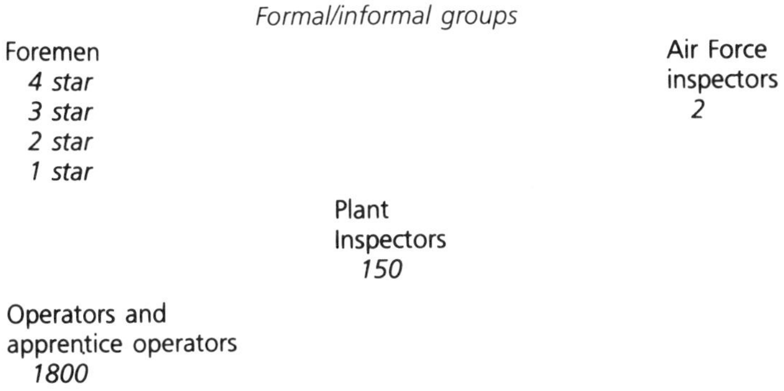

Formal/informal groups

Foremen
  4 star
  3 star
  2 star
  1 star

Air Force
inspectors
2

Plant
Inspectors
150

Operators and
apprentice operators
1800

Figure A.1 *Case of 'the tap'*

groups are: foremen (one, two, three and four star) and plant inspectors and operators
including apprentice operators.

Issue 2

The formal response throughout the company is that use of the tap is illegal, save in
very special circumstances, when an authorisation procedure may be activated, but this
causes much delay and loss of production.

The formal rule is soundly based on the grounds that use of the tap gives rise to an
aircraft being built weaker than specification. Problems are likely to arise later when
engines are changed or wings are under maintenance. Potentially in such a weak aircraft
the wings could drop off.

Enforcement of this rule is backed up by very severe formal sanctions. The company
could lose the aircraft contract. Company management and employees at all levels could
be dismissed for using taps.

Issue 3

The company culture is a 'produce or perish' environment. Targets are sacrosanct.
If a foreman misses his targets then any prospect of promotion is gone, and it seems
that there is much competition to achieve foreman rank and then rise to a four star
status. If a production stoppage is imminent then it is natural that this generates enormous
peer group pressures to prevent the impact of such a stoppage, hence the consideration
of short-cuts and the use of the tap.

However, it is interesting to note the way in which this illegal behaviour is manifested.
Apprentices are discouraged from using the tap by experienced workers as they fear
that indiscriminate use will increase the chances of detection. Furthermore, there is
a skilled workers' culture, which suggests that the tap may be safely used by the most
skilled. Thus status is acquired by a worker when his peer group accepts that he has
the skill to use the tap in special circumstances.

The foremen openly discourage indiscriminate use of the tap and will ritually beat anyone who flouts the rule and threaten dismissal. They wish to appear to support company policy. However, they also know who in the section can be trusted to use the tap with little chance of making a mess, and on the basis of favours will see that inspectors are nowhere near and that their back is turned so no one can accuse them of officially authorising use of the tap.

In an extreme situation a foreman may beg a worker to use the tap or borrow one and do the illegal action himself, but always on the basis that officially this act was never authorised and, by subtle practice, the illegal act is never detected. Sentinels track the progress of the two Air Force inspectors so chances of detection are minimised. Although official sanctions are severe in the extreme, if there is no detection then there is no hurt. But if a production target is compromised, there is an immediate problem situation.

The plant inspectors — and there are 150 of these — could on the face of it apply the anti-tap rule rigidly. But they do not because there is a mutual dependency between them and the production workers. Inspection is a very difficult and hazardous job and it is not possible to inspect all aspects of the aircraft in the time, without the cooperation of the workers who can indicate the parts which could cause problems when the Air Force inspectors check work passed by plant inspectors. Without this mutual cooperation inspection would be an impossible job. But there is a *quid pro quo* for this mutual cooperation and the inspectors are prepared to connive at illegal use of the tap.

Issue 4

People's behaviour is dependent partly on the need to avoid pain. Where in the work situation are there threatening sanctions? How immediate are these sanctions? Can they be avoided? Sanctions from the informal system can be much more immediate and painful to the individual than the sanctions which can come from the formal system, hence it may be easier to indulge in illegal action and go along with the peer group culture than to follow official but unpopular company policy.

It might be helpful to think through what the company should do to retrieve this dreadful situation. It is to be hoped that readers will not now abandon any idea of flying as a result of reading this case study, which was taken from the pressurised period of the Korean War when there was a pressing need to get aircraft built and operational as soon as possible!

The first strategy must lie with the design engineers. Could they not redesign the wings or material or specify a change in process which would eliminate the need for using the tap at all?

Another strategy would be to rewrite, with agreement from interested parties, the official authorisation procedure for using the tap so that it could be activated without loss of promotion prospects. This would be a more lengthy approach, involving changes of target setting and monitoring, and striking right at the heart of the existing line management 'produce or perish' culture. It would demand the setting up of a much more sophisticated reporting back system.

The third strategy would be to break the dependency of the plant inspectors with the production workers by increasing their establishment, so that they can comfortably complete the inspection job without needing to rely on worker goodwill and mutual favours.

Thus by tactics of change or reinforcement of the formal organisation structure and policies it should be possible to neutralise the informal practices.

Exercise 20.2   The improvised drama

First experience

Outcome of the lots
The observer had played the observer role before and felt comfortable in it. The leader was a natural buffoon, a production controller in real life.

First session
Within a few minutes a topic was selected. An article had been written two weeks before giving another Polytechnic credit for developing a Master's programme before Glasgow.

And the problem, it was to be a production manager under stress! The group quickly rallied to both these suggestions and there was to be no going back from then.

However, it seemed to be ages before the scenes could be constructed. Some group members were silent for a long time; two other leaders emerged and started the direction.

A third member had a brilliant idea of a skit, but when presented it fell flat. That member was silent for the next thirty minutes. A fourth member then adopted a 'narrator role' to provide continuity between the scenes and summarise group position. The leader then resumed control and rehearsals began.

There was rather a scramble for parts for everyone; some were disappointed as they could not see a role for themselves, but the leader's social skills operated and all eventually had roles. Two members luckily had some amateur drama experience and this was incorporated.

Second session, next morning
There was some initial panic; the star was still in bed, but one of the group did a policeman's job and soon the full team were operating. The narrator member achieved continuity and structure, while the leader buffooned his way creating the dialogue and material. Morale was very high, all were ready for the group presentation. The theme was good, but the problem was rather lost.

Third session
There was much mirth at the presentations of the other groups and no disaster when this group presented.

Fourth session

The observer read the diary and discussion ensued on leadership problems and the way they were tackled. The predominant style adopted was that of democratic leadership and a natural acceptance of the leader in the role, but some opting out as he found himself out of his depth. As time got short the narrator member tended to usurp and take control with a more task-oriented posture, but with sufficient tact for this to be accepted. The lady with the skit idea, which went flat, admitted that after the rejection of the new idea she withdrew from the group temporarily until a new opening could be found.

The exercise was generally well received, with acceptance of the group that they understood better the dynamics of groups.

Second experience

Outcome of the lots

The observer had never done this before and was distinctly nervous, but was soon put at ease by the group tutor. The leader went white when he picked the leader lot and would gladly have relinquished it.

First session

This was very difficult for a long time. Gradually two ideas for a theme were brought forward from two members and there was a slight power struggle from them. The leader found difficulty in refereeing the contest. Eventually, one gave in and started supporting the other member under pressure of time; a new leader had really emerged. The structure of the scenes and roles had not been completed by the end of the session. One member, who had been silent for an hour, would also gladly have disappeared but for some reassurance by the tutor.

Second session

The appointed leader was still uncomfortable, but the emergent leader, with some tact and skill, got on with the scenes and roles and the leader then supervised the rehearsals. All had a role by now and the atmosphere was suddenly much friendlier. There were two brief rehearsals and the group was ready for production. There were no more threats of withdrawals from the group.

Third session

The performance was good and well received by the other groups; everyone's morale was high!

Fourth session

The observer grew in the role and reported well. The leader admitted his discomfiture: with no previous drama experience and no previous unstructured project task experience so much was new to him. The members were generally supportive of the group; the fear of a group fiasco kept the group together. The member who had wanted to leave the group later admitted that once she could see a role for herself then she enjoyed the exercise, but again she had no previous drama experience and came from a highly structured professional environment, which was very different to the organic unstructured environment of the drama improvisation. All admitted that the exercise had been a valuable learning experience, but with some discomfiture from the learning process.

Tutor observations

This was a revealing experience to see two such contrasting groups in action and the impact of differing levels of knowledge to the task at hand, yet with the pressures of time and fear of failure both groups produced a very acceptable final product. It was very noticeable how leadership style needed to change as the project moved through different phases. It seemed that leadership tended to move to the one that had the greatest competence for that particular phase to the extent that the leadership role was usurped, albeit temporarily.

Case Study 22.1 The problem of the warehouse

Method

What we are looking at is a business problem. We thus are advised to follow the case study method. Salient features of this are as follows:

1. Interpretation: Do a thorough study of the memos and operating data to build up business pictures of the company.
2. Analysis: Analyse these pictures against normative management models to get a clear perspective of the company and its problems.
3. Response phase: This is about how to close the gaps. This suggests alternative courses of action for evaluation.

The main alternatives

Firstly, for the operating data relating to the two divisions we need to do a financial analysis.

A previous example was given in Case Study 4.1, where it was possible to put in perspective the financial ratios and get a feel for profit and liquidity issues.

For this case there are major points of concern arising from a financial analysis based on the given operating statements as follows:

1. There is an appalling delivery record in both divisions.
2. There are weak and deteriorating profit margins and return on investment figures, despite buoyant market conditions.
3. There is poor labour utilisation.

4. Large amounts of obsolete stock are scheduled for write-off.
5. Inventory turn figures are weak for an organisation supported by an MRP
   system.

Secondly, we need to select normative models to be used for analysing the memos.
Four models look likely to offer guidance. These are as follows:

1. The MRP system.
2. The corporate planning system, with the forecasting input.
3. The MbO system.
4. Models relating to choice of organisation structure.

The MRP system

We need to know what an MRP system should do and what it needs as preconditions.
This is primarily a clean database of both forecasting data, clean engineering data and
clear business policies which reflect competitive realities. With MRP working properly
there should be high labour and plant utilisation, quick response and an inventory turn
of up to twenty-eight times.

There are many mismatches here with the norms. The level of executive teamwork
as manifested between marketing and manufacturing is very poor. Queuing logic clearly
is a problem. There is a threat of loss of export business unless the first come first
served rule is established as general guide. The rule which attempts to maximise profit
by queue-jumping of domestic orders acts so randomly that the whole fabric of the
export business is threatened. This, luckily, is a policy rule easily changed in a computer.

Exceptions need to be accommodated. The spares problem would still exist in FCFS
rule. VDUs could help here to check the progress record in the sales branch. However,
if another customer has been allocated stock, intervention must be done in a controlled
and informed way. A marketing coordinator could be put into the Glasgow customer
services group to administer 'overrides'.

With VDUs in operation at both Crawley and Glasgow much of the £750,000 telephone
bill should disappear. The underlying problem will not go away, however, until there
is enough stock in the system to sustain the delivery policies laid down by marketing's
specifications.

The corporate planning system

The major mismatch is the absence of a corporate planning team, so many of the
corporate policies are just not reconciled. There are major difficulties in determining
and applying a marketing posture. Stock levels are needed to sustain a delivery policy
which is simply not understood or really discussed jointly by marketing and
manufacturing.

Market research should determine competitive pressures concerning delivery
expectations. No obvious market research presence reports on this. Where the
competition would suggest 'at once' delivery then this would indicate treating the item
as a stock item. To ensure 95 per cent success then theorists would suggest that the

company holds enough in stock to cover two standard deviations of the variance between actual and forecast amounts. The more accurate the forecast, the less stock is required.

For items not required on a stock basis one needs to aim for a production technology which can respond fast enough to satisfy delivery. This may mean holding many common components in stock with appropriate safety stock calculation. This approach gives a minimum stock for customer satisfaction. The more the production lead-times are reduced by product simplification and the use of numerically controlled tools with very short set-up times, the less need there is to hold stocks. In the ideal world of just-in-time systems stock could be eliminated altogether, but lead-times for hi-tech items cannot be eliminated altogether, and if there is any seasonality in demand patterns, then it is preferable to have stock as the buffer rather than people and overtime working, or leaving the customer as the buffer and making late deliveries.

This additional stock for the factory is called 'levelling stock' to take the shock out of the system to achieve good labour and plant utilisation. Normally this is set at an agreed figure by assembly-line to prevent overstocking. There are no formal methods here. Guidance from industry-established norms is best.

The product range in the company seems to grow far too rapidly. There is a great need to apply corporate planning techniques such as value analysis. That will profile winners and losers in both the product and customer base, and allow the company to cut out the losers and improve the winners. If they do not do something like this then the telephone bill may erode more than their whole profit.

With the forecasting part of the corporate planning system there are major mismatches here. The forecasting manager seems to work in isolation and there is no evidence of monthly or quarterly reviews with the corporate planning team to establish realism, validity and company support. Haddington does make the plea to get these sessions set up. This idea needs adopting quickly.

The MbO system

There are major mismatches here. The executive team does not seem able to get together to discuss objectives and policy rules for company agreement. There is no obvious appraisal process in place to review achievement against target in any methodical way between managers and subordinates, and particularly for coordination of manufacturing and marketing. The company does have a forecasting manager, but they do not seem capable of letting him get on with his legitimate function to ease this coordination problem!

Choice of organisation structures

The company seems to have adopted an unnecessarily complicated structure. This fails badly when attempting to service the very wide product range of make items from two locations 400 miles apart and with poor communications systems. The suggestion to rationalise and relocate the two divisional purchasing sections away from the very factories they serve is completely misconceived. There could only be advantages in rationalisation if the two divisions were mainly purchasing similar items, but the case material does not support this.

Alternative solutions

Maintain the status quo

The company will have to live with the perceived problems. If they are not treated the company may be obliged to cease trading.

Relocate the warehouse to Crawley

The likely consequences are as follows:

1. Increased transport costs for Scottish and North of England customers.
2. There are two warehouses instead of one.
3. There is a further delay in processing all make orders.
4. There is no relief of the forecasting problems.
5. The telephone bill will only be marginally reduced.
6. The impact on stock deliveries is uncertain and depends on stocking levels and forecasting accuracy.
7. Improvements in corporate planning are unlikely.
8. The proposal is costly and risky to implement. There are relocation expenses; another computer is required; training is needed for new staff and there are redundancies at Glasgow.

Improve the system

Follow the mismatches against the norms outlined above and close the gaps. The major new equipment required is the VDUs for installation at Crawley and Glasgow. Adopt the outlined improvements in planning suggested by Haddington. Establish an organisation development team to implement this change strategy. This team could with advantage follow more closely the guidelines on implementation offered in Figure 22.3.

Conclusion

By adopting the option to improve the system above all the perceived problems are treatable.

What actually happened in the company

The company was not capable of taking a dispassionate view. They went ahead with the relocation of the warehouse and the crisis worsened. After two years of declining fortunes they relocated back to Scotland. Fortunately, market conditions improved and the parent company prospered. The UK subsidiary then introduced the VDUs and cut the telephone bill. They took a long time to improve the corporate planning systems.

Class experiences

The following strategies were suggested by an undergraduate class. Basically they followed the method outlined, initially looking at the company problems and putting them into perspective using the normative models. The three best answers were better than answers delivered by experienced managers when this exercise was done. On another occasion experienced managers tended not to be able to look at the issues from a fresh standpoint as easily as degree students. They failed to recognise the fundamental weaknesses in the corporate planning system, which left the MRP system operating very poorly.

The following weak strategies were suggested by an undergraduate class:

1. Blaming the computer system rather than the data or rules of the system. If the system is not right you must highlight the structural weakness or policy inconsistencies.
2. Replacing the computer with a more modern one which would do the underlying thinking for the corporation. A thinking computer for unthinking executives! In fact all systems should be updated to take advantage of new technology and new business circumstances.
3. Putting VDUs in the sales offices. In making this suggestion students did not consider how the hard cases could be handled when reallocation of stock was being contemplated. There has to be a dialogue between sales and warehouse staff to cope with such hard cases. It is important to think of the implications of each solution put forward.
4. Two forecasting systems with Glasgow and Crawley acting independently. In fact the whole purpose of an effective forecasting system is to get production and marketing people to work from the same set of volume targets.
5. Reverting to manual systems. In the light of the volume and wide product range this would be very hard to implement.

Appendix 2

A review of decision-making in case studies and exercises of chapters 9–22

Exercise 9.1

In this exercise there are decisions to be made and chairmanship skills to develop. The chairman will generally attempt to follow the rational decision-making process. It is necessary to find a new future for this unit after the premises are subject to a closing order. Representatives gather from several organisations which might be able to absorb this specialist unit.

The reality from the chair is that political, emotional and human factors are very strong and impede the rational decision-making process. The people involved conspire to manipulate the situation to suit the organisation whose brief they carry and sometimes a plethora of their own values and prejudices.

The exercise has been run on many occasions and thus the variety of outcomes from the same data are interesting in their own right as an example of group decision-making processes. This shows up the need for the chairman to develop communication and listening skills as well as directing a meeting with relevance to the business and decisions of the agenda.

Exercise 10.1

This exercise illustrates the quantitative technique of planning networks. A decision-making crisis arises when the company rejects a twenty-eight week solution to the product introduction and insists on a twenty-week solution.

Decisions are necessary about where to make cuts in time and improvements in business logic and about the allocation of further resources to quicken up the process. The network suggests a critical path, and cuts there alone will improve the project time. Networking is an analytical technique to identify the critical path from many other paths. The technique also suggests to the project manager which events are likely to be shortened by extra resources, and although part of that identification is judgemental, the project

548

management environment in which it operates offers the opportunity for realistic discussion of these points.

This technique allows trade-offs of a time/cost/resource nature to be made on an informed basis and is a good example of the rational decision-making process.

Chapter 14 — use of spreadsheets in computer-assisted decision-making

Attention is directed to a spreadsheet model in Exhibit 14.13. This model is set up to compute net present values arising out of appraisals of investment projects. The criteria of acceptance of a project commonly reflect an organisation's expectations in terms of rate of interest, pay-off period in years and possibly other quantitatively-based parameters.

The model provides a good indication of whether any particular proposal is likely to be funded or not. If not the decision-maker may do what-if projections based on other likely possibilities. For instance, for a capital outlay of £100,000 a project might well fail, but another supplier for the sum of £80,000 might make the proposition acceptable. Alternatively, another department might be persuaded to back the project, thus increasing the cash flows of benefit and providing an easy justification for the original £100,000 capital outlay. There are many possibilities and the spreadsheet provides a quick and simple way of evaluating any such choice.

Case Study 16.1 — Decision-making in the purchase of a first computer facility

The case could be perceived as one about decisions of choice in worthwhile computer applications and decisions about selecting the appropriate computer hardware necessary to support this. The case incident is another disaster sequence!

The DOC wishes to extend its capacity for end-of-month accountancy reports. The purchase of accounting machines at an approximate cost of £16,000 is one choice, but the accounting manager wants a computer.

He has delegated authority to spend up to £40,000 on capital and goes ahead and purchases a computer. However, the once-only conversion costs of the existing manual accounting system to computer is £100,000. Actually he is spending £140,000 when the other option was a mere £16,000.

An eighteen-month accountancy project is authorised, but during that time the DOC engineers become curious about what the computer can do. After a familiarisation course some engineers discover that the computer could help them significantly in the seismic surveying and interpretation of reports. They feel that if they apply computer techniques here there will be savings of £70,000 a year, and knowing better where to drill will give DOC a massive strategic advantage over other oil companies.

AGM Production lobbies AGM Finance for time on the computer for the engineering calculations and after some conflict, and arbitration by the General Manager, the engineers get some time.

AGM Finance is annoyed as this puts his accounting project behind schedule. AGM Production is not happy either, as his engineers soon find that the computer bought by AGM Finance has insufficient memory to cope with the engineers' numbers. The computer manufacturer offers a larger model, but that is too big to fit into the air-conditioned computer room, and the engineers are instructed to use a computer bureau for their work. However, the DOC is some 2,000 miles from the nearest bureau and the engineers withdraw their interest with some ill-feeling.

As far as decision-making went, the DOC adopted a low-priority application area for computing; the accounting project as conceived would never pay for itself. They bought a computer which was useless for the more promising strategic application in the interpretation of seismic drilling information.

Where did DOC go wrong in their decision-making process?

Basically, they adopted the rogue intuitive model of decision-making with the invalid assumption that this was a case of decision-making under conditions of uncertainty. They should instead have adopted the rational approach. But for the rational approach to work they would have needed better teamwork — a computer steering committee, a corporate plan and the general organisational processes outlined in Figure 16.1. With that machinery in place the issue of choice of computer applications would have preceded the decision of hardware purchase. The outcome would have been very different.

By using good practice organisation structure and processes, the uncertainty could have been reduced to an insignificant amount. DOC could have had the benefit of putting computers to use at the front end of the business, where they could make the exciting strategic impact.

Case Study 16.2 — Decision-making in systems design

This is a very complex area of decision-making as many stakeholders are involved and the work is completed in a high-tech environment with some uncertainty surrounding the capabilities of the technology and a lack of organisational experience in deploying such technology. Time-scales are typically short and the outcomes may have a strategic significance for the organisation.

Interest surrounds the decision-making of Arnold, the company's purchasing manager, for whom a duty recovery system is being designed. When this is completed and working some £2 million will flow into the company coffers, so the outcome is financially significant.

Arnold is offered a choice of a complex system or a simple system by a well-informed systems analyst, Keith, and advised to go for the simple system. But Arnold rejects this advice, influenced partly by the Data Processing Manager, Fred (who is a completely uninformed nonentity) and partly by a Surveyor of Customs, who feels more secure with the complex approach. His promotion prospects will be improved if he gets an 'elegant' solution approved in London! The decision to go for the complex approach backfires badly. The Data Processing Manager, Fred, fails to resource the project adequately and the systems analyst, Keith, falls ill. Only he understands this complex system and he contemplates a hijack by refusing to maintain a telephone link to his hospital bed.

Fred is sacked and replaced by a new Data Processing Manager, Doreen. Doreen has a sound knowledge of good practice in systems design. She reverses Arnold's decision and then restarts the project almost from first principles, now with goodwill from Keith, the systems analyst. She introduces a project management process with eleven stages of design; she introduces a new role — that of business analyst — and a new form of project structure. (See Figure 16.1.)

The project is recovered and the analyst is able some two years later to say it was like being born again to work in a new, more structured team environment. With the new design team well balanced in experience and knowledge, and the ground-rule of *working to specification* firmly laid down, he was to say that the team had achieved a wonderful capability — 'inegrated bilingualism'.

Arnold's original choice of approach was difficult because he was so poorly informed and he resorted to intuition.

When Doreen arrived on the scene, she set up a good practice process and organisation structure to reduce the previous uncertainty and enable a rational decision-making model to be applied. Once these aspects of good practice were securely in position, sound decisions could be made on systems design and the overall management of a complex project.

Perhaps this difficulty of decision-making in fields of systems design and the introduction of new technology is really a non-problem after all! We should not look upon them as cases of decision-making under conditions of uncertainty, but get on with setting up relevant processes and organisation structures, like Doreen. This will restore a rational decision-making approach to these hitherto maverick areas of decision-making.

Case Study 19.1 and 19.2 — Decision-making in organisation design

In the P & Q Company (Case Study 19.1) the sequence describes the evolution of a family business. Key decisions on organisation structure have to be taken by Major Quaille after he returns to assume control of the business after the war.

There are several choices open to him. He could strengthen the line parts of the organisation; he could strengthen the staff parts of the organisation; he could divisionalise what has become two businesses through the development of a new machine shop during the period of the war contracts. He wishes to build a sound structure from which the business can flourish.

However, Major Quaille runs into difficulties in decision-making. Initially, he wishes to re-establish his personal authority in the firm by maintaining tight control through having daily meetings. He seems to feel threatened by the presence of Keene, the ex-maintenance foreman, who assumed factory manager status during the war years. Major Quaille is a local personality and wishes to make his mark in management groups in his local town.

Having established his personal control he then builds up the staff organisation with a number of key appointments, all of whom report to him directly, and with the daily meetings things get busy for everybody. Keene, the ex-factory manager (and the natural production line manager), is rather left out of things. Instead of being given objectives and authority, he is given instructions and a rather imprecise coordinating role. This is particularly difficult to discharge in light of the daily meetings of Major Quaille and his large team of staff managers.

Line organisation in manufacturing companies is generally conceived as the twin functions of production and marketing. All other functions, such as personnel, accounting, data processing, etc., are regarded as staff functions. They provide a service to allow the line to operate effectively.

Major Quaille has a blind spot for marketing. He simply hires four of his pre-war salesmen and gets them to sell the pre-war style products under his immediate direction. No market planning or product development is done whatever and little attention is paid to the salesmen.

After an initial post-war boom, the company's sales slumped badly. The company's product line was obsolete and the prices were no longer competitive.

To remake the product portfolio would require some sound market research and a concerted effort with R&D to get new products launched, but that would take at least two years, and with a poor cash flow all that time the prospects for the P & Q Company looked grim!

What decisions should Major Quaille have taken to avert this crisis?

He should have built the organisation around a strong line organisation structure. He might have left Keene in the factory management position, which he discharged well in the war years. Meantime he could have got the marketing structure properly organised with a vital new product development programme. Once that was functioning, he could have gone about getting the staff organisation into being, with terms of reference to report at the level in the organisation where they would be effective for the operating decisions and the long-term planning of the company.

With that structure in place normal delegation and planning could go ahead, and possibly the organisation could be simplified with a partial divisional structure to take account of the different business orientation of a machine shop and foundry.

Why are decisions of organisation structure difficult ones?

The problem is that decisions of structure are not recognised as decisions at all! What we saw with Major Quaille was a series of *ad hoc* adaptations to suit his personal management style. He reacted intuitively and in response to the situation, with an excessive desire to dominate operating decisions. He allowed himself to become a one-man band with the illusion of having control. The reality was that the business under his control was destined for liquidation. A more gifted manager would have recognised clearly the need for a pro-active response and identified the options of choice necessary for getting the structure healthy.

Interesting decisions also face management in Case Study 19.2. In this case Ted Michod is sponsored for an MBA programme, at no small cost to his firm. When he returns he naturally wants to spread his wings and do rather more than just technical engineering work. That was why he did the MBA programme, and he is keen that his gifts should be utilised.

However, Midwestern is a traditional line/staff organisation. There is functional specialisation between executives — shown by Lucas the Customer Engineering Manager and Wayne Smith the Computer Installation Manager — and they have no experience of close cooperation with one another and their staffs.

Michod then gets involved with project assignments with both Wayne Smith and Lucas. This would be typical for a manager working in a matrix organisation. Unfortunately, Michod gets overloaded with three projects. All his attempts at reconciling the priorities are to no avail. Neither Lucas nor Wayne Smith wants to know about the overload. As task-oriented line managers they just want to get the job done, no fuss, full stop. Michod is in a real dilemma. There seems to be no organisational avenue he can go down to reconcile the conflict in priorities in his three assignments.

There is a number of alternative solutions depending on the nature of the problem perceived. One scenario is that Michod needs to develop more positive communication skills and confront his seniors without being treated as a doormat. This suggests that he requires some coaching to develop skills in organisational politics.

Another scenario is that the traditional line organisation structure no longer fits the high-tech environment and that senior management should be prepared for a change in structure to matrix. They themselves would need to be exposed to training and development in readiness for a new and different organisational culture.

This case suggests that decision-making generally follows the process of problem-solving, otherwise there is no natural agenda to trigger decision-making. Nor is the theory about organisation structure particularly strong. It is often couched in terms such as 'contingency', thus we really are working in a situation of decision-making in conditions of uncertainty.

Case Study 22.1 — Decision-making in a fluid business policy environment

Initially, it looks as though the issue is an organisational one — whether the warehouse should be located at the factory in Glasgow or with the marketing operation in Crawley.

Several executives have well-developed views on this issue and these are illustrated in a portfolio of memos.

However, other problems are manifest. Firstly, the company telephone bill is a staggering £750,000 a year — more than the gross profit!

Customer delivery performance is appalling. Export customers are threatening to pull out altogether. The company operates a sophisticated computerised production scheduling system based on US good practice, but the marketing people do not seem to understand how this operates. A forecasting manager is in post, but tends to be ignored by the marketing people, so the corporate planning routines do not work properly. Without the planning routines the production scheduling system works no better than a shabby manual system.

The company has two divisions and a wide product catalogue of 1,600 items, many of which are 'make' items, i.e. they are custom-made. The company is typically a very busy company, but the profit record is poor.

Where do we start with decision-making in this situation? That does seem to be a good question, that one

There is no option initially of escaping by saying it is a matter of decision-making under conditions of uncertainty. The mess and chaos are eminently manifest and crying out for treatment. There is little uncertainty and the prospect of closing down is a real one to concentrate the mind.

However, we can look at norms of good practice, find deviations from these and then think through some gap-closing strategies. These open up the priorities for decision-making and action.

The most salient norms are those relating with corporate planning. In this text they are summarised and conceptualised in Figure 17.1.

A further analysis of this case suggests that there are several significant problems with the articulation and integration of management systems in the company. However, once these are put into perspective, it is desirable to follow the overall route forward through the procedure offered by Figure 22.3. This suggests many further points for decision and action. Out of the chaos of the initial company appreciation comes the prospect of reaching towards an enduring excellence in performance and management!

Decision-making about the nature, style and integration of key company systems is probably the most important set of decisions facing any company. There are well-developed norms of good practice in all these areas. Once we accept these as useful, it is possible to pin our faith on a sound rational approach to decision-making, backed up by sound theory.

Summary

Decision-making is a significant part of the management process. From some simple definitions and an exploration of a decision-making process in chapter 8, the analysis developed into the rich and varied management situations contained in this text. In this Appendix decision-making in the cases of chapters 9–22 was the focus of attention. And the predominant finding was that decision-making tended to be a disaster area and of great difficulty to executives in action.

However, armed with the theories of the decision-making approach it was possible to try these out on the salient issues of the cases. The rational approach, supported by other elements of good practice, shone through as a credible and useful approach to decision-making. Time and again the assumption that an intuitive approach was necessary because of conditions of uncertainty was critically questioned and we were to find that management needed to organise themselves better for informed decision-making to be carried out.

Finally, even in a complicated business policy situation the norms of management systems suggested a way forward which would bring order and excellence out of chaos and poor performance — a true victory for the rational approach.

Some sceptics might aver that the cases across the wide range of topics of this text were not representative of the variety of real life. They will still want to escape with the indulgence of the intuitive approach and the assertion that real uncertainty exists. Consequently this summary provides references to other authors on decision-making in action:

1. Harrison E. F. (1975), *Managerial Decision-Making Process*, Houghton. The section on decision-making in the Cuban missile crisis offers a thrilling analysis of a situation which threatened to trigger a third world war. President Kennedy's decision-making skill, sense of timing and selection of strategic options within a group setting in the political/military field were quite brilliant.

2. Johnson, G. (1988), 'Rethinking incrementalism', *Strategic Management Journal*, vol. 9, no. 1, pp. 77–91. This article goes more deeply into complex decision-making approaches in the difficult field of business policy and risk-taking at the highest levels of business.

Index